W9-AJU-454

FLIGHT FROM BABYLON

FLIGHT FROM BABYLON

Iraq, Iran, Israel, America

◆

Heskel M. Haddad, M.D.,
as told to
Phyllis I. Rosenteur

McGraw-Hill Book Company
New York St. Louis San Francisco
Hamburg Mexico Toronto

1 2 3 4 5 6 7 8 9 DOC DOC 8 7 6

ISBN 0-07-025418-4

LIBRARY OF CONGRESS CATALOGING-IN-PUBLICATION DATA

Haddad, Heskel M.
Flight from Babylon.
1. Haddad, Heskel M. 2. Jews—Iraq—Biography.
3. Jews, Iraqi—Israel—Biography. I. Rosenteur,
Phyllis. I. II. Title.
DS135.I713H333 1986 956.7'004924 85-19871
ISBN 0-07-025418-4

BOOK DESIGN BY PATRICE FODERO

To my father, Moshe Haddad, the central figure in my life; to my mother, Masuda Haddad, whose prayers sustained me throughout my life; and to my children, Ava Masuda, Andre Moshe, and Albert Michael, whose existence perpetuates my life.

The author acknowledges with sincere appreciation the help and encouragement of the Haddad family and, in particular, that of his brother Isaac and his sisters Nazima Dallal, Daisy Mouallem, and Tikva (Osa) Zaroor. Special mention must be made of the aid afforded by his late father in reminding him of much that is in the book.

Thanks are especially due his devoted and faithful secretary and right hand, Carol Sorensen.

And most heartfelt acknowledgment to his comrades in the Underground.

August 1, 1953

For the second time in my life, I was on a plane—literally suspended between two worlds. This time I'd taken off in Israel and would end up in America. In Boston, in the exotic-sounding state of Massachusetts.

Sealed in a steel capsule, forced, for once, to relinquish control to others, I tried to relax, but it wasn't something I did well. For years now, there hadn't been more than isolated moments when I could simply *sit,* and now there was nothing else to do. Nothing to do but think back to the beginning.

Three years ago, the first flight had brought me from Teheran to Tel Aviv, but the journey really began in Baghdad, in 1930, when a boy was born to Moshe the plumber, son of Abraham the shoemaker. It all began in Baghdad . . .

1

To understand the how and why of all that happened, it's necessary to know that patience was never my strong point. As long ago as I can remember, the future was always too far off for me. I hated waiting, and everything took too much time—especially growing up. At almost four, which is when I decided to take a hand and hurry things along, I was already sick of hearing "soon". . . "someday" . . . or, *most* irritating, "you'll understand when you're older."

I could accept it from Baba and Uncle Ezra, my father's older brother, and even from Haron, Uncle Ezra's son and my favorite cousin, but it was intolerable from S'hak. Not only did my brother brush me off more often than the others, but he did so in the smuggest, most patronizing way possible. At nine, he implied, he knew all the answers.

A lot of his showing off, I suppose, was just plain jealousy—not unwarranted, I admit. As the eldest son, S'hak was entitled to certain perquisites, but one way or another, I managed to usurp most of them. Though not the baby of the family, I was the smallest boy child, and even at my age understood how fortunate I was not to have been born female. While Iraqi parents cherished all their children, in our culture, sons were regarded as special gifts of God, and nothing was too good for us. I caught on early, and what few prerogatives weren't freely offered, I readily obtained through a God-given gift of my own. Leather lungs. I could scream louder and longer than any kid my size in the city. Baghdad was well known as the noisiest city on earth, and I contributed more than my share to the hubbub.

Needless to say, I was spoiled in the extreme. The only one I couldn't manipulate was Baba—not always, at any rate. Take the way he sometimes treated me when I was sleeping with Nana. My mother had nursed me until I was nearly three, and I guess I still craved the closeness because I crept into bed with her whenever Baba went off to sleep by himself. About half of every month, he bedded down in the guest room, but I never knew when he'd turn up to re-take his place. He'd arrive without warning, pluck me out of my warm spot, slide in beside Nana, and send me off to my own room "right now!" On those occasions, I hardly recognized the doting father who always had time to spare for a small son.

S'hak would snicker when I crawled back into the bed we shared, angrily complaining about my abrupt banishment. Once I said that Baba was being selfish "because Nana's bed is big enough for all three of us," and he laughed so hard I had to sit on his face to shut him up. As usual, he wouldn't explain. All he *ever* said was "You'll understand when you're older."

That was the night I decided to speed the aging process. Going to school would automatically lift me out of the infant class and S'hak would have to treat me with more respect. Mainly, though, school was where one could ask questions and get answers instead of evasions. However, the *raudha* was for five-year-olds and I was still a year shy. Strategy would be required.

Even at that age, I believed implicitly in my own ability to control events. I knew my strengths and the soft spots of those around me—and exactly where and how to apply one to the other. For small favors, I usually fixed on my fourteen-year-old sister. Giving by nature, Nazima Esther indulged everyone, but me most of all. I had only to ask for anything in her power to provide.

When it was S'hak who had what I wanted, I didn't waste time with the wide-eyed, little-boy-lost look that worked so well on women. S'hak had to be worn down, like sand eroding a rock. If nagging at him all day didn't accomplish my ends, I'd pester him in bed, poking him awake at intervals until he capitulated out of sheer exhaustion.

Unfortunately, neither Nazima nor S'hak had anything to say about my schooling. That was my father's province, and I always thought twice about tackling Baba. Screaming, I had long since learned, was worse than useless. His sole reaction was to stare in my direction, but right through me, as if the unpleasant sound existed but I didn't. Since I couldn't bear to be ignored, I had abandoned screaming insofar as my father was concerned. While I could often coax Baba into a minor concession, school was too serious an affair. I couldn't risk a flat "no" from father.

That left Nana—I started to smile. By a logical process of elimination, which in itself pleased me greatly—so grown-up!—I'd arrived at the only possible answer. What made it perfect was that mother was my easiest mark. Nana not only adored me, she also had supersensitive ears. When begging didn't work, bellowing did. Beyond a certain decibel level, which I could reach and sustain with ease, she simply shattered.

With Nana, all sorts of strategies were successful—even doing nothing. From the time I was assigned my first chores around the house, I'd made a tidy profit out of nonperformance. If I procrastinated long enough, I found, Nana would "encourage" me by offering a few *fils* for my services. After the initial payoff, I never filled a water jar or sprayed Flit against the flies or carried a stick of kindling to the kitchen without "encouragement."

Before I could settle on the proper approach to the issue of school, a severe eye infection, followed by mumps, made any plan of action unnecessary. Being sick was sufficient. Nana didn't stand a chance.

Because Habiba, the baby ahead of me, had died soon after birth, I dominated Nana from the second she knew she'd conceived again. According to my aunts, no woman ever worried as much as my mother worried over me, and before I'd even arrived on the scene. When I *did* emerge—two months early and looking, so family legend went, "barely as big as a bird"—she was sure she'd lose me as she had Habiba. If I so much as sneezed, she turned ashen and keened like an Arab.

I knew the story by heart—how, when I was "almost gone," Nana had taken me to a *kari,* who wrote a secret scroll to be inserted into the little silver *k'tibeh* that I wore on a neck chain, and said mystic prayers to purify my body. Then, as insurance, she'd smuggled me (in secret, because both Baba and the rabbi would have forbidden it) to an Arab sorceress famed for her ability to save babies. The *Daya* had recommended that Will of God be added to my other names, and thus I became Heskel Haim Ma-Sha-Allah Haddad. Immediately thereafter, as Nana told it, I took hold of life. Ever since, I'd worn my name and the small, silver *k'tibeh* with a special sense of destiny.

I fingered the tiny cylinder around my neck and smiled again. With all that to build on, plus who knows how long a stay in bed, anything I wanted would be mine for the asking.

Unwittingly, S'hak aided me by adding a severe stomach upset to my other illnesses. The doctor hadn't been gone an hour when he walked in, gnawing on a huge chunk of *h'lawa.* Rich and fatty foods had been stricken from my diet, and S'hak knew it. Since nothing on earth is as richly oily as a slab of sesame seed ground in sugar, once I wheedled a piece, I had him in my power. For the whole seven weeks I was bed-bound, all I had to say was "I'll tell Nana" to assure a steady flow of all my forbidden favorites.

Under the gun, S'hak disgorged goodies on a regular basis. One day it was orange pop and almond *malfoof.* Next he might bring *baklava,* slightly squashed from storage inside his shirt, or quivering *halkoon,* jellied cubes that coated his pockets with powdered sugar. Best, though, were the sticky pools of dark molasses, maneuvered I know not how, which should have been sopped up with bits of bread, but lacking *khibz,* I discovered that the stuff could be scooped with two fingers, or better yet, the whole hand. After the molasses, I had the whole family awake all night, and in an uproar over my acute attack.

Even if I hadn't been sick to my stomach for most of seven weeks, I would have sent my mother's meals back untouched. Probably my pallor and brave suffering would have sufficed, but "starving" myself guaranteed success. Nothing softened Nana up like seeing me not eat, and eventually we reached a point at which I could have, be, do or not do almost anything if I would only swallow a little soup. The time had come to strike a bargain. I'd force down a bite, I promised, if she'd just talk Baba into sending me to school. Standing by my bed, his daily bribe seeping through his pants pocket, S'hak almost choked.

A week later—now completely well—I woke at dawn, as always, to the sound of Baba's voice filtering through from the next room and the equally familiar singsong of the *mua'dhin* floating from the minaret of the Kambar Ali mosque. While both were chanting morning prayers, one in Hebrew, the other in Arabic, church bells began to peal in the Christian Quarter to the south of us. Outside, on Kambar Ali Street, overburdened camels snorted and groaned, and merchants on their way to Hanoon Market swore at their mules in all six Baghdad dialects. Almost every day, I increased my vocabulary of unusable expressions.

An ancient truck rattled toward the house, the pitch of the driver's chant marking its stop-and-start progress. At the exact moment it came abreast of us, Nana shouted her order, as she did every day. Dragging footsteps and deep grunts ended in a loud thud and a clattering tattoo from our tin-lined food chest. We took the biggest block of ice on Kambar Ali Street. As usual, the noise awakened my baby sister, Daisy, who began to bawl—also as usual. Nazima scooped her up and sang to stop her crying. In sum, an ordinary morning.

All of Baghdad was up and about, but S'hak hadn't twitched an eyelid. I was in no rush to rise myself. After baking on the roof all night during the summer, when the thermometer often hovered around 100, and being eaten alive by mosquitoes in spite of the mesh netting and smelly fog of Flit, I was enjoying the slight chill of the cool-weather quarters to which we'd recently returned.

In the hot months, everyone slept on the roof. *Tried* to sleep, I should say, because no matter how astutely Nana selected the netting that draped our beds (not so open a weave as to admit insects, flying or otherwise, but airy enough to invite a stray breeze, yet sufficiently opaque to afford a little privacy), real rest was almost impossible.

The October air was deliciously crisp, and on this particular morning, the bed itself was especially inviting. Every few months, when our mattresses had packed down into solid slabs, *Hadji* Mahmood would bring his long brass rods and stir up the cotton batting until it was soft again. He'd come yesterday, and the pillowy bed was too luxurious to leave. I decided to stay put for just a few more minutes.

Thinking about Mahmood was pleasant too. He was one of the few Arabs I knew really well because he came on a regular basis, and would talk to me, even teach me verses from the Koran, while whipping and twirling his brass wands. For the most part, Jews and *M'silmin* didn't mix outside of buying and selling, but that was something else no one ever explained. Except for his clothes and haircut, and, of course, his dialect and darker skin, Mahmood could almost have been an uncle. The idea of a *hadji* uncle made me grin.

Mahmood was a *hadji* because he'd made the pilgrimage to Mecca, but he needn't have told me. Everyone knew that only a *hadji* could wear the yellow-checked *amama,* which he never removed, though practically everything *but* his head covering came off in the course of work. After he shed the full-aproned *abaya,* along with the wraparound rough-cotton *jubba* and the wide, embroidered belt that anchored them both, his two-piece underwear still covered him from head to foot. The *lebis el t'wil,* too tight at the ankles to roll up, widened all the way to his waist, where I finally got to see the gaudy *tika* worn by *M'silmin.* Men in the streets sang dirty songs about the braided drawstring that held up all male underpants. Someday I intended to ask Mahmood what it meant for a man to lose his *tika.*

If not as informative as Mahmood, S'hak was warm and available, and I turned to nestle against him. It instantly proved to be one of the worst moves I'd ever made. That little twist triggered an eruption somewhere deep inside me, and I knew that the next, smallest shift might set off an explosion I couldn't contain. Twice a year, Nana cleaned us out with castor oil, and while the rest of the family weren't due for their doses until December, I'd had mine last night so I'd be purged and pure for school.

The *raudha!* I'd forgotten that at 8:30 I was starting nursery school.

Stomach churning, I inched my legs off the mattress and fished for my *na'al* with my feet. The tile floor was icy, but my slippers were well under the bed and I didn't dare bend. I'd have had to shake them out in any case, because centipedes liked to hide in the dark toes, and I was afraid to shake even a *finger.*

Barefoot, I headed for the bathroom, down a flight of stairs, on the "summer" floor and all the way over on the other side of the house. Desperate as I was, I dashed past the toilet and into the adjoining room. Decent people didn't relieve themselves where they washed, and washing came first. I couldn't touch anything, even myself, before cleansing my hands and saying a special prayer. Sometimes, like now, it was extremely difficult to be a good Jew.

The faucet at the bottom of the water tank was high over my head, so I made do with the slow drip into the *s'lapja.* Baba was a master plumber—the best in Baghdad—but luckily the faucet leaked a little!

I dipped my hands into the water, prayed, skipped the soap, and shook dry as I scuttled toward the toilet. The brick bowl in the floor looked positively beautiful. Squatting, with my already numb feet on the frigid iron footrests, I said a prayer of thanks that wasn't part of the religious ritual.

Once relieved, however, ritual did demand the use of running water, and I rinsed myself by tilting the enormous, long-necked ewer which stood permanently beside the toilet bowl. The spout was angled so that a thin, steady stream poured out to wash my privates. By the time I'd bathed myself and flushed the bowl, the ewer was empty. The person who used up the last of the water was supposed to replenish it, but that was Baba's dictate, not God's.

Back in the lavatory, I pared a slice of soap from the long brown bar, washed my hands again (this time with the prayer for *after* defecating), dried them on the *khawli l'intila*—the cotton towel for hands only—then scrubbed my face while saying still another prayer and finished by wiping with the towel for faces. As I often had before, I wondered if Allah demanded as much of the *M'silmin.*

On returning to our room, I saw that S'hak still hadn't budged, but I restrained myself. Time enough to pummel him awake after I was dressed. If he saw me putting on my Holy Day clothes, he'd undoubtedly yell for Nana. Aside from that, I liked to be alone when I looked in the mirror. S'hak hooted whenever he caught me at it, and I couldn't explain that it was less vanity than the need to assure myself of my male image, which was still too new to be taken for granted.

Until I was three, I'd seen a pseudo-female reflection, which was bearable only because half the Jewish boys in Iraq were in the same boat, made to wear their hair long, like a girl's, in order to delude the Evil Eye. Should it fix on any of us, all it would see was a she-creature, not worth bothering about. Of course you were never *completely* safe, whatever your age or sex, and no one was more aware of that than Nana, who knew all the remedies against such malevolence.

I wasn't afraid, exactly, but I touched the *k'tibeh* around my neck, and after pulling on my new velveteen shorts and elaborately embroidered shirt, felt for the small bump that told me I was twice protected. Somewhere on everything we wore, Nana or Nazima was sure to have pinned a bright-blue bead, made for the sole purpose of turning aside the Evil Eye. I confess to a feeling of relief when I found it.

I also confess to admiring what I saw in the mirror. All my clothes were homemade and handsome, but Nazima had outdone herself with this outfit. After five years at sewing school, with two more to go to complete her education, my big sister could weave, tat, knit, and do every known type of needlework, but embroidery was her best subject, and she'd put all she'd learned into my shirt.

Now that my curly hair was cut short, I was extremely pleased with it too, and if the deep cleft in my chin meant that God had touched me, as Nana insisted, it would be sacrilegious *not* to like it. All I lacked was a black mustache like my father's, and I meant to have one as soon as nature allowed. Nature was one of those mysteries I was always "too young to understand," but it seemed to be involved with everything adult and interesting.

The thought of Baba abruptly ended my musing, and I rushed down to find him, heavy straw *zinbeel* in hand, already at the door. We went to market together every morning—the only "chore" for which I didn't charge since it was one which I'd invented for myself. I hurried because I had to toe the line with Baba. Much as he loved me, he left no smallest doubt about who was boss.

Baba was a head taller than the average Iraqi, and when he strode along, his black *sadara* sailed above the crowd like a small ship. I could spot him and his hat at any distance. Maybe his height had something to do with it, and he did look very serious, even intimidating, until he smiled, but though Baba never set out to impress anyone, everyone deferred to him.

When we were halfway down the hall, I heard the inevitable "Abu S'hak!" We never left for market without this last "Abu S'hak" from Nana.

"Father of S'hak, don't forget the okra."

Baba resignedly raised his eyebrows. "Mother of S'hak, do I *ever* forget the okra?"

It was as much a ritual as morning prayers.

Hardly anyone called my father by his given name—Moshe—and, at four, I didn't even know that Nana *had* a name. At my brother's birth, Moshe and Masuda had disappeared; since then they'd been identified, according to custom, simply as the father and mother of their first son. That was the only thing I didn't like about being the youngest boy. *My* name was never mentioned.

Our front door was six feet wide, strapped with iron, and so heavy that even Baba had to strain to open it. Once down the three steps to ground level, I usually ran for the center of the street, where I could walk alongside the open sewer and watch all sorts of interesting debris go floating by. Today, however, I was concerned with staying clean for school, and in the dry season, the middle of a busy dirt street was no place to do it. An unending parade of camels, pushcarts, and pack mules kicked up clouds of yellow dust, which not only clogged the nostrils and coated every exposed surface, but also made it almost impossible to see the piles of dung underfoot. When you stepped in one, you were further blinded by the swarms of flies that rose and buzzed angrily around your head. Closer to the housefronts, under the overhang of the second stories, both ground and air were cleaner and clearer.

It struck me, as it did every morning, that *M'silmin* didn't worry as much about where they walked or, in fact, about anything except the immediate moment, and not one second more. As always, all the passing Arabs were either smiling or screaming the most imaginative oaths at their animals or each other, but not one looked just plain worried. Certainly I saw no one nervously picking his path. It's true that a pile of manure, or even a spitting camel or kicking mule, is less than life-threatening; but Arabs acted the same in every circumstance. In the heart of the city, where the traffic never stops and everyone drives as if he owned the street, Arabs crossed at the busiest intersection without even bothering to look up and down the avenue. A truck could practically amputate a man's toes and he'd be just as careless at the next corner.

When I mentioned just such an incident to Mahmood, because the man involved had also been a *hadji,* he said that I was wrong—that the "carelessness" really indicated complete trust in Allah. A true believer, he explained, understands that each man's fate is already inscribed, so worrying about the future—even a fender away—would not only be foolish but also show a lack of faith.

"If I'm to be hit by a car, a car will hit me," Mahmood shrugged. "Whatever Allah wills will happen."

It sounded like an easy way to live, leaving everything to Allah, but what if you were inscribed, say, to be a gravedigger, and you wanted to be a doctor? When Baba was going to do something, he always said he'd do it "with the help of God," and I decided that I liked that better than being helpless in God's hands.

I dodged another pile of droppings and avoided a skinny dog with ulcers on his spine. Maybe he was inscribed to bite me, but he'd have to find an Arab.

Out of the mainstream, I could finally look up and around. Of the few women in sight, all but one were veiled, and without even seeing her face, I knew the undraped one was Jewish and undoubtedly a widow. If she'd had a husband, he'd be out buying food for the family like Baba—like any proper man.

As for the men, they were so distinctive that at one glance I could tell who most of them were, what they did, and where they came from. That's why I found it so hard to believe what Baba told us about the tourists. His plumbing contracts often took him to the hotels on Rashid Street, where the Europeans, he claimed, couldn't tell Jews from Arabs. I thought he was joking at first, because anyone could see that the *M'silmin* were browner, had broader jaws, round bowl haircuts, and noses shaped like the scimitars in the national museum. What's more, Jews wore suits and ties instead of *jubbas* and *dishdashas.* We couldn't be more different, I thought as I looked for Baba, who was lagging behind. I spotted him at once by his black *sadara* rising high above the other headgear.

Hanoon Market was at the western edge of *Mehalat-el'yhud,* the Jewish Quarter, so *sadaras* outnumbered head cloths. Though I saw an occasional *kaffiyah,* something rarer caught my eye—the bright-green turban that only a *Seyyid* was allowed to wear. I tried to get a close look at this direct descendant of Muhammad, but two of the starving street dogs blocked my way. They were snarling over a chunk of meat snatched from a passing cart, tugging it back and forth between them, fangs bloody and mouths foaming with saliva. I hoped it was only because they were hungry. Rabid animals also frothed, like the dog the *shurti* had to shoot a few weeks earlier. Nana wouldn't allow me out until word came that the policeman had killed it.

The *Seyyid,* I noticed, had also given the dogs a wide berth, and I wondered what Mahmood would say to that. Anyway, he was gone, so I stood in place, waiting for Baba to catch up. It was the same every morning. Father had too many friends and had to stop too many times to greet them. Once or twice, he might use the dialect we spoke "outside"—Islamic Arabic—but most of his hellos were in our own Yehudi.

I was more than usually impatient, both because of school and because it was Sunday and the Bedouin would be waiting. I enjoyed the market most when the desert Arabs were there, even though their presence meant the worst stench I ever smelled. Still a block away my nose was already running from the reek.

Another odor—equally strong but not unpleasant—told me that I was approaching the tea shop just before the turnoff to the market. A smoky whiff of it sneaked through the Bedouin stink, and I stopped to wait for Baba and watch the *kahwat al hashish* who sat inside the shop. They sometimes fell asleep at the table, dribbling spit and snoring, or jerked and twitched, then slid off their seats and sprawled on the floor. It was most entertaining.

I was peering in when Baba clapped me on the shoulder and shoved me, none too gently, in the opposite direction. Whatever "addicts" were, he made it clear that he didn't want me anywhere around them. There were several other cafes I was supposed to stay away from, frequented by men who, according to Baba, gobbled up small boys.

"Don't take candy from anyone," he warned. "It's only to make you sweet enough to eat."

S'hak said he knew what "homosexual" meant, but he wouldn't tell me that either.

I didn't mind being dragged off, because we were heading for the Bedouin, who spread themselves almost the entire width of Kambar Ali Street outside the market proper, so that entering or leaving, you had to pick your way through them. They didn't bother with shelves or scales like the stall merchants, but did all their business from stacks of baskets. If a man didn't own a basket, he'd tie his belt very tightly around his waist. This made the top of his ankle-length *dishdasha* into a warehouse, where he could keep incredible amounts of the most unlikely items. An old man once offered us four dozen eggs, and after he pulled them out, miraculously unbroken, there was still something bulging over his belt, alive and cackling.

In front, and downwind of the first desert women, the smell intensified, and I thought S'hak might be right about the camel urine. He claimed the women combed their hair with it to make it shine. Because I saw them every week, I was nonchalant about bare feet, stained red to the ankles, and faces bright blue with tattooed dots in intricate designs. By now, noserings were no novelty either, and lots of women had a baby slung in back, a second one on the arm, and another in the belly, which still left a hand free for selling. It took someone really startling to make me stare—someone like the girl bargaining with Baba.

She must have been wearing the wealth of an entire tribe. Along with the usual bits and pieces—the shells and silver charms and turquoise-colored stones to foil the Evil Eye—her neck and dress dripped amber beads and gold filigree and even wolf fangs. I couldn't count the rings on her fingers or the bracelets and anklets that tinkled and clanked, and the coins attached to her lacquer earrings were so heavy, her earlobes hung halfway to her shoulders. Best of all, she had an even dozen *ulba* balanced on her head, each a foot and a half around, eight inches deep, and filled to the brim with thin, runny yoghurt. When she nodded in agreement with something Baba said, the contents of the top container almost slurped onto the top of his *sadara.* Coming out, he told her, we'd buy an *ulba* and return it, empty, on our next trip to the market.

I was grateful that he hadn't bargained for any Bedouin milk, which came in three flavors, each worse than the others. Unfortunately, Nana and just about everyone else believed that goat's milk was the best remedy for measles and other assorted ailments. If the measles somehow survived goat's milk, mothers made their kids drink donkey's milk, and a really tough case might even require camel's milk, which is evil smelling, disgustingly oily—and often works. I think we got well simply to avoid swallowing another spoonful.

Beyond the Bedouin, we turned to the right, and the entire mile of Hanoon Market, the largest in Iraq, spread out before us. Officially, it consisted of some 400 stalls, managed by the most substantial merchants in Baghdad, but there were at least as many street peddlers who squatted just outside the enclosures, undercutting shop prices, clutching at passing customers, offering impossible bargains, swearing improbable oaths, arguing, imploring, kicking at the cats kept by everyone against the fat market rats, and sometimes even selling something. With all the cursing at competitors, the seizing of sleeves, the waving of fists in each others' faces, I never saw a single blow struck. Seconds after the abuse ended, all concerned would be laughing uproariously. It was absolute bedlam, and I found it all enchanting.

Baba was ahead of me, checking the fish stalls, and it was too crowded and I was too far away to tell whether he was talking to a Jew or an Arab. When I caught a flash of the man's *yashmagh,* I knew it was a *Mislim,* and coming closer, I recognized Kamal.

The *yashmagh* was as Arab as the *sadara* was Jewish, and I must admit, it was more inventive. Though everyone started with the same size square of cloth—first folding it into a triangle, then whipping it into a long strip—twining it around the skullcap, the *arakgeen,* was the artistic part. The kind of people Baba called "sharks" wound it on the diagonal, almost hiding one eye, which lent them a rakish look. Others twisted it into two perfect circles, like halos, and some appeared to have poked their heads through a random pile of rags. How a man used his *yashmagh* was just as individual. Kamal planted pencils in his, and many merchants made change from coins banked between the coils of cloth. In one way, however, all *yashmaghs* were identical. The why of it was beyond me, but every Arab passionately swore his honor on that particular piece of fabric. "By my *yashmagh*" was the best guarantee you could get.

While I was walking toward him, father had found his fish, and I was barely in time to hear the bargaining begin.

"For you, *Effendi,* 100 *fils.*" To a vendor, anyone who wore a clean *sadara* was automatically a gentleman, and so "*Effendi.*"

Baba hefted the big *shaboot* and held it to his nose. Only after pressing its lips apart to look inside, spreading its fins, and finally examining its eyes, did he respond with a slight grimace that plainly said the fish was inferior.

"It's too much for such a fish, but I'll give you forty *fils.*"

Kamal was obviously impressed with Baba's behavior. If father had offered him more, or if he hadn't shown sufficient contempt for the merchandise, he would have lost face. However, he was clearly a worthy opponent, so Kamal, completely ignoring his other customers, snatched the *shaboot* from Baba's hands and, holding it high above his head, appealed to Heaven. If you didn't know better, you'd really believe his outrage as he cried, "May I be stricken blind if such a fish is worth a *fils* less than I ask!"

It was a truly magnificent performance, enjoyed by all, but still the merest start. When Baba pursed his lips and turned to leave, Kamal let him take two steps before calling out, "But for you, *Ustah,* I will sacrifice this fish for eighty *fils.*"

"Ustah" was even more obsequious than *"Effendi,"* and I knew the big *shaboot* was ours. Not yet, of course, but soon. Baba bent to sniff again and snorted, "He must have died of old age. Fifty *fils.*"

At last, after swearing by all the prophets, Kamal turned up his palms in a gesture of resignation and moaned, "By my *yashmagh,* I can't let it go for less than fifty-five."

"By my *yashmagh*" meant the bargaining was over. Father paid, and the fish was wrapped in last week's *Al Ayam.* This morning, he'd been swimming in the Tigris, and tonight Nana would be scrubbing newsprint off his scales.

When shopping, Baba set his own pace, and at the next stop, unmindful of my fidgets, he held a hundred eggs up to the light before he found twenty he could trust. I tried to tug him toward the *Khistawi* dates, so soft and sugary they started to melt before you could close your mouth. The farmers picked them at dawn, and those that weren't consumed by shortly after sundown turned to slime. I should have saved my strength; he wouldn't budge or buy. Baba was stubborn too. *Khistawi* were for *Shabbat,* and he bought them on Friday, not before.

My itchiness disappeared as soon as we arrived at the meat stalls. For me, this was the heart of the market. Because Hanoon catered mainly to Jews, everything hanging from the huge iron hooks was *kasher.* Slung high in the air, the freshly slaughtered, steaming carcasses revolved in slow, hypnotic circles.

As each customer chose his cut, the butcher expertly carved it out. S'hak always averted his eyes when the knife went in, but I stood on tiptoe, admiring the man's technique. Actually, I preferred the Arab butchers because their carcasses still contained all the astonishing innards that ours threw out. I could have studied the intricacies of the sacs and lobes and loops all day. Baba was amused. "My son is studying to be a butcher or a surgeon," he'd say. He thought he was making a joke, but as a matter of fact, I'd already decided to be a doctor.

This morning, as per Nana's instructions, he chose a shoulder chunk of lamb and asked for a large piece of *lieh.* Most of what little fat there was on lamb was in the tail, and sizzling from the oven, the *lieh* gushed deliciously when bitten into. Suddenly I was starving, and Baba's stomach must have grumbled too, because he raced through the rest of the list. Nana would start breakfast as soon as she heard us open the door.

In moments, there was soft, white cheese in the *zinbeel,* and he'd chosen the butter he wanted from among dozens of densely woven canvas sacks. The merchant weighed the empty crock we'd carried from home, then at the first scoop dug out exactly the amount ordered. I marveled at his skill, but Baba was suspicious. When it came to weights, he trusted no one.

The Jewish and Arab traders were alike in that they cheated everyone impartially. Those who used their thumbs or stood so you couldn't see their scales were easy to guard against, but Baba was forever on watch for the more inventive vendors, such as those who unbalanced the balance arms or exchanged the iron weights for lighter alloys. And he swept off the bed of every scale before putting his purchase on. "They're such thieves," he warned, "their *paper* might be made of lead."

In short order, we had rutabagas for baking and beets for boiling, along with tomatoes, eggplants, and the okra that Nana was always sure we'd forget and that—unfortunately, as far as I was concerned—father never did. *Ta'ghouzi* was next, and since it was one of his favorite foods, the selection took a little longer. *Ta'ghouzi* looked like stretched-out, skinny cucumbers, which you ate raw with salt after scraping off the bitter skins. I liked them just a trifle less than okra, and I hated okra. Another one of the many things I didn't understand about growing up was what it did to your appetite. Not one kid I knew could stand okra, but most adults adored it.

From a distance, the fruit stalls were treasure chests right out of *A Thousand and One Nights.* Grapes, tinted dozens of different colors, glinted in the sun like great heaps of gemstones. Baba bought those first, then added apricots, fresh and dried, and tiny, sweet red apples for us and large, green sour apples for himself. The basket was bulging, but even if it burst, I knew we wouldn't get away without some *adas.*

You certainly didn't buy *adas* for their beauty. They were small, black, misshapen, and full of spines, tough as goat gristle and bitter to the taste. Nevertheless, everybody bought *adas* because they whitened your teeth, freshened your breath, cured your cold, and when necessary, set your bowels straight. Nana swore by them, so with the *adas* tucked safely in the *zinbeel,* all we had to do was pick up the *ulba* from the Bedouin girl, and we could go home.

Chopping sounds floated across the *hosh* to the big family room where we men of the house were waiting for breakfast. On the other side of the square open courtyard, I could see Nana in the kitchen, sitting a few inches off the floor on one hard wood *takhta* and vigorously hacking scallions on another. Unloading the *zinbeel,* Nazima had set ten eggs aside, so breakfast would be a savory *ajja b'kerrath.*

By this time next week, we'd be eating in the dining room upstairs instead of here on the first floor in the enormous summer *neem.* This, our ground floor family room, was actually below ground level, and windowless on the street side to shut out the sun. The tile floors of the huge room helped to keep it cool, and a ceiling fan stirred the oppressive summer air enough to make it bearable.

Once we moved to the winter floor above, Nana would have to navigate the stairs a dozen times during each meal, so we stayed below for eating long after we'd moved up a flight for everything else.

Nazima was too busy to mind her, so my infant sister, Daisy, was with us, sitting like a small queen on her handmade *kia'ada,* with the practical little pot that slid in and out at the bottom. Baba was playing with her, and seeing how he beamed, no one would ever suspect how big a disappointment she'd been.

Father had felt that one girl in the family was enough, and when this one appeared instead of the son he expected, he said he was going to name her Yazie, which in our dialect means "enough." For once, Nana put her foot down, but not all the way. Since she had an English friend named Daisy, and Daisy rhymed with Yazie, they compromised on that. Right under my entry in the ancient family Bible, Baba inscribed "Daisy Aziza Ahuva," and immediately forgot that he didn't really need another daughter.

Within minutes, Nana's wooden clogs clattered across the *hosh,* heralding breakfast. She carried one of the three kerosene stoves that could be lifted individually out of the kitchen counter, and Nazima was close behind with the big bowl of omelet mix. S'hak brought up the rear, almost hidden behind a two-foot-wide wheel of *khibz.* One of my jobs was going to the baker to fetch fresh bread every morning, but S'hak generally had to do it. I guess that's why I felt a little guilty when I pulled him away from the table while he was still swallowing. My school was on the way to his, and S'hak had been delegated to drop me off.

We were headed out when someone slammed down the door knocker. No one but Baba's older brother banged like that, but Uncle Ezra never came until after four, when he finished work. I figured he might be stopping by to see me off to school, and I rushed to meet him, my arms extended for his usual bear-hug embrace, but he brushed me aside and went straight to Baba.

Ordinarily, I'd have yelled my head off at such uncivil treatment, but I was silenced by uncle's expression, and by the streak of blood he hadn't quite wiped from his forehead. As he spoke to father—too far off for us to overhear—Baba's face assumed the same expression of shock and despair, then quickly blackened into anger. Something bad, very bad, had happened. On any other day, I'd have hung around until I had at least a hint of it, but I was almost late already.

I had to pull on S'hak's arm to propel him along the hall. Through the open grillwork, I could still see the two familiar figures, heads together in close conversation. A voice rose sharply, a voice so harsh and bitter I could hardly believe it was Baba's.

"If we had good sense, we'd have registered as *M'silmin.*"

I turned to S'hak for an explanation, but my brother's face was just as frightening as my father's voice. I demanded that he tell me what the words meant, but he rushed me out the door and raced ahead. All he'd say was "You'll understand when you're older."

That's what he always said, but when he'd said it before, he'd always snickered. This time he wasn't smiling.

2

The *raudha* was a disappointment from the first day, which is just about as long as I lasted. It was sort of a room-size playpen, and I discovered with disgust that they even *called* it a nursery school. Nurseries were for infants, not serious scholars, and I began to work on Nana again.

The following week, I was attending my first *tambidi.* Preliminary school, while merely an advanced kind of kindergarten, was certainly a step up, but still not the learning experience I'd envisioned. I stuck this one out for about ten days, until the black-and-blue marks were too numerous to hide from Nana. The class bully, who was five and a half to my four, and twice the size of anyone else, sat in the next seat and pinched me viciously at every opportunity.

Other than R'fail's fingers, only one thing made any sort of impression during my stay at this school. In Bible study the teacher said, "When the Messiah comes, the Jews will be delivered."

"Delivered where?" I wanted to ask, but he proceeded without a pause, as if this startling bit of information was already known to all. After class, a boy who'd been there since the term began informed me that it meant the Jews would be the masters over *M'silmin.* "They'll be our slaves," he stated, and walked away before I could decide if he was simply foolish or making fun of me. Anyway, his explanation didn't have anything to do with what disturbed me . . . the idea of delivery. I loved Baghdad and didn't wish to be delivered anywhere but Kambar Ali Street.

When I so declared myself at dinner, S'hak spat his soup out, laughing, but a single look from Baba shut him up. Father's expression was the same he'd worn with Uncle Ezra, as he quietly enlightened me.

"Jews don't make slaves," he said, "but some people try to make slaves of Jews. When the *Messiah* arrives, we will be delivered from those people and live in peace wherever we like."

I was greatly relieved until he added, in the grim voice I'd heard only once before, "The *goyim* ride Jews like donkeys!" Then he pressed his lips tightly together, as if the words had escaped against his will.

While I was happy to hear that I wouldn't have to move, none of the rest made much sense to me. The sheikhs had slaves, though slavery was illegal, but the slaves were black, and I wasn't black or a slave and certainly not a donkey. When I left the house alone, Nana always warned me to "be careful of the *M'silmin,*" but if they were the *goyim* who rode Jews, why did Baba's business friends, who were mostly *M'silmin,* treat me like a little prince?

It's true that we lived among Jews, and all those close to us were Jewish, but the Christians and Shiahs and Sunnahs also had their own quarters, and the well-to-do Arabs who lived in Abbakhana didn't mix with the thieves and beggars of Abu Shibl any more than we mixed outside our own. I argued that we were all Iraqis, and if my cousins and I sometimes played *M'silmin* and Jews among ourselves, it was just to have two sides, like soccer teams.

S'hak thought that was pretty funny too. "When you grow up and get some sense," he snorted, "you won't have to pretend. There's another side all right!"

Baba silenced him with a sharp "Yazie!" Enough! I was old enough to be a slave and a donkey, it seems, but not old enough to know why.

Since the secular school hadn't worked out, Baba arranged for my admittance to a *midrash*—a strict religious institution—where my Great-Uncle M'nashi would be my *m'allem.* As his nephew, I called him *Khalu,* of course, but the others addressed him as *'Stayi,* the most respectful title for "teacher" in our dialect, elevating him even above a *m'allem.*

For a short time, I felt very superior because of my relationship with the master, but within hours I was disabused of that feeling because all the boys laughingly referred to him as *Lulu* behind his back. *Lulu* means "pearls," and in the oblique Iraqi way, they meant the exact opposite. As one of the boys put it, "He spits shit." I would have liked to fight for the family honor, but by the time I heard this appraisal, I was in complete accord.

However, this *midrash* would have been a disaster with Moses himself as *m'allem.* It was located in the basement of a thousand-year-old synagogue, so close to the city's high water table that the atmosphere was almost liquid. With only a few window slits, high on the scabby walls, the dank space was more suitable for mushroom culture than teaching kids. The ceiling "sweep" was smaller than ours at home and nonelectric. Manned by pairs of students in shifts, it barely moved the stale air. The same dust motes and disease germs could have remained suspended for centuries.

We had no desks, and the class of eighty sat cross-legged on long benches a few inches from the floor. When the *'Stayi* entered, we were expected to leap to our feet and stand until ordered to do otherwise. To ask a question, one raised a finger and hoped to be recognized. In any case, the question could only pertain to a precise point in the lesson then under way. *'Stayi* had no "pearls" of his own to bestow. His answers were all taken straight from the text.

What he did have was an awesome temper, a long, flexible stick that whistled when he whipped it, and a standard of discipline that an army sergeant would have envied. At the end of my second week, he unjustly accused me of whispering when, for once, I was innocent. When I rose from my seat to protest, which in his eyes was unforgivable defiance, he hit me with the whistling stick. I'd never been beaten before, and as I ran from the room, I told *Lulu*—and Lulu, not *Khalu,* is what I called him—that he'd never have another crack at me. The weal on my arm was well developed when I reached home, and an angry enough red to send Nana into shock. Of course I'd rubbed it some to strengthen my case.

Without too much argument, I was off to still another secular school, where I was again treated like an adorable infant. Again I rebelled, and

Baba—by now as resolved as I was to see me successfully started—enrolled me at Rachel Shahmoon, which was run by yet another set of relatives. That I kept running into relatives wasn't as coincidental as it seems, since Baba had had eleven brothers and sisters and Nana was one of thirteen. Some of the family had died before I was born, several were in Palestine, and one in Persia, but with husbands and wives and second marriages and assorted offspring, it would have been hard to escape my uncles, aunts, and cousins.

One day at Rachel Shahmoon was more than enough. When I refused to return, insisting that I was ready for real school, Baba agreed to my being tested. To everyone's surprise but mine, I passed easily and was placed in the first grade with the six-year-olds. At long last, after four false starts, I was on my way.

By custom and choice, because education was of such concern to Jews, each Jewish community built, administered, and supported its own schools, both secular and religious, right up to university level. Almost all the *M'silmin* were illiterate, and even in Baghdad, only fifteen percent could read, so parents and teachers routinely spurred us on by asking, "Do you want to be like an Arab?"

Two years after I started school, I had more unanswered questions than on the day I entered, especially as to relations between Jews and Arabs. The differences between us were clearer than ever, and I recognized that differences often led to disagreement, but most grown-up Jews wouldn't discuss the subject, and if they did, they looked around first to see who was listening, as if they couldn't talk openly in their own country.

Naturally no sane Jew would casually stroll around the Abu Shibl section of the city, but you wouldn't walk straight into a pack of jackals either. However, everyone acted as if *every Mislim* was an alien being. No, it was even sillier than that. Sometimes the Jews of Baba's age acted as if *they* were the aliens and not really Iraqis at all. Didn't they know that there were Jews in Iraq long before Islam arrived on the scene?

As for myself, I was a supernationalist. The history texts, government-approved and prescribed for all schools, were as crammed with drama and romance as any of Scheherazade's stories. According to them, Jews and Arabs had always lived in perfect harmony, "even when our beloved country bled under the oppressive rule of foreign despots." When we arrived at the chapter in which Iraq gained independence, my heart pounded and I restrained a cheer only with a supreme effort of will.

I wasn't merely a patriot, but a raging royalist. My special affinity for the King probably stemmed from the fact that Baba had put the plumbing in the royal palace. After a few *M'silmin* had blown themselves up, my father was called in because no one else in Baghdad understood steam boilers.

I often caught a glimpse of King Ghazi zooming about the city in one of his six automobiles, and sometimes I watched from the roof at night to see if I could spot the Mercedes he'd had finished in phosphorescent paint so that it glowed in the dark. My cousin Haron said the Bedouins ran screaming from the fiery demon that scorched through the desert. I missed the Mercedes, but one day on Rashid Street, our broad main boulevard, I saw the King close up in a long black car, and when I waved, our eyes met and he waved back, to me alone. It was the highlight of my whole six years.

So history and my heart said the *M'silmin* and I were brothers and equal citizens of this best and most beautiful of all lands. On the other hand, the entire family was hysterical when I was late getting home one day and they discovered that I'd dropped in to see an Arab teacher on our school staff. Impressed with my reading ability, Karim had offered me the use of his private library. Right off, I'd found an unexpurgated copy of *A Thousand and One Nights*—all those at school were heavily abridged—and four hours later was still engrossed in picking out the pornographic passages and committing them to memory.

By the time I got home, Baba had the *shurta* out searching for me, S'hak and Haron were scouring the alleys that even the police wouldn't enter, and Nana's face was crepey from crying. When I explained where I'd been, Baba echoed, "His *house?* You went to his *house?*" and Nana stopped crying, but only so she could shriek.

I tried to tell them how Karim's mother, who wore a veil even behind her own walls, had plied me with sugar cookies, but Baba interrupted. I was never to do such a thing again. Never! I didn't bother to ask why, because I anticipated the same stock answer: "You'll understand when you're older."

This time, though, I'd have preferred that to what Baba actually said. "You're old enough," he scolded, "to have some consideration for Nana, especially now." I knew he was talking about the baby, which was due to arrive in about a week. By now, I'd found out about babies. I also knew that men often slept by themselves because women were sometimes unclean in a way men never were. I had yet to figure out what way that was, but the mysteries were beginning to unravel.

Exactly a week later, when I zoomed into the house after school, Nazima shushed me in a surprisingly sharp manner. I was to be extra quiet and stay out from underfoot. Baba was home, and Dr. Kahni was upstairs with Nana.

Across the courtyard, I saw Aunt Gourjiah, my mother's next-to-youngest sister, smashing at dough on the *takhta* as if beating off an attack. Having a baby seemed to affect women strangely, even when it was someone else's. With nowhere else to go, I wandered into the kitchen, but hardly to a warm welcome. Aunt Gourjiah was too busy beating the dough to death. A little later, S'hak also slipped in. So he'd been excluded too.

On hearing footsteps hurrying down the stairs, all of us dashed for the door. Dr. Kahni and Baba spoke briefly at the foot of the stairwell before Dr. Kahni departed.

I overheard the word "girl," which was good news for me. I was still the youngest son. Unquestionably, Baba would have preferred a boy, but he hadn't cried when Daisy was born, and I was surprised to see that he was weeping now, though he bent his head and tried to hide it. Maybe two girls in a row were just too much to bear. But my sister was crying too, and my skin started to prickle. Nazima couldn't care less about the sex of a baby; she loved them all.

Now I was scared, and so were Aunt Gourjiah and S'hak. We raced to the family room, so filled with smoke from father's incessant cigarettes that my eyes teared and my nose ran like a river.

Father was huddled with the women, their heads so close, I couldn't catch a hint of what was happening, and when I tugged at Baba's sleeve, he simply shook it free. Nazima finally became aware of me, but all she'd say was that I had a baby sister and that I could see my mother in the morning.

In bed that night I pestered S'hak until he opened up. Nana had nearly died, he told me. "She just kept bleeding and bleeding. It wouldn't stop. Dr. Kahni says she'll be all right, but there must be no more babies."

I lay awake for a very long time, trying to sort out the jumble of emotions that confused and frightened me. I was afraid for Nana, sorry for father, secretly pleased that I would forever be the youngest boy, and ashamed of myself for being pleased. More disturbing than all the rest, because I couldn't connect it with anything I'd ever felt before, was a strange sadness, a sense of loss, knowing that the family was at a sort of end, that what we were was all we'd ever be. No one had ever explained, in so many words, that death was natural as long as there was birth to balance it, but somehow I knew. "No more babies" had a hollow and ominous sound about it, like a heavy lid slamming shut forever.

I moved closer to S'hak, but he was deep in sleep, a million miles away from me. The house was so still, I might have been the only one awake in all of Baghdad. Curling into the smallest ball possible, I pulled the covers completely over me. Growing up was proving to be a harder, lonelier business than I'd bargained for.

Nana regained her strength quickly, and Espirance was a bubbling delight from the day she was born. She was the kind of infant who makes strangers in the street smile. As for the family, while we all adored her, it was soon understood that Espirance was *my* baby. I took the role of big brother seriously, and right from the start a special bond existed between us.

The day S'hak finally let me join his gang, I thought it was in recognition of my new maturity. My previous overtures had always been rebuffed, but this time he responded with an enthusiasm that should have stirred suspicion. I didn't begin to wonder until S'hak's best friend, Anwar, examining me from head to foot, announced, "He's exactly what we need." At fourteen, Anwar generally acted as if *no one* needed a six-year-old.

For once S'hak explained. The day before, one of our group, a boy named Shaool, had been beaten senseless by a bunch of Arab boys. He'd been careless, of course. He shouldn't have been wandering alone on the very edge of a "safe" area, especially in Ramzi's orbit. Ramzi's mob was famous for picking off strays. There were invisible lines which Jewish kids just didn't cross or even come close to without plenty of company. With a few exceptions—such as Abu Shibl—adults could go anywhere, but Arab boys routinely jumped a young Jew who overstepped certain unseen boundaries.

S'hak said they'd knocked out two of Shaool's teeth, then kicked him in the tail when he bent to retrieve them. "With shoes on," Anwar added. "He can't sit down."

Shaool had to be avenged, and Anwar had a plan in which he promised I'd play a vital part. "In fact, it wouldn't work without you," he amended with a toothy smile.

The word he used was "decoy," but to put it bluntly, I was merely bait. Ramzi had been spotted near the rice bazaar. My assignment was to lure him off the crowded street and into ambush. S'hak and the others would be waiting in the narrow alley that opened slitlike, almost imperceptibly, off Kambar Ali Street, twisted in a hundred loops and turns between the houses, branched off into scores of cul-de-sacs, then ended, as indiscernibly as it began, back on Kambar Ali Street, a stone's throw from its start. Along its course, you could exit into several markets. Those unfamiliar with its outlets, however, might wander about for hours and always end up at another impasse. Even the police avoided entering the alley. Only kids like us, who lived nearby and spent their early years exploring had free and easy access.

Following orders, I advanced on Ramzi from the rear, grabbed his belt, and yanked it hard. He grunted, spun around, and raised his arm to hit me; but when he saw how small I was, he hesitated for a second. Afraid he'd let me off, making me a failure at my first engagement, I called him *"kalb,"* then *"ibn'elkalb"* for added emphasis. I saw at once that one "dog" would have been enough. I should have fled at that—and flung the "offspring of a dog" over my shoulder. As it was, he almost had me before I made it to the alley exit. A minute later, S'hak and the others had *him;* they bashed him pretty thoroughly, but stopped before they did real damage and dragged him to within a few feet of the street. As we departed in the opposite direction—only to double back to reach the street some distance away—we heard Ramzi shouting for his gang to get us. Unseen, we watched them gather at the mouth of the alley to grab us as we filtered out. Soon all of us were safely home while Ramzi waited at the empty mousehole.

The escapade was most enjoyable. Even so, I didn't see why we had to sneak around when seeking vengeance. "An eye for an eye" was in the Bible; we could retaliate with honor, I contended. Why couldn't we fight out in the open, I asked S'hak. Fair and square. Six of us and six of them.

Accustomed to evasive answers and often to none at all, I couldn't believe my ears when S'hak said, "Sit down. I think it's time we talked. There are things you ought to know."

I loved to learn new words, but "minority" was one I could have lived without. S'hak defined it as "a lesser group," and like it or not, he said, I was a lifetime member. I didn't like being a lesser *anything.* There were only 120,000 Jews in all Iraq, S'hak told me, which sounded like a lot until I heard the *M'silmin* total. Millions! A great "majority"—another new word for me—"and," he said, "the majority makes the rules." One of the main rules, according to S'hak, was that Jews must stay in their place, and the *M'silmin* would tell them where that place was. For once, S'hak was serious and *I* was snickering.

"That's silly," I scoffed. "No one tells Baba what to do. He's the boss . . . the *M'silmin* work for *him.*"

S'hak replied that our father had powerful friends, "and when you can do what nobody else can do, and you spread the money around so everybody benefits, they leave you alone. No one kills a goose that lays golden eggs."

I countered with Uncle Ezra. If S'hak was right, how had uncle come by *his* business? It was the most profitable gas concession in the city, supplying all the trucks that served the brickworks, as well as Baghdad's power plant. What's more, I added triumphantly, he was right in the middle of a *M'silmin* district.

"And look what happened to Uncle Ezra," S'hak responded.

I remembered then . . . the blood on uncle's face, the bitterness of Baba's voice, the oddity of what he said about "good sense" and registration.

Uncle Ezra had been attacked by jealous Arabs, S'hak explained, Arabs resentful that a Jew was making so much money. His being in their midst just aggravated the "offense." The onslaught had come without a warning, "as it always does," my brother added. It hadn't been the first attack, he said, nor would it be the last.

When S'hak went on to explain about the census, I realized, to my dismay, that Baba must believe as he did. I hadn't known a thing about the census, since I was only three when it was ordered, while S'hak was all of eight, and old enough to take it in.

Until the end of World War I, Iraq wasn't a state at all, but merely part of the Ottoman Empire. When the Turks departed from Iraq, they took with them all the population records, and our government was left no idea of who was where or in what numbers. In 1933, for the first official count since independence, each family head was therefore asked to mark down every member of his household by name, age, sex, and religion. The last item became a loophole for some frightened or ambitious Jews.

In the absence of a checklist, a man could declare himself and his family whatever it was best to be, and in an Arab state—if what S'hak said was fact—it was best to be a *Mislim.* But Baba hadn't made us *M'silmin,* and it was only momentary anger, aroused by uncle's bloodied head, that had inspired him to speak so. Down deep, he *didn't* agree with S'hak. Even brothers fought, as well I knew, but after fighting, we forgave each other. It was the same with us and the Arabs, I contended. S'hak shook his head and sighed despairingly, but I was satisfied with my analysis.

If any doubts remained, they dissipated with the dawn of *Simchat Torah.* The Rejoicing of the Torah was as old as history, and for the last 600 years,

Haddads had kept the holiday right here. We Jews had been around when the area was still called Babylonia, so who could out Iraqi us?

Last *Shabbat,* we'd listened to the cantor read the final verses of the fifth book of the Bible. Next Saturday, the reading cycle would resume and go on for another year, from the first line of the first book to the last line of the fifth book. This *Shabbat,* the entire Torah would be honored before beginning it anew. It took my breath away when the cantor intoned, "From the time the Word was given, in every synagogue across the Seven Seas, and in all the world where Jews reside, the Five Books of the Bible have been read as we have read them, and as they ever will be."

Being downstairs with the men while the women sat up in the balcony was most agreeable, but after making my obeisance to the Ark on the wall facing toward the Temple in Jerusalem, I'd have to settle down and stay there while my stomach rumbled. Since we couldn't eat breakfast before the *Shabbat* prayers, the early service was a test of will.

I held out longer than I had last year—this time until I'd kissed the sacred scrolls—but once again my appetite defeated self-control, and I excused myself. The bathroom, I told Baba. Instead, I headed straight upstairs. Nana always smuggled in some food from home. Though it was cheating, every mother of a son my age brought edibles to tide us over.

Downstairs again, still chewing, I missed a portion of the chant, and Baba bent and brushed away some crumbs I'd let escape. The corners of his lips twitched, and it occurred to me, as it never had before, that Baba had been six himself a century or so ago.

Even with repeated "toilet" breaks, the service seemed unending. For me, the greatest joy of *Simchat Torah* lay just outside the synagogue, and this year's *sukkah* was especially inviting. Essentially, the structure was the same each autumn, a sort of airy arbor erected in observance of the harvest, its three sides made of slender poles placed a hand's breadth apart, with a roof of palm leaves on a latticework of wood, all serving as a framework for the decorations. These made the yearly difference.

There were ropes and braids and complicated skeins of herbs and berries, fans of grain stalks, and bright cascades of every kind of fruit and produce that Iraqi earth provided. Families competed fiercely for the honor of contributing, and Baba's offering was always found acceptable.

The *sukkah* compensated for the hours of stale indoor air. The sky was dustless, at its brightest blue, and everyone, on making the required seven circuits of the *sukkah,* agreed that Baba's garland was the best. Having helped him pick the score of perfect pomegranates, I basked in his reflected glory.

We were in the synagogue again that afternoon, sitting through a second service, after which we kids went wild. Bursting from the building, we tore around the *sukkah,* kicking up our heels like uncaged animals and almost drowning out the singing of the adults with our shrieks. Benignly, and also in his own self interest, the cantor looked the other way and let it happen. With an evening service still to come, the more explosive energy that we exhausted, the less we'd squirm while he was speaking.

Because of Joseph, the final service of the day was unexpectedly the most exciting. The best friend of my cousin Haron, Joseph was a favorite of mine as well. Several days ago, his wife had had a baby, and since it was a boy and since sundown marked the first *Shabbat* before the *brith,* Joseph was standing at the Ark to be acknowledged. If the baby had been female, he'd be sitting here with us, unglorified. Only an *ab-haben,* a recent father of a son, is invited to the Torah, and only infant boys have entire congregations singing hymns on their behalf.

"May he be a member of the faith . . . may the Messiah come in his day . . . may he see peace in the world. . . ."

I hoped Joseph could hear me above the others. From the balcony, the women showered him with candy, shouting, "May he enjoy sweetness from the child." Joseph got redder and redder, and the more he blushed, the more the other men roared with laughter. Leaving the Torah, he passed close to me, and I pressed my last piece of candy into his hand. He smiled and put it in his pocket, pushing it well down, as if the sticky bit was something precious.

Since Joseph also lived on Kambar Ali Street, a few doors past our house, he walked us home, then went on by himself. Hungry after the long and active day, we sat down to dinner as soon as we arrived. While Baba was making *kiddush* before the meal, we heard a sound like the banging of a distant door, and S'hak jokingly remarked, "I bet he woke the baby."

Before Nana had filled half our plates, we were interrupted by another, closer noise. Fists were banging at our door, and when Baba opened it, Haron fell through. Chalk-white, eyes puffed with unshed tears, he shouted, "They killed Joseph! The bastards killed Joseph!"

3

In the following weeks, Baba had to allow twice the usual time to reach the market. Every other minute, someone stopped him to discuss the murder. He'd motion me to go on by myself, and if I dawdled, glare at me until I drifted out of earshot. On looking back, I often saw him reaching in his pocket for a piece of paper and reading from it to the friends who paused to talk. Their faces would turn even grimmer than before, but why they looked that way remained a mystery. I recognized the paper as a letter we'd received from Uncle Eliahu, but Baba's brother was in Palestine. What did his letter have to do with Joseph's death?

The men stood close and spoke in murmurs. I noticed that no more than two or three would gather in a group, and no group lingered long. The muted voices were unnatural and eerie. Once, though, someone waved a copy of the morning paper, pointed to an article and cried aloud, "It's the same as always. They fight each other and the Jews get killed!" Baba shushed him hastily and looked around to see if anyone had overheard. I ducked behind a cart before I realized that he was checking on the *M'silmin,* not on me.

Upon leaving, the agitated man had dropped his paper, but when I picked it up, I couldn't find anything to justify his outburst. The front page, to which he'd pointed, contained a picture of the King, a piece about the army, and another praising our Prime Minister. All it boiled down to was that the army liked the King, and the Prime Minister thought that "nationalism" would be nice. Another word I'd never heard.

After dinner, I continued studying the stories, searching for a clue, and Baba was amused by my intensity until I asked him to explain what the Prime Minister and the King and army had to do with killing Jews, especially Joseph. And as long as I was in that deep—because now, of course, he knew I'd overheard, I also asked about Uncle Eliahu's letter.

Baba stared as if I'd sprouted horns or scales, then blinked his eyes and said the words that I'd been waiting for.

"If you ask such questions, I guess you're old enough to know the answers."

He plucked his *sibha* from his pocket, and from the way he squeezed the beads, I saw the talk would be a serious one indeed. Ordinarily, the smooth, black oblongs slipped along their string like fluid through his fingers. Just for an instant, I was tempted to stop him. S'hak had been serious too, and I'd hated what he had to say.

Baba spoke slowly and without emotion, sounding like a conscientious teacher who disliked the lesson he was laying out. First ascertaining that I knew the meaning of "monarchy," he said the Prime Minister was against that form of rule and wanted us to have another sort of government, with himself as head. Since this required that the King step down, and since the King refused to abdicate, he'd have to be abolished in what Baba called a "coup." But to make a coup and overthrow the monarchy, the Prime Minister had to have the army's support, and the army was loyal to the King.

I was glad to hear it because I also loved King Ghazi, but where did Joseph enter into all of this? Baba held up his hand, halting my attempt to interrupt him. The lesson wasn't ended.

Without the backing of the army, he went on, the Prime Minister had to hatch another scheme to seize control, and he'd decided to create chaos in the country. He'd bring business to a halt in Baghdad and the other cities, and when paralysis set in and people suffered, they'd blame the government and riot for a new regime.

Baba paused to clear his throat, then resumed in such a throttled voice, I had to strain to hear him say, "And that's where we come in. When the *M'silmin* want to kill one another, they begin by killing Jews."

Word for word, it was almost what the man on the street had said, but this was *father!* If he'd screamed it out, I couldn't have been more shocked and scared. My expression must have shaken Baba, because he made a conscious effort to be cool and brisk.

"In Baghdad," he instructed, "the simplest way to cripple business is to keep the Jews at home. Do that and the whole economy will crumble. Start some rumors, spread unrest, encourage demonstrations, and let nature take its course. When the hungry mobs rise up in anger, the King will have to call the army out to keep control, but this will only strengthen the revolt. As soon as blood begins to run, taking over the country will be easy. But the whole thing starts with stopping Jews from doing business."

He hesitated, and I understood that there was worse to come.

Weeks ago, Baba continued, by the Prime Minister's secret order, assassination squads had been assigned to roam the city. Their job was to pick off a Jew or two in different areas of Baghdad every day or so. The deaths were indiscriminate, the intervals irregular. The only reason for the random murders was to terrify Jews into staying off the streets, thus bringing business to a standstill. "Joseph," he said, "was just the latest." Because he was the youngest to be killed, and on his happiest day—a Holy Day, as well—Joseph's death had been traumatic to the entire community, but many families were also sitting *shiva* for their own.

Almost hardest to accept was that I hadn't been aware of anything at all unusual. The morning market was as mobbed as ever, and the synagogue had positively swarmed with people—and suddenly I understood. We hadn't panicked. We Jews refused to be imprisoned by our fear. I felt a surge of pride, and just as if he'd seen inside me, Baba said, "It'll stop as soon as they decide it isn't working."

That left Uncle's letter. Baba handed it to me without preamble, but since I'd never heard of Nazis or the Grand Mufti, most of it made little sense to me. Uncle wrote, "There are as many Germans in Palestine as Arabs, all here to make propaganda, no matter what their passports say." They preached anti-Semitism on the radio and in their magazines; for illiterates, he said, "they even publish 'comic' books about the Jews. And Arab kids have learned to make swastikas on Jewish doors."

But nothing in the letter seemed related to our situation. Then I read, "The Arabs stopped a bus and killed two Jews," and on the second page, "Every month now, hundreds come from Syria and Iraq to join something called the Committee for the Defense of Palestine. They're burning the crops and shooting our women and children."

Coming from Iraq? Watching me repeatedly reread the sentence, Baba reached for the letter. Briefly—both of us now wanting to be done with it—he expanded on the Germans: They were arming and encouraging the Arabs to "cleanse" Palestine of both the British, who ruled under a mandate from the League of Nations, and the Jews.

I tried to shut my ears when he said the man who led the *M'silmin* murderers was an Iraqi, an army officer named Fawzi al-Kawukji. I learned that there were Arabs right here in Iraq who liked the Germans and listened when they spoke. In minutes, Palestine had moved much closer.

Soon after our talk, Baba went to visit Uncle Eliahu. When he told Nana he was going, she wept, and for once father was defensive. Ordinarily he simply acted; he didn't explain his actions. The sudden journey, I assumed, meant that Baba, too, was seeking answers.

I'd been searching for a weak spot in what he and S'hak had been saying, and the night before father left, I thought I'd found one. If he could travel freely, what was there to fear? My triumph lasted only until he showed me his passport. Baba, I discovered, was officially a Persian, along with lots of other long-established, solidly Iraqi Jews.

Originally Iraqi, our family had for centuries shuttled back and forth between Iraq and Persia; Baba had just happened to be Persian when Iraq achieved its independence. At that juncture, any resident could opt to be Iraqi, or retain the passport he already held. Father kept his Persian papers, and now, as a Persian citizen, he was able to embark for Palestine.

"Without this," Baba waved the book at me, "I wouldn't get an exit visa in a million years."

My mother's eyes were wet from the time the trip was first mentioned until the moment my father was safely back. After his departure, but before he passed from sight, she splashed the threshold of the house with salt and water to wash off any evil that might otherwise pursue him. While she worried every second he was gone, I awaited his return just as anxiously, hoping he'd tell me that uncle had been overwrought. Perhaps he'd been reporting rumors or exaggerating minor incidents. Before Baba reappeared, however, those hopes were blotted out—and by the Baghdad press. Overnight, all the news appeared to be from Palestine, and everything I saw supported Uncle Eliahu's gloomy outlook.

Day by day, the papers gleefully announced each new attack on "Zionists who occupy our sacred Arab soil." The tone was always gloating, the destruction gorily detailed.

Although I'd heard the word, I couldn't define "Zionist," but judging from the articles, to be a Zionist you also had to be a Jew. In fact, the way some stories read, "Zionist" seemed to be a synonym for "Jew." That seemed strange, since almost everyone I knew was Jewish, and I'd never known a Zionist.

By the time Baba was back, I had a thousand pressing questions to ask of him, but somehow he was always too busy for a session like our last. That had evidently been more than he'd bargained for. As for Palestine, all he'd say was "It was bad, but it's getting better." As he'd predicted, the assassinations here in Baghdad had been halted, and he dismissed the articles I'd saved to show him as "only propaganda." As Baba saw it—or *said* he saw it—everything was back to normal.

No one but Haron ever spoke again of Joseph, and when I asked him how the members of the congregation could forget so soon, he answered that they hadn't. "They've just learned to live with it." We were talking in the hallway of our house, and Baba couldn't help but overhear. Well aware of that, Haron spoke as if issuing a challenge.

Baba's head snapped up, and for an instant I was sure his eyes were shooting flames. But the light quickly flickered out, and, unexpectedly, he nodded in agreement. "Yes, you're right," he told Haron. "And when you've lived a few more years, you'll *also* learn to live with it."

Haron started to respond, but Baba walked away. I didn't know what to make of the exchange, and my cousin wasn't any aid at all, merely muttering disgustedly, "They're all the same. Even the very best of them are all the same."

For awhile at least, I decided I was through with asking questions. Every answer only muddled me a little more, and my feelings were at odds with almost everyone's. Baba, for example, had Arab friends he much preferred to many Jews, but I noticed that when with them, he wasn't quite himself—not exactly edgy, but extra controlled, as if he couldn't relax that one last muscle. And yet he said that when a *Mislim* was a true friend to a Jew, you could trust your life to him.

"He might kill the next *Y'hudi,*" Baba added wryly, "but he'd fight another *Mislim* to defend his friend. Of course," he qualified it even further, "this applies only on a high-class level."

With that, I thought I really had him. "What about Ali?" I asked. Ali, a bedraggled, unschooled Bedouin, illiterate and hardly upper-level, had Baba's utter confidence. He was a night guard in the Quarter, a municipal employee, but for longer than I'd been alive, he'd also served my family. Every Friday evening, he came to extinguish the cooking fires, and returned to flick off the lights when we went to bed. At dawn on summer Saturdays, he'd switch the fan on from the outside box. Whatever Jews couldn't do on Holy Days, Ali did for us.

Sad-faced, seldom speaking, dragging laceless shoes and dressed in someone's cast-off jacket and a rag of a *dishdasha,* he was less than prepossessing. Still, his simple dignity inspired trust. Even Nana grudgingly agreed. As a toddler, I followed him around, mimicking his awkward gait, not in mockery but admiration. He understood, and sometimes rewarded me with a quick, rare smile.

Confronted with my challenge, Baba found it difficult to answer. "But Ali's not a *city* Arab" was the best that he could summon up.

Neither could I win at school. We had three Arab teachers, all of whom were heartily despised by each and every one of us. That's not to say that Jewish teachers got away entirely unscathed. The major difference, though, was that a Jewish teacher, while he might invite dislike, would do so as an individual. All the *M'silmin* were abhorred as one.

The unfairness of it rankled, undoubtedly because my sense of singularity was very strong. Distinctions *did* exist, as the class itself confirmed. Like me, the others were Iraqi, male, and Jewish. Aside from that, however, hardly two of us had traits in common. Clearly, then, such blanket judgments just wouldn't work. All *Y'hudim* weren't good; all *M'silmin* weren't evil.

Much to my astonishment, Baba approved of this conclusion—in principle, that is. His immediate response was "If everyone believed the same things to be good and bad, there'd be no problem." He paused to formulate a more precise expression of his feelings, but the depth of them defeated him. "It isn't even good or bad or right or wrong," he sighed. "It's the different ways our minds work."

I suspect that Baba took me to a *Mislim* house—his friend Shabib's—to illustrate exactly what he meant. The visit to my teacher's home, he emphasized, had been an aberration. *This* call would show the way things really were. House visits were confined to strictly ceremonial occasions. On holidays, both Jewish and Islamic, we paid our ritual respects; there wasn't any casual, unplanned communion.

We didn't "drop in" on *M'silmin* as we did among ourselves; in all her life, my mother hadn't met an Arab woman on a purely social basis. As for myself, I'd never held a conversation with a *Mislim* my own age. Like the zonal limits—undelineated but rarely overstepped—there were tacit codes of conduct which were rigidly observed.

When S'hak introduced me to "minority," he'd also underscored the fact that the "majority" makes all the rules. Now, as Baba spoke, I began to wonder what would happen if a unified minority refused to play by them?

Before we entered Shabib's house, Baba briefed me. I wouldn't see a single woman, he informed me. The *harim*—the forbidden ones—would be cloistered in their quarters at the rear of the establishment, cut off by a corridor and door from the rooms in which the males lived their lives and entertained their men friends.

We'd been invited to a wedding party, and since our host was well-to-do, the company consisted of important people, dressed in their most festive clothes. *Z'boons,* like caftans, only extra full and belted, were of the finest fabrics—and could have come from any rabbi's closet. Strange, I thought, that orthodox, observant Jews and *M'silmin* who'd been smiled on by Allah should choose to dress alike. Over their *z'boons,* some guests were wearing loose, capacious *abayas,* and I could pick the wealthiest among them merely by assessing the amount of braid.

As always, I was starving, and the meats served smelled delicious, but Baba had admonished me that nothing would be *kasher,* and the meat, he said, might even have been broiled over cow or camel dung. I was to keep an eye on him and eat only what he indicated.

Luckily for me, the sweets were plentiful, and most of them permissible. While sampling some of everything, I noticed that the servants separated every plate we used from all the rest. Heading home, replete with sweets and even puffier with all the compliments that I'd been paid, I asked my father idly if the sorting out of plates had ritual significance. Perhaps it was a special kind of honor?

Baba's head snapped back. He stared at me for just an instant, then looked away before he answered in a flat, impassive manner that appalled me even more than what he said:

"To the *M'silmin,* all *Y'hudim* are unclean—like pigs to us. Any dish we ate from was contaminated, and required *alk*—hanging. Our plates will soak all night, separate from all the others, then be set up on the highest shelf, stored as inaccessibly as can be managed in order that no *Mislim* might by accident defile himself by eating from them."

The cake and candy curdled in my stomach, but on the verge of being very sick at father's calm acceptance of the insult, I saw that Baba was observing my reaction from the corner of his eye. Then of course, it hit me. Of *course* he'd put the matter calmly. Once again, he'd laid it out for me exactly like a teacher, this lesson in relations with our Arab friends. As Baba knew it would, his answer stirred up still another question, the one toward which the lesson had been leading. If *friends* regarded us in such a light, what might we anticipate from strangers?

Uncharacteristically, I didn't ask, but Baba broke the silence. As stoic as before, he said, "Some *M'silmin* won't allow us in the house at all."

What he was really saying was "You'd better learn to live with it."

In spite of everything, I was unconvinced that I had natural enemies. You made your friends yourself, so it was obvious to me that you also made your enemies. You didn't inherit them.

At the moment, my only enemies were Jewish. I'd just flunked Bible study because the class was taught in Hebrew, and I thought it ought to be in Arabic. I wasn't being petulant about it, nor had I problems with the Hebrew. It's just that Hebrew was a lost, dead language, and instruction, I felt strongly, ought to be offered in the language of our daily lives.

Convinced my argument was valid, I still knew better than to voice it. Pupils didn't express opinions, but unhesitatingly accepted what the school and teacher offered. The response to any questioning of school authority would be a slap and not an answer, so I simply didn't do the work. They warned me that I wouldn't be allowed to take the national exams unless I buckled down to Bible study, but that simply stiffened my resistance. We were all aware that government exams ignored the Bible.

Furious with me, Baba found and hired Baghdad's toughest Hebrew Bible tutor, who made me work exactly twice as hard as Bible class required, and sweating out his exercises, I re-examined my approach. While being right should automatically mean victory and vindication, this experience proved otherwise. Being right without the power to present, much less enforce, your arguments was only whistling in the wind. Those sessions with the tutor taught me more than Baba bargained for.

As for Hebrew, soon after starting with the tutor, he told me something that lessened my hostility toward "wasting time" on it. Now that Hebrew had come to life in Palestine, he said, our government had banned it in Iraq. Except for Bible study, teaching Hebrew was execrated as a great offense and totally forbidden. At that I bridled, and just as I'd rebelled against intimidation by the school authorities, I mutinied against the government's decree, buckling down to Hebrew as I never had before.

When I asked my tutor, whose major source of income had been threatened, if he meant to lodge a protest, he stared at me in disbelief. Government decrees were not discussed, and certainly not challenged.

Even if he hadn't been so scared—even if he'd been dying to talk about the situation—it wouldn't have occurred to him to talk to *me.* Except for Haron and my father, grown-ups only asked how school was going or told me I was getting tall. Once or twice, when someone was especially inane, I was tempted to start quoting from the paper I read every day—every day increasingly aware of the stories of sabotage and murder coming out of Palestine.

An airport had been bombed; an oil pipeline and a refinery had been blown to bits. There were detonations under troop trains, orchards set ablaze, settlements demolished. And daily, in a place of prominence, a running tally of the Jewish and the British dead.

Since every conflict was supposed to have two sides, and the Mufti murdered both the British and the Jews, I concluded that the British and the Jews were on one side and the Mufti on the other. Now, though, a third element I'd first learned of in Uncle Eliahu's letter entered in.

The Mufti bragged about his close association with the German News Bureau, and I saw pictures of Nazis in Palestine honoring the Prophet's birthday by flying German flags. Muhammad was revered by *M'silmin* everywhere, and in a hazy but disturbing way, the stories, run so closely together, created unsuspected bonds between the Nazis and the Mufti and all the *M'silmin* in the world, even in Iraq.

For awhile, I stopped reading the papers, but the radio was equally disturbing. By now, half the programs were purely German propaganda, and since the government controlled the air, I knew they'd all been authorized.

If "Zionist" had once been an unfamiliar word, the broadcasts now hammered it indelibly into every mind. "Zionist" was never used alone, however. It was always accompanied by adjectives—all vicious, some unspeakable though loudly spoken. It would seem that Zionists spent every second "scheming," and invariably, their schemes were "sinister."

All at once, these words were everywhere, unmistakably arising from a single source. When our Prime Minister, Nuri-es-Said, suddenly announced that he was anti-Zionist, I couldn't believe my ears. It made no sense. Nuri was in office now because he'd led a successful counteraction against an army coup, and at that time the army had announced that it was anti-Zionist. Since the Prime Minister backed the British and the army looked to Germany, they'd been poles apart. Now, somehow, both occupied a common ground against the "interlopers on our sacred soil": the Zionists.

Our history texts said that "two groups with a common enemy must act as one," so I waited for the English to object to Nuri's anti-Zionist expression, and demand an end to airing of the German filth. When the Mufti's followers, encouraged by the Nazis, were slaughtering both Zionists and British, how could Nuri be pro-British and at the same time hostile to those who died alongside the British? By every rule of logic, the British had to protest in the strongest terms.

Time passed, and not a peep was heard from them. "Politics" was Baba's one-word explanation. Dissatisfied with that, I asked Haron, who obscured the matter even more with his response.

"Never trust the British, and you'll never go wrong," he said.

Taking pity on my puzzlement, my cousin amplified with, "Only Jews help Jews. Remember that, and don't depend on anyone for aid, *especially* the English."

We appeared to be discussing different topics altogether, and I reminded him that Zionism was the issue I had asked about.

Haron looked amused. "Don't you know? Don't you know that when they say 'the Zionists' they mean 'the Jews'?"

Naturally I knew they meant the Jews in Palestine, but Haron interrupted me impatiently. "No. They mean 'the Jews.' Period."

He loved to tease me. In a moment, he'd break into his biggest grin, delighted with his hoax. I waited, but his expression didn't change. Haron, I realized, was deadly serious. He honestly believed that our government, tacitly supported by the British, was plotting against Iraqi Jews. It hurt me to know he felt himself the object of such hatred, and I couldn't imagine how he'd come by his ridiculous conclusions. Poor Haron!

Although I was intense in everything I did, I could put aside a problem and turn to something else entirely until I had the time and urge to tackle it again. Temporarily, to everyone's relief, Palestine and politics gave way to more involvement with the usual pursuits of boys my age.

I had lots of excess energy, and like all the smaller kids, vented some of it by chasing after bicycles and hitching on behind. Good-natured cyclists let us drag along until their strength ran out. It was a recognized activity in Baghdad, and riders rarely raised objections.

One day I saw a likely looking prospect wheeling past the house, and I dashed to grab the carrier of his bike. (We were in the Jewish Quarter, of course, and it never crossed my mind that the man might be a *Mislim.*) With a wicked backhand swipe, the cyclist knocked me to the ground and spat out, *"Khara ala Mousa!"*

I'd heard "shit" before, but the shock of having it attached to Moses stunned me more than being struck. At least a dozen Jews were walking by when I was hit, and lying in the dirt, I watched in vain for any one of them to settle up the score for me. No one raised a hand. No one even raised his voice. All that happened was that someone picked me up and brushed me off. I fled, angrier at them than at the *Mislim.*

When I was eight, a new element in the curriculum was introduced at school which eased my mind about the incident and life in general among the *M'silmin.* On a regular schedule, officials from the Ministry of Education were sent to speak to us about our role as good Iraqis and to assure us that we all were brothers. Benevolence washed over us in warm and gentle waves.

Countrywide, and almost overnight, the army organized a quasimilitary institution which every schoolboy was obliged to join—*every* boy, both Jew and Arab. No such policy of integration had ever before been suggested, much less implemented, and it clearly marked the start of better days.

Whenever possible, I proudly wore my *al'Kashafa* uniform. Although we bore the name of Boy Scouts, we had no association with the Baden-Powell group I knew about from British magazines. From what I'd read, it seemed to me that ours was much more fun. Instead of tying knots and rubbing sticks together, we did military drills and learned to march in step to snapped commands. Best of all, we got to shoot. While ours were only BB guns, some older boys were using real ones. Soon we would too, the leader of the troop assured us.

The theme throughout was "Arab brotherhood," and to the consternation of the school staff, the envoys from the Ministry kept telling us, "You're Arabs in an Arab land. Only in religion are you Jews."

Though Baba was aghast, as long as I could be a Jew religiously, I didn't much care what else they called me. In the *M'silmin* schools, the Ministry was telling Arab boys that Jews were brothers, and what but good could come of that? I was all aglow with patriotic fervor and smugly full of self-content. I'd been right! All along, I'd said that loyal citizens were equal in the eyes of government.

The press, of course, was echoing the message. Iraq was one big fellowship: Jews, Christians, *Mislims,* "who'd always lived in harmony except when outside forces interfered." Anything that came between us must be ruthlessly rejected.

And then the snake appeared in Eden. "The Zionists alone are obstacles to perfect peace." The Zionists again! Every mention chilled the air a little, and basking in the warmth of brotherhood, I wished we could ignore them. Far away in Palestine, they really shouldn't affect us here, but since they did, I started to resent them. When I said as much, Haron was furious with me, which just confirmed the Ministry's contention. For some mysterious reason, the Zionists were troublemakers everywhere, causing even friends to quarrel.

Haron was certainly no Zionist—he lived right here in Baghdad—so I was baffled by the depth of his distrust and anger. At Uncle Ezra's house I overheard him say, "They're smart, the bastards. They're playing both sides of the street and down the middle! Right now, Nuri doesn't want a bloodbath, so he tells the *M'silmin* that the Jews are brothers, and you mustn't spill a brother's blood. If there are no pogroms, he can tell the world we have no Jewish problem. And to sew it up, he tells the Jews they're Arabs, and since they already live in an Arab state, why would they need another state to call their own?"

Haron was even more wrought up than I'd suspected. Now he saw a vast conspiracy involving millions! It was too ridiculous to stew about, so I dismissed it—all but the final phrase. "A state to call their own" kept niggling at my mind.

There was something very wrong with it, but what? It couldn't be the concept, because irritated as I was by their intrusion on my bliss, I understood why Zionists in Palestine would want a state. Like people everywhere, they needed someplace that belonged to them—that they belonged to—the way that I belonged to Baghdad and Iraq.

And then it hit me. When Nuri said those words, he wasn't *talking* to the Zionists in Palestine. He was speaking to the Jews right here—to Jews who might be harboring the same idea.

Until that moment it had never crossed my mind that anyone could be a Zionist unless he lived in Palestine. Piecing everything together, it was evident that Nuri knew, or thought he knew, that some Iraqi Jews were Zionists. I couldn't conceive of it. Despite some difficulties, which we were even now resolving, we lived like kings compared to Jews in Palestine—and, for the most part, to *M'silmin* in Iraq. Why would anyone exchange what we had here for the chance to break his back in some forsaken sandpile? Baba said the land was barren and the sea was made of salt. And in a Jewish state, off by ourselves, we'd have to do demeaning things like digging sewers and driving garbage carts—all the dirty Arab work.

Nuri, I concluded, had been badly misinformed. Iraqi Jews were much too smart to fall for such an idiotic scheme as separate statehood. And, like me, they were also much too loyal to the state we lived in.

Every day, life was looking up a little more, especially for schoolkids. Among the new activities in which *al'Kashafa* was involved were semimilitary competitions, held in Baghdad's biggest stadium. Bands played without a pause, miles of gold braid glittered from the seats of honor, and the King himself presented trophies to the winning teams. Just one thing marred my total joy on these occasions. No Jewish school was ever judged the best. Even when the crowd roared uncontrollably at a display of skill by Jewish students, the award they should have won went elsewhere.

Determined that we'd take a prize, our team began to train intensively. In addition to required drill time, we put untold hours of our own into polishing the team's performance. With weeks to go, we were already at a point no other had approached.

Seeing me drag in one day, half-dead from drilling in the heat, with dried-up sweat tracks cutting through the caked dust covering me, Baba put his foot down.

"No more," he ordered. "You'll kill yourself for nothing. No Jewish school will ever win."

I tried to tell him that there wasn't any way that we could lose, but father wouldn't listen.

"Don't you understand?" he shouted. "It doesn't matter that you're better than the others. A *dhimmi* can't be equal, so how can they admit that one is better?"

Clearly "they" were *M'silmin,* which left the *dhimmi* to be me, but *"dhimmi"* was another of the unknown words. Baba clutched his *sibha* beads so tightly that I thought the tendons of his hands might split the skin.

"They think that we're inferior." It was his lesson voice again. "To the *M'silmin,* all but *M'silmin* are inferior. Infidels. Both Jews and Christians. In Islam we rank above idolaters, but far beneath the lowest follower of Allah. They only tolerate *Y'hud* because the Koran took so much from us that in a way we *are* related. We're also *ahl el-kitab*—people of the Book. Because of that, they let us live among them, and because they need us, sometimes they even let us be successful, but never"—and here his voice rose sharply—"never *ever* at the expense of any *Mislim.* Do you know now why you'll never win?"

The question was rhetorical, and Baba didn't pause for my reply.

"*Dhimmis* means 'protected ones.' We're a special class of citizens. Lesser, second-rate, but very special." Baba grimaced. "We're under the protection of the state, but it's a *Mislim* state. They don't allow you to forget it. Don't *you* forget it!"

Baba had never spoken with so much vehemence before; his intention, I realized, was less enlightenment than solemn warning. As a *dhimmi,* if I accepted what he said, my temperament could lead to trouble. With my healthy ego, I'd never settle for a secondary place.

Knowing me so well, Baba braced himself for a debate, but I surprised him by remaining silent. I loved him far too much to ask why he allowed himself to be a *dhimmi*—if he was, that is.

As far as I could see, Baba lived as well as any *Mislim,* and much better than the great majority. Maybe he was right about our being *dhimmis* in the old days, but another, a better, era had begun. Baba was behind the times, still seeing bias that had been erased. Take the competitions. Some judges might be blind, some probably accepted bribes, and undoubtedly a few were prejudiced against *Y'hud,* but for that you didn't condemn a country.

I'd always been the one "too young" to understand. Now Baba was apparently too old to take in all the changes. When we won the trophy, he'd see how wrong he was, and I decided not to rub it in.

Baba's pessimism couldn't cloud my sunny mood. My grades were good, I'd grown another inch, and Nana now entrusted me with Osa for her daily airing. The baby's first attempt at "Espirance" had come out "Osa," so Osa is what everybody called her. She had all the air she needed in the *hosh,* of course, but I loved to wheel her out where people could express their admiration. She was adorable, extracting smiles from everyone who passed her carriage, and strutting proudly in my Boy Scout uniform, I also drew approving looks.

Slowly pushing her along, enjoying the attention, I saw three other Scouts cavorting down the street, coming toward us in a casual game of touch-tag. Some yards in front of us, they slowed then stopped, I thought, to say "hello." When no one spoke, I said it first, to no response but hostile stares, and I tensed my grip on Osa's buggy.

My uniform had thrown them off. Our khaki outfits supposedly made us all compatriots, but my Jewish dialect had cut right through the new conditioning, rousing all the old responses. Advancing on us, they spat and shouted, *"Jalak-Allah"*—Discard of God. "Shit on the Jews. Shit on your mother."

As they danced around, cursing, coming ever closer to the carriage, then darting in to rock it, I snatched up Osa before it overturned. With my sister in my arms, I was powerless to fend them off, and seeing me immobilized, they covered her face with their spittle. Only then did Osa start to cry. I yelled that I was in the *al'Kashafa* too, as if they might have missed the uniform. I was a fellow Scout, I shouted. An Arab brother.

Circling us, now coming in to punch and kick at will, they jeered, "You're just a Jew, nothing but a dirty Jew. No Jew is brother to a *Mislim.*"

Clutching Osa tightly, I could only duck and weave. Luckily for us, an adult intervened before they beat me to a bloody pulp. Physically, I got away with nothing but some bruises and a badly tattered shirt. The real and lasting damage had been done to my convictions.

I told Nana that I'd tripped and fallen, but S'hak, streetwise as he was, recognized the signs of combat. Sympathetically, but with a certain smugness in his tone, he gently touched the largest of the blackening bruises.

"Welcome to the world," he grinned. "Now you know it all."

4

Our team didn't win and Baba didn't say, "I told you so." Long after all the bruises healed, I still refrained from picking up the papers or turning on the radio. I'd had enough of propaganda. I wore my uniform only when required; otherwise, it hung as far back in the wardrobe as my arms could reach. I couldn't bear to look at it. So much was going on inside the family itself that my sudden lack of outside interests went unnoticed.

Our main preoccupation was with Nana's pregnancy. Once again, and with the utmost urgency, Dr. Kahni said she mustn't have another baby. Afraid for my mother, and inflamed, as always, with the need to know, I hung around, absorbing every word as he advised a drug-induced abortion.

"It's early enough," he announced with visible relief, but Baba shook his head. He kept shaking it and saying "no" until Dr. Kahni, abandoning his cool and scientific stance, stated bluntly, "You're condemning her to death."

Horror-struck, Baba couldn't speak, but he stopped shaking his head. A moment later, he closed his eyes as if in pain and nodded. But the battle wasn't over, and Dr. Kahni knew it. As a good religious Jewess, Nana's scruples were as strong as Baba's, and her maternal instinct was even more resistant to abortion. When she finally agreed, she looked shattered. Fearful that she'd circumvent him, Dr. Kahni stayed until she swallowed the initial dose. She was to take another powder in the morning, and he handed it to

Baba with a stern command: "Tomorrow morning at breakfast." Baba was to see that she obeyed.

As I watched my mother choking down the dose that would begin the end of life in her, I felt as lost as I had on the night of Osa's birth when Nana nearly bled to death. What made it worse, though, was my interest in the whole event *apart* from Nana's welfare. All things medical increasingly intrigued me, and my conscience hurt because my curiosity was almost equal to my deep concern.

That night I dreamt so vividly that I could hardly wait to tell about it at the breakfast table. As soon as I sat down, I saw the second paper capsule, still intact, at Nana's place. The unaccustomed quiet invited me to plunge into my story, and everyone seemed grateful that I broke the silence. A man had come to me, I started. He had told me that his name was Abraham. I was, he said, his grandson.

In the midst of my description of his full white beard, the springy way his hair grew, and the size of his tremendous, sinewed hands—"huge hands, Baba, twice as big as yours"—I saw that Nana's eyes, as round as buttons, were fixed unblinkingly on me and that Baba's mouth was hanging open. Bewildered by their rapt attention, I stopped abruptly. Ordinarily I had to fight for center stage at breakfast.

"He was tall, much taller than anyone I know, and very fair, much fairer-skinned than Baba, with red, red cheeks. He kept his head bent, but I could see his nose was strange. Very narrow. Not at all like ours."

Nana stifled a sound midway between a moan and scream. I stopped again, but my father motioned me to finish.

"He was holding Baba's Bible, and it was open to where all the family names are written."

At that, Nana uttered a piercing cry. "It's a sign, a sign from Heaven," she said, and Baba nodded.

"The baby must be born, and his name inscribed with all the others. It will be a boy, and his name will be Abraham." Baba spoke with the certainty of someone reading from stone tablets on a mountainside, and bumps broke out all over me. When he stretched out his hand to crush the capsule, beads of sweat rolled down my spine.

I'd been the medium for whatever Heaven had in mind for Nana and the unborn infant. A female's dream would not have been acknowledged, and since S'hak had known his grandfather, his description wouldn't have carried any weight. However, I'd been barely three months old when Abraham had died, and no photograph existed that I could have seen, yet I'd been accurate in every detail.

In due course, as Baba had predicted, a baby boy was born, named Abraham and called Avram. I was no longer the youngest son, but much to my astonishment, it didn't bother me a bit, perhaps because I'd played a part in Avram's actual being, or maybe I was merely growing up. Assessing my atypical approach to Uncle Kh'dhouri's wedding, I believe it was the latter.

In the past, my interest in such a ceremony would have centered on the food. While I did check out the kitchen, I was more concerned now with the social aspects of the occasion.

Because my mother's brother owned a coffeehouse, situated in a crowded section of the Jewish Quarter, he knew absolutely everyone. Since we had the only house in all the family that could even hope to hold his friends and relatives, the wedding was to be at our place.

The canopy had been erected in the *hosh,* and brilliant Persian rugs covered the entire courtyard. Uncle Kh'dhouri was already sitting in an upstairs room, attended by his closest friends, fresh from the bathhouse, with red-brown *hinni* painted on his feet. In the days of Omar, the second Caliph following Muhammad, Jews were not permitted to wear the red shoes that showed status. Ever since, every Jewish bridegroom put *hinni* on his feet to symbolize the shoes that hadn't been allowed his forebears. When the bride arrived, she'd have *hinni* on her hair and on both her hands and feet, but that was mostly to protect her from the Evil Eye.

From outside, the sound of music and the scent of rose perfume heralded the coming of the bridal party. After the lengthy bathhouse ritual, Victoria, soon to be my aunt, already looked exhausted. S'hak, who got it from Nazima, had told me of the washing, the combing, and the application of cosmetics, and of the drumming and the singing, and the ceremonies stemming from the start of Jewish history. According to custom, my sister had attended, along with almost all the other women in the family.

Under the snowy powder and the round red spots of rouge, S'hak announced, there wasn't a single hair remaining on Victoria's cheeks and chin. With a strong taut string, a trained professional had snapped off every hint of fuzz. She was smooth as an egg, said S'hak. Naturally, I had to try it on myself, scraping a thin cord across my calf, leaving it flamingly sore and scarlet, but bare of hair. I only hoped Victoria's face didn't hurt as much.

Guests overflowed our home, first filling up the *tarabzoon*—the gallery that ran around the inside of the house on three sides of the second floor—with late arrivals standing on the roof, all looking down into the courtyard at the round silk *chupah* sheltering the bride and groom.

Victoria's white silk gown was so encrusted with gold and silver stitchery that it could have stood up by itself. Uncle Kh'dhouri, equally resplendent, but looking rather pale and drawn, still had a hectic week ahead of him. The wedding party wouldn't stop for seven days, but for those seven days, he'd be a king, complete with courtiers. No one, except the father of a son, was as honored as a Jewish bridegroom.

Everyone stood up throughout the lengthy ceremony, and as our legs gave out and savory kitchen smells began to overpower the perfumes, a silent little prayer was added to the liturgy. "Let it end, Oh Lord! Oh, let it end!"

Nana, Nazima, and assorted aunts had started cooking twenty seconds after uncle signed the marriage contract. Bushels of onions, raisins, and dried apricots had been brought in to make *torshana* sauce, the most succulent of all fish dishes. Weeks ago, Baba had reserved half the lambs at Hanoon Market for *kuba burghoul, kuba schwandagh, kibbah mehwi,* and other inventions involving lamb. Lamb with nuts and onions, with beets and parsley, wrapped in dough balls, spiced with cumin—endless possibilities and permutations.

One aunt minced and diced. Another had assigned herself to grinding almonds and, when wearied of grinding, to pitting heaps of dates that Baba kept replenishing. An entire flock of fowl had perished to provide the *t'bit* that my mother made. A mountain range of chick-peas had been mashed for *sembouzak,* and the spiciness of cardamon mingled with the slightly fetid smell of steaming cabbage. The cabbage meant *mehasha* was also on the menu. A haze of rice and flour dust hovered overhead as if suspended on the layers of luscious odors.

To fill in any chinks, there were platters full of jellied candies and pastries stuffed with richly sugared dates and nutmeats. Heaps of sweet and oily sesame confections surrounded pyramids of light-as-air *baklava* and *malfoof,* borrowed from the Turks, and bowls the size of cisterns overflowed with every fruit Iraq afforded. There was *arak*—"tiger's milk"—for the men to drink, and *sharbat* of a dozen different flavors for the women.

Just as I was thinking that I couldn't stand it for another second, the ceremony ended. As the reception started, still more guests streamed in, and since the extra chairs were set so as to leave a central area uncluttered, I knew we'd have some special entertainment.

The *chalghi Baghdad* played without a pause. Instead of the four or five musicians found at less impressive weddings, we had eight. I adored music, and the louder it was, the better I liked it. The *dinbeck*'s throbbing beat was what I loved the best—an inherited taste, perhaps, because my grandfather had been the foremost drummer in Iraq. Then I saw that Baba had engaged just seven men. The eighth was Uncle Shaoul, Uncle Kh'dhouri's older brother, who was honoring the bridegroom by performing. Cutting through the babel of the crowd, Shaoul's *santour,* with some sixty metal strings, was almost as effective as the *dinbeck.*

The *rebaba,* made from half a coconut, was being bowed with energy and undoubtedly with skill as well, but the sound was swallowed up in all the din, and even the metallic clash distinctive of the *daff* only reached the ear at intervals.

The hum and buzz of human voices was only overridden by the *oud.* Pulsating like a heartbeat, the sound resonated through my flesh. The rounded *ouds* reminded me of pregnant women, and the players, hunched above their instruments, fingers lightly wielding feather quills, seemed to stroke the strings like lovers.

The violinist sawed away like someone in a silent movie. The *kanoon,* a lesser sort of *santour,* was equally unheard. Only the whistling *nai,* which looked exactly like the pipes of Pan, was as audible as Uncle Shaoul. However, with the entry of the male singers, the guests began to quiet. Finally, both food and songs were done with, and the women went upstairs to watch the coming fun from the second-story *tarabzoon.*

I was supposed to stay with Nana and the other youngsters, segregated from the adult males, but I sneaked away and found a vantage point from which to view the dancers. Until I was *bar mitzvah'd,* when I officially became a man, I wouldn't be permitted to participate.

In accordance with tradition, the bridegroom was the first to take the floor. Uncle Kh'dhouri undulated to the beat of Shaoul's *santour,* and gradually the others joined him. As the tempo quickened, the women ululated loudly in admiration of their nimble-footed menfolk.

Flushed with *arak,* and well aware that he was being watched and judged, though never once acknowledging the audience, each man tried to outdo all the others. The whirls and leaps of one were matched and then surpassed by someone else's swoops and reels. Glasses almost full of *arak* teetered on slick and sweaty foreheads as the celebrants bent backwards, balancing as they danced in place.

A short time later, as if some signal had been given, every mother ordered her offspring off to bed. The guest room had been carpeted with cotton mattresses and set aside for them to sleep in. Nana spotted me and motioned me upstairs, but while the others left, I lagged behind, hoping Nana would relent and let me stay. When Baba wasn't there to back her, my wheedling almost always worked. This time, though, my mother wouldn't be moved, and from the way she laid the law down, uncharacteristically insistent for Nana, I knew my hunch was right: Something was about to happen that we youngsters weren't meant to see. I let myself be sent away, but doubled back and squirreled myself behind a corner column.

The orchestra abruptly picked up pace, and out of nowhere, there were seven women in the center of the *hosh,* twisting, dipping, bending to the beat, their bright skirts billowing in self-made breezes. From above, they looked like frenzied butterflies. The cadence changed. The rhythm slid from brisk to slow staccato, then to sensuous, and the women snapped their fingers to the shifting syncopation, hips and bellies surging to the beat. I was leaning so far over that I nearly fell, and the railing trembled when I grabbed at it to save myself, but no one noticed. The women watching from the gallery were as rapt as I.

Down below, bare midriffs shone with sweat. Tiny jackets, trimmed with clinking coins and hardly closed across the breasts, caught the light and sent it skittering around the courtyard. The men looked blinded by the random rays.

In the center of the troupe, oscillating without a second's stop, the star had shaken off her backless, high-heeled shoes, and at the strangulated sounds of shock from where the women watched, she flung her *hinni*-tinted toes directly at them.

The baring of her feet had been a daringly erotic act, unacceptable at such a ceremony, and all the decent women were indignant. Of course, they knew the dancers sold themselves, but usually they didn't solicit in the sight of wives. Nana was the color of a desert sunset. In the buzz of words that floated from the balcony, I heard some juicy new expressions. And from my aunts!

Excited as I was—and I *was* excited in a curious and unfamiliar fashion—I couldn't keep my eyelids open. Even as I heard Aunt Gourjiah say, "I don't believe she's wearing any underwear," I fell asleep.

5

In 1939, along with Uncle Kh'dhouri's wedding and the birth of Avram, we'd had a deadly epidemic to contend with. Influenza swept Iraq; in Baghdad alone, a thousand died. Baba almost fattened the statistic when, overnight, his mild case became a serious pneumonia.

Since Nana cried and lit *k'nadeel* if one of us so much as scratched a finger, her tears and prayers made no particular impression on me. Other people died, of course, but at the start, it didn't occur to me that Baba *could.* Like the sun, father was a fixed, immutable, eternal star. A world without him was simply inconceivable, so I worked at self-deception while his illness worsened.

Dr. Kahni's grim expression I attributed to overwork, and as for Uncle Ezra, he always wore that worried look. I couldn't allow myself to cry—that would mean admitting the unthinkable—so I bottled up the fear by day, releasing it in such horrendous nightmares that I struggled not to sleep. Tense and jittery, I snapped at everyone, even Osa, and my awareness of the extra pain I was inflicting just increased my misery and made my temper even more atrocious.

Only Haron saw and understood my anguish. My cousin, years older than I, had "adopted" me, and our relationship was something special. Unencumbered by the rivalries of "born" brothers, and close without the constant physical proximity that causes friction, we came together only when we wished to, and so were always at peace with one another. I could expose my deepest secret self and know that the secret was as safe with Haron as in my own possession. I admitted my terror to him, and spilling it out left me exhausted but immeasurably improved.

By an odd coincidence, Baba, too, began to feel much better. Haron was at the house as much as possible, bringing Baba all the street news, and relieving Nana and Nazima by taking the kids in tow. When Dr. Kahni ordered Baba to "a decent climate" to recuperate, he chose to go to Lebanon, and took Haron along.

If *shamash* had not demanded my complete attention, I might have moped about, missing both, and driving Nana mad. This school, however, wasn't like the others. These intermediate and secondary classes were specifically designed to weed out all the weaker students. At the end of five years of study, the all-important baccalaureate exams awaited us. Only the survivors of those dreaded tests would find employment with the government or be permitted to enroll at any institute of higher learning. Failure marked the end of aspiration.

With that in mind, I'd buckled down to business from the day the term began. Before they left for Lebanon, I'd talked at length with Baba and Haron—sober consultations, not the disputatious dialogues we'd once conducted. A death of sorts *had* taken place. My patriotic fervor had expired. I listened now when either spoke about the "realities" of life.

"A Jew must be twice as good to achieve half as much" was one such sober message, and the first step toward achieving anything, they said, was education. If I harbored any government ambitions, Baba told me flatly to abort them. "The Civil Service started to get rid of Jews in 1931. In 1935 they kicked some more out. When *this* is over, there won't be any left."

By "this," he meant the propaganda—pro-Mufti, pro-Nazi, and intensely anti-Zionist—which once again was washing over us. The epidemic had temporarily diverted everyone's attention, but as it died away, the press and radio increased their scurrilous assaults on "Zionistic scum."

When I assured my father that I'd never thought of Civil Service, he asked, "It isn't medicine?" sounding as incredulous as if I planned to run for King. He knew that medicine had always been my major interest, so I didn't answer. Something more was on his mind, and he was stalling, searching for the words to say it.

"Starting *shamash* is a milestone," he began. "It's a time to stop, to examine all the paths that lie ahead. Is it wiser to go one way or another?"

I couldn't tell anything for sure, except that medicine, quite clearly, was not the way he wanted me to go. Haron, who'd been standing by in tight-lipped silence, suddenly could stand no more.

"Why not tell him?" he exploded. "Tell him there's a Jewish quota. Tell him ten Jews in the country are admitted to the college—ten Jews each year from all Iraq!"

I looked at Baba, and his face confirmed it. In all the months of illness, he hadn't looked as sick and gray as at this moment. To conceal my shock and spare him further misery on my account, I flippantly retorted, "Five years is a long, long time. Who knows *what* I'll want." Baba brightened, and Haron indicated his approval.

They'd already left for Lebanon when I was stricken by the aftershock. Out of the blue, it hit me that the quota was for Jews, not Zionists. That being so, Haron was right again. Among the *M'silmin,* the terms were interchangeable.

The *shamash* was only minutes from the house, but starting out immaculate, I reached it yellow-white with dust each day. At the end of summer, everything was parched and pale. An all-pervasive film of powdered sand obscured the sharpest outlines, and the air itself seemed made of microscopic grains that rasped the skin and grated on the mucous membranes. That's why Baba had to leave the city. Sick lungs had no resistance to the grit, or to the dessicating desert winds that drove it deep within one.

When the *lahf* was really raging, it was dangerous to more than lungs to be outdoors. On every rooftop, sheets of corrugated tin provided privacy for summer sleepers, and from time to time, the wind would tear a sheet away and whirl it through the city like a giant's scimitar. Pedestrians had been decapitated as cleanly as by guillotine.

This morning the wind had gentled down, but at eight o'clock, the temperature already hovered at the hundred mark. Yesterday's high had been 120; at the current rate of rise, we'd reach and pass that mark. I wasn't sweating though, because the sun, a white-hot shapeless glow behind the haze, evaporated every trace of moisture as it surfaced on the skin. Even now, in the least oppressive part of day, I couldn't have summoned up a decent spit.

On reaching school, I headed for the water jugs, like the thousand other boys enrolled in my *shamash.* The clamor in the mammoth central *hosh* would have deafened any but a born Baghdadi, and I remembered reading in a British magazine that "Baghdad is the modern Bedlam. Its citizens endure a noise level that would drive the occupants of any other city quite insane."

I found the uproar energizing. It released adrenalin in me, every ounce of which I'd need. Six days a week, from early Sunday until Friday afternoon, we had classes in geography; algebra; solid geometry; chemistry; physics; Arab history, language, and literature; and English language and literature. The curriculum also included art and gym, biology and chem labs, and an hour of religion every week. Although the baccalaureate exams would be in Arabic, all our classes were in English, which had been my foreign language from the first grade on.

While the *shamash* and the synagogue occupied the same stone building, they were entirely separate entities. From the *hosh,* we entered our allotted space through double wooden doors, so wide that twenty adults, side by side, could easily have marched on through. Beyond them was a smaller door of tempered steel. Most Jewish institutions had such extra doors, and I was now aware enough to know why they were necessary.

Once more, however, I had no time or thought to spare for politics or personal safety. Anyway, as Baba said, intellect, not double doors, ensured survival. Though five years in the future, the baccalaureate exams loomed over us like an ever-darker shadow which one day would descend and try to snuff us out.

Between periods we had a twenty-minute recess, and while others fled the classroom, seeking temporary succor from the strain, I stayed behind and studied. Let Baba be at peace—but I hadn't yet abandoned medicine. As long as there was any chance at all, I planned to plug away, but merely passing the exams was insufficient for my purpose. I had to pass so high that the authorities would be unable to ignore me. Another axiom of the

Quarter was "If you're indispensable, you can even be a Jew." I'd be such a shining light that the *M'silmin* would be blinded to the Jewish body and see only the superior brain.

By the time Haron and Baba reappeared, I headed up my class of sixty and had a following. A quarter of the class was known as "Heskel's crowd," and they looked to me for tutoring. Although the youngest, I felt almost fatherly when "one of mine" did well.

Samy, though, was doing well without me, so I wondered why he hung around our catch-up sessions so persistently. He was a short and slightly squint-eyed kid who listened while the others questioned me, but never asked a question of his own. He didn't have to—his marks were almost up to mine—but he never missed a meeting. Whenever I looked up, there he was, grinning at me. It began to be unnerving, but I glared at him to no effect. No matter how I scowled, his expression never changed. Samy, I eventually discovered, couldn't focus farther than his foot. He was so myopic that he simply didn't see my sullen frowns. I noticed too that Samy always smiled; he was just a happy kid who liked to be with people, especially with me.

For reasons of his own, Samy had decided we'd be buddies, and short of spitting in his eye, there wasn't much that I could do about it. He was at the entrance when I arrived each morning and at the exit after school, smiling patiently until I said my last goodbye to others in our class. He was the only one whose home was in the same direction as my own, so I could hardly say he couldn't share the sidewalk, and since his father was in hardware and mine in plumbing, if all else failed, we had faucets to fall back on.

My snideness dissipated very quickly. While Samy stayed as shy and diffident as ever, when he did say something, it was well thought out and worth attention. Soon I was looking forward to our daily walk, but some time passed before I recognized his extraordinary understanding of Judaic history and orthodox religion. It revealed itself slowly, by degrees, almost accidentally. Unlike most of us, Samy wasn't one to flaunt his learning.

I went home with him one day, and when he rang the bell, I saw an opportunity to strut a little and show my own acquaintanceship with Jewish law.

"You know, you aren't allowed to ring that thing on *Shabbat,*" I said, then added rather smugly, "that's why we have a knocker. We can use a knocker all the time, even on *Shabbat.*" Small, I thought, but still a triumph.

Samy squirmed and looked embarrassed, as he always did when anyone required correction.

"You can't, you know," he scarcely murmured.

I stared at him in disbelief, and Samy, in acute distress, explained that plate and knocker were both made of metal, and that metal striking metal can create a spark. Now barely audible, he finished with "and that's like making fire, so it's not permitted."

Still dubious, I checked it with our rabbi. Samy was correct, of course.

Next time I saw him, I asked point-blank exactly how he'd come by so much esoteric information. Our schooling was the same, but he constantly surprised me, and even Baba's eyebrows lifted at some of Samy's abstruse expositions.

He told me that his father was a rabbi who chose to make his living in the hardware business. For the love of it, however, he conducted a *k'hila,* an informal congregation of at least ten men who met to study Torah.

Shyly, Samy asked if I'd like to look in at a meeting, but I declined with thanks. The last thing I was looking for was extra Torah. What I did require of Samy, he had just supplied—the reason for his knowing more than I did. With a rabbi for a father, he could hardly help it, so I needn't feel inferior.

Still, the business of the knocker bothered me, and though I couldn't solve its sparking problem, I did devise a timing mechanism to turn the lights off on *Shabbat.* Using an alarm clock, which I set to ring at 10 P.M., and experimenting until I found the length of string that did the job, I tied one end around the knob controlling the alarm and the other to the light switch. When the alarm went off at ten, the turning knob took up the slack, tugging at the switch and switching off the lights.

Baba was impressed, but Ali, he reminded me, had always manned the *Shabbat* lights; he'd miss the extra income. Thinking fast and defending the validity of my invention, I answered, "We shouldn't be hypocritical. If something's wrong for Jews to do, it's just as wrong for Arabs."

I'm sure that Baba could have found a flaw in my rebuttal, but my sudden moral stance amused him, and he "fired" Ali but continued tipping him. Baba's morality was both ethical and understanding. He knew I needed his approval as much as Ali needed money.

When the lights went out that Friday night, he nodded with a smile of satisfaction, and I went to bed as happy as I'd ever been.

With the approach of Purim, I reflected on the fun to come. Some of the best of being Jewish, I thought again, was in our dazzling parade of Holy Days. In a history as long as ours, there was a lot to celebrate, but then, of course, there was at least as much to mourn. However, Purim was for food and gifts and not for tears or fasting.

This year, the holiday arrived especially early in the month of March. In the lunar calendar, it often fell on widely different dates, and would have caught me by surprise this time around except that suddenly the whole house smelled of sesame and boiling syrup, the distinctive scent of Purim.

From the nonstop clack of Nana's clogs, I knew she wasn't sitting down a second in the kitchen, and in an upstairs room, Nazima was just as busily engaged in folding, packing, tucking, wrapping—putting all the final touches to the Purim presents. S'hak and I, as always, would divide deliveries.

On the holiday, each family unit sent gifts and sweets to all the others via their assorted offspring. It was the only chore I didn't object to, and about the only one I didn't charge for. When I left a package, I knew I'd pick one up—one for the entire family, in which I'd share, plus a little something for myself alone. Among the staples were gold and silver coins and quantities of crisp *zingula.* These "ears of Haman" were very large, extremely delicate and crush-prone cookies, and I'd achieved a certain fame for arriving home each year with every one intact. No one ever realized that because they were so big and brittle and so swirly and irregular in shape, you could break a dozen bits off all around the edges and do nothing but decrease the sweet's diameter, while actually improving on its overall appearance. If strangely small, the *zingula* I brought home were always beautifully symmetrical.

On dividing the delivery list, I would normally demand the names of those who gave the richest gifts, so S'hak was astonished when I asked for Uncle Ezra. Uncle, to be truthful, was a tightwad. Naturally I didn't tell S'hak that I had a kind of crush on my older cousin. A gay, good-tempered girl who made me laugh, she was as open-handed as my uncle was penurious. I loved to gamble, especially at backgammon, and if my luck was bad, I could count on her to underwrite my losses, but what I won was mine to keep. It was an excellent arrangement!

I saved uncle's house for last so I could spend the afternoon with my obliging cousin. After rescuing me from Aunt Habiba's bear hug, and whisking me upstairs to meet some friends, she promptly lost me to another woman.

Vivian was so small and slight, I assumed she was my age or even younger. In almost totally brunette Baghdad, her long and lemon-yellow hair against the glowing gold-bronze skin would alone have been enough to stun me speechless, but what truly mesmerized me were her wine-dark lips, as richly purple as the lips of Western women stars on movie posters.

Before the afternoon was over, I'd worked up several fantasies involving Vivian and me, but at my cousin's casual remark, they all dissolved in smoke. "You wouldn't believe that Vivian was eighteen, would you? It's her heart, of course."

My lack of comprehension was apparent, and my cousin, heretofore so sweet and sympathetic, sneered, "And you're supposed to be the doctor in the family. Didn't you see her lips?" I nodded, but with no assurance, ashamed because I still didn't understand, and I'd always been the one who bound up everybody's cuts and bruises.

When I began my "practice," all we had was iodine and aspirin tablets, but gradually I'd added rolls of gauze, squares of cloth for slings, and Nana's sharpest needles for excising splinters. Once, when Osa slipped and sliced her leg, I'd stopped the spurting blood and sterilized the wound with ashes from a blazing charcoal brazier. When Dr. Kahni finally arrived and checked it out, he'd solemnly referred to me as his "esteemed associate."

I headed for the library as soon as possible, and on closing the cardiology text, sighed for Vivian and myself. The lips indeed were symptomatic. A classic sign of heart disease.

Aside from Vivian's purple lips, Purim had been very happy. Haron reminded me that the rarest things are always prized most highly—"so a Jewish victory is something we should really sing about." Unfortunately, however, Mordecai and Esther were extremely ancient history. They'd defeated Haman, but evil doesn't die. This, too, I had from Haron. Evil only sleeps, he said, and gathers strength until the time is ripe to rise again in other guises. I guess sufficient time had passed, for Haman's incarnation had arisen, and his name was Hitler.

On April 1, 1941, another coup d'etat took place in Baghdad. Fearful for their lives, the King and Regent fled the city, and the power-hungry Rashid Ali al-Gailani proclaimed himself the head of government. Within a day, all key posts were occupied by known pro-Nazis, who looked to Hitler and the Grand Mufti for inspiration. We didn't know it then, but the Germans were supplying aid to Iraq in the form of a military mission and the loan of a million reichsmarks.

For an entire day following the successful putsch, Iraqi radio offered only martial music and impassioned oratory, interspersed with messages from every Middle Eastern state, applauding the uprising. The Arabs wanted all the foreigners out, but the aliens they named were French and English. Overnight the Germans had become their "brothers." That amused me, since not so long ago I'd also been a "brother."

Caught in a war a continent away from home, the British couldn't afford to lose their bases in Iraq or the oil from Kirkuk, but al-Gailani laughed off warnings that they'd fight to keep them. At first I searched the papers for some sign of British forces massing, but buying papers or turning on the radio was only wasting time and money. The same regurgitated garbage spewed out every day, increasing as the new pro-Axis government took firm control. By this time, though, none of us paid much attention. It was just like living with an evil odor. When your nose gets acclimated to a stench, you cease to smell it.

I could recite the articles about "atrocities" in Palestine almost word for word. The only change was in the numbers of "Zionist butchers slain by brave defenders of Islam." With each dispatch, the sums were larger; adding up the figures, there shouldn't have been a live Jew left in all that bloody land.

I soon became aware that Baghdad radio was routinely saying "Jew" instead of "Zionist." The two words had become synonymous in all the media. There hadn't been a proclamation, but all at once it was open season in Iraq on *el-Y'hud*—the Jews. Jew and Zionist were one, and no distinction now existed.

Intellectually I could appreciate the skillful manner in which it was accomplished, as cooly and precisely as I'd set up an equation in the classroom. Had al-Gailani expressed it to himself in just such a way, I wondered. "Let Zionist stand for Enemy. Since Jew is known to equal Zionist, Jew clearly, then, equates with Enemy."

The most illiterate *M'silmin* could follow that with ease, and since it hadn't been officially set forth, whatever happened when the masses reached the "right" conclusion, the government could claim its hands were clean.

Al-Gailani would also have the world believe that Arab students in every city in Iraq had decided—on their own, and all at once—to form the Fascist-style youth groups that were strutting through our streets. Of course, their guns were army issue, which somewhat compromised the spontaneity of their uprising, but as long as they were on the scene, who could quarrel with the noble work that they were asked to undertake. As patriotic citizens, they'd simply help to keep the peace and, oh, yes, keep a sharp eye out for "traitors." No definition of a traitor was enunciated—and none was needed.

Jews with any sense at all stayed off the streets as much as possible, and the gangs that roamed the Quarter had little opportunity to use their guns. Unlike the secret execution squads, these operated in the open and required *some* excuse to shoot. Therefore, when we did go out, it was quietly and quickly, calling no attention to ourselves in any way.

On one occasion, Baba sent me back upstairs to change my clothes. I'd been wearing a resplendent shirt, sewn expressly for the holiday. "Your oldest clothes," he ordered. With Nana standing by, already scared for us, he didn't go into details, but I understood. A *Mislim* kid might like a nice embroidered shirt, even slightly blood-stained.

With the arrival of Passover, the atmosphere grew tenser still. Of all the Holy Days, this one, we knew, would be the most inflammatory to an angry Arab. Here were Jews, celebrating the escape of Jews from other Arabs. Even as I thought it, I heard scattered shots not too far off, and it occurred to me that sometime in the future, other Jews might be commemorating *us.* If that should come to pass, I prayed the day would call for feasting, not a fast.

For Passover, every family ordinarily baked its own unleavened bread, beginning long before the break of dawn. With a blackout in effect, however, any lights or sounds that could be misconstrued might bring a rain of bullets.

Since *matza* was essential to the *Pesach* celebration, the local baker volunteered to do the total job, but though he overfired his ovens and almost dropped from dehydration and fatigue, he couldn't supply enough for all of us. In the spirit of the holiday, we shared what was available so that everyone would have at least a token bit to grace the table.

Apprehensive as they were, I was proud to see that the entire congregation had gathered for the *Pesach* service. Synagogue attendance hadn't been proscribed. In fact, the government had made a point of saying that policemen would be posted to "protect" us. Sure enough, the *shurta* ringed the building, but if anything, the sight of them increased anxiety. Supposedly, they'd been assigned to intervene should any of the gangs go on a rampage, but the same misgivings were uppermost in every mind. If young *M'silmin,* who well might be their sons or nephews, started shooting, would our "protectors" turn on them or turn away? Or in the melee, maybe turn on us?

Baba's cautioning me to keep my head down didn't do much to reassure me. Now his whispered warning was being passed along to everyone.

"Don't look up. Pretend you're praying. Don't let them see your faces."

The Chief of Police was one of father's *Mislim* friends, and familiar with his methods, Baba knew his men were making note of everyone attending services. In their acknowledged role as eyes and ears of the regime, the *shurta* would identify us for official files. I sneaked a look. Some looked abashed, I thought—not for doing what they did, but for *whom* they did it. Only weeks ago, these same police had served the King.

Inside the synagogue, my mind kept wandering from prayer. Just a short time back, everything had been so simple, so easily defined as good or bad. Loyalty, for one, was always on the "good" list. It was only when you asked, "Loyalty to what—and why?" that life became impossibly complex.

Baba poked me, and I joined in prayer again.

The tension lessened when the British landed troops at Basra. As al-Gailani had been warned, they'd fight to hold the bases that were vital to the bigger war in Europe. Although the gangs were still around, the government's priority now shifted to the British threat. Instead of sending troops to Basra, the decision was to strengthen forces here and hold at Baghdad.

For the next two months, official sources told us nothing, and there was little on the BBC about Iraq. The major news was being made in Africa and Europe. Most of what we learned was pieced together out of snatches overheard in coffee shops or on the streets around the Ministry.

We didn't have much to smile about, so one afternoon when Haron walked in wearing such a grin I thought his face would split, I jumped to the conclusion that the King was back. He shook his head, burst out laughing, and exclaimed, "It's almost better."

As he told it, the Nazis had sent three fighter planes to Baghdad airport to beef up al-Gailani's air strength. However, no one had alerted the Iraqi troops on duty, so they shot them down as they were coming in to land.

"The Germans are so mad, they might just bomb Baghdad!" Haron was heaving so with laughter, he could hardly speak. "The mistake was bad enough," he managed, "but what's really driving them insane is that Iraqi soldiers did it with their little rifles, not even antiaircraft weapons. They shot them down with popguns!"

Despite the incident, the Luftwaffe sent another score of planes, and at least four shipments of assorted arms came in from German sources. The railroad ran between the busy brick mills and the slaughterhouse, and train arrivals could be spotted from the Jewish cemetery, so no attempts at secrecy succeeded. We even knew about the fifty German planes that landed at Mosul, sent to strafe a major British camp at Habbaniyah. The reports that filtered through said that almost everything had been destroyed.

While I was playing on the roof one day, I saw a battle over southern Baghdad between a British Spitfire and an Arab plane. Stomping and yelling,

I shouted tactical advice and cheered the English pilot on. As the Iraqi plane went down in smoke, Baba charged up the stairs to snatch me off the roof. I'd never seen such blazing fury in my father's face.

Was I stupid? Didn't I understand? *El-Nazyi'in* were running things. England was their enemy, and there I was, screaming for the enemy to win What would that make me? A traitor! That's what they'd say before they shot me!

All the way down from the roof, he asked his questions and answered them, shaking me for emphasis on every step.

"In all this craziness, they could say that you were sending signals to the British." Baba's booming voice was high and strident now, and suddenly it cracked. Instead of shaking me, he held me very tightly for a moment. What I'd thought was fury was profound and naked fear for me.

On May 30, a British force reached Baghdad, but Rashid Ali and the entire Fascist group in government had fled the city. For once, *we* were the big news on the BBC, and our own, and now uncensored, radio also came to life again.

"Thousands of British troops are pouring into Basra. The Iraqi Regent, Abdul-Ilah, has left Transjordan and is on his way to Baghdad. The crisis is over."

Baba said a low "Amen." I would have loved to cheer, as loudly as I'd cheered the English pilot, but life was making me more cautious all the time. Still, the *Nazyi'in* were gone, and we were here, all healthy and unharmed. What's more, tomorrow evening we'd start to celebrate *Shavuot.* Surely cheering was in order, but a glance at Baba stopped me. Though lulled and much diluted by the day's events, the fear, I saw, was still alive.

6

S'hak was the best thermometer in Baghdad. When the mercury went up, I could always tell exactly where it was by the rising pitch of his complaints. On this first day in June, however, he perspired in unaccustomed silence as the temperature soared. Obeying Baba's orders, all of us were trying to be extra quiet. Even Avram seemed subdued, although he wasn't old enough to understand the situation.

On *Shavuot* eve, the entire area would ordinarily be bustling. This time last year, when I'd gone to buy the bread for dinner, great streams of people had been surging to and from the Quarter. With sunset hours away, they still had time to stroll the streets, stopping to exchange good wishes for the holiday with friends and neighbors. I must have heard *"Sbah elkhair"* a hundred times before I reached the bakery.

Today, there hadn't been a single woman on the scene, and just a scattering of quickly moving men, all headed toward the *M'halat-el'Yhud.* Not a soul was coming *from* the Quarter, and no one sauntered leisurely along or made a sound that wasn't strictly necessary. The men moved swiftly, hugging close to house walls, hiding in the narrow strips of shade beneath the second-story overhangs. Clearly, others shared my father's feeling that Jews should shrink into themselves this day and try to cast no shadows.

True, he said, al-Gailani's coup had been undone and the upper echelons of insurrectionists had fled, but their admirers remained—under no control at all now. "Until the King is back in Baghdad," Baba warned, "we have to watch our step."

As my father often said, he understood the Arabs well enough to know that even Arabs didn't understand the Arabs. For the last two months, the *Y'hud*-haters had been running freely and unfettered, and they knew as well as we did that the fun with guns was coming to an end. Al-Gailani's rout would be seen by them as victory for us, and who could tell how they'd react?

Apart from exercizing caution, preparations for *Shavuot* fell into the old familiar pattern. Before *Shabbat* and all the other Holy Days, the house was not just cleaned, but scoured. As usual, I helped Nazima hose the *hosh,* and, as usual, I soaked myself from head to foot before we'd wet a wall. As always, father pointedly remarked, "A woman your age should be working on her *own* walls."

The jibe was as much a part of every holiday as any prayer. For as long as I could recollect, Nazima had refused the marriages that Baba wished to bring about, while he continued to reject the only man she'd ever wanted. Nana offered no support; it was a father's duty to decide his daughter's future.

Elsewhere my mother might be self-effacing and submissive, but in the kitchen, she was absolutely autocratic. Even *I* thought twice before invading her domain. The *Shavuot* meal was mother's yearly masterpiece, and with every passing hour, the smells grew more enticing. Usually we ate at six, but on the holiday, dinner was considerably delayed. The summer sun seemed nailed to the sky, and before it sank, I'd have settled for a piece of bread. The round, flat wagon wheel I'd brought home from the baker's might not look like much, but when *khibz* was pulled apart—it wasn't to be sliced—I knew how doughy and delicious it would be, especially sopping up my mother's spicy meatballs!

I could smell them now, simmering in the pea soup. And envision the *khibz* soaked with thick lamb stew . . . the rich brown rivulets of gravy surrounding small but juicy "sparrows." At sixteen, practically adult, S'hak was probably above our customary squabbling over the bird-shaped bits of lamb, and Avram, barely three, wasn't big enough to be a threat. The girls might look on longingly, but being females, they couldn't contest my claim. For once, I'd have all the *asphourria.* Anticipation helped to sooth the hunger pangs.

At last the action left the kitchen for the ground-floor summer living room. The ceremonial vessel, filled with oil and water, hung above the center of the massive table. Of dark mahogany, it easily sat fifty, and laying the embroidered linen cloth required the coordinated effort of every family member.

Since work of every sort was forbidden after sundown, and Nana was concerned about encroaching on the holy eve, she'd quit the kitchen thirty minutes early, but everything, I knew, was safely simmering away in warming ovens. Although the pots were covered and clear across an open court, ambrosial odors swept the room every time the ceiling fan revolved. I didn't think that I could stand it for another second.

Then mother took the "servant" lamp and touched its flame in turn to each of seven hand-rolled wicks that made up the *menorah.* As she began to speak the prayer "*Baruch ata adonai*"—Blessed art Thou, O Lord—the gnawing in my stomach stopped. As always, the solemnity and splendor overwhelmed all else.

In the light of the seven golden flames, Nana's face looked young and fresh, and their glow erased the deeply graven lines in Baba's brow as he intoned the *kiddush.* An elation as old as history eliminated all the strain and fear we'd lived with for the last two months.

When Avram, as the youngest son, finished up the blessing, then broke the bread, the mood turned festive, and food again was all-important. Along with Nana, every mother in the *M'halat-el'Yhud* was heaping plates and urging all, "Eat. You'll need your strength."

Fortification would indeed be necessary. In Iraq, as nowhere else, Jews stayed up all night to celebrate *Shavuot.* In every family, all male adults would take turns reading chapters of the Torah from the first word to the last. Only here was observation of the day so much more than merely ceremonial, for what others learned from rabbis, our families had lived. For Iraqi Jews, each *Shavuot* added still another link to a long, unbroken chain attaching us to ancient *Yisrael.* It was a very personal attachment.

All other Jews had split and scattered. We remained the only undispersed descendants of the exiles. Driven from Yerushalayim after the destruction of the Second Temple six centuries before the birth of Jesus, our forebears fled to Babylonia—Iraq of old—and here we'd stayed until this day. When we read the Ten Commandments, I could close my eyes and summon up that long procession, ancestors stretching back to those who might have heard these self-same words from Moses.

By the time dessert arrived, Osa and Avram were much too sleepy, and the rest of us too stuffed, to care. Only Baba reached out toward the bowl of polished fruits. Full or not, my father never could resist a date. His hand stopped short, however, and his fingers made a fanning gesture, shushing us. He seemed to hear some distant sound, but though I strained my ears, they picked up nothing. However, people said of Baba that he could hear a fly buzz at the other end of Baghdad, so I listened hard, and then there *was* a sound . . . the merest spatter of a shower, so I thought. But rain in June? No wonder Baba's ear had been alerted. It was unnatural, a true phenomenon. This time of year, the air in Baghdad was as dry as dust.

Now I heard another distant noise, like the muffled thrum of thunder.

"People. Lots of people." Baba's lips had barely moved.

Suddenly a high-pitched howl pierced the hum. Before it faded, my father's ear was at the outlet of the ventilating chimney.

"It's moving this way."

When Baba started for the roof, we fell in line behind him, but on arrival, he waved us from the six-foot wall that overlooked the street. The drone was louder now, the crowd that caused it closer. The few words we could clearly hear were in a *Mislim* accent, and the soft spatter had become a crackle. In our own dialect, an anguished voice cried out.

"God save us!"

"Us" quivered in the air, trembling above us, as frightening as a sword suspended on a fragile thread. "Us" meant more than just a single Jew in jeopardy. This wasn't just another sickening but isolated outrage. The unseen sword hung over all of "us."

S'hak and I joined Baba at the wall, and he allowed us to remain. By standing on the ledge, we could see that Kambar Ali Street was empty, but the overhangs of other houses hid from sight whatever might be happening on either side of us. Not that a wider field of vision would have helped a lot. The blackout of the last eight weeks was still in force, and Baghdad was a stygian black.

Over the ghetto, though, a grayish pall appeared to be expanding, and as we watched, two straight new plumes of smoke shot up. A hail of bullets from a nearby alley told us that the trouble wasn't only in the Jewish Quarter but a whole lot closer to our house.

Baba snatched me from the ledge and Nana wailed, "They'll kill us all." All we knew for sure was that "they"—whoever they might be—had automatic weapons. That, and that the ghetto was afire.

S'hak and my father had their heads together, and Nazima had the kids in hand. No one seemed to need me. There was nothing I could think to do except perhaps divert my mother.

Even in the dark, it took me just a minute to discover she was missing. Since she had to be inside, I headed for the stairs full speed. Going anywhere without the baby, especially if danger threatened, was so alien to my mother's nature that it scared me more than anything I'd seen or heard all evening.

Nana wasn't in the kitchen or the courtyard, but cutting back across the *bosh* and looking through the grillwork, I saw her in the family room.

Appearing very small and vulnerable, she was standing at the far end of the massive table, twisting cotton wicks for the saucers filled with oil before her. Head bowed, she touched a flame to each of the *k'nadeel,* first asking that Ezekiel the Prophet intervene for us, next invoking Ezra, the Second Temple's architect, and finally imploring aid of Rabbi Meir Ba'al Haness, the miracle maker of Tiberias and one of Nana's favorites in the courts of Heaven.

Her murmured words were much too faint to catch, but I could see the fear drain from her face. For reasons that I couldn't explain, I ducked from sight as Nana left the room and headed for the roof again. Her pact was private. She'd done her best. The matter rested now with God.

I looked back at the three *k'nadeel.* As the ceiling fan swept over them, all the little flames would flicker. However, when each disturbance ended, the tiny lights were still alive, defying darkness.

Following my mother to the roof, I realized that the window on the landing of the second floor allowed a look straight down the street. The ghetto was a little beyond and to the right. With any luck and a minimum of moonlight, I might just make out *something.*

I stared into the blackness and, as my eyes adjusted, my hands locked on the sill. I wanted to run screaming to the roof for father, but what I saw glued me to the spot.

Every entrance to the Quarter was awash with Arabs, two streams to every street. Those entering the ghetto were moving swiftly, but those departing inched along like overladen ants. Some of the *M'silmin* carried lanterns, and I could see what slowed them down.

I shut my eyes, but that was even worse. Divorced from sight, you'd say it was a great big, joyous jubilee, the gayest, most extravagant of family gatherings. Bursts of laughter floated on the air, feminine giggles mingling with the bass and tenor of the men and boys.

When I looked again, I saw infants slung in shawls and kids of every age following in their parents' footsteps. One youngster, no older than Avram, was clinging to his mother's *abaya,* crying; the mother's arms were fully occupied and unavailable to him. She was carrying a mammoth copper pot, exactly like the one in Nana's kitchen. Whose kitchen had it come from?

My mind was functioning, but the rest of me was frozen stiff, as in a nightmare. The scene assaulting me was eerie as a dream. There were squeals of pleasure and sounds of scuffling. Metal clinked, something crashed, and several times I heard a baby—babies?—bawling. Each sound was magnified in rising to the roof, but none was synchronized with anything that I could see.

In the light of swinging lanterns, disjointed fragments flashed before me from the blackness. For the briefest instant, every detail was disturbingly defined. In the strange illumination, ordinary objects were unreal. Colors fluoresced and steely edges glittered evilly. At times it seemed that precious stones were sparkling in the dark.

I shook my head to clear it and made a conscious effort at control. My imagination had been running riot; I couldn't report such fantasies to father.

However, when I focused on the scene again, I saw that jewels *were* blazing, and the glinting edges were the edges of an axe that *did* exist. A man with many gem-set bracelets hanging from his belt like trophies of the hunt had set his lantern down and stood now in a stationary pool of light. The precious stones refracted it in fiery rays.

Another paused within the pool to shift the heavy linen chest that bent his back. When he straightened up, I knew that nothing was illusion, but nightmare formed of flesh and blood. From neck to knee, the man was one great smear of gore, spilled so recently that it was still a rich and healthy red. And it wasn't his.

I raced upstairs, too late to sound the first alarm. Word from the Quarter had passed from roof to roof until it reached us on the outermost perimeter of Jewish homes. Baba said the mob was leaderless and mainly after loot, but it was also armed and in a mean, explosive mood. Trying to protect our property would only mean more burning and more bloodshed. Our wisest course would be complete inaction. Stay silent, out of sight. Save your life and let them *have* the loot.

It was the same advice that Jews had given Jews since time began. Someday. . . .

Baba broke into my musings with a curt command. "Go help S'hak get the bedding." He'd decided we'd be safest where we were. In normal times, we'd have started sleeping in the open weeks ago, but the revolution had kept us off the roof. Too many sleeping Jews had fallen prey to prowling cutthroats.

We'd stay awake tonight but not, as planned, to read the Torah. Baba had long since doused the lights. Downstairs, the *k'nadeel* burned, but they couldn't be seen by anyone outside. Thinking of those three small beacons raised my spirits, but I couldn't help wishing that we had as many guns.

Even if we'd wanted to, we couldn't have closed our eyes. Drunk with banditry, and some, undoubtedly, with *arak,* groups of stragglers wandered through the side streets, shouting out their daring exploits to each other. Directly underneath our overhang, several almost came to blows over a stolen sweater.

Shots and intermittent screams kept coming from the Quarter, and then—much closer—from Kambar Ali Street itself, an old, old voice, a Jewish voice, called weakly on the Lord to send him water.

When I started for the stairs, Baba grabbed my arm and yanked me back. His face was haggard but, silently, he shook his head and held me fast. We couldn't help anyone. We couldn't even help ourselves.

He hadn't said as much, but I'd seen his eyes sweep ceaselessly around, searching every inch of rooftop, seeking any means to save us. There was no concealment, no escape. Surreptitiously, trying not to scare us even more, he'd bent to pick an object from the rooftop—all it had to offer as a weapon. I'd seen him shove it up his sleeve, and all night long he held the heavy length of pipe against his arm so he could slide it down for instant use.

Periodically we'd monitor the stairwell window and watch as, hour after hour, the endless streams surged through the ghetto. In the glow of burning houses, I began to recognize familiar figures in the flood of rabble. Many of the same marauders reappeared at intervals throughout the night. Energized by greed, they'd dumped their booty elsewhere and returned to ravage.

Close by, Baba muttered to himself, "Those *mamzerim.* Don't they ever sleep?" It jolted me as much as any of the night's alarms. Baba never used a word like "bastards."

Unceasingly, seeping through the other sounds, the old voice from the street below begged and wept for water. His wail grew fainter as the night wore on, but I could hear him all too well. If I hadn't been ashamed to do so, I'd have stopped my ears. As the first flush of the sun appeared on the horizon, the entreaties ended, and the silence was more awful than any scream I'd ever heard.

Dawn broke quickly, and in the glare of day, each of us was shocked to see how sallow-faced and leaden all the others looked. With the exception of the kids, who'd slept like angels, we were hollow-eyed as much with horror as exhaustion. At dawn on a normal *Shavuot* morning, Nana and Nazima would be in the kitchen, making mounds of *kahee* as quickly as the batter could be poured. A whole night's reading of the Torah would have left us ravenous. Today, instead of sugared pancakes, we had only tea and milk, but no one minded. With the old man's cries still ringing in our ears, we could hardly swallow that.

By 8:00 A.M., however, even Baba was beginning to relax. For an hour now, we hadn't seen new smoke or heard a sound apart from normal city noise. With the rising of the sun, the hordes had thinned and melted off. The daylight had dissolved the nightmare.

Before allowing us to leave the roof, Baba went for one last look. On his return, a moment later, his face had aged a decade.

"Shiblawiyin!"

Daisy burst out crying, more alarmed by his expression and the way he spat the word than by the word itself. For the rest of us, the single word explained it all.

"Shiblawiyin" was a synonym for evil. It stood for thugs and thieves and casual assassins, savages who'd steal a piece of bread or rape or kill with equal equanimity.

Abu Shibl, the district of the city that had spawned the name, was the rankest, most corrupt in the entire country—and it almost touched upon the Jewish Quarter. No one was safe from the *shiblawiyin,* not other Arabs, not even their own neighbors, but the ghetto was their favorite place to pillage. Last night, along with all the other *M'silmin,* they must have picked it clean, and now, their lust for loot unslaked, they were coming after us, on the outskirts of the Quarter where the wealthier Jews had built their houses.

Father tried to stop me, but I had to see. Out there, in the hot white light, the nightmare started up again. Instead of last night's crowd of scrambling and haphazard hotheads, I saw an army, well equipped and disciplined. The rabble had acquired leaders and a plan of action.

In their first concerted effort to effect an entry, they were unsuccessful in battering the door down. The street was much too narrow for effective ramming, but the door, in any case, would have stood against the heaviest assault. They couldn't know, as I did, that on Kambar Ali Street, the entrances to all the Jewish homes were strongly fortified. A tempered metal strut, anchored deep within a wall, braced an iron bar across the six-foot width of each front door and frame.

My heart began to race when I heard a call for axes. The leaders had already learned what *wouldn't* work. One sharp command, and blades were biting through the wood. Some hit the bar and broke, but others chipped a hole through which a hand could reach and disengage the barrier.

The initial break-in took an hour, with all of them at work. The second was accomplished in a quarter of that time, and by a team of only five. With an efficiency that chilled me, the mob split up into a score of smaller groups, each taking on another house and making ever quicker entry. Not that minutes really mattered much. Weaponless, if we had a week, we'd still be at their mercy.

Beside me, Baba said, "At least there aren't so many of the *mamzerim.*" The earliest invaders, staggering under loads of stolen goods, were going home, but Baba knew as well as I that, given our position, fifty were as powerful as fifty thousand. The feeling of complete and utter impotence enraged me more than all the *mamzerim* outside.

They were next door now. We could hear the splintering of wood, then a heavy thud as the iron bar, forced up and out of place, fell to the floor. Father spread his fingers, signalling silence. When they got to us, we couldn't stop their sacking of the house, but we still might save ourselves. Since everything of value was inside, they might not bother with the roof. About the best they could expect to find there were the water jugs and bedding, and they'd be rich enough already with everything else we owned in their possession.

When we heard our front door go, father ordered that we speak in whispers only. The pipe he'd clutched all night lay seemingly forgotten by the streetside wall. I picked it up, but when I took it to him and he turned to me, I understood why he'd abandoned it. His hand now held the longest knife in Nana's kitchen. S'hak also had a shiny something he was trying to conceal from us.

During the night, father must have crept downstairs instead of staying at the second-story window, but he hadn't brought a knife for me. Did he think that I was scared? Was he afraid that I might shame him?

My stomach turned with such a sickening mix of anger and humiliation that I thought I'd vomit. Dear God, I begged, I don't mind dying, but save me from disgrace. Don't let me be a coward. An outcry from the house next door diverted my attention from my own despair.

"They're in! The murderers are in the house!"

Like us, the Eizer family had taken refuge on the roof, but now that gutless Akram had exposed them all by shrieking out. The raiders could have heard him if they'd still been in the Quarter. And, of course, he'd put them on to us as well. The wall between our roofs was only one brick thick. Built for privacy rather than protection, it wouldn't shield us from the *shiblawiyin* for even seconds. They'd investigate the shrieks, and once they finished with the Eizers. . . .

My stomach heaved again, but this time from the impact of a wild idea that hit me like—like a *brick.* The *shiblawiyin* must be stopped before they reached the Eizer roof, and the wall would be our weapon.

I seized the pipe again and slammed it hard against the flimsy structure. As I suspected, the winter rains had eaten at the mortar, and a single blow broke through. Baba and S'hak swiveled at the sound, but the fury faded from their faces when I waved a brick and yelled out "Ammunition!" They understood at once. I was already on the Eizer roof, with bricks in both my hands, and they were just a step behind. Without a word from anyone, the women battered at the wall and built a mound of bricks within our reach. Each of us would be a missile launcher.

Drawn by Akram's outburst, scores of the *shiblawiyin* were congregated on the street outside, and at least another hundred were already in the Eizer *hosh.* Since these had easiest access to the stairwell, we opened up on them.

As if we'd drawn a plan and practiced, we spaced ourselves to cover the entire courtyard, then flung our bricks at Baba's signal. While the first barrage was on its way, we launched a second salvo—and a third and fourth. From below, a yelp of pain became a roaring chorus, and someone screamed, "The *dhimmiyin* are killing us!"

Packed tight, the *M'silmin* panicked. The only exit open to them was the narrow L-shaped foyer leading to the door they'd forced, and as they scrambled for the safety of the road outside, we rushed to take our places on the parapet commanding Kambar Ali Street. Hidden from their view, we continued the attack.

Battered by the raining bricks, the *shiblawiyin* below us, already shaken by the shrieks of their companions from the courtyard, stampeded like the buffalo in cowboy movies. Those fleeing from the house ran head-on into crushing hail. Deranged by shock, they lost all reason, and we pelted them at random. Imagination did the rest. Eerily invisible, they mentally perceived us as an awesome army, and screeched to Heaven and each other, "*El-yahood!* They're slaughtering us! Hundreds of *yahood!* Thousands! All around us! The *Jalak-Allah* are all around us!"

As they fled, we wordlessly deployed again. I checked for stragglers while S'hak took the street side and Baba scanned the roofs around us.

Unlike the wall that ringed the outside of the roof, the one that ran around the *hosh* was hardly four feet high and made of metal bars instead of solid masonry. Through or over it, I could see each inch of Akram Eizer's courtyard. The *hosh* was empty, except for several Arab sandals. Some of the *shiblawiyin* had literally leaped out of them!

And there was something else on the otherwise untainted tiles, newly scrubbed in honor of *Shavuot:* from wall to wall a scattered pattern of a thousand tiny polka dots, some larger patches of the same rust-colored stain, and a few still-widening, still-crimson pools. Blood. This time, though, it wasn't Jewish blood.

The sight was satisfying, and yet I felt no sense of pleasure. I was sorting out the odd emotions that the scene evoked when something caught my eye in Eizer's place. There was someone in their storage room. All the Eizer's though, were still with us.

The shadowed figure made a half-turn toward the window. It was a muscular young *Mislim,* hacking at a heavy brass-bound chest. Two candlesticks I'd often seen when visiting the Eizers were stuck like matching sabers through his shabby belt, and Akram's brand-new shoes were slung around his neck by long brown laces.

Unbridled avarice explained his presence. The chest was much too large to haul away and much too rich a prize to leave behind. Such chests contained the family silver, and overwhelmed by lust, he couldn't let it go. I watched his fingers scratching frantically at burnished brass while his dirty face dripped sweat, and an enmity I hadn't heretofore experienced washed over me.

With the others, all I'd wished to do was drive them off. If I had to hurt them, it was only as a last resort to save myself and mine. This was different. I *wanted* him to suffer. En masse, the others had been abstract evil. He was all too human. He looked like any adolescent male. Like me, in fact, except some five or six years older. Perhaps that was the horror.

Without my knowing how they got there, the bricks were in my hands. I threw one and the window shattered, spraying him with glassy shrapnel. Blood was trickling down his cheek when my second missile struck him on the upper arm and laid it open. He screamed and made himself as small as possible, cowering on the floor. I knew that he could see me standing on the rooftop, arm upraised. Staring up at such an angle, half-blinded by the sun behind me blazing in his eyes, I must have looked like a colossus—or maybe an avenging angel.

Certainly no *Mislim* would otherwise be screaming *"el-khater-Allah!",* appealing to a lowly Jew, and a lowly Jew of just eleven. The lovely irony of it! Pleading "for the sake of God." First ravaging *Y'hudim* in Allah's name, now begging mercy of a Jew for the sake of that same Allah.

Our eyes had locked and neither of us moved a muscle. Slowly then his hand reached up for Akram's shoes. At first, I thought he'd fling them at me, but he slid them to the floor and placed the candlesticks beside them. I realized only then that I had another brick in hand—that I'd been holding it with elbow bent, all set to heave it at his head. He knew I had him in my sights.

Eyes never leaving mine, he inched his way across the room, backing toward the door of the *jam-khana.* When he disappeared, I shouted to the watching, wide-eyed S'hak, "Let him go." It was enough to know I could have killed him.

When *Shavuot* came around again and the time arrived to read the Ten Commandments, I could still say, "Thou shalt not kill," and thank the Lord I'd kept the Law.

7

It was about 11:00 A.M. when the remnants of the mob retreated. On Baba's orders, we remained in place while he went down to try the radio. Returning, he had some hopeful news for us. The Kurdish brigade, which was loyal to the King, was in the city and enforcing order. However, until the soldiers reached us, we'd remain up here and on our guard. At any moment, the bandits might regroup for one last foray. As for the fate of the other members of the family, he had no information. The phone was dead. The lines had probably been cut.

For the next three hours we existed in a passive, stagnant state, physically too tired and emotionally too drained to move or talk. A spooky silence enveloped the entire city, as if the night's events had dissipated all its energy.

"Stop or I'll shoot!"

A shout cut through the stillness, and the Kurdish accent acted on us like adrenalin. Rushing to the wall, we saw men in uniform converging on the Quarter. In the distance, army vehicles were turning into Kambar Ali Street, and orders blared from mobile speakers.

"Stay inside your homes. Anyone outside will be stopped and searched."

Still wary, Baba watched and waited. Only when he saw them flush a *Mislim* from his hiding place and haul him off in handcuffs did he let us leave the roof.

Nana headed for the kitchen. The rest of us clustered at the radio. From every sector the military made the same report. "The coup is crushed." Until further notice, a curfew was to be observed throughout the city, and people were forbidden to assemble in groups of more than five.

The official statement was read repeatedly, without a single word changed, and it mystified me that Baba listened more intently every time. Satisfied at last, he switched the set off and explained, "I had to see if they kept saying 'throughout the city' and 'any assembly.' " So that was it! He'd wanted to be sure that everyone was covered, not only Jews.

Sometime later, the Regent spoke, announcing that the King was back in Baghdad, and, in his name, expressed profound regret that such "unfortunate occurrences" had taken place. While making no specific reference to whom the damage had been done, he pledged the government to safeguard all its citizens. I was relieved but not entirely convinced. Experience was teaching me that safety lay in being just a bit suspicious. Only time would tell if we could trust the Regent.

Although we hadn't eaten since the day before, we barely picked at Nana's dinner. Even if we hadn't been too nervous to relax, and so fatigued that chewing was an effort, we wouldn't have made a dent in it. Fresher worries had killed whatever appetite we might have had, but no one wished to be the first to bring them up. Better to assume the family had all come through as well as we had. But, of course, we nearly *hadn't.* And, except for Uncle Ezra, my aunts and uncles lived in far more dangerous zones than we did. Aware of what was troubling us, Baba laid the law down. "Everyone to bed. We can't do anything until tomorrow."

It was safe now to start sleeping on the roof, but torrid as it was, each of us decided on his own to stay inside. Without expressing it, or even knowing it perhaps, we wanted the security of solid walls around us.

Everyone was up much earlier than usual, but with the curfew on, we couldn't leave the house. The telephone was still disabled, and broadcasts wouldn't begin for several hours. By 6:00 A.M.—the end of curfew—we were snapping at each other in our impotent impatience. Then the radio came alive and advised against our going out. We'd heard sporadic shots all morning as oddments of the mob were rounded up, but Baba brushed off all attempts to stop him. In spite of Nana's tears, he was heading toward the door when someone knocked at it.

I raced to get there first, but he pushed me back as fiercely as he'd pulled me off the roof. Of course. This couldn't be a normal call—not at 6:00 A.M.

He braced himself and cracked the door just far enough to see outside. A second later he yanked it open, and his youngest brother almost fell into the foyer. A stutterer, Uncle Kabi was the shyest figure at any family gathering. He was the *last* one we'd expect to brave the streets today. Father started to rebuke him for his rashness, but he didn't seem to hear. Looking dazed, and in a dull, flat voice, he interrupted.

"They got Haron."

Baba demanded details, but Uncle Kabi kept repeating, "They got Haron." Impatient with my uncle's slowness at the best of times, Baba seized his scrawny shoulders and shook him till he stammered "They stabbed Haron."

"Stabbed" was some improvement over "got," and I began to breathe again. My cousin wasn't dead. Haron was in a hospital, wounded seriously but still alive. In fits and starts, we drew the story out of Uncle Kabi.

Yesterday, before the full-scale riot started, Haron was walking with his friend Shaoul not far from home. A gang of Arab hoodlums had appeared, intent on trouble. Having grown up coping with this kind of thing and knowing he could hold his own, Haron's concern was solely for Shaoul. Frail and undersized because of asthma, he'd never learned to fight; the least exertion led to an attack.

As the boys approached, Haron thrust Shaoul aside and prepared to parry an attack. Expecting fists and feet, as in many past encounters, he was wholly unprepared for knives. The blade flashed out before he could recoil and run.

As soon as Haron fell, the boys had fled. Gasping like a fish, Shaoul had run to Uncle Ezra's, turning blue before their eyes as he wheezed out what had happened.

Uncle Ezra and Haron's two brothers had brought my cousin to the house. They stopped the bleeding and bandaged him as best they could, but Uncle knew the slashes needed quick and skilled attention. The house, however, was on the outer edge of Abbakhana, an Arab section, and five miles from the Jewish Hospital.

The streets by then were full of *M'silmin,* not yet a mob but working up to being one. Because of the danger and the distance, Haron had been carried to a nearby clinic owned and operated by a Christian Arab.

"He didn't want to take him in," Uncle Kabi told us, "but Ezra bribed him."

Baba was out the door before his brother finished. He was gone for hours, and the news he brought was bad. Haron was incoherent and burning up with fever. No one seemed to be attending him, and Baba had returned to get a doctor. "One of ours," he emphasized.

I begged to go back with him, and clung to him until he threw me off. All day long, I either hovered at the door or hung around the roof to see if I could spot him coming. Haron would be all right. Like a litany, I kept repeating all the reasons. After all, he'd only been out walking . . . they'd simply stumbled on him . . . senseless accident. . . .

Hearing Baba's footsteps, I clutched so hard at my *k'tibeh* that I broke the chain, but neither amulets nor prayers had helped. Though Baba didn't speak or even shake his head, Haron, I knew, was either dead or dying. Father looked as if his very soul was sick.

Haron was dying, and in agony. The septicemia was so advanced he couldn't be moved. My cousin was suffering and dying among *M'silmin* because the so-called "Christian" Arab hadn't made a move to save him. Our doctor had discovered Uncle Ezra's makeshift bandage still in place. The wounds had never been examined, never stitched or even cleaned. No drugs had been administered to ease the pain. Baba's voice had risen steadily, and now it broke. "The bastards didn't even feed him!"

Haron died the following day. As we later learned, the Christian Arab was known to be pro-Nazi. "But it wouldn't have mattered where you took him," Baba tried to comfort Uncle Ezra. On the night it happened, no Jew had been admitted to any public hospital.

The funeral was held that afternoon, but only grown-ups were allowed to go. The girls were staying with the neighbors, and, home alone, I crept off to the corner room we used for storage. Huddled there, I pictured the proceedings.

Right this minute, all the adults in the family were at the house in Abbakhana. Soon the pallbearers, followed by a line of mourners, would lift the coffin and carry it to where the Jews of Baghdad had been burying their dead for more than twenty centuries. The walk would take more time today. In a single night, 900 Jews had died. Twelve hundred more were wounded, with several hundred others unaccounted for. The Haddads would have a lot of company along the road. Luckily, Jewish custom only called for carrying—not burying—the dead in coffins. Otherwise there wouldn't have been enough to go around.

Secluded in the corner room, I conjured up the cemetery scene. The teak-and-rosewood box, carved and softly quilted, but without a cover. The corpse, face up to Heaven. At the gravesite, the closest relative, Uncle Ezra, would sift some earth on both the corpse's eyes and on the body. Next, the body would be lifted out of the ornate *aron,* laid into a shallow grave, and sealed beneath a layer of soil. At a later date we'd build a dome of brick above it. Till then, all Haron would have was a covering of dirt from the country that had killed him.

I'd been saying "corpse" and "body" to myself to stave off the reality of Haron's death, but having said "Haron," I saw his face. It was my cousin's face that stared up to the sky, and racking sobs replaced my stoic self-possession. In the isolation of the storage room, I cried myself to sleep.

I woke abruptly, knowing what I had to do. The decision had been made in sleep, without my conscious input, and awed by my intent, I crept silently downstairs, heading for the cupboard where Baba kept our Bible. For the past 600 years, all family births and deaths had been recorded in this book, and because of its fragility, Baba had forbidden us to touch it. What I had to do, however, demanded that I disobey.

The book was on the highest shelf, cocooned in Nana's best embroidered cloth and pushed well back for safety and concealment. I had to mount a stool to reach it, and tease it to the shelf edge with the handle of our largest ladle. It was heavier than I expected, and my hands were trembling when I took it to the dining table.

Unwrapping it, I held my breath and turned its aged pages with exquisite care. The ancient Hebrew script made it difficult for me to find what I was after. At last, it leaped up off the page: "Whosoever sheddeth the blood of man, by man shall his blood be shed."

With my hand upon the Torah, I took a solemn oath. To avenge Haron, I swore that I would execute an Arab.

That night the immediate family started to sit *shiva* for Haron. For seven days they'd sit together on a rug-strewn floor, praying for his soul, while friends and relatives stopped in to offer their condolences and cook for them. As the week progressed, it grew ever plainer that sitting *shiva* would be all they did. If *all* their sons were slaughtered, they'd simply sit and pray.

When I asked my father why we couldn't organize to fight off future threats, his eyebrows lifted and he laughed.

"You're joking!"

I wasn't and I said so.

Smile gone, Baba snapped, "The Jews of Baghdad are afraid of their own shadows."

I wasn't satisfied with that, and throwing up his hands at my persistence, he attempted to explain. I wiggled with impatience when he started with the Ottomans. What I wanted was the *now,* not the centuries of Turkish rule, but his expression said that it was all or nothing. Resigned, I settled back to listen—and learned some things our school texts never touched on.

He told me how, when the Ottoman Empire held dominion over half the world, the Turks oppressed the *M'silmin,* who, in turn, oppressed the Jews. Jews were not permitted to own property outside the ghetto or to leave the ghetto after nightfall. In every respect, a Jew was made inferior to a *Mislim.* Meeting on a narrow street, the holiest Jew would have to step aside for any ragamuffin Arab; age or station didn't make a difference. Jews might open shops, but the majority of crafts and most of the professions were closed to them.

I interjected, "But what about you, Baba?" Until father, there hadn't been a Jewish plumber in Iraq. Wasn't it a matter of ability, plus guts enough to back it up?

Baba was exceptional and knew it, but he reminded me that luck had played a part. As the holder of a Persian passport, he'd had a little extra leeway. And if it suited him, he could also pass as a patrician Arab. Mainly, though, he depended on his skills and the respect that he inspired. Very tall for an Iraqi Jew, clearly powerful, and commanding in his attitude, he didn't invite abuse.

"They know I'm not afraid," he said, "but the average Jew has forgotten how to make a fist. First the *M'silmin* crippled Jews, and now they say that 'Jewish hands are paralyzed.' When a lie's repeated long enough, people will believe it. After all this time, both the Arabs and the Jews believe it's true."

I had my answer, as unpleasant as it was, but Baba still had more to say. He'd arrived by now, at 1917—the beginning of the British occupation. With the English on the scene, Iraqi Jews acquired a certain measure of security. They felt so safe, in fact, that Zionists from Palestine were teaching Hebrew in the Quarter and collecting money for the Jewish National Fund. Eight years later, Palestine exploded, and following the Arab butchery of Jews in Hebron, riots against Iraqi Jews had broken out in Baghdad. King Faisal was willing to protect our people but they'd have to pay a price: disavowal of the Zionist movement.

From Baba's face, it was hard to tell if he approved of his compatriots' compliance, and when he spoke again, his attitude still struck me as ambivalent.

"For awhile we had peace, so now that *this* revolt is over and the British have come back again, if only on a treaty basis, the community believes that all is well, that another golden age is on its way."

But did *he* believe?

"And who can blame them?" He answered my unspoken question with an indecisive sigh. "The British troops will help the whole economy, and when things go well, we also benefit."

I noticed that he'd switched from "they" to "we." And when he ended with "And you think these Jews will make a fist and fight?" I wondered on which side he stood, or if he knew himself.

I had a hunch that all the adults, even Baba, could be counted out. They'd grown too used to compromise. They couldn't conceive of unrestricted freedom, of entitlement to equal rights. Instead, they'd let the *M'silmin* make them *dhimmis,* with the quality of life, and even life itself, dependent on an Arab frown or favor.

Perhaps, as father said, I couldn't fault them, but neither could I trust my future to hands that couldn't or wouldn't make a fist. I didn't plan to be a *dhimmi* or to die before the Lord intended. One day, along with others of my age, I'd surely have to stand and fight. And toward that time, we'd have to organize an army, invisible to both the Arabs and the older Jews. I'd known it since the day that Haron died.

8

Officially everything was once again in order. The restored regime was striving to assure us of our safety under its administration. Although the major criminals had long since fled, a few unlucky, laggard officers were executed as evidence that, with the King's return, righteousness had also been recouped. Overnight the anti-Zionist diatribes gave way to earnest dissertations on "the age-old spirit of Iraq, our beloved land which values all its citizens alike."

It's possible that, even then, I might have been persuaded, but they didn't have the sense to stop with such as that. Someone in the upper echelons of government selected a quotation from the Koran for repeated broadcast. It was meant to underwrite the promise of a perfect, shared society, and the phrase they picked to blueprint this utopia was "Muhammad commands us to protect the Jews."

They played the message every other minute, and every repetition made me angrier. If truly equal, no citizen required such a special service. What the *M'silmin* were protecting was their power. From all appearances, however, I was alone in opposition. The community was more than willing to accept the same old system. I couldn't believe how quickly they had wiped away the last few months. They buried memories as fast as they interred their dead.

If Haron were here, I knew what he'd be saying. "Of course they're hopeful. They know the British laid the law down." Unlike me, Haron did not admire the Empire. I could almost hear his voice; by now, it would be rising, telling me that "riots are disruptive to the interests of the English in the Middle East, and this regime depends on English arms. Actually it doesn't have a thing to do with us. We're just some pawns for them to play with."

Thinking of Haron recalled my oath to mind. As yet I hadn't made the smallest effort to effect a plan, and while I *would* dispatch an Arab to avenge my cousin, to date I hadn't even set a deadline for the deed.

The truth is that I liked the Arabs in my life, and even though I looked at them with new and deep distrust, I didn't want to see them dead. Haron's Arab would have to be a stranger. Since I'd made my pact with God, I guess I was awaiting help from Him to pick my victim. When He caused the proper man to cross my path, I'd keep my promise.

In the period immediately after Haron's death, our relationships with *M'silmin* were extremely awkward. Arab friends expressed their sorrow and the family accepted their regrets, but guilt and horror hung between us, tainting each exchange to some degree.

The grown-ups, intertwined in commerce and dependent on each other, told themselves that everything would be the same "in time." I was afraid it would. Baba and his friend Tawfik, a building contractor with whom he'd worked for years, were already back to normal. Tawfik came to see us as casually as a member of the family. In fact, I'd always called him "Uncle," and run to him, as to my Uncle Ezra, to be hugged.

Following my cousin's death, he'd paid a consolation call, and at first my father had been overly polite and formal. However, Baba's face began to thaw when tears filled Tawfik's eyes. From across the room, Tawfik held his arms out for our usual embrace, but I didn't make a move. I'd said my final "Uncle" to an Arab.

Father never mentioned my rejection but when another Arab friend, Bahjat Baik by name, phoned from Basra to express his shock and ask if he could aid in any way, Baba quietly observed that "it's better to have *Mislim* friends than enemies." Especially a friend like Bahjat, I reflected.

His actual name was Bahjat al-Delaymi, but everybody called him Baik, an honorary title—Turkish for a rank exceeded only by a Pasha. He was a handsome, blue-eyed blond from north Iraq, who had married wisely and with an eye to his career. Both intelligent and backed by monied and important people, he'd already reached the post of Assistant Chief of Police of Baghdad when Baba met him.

At the time, the Baik was just about to build a house, and, able to afford the best, he'd hired Baba. From the very first, my father knew the man was bound to rise, and, looking toward the future, he refused to bill him when the work was done. However, Bahjat made a point of paying. He wouldn't accept *bakhsheesh,* he said, because Islamic principles forbid it. Father was impressed. In Baba's whole experience, such religious scruples had never stopped another *Mislim.* The Baik was equally impressed with Baba, and soon the two of them were close enough to call each other Abu Tarik and Abu S'hak.

New administrations came and went, and with every change the Baik had moved on up another notch. Now Inspector General of all Iraq, he was calling to apologize for *M'silmin* murderers, telling us his heart was bleeding for the family. Almost incidentally, he mentioned that we'd see his sergeant shortly. He was sending him to pick up Baba and escort him to the house he'd built. Would Abu S'hak please prepare it for his imminent return? Bahjat valued Baba, well aware that a master plumber was even rarer in Iraq than an honest government official. It was a "working" friendship in which, in father's words, "one hand washed the other."

I couldn't be as tolerant as he was. I didn't *want* to be that tolerant. In school and in the synagogue, they'd drummed it into me that man should seek the right, not settle for the realistic. Therefore, I was growing ever more conflicted while those around me were relaxing back into the status quo.

It was question time again, but this time I had harder questions than those I'd asked of Baba about Jews and *M'silmin.* These had to do with God and man. I was baffled by a God who could allow such injustice and suffering as we endured, a God to whom Haron had prayed with love and trust.

The *yeshiva* was the source of answers to such questions, but I couldn't study in religious school until I made *bar mitzvah,* and I couldn't make *bar mitzvah* before I reached thirteen—except, if I remembered rightly, the age requirement was sometimes waived.

When I broached the thought to Baba, he rejected it, but since *bar mitzvah* was the province of the rabbi, he agreed to put the matter up to him and abide by his decision. After quizzing me, the rabbi said that I was ready, and Baba set the ceremony for July. I hadn't mentioned the *yeshiva.* That would be a higher hurdle.

The chaos of the past few months had closed our school before the normal summer recess, and before our final tests. Tomorrow it would open, but only long enough for those exams, then shut again until September. The timing couldn't have been more perfect for what I planned to do.

Since Haron's death, I'd racked my brain for a fitting way to say a last farewell. I hadn't been there when he died. I wasn't with him when they put him in the ground. I didn't sit *shiva,* and I couldn't stop shaving for a month like Uncle Ezra because I hadn't even started. Anyway, one did that for a father. For cousin-brother-friend and mentor, there weren't any rules to guide me. I could forge my own farewell, but it had to be one worthy of Haron, something special, something that he'd hug me for if he were here. The reopening of school offered me the ideal opportunity. Suddenly I knew exactly what to say and where to say it.

We had two *Mislim* teachers; with one of them I had a real rapport, and I chose his class to act in. He, at least, was capable of understanding. 'Mrewah taught us Arab history. He was a decent, thinking man, an activist whose monthly broadcast had been sponsored by the government, before the Nazi coup. With the Fascists gone, he'd undoubtedly be on the air again, lecturing about Islamic grandeur as he did to us.

Before history we had five periods with Jewish teachers, and each one made me more despairing of my elders. None said a word about the pogrom. One even made a joke about our long "vacation." It took all my self-control to keep my mouth shut. What I had to say, I had to say in history class.

I was 'Mrewah's favorite student, so when I asked if I might read a paper I'd prepared, he smiled and waved me to my feet. Since the term began, I'd delivered several compositions that delighted him. The one he liked the best had been on "Justice in Islam"; it was a laudatory essay on Caliph Ali, Muhammad's nephew.

On this first day back, every classroom had been noisy, the students squirmingly impatient to be done with school again. History was no exception. Samy, though, was sitting at attention, undistracted by the others, so I fixed on him and started speaking.

"Much has happened since we last were here together. The last time that I spoke to you, I spoke as an Iraqi"—from the corner of my eye, I saw my teacher's smile slip a little, then fade away entirely as I continued—"but now instead I speak to you as one Jew to another."

The shuffling and whispering had stopped, and every pair of eyes was on me. All but 'Mrewah's. His were focused somewhere out in space. He was trying not to see me and succeeding, but I didn't care. He couldn't turn his ears off.

"Last year," I said, "I spoke to you of justice in Islam. Now I speak to you of bloodshed in the streets of Baghdad." There were gasps, for I'd turned my back on Samy and my classmates. What I was saying now was mainly for 'Mrewah.

I aimed directly at him. "Where now is this Islamic justice? Is the glory of Islam to rise up on the ruins of Jewish homes? Will it bloom upon the broken stones of synagogues? Will it boast of cutting off the feet of Jewish babies so the faithful may have offerings of ankle-rings for Allah?"

The whole class caught its breath as one. 'Mrewah's face was waxen, and he'd closed his eyes.

"If that is Islam's thinking, this Jew will tell you that those days are over." My voice was getting reedy with emotion, and I struggled to control it. The more dispassionate my tone, the more attention would be paid my message.

"The next time," I said slowly and distinctly, "the next time Jews will be prepared. We will defend ourselves by any means at our disposal, and for every Jew who dies, an Arab will be dead as well."

Before the last word died away, I was trembling like a rubber band released from tension. The room was absolutely still; no one even shifted in his seat. 'Mrewah broke the silence, speaking in a strange, constricted voice.

"I can't dispute your every word," he started, but the natural pause to marshal arguments prolonged past normal limits as he searched in vain for anything to offer, but, a sensitive and honest man, he had no real rebuttal. Lamely and ashamedly, he ended with the words I'd heard from all our Arab friends, "but not all of us are guilty." Fifteen minutes early, with his eyes averted, he rang the bell for our dismissal.

I ran for home alone. Samy and the others shouted after me, but for once, I wasn't interested in anyone's opinion or applause. Haron had had his funeral oration. At the moment, that was all that mattered.

By morning, the entire school had heard about the speech. On entering the *hosh,* I was surrounded by a mob of screaming students. Several grabbed at me, and there was such an uproar that I feared at first the whole *shamash* was up in arms against me. At home last night, I'd wondered what reception to expect. Some approval, and a good deal more of sitting on the fence, I figured. Probably a few would call me stupid for stabbing at a sleeping beast, but I hadn't counted on hostility in wholesale lots.

When I could make out words, my mouth fell open in astonishment. The clamor was composed entirely of compliments! Haron's farewell had kicked off a recruitment drive. They wanted me to tell them how to join the Jewish army! How could I confess that it was nonexistent? The bell reprieved me, but during recess, I'd have to put a plan together. *Someone* had to make a start. There'd never be a better opportunity—almost Heaven-sent, it seemed—as if Haron had made it happen.

At the break, an audience assembled quickly, and to start things off, I tried out titles. Underground was greeted with the loudest shouts, Defense Corps drawing only slightly less enthusiasm. When I began to speak of knives and guns, however, some who'd been the most vociferous grew silent. Others backed away as I informed them of the measures we might have to take. When recess ended, I was practically alone.

All afternoon I brooded through my classes, contemptuous of those around me. They'd take a stand as long as war was waged with words, but put some weapons in the picture, add the possibility of combat, and see how fast they'd cut and run. It's not as if I'd spoken of attacking others. Since our sole concern would be our own defense, they couldn't excuse themselves by questioning the ethics of an underground. It couldn't be anything but cowardice.

I must have shown my scorn, because when school let out, Selim, an upperclassman, stopped me and insisted that he wasn't scared. At fourteen, he was twice my size. His voice was in the bass range and extremely resonant, and before I realized what he was after, he controlled the conversation, speaking less to me than to the audience his voice attracted. Too late, I recognized the signs of well-rehearsed and highly polished exposition.

"Do you think that we're the only ones who suffer?" On that he turned and talked directly to the others. "People are oppressed in every country, on every continent. Alone, in little enclaves, all of them are easy prey, but united in a worldwide brotherhood. . . ."

I grimaced. Again, "brotherhood"! But his audience was buying it. The word itself was soothing, much more so than "underground" or "guns."

When I spoke to Selim later, he confirmed what I suspected. He *did* belong to *Hizb al-Shuyui'i.* The Communist Party was illegal in Iraq, so his openness about it made me blink—and more surprises were in store. I assumed he was the one and only member in our school, but in the next recess, he introduced three others, and another six the morning after. By the time school closed again, our class divergences were clear. Of sixty students, about a third were Communists or followers, seven or eight agreed with me, and those remaining were too fearful, or too starry-eyed, or just too indecisive to opt for anything but breathing in and out.

I was startled by a showing of such strength. Our school curriculum ignored the Russian revolution, and all I knew about the Party, I'd picked up on my own. All Reds, I'd heard, were barbarous and blood-stained anarchists who tossed their bombs at random and wanted to abolish marriage. They were also said to be against religion, but that was patently untrue, or how could Jewish boys be so involved?

Deciding that I'd check it out myself, I searched but couldn't find a single book on Marx or Lenin in the library. Always seeking converts, Selim lent me his, and I was utterly convinced. Communism offered nothing to the Jews or to any group intent on keeping its identity intact.

Selim's tracts spelled out the main objectives of the Party in the simplest and least subtle terms, and dissolution of religious ties was one of them. Selim laughed, however, when I told him that he'd have to choose between the hammer and sickle and the synagogue. In the Party's perfect world, he said, all people would be truly equal, and when everyone was equal, no one had the power to enforce his will on someone else. How, then, could the way a person worshipped be affected?

Selim was lost in dreams of earthly paradise, and unreachable as all the other Party members. Everyone had been recruited since the riots and imbued with the illusion that the Russians had the answer. The pogrom had been a blessing for the Party. Selim and other disillusioned Jews had simply fallen to it by default. No one else had held out either help or hope. I bound myself to offer an alternative after my *bar mitzvah.*

Aside from the *yeshiva,* which as yet I hadn't mentioned, I wanted to *bar mitzvah* early for another reason. If I waited, I'd have to suffer through a huge affair, like S'hak's, and I wasn't in a merry-making mood. However, Baba loved to entertain, and only in the wake of the pogrom—which meant right now—would he consent to keeping the festivities confined within the family.

There wasn't time enough to sew a new *bar mitzvah* suit for me. Nana and Nazima were pushed, in fact, to put the final touches on the prayer shawl; it was extra wide, fringed at either end, with knotted tassels at the corners, and provided with a beautifully embroidered pocket. Now that I'd be wearing the phylacteries, my boyish shawl would be too narrow. Baba had reminded me a hundred times that putting on *t'filim* is a private act, which only God may witness. The shawl, therefore, must be voluminous enough to hide the head and arms.

As I stood before the family, I again reviewed his teachings on *t'filim.* First, there were the two fine deerhide straps, natural tan on one side, dyed black on the other, and of differing lengths. The light side was always to be worn against the skin. The light and dark represented day and night, as well as God and man, and the straps themselves signified the Levis and Cohanim, the two tribes of the twelve which were singled out especially to serve the Lord.

The two *hazozrah,* though the tiniest of boxes, only an inch or so on every side, were exquisitely constructed of five thin layers of leather, each containing lines of text taken from the five books of the Pentateuch. From tomorrow morning on, for as long as I would live, I'd wind the straps and place the cubes, one on the arm, the other on the brow, as Jews had done for more than five millenia. In time, my father told me, donning the *t'filim* would become such second nature that I couldn't make an error if I tried. And yet, he warned, the sacrament must never be an automatic and unthinking process. Always and forever, *Kavanah* must be uppermost in mind. He'd cautioned me repeatedly, "Attention and intent . . . attention and intent."

I began the ceremony by kissing the phylacteries. Sitting down and pulling up the shawl to make a tent, I concealed myself so only God could see me, then proceeded with the ritual. Baba's voice reechoed as I did so. "The first *hazozrah* on the bicep of the arm, the left arm, nearest to the heart." Take one turn of the strap "for the seven days of the Creation," three more "for Abraham, Isaac, and Jacob." For "the four corners of the universe," the four dangling corners of the shawl. Finally, in the center of the brow, the second of the cubes, symbolizing knowledge: "Torah, given by God to crown the head of man."

I'd risen, as prescribed, to place the second cube. In sitting down again to pray, I shook beneath the shawl, overwhelmed by the immensity of the occasion. In this, the single biggest step I'd ever take, I'd bridged the gap between the boy I'd been and the man I'd now become. In this single act, I'd taken on the obligations of adulthood—those of man to man and those of Jew to God—and I prayed to God that I was really ready.

On standing up and kissing Baba's hand, I saw his pride in me—and also sadness that I'd grown up sooner than he would have wished. His speech was very short and emphasized what I already knew. From this day on, I was accountable.

I swallowed hard, fingered my *k'tibeh,* and answering my father, announced my first decision as an adult. When I said I wanted to attend *yeshiva,* a shock wave ran around the room. Our family was observant, but not as utterly committed as, say, Samy's. We didn't run to rabbis, and in Baghdad, one only went to a *yeshiva* if the Rabbinate was what he wanted.

Baba looked as if I'd punched him in the stomach, and I wished that everyone would go away so I could speak to him and ease his mind. I had no intention of ever entering the Rabbinate, and I'd continue to attend my present school. All I wanted from *yeshiva* were some basic facts about the pact between the Jews and God. What I had to know was why we Jews were singled out for so much bloodshed. Perhaps there wasn't any answer, or perhaps the answer was so mystical that only certain of us were allowed to share the secret. I might not like what I would learn, but religious school was where I'd learn it.

9

The next morning, while winding the *t'filim* for the first time on my own, my mind, I realized, was already wandering from the ritual. No matter how I concentrated, thoughts of the *yeshiva* kept intruding.

The night before, I'd tried my best with Baba, but he still objected, and the basis of his opposition so astounded me, I'd simply given up and gone to bed.

Baghdad's sole *yeshiva* was, of course, connected with the Rabbinate, and the religious court, according to my father, had descended into dire disrepute, so serious, he said, that I'd be tainted by the slightest tie. Expecting something lurid, I could hardly wait to hear the story, but the sordid matter only had to do with meat stamps.

To a large degree, the Rabbinate depended on the fees collected for the *kasher*ing of meat. Seven years ago, a rumor started circulating in the Quarter that the proceeds ended up in private pockets. Fingers pointed to the highest-ranking rabbi. While he indignantly denied it, something even worse had surfaced to indict him. Our meat was stamped to show its suitability for Jewish use, and his accusers said he sold the usage of the stamp. That meant that *trefa*—unclean—meat was on the market, and unsuspecting Jews were eating it.

The religious court eventually expelled him, but instead of putting things to rights, the action aggravated an already sorry situation. The Iraqi government and many of the country's richest Jews sided with the ex-Chief Rabbi, and since these Jews controlled the Jewish Council, and the Jewish Council controlled the treasury of the court, they were able to withhold the salaries of all the other rabbis. They, in turn, halted all the *kasher* slaughtering in the city.

Baba said the impasse lasted seven months, until the people rose in wrath and started demonstrating in the streets. Although the slaughtering resumed, the affair, he warned, was not forgotten. Father claimed the whole community still shied away from anyone connected with the court. He added hastily that individual rabbis were as honored and esteemed as ever, and the *yeshiva,* he acknowledged, hadn't been involved at all, but when Baba had his mind made up, he tended to lose sight of logic.

My only hope was Rabbi Ezra. *Hakham* Ezra taught at the *yeshiva,* and if anyone could win my father over, it was he. Baba often spoke about the brilliant Talmudist—a man, he stressed, not only learned in scripture, but lion-hearted and completely incorruptible. However, before I started in again on Baba, I had a selling job to do on *Hakham* Ezra. His class had been in session for a year already, and he'd have to be convinced that I could catch up and keep pace.

By September, I'd brought the two of them together, and both reluctantly agreed to let me enter the *yeshiva,* though the *Hakham* was concerned about my schedule. To an adult, I suppose it looked impossible, but at almost-twelve, I was untiring—or so I thought.

I was the only boy at the *yeshiva*—'Slat Zilkha was its name—who also went to secular school. The *yeshiva*'s morning session ran from five to seven, so I could sleep until 4:30 at the very latest. At 'Slat Zilkha, morning prayers were said exactly as the sun rose, so we sometimes studied Talmud first, with one eye turned to Heaven to distinguish dawn. When early classes ended, all of us went home for breakfast and, except for me, returned at nine to take instruction in such down-to-earth affairs as *kasher* slaughtering, the proper upkeep of a synagogue, and the conduct of a *brith. Hakham* Ezra permitted me to skip these sessions, so after gulping down a hasty meal, I headed for *shamash,* my other school, which ran from 8 A.M. to 2 P.M. Lunch at home was also on the run, because from three to five, I claimed involvement in activities connected with my classes.

While I couldn't tell bold-faced lies to Baba or the rabbi, neither could I tell them the entire truth. In a way, what I did from three to five *was* associated with the school. All seven members of the underground, which met each afternoon, were fellow students. As I said I would, I'd begun to organize for our defense as soon as my *bar mitzvah* was behind me.

At five, I hurried back to the *yeshiva,* and, at eight o'clock, left the building like a bullet from the barrel of a gun. The others dawdled, exchanging idle talk among themselves while waiting to accompany the rabbi wherever he might have to go.

In speeding off, I wasn't being snobbish or aloof, but at 8 P.M., every second was extremely precious. That's when the BBC began to broadcast. Since our papers were completely biased, listening to the BBC had been a necessary part of life, like food or drink, since I first became concerned about "the Palestinian problem." Eating—even greeting anyone at home—had to wait until the broadcast ended. Ravenous by then, I'd shovel dinner in as fast as I could spoon it up and swallow. I still had several hours of studying ahead, and rarely got to bed before eleven.

I thrived on the regime, and though enlightenment along religious lines was slow in coming, I was learning facts of life at the *yeshiva* that I'd never been exposed to at any of my other schools. Until 'Slat Zilkha, I'd only met with other boys much like myself, from families with no financial worries, and since everyone around me lived the same abundant life, I'd never felt unduly lucky.

Until now, I'd taken all I had for granted. Now, though, I was made to measure it against existence for the other kids in class. The contrast was as stark as that of slave and sheikh, and I was sheikh, not because of anything I'd yet accomplished, but only by an accident of birth. Glad, admittedly, at being so well-born, I was also, for the first time in my life, truly grateful for my great good fortune. And mixed with gratitude was a certain new humility and almost shame. I had so much. So many had so little.

Most of the *yeshiva* students were there because they *were* so poor. At

'Slat Zilkha, unlike expensive secondary schools, they received a practical as well as a religious education. Maybe two of the entire class would wind up full-fledged rabbis. Many would be *shohets* and spend their days in ritual slaughtering of animals for food. Others would be *mohels,* hoping every pregnancy produced a boy because the *mohels* handled all the circumcisions in the Quarter. Those who had melodic voices might aspire to be *hazans* and officiate at services. The remaining students would either wind up *ozers,* aides to cantors, or on the lowest rung of the religious ladder, act as ushers in the synagogues or odd-jobs men.

At this early age, their entire lives were predetermined, while my major problem would be weighing which of many options to adopt. To justify the headstart I'd been given, I'd have to work a whole lot harder than the others and learn enough to make a larger contribution. It was the only way to even up the score.

In view of the discrepancies between us, I expected some resentment from the other boys, and was embarrassed when, instead, they openly expressed their admiration. At the very least, I anticipated taunts about my custom-tailored schedule, but this too only served to make me seem the more exceptional. While I thoroughly enjoyed a contest, I found it difficult to cope with this unearned, too easy approbation. Their lack of envy was amazing. If I'd been in their shoes—in their old, scuffed shoes, in patched up clothes with empty pockets—I'd have hated me with all my heart.

Though Rabbi Ezra seemed oblivious to the situation, I'm sure he was aware of what was happening. I believe, in fact, he meant for it to happen. I must have struck him as supremely cocky when I came to him to ask to be admitted. Had he accepted me in *spite* of my "superiority"—to shake me up and force the sort of insight I was finally achieving? At that initial interview, when he asked why I was there, I told him that I wanted him to teach me "all about the Lord and our religion." At the time, I thought his answer was evasive.

"Before a man can know the Lord, he must know his fellowman. And to know your fellowman, first you have to know yourself. You must look inside yourself with honest eyes."

I was looking now as never in the past, as he undoubtedly intended that I should. The system at the *shamash* actively encouraged competition and measured one's success in marks. Here I saw my standing in *Hakham* Ezra's smile or frown.

In things like history and math, the answers were exact and unequivocal. All I had to do was read a book and throw back what the text had taught me. I was finding, though, that answers at *yeshiva* were elusive. Rabbi Ezra and the Torah were supposed to be my shortcuts to the truth, but I could tell already that attainment of the truth could take a lifetime.

Each school demanded different things of me. They were dissimilar in every way, including their design. Each *yeshiva* classroom, for example, was in a sense a little synagogue, laid out so its western wall would be intact.

The wall, which faced Yerushalayim, was never broken by a door, and any absolutely necessary opening was always curtained. When we prayed, we faced the west, toward what remained there of the desecrated Second Temple. The Torah, central to all teaching, was supported by a wooden lectern in the center of the classroom and surrounded on three sides by several rows of hard, bare, wooden benches. Cross-legged, sometimes rocking on my haunches to relieve the pressure, I listened more attentively to Rabbi Ezra than to anyone I'd ever known.

Hakham Ezra was all and more than I'd anticipated. Asked for a description in the first few days, I would have said his eyes were like an eagle's. The rest was simply aura. When we met, his eyes had seemed to auger into mine and link directly with the seat of all my senses. A current flowed between us on a narrow focused beam, and everything beyond it was a blur. Only in the classroom, when his eyes were concentrated elsewhere, could I really see the rest of him.

He was even taller than my father, with a creamy skin and heavy, ink-black hair, waving off the highest, widest brow a man could have. Unlike most Iraqi rabbis, who were "modern," *Hakham* Ezra, in accordance with Talmudic law, left his beard untrimmed. Even blacker than his hair, billowing out and streaming down, it blanketed his upper body like a living shield. His towering height and striking coloration, together with those startlingly incisive eyes, would have added up to someone awesome, even scary, except that both his head and back were bowed from years of poring over scrolls and bending down to better hear the lesser men and students who consulted him.

In our first encounter, I'd given up all hope of quick and easy answers. When he informed me that I'd start with study of the Torah, I argued that I'd long since finished all five books; he shook his head in disbelief. Plainly, I'd already disappointed him.

Sighing, he explained. "Everybody thinks the Torah is only those five books of Moses. The Moses Torah is merely one of three parts of the Bible, and the Bible is only one of five parts of the Torah. In any case, reading the Bible is not knowing the Bible. To understand its meaning, the Talmud must be studied too."

Utterly demolished, I listened to a further inventory of unknowns: the Mishna and G'mara, the two components of the Talmud . . . the Midrash, the third segment of the Torah . . . the fourth, the Mashal . . . the Haggadah . . . On hearing Haggadah, I brightened up and burst in with the news that I *did* know something! I was acquainted with the Haggadah, and proclaimed, as proof, "Passover! That's the story of Passover."

This time I was truly shocked when he shook his head and smiled sadly. I'd been so sure. The Haggadah, I learned, consisted of a *thousand* stories. My head was swimming, and we still had one more segment to explore.

The fifth part of the Torah, said Rabbi Ezra, was the Sod. He'd amplified on all the others, but here he stopped with such abruptness, I could tell he wouldn't continue. "Sod," I knew, meant "secret," and the word itself, along with his reluctance, piqued my interest. Curiosity, as always, conquered caution. I asked him to describe the Sod, but saw at once I'd made a major error. His lips compressed as he rose to end the interview, stating as he did so, "The Sod is not for everyone"—it sounded like a warning—"and certainly not for someone who's just starting in to study."

As he walked away, I wondered if my *big* mistake had been insisting on attending the *yeshiva.* Instead of solving the uncertainties I'd come with, all I'd done was turn up new enigmas—and I hadn't even been enrolled yet. I couldn't back out because I'd been too stubborn about getting in. But what was it I'd gotten into?

As instructed, I studied Torah. Along with being wise, benevolent, and understanding, *Hakham* Ezra was also the supreme, all-powerful authority at 'Slat Zilkha. We might ask a thousand questions about anything he ordered us to do, but there wasn't any doubt about our doing it. To his students he was more than guide and mentor. "As God is to the Rabbi, so the Rabbi is to us" was the way that we expressed it.

At the *yeshiva,* every rabbi was the absolute, unchallenged ruler of his classroom, but none was served as slavishly as *Hakham* Ezra. Students fetched and carried for him endlessly, and on private or religious errands, they battled for the honor of acting as unpaid attendants. When he sat, someone ran to slip his shoes off the second that his feet had left the floor. At the slightest indication of his wish to stand, the closest student leaped to slip them on again. He could hardly lift a finger on his own behalf. All he was allowed to exercise was intellect.

In addition to his teaching, *Hakham* Ezra also functioned in the customary roles assigned to rabbis. Happily for all his hungry students, he officiated at many festive weddings and almost daily lent his presence to some sad or glad occasion, all of which included food.

The pupils who escorted him would stuff themselves and bring back what they couldn't eat to those of us the *Hakham* hadn't taken. In the early days, I'd grab along with all the rest when they returned, but after watching the voracious way the others ate, I quit the competition. What was just a tiny extra treat for me was vital sustenance for some of them. Rabbi Ezra never mentioned my renunciation, but I think that he was pleased with me.

Early on, when he'd agreed to let me skip the ritual slaughter sessions, I remember he'd remarked, "So the *shohet* comes to you to kill a lamb." Now I knew it hadn't been a casual comment. He'd been telling me how fortunate I was. I'd already seen firsthand what the other boys would have to learn from lectures. Their families could barely feed them, much less buy entire lambs, then send for *shohets* for the slaughter. They *couldn't* be as well informed as I was, or, not so incidentally, as strong and healthy.

Inasmuch as I'd been given to the family that God selected, I felt that shame was futile and uncalled-for. If I harbored any self-reproach, it had to do with Haron, not my heritage.

Since my oath to kill an Arab, all I'd done was fantasize about the act. I'd looked at every adult male *Mislim* as a candidate for execution. In the market and on every crowded street, I assessed the men I saw, but if the time and place were opportune, I couldn't find the proper person, and if the place and person fit my plan, I wouldn't have a weapon with me.

If I killed amid a crowd of *M'silmin,* I'd be killed in turn, and if I did it in a Jewish section, every Jew around would be accused as my accomplice. Every time I narrowed down the possibilities, I came a cropper. This Arab was too old, that one much too mean and sickly. He wouldn't be missed, I told myself. It had to be a young and vital man whose death would leave a hole in many lives, as Haron's passing had.

Not a day went by without my saying, "Almost." How many "almosts" had there been since early June? I was starting to distrust my judgment and, more jolting still, my dedication to the job. Was I making rational assessments or seeking out excuses? Every day the doubts gnawed deeper.

The night the BBC reported from Bengazi on the butchery of Libyan Jews, the doubts about myself expanded to include the Lord. My pledge to Him was overdue, but His to us was more than merely unfulfilled. This latest incident was only one of many thousands He'd allowed. He'd made us chosen people, but He'd chosen us, apparently, as whipping boys for all the world. I wasn't ready to renounce him—yet . . . but sometime soon . . . unless He gave me insight into what He had in mind for us. . . .

The hair raised on my head, and sweat ran down my spine. *I* was giving *God* an ultimatum! If *Hakham* Ezra knew, I wondered if he'd laugh or cry.

With Haron weighing on my mind, I decided to retreat from revelation for awhile and concentrate my major effort on revenge—and with *Hakham* Ezra's help. Since the subject crops up often in the Book of Moses, it wasn't difficult to introduce, and though my mind was all made up, the Rabbi's affirmation had become important to me.

The tale of Jacob's daughter, Dinah, whom Hamor took against her will, afforded me an ideal opening. When we reached the point at which her brothers vowed to kill the violator, I asked, "Can anyone condemn them?"

Rabbi Ezra could, and in no uncertain terms. He categorically disowned reprisals by anyone but God. "Vengeance is mine, saith the Lord" was his immediate response. However, I rebounded briskly. "But He didn't say '*only* mine.' Was that an oversight, or was He leaving room for special cases?"

The whole class murmured in approval, and even Rabbi Ezra gave a grudging nod. Although my thesis was unsound, he said, my argument was interesting. But assuming that I *had* a case, he added, Dinah's brothers couldn't be used to bolster it. Moses, he reminded us, had not yet brought the Law when Hamor did his dirty deed, "and none were bound before the Law—but we are now."

Chastened, but only for a second, I countered swiftly with the story of the Prophet Samuel, who commanded Saul to "kill even the animals." When Saul allowed the animals to live, hadn't Samuel thundered, "God will tear the Kingdom from you"? Rabbi Ezra bobbed his head. "That's what I said. Vengeance is divine, the prerogative of God, and God alone. '*God* will tear the Kingdom. . . .' "

I retaliated with my best and last remaining reference. Then please explain, I asked, the order Moses issued to the Israelites: "An eye for an eye, a tooth for a tooth, and a life for a life."

I sat back, satisfied I had him, but he responded even faster than before. "That's justice, not revenge."

Hakham Ezra waited for another sally, but I'd spent my ammunition and to no avail. I couldn't convince him, but neither had he overturned my own conviction.

After this exchange, the forbidden Sod was more than ever on my mind. The classroom shelves were crammed with every size and shape of book, from ancient Aramaic texts to tomes in modern Hebrew. Among the thousands, there had to be a copy of the Zohar, which explains the Sod, and whenever I could do so unobserved, I searched for it. Alone one evening, I found it thrust behind another book, and defying Rabbi Ezra, opened it and started reading.

The mystic Zohar interpreted the two main streams of Jewish mysticism. At first, I only skimmed the section on Cabala. Defined as "inspiration straight from God," Cabala, once established, couldn't be questioned. Cabala, it appeared, hit one like a bolt from Heaven. From the blue, a rabbi would be struck with revelation, and while one might doubt a rabbi had received Cabala, when and if the inspiration was authenticated, his vision had the force of law.

Skipping quickly, afraid that *Hakham* Ezra might discover me, I found, by sheerest luck, a passage that erased the fear, replacing it with such excitement that I took the book and boldly spread it open on the lectern where the light was better.

By chance—or perhaps by preordainment—I had come upon a kindred spirit. Eighteen centuries ago, Rabbi Elisha 'Aher had been a questioner like me. The concept of a God encompassing both good and evil bothered him. His dilemmas were the same as mine, and I avidly pursued the text to see how he'd resolved them.

To my dismay, he ended as confused as ever, but continuing to read, my hopes revived. His pupil, author of the books said to be the basis of Cabala—and all ten together called the Zohar—seemed to strike a chord in me.

Now I could abandon Sod and not be insubordinate to Rabbi Ezra. He hadn't said I couldn't study Zohar, but of course he hadn't known I'd ever *heard* of Zohar. He couldn't know the certainty that filled my soul . . . that made this small evasion a necessity I couldn't deny.

One day, *I* would have Cabala. In one great thunderclap from God himself, I'd have the answers!

10

Life was getting very complicated. Like the Torah, mine was now divided into five distinctly separate segments. As if home and family, *shamash,* Rabbi Ezra, and my underground activities didn't fill the day quite full enough, I started up a business with my brother S'hak. Unknown to Baba, we ran a sort of store, operating from our bedroom with the cupboard as our warehouse and our stock concealed behind our clothes.

S'hak had a head for figures and understood the ins and outs of trade. He did the buying—mainly school supplies and common household items—and kept the firm's accounts. I handled sales, and with a captive clientele of family and friends and S'hak's cut-rate prices, we were prospering.

In financial matters, S'hak and I were almost always in accord, but otherwise had few, if any, common interests. Having finished all of school he wanted, he was keeping the accounts for Baba's plumbing business and would undoubtedly go on to great success in some commercial sphere. Ideologies and arcane aspects of religion didn't excite him in the least. Business was my brother's true belief; it was only trade, he argued, that would ever bring the Jews and *M'silmin* to an understanding. When he heard about the underground, he scoffed, "You see too many movies."

As the weeks went on, however, and my ardor didn't abate, his mocking stopped. Now he spoke more soberly. The underground was dangerous, he claimed, not only for its members but for every Jew. He stated flatly that kids couldn't keep a secret and that, once exposed, a secret group invited grim reprisals even if it hadn't done a single thing.

I yelled at him. He threatened me. He said he'd go to Baba and tell him all about the underground, but I knew better. No matter how he felt, he wouldn't inform on me to anyone, not even to our father. We never spoke about the group again.

Newly named, the Brotherhood for Jewish Defense had six enthusiastic members, all carefully selected. While I'd die before admitting it to S'hak, many of my classmates *couldn't* keep a secret. Take Samy, for example. I'd wanted Samy with us, but he backed away from every invitation. When he said his mother would be worried, I stopped pursuing him. We couldn't use anyone who'd tell his mother.

Shlomo Menashi was my first recruit. At fourteen, the oldest of us all, he was built as broadly as a bear, but moved his body like a cat. Once he'd fallen from a roof and bounced back to his feet without a scratch. Women were still screaming when he sped away.

His brother Shipath was a carbon copy, one size smaller. Shipath was a close friend of my cousin Sion, who was also in the Brotherhood. Like the two Menashis, Sion was a brawny type, a little short on brains, but I liked him and we'd played together all our lives.

Abdallah Safi, a friend of mine from school, was of another sort entirely. His mind moved faster than his muscles; I made him second in command.

The others wondered at my eagerness to have Hiyawi with us. His hidden asset was an older brother, the owner of a pharmacy. The day might come when we'd have need of him.

Naturally we took an oath, pledged ourselves to secrecy, sealed the bond with drops of blood, and swore to fight unto our deaths when Jewish lives were threatened. As I led them in the solemn chant, I reaffirmed the other vow that I alone had taken. Haron, in spirit, was our seventh member.

Aside from earnestness, we didn't have much to work with. We couldn't wear uniforms, of course. Insignia were also out, and even recognition signals would be risky. All I could dispense was status, so I gave them fancy titles. I planned to train this cadre first, then send each member out to mobilize another unit. Starting at our own *shamash,* in time we'd sign up every close-mouthed and courageous Jewish boy in all Iraq!

At the moment, though, what we had were six know-nothings and a Boy Scout manual, which didn't have much to say on secret combat. At the library, where I foraged for military information, I waded through a thousand raids, crusades, and tactical campaigns, from the Alamo to Indochina, storing up ideas to draw on. Among the six of us, we saw every war and Western movie that was shown in Baghdad, each making notes to bring to meetings.

Every member also had to arm himself. The Menashi brothers brought a scimitar from who knows where and a pair of homemade iron knuckles. Hiyawi swiped a cleaver from his mother's kitchen, and Sion made his own *tapooz* by whittling a heavy wooden club, tipping it with viscous tar, then lovingly imbedding rows of brutal-looking nails. He dubbed it his "Majestic M'silmin Mincer." My contribution, courtesy of Baba's warehouse, was a length of iron pipe with a massive angled ell screwed onto its end, and the biggest ball-peen hammer I could lay my hands on.

Abdallah took the honors with an airgun, "liberated"—a word we'd learned from movies—from the *shamash.* Before the riots, it was used for target practice in the sports curriculum, but the school had stopped the program as even popguns might antagonize the Arabs. They'd shoved the gun so far from sight and mind, it wouldn't be missed. We used it as a training tool, to get the hang of drawing fast and squeezing off a shot.

On the day Hiyawi slipped and sliced his elbow and I wrapped the gauze so tightly that his arm turned blue, I'd suggested that some training was in order, and nominated me to take it. Since the gushing blood had sickened all the others, there was no dissent. With profits from our bedroom store, I swapped for English pounds and sent a money order for the correspondence course described in *Reader's Digest.* The British edition was available at every kiosk near the big hotels, and I'd been reading it since I was eight.

When the lessons started coming, I borrowed side-poles from our summer beds, by now in storage, and, following instructions, slipped them through the sleeves and pants of Sion's suit to improvise a stretcher. I'd splinted both his "broken" legs and tied a sling to keep his "splintered" clavicle together. Each week brought another new technique, and with the Brotherhood at my command to wrap and patch at will, I soon felt capable of coping with most common injuries.

While I was in my element, the other boys were getting bored with doing drills and being bandaged. I could almost hear my brother jeering, "I told you that they'd drift away." To keep them interested, I'd have to offer more than Boy Scout exercises—more than iron pipes and ball-peen hammers. It struck me that a gun, a *real* gun, steely cold and deadly serious, would do the trick. And by the time we'd taught ourselves to handle it, I'd have more ideas to hold them.

S'hak himself had always hoped to own a gun, so, making no allusion to the underground, I said I knew where we could buy one which we'd own together. I had sufficient money; what I lacked at eleven was the physical authority of S'hak's age and height and heft. The sergeant wouldn't laugh at *him.*

A certain sergeant of police was practically on Baba's payroll. For every little "favor" that he did, father would discreetly slip him tips. The small *bakhsheesh* probably exceeded what the city paid him. Ismail had excessive appetites, an overweening ego, and an abject fear of his superiors. All in all, he was the perfect "pigeon"—another useful word provided by the movies.

It was illegal for any private citizen to own a gun, so we couldn't ask him openly if he would sell us his. Even Ismail had his standards. However, there wasn't any law against my looking up at him, seemingly bedazzled by his splendor, while S'hak flattered him outrageously about his shooting. He always wore the medal won for marksmanship and was, in fact, a most proficient man with firearms. Indeed, he was a better man than most in other ways as well, which is why he suffered qualms for failing to protect us in the course of the pogrom.

By working on his guilt and ego, we'd gotten him exactly where we wished—on the outskirts of the city, teaching us to shoot. For targets, we'd brought along an armful of *ta'ghouzi,* some as much as two feet long. Stuck in the dirt, the skinny cucumbers called for an unerring eye. Ismail took a stance, and in a sustained burst that sounded like a single shot, demolished six of them. My phony admiration turned to real regard; only in films had I seen such rapid fire. Asking him to teach us had simply been a ruse to gain his gun, but we could learn a lot from him.

After several sessions at our makeshift range, some small *bakhsheesh* "to buy the bullets," and a thousand sugar-coated compliments, we asked if we could keep the gun to practice with when he was busy. Before he could refuse, S'hak's hand was full of silver. From the heap of heavy coins, he clinked out eight *dinars.*

"So you won't be worried that we'll lose it," my brother's voice was brisk and businesslike, "we'll give you what it's worth."

Ismail was wavering, and S'hak clinked another coin to make it nine. As if the matter had been settled, he held the money out. The sergeant couldn't resist the cash, and with the gun in our possession, we beat a quick retreat.

When a week went by Ismail asked to have his weapon back; I tried to talk him out of it, but S'hak waved me off impatiently and bluntly told the sergeant that he'd tell his boss if he persisted. "Not only will you look a fool," he promised, "but you'll lose your job and go to jail."

The plan was mine, but S'hak made it work. "All you have to know is how to handle them," he said, and I agreed with him—up to a point. One on one, a Jew could deal with almost any *Mislim.* With their millions, though, and with the arms and the authority to make and break the laws, they had us licked—if, that is, we played it S'hak's way. However, I was past the point of wrangling. Only time would tell which one of us was wiser.

With the sergeant thoroughly intimidated, I had little trouble getting ammunition and a second weapon, this one strictly for the Brotherhood and me. Assessing every member two *dinars,* I bought a Mauser and, for S'hak's sake, handled the transaction on my own. In case the gun was ever traced to me, he wouldn't be involved.

I'd come to a decision on the day I'd hit my first *ta'ghouzi* and the sergeant said I'd someday shoot like him. In pledging to avenge Haron, the *why* was clear, the *how* had been elusive. I'd more or less eliminated knives and fists or any face-to-face encounter, since that would either get me slaughtered on the spot or caught, and tried, and taken by the neck and hanged. Instead of settling the score, the balance would be even bigger on the *Mislim* side. The gun would give me distance and ensure the man a quick and easy death. When I was good enough to put a bullet right between a pair of Arab eyes, I'd do it. Unlike Haron, the victim wouldn't suffer.

Considering my schedule and the crazy incompatibility of my pursuits, it's surprising that I wasn't schizophrenic. My day was laid out like a ship, divided into watertight compartments, each section safely self-contained. I could fill a morning with the prophets, an hour with Islamic lore, another oiling my Mauser, and swiftly move from each to each, shutting one off from the other as I went. Only by such isolation was I able both to plan a killing and to pray I'd have Cabala.

In one arena or another, even the most mild-tempered, average kid inclines to be extremist at eleven. I wasn't any different, merely more so. I went all the way in *everything.* At the *shamash,* I had to have the highest marks. At the *yeshiva* I worked to be the best of Jews. I might question God, but God would have no cause to question me.

Checking my progression against the seven steps of man, as set forth in the Talmud, I was well ahead of the agenda for a pious Jew. Eight days after birth, the *brith;* at four, the introduction to the Torah; swimming lessons at the age of six. ("If a man should drown, and his father had not taught him how to swim by six, his death is on his father's head.") With the fourth step taken—my *bar mitzvah*—I had more than half the requisites behind me, and was two years in advance of all my peers. Still to come was work at age sixteen or further study, the *chupah* when I reached eighteen, and fatherhood by one year after wedding.

Though women weren't to be seen at the *yeshiva,* they were ever-present in our thoughts and in the Rabbi's rote of prohibitions. Each time he echoed them, he stared directly at the older boys, who squirmed a lot.

We were barred from lingering in conversation with a female, except for family members. Succinctly, and without allowances, *Hakham* Ezra stated, "Talk leads always to enticement." Even worse was unclad female flesh, face included: "A one-square-foot exposure is the same as showing sexual organs." But since the most punctilious man will see unveiled women in the streets, we were told to drop our eyes when in their presence. Thinking back to Uncle's wedding and the bare expanses of the belly dancers, I couldn't remember seeing any eyes averted. I meant to ask if women such as these might be excepted, but in view of Rabbi Ezra's stern injunctions, staring seemed too trivial to talk about.

He warned us that we couldn't know when females walked among us in an unclean state; we therefore ran a risk in touching any woman. We were all aware that women were unclean at times, but not till now had anyone explained it.

During *nidda*—the four days which preceded onset of the menstrual flow, the period of flow itself, and four days following its finish—the female was unfit to touch, the *Hakham* told us. I did a hasty calculation, and was horrified to find that for half of every month, every woman was polluted.

Near me on the bench, one boy nudged another and whispered with a snigger of disdain, "They're filthy as a pig!" In any other place, I would have punched him. There wasn't any doubt that women were unclean, but not the dirty way that he was saying. The unclean state was somehow necessary, or my mother and my sisters would have been exempt. At least I now knew why I'd sometimes been allowed to sleep with Nana and why Baba sometimes slept all by himself. At four, I hadn't been adult enough to be contaminated.

It came as no surprise that casual fornication was forbidden, but even in marriage, sex, we learned, was ringed with regulations. His eagle eyes transfixing one boy, then another, resting here a moment longer, drilling deeper there, Rabbi Ezra laid the law down. In the sight of God, he gravely stated, sex was evil except for purposes of procreation. The aim of every sexual act must be the siring of a child; since that was so, no means of contraception could be used. "*No* means," he emphasized, but the emphasis was lost on me. I didn't know that anything but abstinence might be employed.

At eleven, though, none of this presented any major problem. What concerned me more was what he said about the sin of wasting time on frivolous activities. I was afraid that might embrace the movies. If I asked and he replied in the affirmative, I might argue that the films improved my English or that the Talmud didn't have a word to say about the cinema. On the other hand, I could just sit back and wait for him to be specific. If Rabbi Ezra said the cinema was out of bounds, I'd give it up, but since he often made the observation that exercising self-control was virtuous and, for me, not asking questions was the toughest test of self-control, it might be virtuous of me to drop the movie matter. Quite conscious of my sophistry, I kept my mouth shut and continued to attend.

If my conscience twinged at all, it had to do with how I felt, or didn't feel, about my classmates. I didn't dislike them. I just didn't think about them much. The *yeshiva* students caught on quickly; I was there to study—that alone—and my social life revolved around the *shamash.* Except for 'Fraim, none sought active friendship.

Like Samy, he'd attached to me without my least encouragement. He lived a long way off, though, and in the opposite direction, so we couldn't walk home together, even if I'd had the inclination. In spite of numerous polite refusals—because of time, I told him—he kept asking me to visit. It was true I had no time, but I also knew that I could find an hour if I'd cared to make the effort. What bothered me was why I hadn't. While I doubted that I'd act much differently if he were better dressed or from a more distinguished family, I didn't know for certain. To atone for my disinterest, I'd decided to do something nice for 'Fraim before the year was over—and very little time was left.

It was almost Rosh Hashonah, which meant the *shohet* would be coming. For the moment, 'Fraim fled from mind and slaughter filled it.

The ritual had added meaning for our family. In his childhood, S'hak had contracted smallpox, and Baba vowed that if his son was spared, he'd sacrifice a lamb on the eve of every Rosh Hashonah and divide its meat among the needy.

During the holiday season, with lambs in big demand and busy butchers undependable about deliveries, Baba played it safe by buying ours before the rush. A knob-kneed, nuzzling lamb had been tethered in a corner of the courtyard for the last two days, and disobeying Baba, all of us had slipped him bread and cookies on the sly.

I thought Baba was afraid we'd overfeed him, and if we made him sick, he'd be unfit for sacrifice, but by the time the *shohet* and the two required butchers came, I knew the ban was based on something else, and I wished we'd followed orders. Father understood how fast a kid could grow attached to any living creature, especially a wooly one that nuzzled with a soft, wet nose. I wouldn't disgrace myself by blubbering because I'd seen the ritual so often, and in accordance with *halachic* law, the lamb would die a painless death. But Baba was correct, of course; it was better not to know the victim. That's why the *Mislim* I was stalking had to be a stranger. Unsolicited, the thought had sprung to mind. More and more, the oath impinged on every element of my existence, but I shunted it aside for now and concentrated on the ceremony that was just about to start.

This time I'd set myself the task of trying to anticipate each move the *shohet* would be making. And along with all religious aspects of the ritual,

I'd be checking on my knowledge of anatomy. Although the books I'd read concerned the human body, I assumed that all the vital organs of another mammal would be much the same as ours. Medicine continued to intrigue me, even more so since I'd sent off for the first-aid course.

The *shohet* was about to test his knife. The steel was almost two feet long and looked as sharp as Dr. Kahni's scalpel. The *shohet* plunged into his beard, plucked a hair and drew the edge against it, slicing it in two. Satisfied, he slowly passed the blade across his "testing" nail, inspecting it for nicks. For the sake of cleanliness, rabbis kept their nails clipped, but you could always spot a *shohet* by the lengthy nail he nurtured on his left-hand thumb.

Had the blade contained the tiniest irregularity, he would have had to substitute another knife, but this one had a perfect edge and passed. The slash would be so swift and smooth that it would sever every nerve before it signalled pain. The lamb would never know what happened. Like my Arab. Once again, I wiped him from my mind, and applied myself instead to S'hak.

He was crouching in the center of the *hosh,* and as the *shohet* said the prayer, the bigger of the butchers held the animal aloft and circled S'hak's head with him. My brother, having done his part, retired to the sidelines, and the animal was taken to the drainage hole. The lamb was held, neck extended over it, and the fleece combed back to bare a patch of skin. The *shohet* swung. As required by the ritual, the single cut had parted both carotid arteries and trachea, and without a second's suffering, the lamb was lifeless. The butcher had positioned him precisely, and the gushing blood poured neatly down the drain hole.

More relaxed now that the lamb was dead, I sidled closer than the *shohet* really liked. As often as I'd seen it, the first step in the three inspections always made me catch my breath.

The second butcher made a small incision in the lamb's left foreleg, then bent and blew into the slit. As he did so, the fleecy hide separated from the flesh, smoothly and intactly, over the entire body of the animal. He peeled it like an egg, and it was just as bloodless. Every drop had drained away.

The first inspection was external. Inch by inch, the *shohet* checked the carcass, on the lookout for discoloration or any lumps that evidenced disease. Muscle cysts, for instance, might mean tapeworms, but our lamb was pink and perfect. At the *shohet*'s signal, the butcher opened all four knee joints. Fluid here would point to possible tuberculosis, but the capsules were exactly as they should be.

For the second inspection, the abdomen was slit, and the *shohet* felt inside for masses in the kidneys and intestinal adhesions. Next, I knew, he'd check the spleen and liver. Thrusting upward he grasped the trachea, and when he pulled it down and out the small incision, the heart and lungs came with it. Collapsed, the lungs were like two tiny squashed tomatoes, but when the butcher blew into the trachea, they bellowed out, becoming huge balloons.

I moved in closer and grabbed for my *k'tibeh.* At the same time, Baba pulled his *sibha* from his pocket.

Yes, the surfaces were sleek as silk, and no, there weren't any hissing sounds. The *shohet* nodded, and Baba let his breath out in a gust of great relief. Last year we'd had to put aside the first three lambs before we found one that would satisfy the *shohet.* The third had been all right until we reached this point in the proceedings, and then the lungs had hissed. So far our luck was holding.

The butcher squeezed the lungs, expelling all the air, and ripped them open so the *shohet* could inspect the bronchi. These ruled healthy, the heart was next. After stripping off its membrane, he sliced it twice from top to bottom. To my delight, I recognized the ventricles from textbook sketches.

The last inspection was the shortest, but before it could be made, the butcher had to lop the head off and open up the skull. Plucking out the brain, the *shohet* looked for signs of hemorrhage or pus. The butchers were awaiting his decision as anxiously as we were. If he declared the lamb unfit, they'd have to cart it off and sell it to the Arabs for a lot less money than we paid for *kasher* meat.

The *shohet* took his time and tension mounted. At last he turned to Baba, smiled broadly, and wished him "Happy New Year!" The women shrieked with joy and Baba put his beads away. The butchering began.

With Baba's blessing, I picked a large, choice chunk of lamb to take to 'Fraim's family. His house was in the oldest part of Abu Saad, the center of the ghetto, where the unpaved streets, so pinched and narrow that a pair of mules could barely walk abreast, were moats of mud all winter. The doors in Abu Saad were even heavier than ours, and reinforced from edge to edge with massive metal straps. Each night, and during troubled days, the Quarter's every opening was bolted closed.

Since it was common in the ghetto for several families to share a building, I thought I'd see some six or seven females in the courtyard when I arrived within the *hosh* of 'Fraim's house. Instead, the courtyard *swarmed* with women. Disconcerted by the sight, I shouted, "Where will I find 'Fraim?" and was flummoxed even more to hear, " 'Fraim who?" "Which 'Fraim are you after?" At home, if someone asked for Heskel, there was only me.

" 'Fraim from 'Slat Zilkha," I replied, and received in turn a chorus of directions. I paused to look around before advancing. Many unmatched shabby blankets were airing on the *tarabzoon,* and I also saw that faucets had been spaced at intervals, alongside every door. Each had been installed to satisfy requirements for ritual washing, one faucet to a family. I counted doors and faucets. Six families were living in a house not quite as large as ours.

'Fraim answered when I knocked. Behind him, in the single room in which the family resided, five thin mattresses were ranged around the walls. Resting on the bare brick floor, they were the only furniture except for one big wooden cupboard. I felt sick with shame that I should have so much while others lived like this.

'Fraim's eyes lit up on seeing me, but he was too surprised to ask me in at once. In another moment, though, he would, and wanting only to evaporate, I wished him "Happy New Year," thrust at him the pot which held the meat, and said I had to hurry home. He turned to take the package out and put it down, and when he swung around again and handed me the empty pot, his face was wet but smiling. Unable to contain his tears, he told me that the lamb would be the only meat they'd had all year.

I fled before the flood of thanks began. I could have handled anger or reproach, but not the kind of abject gratitude he offered. The meat was meant to be a minor gift between two classmates, bringing us, I hoped, a trifle closer. Instead of helping bridge the gap, however, it only showed how wide a gap existed.

Late on Yom Kippur, full of turmoil and light of head from fasting, I was in the synagogue but out of touch with everything around me. I don't recall the services at all, though I must have made the right responses or Baba would have poked me black-and-blue. My mind was occupied with other words which overrode the Rabbi's. "Haron . . ., 'Fraim . . ., vengeance . . ., justice . . ., Haron . . ., 'Fraim . . ., vengeance . . ., justice. . . ."

Without a pause, the sequence kept repeating. I tried to block it out with Rabbi Ezra's admonitions and S'hak's businesslike advice, but my brain refused to play back anything but this refrain until I fell asleep. In the dream that then took over, Haron and 'Fraim each had me by an arm. Between the two of them, they were tearing me apart.

11

Shortwave radio was our major link to everything outside Iraq. Throughout the winter, the Voice of Jerusalem and the BBC had been informing us that Jews were being rounded up in Germany and placed in camps. Just that. In March 1942, therefore, when our Rabbinate announced a special *slihot* for the Jews of Europe, a shock wave galvanized the ghetto. In the ordinary course, a *slihot* would only be convened in the ten-day period between Rosh Hashonah and the eve of Yom Kippur. Except in some extreme emergency, this assembly simply wasn't held at any other time.

The Great Synagogue of Baghdad was so enormous that it looked a little empty even when a dozen different congregations were in simultaneous attendance. This synagogue was the oldest in the world, erected almost six centuries before the birth of Christ, in the reign of Nebuchadnezzar, the King of Babylonia and conqueror of old Jerusalem. The edifice was built to hold 20,000 people, celebrating twenty separate services, each confined within a spacious vaulted area of its own.

On the day designated for the *slihot,* 30,000 crowded every inch. Without a shred of solid information to explain the sense of urgency that seized us, all who could had come. The calling of the *slihot* in itself compelled our presence. Inside the synagogue, the very air appeared to shiver with suspense.

When the chanting of the prayer was over, and the *shofar* had been blown, Rabbi David Ben Yossef Haim rose slowly from his seat and, more slowly still, approached the lectern. It was plain that what he had to say was eating at his vitals.

"My masters, the children of Israel"—he addressed the congregation in a voice that trembled with intensity—"I must say to you that many men of faith have perished." He went on to tell us that the truth about the concentration camps was worse than even the most monstrous rumors. A sound between a groan and sigh escaped from 30,000 throats. The Rabbi raised his hand and instantly the synagogue was still as death.

"In these camps Jews are being slaughtered like so many sheep, but so obscenely, so atrociously, in ways no animal would be allowed to suffer." Again a gasp arose as from a single body, and the Rabbi waited for the cry to die away. There was more to come—and more—and more. We heard about "selections"—the women singled out to serve the German soldiers, the "useless" infants bashed to death before their mothers' eyes, the medical experiments so bestial that the Rabbi gagged—and the desecration of the Scrolls in such foul and loathsome fashion that he sickened as he spoke. Though his voice, grown hoarse with horror, cracked, he persisted with the ghastly list of indescribable atrocities as the women of the congregation wailed and their husbands wept.

"We are powerless," he ended. "Only God can help."

In growing disbelief, I listened to this good man as he gravely gave instructions. We were to aid our fellow Jews by fasting! On the two days of atonement in the Jewish week, we'd refrain from food and offer special prayers, beseeching God to save them. On Mondays and Thursdays, as Jews died by the thousands, that's all that we would do. Was it possible that 30,000 people had nothing more to mobilize than piety and hunger pangs?

Baba, S'hak, and I, sitting near the lectern, were unable to get up and out until the rows behind us emptied, so we spent the time discussing what we'd heard. S'hak hadn't been convinced. "Jews wouldn't let themselves be butchered," he insisted. I reminded him of what had happened here in Baghdad, and he answered hotly, "We fought them off, if you remember."

"We should have seen it coming," I rebutted, but it only drew a shrug. We'd been over this so often, it was simply rote.

Baba's head was bent. I couldn't see his face, but I knew he'd heard us speaking. Deciding to make one last effort to enlist him, I opened with a safely cautious quote: "Rabbi Hillel said it. 'If I am not for myself, who is for me?' "

Baba raised his head and turned in my direction. He sensed that I was building up to something, and I rushed along before I lost my nerve.

"Unless each of us is ready—unless all Iraqi Jews are organized—"

He reacted to the words with fury and wouldn't let me finish.

"It's idiotic! It's the surest way to stir up trouble! Don't ever mention it again!"

I recognized finality in father's steely voice, and no one spoke again until we reached the street. In the stir of greeting friends, I slipped away. Baba was as adamant as ever, still confident that we could "work it out." A million German fathers must have said the same. And if *Baba* felt this way, would lesser men be more inclined to action?

In my heart, I'd always known the answer, but Baba's last command to me extinguished any lingering hope I might have had. We couldn't depend on any adult help at all. My big job now would be to keep the boys involved.

We'd enlisted only three new members in the Brotherhood, and week by week, the interest of the group had waned; soon they'd start to drop away. Every waking moment free of family or school affairs I spent in seeking ways to make the underground a more attractive and effective operation.

On Rashid Street one damp May morning, while slapping at mosquitoes and brooding on the Brotherhood, I saw two youngish Europeans who also seemed to have a problem. They were stopping passersby, speaking to them briefly, then moving on, as baffled looking as before. The shorter, stockier man, somewhere in his middle twenties, with white-blond hair and the bluest eyes I'd ever seen, was more aggressive than the other, accosting Jews and Arabs both, apparently at random. He spoke in English with a heavy accent, and those he stopped either stared at him in silence or, distinctly startled, scurried off. From where I stood, "synagogue" was the only word I could distinguish, and it made me wary. He was plainly Aryan; why was he inquiring about a *'slah?*

Appraising his companion, I assumed the question was on his behalf. A slightly moon-faced man and also in his twenties, he had a Jewish "look" about him. Both were wearing uniforms of some description, but bearing no insignia of any sort.

As I passed abreast of them, the second fellow—Moon-face—stopped a *Mislim,* and spoke to him in British English, which I understood. The Arab didn't, but assuming that he knew what two healthy young men were seeking, he pointed to a building down the street—the public brothel. At that, I intervened. It was approaching sundown, and Moon-face had been asking for a place to pray, not play.

Both men, I found, were Jewish. Josef had come from Poland, which accounted for my inability to understand his English. Zev was born in Germany but bred in Palestine. *Ashkenazim,* the first I'd ever met. I could have kept them busy for a week just with the questions that had come to mind the last five minutes. They were showing signs of restlessness, however, or was it apprehension? Then I recognized what they were wearing: uniforms, all right, British army issue, but with everything removable removed. No *wonder* they were nervous! This part of Baghdad was forbidden them. The British troops were bivouacked across the Tigris and restricted to the western bank. Sooner or later, someone would report them if they stayed on Rashid Street.

During our exchange of names, we'd been walking toward an intersection. On reaching it, they turned off to the right—but, here, the right was wrong. I had to pull them back and tell them that was Arab land and that it wasn't safe for Jews to stray in certain sections.

Josef threw his hands up and exploded, "Oh, God! The same thing here?" I laid the situation out for them, and at the next safe corner signalled them to follow me into a narrow, twisting alley, used exclusively by Jews.

Zev asked if we were heading for the synagogue, and I explained that it was shut up tight except when services were scheduled. The hoodlums didn't attack if all the congregation came together, but arriving one by one, the cowards jumped us.

Josef swore at length, in Polish, I presumed. I'd never heard it spoken, but in any language, swearing has a cadence you can recognize. Zev was less vociferous. All he said was "Germany again!" but he spat it out like stored-up venom.

In the alley I suggested that they roll their sleeves and stuff their military caps inside their jackets so they'd pass as workmen when we made our exit. We were heading home via Shorja Market, which was always mobbed. Half of Baghdad bought its rice and spices there. Later, I assured them, I'd take them to the *'slah* for services. We had time to kill, and this way I could also get civilian clothes for them so they could wander freely. Especially a cap, I thought. That white-blond hair of Josef's caught the eye like snowdrifts on a desert dune.

A plan was forming in my mind, but I had to find out more about their backgrounds and availability before proceeding. What inspired me was their being in the Corps of Engineers; the Corps, I soon elicited, would be around for several months before it went to Mosul. By treaty, British troops had long been posted at the port and west of the Euphrates, but not, till now, this close to Baghdad. I could thank the coup for bringing me the men we needed.

More exciting still was hearing that their whole brigade was Jewish—each man a volunteer, Zev told me, and each enlisted as a citizen of Palestine no matter where his mother was when he was born. So Zev and Josef shared my view that Jews should join with other Jews.

I steered them slowly through the market, tacking back and forth on the crookedest of courses, trying to prolong the trip and pumping them at every turn.

Yes, I found, they *did* have access to a great variety of military field guides and assorted information. And they *had* been issued the official army manual; a giant step beyond the Boy Scout manual! They mentioned building bridges; the Brotherhood could use construction skills. They were also demolition experts, experienced with high explosives. And before their present service, both had been in other armies, Zev in Palestine, Josef in Poland. The two of them could teach us almost everything we had to know, and by the time we hit the house, I'd mapped a whole curriculum.

If God was with me, Baba wouldn't be home to shut the door on them.

Once inside, I'd have some leeway. He wouldn't push them out until I offered him an explanation. As yet, I hadn't thought of one that he'd accept.

It was tempting fate for us to entertain a British soldier, especially a Jewish British soldier, and I admitted to myself that bringing home *two* Jewish British soldiers, out of uniform, and in the city in defiance of both English and Iraqi orders, might be stretching matters past the point of reason. In addition to inviting trouble for my father, there was also Nana to consider. At this late date—actually, while opening the door—it struck me that she'd never seen a foreign Jew, but relying on her ingrained hospitality to overcome her fear, I beckoned Zev and Josef in.

I was jittery, and they were even more so. From the way they stared, it was plain to see they'd never been inside a house like ours. Baba didn't seem to be around, so with a confidence I didn't feel, I called to Nana, "I'm home with friends." On catching sight of my companions, she smiled uncertainly and looked to me to be enlightened.

"They're Jews like us," I soothed her, and, extempore, I added, "They're here to teach me Hebrew." All three of them looked startled, but her response, as I expected, was "Will they stay for dinner?" If Hitler turned up hungry, she'd have to fight the need to feed him.

At my nod she asked, "Do they eat like us?" To mother, they were aliens from another planet, and if *M'silmin* gobbled locusts and Frenchmen swallowed snails. . . . I quickly reassured her, and she left us for the kitchen.

From the family room, I heard the front door open and, recognizing Baba's footsteps, braced myself for trouble. He identified the uniforms at once and, though aghast, was gracious in his greeting. Guests were guests. A glance, however, told me what I'd get when they were gone.

Except for prayers, the extent of Nana's Hebrew was *"Shabbat shalom,"* but Baba could communicate in fits and starts with what he'd picked up on his several trips to Palestine. I relaxed, satisfied that things were going well, until Nazima entered. Josef took her hand and kissed it, while Zev, all smiles, exclaimed about her beauty.

Nana flinched in horror, Nazima tore her hand away, and I half-expected father to go up in flames. His face was purpling, and my soldiers must have thought that we were all insane. Hastily, before they fled or Baba threw them out, I alternated explanations, both in Arabic and English.

A misunderstanding, I informed the family. On the continent it was customary for a man to kiss a woman's hand on meeting, and women *welcomed* such remarks. "They meant to honor you," I told Nazima.

I was more explicit with the soldiers. "You can praise my mother's cooking or my sister's needlework, but you must never compliment a well-bred girl on her appearance." When they still looked blank, I made it plainer. "We only say such things to women we expect to sleep with—to prostitutes. It's the worst of insults to tell a decent girl you think she's pretty. She'll think you think that she's a whore."

As what I said sank in, both Zev and Josef blushed like schoolboys, and the ice was broken. Bless the movies! They'd taught me most of what I knew about the outside world. Till Josef actually performed the act, however, I thought that kissing hands was strictly for the cinema.

In his broken Hebrew, Baba waved apologies aside. The men's acute embarrassment was proof enough of their intentions. At the table he even showed them how to break off pieces of *khibz* and sop the last delicious drops of Nana's lamb and rice. After lunch, as he always did, Baba led the Sabbath singing. "God has blessed *Shabbat* and sanctified the day," he started, and when Zev and Josef joined him, both richly deeply baritone, he thawed completely.

For the next three hours, we had a family-style songfest, and after all the old familiar melodies had been exhausted, our now good friends announced one that was new to me. Though Baba nodded at the name and clearly recognized the rhythm, he let them sing "Hatikvah" by themselves. I wondered why—it was such lovely, haunting music, just the sort he favored—but when the final note had faded and Zev announced it as the anthem of the Jewish homeland, I understood his silence. "Homeland" had to do with Zionism, and for Iraqi Jews, Zionism offered only punishment and pain.

If Baba asked if they were Zionists, and if they were—and I was sure they were—that would put an end to all my epic plans. He'd never let them come again. Luckily, our table was a long one, and sitting at the head of it, he was far enough away for me to whisper "Don't talk politics" to Zev and Josef. Catching on at once, they changed the mood by turning to the younger kids and teaching them a clap-hand chant that set the dishes dancing.

Then Zev was looking at his watch and saying that they had to leave. We'd been having so much fun, they'd missed the service at the synagogue; as for me, I'd missed my opportunity to talk to them alone. One chance remained. If I took them to the bridge, I thought that I could sell them on my scheme by the time we reached the Tigris.

Baba was about to put his foot down, but before he gave the order that I couldn't go, I trotted out the reasons why I should. By themselves, I said, they'd either wind up in a cul-de-sac or stray into an Arab enclave such as Abu Shibl. They might be caught and put in prison, or maybe only beaten bloody. As Zev and Josef grimaced, he reluctantly agreed to my escorting them; he even lent them two old jackets, and Nana packed their khakis in a paper sack. Once across the Tigris, they could change.

The second we were on the street and out of Baba's earshot, Josef opened up. "Why's your father so afraid of Zionism?" he inquired. I answered him indignantly. It wasn't fear, I said. "He simply thinks it's not for us."

Josef snorted, sounding much like S'hak when he scoffed at me. "I bet he says that 'we can work things out.' "

On seeing my discomfort, Zev shook his head at Josef and tried to soften it for me by saying, "Many of the finest men who ever lived have felt that way." But Josef wouldn't be squelched. "And how many of the finest men have died *because* they felt that way?" I seemed forgotten in the cross-talk, and something told me that the two of them had argued this before.

All of us had questions. Zev was curious about my telling Nana that they'd teach me Hebrew. It had just come out of me, I said; it was all that I could think of to explain their presence. Grabbing at the opening he'd given me, I told them what I really wanted.

Zev, I saw, was negative, but Josef whooped and clapped me on the back in glee, exclaiming, "*That's* the way!" He looked at Zev as if he'd scored a point against him in a vital game. To my astonishment, they stopped there on the street and battled over me—in Hebrew. Without consulting me at all, they struck a bargain. They'd teach me Hebrew first, and then we'd talk about the other things I'd asked for. I protested that I had no use for Hebrew, but Josef didn't back me up as I expected. Their differences were centered on the use of force. Zev advocated *havlagah.* "Translation: self-restraint," he offered over Josef's tart assertion, "*Some* Hebrew he can live without."

Since the only area of their agreement was my need for Hebrew, I had to go along. If I learned the language, they promised that they'd teach me tactics. I felt manipulated, and a million questions bubbled up, demanding answers, but we'd reached the bridge and everything would have to wait until we met again. Hastily, we made arrangements for the following week, and off they went.

On the bridge, Josef snapped his fingers and his face lit up. Rushing back, he fished a booklet from his pocket and handed it to me. "I forgot I had it. It's in Hebrew. See how much you understand and mark the words you can't make out."

I slid the book from sight and waved goodbye. Next week I'd have to warn them. Except for purposes of worship, Hebrew was illegal in Iraq.

At the designated hour, I was at the bridge to pick them up. For a few days now, Baghdad had been full of British soldiers and, even as I watched, others straggled over. Either the police had been instructed to ignore the prohibition or they were being bribed. Both, I guessed. Certainly the merchants of the city wouldn't squeal. Soldiers spent and money talked—louder than the law. While waiting, I tried to spot the Jews among the servicemen, but I couldn't tell an *Ashkenazi* from an Irish Catholic.

Zev and Josef arrived exactly on the minute, and before we reached the house, I'd entertained some second thoughts about the whole idea. The two of them were certainly divided, not so much on aims as on the methods of achieving them. Each was trying to convert me to his own conviction, and I didn't want to be involved in any differences between them.

As I suspected, both were Zionists, and spoke of *Eretz Yisrael* instead of Palestine. Up till now, I'd only heard those words pronounced in solemn prayers, and they sounded strange and out of place in English conversation on a crowded street.

Josef explained, "Palestine is *their* name. Ours is *Eretz Yisrael.* And *Eretz Yisrael* is ours."

He was passionate about a Jewish homeland, and though Zev expressed himself with less abandon, he was equally committed. But a chasm yawned between them as to how to make it happen. Zev believed in Jewish education and bringing in more immigrants, declaring that "a Jewish State will have to happen. It's inevitable, preordained." Josef glowered at him. "Only death is preordained."

Before they squared off for another fight, I set them straight about the Brotherhood and our beliefs, informing them that no one in the underground was anything resembling a Zionist—I least of all. *Eretz Yisrael,* of course, was ours in spirit, I assured them, but we *had* a homeland.

"You *Ashkenazim* have been pushed around so much," I tried explaining, "it might be difficult for you to understand, but we've been settled here for twenty centuries, since the Second Temple. This is home. We have the right to be here, and if we have to, we'll defend that right. We need your help, not your ideology."

Josef looked astonished at my outburst, but not at all antagonistic, and all Zev said was "Home is where the heart is." I thought my bluntness might estrange them; instead, the strength of my conviction seemed to make them like me more.

At the house, after greeting Nana briefly, we went upstairs to work. Looking at the booklet he had given me, Josef roared with laughter. The whole first page was one big pencil mark. I'd had to underline every word that wasn't in a ritual. All I knew was Bible Hebrew. I could speak to God but not to man. Zev's lips were twitching too, but he restrained himself. In the living language Hebrew had become, he solaced, even scholars had to start from scratch. Still chuckling, Josef said, "You'd starve to death in *Eretz Yisrael* unless you planned to live exclusively on milk and honey. We're a little short of manna."

Eretz Yisrael again. Both, I saw, expected some reaction but I didn't respond. Having failed to involve me in a fresh debate, they got briskly down to business. From this point on, they ordered, we'd only speak in Hebrew. I snapped back, *"Tov"*—good—and grinned. One for me.

Josef pointed to a chair. *"Kisseh,"* he said; in Jewish Arabic, *"kigshi."* So far, so good. Next was "table," even easier: *"shulchan"* in Hebrew; for us, *"shulhan"*—more gutteral in Hebrew, but no problem. As in every Jewish home, the table always held a salt bowl and a plate of bread. Zev gestured toward the salt, and my *"milh"* merged happily with his *"melach."* I hadn't dreamt that so much Jewish dialect derived from Hebrew. This would be a breeze! For Zev, pepper was *"pilpel";* for us, *"filfil."* Josef tipped the pitcher, and pointing to the water, I declared it *"mai";* in Hebrew, it was *"maim."* In *Eretz Yisrael,* Zev's nose was *"af": "inf"* on Kambar Ali Street.

Buoyed by my performance, I didn't flinch when Josef asked, *"Efoh lechem?"* I knew it was a question from the way he said it. *"Efoh"* I knew was "where," and it was child's play to figure out the other. *"Lechem"* could only be *"laham,"* which in Jewish Arabic means meat. He was playing tricks, trying to confuse me, but since Nana hadn't furnished us with meat, I responded with a smug *"En po"*—it isn't here.

He grinned from ear to ear, grabbed the bread and shook it at me, shouting gleefully, *"Lechem, lechem."*

The man was devious! So he knew a little Arabic—enough, at least, to know *"laham"* was "meat." He'd set a trap for me. By allowing me my early triumphs, he'd made me overconfident and simple to ensnare. A military strategy enveloped in a Hebrew lesson! Rapping out *"lechem, lechem,"* he tossed the bread to me, and catching what I'd always called *"khibz,"* I hastily recalculated. It might not be as easy as I'd first believed.

"Sakin" for "knife" was reassuring; it was also that in Arabic. Then Josef held a fork aloft, and when I offered up "*shikacha,*" he shook his head and grinned. *"Mazleg,"* he said to my dismay. I couldn't help exclaiming, "But it doesn't even *start* the same."

"Which is why we brought you this." He handed me a Hebrew dictionary and admonished me for breaking into English.

To thank them for the book, I sifted through the prayers I knew that might provide the proper words. On rising every morning, I gave thanks for having passed the night in peace, so I started, *"Mode Ani,"* and they laughed so hard they had to hold each other up. Gasping, Josef said, "We really don't deserve it. That's a form of thanks you give to God alone. Even for such noble souls as us, you say a simple *'toda raba.'* "

We met for lessons once or twice a week for several months, and as my fluency increased, they suggested that we spend some time on Jewish history—*current* happenings, they emphasized. Both seemed to think my knowledge stopped at ancient Israel, and I informed them rather haughtily that I was well aware of what was going on in *Eretz Yisrael* and in the concentration camps (I'd long since switched from "Palestine" to please them).

It was Zev this time who challenged me with unexpected vehemence. "You know *nothing,*" he erupted, "tell him." And he turned to Josef, who was nodding acquiescence.

"You really had to be there." Josef said it jokingly, but the icy little smile seemed to hurt his lips. As if nailed on, it stayed there through the audit of abuse that followed. He started with his own humiliations in the Polish army, relating each abasing incident without emotion, saying only, "They can teach the *Germans* anti-Semitism." He continued with a flat, dispassionate recital of obscenities, compared with which the *slihot* revelations were but minor peccadillos.

In the middle of the awful litany, I shouted out, "They should have fought. Why didn't they fight?" and through the ghastly little grin, he answered that they couldn't believe such things could happen—even when they happened.

Josef's throat had tightened; eventually he couldn't speak at all, and Zev took over. "By then it was too late. Some managed to escape, though—like those aboard the *Struma.* You know about the *Struma?* No," he answered for me, "no, of course you don't."

The *Struma* was a ship, he said, built to hold, at most, a hundred people, and designed to sail in tranquil coastal waters. When, battered by the open sea, it put in for repairs at Istanbul, it carried eight times more than its capacity, all Jewish refugees from Europe.

The engines were beyond repair, the Turks refused a plea for sanctuary, even for the children, and for eight long weeks, from December 1941 to February 1942, just last month, the *Struma* and its human cargo lay there in the water, dead and dying. Food was running out, and the refugees implored the British to allow them to go overland to Palestine. The British were implacable, however, and on February 24, the Turks had towed the ship outside the harbor and turned their backs on it. The *Struma* sank and all aboard were lost.

"428 Jewish men, 269 Jewish women, 70 Jewish children." Josef had found his voice again.

After that, in session after session, they filled me in on all the BBC had censored from its broadcasts and all our government had excised from the history books it issued to Iraqi students.

"You have to know the background," Zev began. He ruminated for a moment, putting the events in order. "Maybe 1922," he murmured to himself, and then aloud, "yes, 1922, starting with the Mufti. To understand, you have to hear about the Mufti and the British . . . how Palestine was caught between them."

I sat transfixed as Zev reeled off a tale of international intrigue and double-dealing. In 1922, Haj Muhammad Amin al-Husseini, the Grand Mufti of Palestine, was, with the backing of the British, elected lifetime President of the Supreme Moslem Council. What strained credulity was that just the year before he'd been sentenced by the British to ten years of imprisonment for instigating bloody anti-Jewish riots.

Josef muttered, "Mideast politics," but paying no attention, Zev continued. Because of Uncle Eliahu, who'd been in Palestine in 1929, I already knew about the pogrom he described, the one incited by the Mufti in which 500 innocent civilians had been slaughtered. I hadn't heard, however, that the Mufti had been purged of guilt by two commissions. Both, of course, were British.

"But *why?*" I interrupted, and Josef growled again. "Politics, I told you. British interests. Saving British skins. Keep the Arabs off the backs of Englishmen. Throw the dogs a bone—a Jewish bone."

If that was it, apparently it hadn't worked too well. In the 1930s, Zev resumed, the fighting escalated and Jews and British suffered almost equally. There was sabotage and outright murder by the Mufti's men. The airport was destroyed, troop trains wrecked, pipelines smashed and blasted. Jerusalem was close to capture by the Arabs. In the midst of this, the Mufti also killed off many of his *Mislim* rivals—among them, the mayor of Hebron and the *mukhtars* of Caesaria, Ein Razel and Beit Maksir.

The only happy note emerging from this dirge was that the Haganah, first an underground defense group, then a localized militia, had turned into a potent fighting force—a real, if unofficial, Jewish army.

Unbelievably, in view of all their anti-British actions, in 1938, the British had not only freed the interned members of the Mufti's High Command, but had also accepted them as full-fledged, honored delegates to a conference concerning Palestine. In London, as in the Middle East, they received their orders from the Mufti, temporarily in Lebanon, in exile.

I couldn't contain myself. "He was here!" I blurted, "here in Baghdad. He was with the Nazis against the King. He's just as much the enemy of England as he is of Jews."

Zev nodded. "But that was later. He was in Iraq in 1939. Even then, the British tried appeasing him. They needed Arab help against the Axis."

"And they'd do anything to get it"—that from Josef.

What they did, Zev continued, was disembowel the Balfour Declaration, selling out the Jews to keep their Arab clients happy.

Josef broke in once again. "That bastard Chamberlain! That *stupid* bastard! The same mistake he made at Munich!"

In the White Paper of May 17, 1939, the English, in accordance with their clients' wishes, set quotas and conditions which assured the final failure of the *Yishuv.* Henceforth the Jews of Palestine could purchase land only in a barren and restricted area. Acquisition in the fertile sections was forbidden. But the killing blow was in the human quota. For the next five years, a maximum of 15,000 Jews a year would be admitted. After that, not a single one would be allowed to enter unless the Arab leadership agreed.

"So the British fight the Germans while they're turning back the Jews to die at German hands." Zev folded inward like an empty sack and shut his eyes. Head in hands, Josef stared at space. Neither of them saw me, and I'd never felt so all alone.

When I broke the silence, they twitched as if I'd touched an open wound. "But you're *with* the British." To my complete confusion, both began to grin.

"Of course we are. So are all the Jews of *Eretz Yisrael.* You never saw so many volunteers. And such good soldiers! Just ask the English how quickly we catch on."

My bewilderment amused them, and I was getting mad when Zev enlightened me.

"Don't you see? We're joining them against a greater evil, but when the Germans are defeated, all these volunteers will fight with us. Instead of raw recruits, we'll have seasoned men with military skills. The Jews of *Eretz Yisrael* will have the benefit of British training. After all, it's only fair." He grinned again.

So the situation did have elements of humor. Still, I found it difficult to smile. I'd long admired the British, and losing one's illusions is a painful process. Not too long ago, I'd cheered an English pilot, even though he'd been opposing one of—

I paused, the thought unfinished. Once I would have ended it with "us," "one of us." An Iraqi. But this time, what I almost said was "them." More and more, I realized, "us" had come to mean my fellow Jews. All Jews everywhere, not just those I knew or knew about. And yet I wasn't ready, not quite ready yet, to cut the cord that bound me to the country of my birth.

Josef and Zev had fallen silent. Sometimes, as now, they simply sat and let me cogitate about a lesson. I was thinking now, however, of something said a while back. We'd been speaking of the Jewish Agency, which, as I knew, had represented Jewish interests in the Holy Land ever since enactment of the British Mandate. Zev divulged that it was branching out. Zionist volunteers, trained in teaching Hebrew, were being sent in secret to every country with a Jewish enclave. Two, he said, were already in Iraq.

At that, he clamped his mouth shut, and both men left without another word.

12

Hakham Ezra was pleased by the remarkable improvement in my Hebrew. To him it meant that I was serious about my studies—as indeed I was, but not for reasons he would recognize as valid.

Because I truly loved the Rabbi, I hated to deceive him, but while I wouldn't lie to him, I did withhold the truth. It was either that or leave the *yeshiva.* In spirit we were perfectly attuned, but our intellects were incompatible. I questioned everything; he was unequivocal in his beliefs. The rigidity of his convictions was equalled only by the depth of his compassion, so even when my mind rejected what he said, my heart responded.

He directed me to stay one day when class was over. Anyone aspiring to the Rabbinate, he said, was expected to acknowledge his misdeeds to God and seek to expiate them. One truth I'd never told the Rabbi was that I didn't intend to *be* a rabbi, but since my sins were known to God already, I indicated that I understood and would obey. I awaited his dismissal. Instead, he ordered me to start. "Confess to God," he said, but of course the *Hakham* also had to hear; unless he knew the size and scope of all my sins, he couldn't assign a proper penance.

Instantly, I started sifting and excising. I was willing to inform the Lord of every aberration, but *Hakham* Ezra was another matter. For instance, I could hardly tell the Rabbi that I was even *then* deceiving him. The big omission would have to be my oath to kill an Arab. To the *Hakham,* it would be intent to murder; God alone could weigh my motivation and absolve me.

Rabbi Ezra cleared his throat to indicate that he was waiting. After all my pondering, he must have been prepared for Sodom and Gomorrah, so was pleasantly surprised when I told him that I'd broken the *Shabbat.* It was true. I'd turned the lights on several times. My clock device didn't always work, but rather than admit to Baba that it wasn't perfect, I'd sneak outside and pull the switch.

For violations of the Sabbath, I was to fast two days a week for twenty weeks or else contribute what my food would cost for forty days to those less fortunate than I. Since the *slihot,* I'd been fasting on behalf of Jews in Europe, so I added up those days and applied them to my penance.

My cynical reaction to the *slihot* fast had modified somewhat. It did make sense of sorts. Self-denial showed concern for fellow human beings, but I still believed that it belittled God to even dream that we might influence His actions by not eating. And if we could, that would truly be unbearable. The God of Jews should not require extra prayers and penance to protect His people.

On leaving the *yeshiva* I was too roiled up to talk to anyone and much too tense to study. Outside, the sun was hot enough to cook an egg the chicken hadn't *laid* yet, and instead of heading home, I turned off toward the Tigris. I'd be breaking all the rules by swimming at this hour of the afternoon, but doing so precisely suited my rebellious mood.

In itself, my swimming wouldn't cause concern to anyone. Every day in summer since the age of eight, and with Baba's blessing, I'd taken off at sunrise for the public beach, about a fifteen-minute walk from home. I was such a fish in water that not even Nana worried, as long as I abided by the rules.

Since it was after 2 P.M., I was fracturing the first of those commandments. Naturally the *M'silmin* chose to swim when the day was at its scorching worst, so in order to avoid "unpleasantness," Jews restricted their activity to early morning hours. That meant there wouldn't be another Jew around—and the second rule was "never swim alone." That, however, had to do with danger from the river rather than the Arabs.

In its twisting, snaky course, the Tigris could be wildly unpredictable. At its calmest, the water roils at the many spans across it, and crazy currents intersect even in the straighter stretches. Flood time sees it raging full of rips and whirlpools, aggravated by the runoff of the heavy winter rains. In a single night in spring, the river often rises twenty feet; then half the stories in the papers are reports of drownings. On occasion, sharks originating in the Persian Gulf were sighted right off Rashid Street.

I'd learned to swim at six, in the shadow of the barge-supported pontoon bridge. Except for its replacement by a shiny modern span, nothing else had changed. Every spring the swim instructors rented sections of the beach—in reality, a mudbank—and erected flimsy skeletons of structures in which adults changed their clothes. The *jardagh,* though a hundred feet or more in length, were strictly temporary, consisting of some poles stuck in the mud, with walls of woven palm leaves and nothing overhead. Knocked down at the end of summer, they were reassembled when the springtime floods that swept the bank subsided. To save the few *fils* charged, we kids wore bathing trunks instead of underwear, and simply stripped.

The instructors were equipped with lengths of rope and piles of foot-long segments cut from palm-tree trunks. Three buoyant slabs, lashed securely to his upper body, would float a small beginning swimmer. You could tell how well a kid was doing by counting up the wedges he was wearing. As proficiency increased, they came off, one by one. When a boy could swim across the river unassisted, a formal graduation followed, complete with feasting at the riverside. Since he'd told my father it would take two summers to teach me how to swim that well, the instructor was chagrined when I shucked my palm-tree sections and soloed after six weeks' worth of lessons. I made a tentative suggestion that Baba split the fees he'd saved with me, but one look shut me up.

By now, I was close enough to smell the *samak masgouf* cooking. Along the whole embankment, the delicious fish, only minutes from the river, were roasting over tiny fires, fed sparingly with twigs and straw. Wood was hard to come by and could eat up all the profit. Old Arab men, for whom this was a way of life, waved little raffia fans to make the flames leap up and lick the *masgouf.*

As I'd hoped, the beach was virtually deserted. A few ambitious souls were dunking near the shore, but there was no one in the river, really swimming. I'd have the Tigris to myself, and as I did each day, I set about to break the last of the unwritten rules.

Like the city, the river and its shores were separated into "theirs" and "ours." Resafa, which was "our" side, was considered fairly safe, but the final rule was that Jews avoid not just the other bank—Karkh by name—but the river water washing it. Our orders were "stay on our side"—as if a line ran down the Tigris, splitting it in two. Once, when S'hak "crossed" the line and swam too close to Karkh, Arabs on the shore had stoned him, but I still persisted. Streets were made by men, so maybe men could argue over who belonged on them, but God created rivers, and this was mine as much as any *Mislim*'s. I swam from shore to shore each morning, and today would be no different.

The beach sloped sharply and was first elastic underfoot, then oozy. Two steps in the stream, as it was running now, and a boy my size would be neck-deep. I paused, as always, to estimate its swiftness, both for safety's sake and because I played a little game, betting with myself about how close I'd come to hitting shore exactly opposite from where I started. With the water at its normal stage, I could usually restrict the drift to less than forty feet.

When there were *guffahs* on the river, I gauged the rate of flow and noted where the water swirled by watching them. More raft than boat, woven out of reeds and circular in shape, they rode atop the water rather than immersed in it. Captives of each current, they bobbed along like corks. However, the stretch ahead of me was empty. Some buffalo were wallowing below the bridge, but too far off to tell me much. I'd have to judge the water by the island. Jazeera was a measure of the river's elevation.

Though always called an "island," the description only fit Jazeera at isolated intervals. On the map, and during dry spells, it was just a mounded spit of sand off Bataaween in southwest Baghdad. Except at flood stage, the river bent around it. When we'd visited in Bataaween the previous week, Jazeera *was* an island, cut off at its neck by rising, rushing waters. I knew, therefore, that currents would be extra strong today, but I didn't expect to catch one quite so close to shore. A few strokes out, and it was sweeping me downstream. Face submerged, I dug in deeply, employing every ounce of strength against the drag.

Exhausted, but near enough the other bank to know I'd make it, I raised my head to orient myself. To the left of me, something thrashed the water. I heard a strangulated shriek, and suddenly a face emerged, all bulging eyes and sucking fishlike lips, but the apparition sank without another sound, and bubbles broke the surface. The undertow was sucking someone down and to his death. A man was drowning, a *Mislim,* and on the shore a score of Arabs watched, but no one made a move to save him.

My mind was churning like the *Mislim*'s windmill arms beneath the water. *Letting* someone die wasn't quite the same as *causing* him to die, but die he would unless I intervened. The debt to Haron would be wiped out by the water and the will of God. I wouldn't have done a thing, and yet an Arab would be dead. A simple lack of doing—surely not a sin.

Weakened by my fasts, with the river running rampant, I told myself I couldn't make the Karkh embankment with a large dead weight to drag. Insane to even think of it . . . completely crazy . . . just see his brother Arabs anchored to the bank. Not one would risk the swollen river.

Unaware that I was doing so, I dived to fish the *Mislim* up. Before my conscious mind had come to a decision, I had him on the surface. Luckily, he didn't have the strength to struggle, and I cupped his chin to keep his head above the water while I stroked for shore. The undertow continued clutching at our legs, and energized by terror, he kicked convulsively and almost tore away. While my swimming arm became a limp and leaden noodle, I talked to him to calm him down.

More *M'silmin,* dozens more, had gathered at the waterline to watch. Fifty Arabs screamed encouragement and asked the aid of Allah. Not one, however, waded out to help us in. In all the clamor over Ismet, no one paid me much attention when I hauled him up the bank. The crowd assumed that I was Arab, and I slipped away before they looked too closely. Ismet knew I wasn't *Mislim.* When I'd spoken to him in the water, it was in our Jewish dialect, and his eyes had widened till the whites showed.

Back on the Resafa side—by bridge this time—I grabbed my clothes and ran like fury for the synagogue. The service was already underway when I arrived, and Baba glared at me, as angry as I'd ever seen him.

Outside, when he could speak, I understood. Taha, one of Baba's workmen, had been on the beach at Karkh. He'd recognized me in the water and had raced to tell my father while I struggled toward the shore. Though he'd known me all my life, Taha hadn't stretched his hand out either. Instead of helping me, he'd run to tell the *usta* where his son was, and extend his hand instead for Baba's *bakhsheesh.*

Baba's rage was monumental, and he blistered me the whole way home. I recognized that fear for me was, in the main, responsible for his explosion, but it wasn't only that I'd risked my life that angered him, or even that I'd risked it for an Arab; he was furious because I'd fallen for an Arab trick. Deadly serious, he said, "You should have been suspicious. They're sneaky bastards, especially there in Karkh." Baba honestly believed that the drowning man had been a decoy, his "act" designed to draw me close enough to kill!

I could hardly tell him that the only thought of murder was in *my* mind. Right then, I couldn't have told him anything because the sentiment he'd just expressed had shocked me speechless. For all his surface friendliness, for all his "we can work it out" insistence, my father, I discovered, had a deep and visceral distrust of Arabs.

He concealed it well, and if he hadn't been distraught already, I'm sure he wouldn't have said a word about the *hadji. Hadji* Umer was one of father's friends, the one who'd wept the hardest when Haron was killed. In a flat, metallic voice, Baba told me he'd been in the *Hadji*'s home today.

"The room was draped with silver chains, dozens of them, the kind we use with *Shabbat* oil lamps. And against the wall, I saw the pillow Nana made for Liaa when she married."

My mother's needlework was so distinctive that it couldn't be mistaken, and a gift of hers would never willingly have been relinquished to an Arab. *Hadji* Umer's house, Baba said, was full of Jewish objects. During the pogrom, his sons, if not Umer himself, had stolen wedding pillows and ripped the chains from prayer lamps. Who knows what other crimes had been committed by our *Mislim* "friends."

Exhausted as I was, I lay awake a long, long while, mulling over all the day's events. How was it possible for Baba, feeling as he did, to fool himself into a false security about the future? I tried to keep my mind on that, to keep it off the Arab who was safely home instead of bloating on the river bottom.

Conditions couldn't have been more perfect, yet I hadn't kept my pledge. My natural impulse was to help, not hurt, and I knew without a doubt now that I couldn't destroy a life, any life at all, except to save another.

At last, for what little comfort it afforded, I was rid of all the "whos" and "whens" and "wheres" and "hows." The problem had been stripped to its essentials.

I'd made a sacred oath.

I hadn't honored it.

I never would.

I must have slept because I jerked awake, trembling in the aftermath of nightmare, and knowing that I had to talk to someone quickly or I'd tear myself apart. From Rabbi Ezra, I'd get warmth and dogma, but I needed someone uninvolved, someone who could stand off from the issue and from me. To help, he'd have to be dispassionate but sensitive, someone close to God but very much in touch with human frailties and feelings.

Out of nowhere, Samy's father came to mind. He was a scholar and a spiritist, a businessman and rabbi—and we'd never met. The very man! At my request, Samy made a date for me to see him.

On approaching him, I felt a pleasant shock of recognition. He had Samy's face and smile, and wasn't in the least intimidating. My relief was mixed with just a bit of disappointment. He looked too ordinary for a mystic. When I addressed him as *Hakham* Ya'akoob, he graciously dissented. "Call me Abu Samy. My son has told me all about you." He assumed I wished to study with him and was there to make arrangements.

I couldn't begin by lying, so I shook my head and said I'd come because I had a problem. With only that preamble, I poured the whole thing out in one great gush. Rabbi Ezra would have interrupted me a dozen times to disagree or interject a quote or comment, but Samy's father, listening intently, let me race right through to my conclusion.

He wore a thoughtful look throughout, but when I stopped, I was stunned to see a lively smile light his face. "It's serious!" I cried indignantly. "It was a sacred oath!" But Abu Samy's smile widened.

"First, there was no oath. You were just a boy. It's impossible to make a binding oath before *bar mitzvah.*"

A weight within me shifted and began to lift.

"Secondly"—Samy's father hadn't finished—"even if it had been binding, Yom Kippur arrived between the time you made the vow and the time you spared the Arab, and on *Kol Nidre* night, all vows become invalid. They're stricken from the record." Leaning forward and fixing me with eyes as piercing now as Rabbi Ezra's, he repeated, "They're stricken from the record. They don't exist."

I'd held my breath ever since he'd said *"bar mitzvah."* With Abu Samy's final words, it all whooshed out, and I was feather-light, the whole load lifted from my heart and mind. *Hakham* Ya'akoob's eyes had never left me, and his face retained the shadow of a smile. As I would learn, a trace was ever-present, for Abu Samy's soul knew true content.

As if he had a marker in the book, he opened up his Bible right to Judges and began to read to me of Yiftah. In the twelfth century before the Christian era, following his victory in the fight against the Ammonites, Yiftah promised God a sacrifice to show his gratitude. He pledged to offer up the person who approached him first. The first to greet him was his daughter, and to keep his vow, he killed her.

It was the last such act recorded in the Torah. Abu Samy closed the book, and fixed his eyes upon me even more intently. The community was so appalled, he said, that human sacrifice had been forbidden. From that day on, no vow demanding it was valid in Judaic law.

"So you see, if such a vow is made, even in the best of faith but knowing nothing of the ban against it, it isn't binding."

He was saying I was in the clear in every way that he could think of. Though he'd seen my body's swift reaction, he was seeking ways to satisfy my intellect as well. Samy's father seemed to understand that hearts and minds are often worlds apart—that one might honestly believe implicitly in what the other won't admit exists. As both a man and Jew, I wanted more than anything for all of me to mesh—and maybe he could make it happen.

One evening, not long after, I slipped inside the Shahmoon synagogue where his *kehilla* group was meeting. Squinting through his owlish reading glasses, he waved me toward a seat and gently censured me. "You're late. Sit down." He'd been expecting me.

A small red book lay on the lectern, and each man in attendance read a paragraph aloud. *Hakham* Ya'akoob then explained the hidden meaning of the text in question, exploring every shade and subtlety. Finally the time arrived for me to read. Though the youngest of the others was over forty years my senior, they accepted me as one of them because the *Hakham* had, and as I recited, they listened with the same attentiveness they'd shown the men preceding me.

"Man is privileged to study Torah in order to learn the secrets of Heaven, and so enter the Second World cleansed of sin. What man should strive to know is first about himself . . . then he must seek to understand the secrets of the soul. Even if they do good deeds, all those who live without attempting to inform themselves about these secrets will be excluded from the gates of Heaven. God will ask the spirit, 'What are the secrets that you studied?' If the spirit answers that it wished to learn but could not, it will be forgiven."

I was reading from the Zohar!

Walking home with Samy's father, I was still exhilarated. My spirits soaring higher than they ever had, I thought I couldn't be happier. We'd been walking briskly, discussing what we'd cover in the next *kehilla* session, when *Hakham* Ya'akoob slowed and stopped. His face, though mostly lost in shadow, looked more solemn than I'd ever seen it, and when he spoke again, his voice was grave.

"What happened in the water was more important than you know. It wasn't merely that you let the Arab live. You saved his life. In the eyes of God, so says the Talmud, 'He who saves a life is the same as one who saves a world.'"

Head to toe, I shivered uncontrollably, thankful that the darkness hid me. Abu Samy couldn't know, but I'd been thinking more and more about a medical career, about defending life in general, not just endangered Jewish lives. For him to quote exactly what he had, and on the very day I ventured into Zohar—I had icy bumps all over me. If not a thunderbolt, if not Cabala, it was certainly a sign of sorts from Heaven.

13

The Brotherhood had been meeting less frequently and to little purpose for a long time now. It was teetering on the brink of breaking up, and I wasn't in the most receptive mood when Eli introduced himself, even when he said that he'd been sent by Josef. Both Zev and Josef had been shipped to Mosul, and I felt abandoned. Eighteen, acne-scarred and gangling, Eli looked to be a poor replacement. He'd been told, he said, to take good care of me, and asked if I would meet with him that evening. My curiosity was piqued; I couldn't resist a mystery and Josef knew it.

Eli took me to a house in Bataaween, not far from where my father's partner lived. Familiar with the section, I recognized the somewhat ostentatious building as belonging to a Jewish banker. The wealthiest and least observant Jews were clustered in this newer Quarter; I couldn't imagine their relationship to me or Josef. The mystery increased when Eli tapped the door in what was clearly code. It opened just a crack, until a whispered password gained us both admittance. Eli led me to a bench and disappeared.

As my eyes adjusted to the dimness, I saw that other seats around the room were occupied. I counted five young men, who ranged in age from fourteen, maybe fifteen, to the early twenties. Every face was fixed and mask-like, and we all sat poker-stiff. I had qualms, and all the others evidenced the same unease and shame on showing it. While no one spoke, each of us was furtively examining the others. I'd never seen a single one of them before.

Without a sound to mark their coming, two slightly older men were suddenly among us. One offered us *"Shalom"* in greeting, and when the other spoke, I knew for sure that they were Zionists. He said *"hala,"* like Zev. It was Arab slang, he'd told me, picked up while he lived in *Eretz Yisrael* and used only by the *M'silmin* in the Mandate.

The older of the men addressed us. "We're Zionists," he stated crisply. "We've come from Palestine. We know you're all involved in some way with The Movement."

It was the certainty with which he spoke that set my pulses pounding. I'd never heard of any "movement"; but my brain was racing like my blood now. This meeting was clandestine, and my only secret business was the Brotherhood. By "The Movement," then, he could only be referring to an underground, and that could only mean the other five had also been engaged as I was. There had to be a half-a-dozen going groups, and each unknown to any of the others!

Judging from the way our jaws went slack, the six of us had reached the same conclusion. Enjoying our excitement, Nadji grinned at us. Nadji, he'd informed us, was his code name; his true identity would never be revealed.

"You're right in what you're thinking," he announced. "That's why we're here. We want to work with you, not only here in Baghdad, but in Basra and Mosul, in Arbil, Kirkuk, Sulaimania, in all Iraq." So jubilant I could have danced for joy, I shook his hand instead. Arbil, Kirkuk, and Sulaimania were Kurdish towns, so after centuries of meek subservience, even the most isolated Kurdish Jews were stirring.

Nadji had been sent by Mosad Ha'aliyah, the Jewish Agency's highly secret immigration arm. Organized to circumvent the Arab-British quotas, it smuggled Jewish refugees—"illegals"—into Palestine.

As he continued, that first elation faded. Defense, as far as Mosad was concerned, took second place to immigration. The Jewish Agency would aid in our survival, but toward the end that we would one day make our *aliyah* to *Eretz Yisrael.* A murmur of dissent arose, and Nadji rushed to reassure us.

"We don't require that you be a Zionist. It's enough that you're a Jew. However, if we're going to work together, you ought to know what Zionism is. That's all we ask. In the last analysis, you'll make your own decision, but without our help, you have no choice at all." He challenged us. "How many of your units are intact? How many members have you added? How many have you lost?

From our faces, it was obvious that all the troops, not only mine, were cracking up.

Taking silence for assent, Nadji plunged ahead, identifying both himself and silent partner as *sh'lichim,* messengers of Mosad. For reasons of security, he said, each *shaliyach* would spend, at most, a year in any country. On his recall to Palestine, another would be sent to take his place. "I'm the new boy here in Baghdad," he announced, and briefly grinned again.

"We've come to organize a strong, cohesive underground. The Movement's name is *T'nu'ah,* and the six of you will be its nucleus."

The room was now electric. Naming it had made it real. The project would be launched, he said, with two weeks of intensive training in the Hebrew language and the history of Zionism. After finishing the formal course, each of us would head a cell, consisting of at least six others but limited to twelve. Recruits must be at least fourteen. (On saying this, Nadji stared directly at me, but refrained from further comment. Even for a twelve-year-old, I wasn't very big.) Each recruit would have a code name—mine was Haim—and only those would ever be employed. The leader of a cell would be referred to as *madrich.* The six of us would choose additional *madrichim* from among our members and teach them how to start new cells; they, in turn, would choose and teach more leaders, thus widening the network.

"Each year, a *mazkir*—a secretary—will be chosen from among the *madrichim.*" Nadji's voice, I noticed, had taken on a more portentous tone. "He will act as overall coordinator and maintain the records, and when his year is up, he's pledged to go to *Eretz Yisrael.*"

He paused, expecting protests, but we waited for an explanation. "As I told you, we encourage *aliyah,* and while we can't insist on it for everyone, we have the right to ask that leaders serve as good examples. That's reason number one, which I know you won't approve. The second reason you'll agree with. With luck and care, a *mazkir* may escape detection for perhaps a year. After that, the odds are all against him. He's the easiest to spot because he has to meet more often with more members of the underground than any other individual. And if they catch a *mazkir. . . .*" We could finish that ourselves. We'd *all* go down the drain.

He was about to end the meeting, and without another mention of defense. I began to rise to bring the issue up but someone beat me to it. "We'll learn Hebrew if we have to, but first we'd like some arms instruction."

From the swiftness of his answer, Nadji had foreseen the question. "Your defense instructors will be coming here from *Eretz Yisrael.* Most speak only Hebrew, or Hebrew and a Western language, and without communication, there can't be any lessons."

From the time he'd said *"Shalom,"* the entire meeting had only taken twenty minutes. Our *shaliyach* impressed me with his frank approach and brisk responses. He'd anticipated every problem and wrapped up all the straggling ends. How many times, I wondered, had he done this? How many of us were there in Iraq? And elsewhere in the world? Wherever there were Jews, he said, an ever-widening network.

We worked with Hebrew primers especially designed for adult immigrants, and I concealed the fact that I already knew the whole vocabulary we would cover. I prized the little book because I'd learned phonetically and lacked the grammar. I would have liked to take it home, but we were short of copies and several students shared each one. And then, of course, all nonreligious Hebrew books were banned by law; one that taught the language would utterly incriminate the person who possessed it. I'd have risked the danger, but the opportunity eluded me. At the end of class, we had to turn the primers in. I was cudgeling my brain for a reason to retain a book when the *shaliyach* himself made argument unnecessary. He decided that my house should have a book *slik.* I was only plotting for a lonely primer, and he was giving me a library!

Slikim were hidden crypts hollowed in the floors of private homes to hold illegal books. To protect the owners of the buildings—mainly parents of the *T'nu'ah* members who knew nothing of The Movement and were unaware their offspring were involved—we constructed them in secrecy. Insofar as possible, books would be deposited where members of the *T'nu'ah* met. Since I'd volunteered our storage room—Nana was accustomed to my "studying" with friends—it was logical to build a *slik* at our house.

An even more important factor was the house itself and where it stood. The water table underlying Baghdad was so near the surface that most buildings in the city had no basements; they would have wound up swimming pools instead of cellars. Because Kambar Ali Street was slightly elevated, and our house was three high steps above the level of the street, Baba had been able to construct a storage space, barely five feet deep, beneath the dining room. We could therefore dig a *slik* without disturbing anyone and without the risk of hitting water.

I'd have to lift a two-foot square of flooring, which in this case was a single tile, dig a pit the same dimensions, tar it, line it with cement, sheathe the bottom and the sides with sheets of tin, and top it with a wooden lid, also lined with metal. This cover, which I'd cut ahead of time to fit the opening, would have a length of strong steel wire threaded through its center. When the lid was on, and before I put the tile back in place, I'd drill a tiny hole and pull the wire through the tile too. A plug of clay, the same the tile was made of, would conceal the cavity. To open it and get the books, all one had to do was pry the plug out, fish the wire through, and tug both tile and lid off.

In the winter it would have been more difficult to do the job, but everyone was sleeping on the roof now, out of earshot. The others went to bed at ten, but since I often stayed downstairs to read, my absence wouldn't inspire any questions.

With a list of what I needed, I'd been dropping by at Baba's building sites and doing some judicious swiping. In the dead of night, when the crypt had been completed, the Menashi boys came by as planned. We packed the excavated earth in old cement bags which we hauled outside and heaved between the houses. All the buildings were a little out of line, and every indentation harbored heaps of refuse. Though a garbageman came daily, some festering debris was uncollectable. People walking in the street would spit out seeds and fling down rinds and other rubbish with unerring aim at jogs between the building walls. Clogged with bits of rotted food, they were also used as urinals. Our nice clean dirt was never noticed.

Before the training sessions ended, I'd signed up twenty new recruits. Nadji—from whom "not bad" was practically a Nobel Prize—signified his satisfaction with a grunt. Our *shaliyach* was not a man who made a show of his emotions, except where Zionism was concerned.

He was impassioned on the subject, even lyrical, and I always found the transformation touching. I was envious too as he expressed his almost mystical belief in *Eretz Yisrael.* Once I'd felt as sure about Iraq. But at least Iraq was real; you could find it in an atlas. During our indoctrination, I'd defied Nadji to show me *Eretz Yisrael* on any map. As if explaining to a backward child, he'd answered quietly, "We'll *put* it on the map."

I'd told him from the first that I would not be emigrating and, faithful to his promise, he never pressured me. I, on the other hand, was growing more insistent on the matter of defense. At intervals I'd ask him, "When?" His unvarying response was "When the time is right."

While waiting, we continued to recruit new members for The Movement and also organized another arm, called *Noar*—"youth"—which kids could join officially at nine. As I was underage myself, and no one ever raised the issue, we enrolled them even younger. I enlisted Daisy, but at four and seven, Avram and Osa would have to wait a little longer. In the meantime,

I began to teach them Hebrew on my own, warning them that they were not to practice when our parents were around. Baba would have had a stroke.

I wasn't sure myself why I involved them, except that I enjoyed the role of teacher, and while I wouldn't admit it for the world to Nadji, I was liking Hebrew more and more, perhaps because I liked our government's suppression of the language less and less. Nothing was forbidden to the Arabs. They could study anything from Afrikaans to Esperanto, but Jewish citizens were not allowed to learn a Jewish language.

I'd already shaved *yeshiva* time to study Zohar. Now I did my homework even quicker to accommodate the *T'nu'ah* meetings, and squeezed some hours from sleep for Hebrew classes. Nana said she never saw me eat; S'hak said I ate as much as ever, but faster than the human eye could follow. Both were right; I swallowed on the run.

Of necessity, I perfected my "division-of-attention" trick, in which my mind was made to operate exactly like a radio. When tuned in to the *T'nu'ah,* nothing but the *T'nu'ah* reached me, but I could switch at will, and instantly, to Zohar, *shamash* or *yeshiva.* Whatever wavelength I selected would suppress the rest until I chose to change. Sharply focused, I could filter out both large and small distractions and concentrate my total being on whatever lay before me at the moment.

Because of that technique, my grades stayed good, my group made progress, and my pupils picked up Hebrew like a bunch of little blotters. I was less receptive. For the last six months, Nadji had been soaking us in Zionism, but I still resisted. As a fantasy, a wish fulfillment, I understood the strength of its appeal; at times, I even felt the pull of it, but stood my ground against it. Having suffered from the loss of old illusions, I was wary of acquiring others. Disavowing *aliyah,* I felt that Jews should fight for justice where they were, not run away like frightened rabbits. Nadji's even-tempered answer was "We aren't running *from,* we're running *to.*"

My reservations notwithstanding, anyone who wished to go would have whatever help I had to give. On at least one issue—our entitlement to enter Palestine—the Zionists and I were in accord. The British had no right to bar a Jew from any place but, possibly, Great Britain. If they pointed to the Mandate, we could counter with the Book of Moses. Where, I'd ask, does "Englishman" occur in any Bible? The Holy Land was much more ours than theirs, and I was proud of what my kinsmen had accomplished there. I was surprised, in fact, to find how proud I was.

When Nadji, who'd been briefed about my medical activities, told me that trachoma and malaria had almost been eliminated in the Jewish sectors, my elation must have shown. No other Mideast country had ever freed itself of these diseases. Nadji nurtured my increasing interest in the area with random bits of information. The Arabs had destroyed 200,000 trees—the Jews replaced them with a million. There were miracles of cultivation on land considered dead. Modern plants were making chemicals, and quantities of minerals were being processed.

"For us," he said, "the Dead Sea is alive and well—like the language.

When we started speaking Hebrew," he reminded me, "the whole world laughed. That, too, was dead, they told us, dead and buried in the Bible. Well, it's been reborn, just the way we'll bring back *Eretz Yisrael.*" When Nadji spoke, it sounded possible.

One day he handed me a book that looked as if he'd read it through a thousand times. It was his own, he said, not *T'nu'ah*'s, and he thought I'd find it worth my while. Since Nadji hadn't struck me as a literary type, I could hardly wait to see what he indulged in. A cops-and-robbers or a Western, I'd have bet, but it proved to be *The Jewish State,* written by a bearded man named Herzl. His eyes, in the picture opposite the title page, were even more intense than Rabbi Ezra's. You could see that something burned in him.

I couldn't ignore a book of any kind, but I opened this one mostly from a sense of obligation, figuring I'd skim it quickly. What could Herzl say that Nadji hadn't said already? My enthusiasm waned still more on making out the date of publication: 1896—ancient history! And the author was an *Ashkenazi,* an Austrian Jew, an alien. His views could hardly have much relevance to me. Powerless, however, in the presence of a printed page, I started reading.

By the time I closed the book, the dawn was breaking. I couldn't believe that I could feel such deep affinity for someone seemingly so foreign. Different as we were in every surface aspect, inside we were the same.

As Austria had been to Herzl, so Iraq had been to me. Like me, he'd been a patriot, a supercitizen, whose birthplace was a source of pride. Like me, though later in his life, he'd found himself an alien in his native land. Like me, he'd learned that Jews in many lands, not only his, were looked upon as less than human—and, again like me, he'd fought the knowledge.

On the day my cousin died, I conceded that the evil did exist. For Herzl, it was the Dreyfus trial in France that forced him to accept the ugly facts.

Lying there in bed, his book in hand, I faced up to the latest evidence that Jews were hated just for being Jews. The Dreyfus farce had ended more than fifty years ago, but even at this moment, the Jews of France, like all the Jews of Europe, were being winnowed from their countrymen for killing—in all too many cases, with their countrymen's cooperation. Without the covert, and often open, aid of others, Hitler couldn't have swept the continent of Europe "clean" of Jews.

Nothing but some names had changed, and nothing *would* be changed as long as we were weak and scattered. Herzl hadn't needed Hitler to convince him, and it shamed me that I hadn't seen the truth much sooner. Stateless, Jews were at the mercy of a hundred states. Therefore—it seemed so simple now—Jews must have their own state. And since the exodus began in Palestine, ending there made perfect sense historically. Both logically and biblically, the land was ours.

In a sense, I'd just become a Zionist, but a Zionist for other Jews. I knew without a doubt now that a Jewish state was needed for the cast-outs of a score of countries, for those of the Diaspora who hadn't really sunk their roots in centuries of roaming. In Iraq, however, we had rooted deeply, and I intended to remain—and make some changes.

When I returned the book and asked if he had any more by Herzl, Nadji knew he had a convert, but he didn't know what kind. While pleased with me, he put me off again on the issue of defense; when pressed, he finally admitted that only boys eighteen and older were admitted to intensive training.

I reacted angrily, of course, but when the import of the words sank in, I stared at him with more respect than ever. So all along he'd been schooling some of us, and none of us suspected. With security that tight among our own, our secrets should be safe from anyone outside The Movement. Still resentful, though, I argued that assigning boys to training on the basis of their birth dates was merely one more form of bias. All Nadji said was that he'd think it over.

A few days later, a new *madrich* approached me, and invited me to join a special unit. I accepted, but he clammed up tight when I began to question him. His instructions, he informed me, were to give me only date and time and place, and password.

On the night he named, another door in Bataaween swung open, and another silent stranger motioned me to slip inside. The room in which he seated me was eerily in shadow, and I sat alone. Only seconds passed before a figure beckoned me along a passage, pointed to a door ahead, and stood aside.

I braced myself to face whatever lay inside and pushed through smartly, but all I saw was a scintillating blue-white circle. I flinched from the spotlight stabbing at my eyes. From the black beyond the blinding glitter, an unknown voice was asking me my name. Though shaken, I responded, "Haim." Someone chuckled, and a second voice said, "Good! But now let's have your real name." I hesitated, but if they knew I'd given them a code name, they had to be involved with us. I'd have to trust them, all three of them, for another man had made his presence known.

They quizzed me up and down on everything from personal relationships to politics. What was I studying and why? Was I intimate with any Arabs? Had I told my family about my feelings? Describe the last pogrom . . . the members of my cell . . . my relatives in Palestine.

For hours, it seemed, I stood there, the questions coming at me like machine-gun fire. My mouth grew dry, and the blazing light was giving me a migraine. The voices talked among themselves, too low for me to overhear; then the one who'd sounded most decisive spoke to me again.

"Just two more questions, but be very sure before you answer them."

Involuntarily, I held my breath. When he asked me if I'd sacrifice my life to save my fellow Jews, my "Yes!" exploded from ballooning lungs. I heard another smothered chuckle, an impatient shush, and the same voice put the second question.

"If you join us, will you guard our secrets even if it means your life?"

Surprise, not indecision, made me hesitate. This was something more, much more, than a defense course, but if my "yes" this time was slower, it was equally sincere.

Suddenly the light blinked out, and when my eyes adjusted, three men were smiling welcome. The most pedantic-looking person at the table proved to be the owner of the most portentous voice. In front of him, a large revolver rested on a Bible.

"We are the *Shura,*" he announced. "In Iraq, we represent the Haganah."

From Boy Scout manual to Haganah! The Haganah's exploits were already legend. Tactical instruction by its members was like being taught the Ten Commandments by the Prophet Moses.

I was told to place my hand on the revolver and repeat the oath as it was given me. In Hebrew, I promised to resist the enemies of *Eretz Yisrael,* and silently, in dialect, I added, "and the enemies of all Jews everywhere, especially in Iraq." I also vowed to keep the *Shura* secret "to the end of my endurance and beyond—to death, if necessary."

By all Judaic laws, these oaths were valid. These, I'd keep.

14

In the last twelve months, the *T'nu'ah* had expanded at a steady rate; 2000 young Iraqi Jews were currently enrolled. As for the *Shura,* no one knew its total membership. None, in fact, but those recruited knew of its existence. I now had secrets hiding secrets from still other secrets.

Nana was the only one outside The Movement who never worried me. Even in a city where every male offspring ruled his mother, I was recognized as king of all such autocrats. My absolute control had made our house the safest place for meetings, and it soon became a center for defense instruction. Because it froze my mother's marrow when I screamed in fury, she'd long since learned to leave me to my own devices, and she never entered any room I occupied without an invitation.

We used the first-floor family room for training that required an extensive space. To explain the thumps and grunts and smothered outcries that escaped the room, I said that we were learning special exercises, and so we were. Of course, she thought they had to do with school.

We learned to fight with knives, sheathed to start, bare-bladed when we'd gained sufficient skill. Our instructor was as agile as an eel, and before we reached his stage of expertise, I also got some added first-aid practice. Since we hadn't honed the blades, the cuts sustained were superficial, but even so, they could have done us in simply by attracting the attention of our elders.

Menashi's mind was wandering one day—he'd just discovered women—and he wound up wounded in both arms and legs. Annoyed with him, I sloshed on iodine and did a bumpy job of bandaging. He left the house wafting clouds of antiseptic and looking like an ill-wrapped mummy. Nana must have noticed that Menashi had arrived unblemished and departed bloody, and whatever she suspected, she conveyed to Baba. Late that night, I heard him fumbling for the niche inside the air shaft where he hid his knife. Finding it exactly where he'd left it, he went off to bed. It never crossed his mind that I might have my own, and he never asked about Menashi. Nonetheless, I made my patching inconspicuous from that point on.

The same instructor saw us through the judo and jiujitsu courses. By the time we finished, I could handle someone twice my size and come up smiling.

We arrived, in time, at guns. Experts taught us how to ream and rust-proof, how to file sights and reset triggers. We learned to "break" a weapon, and anything we took apart we had to reassemble wearing blindfolds.

Our arsenal was what you might call motley, and we never knew what kind of gun we'd have in class on any given day. Bought or "liberated" one by one, they stemmed from half-a-dozen different conflicts and twice as many countries.

To practice shooting, we went out in groups of four, with well-filled picnic baskets on our arms and with girls along to add a final touch of authenticity. Our favorite spot was twenty miles south of Baghdad, where a sharp bend in the Tigris left a long, low strip of countryside deserted. It was off the beaten track, and our shooting went unnoticed. Not that there was all that much to notice. With bullets so expensive and so hard to come by, we aimed a lot more than we shot; and since our tiny stock of hand grenades was even less expendable, we practiced pulling out imaginary pins from rocks the size of the grenades, counting off the proper time before we tossed them at the target.

I had no idea our training was to take two years. My definition of defense, I found, was far too limited. Mere resistance meant, at best, an endless war. To win a peace, you had to hurt the enemy a whole lot more than he hurt you.

We learned that fighting off attack was often costlier, and always less effective, than mounting a surprise assault. Even fearfully outnumbered and outgunned, a tiny, well-trained force could keep the enemy off balance and in disarray. Our instructors taught us when to lie in wait and when to seize initiative and strike. We studied strategy and mapped elaborate maneuvers. A lecture on guerilla warfare might be followed by discussion of survival tactics under seige. All in all, it was intensive education, if not the sort my schools, or Baba, would approve.

Surprisingly, I felt no conflict with the Zohar. All through training, I'd continued to attend *kehilla*—also undercover. Should Rabbi Ezra find me out, I'd have to take my leave from the *yeshiva.* However, Abu Samy and the others had agreed to keep my secret. What was one more secret, and an earthly one at that, to students of the small red book?

The Zohar opened to another world, an afterlife existence of the spirit-soul. At *kehilla,* I was close to God, and often close, I felt, to revelation. I caught tantalizing glimpses of a total truth, but the book concealed as much as it unveiled. As *Hakham* Ya'akoob warned it would, for every mystery the Zohar solved, it shrouded several more in deeper shadow.

Still, several fundamentals came through clearly. The hardest for my ego to accept was that the history of man—the whole of it—was but a blink in time, and all the places that we occupied and thought enduring and important were as specks of dust.

Ants scurrying around their little anthills was my first reaction, and I wondered why such knowledge made the *Hakham* happy. Did the ants believe in God? A God who made the ants His people? Who made them promises? And when someone crushed their anthills, did they feel forsaken?

For awhile, I was wretched and confused, but so caught up in study of the Zohar that I couldn't quit. When the revelation came, it wasn't like a bolt from out the blue at all, but rather like a seed of knowing, dormant deep inside me since my birth—a seed the Zohar stirred to life.

When it blossomed, all the doubt was driven out. I knew now that the Lord would keep His covenant. My error lay in thinking that His promises applied to our existence here on earth. His pledge would be fulfilled in the foreverafter. To redeem the pledge, to win a place in Heaven with the Lord, one only had to live a Jewish life and, if necessary, die a Jewish death—a tiny price to pay for peace and joy eternal.

I never questioned God again, but nothing in the Zohar said I couldn't look askance at people. The complacency of older Jews, including Baba, kept me at a constant boil. "Don't make waves," they warned. "Look how well we're doing."

Prosperity was at an all-time high. War was raging to the west of us, and with Turkey neutral, only north Iraq and Persia blocked the Nazi pincers. Our location made Iraq essential to the Allied effort, and more than half a million troops moved in and out of Baghdad. Most were from the British Commonwealth, but Sikorsky's army—150,000 Poles—and even some American liaison officers were here as well.

Despite the efforts of the government to keep it quiet, the Quarter knew that Jews from Palestine were camped across the river and that the Star of David flew defiantly above them. The Star had been forbidden to Iraqi Jews, so even those who scorned the Zionists exulted. In Palestine, the *Shura* said (as I already knew from Zev and Josef), Jewish settlers by the tens of thousands had volunteered for service in the British army. Some, like those across the river, insisted that they fight as Jews, and since the British needed them, the Star of David decorated three battalions.

With such heavy traffic in the city and so much new construction, trade was brisk and money plentiful. Both Jews and Arabs prospered, but the Jews, because of broad commercial interests, were reaping bigger benefits. There was muttering among the *M'silmin,* nothing more, but I worried over what would happen when the boom went bust. No one else appeared to see an end to it.

The city, lively and exciting at the worst of times, was now a seething hive of fevered fortune seekers. As goods began to disappear, the frenzy to obtain them burst all normal bounds. Minor bribery became corruption on a massive scale. Black markets flourished, soldiers stole to order from Supply Corps, and for cash in hand, anyone and anything could be procured.

Made euphoric by the swelling of their pocketbooks and the presence of the Allied troops, the older Jews felt more secure than ever in their lives. Reminded that the laws restricting Jews were still in force, they simply shrugged, and the few who knew about the underground regarded us with much more trepidation than they did the average Arab.

As subjects of the Ottomans, Jews my father's age had been conditioned to accept their secondary status as the price of life itself. Pogroms had been part of life, so much so that some regarded them as natural disasters, much like locust plagues or sandstorms. They struggled to survive, and simply prayed catastrophe would skip them on its next occurrence. In the present atmosphere, they were starting to believe that further pogroms weren't possible, and I understood their self-delusion. They'd suffered under such restraints, this loosening of bonds must feel like freedom.

While many of the younger Jews were flocking to the *T'nu'ah,* and to Communism, few left for Palestine. Some who'd made the trip returned, telling such alarming stories of the hardships that others were discouraged. Soft-handed city boys couldn't stand the sweaty labor of the *kibbutzim,* and they resented taking orders from the *Ashkenazim.* Conditions, they complained, were as bad as in the poorest Arab Quarter, the food was worse, and there were hardly any women. Instead of the excitement they'd expected, what they found was unremitting work and deprivation.

By bribing drivers, we could have sent out emigrés on every British convoy headed for Suez. Access to the Holy Land would never be as easy to attain again, but all too many convoys left with space to spare.

By sheerest accident, I stumbled on a solid block of eager would-be emigrés, enough to fill those trucks to overflowing. Since meeting Zev and Josef on the street, I'd made a habit of approaching any foreigner in uniform, ostensibly to practice English. When I discovered that a large majority of foreign Jews wore neck chains with the Star of David dangling, I watched to spot the glint of gold. Although the pendant often proved to be a cross, Menachem's was a *Magen David.*

He'd been extremely wary when I greeted him on Rashid Street. As he told me later, he thought I was an Arab kid setting up some sort of swindle. He didn't relax until I spoke to him in Hebrew, so softly that he had to bend to hear. What I said was that it wasn't safe to speak the language I was speaking, and at that, he burst out laughing. "You're a Jew, all right. I recognize the paranoia." I didn't know what the word meant.

At home—because, of course, I took him home—Menachem told me he'd been serving in the Polish army when Russia was a German ally; when the Soviets switched sides, he'd been a prisoner of war in Russia. At Churchill's urging, the Russians let the Polish POWs leave the country on condition that they join Sikorsky's Polish Freedom Fighters, en route to Africa and active combat.

"We came," Menachem sighed, "because we hoped to get to Palestine from here, but the only way is with the British, and you have to be a Jew from Palestine, with all the proper papers, to join the Jewish unit."

As Menachem let off steam, I felt the old familiar prickle of a hatching plan. I asked if there were many more who wished to emigrate, and he staggered me by answering, "At least a thousand." Concealing my excitement, I invited him to visit us again. "Two weeks from now for dinner." If all went well, I might have more than food for him. For the moment, though, I had to keep my scheme a secret, one reason being that he would have laughed and stayed away. I was a sympathetic listener, but still a kid. Anyway, I wasn't sure that I could swing it. The moment that Menachem left, I was on my way to see Sireni.

When Nadji finished out his year and Mosad sent Sireni, I decided that I'd keep relations casual. Nadji's going left a painful gap, and when this new man went, I didn't intend to hurt again. From all reports, this new one wasn't after bosom buddies either. The word was that the man was very cool, almost to the point of coldness. He was also said to be a bit despotic and a stickler for detail.

When we met, I didn't recognize the monster. What I saw was a smoother, older me. Somehow, I knew at once that this Italian Jew and I were temperamental twins, but his intensity was much more tightly reined than mine. When I was twenty-four, I hoped I'd have the same control of my emotions. He was unequivocal because command required it, but coldness wasn't in him. Like me, I was to learn, he covered up his innate shyness with an air of great authority.

As time went on, other similarities began to surface. Sireni was an architect, and if I hadn't chosen medicine, I would have been a builder. Both of us were interested in archaeology, and he too studied Talmud. His fluency in English challenged me to better mine, and he, in turn, improved his Arabic. Although they weren't anything alike, I felt about Sireni almost as I had about Haron.

I told him of my meeting with Menachem and the situation of Sikorsky's Polish Jews. If I rounded up the soldiers, could we slip them into Palestine? Yes, he said, the *T'nu'ah* could and would.

False papers first, then, ticking off the necessary steps, safe houses. He asked if I could line up three, in case they had to hide awhile. And clothes. Civilian stuff. I was to spread the word to start collecting clothes. We could need a lot of them. He was off and running before I fully comprehended. Not only had my project been approved, it was already underway.

By the following evening, I had all the houses set. One was ours, of course, but selection of the others weighed more heavily than I'd expected. AWOL soldiers could be shot, and those who harbored them faced jail, at best. In Baghdad, Jews in league with Jewish AWOLs were in double trouble. I was jeopardizing other lives, not just my own, and if any element of this had ever seemed like fun and games, that feeling fled forever.

On wrapping up our weekly meeting on the night before Menachem was to come, Sireni motioned me aside. "Alert your soldier," he instructed. "We have his papers ready."

My Polish friend arrived as planned. To my dismay, however, three friends of his had tagged along—not for dinner, he hastily explained, just to meet me and to see inside a Jewish home. Nana, need I say, insisted that they stay to eat. The machinery had hardly started, and Menachem's pals could stop it cold.

Hours later, as they all prepared to leave, I got him off alone and asked how much he'd trust the others. His flat, unhesitating "With my life—but why?" resolved the crisis, and I told the four of them our scheme. Eventually, I promised, we'd get them all to Palestine, but tonight it was Menachem's turn. He'd have to stay here, and they could help by covering his absence at the camp. They could aid us even more, I added as an afterthought, by acting as my liaison with other Jews who wished to emigrate. I tried to sound exactly like Sireni, and the words emerged with crisp conviction.

No doubt inspired by my cool assurance, little knowing why I clung to my *k'tibeh* (or even what it was), they all agreed. As for Menachem, he was stunned and silent. "All my things," he said at last, "everything's at camp." A second later, as the news sank in, he beamed from ear to ear. "Never mind. I can live without them. I left a whole lot more in Poland."

The others went, and I told my mother that Menachem would be sleeping overnight with us, and possibly tomorrow too. Baba quirked an eyebrow, but he asked no questions. Since Menachem had to stay inside as long as he remained, which might inspire even Nana to inquire, I decided that we'd cover up by saying he was sick; we settled on a bellyache. Menachem proved to be a real performer, moaning so pathetically that by the second day I was fighting down the urge to purge him. Poor Nana kept apologizing. Everybody knew that our Iraqi food was much too rich for *Ashkenazi* innards, and still she'd fed him seconds, even thirds. Trapped between the two of them, I was happy to escape to school. My hands were tied until I had instructions from Sireni.

The orders finally arrived; following them, I phoned the one-time-only number he provided at precisely the appointed hour. As Sireni said he would, a "Selman" answered, with his name and nothing more. I responded, "The merchandise is ready," and we both clicked off. Sometime later, at his own discretion, Selman would connect with me again.

To avert suspicion, I had to go about my normal business. Menachem, imprisoned in the house, was beginning to be dubious, when Nana finally announced that a man had called to see me and would come again at 8 P.M.

I was at the door awaiting him, Menachem at my side, arrayed in some of S'hak's outgrown clothes. The man arrived, identified himself as Selman, and exhorted us to hurry. Menachem had been fumbling for an adequate farewell, but settled for *"Shalom."* With Selman so impatient to be off, he didn't have time for all the niceties, like thanking Nana. I had worries of my own to face. Baba couldn't have helped but hear the knock, yet hadn't moved to answer it. It wasn't like him.

I was certain now that Baba knew about the underground—knew, at least, that it existed—and knowing me, he had to know that I was in it. He was *allowing* me to keep my secrets. Lately I'd been braced for lots of questions that had never come, and not because I'd covered up my tracks so well. He simply hadn't wanted answers that he couldn't ignore. For the sake of peace between us, he had chosen to be deaf and blind to anything I did that might destroy it.

A rush of love and gratitude enveloped me. Though hostile to the idea of an underground, he was according me the right to make my own decisions. I determined to be extra vigilant for his sake. The less he saw and heard, the less he'd be endangered by my doings.

In a week or so, Menachem was reported safe in Palestine. Aside from those who set them up, no one knew the details of the separate operations, but I supposed that he'd been introduced among the convoy troops, wearing the regalia of the regiment. With well-forged papers and an excellent command of English, he could have ridden in the open all the way. Most had to make the trip hidden under tarps. We relied on bribery, good luck, and God, knowing that the British rarely gave their own equipment more than cursory inspection.

Menachem's friends sent a steady stream of Polish "visitors" to see me, en route to Palestine via Kambar Ali Street. When the total topped 300, I lost count of them. The three who acted as my contacts with the camp remained until the last, and, at my request, Nana made a feast for them the night they left. When my father marveled at the way she stretched our rations, I had to turn away to hide a smile. He never knew that every soldier brought a little something from the larder of the British army.

My admiration of the English had begun to dim with Zev's and Josef's exposé of British policies in Palestine, and it sank a little lower every time I talked to someone else who'd suffered under them yet served now in a Jewish unit of the British army. What struck me was the utter lack of loathing when they spoke about the English. They were bitter, certainly, and deeply angry, and without a doubt would fight against the British when they finished with this current war, but with Hitler on the scene, they had no hate to spare. In a way, though, what they felt was even worse. As a Polish Jewish Palestinian expressed it, "With Hitler, we never had illusions."

It was true, I thought; enemies don't ever disappoint us; to be disillusioned, first you must be friends. I recalled the soldier's comment on the evening I apologized to Churchill's picture as I stripped it off the wall above my bed. I'd had it up so long that it left a pale square to mark its passing. Though British, Churchill still retained his hero status in my eyes, but someone else had superseded him in my affections.

His replacement had been scissored from a publication smuggled in from Palestine some months ago. Although I'd made a frame for it, I hadn't hung it at the time. I didn't want to put it up simply as the object of an adolescent's hero-worship. While that would serve for movie stars or even statesmen, when and if I ever hung *this* portrait, it would signal my conversion to a cause.

I made my mind up in the middle of the Polish exodus. Now Herzl hung above my bed, and I swore—at last—allegiance to the idea and achievement of a Jewish state.

15

For someone who'd started life so undersized and puny, I'd been a pretty healthy kid. Naturally, I'd had the normal cuts and colds, but I craved some kind of chronic ailment—a painless one, provocative but non-impairing—and just pronounced enough to gain me ready access to the doctor's office.

Dr. Kahni was very good about discussing medicine with me, but I only got to see him when someone in the family was sick. My first-aid course had long since been completed, I'd plowed through all the textbooks I could buy or borrow, and the more I learned, the more that medicine intrigued me.

My zeal was such that I was much more stimulated than disturbed when my cousin said my neck was swollen. This swollen neck would get me to the doctor's office and allow for lots of talk between us.

On seeing the distention, Nana shrieked and Baba winced. I smiled, however, when he said that he was taking me to see our other doctor, Salih Hakim, instead of Dr. Kahni. Even better! Hakim could be a mine of information and he hadn't been explored at all. While he probed my neck, I planned to pick his brain.

The waiting room was crowded, but a glance around assured me that we wouldn't be waiting long. Although we were the last ones to arrive, we'd be ushered in before the others, and no one would object. In Baghdad, the best-dressed patients, those prosperous enough to pay in cash, automatically took precedence.

I could predict the order in which every person there would be admitted to the doctor's presence. After us would come the Jewish women, the only ones, aside from us, who were wearing shoes and sitting on the straight-backed chairs. Next would be the barefoot *M'silmin* squatting on the wooden floor. The single Bedouin, a basketful of dates beside him for the doctor's fee, would certainly be treated last. Apart from being poor and supersmelly, he was breaking an unwritten rule. When patients paid in meat or produce, the fee was properly delivered to the doctor's home.

The examination was a brief one, and Dr. Hakim didn't talk to me at all. He'd barely touched my neck before he turned to Baba and said that he was sending us to see a specialist in *ghudad.* With that, my pique completely disappeared. What an opportunity! Glands were something strange and new, and so were specialists.

Dr. Grobak agreed that it was *ghudad,* and like Dr. Hakim, addressed himself exclusively to Baba. Luckily my hearing was acute enough to pick up "operation." If I hadn't heard, if I'd only seen my father's face go white and frozen, I'd have figured it for something fatal. But of course to Baba, as to most Baghdadis, an operation meant exactly that. In his opinion, the specialist had sentenced me to death.

I knew it wasn't so, and I could prove it with statistics. The scalpel didn't scare me. If surgery was indicated, I'd consent without a qualm except, that is, for one which had no sensible or scientific basis. Intellectually, my faith in surgery was strong, and I'd willingly submit myself. However, I was just as sure as Baba that I wouldn't survive. I couldn't explain it, but I knew without a doubt that I would die.

Dr. Grobak made a phone call, and an hour later we were in the surgeon's office at the Jewish Hospital. On entering, my overriding thought was that I'd die in style. The waiting room was furnished like a palace—an empty palace. His Eminence saw patients by appointment only, a concept that I found exalting. Or it might have been the air of perfect peace that so impressed me, accustomed as I was to pain-filled, overcrowded anterooms, always odorous and noisy. Here, there were no keening women or bawling babies digging at their fly-infested eyes. For this unruffled calm, his fee was 20 *dinars,* ten times that of Kahni and Hakim. I'd never seen this side of medicine or even dreamt of its existence.

Not only did the surgeon echo "operation," he advised that it be done at once. If he'd had his way, I would have been admitted then and there, but Baba wanted time to tell the family. Phoning from the hospital, he broke the news to Nana. Her "No!" was so explosive that he almost dropped the instrument. Crying was to be expected, but Nana never contradicted him.

By the time we reached the house, Nana had recruited all the relatives to back her up. In the melee, I managed to escape upstairs. On an ordinary day, I'd have been delighted with the mob scene, especially since I'd be the center of attention, but this might be my only opportunity to draw a will. Seeing everyone's concern intensified the certainty of death.

I chose the most expensive sheet of paper from the stock we had for sale, and after filling my *bar mitzvah* pen with blood-red ink, I set down the date—October 5, 1943—and started to inscribe my final testament.

With misted eyes, and extra care for my calligraphy, I allocated all I owned to family and friends—with one exception. The underground would get my gun and dagger, and I gave directions: "These will be discovered suspended from a nail, exactly two feet up on the inside front of the ventilation shaft in the summer dining room." That was one I'd learned from Baba. A tear crept down my face and fell. I blotted it, but the ink had blurred and spread. It looked exactly like a bloodstain.

Books, some stones and artifacts from ancient diggings, my gold and ruby ring, my *tallith* and *t'filim,* the *k'tibeh* that I'd never taken off, the *kaf* I also wore around my neck. I fingered the little silver hand, feeling for the small blue stone set into it to ward off evil. I knew they wouldn't let me wear it when they operated. The incision would probably be made along the very line on which the neck chain lay.

Just as I was willing it to S'hak, he appeared to say that I was wanted. When he turned to leave, I lifted up the mattress and shoved the sheet of paper under it as far as I could reach, though it really wouldn't matter if my mother found it when she made the bed. She couldn't read, and as long as I was living and in shape to scream, she wouldn't show it to another soul.

In the family room, they'd reached consensus in that everyone was equally uncertain. The only point on which they all agreed was that we ought to see another doctor, so off we went again, this time to the sumptuous office of a Dr. Malekovski. I noted that his given name was Max, the same as Dr. Grobak's. My second European doctor and my second Max. On gaining their diplomas, did they all adopt the name? Was I feverish, I wondered? Such silly, wandering thoughts. Had the swelling pinched off blood that fed the brain? Whatever was to happen, I wished that we'd get on with it.

This second Max had several waiting rooms, and a well-dressed servant named Saadoun who separated patients at the outer door by their appearance. He steered the poor ones to the left and the wealthy to the large room on the right, which offered pillowed chairs and Persian rugs and icy *sharbat.* Probably his price went up with every sip. It's true that I was learning more about the medical profession, but nothing that would profit *T'nu'ah.*

In the inner office, with a grunt for greeting, the fattest man I ever saw approached me, put his swollen-penis fingers on my swelling, palpated once or twice, then snorted, "*Hawa.* Nothing but a little *hawa.*"

His Arabic was awful, and before I knew for sure that he was saying "air," an oversized syringe was sticking in my neck. When he drew it out, he turned triumphantly to Baba, ignoring me as had the others. "*Hawa,*" he repeated, "not *ghudad.*"

In Iraq, all diseases were attributed to spheres of influence, of which the major three were air and glands, and water. *Hawa, ghudad, mai.* I'd been diagnosed, so far, in two divisions, and substantial doubts were stirring. Both doctors were supposed to be among the best, so why the big discrepancy in diagnosis? If air could be confused with glands, then doctors were as fallible as other men. They weren't demigods at all. I felt a sudden pang of pain, and not in my distended neck.

Yes, the neck was still distended, but though the swelling was as bad as ever, every time I tried to say so, Baba stared me down. Air was fine with him. With air, there wouldn't be any operation. All I'd have to do was take some medication for the next two weeks.

When the pills were gone, however, the swelling still remained, and surgery was once again an issue. In spite of my conviction that I wouldn't come through it, I almost hoped I'd have to undergo the operation. What an interesting experience! And assuming that I did survive, how enlightening that inside look would be. I really had my heart set on the hospital.

I got my wish, but by way of Radiology rather than the operating theatre. It was *ghudad* after all. At the Royal College they called it goiter—an enlargement of the thyroid gland—and prescribed a course of X-rays. "A simple matter," the department chief assured my father, and I resigned myself to something less spectacular than scalpels and incisions. On the other hand, this radiation, invisible but capable of either killing or effecting cures, was even more mysterious.

So I wasn't going to die, but it suddenly occurred to me that living wouldn't be worth a lot if Baba ever read my will. He might close his eyes to secret meetings, but guns and daggers were another matter.

My mattress wasn't on my bed! I'd forgotten Nana's habits as the best of housewives—how frequently she hauled the bedding to the roof to air it and how often Baba helped her! I dropped down at my desk, sick at my stupidity. Through eyes half-shut against the onset of a headache, I saw an edge of paper showing under my encyclopedia. Nana, having found my will, had neatly centered it and safely weighted it!

The vellum was resistant, but I ripped it to a pocketful of crisp confetti. All the following day, I sprinkled little scraps of it throughout the city and dribbled out the last on entering the library. Before embarking on a project, I always did a research job; this time it was glands and X-rays. By the middle of my course of treatment, I could talk the language, or at least enough of it to entertain the doctors. They started out amused at my precocity, but ended by explaining all the thousand things I asked about.

However, I withheld a vital question for another year. By the spring of 1945, I finally felt firm enough in my resolve to ask it of a teacher at the *shamash.* Could I hope to be a doctor? Yamen Michael taught biology; he could tell me what my chances were. Though undoubtedly the quota system still existed, the numbers might be more propitious now.

After class one day I blurted out the question. There wasn't any tactful way to ask, and I knew the answer from the way he flinched. The Jewish quota was the same as ever—only ten a year—but Haron had merely skimmed the surface. As Michael filled me in, all hope evaporated.

In the entire country, we had a single school of medicine. Only 200 students could matriculate each year. Ten thousand took the baccalaureate exams. It was difficult for everyone, but not unfair, except to Jews. Though Jews were less than one percent of population, more than half who qualified to take the tests each year were Jewish, and more than half who passed were Jewish. Fifty-plus percent of all who made the grade, we had to fight each other for five percent of freshman places.

Good marks alone were not enough. With so many Jewish students scoring at the same high level, Michael said a Jew must have a sponsor to ensure a spot. So first we had to kill each other off in class, then find an influential Arab who would do a Jew a favor—for a price.

Michael tried to cheer me up. Just sixty freshmen would survive the first semester, he informed me, but no Jew, once enrolled, was ever winnowed out; each earned his medical degree. He said this with enormous satisfaction, and I stared at him in disbelief. After beating out our brains in school, then paying bribes and licking *Mislim* boots, he truly thought that we were putting something over on the Arabs by becoming doctors?

If medicine was out, what *was I to do?*

Weighed against the agitation of my private life, the routine of the underground was almost restful. When I wasn't teaching in the *T'nu'ah,* I was learning in the *Shura.* Between the classes and the meetings, we were getting the "illegals" out with disciplined dispatch. Our security proved sound, and with every project panning out, we soon became complacent. The jolt, therefore, was all the more disturbing when the *Shura* leadership discovered something missing. We had no city map nor did anybody else in all Baghdad. The Jewish Quarter was entirely uncharted; and without a map, we couldn't deploy our insufficient men and weapons with any hope of holding off a *Mislim* mob. Ergo, we'd have to make our own.

I got to be cartographer because I was the smallest and still looked like a carefree kid. Doing what I'd have to do, an adult would have drawn too much attention to himself. If I hadn't been selected, I'd have volunteered, since I knew exactly how to go about the business. Quite by chance, I'd stumbled on the method in my reading.

In 1936 a commander of the Haganah had drawn a map of Old Jerusalem by walking the entire area within the ancient walls and counting off the steps he took between the salient points. By measuring his stride and multiplying by their number, he could figure out the distances for mortar fire. I aimed to do the same for Baghdad's ghetto, but with more embroidery. Because of our communications problem, we'd also want to know the time it took to get from place to place. Lacking wireless equipment, and with telephones so sparsely scattered, we'd have to trust to runners.

I began by sketching in the major arteries and indicating known attack routes—information drawn from past pogroms. Coming from Abu Shibl, the mobs would stream up Ghazi Street, while *M'silmin* from Al'adhamiya would swarm along Rashid. If we commanded those approaches, we could turn the tide before the ghetto was engulfed. According to our action plan, each *Shura* team of six would rush to its defense position when the coded word went out. At every post we'd have a hidden cache of hand grenades and guns. On my map I'd underline the likely sites for these positions.

It took a full four months to get what I was after. At the start, I thought I knew the Quarter well, but when I walked it street by street, unsuspected nooks and crannies came to light. *Mehalat-el'yhud* was as quirky and complex as its inhabitants. I always had a schoolbook with me, a sheet of paper stuck between its pages; when I stopped and pulled a pencil out, I'd be the picture of a conscientious schoolboy scribbling notes to study. Stroll by stroll, I indicated every passage, specifying which were paved and which would be a mud morass when wet. I also marked the spot where any roadway narrowed down enough for easy interception of a moving vehicle. Every barricade and ambush point was asterisked, as well as openings between adjoining structures. Some offered hiding places, others were escape paths.

On the outskirts of the Quarter, where Jewish buildings intermixed with *Mislim,* I invented symbols to show which shops were safe, which houses hostile. I called attention to the dumping grounds for garbage; in emergencies, they'd be a source of ammunition. Where entry steps went down instead of up, I showed the "trenches" as emplacements for machine guns, and by means of color coding, traced the sight lines for our lookouts and the shortcuts for our runners.

This was to be my last assignment before the baccalaureate exams, and I was satisfied, for once, with what I'd done. So satisfied, in fact, that I signed my masterwork, hiding "Haim" in microscopic script in the middle of a twisting alley.

16

Hitler died the same day I received the letter telling me the time and place of the exams. April 30, 1945 also marked the start of my reluctant split with Rabbi Ezra.

The news of Hitler's death only aggravated all my stored-up anger. He'd escaped us. "What happens now?" I demanded of the *Hakham.* What would be his punishment? What *could* it be for sin on such a massive scale? All the *Hakham* said was "God will deal with him."

In pain and rage I shouted, "So he's standing now before the Lord, telling Him, 'Since the dawn of time, you the Lord could only keep some 18 million Jews alive, but I, in just a few short years, have killed a third of them.' "

The Rabbi's lips had tightened. Would *nothing* goad him into more than meek acceptance? "Tell me!" I insisted. "Who *really* rules then—God or Hitler?"

"Blasphemy! That's blasphemy!" His black eyes flamed, but nothing followed. What Rabbi Ezra labeled sacrilege, I looked upon as seeking truth—and it was God Himself who'd given me my questing mind. If He'd wanted blind obedience, he would have made me in a different mold.

In Rabbi Ezra's world, everything was straight and narrow, all the boundaries defined as clearly as if carved in stone. Life, though, like the Quarter I'd just mapped, was much more treacherous to travel, replete with crazy detours and confusing twists and turns. There were a hundred different ways to get where one was going, and while the Rabbi's way was safe and sure, it simply followed others' footsteps. Some of us were destined to explore, and even temporarily to lose ourselves. By any road, however, as the Zohar said, we'd join together at the journey's end. Maybe then the two of us could talk.

The baccalaureate exams were only weeks away, and almost everyone at school was in a state of zombielike exhaustion, sunken, bloodshot eyes a testament to nights of frantic cramming. Our futures were dependent on the test results. Those who passed could go to college; the others kissed their dreams goodbye and went to work.

Throughout Iraq, students qualified to take the tests would spend six days with sweaty palms and quaking stomachs. The strain would be too much for some; every year, a few would physically collapse or sink into a deep depression.

Exams had never scared me, but the site of this one did arouse some apprehension. Each of us had been assigned to a specific seat and classroom in the high school closest to his home. Mine was in the north of Baghdad, in the middle of a *Mislim* quarter; in those surroundings, any Jew would be uneasy. On the other hand, according to our teachers, the exams themselves were fairly judged. Each sheet would be identified by number only, and since no one knew whose paper he was handling, no one could be bribed to give a better grade. While not primarily designed to hinder bias, the system kept the *Y'hud*-haters from eliminating us.

Then we discovered that the first exam was set for our *Shabbat.* The official line was that we Jews were free to choose. We could violate Judaic law or relinquish any hope of a career. And no—we *couldn't* take the test another day.

I went to Abu Samy for advice; he said that I must think the matter through myself, remembering always that I had free will. As long as I could be at peace with God, he added, he wouldn't condemn whatever I decided—which was tantamount to telling me to take the test. When I approached my father, expecting thunderous resistance, not only did he fail to forbid it, he insisted that I go ahead. Right along, I realized, he'd been afraid that *Hakham* Ezra's influence might turn me toward the Rabbinate, and if I passed up the exams, little else would be available. Baba had his own ambitions for his scholar son.

Just to close the circle though, I went once more to Rabbi Ezra. Without discussion, and without a moment's pause to weigh the matter, he said *Shabbat* was sacrosanct. I couldn't take the tests. I loved the man, but when I left this time, it was for good. I wasn't coming back. Not ever.

On the day exams began, I was to meet with Samy and my cousin Sion at the bus stop. Even if the high school hadn't been so far away, we wouldn't have dared to walk through Arab streets, but the bus required still more compromise with our religion. To ride, we had to carry money, and that, as well as riding, was a violation of the Sabbath law.

Since we'd been assigned to different sections of the high school, we separated on arrival. Six to seven thousand students milled around the several entrances, waiting for the bell to ring them in. Every one of those around me was a *Mislim,* and they pointedly encircled and appraised me.

"Aren't you from *shamash?*" It was more a declaration than a question, but I nodded. Someone asked what room I'd been assigned to, and someone else, the number of my seat. The two then huddled with the others, and I heard their grunts of disappointment on discovering that none of them would sit nearby. I tried to look as if I didn't understand and willed the bell to ring before they found a friend who'd been assigned to sit by me in class. Jews, they knew, received a sounder education, and the Arab kids would always seek us out and copy answers. Every year, *shamash* students scored among the highest in the city, so I was automatically of special interest. Undoubtedly, Samy and Sion were also undergoing this attention.

Refuse to show your test sheet, and a gang of boys would lie in wait and beat you bloody. If you hurt enough, they figured that you'd help them out the following day, but since your brain cells had to function, they were careful not to hit you in the head.

On the other hand, allowing them to look could lead to summary dismissal and disgrace. All classroom monitors were *M'silmin,* so if a Jewish student claimed duress, he didn't stand a chance. Even total innocence was no defense against an accusation. Without a shred of evidence, Jews had been denounced for cheating and disqualified forever. Because of such occurrences, we'd all been briefed about the best way to conduct ourselves—in essence, "be invisible."

In the classroom, I sat completely still, eyes front and down, afraid to make a move that might be misinterpreted. Exactly on command, I flipped the test book open, and within an hour, I was handing in my answers. As I left, a murmur rose and followed me. "The Jew . . . the Jew's already finished." The jealous whispers warned of trouble.

At *shamash,* we'd been told to take our time. "Don't call attention to yourself," they'd said, but time was much too precious to be twiddling it away, and in any case, I was constitutionally incapable of sitting like a lump.

On the second morning, though, I wished that I had listened. They were waiting for me—seventy-eight of them—everyone who'd seen me finish early. Those seated closest said that they expected me to slip them answers; swallowing hard, I answered that I wouldn't. "For all our sakes," I added. Anticipating this, I'd framed a very careful counterargument. I told them that we'd all be caught, disqualified, and worst of all, dishonored. Would they want it known they needed help from me? And when that sank in, I said that they were smart enough to do it by themselves. The shame of seeming dumber than a *dhimmi* worked for some, and the frank appeal to ego freed me of another few. Unhappily, however, the majority put pride aside. I'd help or else. This time, I'd *have* to finish first so I could catch a bus before they caught and clobbered me.

Except for ever-growing animosity, almost dense enough to touch by now, the next four days were little different. Like me, Samy made his exits fast. Taking the opposing tack, Sion saved his skin by acting stupid. One boy we knew from *shamash* was beaten up so badly that he skipped the last two tests.

At 8 A.M., on the day the pass-and-fail lists were published, *shamash* students poured into the courtyard of the school to check the posted roster. Each was achingly aware that a single printed word would shape his future. This morning, in every secondary school throughout Iraq, the scene would be the same. Probably more prayers were said in Arabic and Hebrew than on either of our Sabbaths.

Posting day was also graduation day at *shamash.* Positive I'd passed, and afraid some friends had flunked, I decided that I'd stay away until the ceremony was about to start. By then, the principal would have our grades and ranks, not only in the *shamash* class but in the country.

On winding up his speech, the principal reminded us to have our money ready for the Welfare Fund as we approached the podium. Diplomas would be handed out according to our scores, beginning with the highest.

I was so intent on digging out some money that I didn't hear him call my name.

"Heskel, *listen!*" Samy poked me hard enough to make me leap upright, and all around us people laughed and then applauded. Conscious that my face was turning crimson and still fumbling for the money, I sprinted toward the principal to get this over with as quickly as I could. I loved applause but laughter disconcerted me. I was, in fact, in such a state that everything my fingers closed on went to Welfare.

When I took my seat again, Samy pounded me. He was pounding me and grinning in the purest, most unjealous joy. It only hit me then that my name had been the first announced. I'd expected highest honors in my class, but there were four senior classes at the *shamash,* and heading all of them was more than I'd foreseen.

Several rows away, Sion waved his arms at me like windmills, and beside me, Samy carried on as if I'd won the Nobel Prize. I thought that they were overdoing it a bit. Then the principal was standing at my seat, looking rather puzzled and asking me if anything was wrong. I said that I was feeling fine, which only seemed to add to his confusion.

"I just don't understand you!" he exploded. "Aren't you at all excited? When a boy ranks first, he ought to show a little more enthusiasm!"

For an instant, I was sure I'd faint.

"First in the Country!"

I'd licked the quota! If I elected medicine, how could they keep me out of college? To be absolutely certain, though, Baba said he'd pull some strings. Important people owed him favors. And I hadn't asked. He'd made the offer of his own volition.

Architecture had been Baba's dream for me, and he'd abandoned it because it wasn't mine. With his capitulation, I was forced to face my hidden fears. The fact is, I was overawed in spite of my bravado. In Baghdad, in a family like ours, doctors were regarded as exalted beings, members of a pantheon that one was born to. I'd been born to builders, so architecture was achievable. Maybe medicine was out of reach. Suppose I reached and didn't make it?

I believe I would have risen to the challenge on my own, but Baba settled it by telling me to try it for a year, "and if you drop out then, I won't consider it a failure or defeat." That really did it! I might doubt myself, but it was insupportable that *Baba* doubt me. In five years' time, I starchily assured him, there'd be a doctor in the family.

The decision made, the battle with bureaucracy began in earnest. Application to the Royal College required lots of documents and legwork. In addition to my baccalaureate certificate, I'd need a letter from the *shamash* principal, a Police Department deposition attesting that I had no record of arrests, a financial statement guaranteeing my ability to pay tuition, three recent photographs, proof of citizenship. . . .

I was certainly a citizen—but then it struck me that I hadn't been one *long* enough. My birth certificate would show that I'd been born in 1930, making me fifteen. Eighteen was the legal minimum for entry to the College. I was out before I'd even started—or I would have been if not for Baba. He didn't blink an eye. "Don't worry" was his only comment, and when Baba said "don't worry," you could safely stop. One way or another, I'd be old enough when father finished. Jews survived in business in Iraq by knowing how to manage, and Baba was a born survivor.

While he was managing my birth, I went about the other matters, and one by one acquired all the necessary items. At police headquarters, the last of all of the offices I had to visit, I answered every question on the four-page form and stood in line to leave it with the officer in charge. When he'd checked and stamped it, I'd be set for school. I'd heard him tell the applicant ahead of me to "come back in tomorrow," which relieved my mind. Most mills of government ground very slowly, and the deadline for applying was just days away.

The lieutenant took my questionnaire and skimmed it. I saw his eyes stop briefly at "Religion" and again at "Reason." Why, the form inquired, did I want the deposition. Since my response—"for medical school"—appeared to be of interest to the officer, I said that I'd appreciate his quick disposal of the matter. Wednesday, I explained, was the final day for filing. When he smiled understandingly and told me to return on Tuesday, I was pleasantly surprised. At his tiny hesitation over "Jewish," I'd braced myself for some harassment, but I'd read him wrong. The man was being most cooperative.

On Tuesday, on my way to get the document, I bumped into my uncle on the street. When he heard where I was heading, he tried to lend me ten *dinars* to take along. I thanked him but refused the offer. I didn't believe a bribe would be required.

The lieutenant, I was gratified to note, remembered me at once. However, he couldn't seem to find my file. After searching unsuccessfully for several minutes, he asked me to return the following morning, assuring me he'd have it when I got there. As I turned to leave, he cleared his throat, and much too casually inquired, "Aren't you the son of Moshe el-Haddad?" Moshe, the plumber. He knew darn well I was, having read it on the first line of the form. The man had something up his sleeve, and when he said his sink was broken, I knew exactly what it was. If Baba fixed his sink, he'd find my deposition. Fuming inwardly, but knowing I was licked, I nodded. Father sent his best man out as soon as I reported.

In the morning, instead of validated papers and a smile of thanks, the lieutenant gave me hell. In a phony rage he roared, "Your father ruined my sink. He'll never get a *fils* from me."

He knew I knew that he was lying—no bill had been presented and he hadn't even tipped the workman—but I held my temper and my tongue. Until I had the document, I couldn't trust myself to speak. Let the big man play his small charade. When the others in the office were impressed enough, and I looked scared enough, to gratify his ego, I figured that he'd "find" my file. This time, though, he didn't even simulate a search.

"If I find it, you'll know soon enough," he snapped.

Not "when" but "if"—and that was ominous. He wasn't satisfied with just the sink. Uncle had been right. I should have offered ten *dinars* on handing him the filled-out form, but in the state this man was in, he might even then have crossed me up. What was eating the lieutenant was a good deal more than ordinary greediness.

"What difference does it make? So you *don't* get into school. You Jews are rich enough already." His voice was shrill with hate and envy, and his bogus rage was real now. There wasn't any sense in staying at his desk a second longer. This was something else I'd have to hand to Baba.

Father's friend, Bahjat, the Inspector General, must have cracked his whip or maybe waved a magic wand. In any case, an hour after Baba called him, all my papers were delivered to the door. And in those sixty minutes, I'd somehow gotten four years older. Officially, on every record, I was nineteen years of age. On my birth certificate, the original "1930" now read "1926." I'd needed only three more years to make me eligible, but on looking closely, I could see why I'd been given four. In Arabic calligraphy, 1926 had been an easy alteration; 1927 would have made a smudgy mess.

Finally—by honest effort and a touch of fraud—my foot was on the threshold!

17

The medical school was part of the Royal Hospital complex, located on the right bank of the Tigris at a sharp bend in the river. In the northernmost section of the city, beyond the intersection of Rashid Street with Ghazi, it was way outside the limits of most Jewish lives, almost foreign territory.

The nucleus of the hospital had been built in 1917 when the British captured Baghdad. The greater part of it was made of white mud bricks like most of Baghdad's buildings, but a portion of the southern face consisted of the remnants of the ancient Turkish wall that once surrounded the entire city. In sporadic bursts, the Iraqi government, in tandem with the British, had added to this central core, expanding randomly in all directions. Now the complex sprawled across a quarter of a mile.

The original building was divided into large and crowded wards, which held a total of a thousand beds. It also housed a clinic with an average daily patient load of several thousand sick and injured. For the majority of *M'silmin,* the clinic was the family doctor. Attesting to the British presence, the choice adjoining tract, also fronting on the Tigris, was given over to a dozen tennis courts. From the other structures, which lay behind the hospital, detached from it and dwarfed by it, the view was less agreeable, overlooking, as they did, a stretch of undeveloped fields and the burial ground for unclaimed bodies, amputated limbs, and other human miscellany.

To reach the Royal College of Medicine, which was the largest of the newer buildings and the farthest north, I had to pass the Mental Hospital, the Dental College, the School of Pharmacy, and the Nursing School. I stopped to look at that one for a speculative second. If what I heard was true, it was full of Jewish females, allowed to enter training unrestricted by a quota, the reason being that Arab women didn't seek admission in sufficient numbers. Most of them still wore the veil, and to study nursing, a woman had to be emancipated.

I was only going in today to leave my application and credentials, but all at once, I was acutely conscious of disease and disabilities. The city was a sea of sickness. Everywhere I looked I saw eye infections, scabrous lesions, and the sweats and shivers of malarial fever. Fifty thousand deaths each year from malaria alone. In the last few days, I'd seen a hundred "Baghdad boils"—ugly suppurating ulcers—and on the bus just now, the man in front of me had crawled with lice. They were healthier than he was. Overnight, everyone I saw was ill in one way or another, and Abu Samy chuckled when I asked him if he'd noticed.

"No," he said, "that's *your* department. If you were going into plumbing, you'd see a city full of rusty pipes and stuffed-up drains. What involves you will attract your eye."

At the school, a secretary took my application and told me to report on Monday for the English test; all classes, he informed me, were in English. Grammatically, I had a better grounding than the Arab boys, and speaking with so many foreigners had made me fluent. I'd be starting out a length ahead.

The exam was easy, and nothing more remained except an interview, a mere formality I understood. Following the test, I sat with fifty others waiting to be summoned, one by one, before the Board. All this group were *M'silmin,* and most were showing signs of panic. I watched them with amused disdain.

Anyone who'd reached this stage was safe, and I lounged back in my seat, cool and in complete control—until I heard my name called.

Even now, I can't explain what happened. All that I remember is the rush of bile and the sudden inability to draw a breath. Inside that office were unknown men on whom my life, at least in medicine, depended. My mouth was arid as the desert, but the rest of me was soaked with sweat. I *hoped* that all of it was sweat. When I arose, the seat squished under me and someone tittered.

Of the interview itself, I can only summon up a single memory. I was standing there, facing the professors, perspiring from every pore, and wishing I would wake up from this dreadful dream, when the Dean himself asked me what my strongest subject was. Instead of any of the sciences, *anything* that had to do with medicine, a strangulated voice—my own, I recognized with horror—squeaked "English." The Dean repeated, "English?" arched his eyebrows, exchanged a glance with others at the table, and after that the interview became a blur. When the fog began to lift, I was fleeing south on Rashid Street, the hospital and school—everything—behind me. In a minute, I'd undone a decade's work. I'd never be a doctor now.

I didn't have the heart to tell my father. He'd find out when the freshman list was published, minus me. By then, however, I'd be otherwise engaged. His disappointment would be lessened—and some remnant of my pride preserved—if I could make him think that I was interested in something else. In fact, he'd probably prefer my fallback field. If I couldn't be a doctor, I'd be the best damned builder in the history of Baghdad.

I had to find a job and find it fast; otherwise, my father would insist I work for him. To my deep chagrin, however, I was almost unemployable. Despite my fine, expensive education, I hadn't any skills to offer. Loathing every second spent on them, I started typing and accounting lessons with a private tutor.

Two weeks later, I was flat out on my bed, bored into extreme fatigue and resting from the dreary rows of figures, when I heard a roar from Baba, followed by the clatter of my mother's clogs. As she came running up the stairs, screaming "Doctor!" I rushed to meet her with my first-aid kit in hand. Nana sometimes cut herself and Avram often skinned his knees. But to make my father bellow, it had to be much worse. Heart attack? . . . rabid dog bite? . . . or had the stove exploded?

Nana threw herself at me, so choked with tears I couldn't catch a word she said, and Baba wore a strange expression. On any other face, I would have said it was a silly grin, but Baba never grinned like this.

"Did you hear me?" The grimace grew absurdly wide. "It was on the radio. They read the lists. You've been accepted!" I could only nod in answer, and hug my mother hard.

Baba squeezed around us, heading for his bedroom, and was back in seconds, almost shyly holding something out to me. I couldn't imagine what was in the box, but from the speed with which he hauled it out, it had to be right on his bedside table, waiting for exactly this occasion. When I saw the stethoscope, my eyes brimmed over. He'd been so sure of my acceptance! As I discovered later, he'd bought it on the day I made my application.

Profoundly touched by Baba's faith in me, I was also staggered by the gift itself. To the layman in Iraq, the whole mystique of medicine was represented by the stethoscope, and those who wore it were regarded with the reverence reserved elsewhere for royalty.

In my room that night, I practiced with the instrument. Not using it, but wearing it to best effect. Around my neck, dangling from my ears, hanging from a pocket, looped and held in first one hand and then the other. S'hak caught me looking in the mirror, but he didn't smirk or make a snide remark. Even S'hak was impressed, and that impressed me more than anything.

As something extraordinary seemed in order, the family decided to present me with the "wolf-dog" that I'd always wanted. Among the ultraorthodox, dogs were lumped with other "unclean" animals, but everyone was smitten with the sweet-faced puppy with the long pink tongue and paws as soft as pillows. From the dimensions of those paws, I knew that she'd be big enough for what I had in mind.

Lassie's life was all mapped out; she'd be the first four-legged member of the underground. By adoption, the German Shepherd pup was Jewish now. In any new attack against the Quarter, my little German friend would fight with me against the Arabs who admired Hitler. While she was worrying my finger with her milk teeth, mewling like an infant and licking me between the "bites," I looked ahead to long, sharp fangs and fearsome snarls. She'd spring at my command, and the boldest of assailants would become a cringing coward. If slightly over-colored, the picture in my mind was pretty accurate. The *M'silmin* feared the "wolf-dog" more than any man-made weapon. As soon as she stopped kissing me and peeing when I patted her, I planned to start her training.

At a meeting of the *madrichim* shortly after my acceptance, I asked to be relieved of all my teaching duties. College, I explained, would take more time and effort than both *yeshiva* and *shamash,* and I didn't feel that I was really needed any longer in the *T'nu'ah.* By now, the tail-end of summer, 1945, the underground had upward of 4000 members. Of the many hundreds that I'd trained myself, one could easily be found to take my place. While I didn't say so, I wished to concentrate my energies on *Shura* instead of shuttling between the two.

Life closed off in other areas as well. I didn't relish seeing Rabbi Ezra to say that I was leaving the *yeshiva,* but to my surprise, he gave me his reluctant blessing. I'd been afraid he'd turn from me without a word. More amazing still, he declared that doctors, "even student doctors," were absolved from certain obligations of Judaic law. He knew I'd have to break *Shabbat* to go to school, and do other things he found abhorrent, but at last he'd bent a little. He could have burdened me with guilt, but had lightened it instead—and counter to his own convictions. Sending me away absolved had been an act of love, if not approval.

I'd be cutting out *kehilla* too, but telling Abu Samy was much easier; our relationship was less intense. The group would welcome me whenever I could come, he said.

My life was squared away, with everything on hold until September 1, when classes would begin. That left me barely time enough to wind up one last project: my matriculation present to myself. From the age of four, I'd wanted a mustache like Baba's and now I had a good excuse to grow one. I had the shoulders of a full-grown man, but the rest of me was fifteen-year-old skinny schoolboy. The extreme discrepancy called far too much attention to my youth, and I figured that some facial hair would age me. As the fuzz appeared in scraggly patches, S'hak made my life a misery. He knew every unwashed-upper-lip joke and delivered the entire repertoire at my expense. By the start of the semester, though, he had to stop. By then, I had a very big and very black mustache. So did almost every other student. In the Middle East, a mustache was *the* mark of manhood.

Since Friday was the *Mislim* Sabbath, the college week began on Saturday—*Shabbat.* Even with the Rabbi's semidispensation, I felt sinful as I checked in with the Registrar. To some extent, I always would.

Armed with lists of instruments and textbooks that we had to buy, we new boys headed for the lecture hall to hear our first official words as freshmen. On the dot of 8 A.M., the Dean, a snow-capped, sour-faced old Scotsman, strode behind the lectern and laid it brusquely on the line for us.

Lectures 8 A.M. to noon, labs 2 P.M. to 6:00, six days a week. And if we hoped to pass, we'd be swotting at the books till 2 A.M. Absenteeism wouldn't be tolerated; no matter what the reason, more than twenty percent meant automatic washout. The honor system would prevail, with students signing in and out of labs and classrooms.

Since all of us had slaved to get here, none of this had any negative effect. The thunderbolt was yet to be released.

"The class ahead of you," he said, "has only sixty places open, which means that most of you will not be with us when we meet next year." He smiled thinly as shock stiffened all 200 spines. So Michael had the number right, but not the reason. He'd said that only sixty would survive, but only sixty *could* survive. One letter made a world of difference.

The problem wasn't flunking out, but being crowded out. We'd be competing against each other and not against a gauge of grades. Pass-fail wouldn't apply here. However high one's marks might be, if others' marks were higher, it was "Go, and God be with you." One hundred and forty of us were doomed to be discarded, even if superior by normal standards.

The Dean stood silent while the words sank in. Only when completely satisfied that we'd absorbed the implication did he introduce our teachers.

Boswell, with whom we'd take Biology, was a cheery-looking Englishman, a plump small pigeon of a person, who spoke to us as reassuringly as possible about "our work together." The tension lessened as he talked. The Anatomy professor, an Egyptian named Amin, also seemed unthreatening. A Fellow of the Royal College of Surgeons in Great Britain, his credentials were impressive and his manner almost fatherly. A second plus for us, quickly followed by a major minus. Fuad Said, the Iraqi who taught freshman English, was a frank disaster. His accent was atrocious, and in the minute that he spoke, he managed to misuse a word and stress some others incorrectly. My English was a great deal better, but though his class would be a total waste, I'd have to take it. The Dean had made it crystal clear that every cut would count.

The next man up was Startub, another Englishman, and I sincerely hoped he had a firmer grasp of Physiology than fashion. In a city full of ill-assorted outfits, it took something special to assault the eye, but Startub made me blink in disbelief. With a light and crinkled cotton jacket, made of multicolor "bleeding" madras, he wore heavy woolen trousers, greenish-black with age and bagging at his knees and bottom like a baby's well-filled diaper. When he spoke, the movement of his Adam's apple bounced a gaudy bow tie, a butterfly half apple-green, half orange. I half expected it to spring its bonds and soar away. His pants cuffs barely reached his ankles, exposing two quite different socks, and the jacket stretched across his stomach like a sausage casing just about to burst. As the term went on, we were to find that Startub's opening ensemble only hinted at the horrors in his closet.

When Lindsay Rogers was presented, I leaned forward in my seat and stared. Although he couldn't have looked more commonplace, I knew that Rogers wasn't ordinary in the least. While swapping stories in a "safe" house, a couple of the Polish soldiers had talked about a certain doctor from New Zealand who'd spent several years with Tito's partisans in Yugoslavia. "And now he's here in Baghdad. That Lindsay Rogers sure does get around!" one laughed.

The name stuck in my mind. Mild-looking Lindsay Rogers—and guerrilla warfare. When he stood to speak, the apparent incongruity promptly disappeared. He leaped up from his seat, and teetered back and forth while talking, like a car with too much motor for its modest frame. Just standing there, he thrummed, and I recognized my own metabolism. This man would be impatient with stupidity or slowness. "Clinical Introduction." I found it on my list and checked it off—in red. Another plus.

On the other hand, the moment Hawkins stood, Chemistry became a minus. But "stood" is incorrect. He unwound. Accordion-pleated arms unfolded, boneless legs unbraided, and up and up he went until I had to crane my neck to keep his face in focus. Six-feet seven, sunken-cheeked, with tallow skin and hairless scalp, he was scary merely standing there. And then he spoke.

"The first year I will teach you Chemistry. The second year"—his thin lips started spreading in a grisly death's-head grin— "the second year, Biochemistry . . ." he paused again, but the sentence hadn't ended ". . . to those of you who slip through *these!*" With that, he shot his hands out, and his long and fleshless fingers curved to clutch us.

It was well into the afternoon, but the Dean announced that several classes had been scheduled. Biology went well—and then came English.

In front of students, Said was far less careful in his speech than he'd been before the Dean, and I could scarcely follow what he said. While the Arab boys appeared to understand him perfectly, the other Jews were just as lost as I was. In Said's class, we realized, our *shamash* education was a handicap.

We'd been taught an *English* English, crisp and classically correct. Said and the Arab students spoke a sort of bastard English, whose rhythms and locutions were an insult to the educated ear. We were stuck with him, however, and to put it as the English would, it was a sticky situation. We didn't want to unlearn what we knew, but we couldn't antagonize our teacher by objecting to his every word.

While I was pondering the problem, another of the Jewish boys had raised his hand and was asking most politely that Said repeat his opening remarks. On hearing David's polished speech, our teacher's face flushed red with rage. His immoderate reaction clearly indicated he was conscious of his own defects, but the Arab boys looked up to him, *admired* his English. I could almost hear his mind at work: ". . . those *others,* trying to embarrass me. . . ."

His eyes didn't rest on David, but darted all around the room, searching out the Jewish faces. When they came to mine, he locked on me, . . . the last of *them* . . ., and having found us all, he finally responded.

"So you think your English is more good than mine."

I struggled to subdue a laugh, but Said saw the effort and it sealed my fate. He couldn't flunk us all, but he certainly could manage one—that cocky little one who laughed.

With only ten of us in school, I'd been hoping for equality as individuals. Deliberately, on signing in, I'd mingled with the *M'silmin.* At assembly I hadn't sought out other Jewish students. I told myself that this school would be different. All of us were brighter than the average, better able, I'd convinced myself, to coexist in peace, if not in perfect harmony. Here, we wouldn't be Jews and *M'silmin,* just pupils and professors. And before the first day ended, Said had brought me back to earth. Again.

For someone brighter than the average, I'd taken far too long to learn a simple lesson. Anywhere we went, Jews would always be the "them" among the Arab "us." In school, as in the underground, we'd have to stick together to survive. Aside from Samy and Sion, I hardly knew the others, but all of us were bonded by our being Jews. We might not even like each other, but it didn't matter. Enduring was the issue.

I made arrangements with the other nine to meet me in the locker room at lunch break, and on the second day of school I put the matter squarely to them for a quick decision. The pattern of the next five years depended on their answers. Did we work together or was it each man for himself? In the latter case, I warned, we'd be more alone than ever in our lives, and very easy pickings.

Only two withdrew—the Communist and the assimilationist. Neither would involve himself with something strictly Jewish. As it happened, this tidied up the enterprise I had in mind. We'd been ordered to establish four-man lab teams, and with eight of us, we had exactly what was needed for a couple of cohesive cliques. (I barely stopped myself from saying "cells.") Cooperating in our classes and studying together after school, we'd keep each other on our toes and see to it that no one fell too far behind. By setting us apart, they were *forcing* us to be superior. In five years, I predicted, we'd be taking all the honors.

"And then, you know, they'll hate us all the more."

David said what I was thinking, what all of us were thinking, and all of us reacted with the self-same shrug. Dumb or smart, we'd still be *dhimmis.* If we couldn't be equal, being better was our best revenge.

18

On the second day we started by dissecting frogs, and with the first insertion of the scalpel, I discovered that I loved to cut. Book beside me, open to "Amphibians," I'd taken up the instrument with trepidation, but it fit between my fingers as if meant to be there. At a touch, the skin and tissues of the frog parted with a smooth precision that delighted me. At other tables, some few, I saw, were sharing my experience. Most, however, stabbed and gouged and hacked—some with eyes shut tight against the sight of their incisions. There were sounds of someone being sick. Another student shrieked on slicing through his finger, but I seemed to know instinctively what pressure to apply and when to lessen or increase it. Once inside the small green creature, I was so engrossed, I didn't know that Boswell had come up behind me. He told me that my work was "most meticulous." I must "practice, practice, practice."

Inspired by his notice, I acted on his good advice that very afternoon. The creek where Baba used to take the family on picnics was full of frogs, and I scooped a basketful—a month's supply of "homework." In a corner of the *hosh,* I improvised a royal frog environment, and paid the kids to catch them flies; no frogs had ever fed as well. Their lives were limited, but lush. I felt it was the least that I could do.

Every night another disappeared. The kids were in a quandary and of course I couldn't explain. Avram finally concluded that the pup was eating them. Poor Lassie! In my room at night, she'd nuzzle at my latest victim, wondering why he wouldn't play.

By the time the last and fattest frog had ceased to be, the scalpel followed my instructions like a flesh-and-blood extension of my body. Out of gratitude and guilt I always wrapped the small remains and gave them decent burial. It was silly, I suppose, but it eased my mind to do it. Slaughtering a lamb was different. One slash and he was dead. The frog was living while I sliced and probed. I felt him pulsate and I also felt his life depart. Anaesthetized, they hadn't suffered, but I couldn't dull my own discomfort.

My studies were at constant war with my religious training, and I knew that this dichotomy could do me in. Like proper English, *yeshiva* learning could impede my progress. Cutting up a human body was next on the agenda. I'd have to desecrate a corpse, knowingly commit a sin against the teachings of the Talmud. By Jewish law, a body has to go to God intact. Both embalming and autopsies are forbidden.

Before I was prepared for it—if, indeed, I ever would be—twelve cadavers were awaiting our attention. In this first of six anatomy semesters, we'd be working on the head and limbs, and for this course only, the four-man teams increased to twelve: two students to each arm and leg, four to every head and neck. Those of us who made it to the next semester would do the chest and abdomen and genitalia. Lab procedure called for members of the team to switch around at intervals, so each would work eventually on every segment of the body.

As I walked slowly toward the lab, trying to suppress my qualms, I noticed that the other Jews were also lagging. Nor were the Arabs rushing to arrive. At Lab Room 8, we milled around the entrance, all equally uneasy, shrinking from that final step across the threshold. Stripped to its essentials, there was death behind the door. Given time, we'd cultivate detachment, but for now, the fear was visceral, though no one would admit it. While I told myself that my reluctance was entirely religious, I was lying, and disgusted with my own dishonesty and apprehension, I marched up to the door and flung it open.

Although I'd braced myself to face the naked corpses, I hadn't counted on the smell. It was a solid wall that stunned me when, a step inside the room, I struck it. As they straggled in behind me, the others gagged and grabbed for handkerchiefs against the foul odor of the formalin. That, in turn, was blanketing another stench, but not completely. A faint but terrible putrescence drifted lazily around the tables holding the cadavers. Though it would worsen as the weeks went on, as flesh imperfectly preserved decayed, our level of acceptance would adjust as well. The day would come when we would even *eat* in Lab Room 8.

The body I selected had a stony face without expression. I'd sped by one whose teeth were showing in an evil snarl, even though I knew that it was due entirely to muscle stricture. Mine was strongly muscled, and I chose a sturdy leg, probably because the textbook started with a leg—or perhaps because it was the farthest from the head and heart.

The team of twelve I'd put together was assembled at the table; three Arabs and a Kurd had joined our Jewish group. Tawfik, the Kurd, was one of only three at school, and it amused him to be on a team with us. He liked to say that he was more of a minority than we were. While he wasn't all that keen on Jews, he really hated Arabs. The enmity between these groups was ancient and enduring.

I'd had my pick of Arabs. The *M'silmin* might not like us, but they clamored for inclusion. We *dhimmis* didn't flunk out, so working with a Jewish team was almost an assurance of success.

I selected Salah, who despised us, because he was the brightest of the bunch. Abdul Sahib, almost as intelligent, was less antagonistic. Of the four, however, Rashid promised most. Like many Arabs from the north, he was fair-complected, with blondish hair and eyes the color of a lucky bead. It was more than his appearance though that set Rashid apart. He had a talent for enjoyment, and was naturally an arbiter, the oil on the often troubled waters of the team. He liked the world and all of its inhabitants. Except for Samy, I'd never seen a person smile so much. I distrusted such euphoria, but against my better judgment, I was drawn to him.

David was my partner on the leg. With two of us to every limb, one would wield the scalpel while the other checked the textbook. The other pairs were flipping coins, deciding who would cut, but we didn't have to do that. One glance at the cadaver, and my teammate turned a sickly green. He seized the textbook like a lifeline, leaving me the knife. Our text was Cunningham's *Anatomy,* and shakily he started reading: "Incise along the sacro-pubic ligament. . . ."

Checking reference points, I drew the blade along the fold line in the groin. Saturated as it was with the preservative, the flesh resisted like a slab of solid rubber, and I had to press much harder than I had on frogs. As I grunted with the effort, David swallowed hard and kept his eyes averted. The fumes of vomit were already in the air on every side of us, and I felt a little sick myself. For me, though, it was just the smell. The cutting came as easily as spooning soup, and bothered me about as much. Because the texture of the leg was so unlike the living flesh, one could hardly think of it as human, and that helped a lot.

David sneaked a look and retched. When he was able to resume, I pulled the skin back, as Cunningham directed, to expose the femoral canal. Around the artery I saw a ligature that shouldn't have been there. On close inspection, I found a small incision at the femoral joint. Aside from that, the leg was absolutely normal, and in the whole of Cunningham, we couldn't find a clue to this particular procedure.

Immensely curious about the cause of this incision, I looked around for someone to enlighten me, but no instructors were in sight. When I checked the corridors to see if I could spot them, halfway down the hall I saw a door discreetly marked "Anatomy." Since no one answered when I knocked, I tried the knob. The door swung open, and the stench that made me stagger back put Lab Room 8 to shame. Handkerchief to nose, I ventured in, only to be stopped again, this time by the sight that met my eyes.

In a concrete pool, dug four feet down and filled with stinking liquid, six cadavers floated, faces up, bumping gently and rebounding. Underneath them lay another layer of bodies, barely moving.

They were deceased—oh, indisputably deceased!—but still I heard a heart-beat sort of sound. Stepping closer, I noted that a rubber tube was tied into the groin of each cadaver in the topmost tier. The heavy bodies at the bottom had scalpel scars where tubes had been. That solved the mystery of the small incision.

Each slender tube stretched upward for about five feet and there connected with a metal pipe that spanned the pool. This terminated in the source of the pulsations, a pumping mechanism. From the pump, a second pipe led to the pit, and coming nearer, I heard a snuffling, sucking sound. A plumber's son, I understood. What the pump was draining out was being pressure-pumped back in the bodies. They were swimming in the fluid that filled them! Formalin. The sunken ones were saturated, ready for dissection. I was watching the embalming process taking place, too stunned to turn away.

At the far end of the room, two young men were tinkering with the apparatus. On catching sight of me, they scrambled to their feet and, addressing me respectfully as "Doctor," asked if they could be of any aid. Mustafa, the older of the two, was especially solicitous. Would I like to see a tube inserted? Or was I interested in watching how they forced the fluid in when the arteries were clogged? On asking this, he reached behind the pump and produced a huge syringe. The thought of seeing it in action made me nauseous, though I couldn't explain exactly why a hand-held hypodermic should be so much more offensive than the same procedure by machine. Perhaps it was Mustafa's unconcealed enjoyment as he pushed and pulled the monstrous plunger.

Queasy as I was, an idea had occurred to me while standing at the pit, and Mustafa's attitude encouraged me to speak.

"What happens with the bodies when we finish our dissection?"

He was on to me immediately. Scores of students must have made the same approach. He knew exactly what I wanted, and without ado, he asked me if I'd care to have a skeleton.

Mustafa and his silent partner had a modest little business on the side. Boiling bodies. For ten *dinars,* they'd turn a used cadaver into nice, clean bones. "In a little box," Mustafa added grandly.

Three days later, I had the last remains of someone middle-aged and male beneath my bed. I thought that I'd be ill at ease, but unassembled, the bones were simply building blocks. Three hundred and thirteen pieces of the human puzzle, the basic structure of the species. What other architecture could compare with ours!

To make it to the synagogue for morning services, I had to start my day at 5 A.M. Since I studied until after one and still maintained my *Shura* schedule, by the middle of the term the lack of sleep was starting to affect my mental state. I was unaware of just how edgy I'd become until the afternoon I blew my top and blasted my astonished teammates.

As I lived closest to the Royal College, we always met at my house for our study sessions. Before we buckled down to business, we'd horse around awhile to unwind. This day, however, with the quarterly exams just weeks away, I told them that I wanted to begin at once. Even to myself, I sounded somewhat shrill and dictatorial.

Catching Alber's eye, Samara pulled his mouth down with his index fingers, aping my expression. With indulgent smiles in my direction, both returned to teasing David. Older than the rest of us, skinny as a string, bespectacled, slightly prissy in appearance, and extremely shy, David was accustomed to their kidding, but in my present mood, it bothered *me.* David's hickey was his own affair. David's *hickey?* I looked at him and, sure enough, he had one.

"She really gave it to you, didn't she?" Alber leered.

When David's mouth began to twitch, I thought he was about to tell them off. On seeing his reaction, Alber and Samara grew increasingly obnoxious.

Was he hiding any other hickies? . . . Was she worth it? . . .

I sat there steaming. If David didn't shut them up, I'd do it for him. Then he broke his silence—and I almost choked.

"She was *unbelievable!* Wouldn't let me sleep a wink!"

Samara whooped and my "unworldly" teammate took the floor. Grinning broadly, eyes gleaming through his glasses, he described the girl inside and out, from every angle, and from one end to the other, a living lesson in anatomy. I was in a state of shock. Shy David! Dead bodies still disturbed him, but clearly he could handle live ones. Naturally the others had to top him. Ignoring me and all my careful lecture notes, they lolled around, laughing and comparing prostitutes and brothels. We had licensed houses everywhere in Baghdad, and apparently they'd paid them all a visit. Once Samara turned and winked at me. He knew that I had nothing to contribute.

I was growing madder by the minute; at this iffy stage in school, wasting study time on anything was stupid, but throwing it away on garbage was a sin. And they were dumping all their dirty little business *here,* in my family home, with my mother and my sisters just a wall away. I tried to steer them off the subject by reminding them again of the exams, but Samara simply brushed me off and started a repulsive story that even in a whorehouse would have raised some hackles. I finally exploded.

After I'd subsided, apologies were offered and accepted. The incident was over, but though I should have been at peace, an hour after the eruption every pulse still pounded. Since the start of school, Samara had been saying, "You're too tense. Relax a little!" I used to answer lightly, "You're loose enough for both of us," but long ago I'd stopped responding. It simply wasn't funny any more.

"Relaxation, the release of tension." I knew the definition, but even as a kid, I couldn't sit still. At puberty, more intense than ever, I'd gone to books to seek an explanation of the strange new set of stimuli that shook me. After reading up on all the symptoms, I'd diagnosed myself as a normal adolescent, on the hyperthyroid side, heaving with hormonal urges. Between religious ethics and my itchy flesh, I'd suffered through some stormy moments, but until today, I'd kept the tumult under strict control.

Later in the week, when I pressed the boys to tell me just exactly how I'd acted, they said that I'd been almost incoherent. "Your face was purple and your eyes were bugging out." Samara said that he'd been scared. "I thought for sure you'd burst a vessel."

Now *I* was scared. What they described was someone on the brink of breakdown. Those simmering male hormones had merely added one more burden to a load already much too heavy.

Four hours' sleep was all I ever got. Some mornings when I woke, I could almost feel each nerve end individually exposed. Noises which I'd never even noticed now set my teeth on edge. Several times, I'd blanked out for a second, and once, when Osa interrupted me, I'd come within an inch of striking out at her. If I didn't ease up, I'd simply fall apart.

The first priority was sleep. By skipping synagogue, and saying morning prayers at home, I could stay in bed at least another hour. Since early service was my special time with Baba, I expected him to argue. When he didn't say a word, I knew that he was worried too. He must have been aware of the increasing strain.

School was asking more of me than I'd anticipated. In retrospect, *shamash* had been Easy Street. At *shamash,* an agile mind allowed for lots of corner-cutting. At the College, though, I couldn't approximate or improvise. In the sciences, every answer had to be exact, each procedure by the book. I'd had to buckle down to textbooks as never in my life before.

My ego wouldn't admit that my capacity had any limit; luckily, my body was a better judge. Except for absolute necessities, I eliminated everything but study.

19

The only relaxation I allowed myself was training Lassie, and even that was not entirely amusement. She was a loving pup, and in a better world would probably have spent her life in chasing sticks and licking children's faces. Instead, I had to teach her to attack. While Iraq was fairly quiet on the Jewish front, *Eretz Yisrael* was heating up, and by their recent actions, the British had made certain it would boil over. Trouble there most certainly meant bloodshed here.

In 1939, before the mass atrocities took place in Europe, the British made a promise to the Arabs that Jewish immigration into Palestine would be restricted. Now, six years later, when the European war was won—with the Arabs, in the main, having sided with the enemy and in spite of what the Nazis had already done to decimate the Jews—the English were intent on honoring their promise. They'd just increased their coastal forces, adding four destroyers, several cruisers, and squadrons of patrol planes to sweep the waters even more efficiently. Palestine must be preserved from Jews! Not a refugee must reach the shore!

Intercepted within sight of their ancestral land, the survivors of the death camps were denied admission. The leaky, stinking tubs, unfit to put to sea, but overflowing with pathetic remnants of the Holocaust, were halted by the bright-white British cutters. Like German officers before them, their clean-cut captains "only followed orders."

The Iraqi press, of course, never printed any pictures of these hollow-eyed and skeletal survivors, but when the new commander of the *Shura* came, he brought a pocketful of clippings. Though stained with desert sweat and split along the creases, the images were clear enough to make me cry. Some of them looked less alive than our cadavers at the College.

Since seeing them, I'd searched the papers constantly for any hint of action from an outraged world. At long, long last, the conscience of the Western world was finally aroused enough to set up an exploratory council. The question was—could Palestine accommodate 100,000 Jews still herded, cattle-like, in makeshift camps—camps operated by the Allies? The Commission would decide.

On a hazy morning in May of 1946, I stopped, as always, on my way to school to buy a paper. For news outside Iraq, none was really worth the reading, but since I had the reading habit, I'd select the least intemperate and catch up on the local stories. Today, however, a huge black headline screamed at me, and I grabbed instead at *Al-Sha'ab*—supernationalist and the worst example of the anti-everyone-but-Arab rags. To *Al-Sha'ab,* Great Britain and America were just as evil as the Zionists. The banner headline read, ANGLO-AMERICAN COMMISSION BETRAYS ARAB WORLD.

Anything that made *Al-Sha'ab* unhappy had to be a plus for us, I figured, and the first words of the article confirmed the feeling. The Commission had declared itself in favor of admitting the disputed Jews. With the final paragraph, however, my elation petered out. After columns of the usual abuse, the paper called upon its readers to demonstrate against the British and American imperialists. At 2 P.M. on Thursday, everyone must mass at Hamam Circle and make their anger known.

That, I knew, would only be the start. By now, the other camp undoubtedly was stirring up its own adherents. In Iraq, as elsewhere in the area, the Communists and Nationalists were at each other's throats, fighting for new followers. Since the Nationalists had called a rally for the afternoon, you could bet the Communists would jump the gun and make their move that morning. Because the Party was illegal in Iraq, it called itself the League to Combat Zionism, and in this disguise, avoided interference from the government. It was a double-edged deception in that the leadership consisted of Iraqi Jews. Anti-Zionism was the safest front that they could possibly employ.

The scheduled demonstration and the one the Communists would soon announce would both require careful watching. Crowds could easily catch fire, and Hamam Circle was just outside the Jewish Quarter. The *Shura* still had several days in which to map a plan, but if they wanted me at once, a message would be sent to me at school. We'd arranged, of course, for such contingencies.

On my arrival home that afternoon, Nana rushed to tell me that a "Hai" had called but hadn't left a number. "Hai" was code for "phone in for instructions." When I did so, I was told that every member of the *Shura* would be on alert at 10 P.M. on Wednesday. The Communists had called a Thursday morning rally. My assigned position was in the Jewish house closest to Hamam Circle. Should defensive action be required, my weapon was to be a Sten, a submachine gun; if I had to shoot, I'd be aiming from a Jewish site and into Arab territory.

On Wednesday after dinner, avoiding Baba's eyes, I said that I'd be studying with a friend and sleeping over.

Seven others were already on the spot when I arrived, all but one unknown to me. I'd expected Ghali, since his job was feeding cartridges while I was firing, but I should have known that such a house, so strategically positioned, would be more than just a gun emplacement. I'd been sent to a command post.

Instructions called for me to reconnoiter when the crowd collected. While I was on the street, three *Shura* soldiers equipped with handguns and grenades would keep me covered. All the others were communications men.

Now there was nothing we could do but wait. With that in mind, I'd brought my books along, and when the others bedded down in boredom, I studied for my finals by a tiny flashlight.

The Communists began to gather early. By 10 A.M., 5000 Red Iraqis, masquerading as the League to Combat Zionism, were mobilized in Hamam Circle. The most gigantic of their waving standards, the one deliberately designed to draw official eyes, was so over-sized that half a dozen sturdy types were needed to support it. The message read, in bright-red letters, DOWN WITH BRITISH-AMERICAN IMPERIALISM AND DEATH TO ZIONISM!

More than satisfied with both the sentiments expressed, few of the police on duty would bother looking far beyond this biggest of the banners. If some were extraconscientious and scrutinized the many smaller placards, they'd also see some shorter exhortations, too innocuous to note unless one was acquainted with the Party line. The most popular of these appeared to be LONG LIVE THE ARAB PEOPLE, THE MASSES MUST BE HEARD, and TOGETHER WE WILL WIN, any one of which could be interpreted to suit the viewer.

Only "Communist" was absent. Never printed on a poster, never uttered in a public place, nonetheless the ideology was undiluted. Though outlawed in the country and anathema to everyone in power, the Party flourished in the very shadow of the ruling structure. The daring deftness of the leaders and the cover of the League had so far kept them safe. It was just the sort of bold but subtle scheme that I admired most, and I only wished the Jewish brains behind it were with us.

When I left the house to scout the area, I saw only Arab faces on the outskirts of the Circle. I'd expected that, however, since the comrades in the public eye were always *M'silmin.* The Jewish principals stayed out of sight as much as possible; Arab membership would drop off sharply if the real authority was seen to be in *dhimmi* hands. At *shamash,* I recalled, the Jewish Communists had spoken, eyes aglow, about the solidarity and perfect oneness of the proletariat. Most were Communists because the bedrock of the Party was supposed to be equality for all, and still they had to hide behind the *M'silmin.*

One aspect of the scene before me *was* surprising. In the middle of the mob, Jabbar, who worked for Baba, was striding back and forth, thrusting up his BREAD FOR HUNGRY WORKERS sign in rhythm with his steps. It was the energetic bobbing that attracted my attention; everything that Jabbar did, he did with all his might. That's the way he worked for Baba, who appreciated and rewarded his endeavors. Jabbar was better off than any of his family or friends and had never evidenced the least unhappiness. I'd have liked to push my way across to him and ask some questions, but, of course, I couldn't expose myself and risk my comrades.

A quick reconnaissance was reassuring. The organizers were exercising strict control. Using bullhorns, they urged that everyone behave himself and stay within the limits set. If they set off on a looting spree, the spokesman warned, the world would look at them as simple outlaws. In their own best interest, the demonstration must be orderly. I reported back that weapons wouldn't be needed. In the time between the rallies, we had other work to do. Waiting for the *Al-Sha'ab* crowd to show, we sent out couriers to test communications; in a subsequent review, we found that each dispatch had been received and all within the time allotted. The system was a thundering success.

The Communists dispersed at noon. As the last of them departed, the others were already filtering in. By 2 P.M., the Nationalists had filled the Circle. When I went out a little later, the only difference that I could see was in a certain few omissions from the signs. While "anti" all the same old enemies the League excoriated—the British and Americans and Zionists—no Nationalist posters spoke of starving masses. Except for that, the aims of both assemblages appeared identical.

Even so, it startled me to see Jabbar again. This time, his bobbing banner read, SAY *NO* TO FOREIGN INTERFERENCE! Then I recognized some other faces from the morning scene. Something odd was going on . . . something, I felt sure, the *Shura* ought to know about. Finding out was up to me, and the safest source of information was Jabbar. How well it all worked out! I could satisfy my curiosity and still discharge my duty.

When he was close enough to hail, I called his name. While he dipped his sign to show he'd heard, he looked distinctly woeful as he wormed his way to where I stood. He was afraid of what I'd say to father, I was thinking, when he shamed me by exclaiming in a worried whisper, "Doctor! What are you doing here? Go home!" The concern I'd seen had been for me; he knew it wasn't safe for Jews to be at demonstrations.

I said that I'd been in the neighborhood and thought I'd take a passing peek, which he accepted; since my infancy, he'd seen me nosing into everything at building sites and Baba's office. While I was wondering how to ask about his own appearance, both now and in this morning's mob, he burst out with the answer, too delighted to contain himself.

"I was here this morning, and they gave me fifty *fils,*" he chortled. "This bunch"—he waved his hand expansively around the Circle—"they gave me fifty *fils*—and lunch!"

We parted, and in seconds his sign was jouncing up and down again among the others. Jabbar was an honest man and always earned his wages.

He, and others like him, were the only ones completely on the level. This demonstration was as phony as the first. The Nationalists—who were actually pan-Arabists—opposed the current government because of its pro-British bias, but knowing they'd be crushed in open conflict, they expressed themselves in slogans. The Palestine Commission had provided them the perfect opportunity to air their views. Any group could safely scream against increasing Jewish immigration into Palestine, whereas a bloody clash with Jews in Baghdad would have caused the government to call up troops. For the moment, exterminating Jews was out of favor. Once again, therefore, the leaders of the pack were pleading with their people for a peaceful rally. It was almost funny. Though Reds and Arabists alike villified us as the enemy incarnate, neither faction could survive without us. Without the Jews to pin their propaganda on, neither would have dared to demonstrate today.

When I returned to say that we could stow our guns, reports were in from all the other *Shura* posts. Deep in the ghetto, there'd been some minor skirmishes. Aside from those, the city was at peace. However, we remained, as ordered, until the Circle emptied.

Heading home, I ruminated that we really ought to send some thank-you notes to the League, the Nationalists, and "Al-Sha'ab". As far as I could tell, their efforts had accomplished nothing except to let us test our network—and it had worked without a hitch. For the *Shura,* and for me, the day had been a big success. I'd even finished all my homework.

20

After eighteen hours of tests, exam week ended, and my brain was like a sponge squeezed dry; I felt emptied of every bit of information ever stored, and sleep rushed in to fill the vacuum. The family was still at dinner when I fell asleep, and I didn't stir again until the middle of the morning. Waking up refreshed for once was more rebirth than mere arising.

Rested and euphoric, I eagerly awaited the arrival of my marks. Grades were mailed by the government, and I pounced on every post like Lassie on a lamb shank. On receiving them, however, my elated state abruptly ended. While excellent, they weren't up to expectations. Of course they never were, and never would be. Less than perfect always disappointed me. I was about to throw the envelope away when another sheet of paper fluttered out, this a letter from the Dean, informing me I'd won the Boswell Prize.

Unworthy as my marks might seem to me, the Boswell meant they were the highest in the freshman class.

Free of school till fall, and completely reinvigorated by a solid week of sleep, I volunteered for anything that needed doing in the underground. Six mornings of the week for the entire summer, I'd be working on my own cadaver—courtesy of an instructor at the school—but my afternoons were uncommitted, and I wasn't used to empty hours. The days had been so full so long, I'd forgotten how to just have fun.

Since the *slik* I'd built for books was almost empty now, Yehuda, the new commander of the *Shura,* suggested that we use it as a weapons store. When I agreed, he said the messenger delivering the weapons would identify himself by asking, "Is Dahood here?"

At the appointed hour, I was hovering in the hallway, alert to intercept the courier before he knocked. The family was still at lunch; with any luck, I'd have him in the house and out again without their ever knowing. I almost missed the footsteps, and when I cracked the door, her hand was only inches from the bell. *Her* hand!

In a single look, I fell in love. We stood there staring at each other until her lashes fell and cut the contact. Her huge, black-diamond eyes had held mine like a magnet. In vivid contrast with the sweeping wings of sable hair that framed it, the perfect oval of her face was richly creamy, barely tinged with rosy beige. She'd feel warm, I knew, like bread right from the oven. She recovered first, and when she spoke, I saw that several of her milky teeth were just the slightest bit aslant, and that too was enchanting. I loved everything about her.

In a shy, low voice, she asked, "Is Dahood here?"

A code response was called for; what actually escaped was "Yehuda didn't warn me!" She should have walked away at once. Instead, she waited while I searched befuddled brain cells for the right reply. On receiving it, she let me take the baskets.

In the storage room, I locked the door behind us. While she was lifting off the layers of food that covered the grenades, I pushed away the cupboard that concealed the cover of the *slik.* By the time I had the lid up, she had taken off her all-enveloping *abaya,* and was tucking up the loosened bottom of her blouse. To do it properly, she'd sucked her breath in, which had thrown her shoulders back and thrust her breasts out, firm and full. Where blouse met skirt, my hands could almost span her. The temptation was so strong, I had to jam them in my pockets. At just that moment, she became aware that I was watching, and both of us began to redden.

Conscious suddenly of something more embarrassing than blushing cheeks, I hunched above the *slik* to hide myself from her. More than blood was mounting. The hormones were unbridled, out of my control, and I sent a silent cry to *Hakham* Ezra. Help me! He'd told us what we mustn't do and why, but I hadn't ever thought to ask if *wanting* to was also sinful outside marriage. And was sixteen-plus too young to think of getting married?

Could anything be more insane? Not only was I instantly and breathlessly in love, but with a soldier, one whose name I didn't know and, for reasons of security, could never try to ascertain.

The sight of armaments, uncovered now, intruded on my trance and restored me to reality. We had to hurry. If Baba found me stuffing weapons in his cellar floor, I wouldn't live to have a wedding *ever.* To reach the bottom of the *slik,* I had to stretch out on my stomach, and the icy tiles helped to quiet the commotion down below.

From the corner of my eye, I saw her kneel beside me. One by one, she handed me the packets holding gauze-wrapped, grease-enveloped handguns.

The grenades were small, and our hands could hardly keep from touching as I took them from her. When she passed the last one over, I grasped her hand and held it gently. Just as gently, she withdrew it, and pretending to be angry, pouted, "I'm Evlene, not a hand grenade." She hadn't simply let it slip; she wanted me to know her name, and I was wildly elated. To violate her *Shura* oath, she really had to like me.

Before she left, I had to figure out a way for us to meet again. Nice girls didn't make dates. In fact, if it weren't for the underground, we wouldn't have met at all. Even if we'd seen each other, the odds were astronomical against our ever speaking, since our families were unacquainted and we had no friends in common. Only prostitutes could be approached without a proper introduction.

In desperation, I asked her how she spent her days. Any girl who joined the underground would have to have a wider sphere of interests than the average. With any luck, our lives might overlap at some point that her family would find acceptable.

When she told me that she taught a kindergarten class, my desperation deepened. Instead of only one, we'd have fifty mothers watching us. Then Evlene added, "But I also tutor private pupils, mostly in elementary French." The fog abruptly lifted.

"You do? That's *wonderful!*"

The degree of my enthusiasm startled her, but it was absolutely genuine. A legitimate excuse at last! Unbeknownst to him, Avram was about to get some extra education. On his behalf, she gave me both her surname and address.

Turning from the door, the precious information in my hand, I spotted Nana. While mother took my male friends in stride, I'd never tried her tolerance with women. Even Nana had her limits, and from the look of her, I saw I'd overstepped them. Before she could attack, I shouted out triumphantly, "I found someone! Finally, I found someone for Avram."

"For Avram?"

"To teach him French." Teaching Avram French had never been a topic of discussion, or not as far as Nana knew. On the other hand, of course, she never knew for sure what I was up to. Throwing up her hands, she scuttled for the safety of the kitchen.

That night at dinner I brought the matter up with Baba. The Alliance

Française Israelite was then the finest school in Baghdad. That fall, I said, I thought Avram should be enrolled. I mentioned, though, that half of those applying were excluded; the school was so selective, a potential student had to offer something special. If Avram studied French, it might enhance his chances. Baba took the bait. No one would reject a son of his if he could help it, and he authorized the lessons.

Since Evlene had no phone, I had to go on foot to make arrangements. I knew from her address that the family was lower-middle class, the *most* suspicious segment of society. Everyone at home when I arrived would peer distrustfully at me and speculate about the reasons for my being there. However, it was Evlene, not a relative, who answered when I rapped, and she smiled at the sight of me.

I was half-afraid to look at her. The Evlene in my mind was just too beautiful to really be—but there she was! My heart gave such a mighty heave, she must have heard it. For whatever reason, she began to blush. Along with *Shura,* that was all I knew for sure we shared. At any provocation, the blood would rise in both of us, but where she reddened like a rose, I boiled like a beet.

Without a word, she slipped outside and shut the door behind her. That meant she welcomed my attentions, but it also meant I wouldn't meet her mother. Though momentarily relieved, I was also disappointed. Evlene's warmth had wiped away my trepidation, and I *wanted* to confront the family. More than anything, I wanted to commit myself.

As matters stood, I'd have to be content with walking side by side with her, back and forth, right in front of where she lived, with everybody watching. Unchaperoned, I couldn't take her to a movie or a coffeehouse or off the street at all. Even what we did was daring. Should we walk too long, too close, too happily together, we'd encourage ugly gossip. In spite of these restrictions, I told myself I should be grateful. If Evlene weren't such a liberated girl, she would have slammed the door with me outside, alone.

As modern as she was, however, the walking would have been the end of it without Avram. Bless my little brother and the dream that led directly to his birth! Because of him, my present dream might possibly come true. I told Evlene that I'd arranged to have her tutor Avram, and we set a time when I could be at home. We didn't have to spell it out; she understood. In two short meetings, we already understood each other's silences. As someone who'd been shouting all his life, that awed me almost more than her adorable appearance.

For the balance of the summer, I was the very model of an older brother, sitting in to monitor each teaching session, more concerned, it seemed, with Avram's welfare than my own. To maintain the fiction, I was learning French myself so I could drill him ostentatiously in front of Baba. Since I'd always been absorbed in education, my zeal didn't strike my father as excessive. I fooled everyone but S'hak, who was now the chief accountant for an import firm and very worldly. Once he saw Evlene, he was on to me, but all he did was raise his eyebrows in approval.

In one respect, Evlene was more to be admired than I might have wished. With all her obligations, she still spent so much time on *Shura* business that I soon began to feel a slacker. Influenced by her activity, I returned to teaching Hebrew in the *T'nu'ah,* and by the end of summer I'd become commander of the *Izrah Rishonah,* the *Shura* first-aid corps. In that capacity, I began to write the underground's official first-aid manual.

With every meeting, my feeling for Evlene intensified. At first, the secrecy of our intrigue excited me, but as the weeks went by, I wanted more than surreptitious snatches. Evlene was taking much too long to introduce me to her parents. Avram would soon be going off to school, and when the lessons stopped, we'd lose our only opportunity to meet. We had to talk and, inadvertently, my mother made it possible.

One Thursday, I was home alone when Evlene came. The family was shopping for our school clothes, or more precisely, picking fabrics. Nana and Nazima made every stitch we wore, but before they started sewing for the season, they'd visit all the finest shops to check the latest fashions. Mother had reminded me to cancel Avram's lesson, but I'd honestly forgotten.

When Evlene arrived, I led her in before announcing that the house was empty but for us. If I'd told her on the outside steps, she might have left, and from the way her smile was fading, she might *still* retreat. I jumped in fast to circumvent it, and explaining as I went, I sort of herded her along the hall. The farther from the door she was, the better chance I had of holding onto her. Finally, running out of self-reproaches, I suggested, "Since you're here, stay awhile and we'll entertain each other."

Her eyes went wide, and when she halted in her tracks, I tried to extricate myself.

"What I meant was, we can read some poetry together, or play some games—well, *something. . . .*" To tell the truth, I didn't know what I had in mind myself, but then she rescued us by running up the stairs and heading for the roof. "It's much too nice to stay indoors," she shouted down. When I saw that she was chalking squares for *gola,* I doubled back to Nana's sewing box and rummaged for the biggest, flattest buttons—the ones that threw the best.

Evlene was waiting with her hand out, and I dropped the finest of the *tuen* into it, now careful not to touch her. She'd picked the game; I'd play it her way. How wise she was! An active child's game would ease the tension. Relieved of pressure for this short, suspended space of time, we romped like eight-year-olds, relaxed together as we'd never been before.

One foot off the ground in accordance with the rules, Evlene teetered in the final square, trying to maintain her balance while she bent to pick her *tuen* up. When I saw her toppling over, instinct shot my arms out. She tumbled into them, and all at once, it was another game entirely. She didn't move at all. As she landed, so she stayed, both of us immobilized and breathless. But if she raised her head or let herself go limp, I'd lose control.

For the longest minute of my life, I waited motionless. Almost imperceptibly, she pulled away. Her hand sought mine, however, and it pulsed to match my heartbeat. Too choked to speak, I couldn't in any case have uttered any of the words that welled up in me.

You could tell a whore that she was utterly enchanting, that you dreamt of her, desired her. No compliment was too preposterous to pay a street girl, but with a proper girl, a man was stricken mute. Forbidden to express my feelings, I could only ask, "Are you old-fashioned? Will you let a marriage be arranged for you?"

When she shook her head and answered, "No, I'm not old-fashioned," my fingers tightened on her hand, but with a gentle tug, she disengaged herself. "But I won't be here," she added. "I'm leaving soon for Palestine."

Though I slept that night in fits and starts, I faced the morning confident that I could change her mind. Because she *was* a proper Jewish girl, she'd listen to the man she loved. Compared with some, she might be liberated, but not enough to matter when it came to marriage. When I actually proposed, she'd put aside her girlish plans. The male did the planning in Iraq. Even in the underground, we gave the orders.

She wouldn't be back until the following Tuesday for the next to last of Avram's lessons, and since I couldn't wait that long, I went to her. On answering the door, Evlene looked startled, but she wasn't angry or she wouldn't have let me in. To visit her at all defied the rules, but to present myself an hour before *Shabbat* was the grossest imposition. Also stupid. Her mother would be frantically at work and in the worst of moods. I couldn't have picked a less propitious moment. I don't recall a word I said except "No, thank you" after Evlene introduced us. It was mandatory that her mother offer food and drink, but relieved at my refusal, she rushed back to the kitchen and her interrupted tasks.

But the introductions weren't over. It hadn't crossed my mind that Evlene might have sisters, and on seeing them, I almost froze. One was so obese, she bobbled. The other was an Evlene who'd been soaked in brine and then in bleach. Both were older than Evlene. Older and unmarried. All else aside, her parents wouldn't consent to Evlene's marriage until the other two had stood beneath the *chupah*—but without the most enormous dowry, which they plainly couldn't afford to pay, what hope had they of finding husbands?

Slightly giddy from the stifling heat inside the small and overfurnished living room, I must have swayed a little. Evlene insisted that I sit, and suddenly a welcome breeze was washing over me. She was fanning me in full sight of her sisters! This attention was bestowed only on one's intimates and family elders, and my hopes revived along with all the rest of me. I had to be at home by sundown, but we'd get this whole affair in order, I decided, just as soon as she arrived for Avram's lesson.

Tuesday came, but Evlene didn't. She'd postponed before because of underground assignments, so I wasn't too concerned. When she didn't come on Thursday either, I set out anxiously to see her. At Evlene's house, the bleached-out sister asked me in. As I was halfway through the door, the mother flung herself at me and burst into a flood of tears. From her ravaged face, I could tell that torrents had been shed already. For an instant, I was sure Evlene was dead, but her mother wasn't wearing black or sitting *shiva.*

I asked where Evlene was, and she drew away and looked at me accusingly. "In Palestine," she wailed. "If you had asked to marry her, she'd still be here." She beat at me hysterically. "My baby's gone," she shrieked. "My baby's gone from me."

Paralyzed in place, I let her pound at me. I was immobilized by shock, but even more by sheer astonishment. Not only did her mother know about our meeting, but she would have let us plan to marry. We could have been betrothed. Could I believe it, though? Was she simply saying it to shift the burden? But if what she said was so, why hadn't Evlene even hinted at it?

What hurt me most was that she hadn't said a last farewell. But that was inconclusive too. Perhaps she didn't trust herself to see me, afraid I might persuade her to remain. Until we met again, I'd cling to that. It was a fragile hope, but all I had.

21

The start of the semester snapped me out of my depression. I told myself that many emigrants came back from *Eretz Yisrael.* Life in Palestine was hardly comparable to ours in Baghdad, and especially now. In the postwar boom we were enjoying, everyone was doing well. Baba said he'd never seen such business, and though Palestine was still a burning issue to the Arabs, they hadn't bothered us unbearably of late. In Palestine, living in the midst of strangers, surrounded by hostility and scratching for necessities, Evlene would see she'd acted rashly. At the moment, *Eretz Yisrael* required *men.* She'd help the cause a good deal more by coming back and serving *Shura.*

With that to solace me, I lost myself in study when the second year of college started. However, as the weeks went by and Evlene neither reappeared nor wrote, I watched my marks slide down with mounting dread. My "trick" of tuning in to one thing at a time would have to be employed again. First things first, and first was earning a degree. On the day I was a doctor, I'd go find her. With that resolved, I set romance aside and concentrated on my courses.

Early in the spring, dissection done, we took the giant step to breathing bodies. Once a week, in groups of twenty, we trooped into the hospital adjoining us; from this point on, we'd do our learning on the living. I'd been avid to begin, but the first encounters were acutely disappointing. All we did was stand around like robots, watching while the house physician indicated—by tracing on the surface of the patient's skin—the position of arteries and organs we already knew. At least with the cadavers we could see inside.

The day I laid my stethoscope on someone's chest made all the difference. Of course we'd listened to each others' hearts since school began, but that was student larking. This was life or death. This heart was sick and stuttering. I'd grown accustomed to the cold and rubbery resistance of a corpse, and when my fingers sank into the living flesh so easily, the shock unnerved me for an instant.

Some weeks later, we ventured into truly virgin territory. Our guide, a gynecology instructor, led us to the female ward, and to the bedside of a wizened Bedouin woman, where he announced the subject of our study would be female organs.

To foreign eyes, the patient would appear to be an aged crone, but we natives knew that constant sun and scouring desert winds had weathered her to this patina. I was up in front, intent on figuring her actual years, and just as I decided she was somewhere in her early forties, the instructor signalled. "Haddad," he ordered, "a vaginal examination."

He spoke in English, and though she couldn't have understood the words, she saw me snap my gloves on. Looking scared to death, she shrank away. Had she known how nervous *I* was, she would have leaped from bed and left the premises! As I approached, she clutched the sheet convulsively, yanking it so high, she bared her lower body. By long-established custom, women were examined under cover, and by touch alone, so I tried to pull the sheet back to the bottom of the bed. Her hands were knotted in the hem, however, and she clung to it so tightly that I couldn't tear it loose. When someone tittered, the instructor spoke up sharply, and ordered her, in Arabic, to let it go.

With the sheet in place, I slid my gloved hand under it, feeling for the mouth of the vagina. While I found the vulva, the patient's thighs were fused together. I fumbled for an opening, but they were solid marble pillars, minus crevices or cracks. When poking didn't work, I pried. The woman was unpierceable! I'd almost given up when Rashid spurred me on by saying in a warm paternal tone, "My boy, by now I'd have her pregnant." His remark had been in Arabic, and everybody whooped with laughter—including my reluctant lady. Her thighs relaxed and I completed the examination.

All in all, the year at school went smoothly. Our problem was at home, and centered on Nazima and her single state. Now twenty-six, she'd been in love with Shua, who lived next door to us, since both were children. For many years, they'd wished to marry, but Baba wouldn't hear of it. It was unheard of for a girl to find a husband for herself. That was her father's job, and Baba kept presenting better candidates with brighter futures. In every other way, the sweetest, most obedient of daughters, in love, Nazima was as stubborn as our father and refused them all. Unless he let her marry Shua, she'd remain a spinster.

The entire winter, we'd been torn apart by bitter arguments that always ended in the same impasse. Matters reached a crisis stage when Nana started having fainting spells, which terrified my father. She didn't want to die, she cried, before she saw her daughter safely married. Finally he threw his hands up and agreed, and as preparations for the big event began, Nana's fits of faintness ended, as I knew they would. I'd applied the stethoscope, of course, but since I sided with Nazima, I'd never said that Nana's fainting spells stemmed solely from emotion.

The house required work before the wedding. Since 1941, when we'd ripped out bricks to toss at the attacking Arabs, the roof had needed fixing. Watching as the *Mislim* masons worked, I couldn't help but wonder if any of these men had been among those mad marauders. The very ones who'd made us rip our roof apart might be repairing it—at our expense.

As I was pondering the possibility, the brawniest of all the workmen paused to rest. I'd been fascinated by the play of pectorals and biceps as he swung his pick; very large, but lithe, he was an animated lesson in anatomy. When he saw me watching, he pointed to the broken wall and asked if I could tell him what had happened. He didn't think it could have been the wind.

It wasn't, I assured him. I told him that we'd picked the bricks out during the *farhood* to use as ammunition. He grinned good-naturedly, but shook his head in disbelief.

"You aren't telling me you fought? Everybody knows you Jews are all *mashlool.*"

It wasn't said with any animus, and he didn't intend to be insulting. Among the *M'silmin,* it was simply an accepted fact that Jews were frozen in the face of danger and couldn't raise a finger in their own defense. I decided to enlighten him.

"If we're all *mashlool,*" I answered with a matching grin, "why don't you hit me with your *fasa?* Go on. You have a pickaxe, I'm *mashlool*—so pick it up and hit me."

The other men had gathered in a ring around us, and I urged again, "Go on and hit me."

He bent to grasp his *fasa,* but let it dangle indecisively until the foreman shouted, "You heard him, Mahmud. If he says to hit him, hit him!"

An order was an order. Mahmud straightened up and took a vicious swipe at me. I'd seen his muscles tense, and as he swung his arm, I stepped inside its arc. In the fluid move developed in the *Shura* drill, I thrust my forearm out to skew the axe aside, and using Mahmud's own momentum, tossed him over me. He landed hard and lay there stunned, but though he'd be a single bruise from scapulae to sacrum, he wasn't really hurt. His eyes looked blank, however, and his mouth was hanging open. A *mashlool* Jew had thrown him, and he simply couldn't believe it.

What now, I wondered? Would the silent watchers jeopardize their jobs and jump me? Then someone laughed, and one by one, the others joined him. I reached for Mahmud's hand to help him up and salved his pride by saying, "It's just a trick."

One thing about the *M'silmin*—they enjoy a joke. Mahmud's grin was back in place when he responded, "It's lucky all *Y'hud* can't do that trick."

With wide-eyed innocence I answered, "But they can. Any one of us can handle *that*"—dismissing "that" as if it were the *least* of our accomplishments. And with "that" I left the roof. Mahmud's jaw had dropped again, and no one now was laughing.

When I told the story at a *Shura* meeting, the Chief of Staff applauded. "The stronger they believe we are, the less they'll want to tangle with us." The flaw in that hypothesis was that it only worked when both sides were about in balance. All by himself, Mahmud might not ever pounce upon a Jew again, but with a hundred Mahmuds at his side, he wouldn't hesitate a moment.

Once the masses were involved, they could wipe us out by weight of numbers. Therefore it was vital to contain each minor clash before it escalated. For the kind of swift, conclusive action that required, each defense position had to be as self-sufficient and autonomous as we could make it. Every six-man unit had its own supply of weapons and was also trained to cope with casualties until we could evacuate them to the sector's first-aid station.

I finished writing the official first-aid manual, which differed from the norm in that we couldn't rely on having the conventional equipment. With ordinary items either scarce or nonexistent, I scrounged around for substitutes and emphasized improvisation. Our motto was "Make Up, Make Do."

We tested out the most unorthodox materials and methods, and those that worked—however weird they might appear—were added to the arsenal. A certain brand of inexpensive *arak,* for example, externally applied, suppressed infection even better than some costly antiseptics. *Arak* was obtainable. So were ashes, and ashes didn't cost at all. With a match and almost anything inflammable, we had a substance that would staunch a wound and also help to sterilize it. And the morning papers, rolled up tight, made rigid splints.

Though the load I bore was heavier than ever now, I hardly felt it. I found that I could call upon a sort of psychic second wind, and I knew with certainty that I could handle almost anything that happened by—except, perhaps, a "proper" Jewish girl.

In the spring of 1947, something happened half a world away that was to end this period of almost perfect equanimity. When I saw the morning paper, I knew at once that we were in for trouble.

In April, tired of pouring men and money into Palestine, the British had decided to depart. When they laid aside the Mandate, the United Nations had assumed responsibility. The news today was that a U.N. delegation would determine a partition plan. To Arabs everywhere, the word "partition" was the foulest of profanities, and here it was, in headlines.

Every story printed in our papers was a vicious smear, indicting all the Western powers, with the worst of calumnies reserved, as always, for the Zionists. The radio was even more inflammatory than the press, and as the hatreds heated up, the most optimistic Jews grew apprehensive.

In this poisoned atmosphere, the government suddenly announced a census, at which nervousness increased throughout the Quarter. Could it be a cover-up for something else, and if so, what? When "Instructions for Iraqi Citizens" were issued, anxiety became alarm, and the *Shura* issued stand-by orders.

On census day, schools and offices were closed. Empty, the familiar streets were strangely alien, and the stillness shrieked a warning. In Baghdad, silence was unnatural and ominous.

According to the government's instructions, we were to stay at home and open up our houses to the civil servants, and the armed policemen, who would come to question us. When Baba heard the knock, he waved us out of sight before he answered. Though the *Shura* had decided on a "wait-and-see" approach, I had my own small handgun tucked inside my shirt, and from where I stood, I could, if necessary, pick off anyone who threatened us.

As three men entered, I sized them up and raised my arm—but just to clap my hand across my mouth to keep from laughing. They were scrawny little mice of men, lower-level, ill-paid government employees entrusted with an unaccustomed chore and very ill at ease with it. One look at Baba and they withered even more. I felt a fool, but only for an instant. Better to be slightly paranoid than unprepared.

The census ended with nothing having happened to concern us, but the propaganda didn't stop; there were daily diatribes against partition and almost daily demonstrations. Students, encouraged by the government, were starting to participate in greater numbers. Though matriculants in other colleges were on the march, my classmates seemed immune to agitation. Perhaps it was the British influence that still held sway, or possibly the lack of time to spare. Medicine demanded more than other disciplines. For whatever reason, the school appeared to be an island of serenity in troubled waters.

Unlike the *shamash,* where we'd argued endlessly on social issues, exchanges here revolved entirely around the school curriculum. Since politics was never mentioned by the *M'silmin,* I stupidly assumed a lack of interest. Undoubtedly they leaned in one direction or another, but not enough, I thought, to make a difference. Take Rashid, for example.

After twenty months of close companionship, I couldn't have told you his political affiliation, or even if he had one. I knew his aims in life, the degree of his commitment to Islam (he was a good but not obsessive *Mislim*), and all about his amorous adventures, but we didn't discuss the "isms" of the world at large. It wasn't that we ducked them; they simply didn't come up in conversation.

Early on, and much to my chagrin, I'd discovered I had more rapport with Rashid than with any of the Jewish students. Propinquity had much to do with it, of course. While initially attracted to each other, it's doubtful that our friendship would have flourished in the atmosphere outside the school, where Jews and Arabs went their separate ways. In anatomy, however, we worked together, close as twins, for hours every week. In doing so, both of us became aware of matching skills and a similarity of interests. Intellectually alike, we soon began to see each other outside class.

Along with love of surgery, we shared a passion for the movies, and as often as we could would catch one. Since Jews and Arabs almost never paired off on the social scene, everyone who saw us stared, most of them with ill-concealed hostility. Since I was dark and Rashid fair, half the time our Jewish and/or Arab critics would be cursing at a coreligionist. It didn't matter much; each group was equally unhappy at the sight of us.

While the Jews at school expressed the same displeasure, they'd always start by saying that they liked Rashid, "but after all, he *is* an Arab. He's like all the rest." The first few times, I lost my temper. Rashid, I snapped, was only like Rashid. He was unique, an individual before he was an Arab. How many *M'silmin* ranked as high in class as he did? They admitted he was bright, obliging, and apparently unbiased, "but. . . ."

When I found that we were going round in circles, repeating all the same clichés each time we argued, I put an end to it by using Rashid's own technique. Next time they started up, I shrugged my shoulders, smiled angelically, and said the magic words, "Everyone's entitled to his own opinion." After that, I locked my lips—for me, like capping a volcano—and pretty soon, the lectures stopped.

I wondered if Rashid was having similar disputes with *Mislim* students. His preference for me would hardly be endearing to his Arab peers. The truth was, he had few to choose from in the *Mislim* group. The handful who could match him mentally were either socially inept or too prosaic to appreciate his style. Rashid took a zesty view of life and loved to laugh, but much that struck him funny wasn't understood at all by fellow Arabs.

With me, as well, it had started as a friendship by default. In the usual course, I'd have looked among the Jews for my companions, but the nine in class had proved to be a painful disappointment. In suggesting, at the start of school, that all of us should work together, I'd been trying to prevent our being swallowed in a sea of Arabs. However, as I soon discovered, the majority of Jewish students were *anxious* to efface themselves—afraid of being Jewish in the midst of *M'silmin.* Instead of fighting for the right to their identity, they turned their backs on it. Because their absence would have been conspicuous, some even went to classes on the highest Holy Days. It wasn't "wise," they said, to call undue attention to themselves, and thought me too outspoken to be safe.

Conversely, Rashid respected me for being forthright, and we spoke about religion as openly and easily as of the school or movies. And yet, in twenty months of talking, we hadn't tackled politics. We hadn't even tiptoed on the outer fringes. Therefore, I was unprepared when, apropos of nothing, Rashid asked me what my feelings were about partition. Startled as I was, I had to smile. He spoke exactly as he used his scalpel. There was nothing tentative about his style; here, too, he cut, without equivocation, to the core. I responded as decisively. "I'm for it."

It was Rashid's turn to be surprised. What shook him up was not so much my pro-partition stance as my candor in expressing it. When he admitted, "I didn't think you'd be so frank," I answered that I wouldn't have been with anyone but him. "If I didn't trust you," I went on, "would I put myself completely in your power?"

The moment it was said, my blood went icy. I'd just confessed myself to be a Zionist, and if he turned me in, he'd be a hero.

During this exchange, we'd both stopped walking. Striding off again, Rashid changed the subject as abruptly as he'd brought it up, and we carried on as if the conversation hadn't happened. In the depths of me, where I thought I'd buried it forever—insofar as Rashid was involved—the same old question quickened into life again.

Was he like the others?

No matter how I tried, I couldn't suppress it. I'd been honest with Rashid, but not myself. As much as I might like a *Mislim,* I'd never wholly trust one.

22

The summer of 1947 marked the start of still another odd alliance, even more illogical than my relationship with Rashid. As medical commander of the *Shura,* I'd have listened avidly to anyone who'd doctored partisans in Yugoslavia, but Professor Rogers also reached me on another plane.

I liked his whole approach, and responded to his air of self-assurance; he inspired confidence, if not affection. Gruff and blunt, he talked precisely to his point, making no attempt to entertain us, and when he finished, all the necessary facts had been abstracted, undimmed by nonessentials. He knew where he was going and he *got* there. Some professors hemmed and hawed and hedged so much, a patient would have died before they settled on a diagnosis. Those, less certain of themselves, were easier on us. Rogers was by far the most demanding, and thus for me, the most impressive of the college staff. In turn, of course, I wanted him to be impressed with me.

Toward that end, and to give myself a running start, I planned to study him in action this entire summer. By the fall semester, when our class in Surgery would start with Rogers, I'd be miles ahead of all the others.

Instead of going for my morning swim the first day of the summer recess, I sneaked up to the observation deck above the operating theatre. In order to avoid the most oppressive heat, surgery began at 6 A.M. or even earlier, and almost no one was around. I thought I'd find the deck deserted, and I did.

According to the schedule, the first procedure was an appendectomy, to be followed by an amputation at the thigh in a case of osteosarcoma. As I settled down to watch, Rogers caught a glimpse of me and asked what I was up to. When I said I was a student, he arched his brows and turned away.

On his next appearance—a splenectomy—I was there again. Though I saw him start on catching sight of me, he made no comment. As the days went on, he grew accustomed to my presence; on occasion, he'd acknowledge it, but just by nodding briefly. Soon, however, he was looking up on entering the theatre to see if I was there. At first he must have thought I'd come to flatter him, but as we ushered in our second month together, he began to understand. Surgery obsessed me.

After watching him at work, I'd go home and hit the books, reading and rereading the description of the surgery I'd just observed until I had it down by heart. At night, imagining my desk to be an operating table, complete, of course, with patient, I pantomimed each move he'd made.

I was minutes late one morning, and much to my annoyance, Rogers had already entered. As I ducked into the deck, hoping I was unobserved, I heard him bark, "Where have you been? Get down here now." When I didn't obey at once—because I couldn't believe my ears—he shouted up, "I said get *down* here! You won't learn much from way up there."

Gowned and masked and throbbing with excitement, I stood the proper viewing distance from the table, leaning forward and listening intently to his running commentary. Occasionally, to test my knowledge of anatomy, he'd ask a question, grunting his approval when I answered it correctly.

The next time he was scheduled for surgery, I climbed upstairs, as usual, to Observation, and Rogers yelled impatiently, "What's wrong with you? I want you *here,*" jabbing toward the floor beside him. From that day on, I went directly to the theatre.

One morning, with the patient on the table and already under anaesthetic, Rogers glared at me and asked with even more than his habitual asperity, "Are you waiting for a formal invitation? Can't you see that my assistant hasn't come?"

Was he telling me to take his place? Booming "Well?" he left no doubt about it. On the roster for the day, this was marked up as an appendectomy. I reached for my *k'tibeh* and offered up a silent "Thanks"; an appendectomy "belonged" to the assistant, as did all the easier procedures. In a minute, I'd be operating!

With Rogers' "Don't be tentative" impelling me, I made my première incision in a living person, and if I had the slightest qualm, that first firm stroke excised it. Rogers stood beside me, guiding every move, and buttressed both by his instructions and the text imprinted on my mind (I could see it on my inner eyelids if I shut them), I felt fully in command. Only when the final sutures were in place did I see, to my amazement, that my gown and pants were soaked with sweat. I'd felt so calm and cool! All Rogers said was "Not too bad." From him, it was the headiest of praise.

Though the lightning never struck again—thereafter, having suffered Rogers' wrath, the assistant was in place when I arrived—from that day on, I always walked him to his office after surgery. At the threshold, as I turned to leave, he'd sometimes ask me in for tea and talk about the morning's cases. I was careful not to overstep the bounds, of course, aware that, as a student, I merely served as audience. Students weren't equals.

In time, on finding that we shared an interest outside medicine, we moved to something more like friendship. Both of us collected stamps. I'd inherited the hobby when S'hak, the original philatelist, concluded it was too much trouble. The collection was impressive, in the main because of Baba's plumbing business. Among his clients were the best hotels in Baghdad, those frequented by foreigners, and I suspected that he bribed the maids to sift their waste for envelopes from all the world.

At first a simple pleasure, collecting had become a bridge. Between collectors, I discovered, there aren't any barriers of age or status. When discussing stamps, Rogers was surprisingly loquacious, and we spoke as peers.

At the start of the semester, I couldn't resist revealing my experience in surgery to David and the others, and all but one reacted with the right degree of awe. Samara made a face and snorted, "I bet he doesn't know you're Jewish." I assumed that it was envy speaking, but the boys affirmed that Rogers had a reputation as an anti-Semite. If true, I figured that I'd better find out fast, while each of us could still back off from closer contact.

I'd ask him outright, I decided, the same brusque way he queried us. The starkness of my question shocked him, but he shook his head in vehement denial. "Once I had a bad experience with someone who just happened to be Jewish," he explained, "and that's all there is to *that.*"

Though entirely convinced of his sincerity, I couldn't help thinking that if all the boys had heard about it, he must have spoken of the incident a lot, always mentioning the man was Jewish. Had the fellow been an Anabaptist or a Roman Catholic, would Rogers have alluded to his faith at all? But all I said was that it didn't take much to get such stories started. Rogers looked abashed; he knew he'd been rebuked without my making it unpleasantly explicit, and what might have poisoned our relationship instead improved it.

In terms of personal fulfillment, this period would have to rank among the richest of my life. With partition in the wind, however, the world outside of school looked less auspicious with each passing moment. The rumblings grew ever louder as a grim new phase got underway and gathered force.

No decision had as yet been reached, but cries for *jihad* were already rising, and recruitment for a Holy War had started in a dozen Arab countries. A bonus fund for volunteers had been established in Iraq; along with pleasing Allah, a holy warrior would also be financially rewarded for signing up to fight *Y'hud* in Palestine.

To meet the monetary quota, the government imposed a heavy levy on the Jewish merchants—and *only* on the Jewish merchants. Iraqi Jews were made to pay the *M'silmin* who would march away to murder other Jews. Since refusal to contribute was considered evidence of Zionism, and Zionism had been made a major crime, there wasn't any way around the edict.

That summer, the last before abandoning the Mandate, the British also dealt the Jews a dirty blow. Ostensibly to keep the peace, they closed the routes to Palestine; somehow, though, the Arabs on *jihad* got through, and only Jews were turned back at the border. More or less our life preservers in Iraq, the English were, as ever, our enemies in *Eretz Yisrael.*

In July, we learned about the *Exodus,* a small converted ferry boat used to carry refugees from France. Off the coast of Palestine, British troops had boarded it by force. With three Jews dead and a hundred others wounded, British Foreign Secretary Ernest Bevin ordered all the rest returned to France. Once there, 4500 refugees refused to disembark. British troops with clubs "encouraged" them to leave the transport, and pried loose at last, they were packed right back to Germany.

In August, though, we'd had a little needed laugh. In spite of Englishmen and Arabs, some Iraqi Jewish emigrants had reached the Holy Land. They'd flown there—and from Baghdad's busy airport. Cleared for takeoff, a chartered plane obtained by bribing an official, had taxied to the far end of the runway, swung around, and idled in the normal manner. No one saw the door swing open or the men who slipped inside. Our *shaliyach* had been among them.

As for me, I wasn't going anywhere but school and *Shura* meetings. My life was spent in study, except for tending to a small and strictly private "practice" on the side.

Naturally, my mother sang the praises of her student-son, and that's how the injections started. Calcium injections had become a craze among Iraqi Jewish women, inducing, as they did, a "healthy" flush. In the ghetto, they were lining up for shots like kids for candy.

My mother's bragging brought a friend of hers to see me. She didn't like her doctor; would I do the job? With Nana's pride in me at stake, I said I would, but only as a favor. After that, I had the two of them acclaiming me, and women started showing up, their calcium in hand, demanding that I "do" them. (No doctor kept a stock of pharmaceuticals. If a woman wanted ten injections, her physician would prescribe for that amount, and the patient would obtain it from the pharmacy herself.)

Friends of friends began to come because I had the best equipment to be found in Baghdad, and could slip my sharper needles in with more finesse than most. If I "shot" a woman once, she'd stay for the entire series. I soon grew quite blasé about my sideline, and I hardly ever blushed at all on looking at an unfamiliar female.

Violet, though, was something else again. The others, like my mother, were mostly middle-aged and anything but sensuous, but Violet was under twenty and a blooming, sexy beauty. Even so, it wasn't her appearance that unsettled me as much as what I knew about her situation.

It was common knowledge in the Quarter that her wealthy husband, who was older than her father, had been impotent for years before he found her. The gossips said he'd checked out every girl the ghetto offered and had finally selected her as best endowed to rouse his dormant passions. And if anyone could do it. . . .

I knew my neck was red, and my cheeks began to burn when she said that she was here to see the doctor. Explaining, as I always did, that I was still a student, I attempted to dissuade her, but she was in the hall before I could forestall her. If she was so determined to receive a shot, I thought I'd better get the calcium in—and Violet out—as quickly as I could. Her husband was supposed to be insanely jealous. With that in mind, I hurried her upstairs. In my "office," I asked her for the packet, but she hadn't come for an injection. Not of calcium, at any rate.

"I want you to examine me," she stated, while starting to disrobe. I kept saying that I wasn't qualified, but by the time I pulled myself together, she was down to bra and panties of some pink and silky stuff. Standing to the rear of her to hide my fiery face, I gripped her hands and stopped the strip. Though extremely well-developed, Violet wasn't very tall, so even from behind, I had an unobstructed view. Till then, the only underwear I'd ever seen was home-made shapeless cotton, so, not surprisingly, I stared. Off guard, I let my arms relax. Before I had a hint of her intention, she'd taken both my hands to hold against her lower belly. As she took a backward step and snuggled into me, she murmured, "Something's wrong down there."

Everything was wrong. Too late, I understood that marriage hadn't helped her husband, and what Violet sought was help from me. God knows, I knew about frustration—and was learning more each minute that she leaned on me! I felt sorry for us both, but not sufficiently to risk my soul—and maybe skin. Sleeping with a single woman would be sin enough, but this would be adultery, more heinous still.

I snatched my burning hands away and heard her laugh.

"So you're another one who can't do anything for me. I might as well go home."

In my confusion, harking back to what I'd said before, I answered, "I'm not qualified." She laughed again, a hard, dry laugh that held no trace of humor.

"I'm afraid you're not."

With that, she slid away as quickly as she'd come. She'd carried off a false impression, and I couldn't correct it. What *could* she think, except that I was ignorant or scared. She might even think I was unable. It wouldn't occur to her that anyone who wanted to, and could have, *wouldn't.* At least I *hoped* I wouldn't, but what if she came back? To protect myself, I let my "practice" lapse. At my behest, Nana spread the word. Her son the "Doctor" wouldn't be seeing anyone; his time was otherwise engaged.

By October 1947, as serious debates about partition started at the U.N. in New York, there were daily demonstrations at the other schools in Baghdad. Though our students weren't marching in the streets as yet, they met informally, and often, to protest. Notices of such assemblies weren't posted, but by word of mouth every *Mislim* was informed. Without Rashid, I wouldn't have known about these sessions, but since the auditorium was open to us all, I saw to it that all the Jews attended. For once we were agreed. In order to protect ourselves, we had to be aware of what our Arab peers were planning.

On this single subject of partition, the Left and Right were clearly in accord. While most of those we sat among were ardent Nationalists, the Communist contingent, even though illegal, was openly in evidence, carrying signs and shouting slogans only slightly edited for the occasion. The Jewish Communists alone were quiet. England, the United States—all who seemed supportive of partition—all were vilified in equal measure. I'd read the same denunciations every morning now for months, but here at school, and from my fellow students, every word had fifty times the hurtful impact. "Jew," I noticed, was never once enunciated. The "swine" were always Zionists, but when "Zionist" was said, I also noticed that the speaker always focused on a Jew.

After one such meeting, as Rashid and I were walking to the lab, he asked, "What have you to do with all those Europeans?" referring to the Jewish refugees in Palestine. He honestly didn't understand. While completely satisfied as to the "oneness" of the Arabs—the Islamic nation—the concept of a *Jewish* people, bound together by their God, was wholly inconceivable.

At a later rally, after Russia went on record for partition, the Communists sat silently and signless. Enjoying their embarrassment, I was too bemused to listen to the speakers, but snapped back to attention on hearing a familiar voice. I saw that it was Rashid at the lectern, a taut, intense, inspired Rashid that I'd never seen before. Pointing to the Communists and taunting them, he ridiculed their loyalty to Russia.

"She plotted with the other powers . . . she sold you out . . . she stabbed you in the back . . . she *used* you. . . ."

Attacking them as traitors to Iraq, he derided them as "cats' paws"—Russian pawns. He slid from poking fun to flights of fervent passion, playing to his audience as artfully as any orator I'd ever heard. As his friend, I wanted to applaud. As a Zionist, what followed made me flinch.

"Palestine is Arab. It belongs to us, and we will never rest until we sweep the interlopers out. The sea will swallow them. When the *jihad* starts, we here will offer up our skills to Allah and bind the wounds inflicted by the infidels."

The hall went wild. My heart was in my shoes. As a teammate, I could trust Rashid, but *this* Rashid, this superpatriot, would certainly betray me. In the heat of holy war, even brother turned on brother.

Rashid approached me, flushed with triumph, and I sat up ramrod straight, awaiting his denunciation with as calm an air as I could manage. He clapped me on the shoulder soundly, but instead of the expected accusation, he exclaimed, "You see there? It's a Commie plot! You're just as anti-Communist as we are, so you *can't* support partition!"

He proclaimed it with exuberant relief at my salvation, and saved I was, rescued once again by Rashid's steadfast lack of faith in my conviction. While touched by his solicitude, I wished he wouldn't be quite as open with me in the midst of other *M'silmin.* To anyone who overheard, his emphasis was unmistakable: if I wasn't for partition *now,* it followed that I'd *been* for it.

Right from the start, I shouldn't have been so honest with Rashid, but here I had the perfect opportunity to rectify that error, and again with perfect honesty. I meant it most sincerely when I answered, "I'm not for anything the Communists can offer." Of one thing I was absolutely sure. Whatever Jews aspired to in Palestine, the Communists were after something else entirely. Currently, it served their purpose, whatever it might be, to back partition, but as the saying goes, though I didn't say it to Rashid, "One may choose to eat of honey even if the devil *also* likes to eat of honey."

In late November, with the United Nations getting set to vote, the Iraqi press and radio again increased the propaganda blitz against partition. For factual information, in defiance of the law—it was illegal, both for them to broadcast and for me to listen—I tuned to Kol Ha Haganah from Palestine.

The first hard news I heard was that the Arab League had vowed to fight forever if partition won the vote. To me, that meant the sentiment was swinging in our favor, but when I smacked my fist in satisfaction, Baba glared at me and shook his head. "There'll be a bloodbath," he predicted.

Although he'd been to Palestine and lived among its people, I felt confident enough to argue. The League, I said, was bluffing for the sake of saving face. They were fanatics, but they weren't fools; they had to know they couldn't win against the world. They'd try intimidation and issue calls to arms, and probably there'd be some skirmishes, but once they blew off steam, I said, they'd start to fade away. After all, the Arabs couldn't begin to occupy the vast amounts of territory they already owned. Baba didn't respond, except to shake his head again as if amazed by my naiveté.

At midnight, Baghdad time, as the United Nations cast its ballots in New York, Kol Ha Haganah reported forces on alert in every Jewish settlement. The announcer's voice had sounded crisp and soldierly, but now it slowed and deepened.

"Our people are in danger. If the U.N. votes partition, the Arabs promise war. If it goes against us, they'll have won, and they'll celebrate by killing settlers. In either case, we're ready for them."

The radio went silent and I reached to switch it off, but the broadcast hadn't ended. There were three words more. "Pray for us."

I lay awake long after station sign-off. When Baba and the Haganah agreed, I knew that it was time to worry. Along with overall concern, Evlene was also on my mind again. The sky was lightening before I fell into a twitchy sleep.

Since the papers would have gone to press before the final vote was tallied, I wasn't in a tearing rush to see them. The radio was useless too. Except on Fridays, and during coups and other state occasions, Baghdad didn't go on the air till 5 P.M., and there was nothing on the shortwave bands but static. Unless the *Shura* had some way of getting word, I wouldn't know where we stood until that evening.

Logy from my short and unrefreshing sleep, I started late for school and shot right by the newsstand. Half a block beyond it, doubting what I thought I'd seen, I doubled back. The streamer *did* say EXTRA! An edition had been printed in the middle of the night, and the headline on it read, VOLUNTEER TODAY TO FIGHT THE ZIONIST STATE.

Resolution 181 was history. Partition had been passed.

23

At school, the students milled around the auditorium, ignoring classes, and the new Dean, himself an Arab, decided to allow us out to demonstrate. If the others marched en masse, the Jews, as members of the student body, would have to march along with them. The school was government-supported, and students were expected to support the government.

Even if I'd had a choice, I would have wanted to be on the street, checking out the temper of the city for myself. It was likely to be chancy, though. If anyone suspected me of sympathizing with partition, I could find myself in trouble.

From several rows away, just as if he'd read my mind, Rashid caught my eye and made a sweeping motion toward himself, mouthing, "March with me." His impassioned speech against the Reds had given him such special status, I'd be more than safe beside him. I'd be his *dhimmi,* his protected one. The word popped up, unsummoned, and my stomach lurched. However, Rashid hadn't said it, and I despised myself for being so unfair to him. Now, as always in the past, he was acting out of friendship, but still the tiny doubt persisted.

The march was loud but peaceful, as were all the other demonstrations taking place that day. Except for larger crowds and more police patrolling them, it wasn't any different from a pre-partition protest. On reporting in to *Shura,* I found that all observers were agreed; no alert was necessary.

On the following Friday, the Islamic Sabbath, when Radio Baghdad broadcast morning services from major mosques, I tuned in idly, betting with myself about the topic of the sermon. As expected, it was *jihad.* If an Arab stubbed his *toe* these days, he hollered "Holy War!"

I switched the sermon off, but before the sound had faded, something new about these stale old denunciations struck me. Today, the mullah hadn't damned the Zionists. Instead, at every juncture he'd said "Jew." The "Jews" must be destroyed in *jihad.* "Kill the infidel! Allah will reward you with a seat in Heaven!"

It no longer mattered whether one was in or outside Palestine, pro-Zionist, or passionate opponent. The mullah's choice of words made every Jew the enemy. To the faithful, no distinctions now existed, if, indeed, they ever had.

Next morning, in the locker room at school, the change in atmosphere was evident at once. At my appearance the excited babble of the Arab students ended as abruptly as a bubble bursts. While Rashid's greeting was as warm as ever, I heard him say he'd see the others after school. The boys that he'd been talking to were mediocre students, some close to flunking out, and all they shared with Rashid was identity as Arabs. Today, apparently, it was enough.

As we soon discovered, the sermon had been just the curtain raiser for a big recruitment drive. Overnight, ARAB LIBERATION ARMY posters plastered Baghdad, and, orchestrated by the government, the media and mosques began a series of appeals geared to the entire gamut of emotions. Religion, . . . hatred, . . . pride, . . . pan-Arabism, . . . lust, . . . and greed. Officially the army was aloof from this enlistment effort, but any soldier who desired to do so was allowed to switch allegiance to the Arab Liberation Army.

The majority of *mujahaden*—fighters in *jihad*—were motivated solely by religious fervor, and the opportunity to slaughter "enemies of Islam" was enough inducement. For the less fanatic there were little extras, like the cash collected from Iraqi Jews and the Jewish women waiting helplessly in Palestine, whom they could rape at will on winning back the land. They were also promised that their raids on Jewish settlements would make them rich.

In the middle of *Muharram,* almost half the city was already in a fevered state, and I suspected that the Ministry had timed its drive to take advantage of the annual frenzy. Commemorating the assassination of Muhammad's grandsons twelve centuries ago, the ten days of *Muharram* saw the Shi'ites go insane. The most hyperorthodox of all the *M'silmin,* the Shi'ites whipped themselves . . . with very real substantial whips . . . into a rabid, seething orgy of religion. On the last three days, their fervor burst all bounds. On public thoroughfares, they scarified themselves with swords and beat their arms and backs with iron chains, howling loudly all the while, but in passion rather than in pain. They didn't seem aware at all of shredded flesh and flowing blood.

Such delirium could all too easily be redirected, and on the tenth day of *Muharram,* a Jew with any shred of sense stayed out of sight of Shi'ites. In the Shi'ite code, "unclean" Jews contaminate by touch, so even in the best of moods, they didn't condone a contact. At *Muharram,* the slightest brush with one of us could detonate a total war.

Despite the overall excitement, to say nothing of the bonuses and ballyhoo, just about a thousand men signed up to fight. The smallness of the figure would have cheered me more if fewer of my countrymen had been involved on higher levels of the "holy war." More Syrians, by far, had volunteered, but an Iraqi general was training them, and another of our generals was Chief Commander of the A.L.A. The notorious Kawukji, also an Iraqi and known for his pro-Nazi stance, was Field Commander. And in Cairo, Saleh

Jabr, the head of the Iraqi government, had served as spearhead of the Arab intervention. With so much input by Iraqi *M'silmin,* the question wasn't *whether* Jews would be affected in Iraq, but rather when and how.

Under Ministry control, the media disseminated daily lies about the progress of the war in Palestine. Grim enough in print, on radio the situation sounded even more disastrous. Announcers didn't merely read the doctored news; they gloated over every Jewish death, and jeered at the *Y'hud* "who flinched and cried like women as our brave defenders of the faith descended on them." All figures were inflated. The death of any single soldier became the snuffing out of an entire settlement. On the day a load of dynamite exploded in Jerusalem, killing fifteen people, the radio reported that a thousand Jews were blown to bits.

Soon the trickle back began. The *mujahaden,* having sworn to fight the infidels forever, excused their flight by claiming that the Jews encountered in the Holy Land were more than mortal. Fearsome tales of eight-foot demons out of hell, accompanied by superhuman, fire-breathing females, circulated in the city's streets and coffeehouses.

The brother of one of Baba's workmen had participated in a raid with twenty other *mujahaden,* and he, too, had a tale to tell. As he related it, unaware of Baba in the background, the village they descended on had been deserted except for one young woman. When they headed toward her, joyously intent on rape, she'd screeched in some unholy tongue—Hebrew, I assumed—at which the hills and trees erupted men. He alone was left alive, left deliberately, he said, to serve as warning to his fellow Arabs. They'd tattooed him with a Jewish Star, he told his gaping audience, and taken him across the border, promising to shoot him in the back if he so much as turned his head to see the last of Palestine.

Baba saw the fellow roll his sleeve to show the crudely rendered star—all five uneven points of it. He'd clearly pricked the skin himself to lend some credence to his story. Happily for him, his listeners had never seen a *Magen David,* so they didn't know that Jewish Stars have *six* points.

With minor variations, this fictional account became a staple of returning Arabs. At market, overhearing bits of it, our lips would twitch, trying to suppress our smiles, but I wondered what we'd have to pay for such a minor pleasure. Every telling stirred up greater animosity among the *M'silmin.* Powerless, the Jews might be endured, but Jewish victories demanded vengeance on any Jew available.

To contravene these stories of defeat, the government increased its propaganda output. Repeatedly, we heard and read the "sacred pledge" of Azzam Pasha, Secretary General of the Arab League:

"This will be a war of total and complete extermination, a momentous massacre like nothing seen on earth since the Crusades!"

On radio this was always followed by a blast of martial music and reports of ever-greater Arab triumphs. In the ghetto, dependent on official statements for the news, the gloom was almost tangible. Convinced another Holocaust was taking place in Palestine and helpless to prevent it, Iraqi Jews were saying prayers and shaking in their shoes. Every time the Ministry announced, "Another hundred of the enemy have perished," the people in the streets appeared to shrink a little more.

As a nightly listener to broadcasts by the Haganah, I had access to more accurate accounts. If I could only pass the truth along—that Jews in Palestine were fighting back and winning battles—at the very least, it would lessen the abject despair that now prevailed. It might even stiffen up Iraqi Jewish spines if we ever had to fight.

I brought a plan to Yoav, currently the *Shura* Chief of Staff, and on gaining his approval, got to work on it that very evening. Every night, from that night on, I wrote down every word I heard on Kol Ha Haganah, and early in the morning, at a predetermined place, I passed the notes to Yoav. Once a week, digested down to its essentials and run off on a mimeo machine, our "paper" was delivered to the *Shura* and the *T'nu'ah.* Each member of a cell received as many copies as he thought he could distribute safely. With a thousand in the *Shura,* and ten times more, including youth squads, in the underground, we blanketed Baghdadi Jews.

Morale improved so visibly, it almost scared us. Anyone at all observant would have to ask himself why spirits in the Quarter had so quickly lifted. Although we'd given strict instructions that everyone destroy his paper after reading it, we sat on pins and needles for the first few weeks, afraid that one would fall into unfriendly hands. As Yoav said, however, "Fear makes people very careful." Not a sheet was ever seen by Arab eyes.

"Yesterday, January 15, 1948, Prime Minister Saleh Jabr of Iraq and Foreign Minister Ernest Bevin of Great Britain signed a treaty at Portsmouth to replace the present treaty between our two countries."

Since I always stayed up late to study and to monitor the shortwave stations, I got the shocking news the night before it burst upon the populace. As inflammatory as partition, this apparently prosaic message might well incite the country to explode. Undoubtedly, that's why Jabr had opted to disclose the signing on this late-night newscast, when just a handful would be up to hear of it. By tomorrow, there'd be troops in place to put down any show of insurrection.

The old Anglo-Iraqi Treaty of Alliance still had years to run, but Nationalists and Communists alike were living for its final day when we'd be "free of foreign domination." Finding that another treaty had been secretly arrived at would almost certainly precipitate a full-scale conflict. "Foreign domination" was the only area on which all factions were agreed. They wouldn't even wait to hear the treaty terms; all they wanted was the British out. Most British troops were, in fact, already out. Only RAF detachments were still at Shuaiba and Habbaniyah, guarding the Iraqi oil fields against encroachment by the Russians, but even these, though operating in Iraqi interests, were opposed.

The more I thought about the probabilities inherent in this pact, the more appalled I was. Instead of fairly passive activists, comparatively few in number, parading with their placards, this could mean a real and rampant outburst by an outraged people.

All else aside, the timing of the treaty was about as bad as it could be. Not only was the war boom over, but locust plagues and scanty winter harvests had dramatically reduced our food stocks. Three million *fellahin* were close to starving, and the middle class was barely managing because of runaway inflation. Everyone, for once, was equally unhappy.

If nothing else, the influx from the lowlands should have given pause to those in power. Every spring, thousands of the rural families that farmed the land around us swarmed into the outskirts of the city to escape the floods. Every vacant lot was dotted with their makeshift shanties. For weeks, until the swollen Tigris fell, they squatted uncomplainingly in squalor, eking out a bare existence on whatever they had brought along. Since they stayed together out of sight of most of us, no one paid them much attention, least of all the government.

This year, though, with every lot already overfilled with crowded hovels, the *fellahin* were still arriving, and instead of merely seeking shelter, they were here this year demanding help. Although the peasants should have blamed the sheikhs—fewer than a thousand sheikhs owned two-thirds of Iraq—their enmity had skillfully been steered away from those, their real oppressors, and toward the English. They believed whole-heartedly that foreigners alone had bled the country. Throw the British out and all their troubles would be over. What would happen, then, when these believers learned their government had once again made treaty with the English?

In an early morning phone call before I left for school, the *Shura* Chief informed me that, at 9 A.M., the High Command would meet at my house. In the meantime, I was to monitor the mood at school. Arriving at the locker room a little late, I found myself alone; on a hunch, I headed for the auditorium. Before I reached it, I could hear the hum of many hundred voices, and the overflow of what appeared to be the total student body was eddying outside the too-small hall. Classes had been cancelled, and rumors flew about activities at other colleges. The law and architecture students were said to be en route already, headed for the Ministry to show their wrath.

In the auditorium, far down in front, a solemn-faced Rashid was conferring with the other leading activists; even from a distance, I could see that there was disagreement. Squirming close enough to signal him, I indicated that I'd meet him in the corridor.

There, with greater ease than I'd expected, I convinced him that our school should stay aloof. Like me, he thought there might be shooting. I argued that we ought to act like doctors; we'd be needed by the wounded. I should have guessed he'd be receptive. Whatever Rashid's other interests, for him as much as me, medicine was first and foremost.

Huddled once again with the decision makers for the student body, he winked at me to tell me that the College wouldn't march. Mission done, I headed home. The Ministry was on my way, and from every corner of the city, streams of people were converging on it. When they merged, the mob would be the biggest ever seen in Baghdad.

I made it to the house only minutes in advance of the Command Staff. All seven, I told Nana, had come from Khanakin, the oil center in the north; they'd been in Baghdad on a short vacation, I explained, and were stranded here because the streets between the ghetto and the station were impassable. I'd invited them to stay, I said, until the crowd dispersed. It was Nana who suggested that they call their families to reassure them. I could have kissed her. We'd been wondering what ruse to use for phoning all the outposts.

Fortunately, the calls had been completed before my father and my brother S'hak unexpectedly arrived at ten. Businesses were shutting down all over town. Baba said the mob was growing bigger by the minute and beginning to act ugly. Outside the house, endless waves of people washed toward Rashid Street, intermixing at the corner with the current flowing north. For a pleasant change, a hostile horde was heading off *away* from us. We knew, however, how easily a crowd could be diverted, and when *M'silmin* marched, no matter where or why, we were well-advised to keep a constant vigil. Since the Ministry was certain to be ringed with troops, and the British weren't reachable at all, the pent-up rage might seek another outlet. All too often, it was spent on us.

Tides had turned before, and the government was expert at manipulating masses. The Iraqi leadership had always used the Jews to take the pressure off itself. The *jihad,* for example, had been artfully employed to draw attention from the treaty talks. Whipped to frenzy over Holy War, who would notice what was happening at Portsmouth Harbor?

Once the document was signed and sealed, Jabr thought the public would accept it. From the roof, where I'd taken the Command Staff for some private conversation, we could see how truly awesomely he'd erred.

At 4 P.M., we heard some random shots. At five, the radio announced that all the students had withdrawn. An hour later, there were shots again, these not scattered as before, but fired, as by snapped command, in systematic fusillades. The radio began to blare out military marches, and at 8 P.M., the expected dictate was delivered.

"Martial law has been declared. Groups of more than five will be forcibly disbanded. Anyone inciting riot will be shot."

Word filtered through by phone that several students had been shot already. One of the deceased had been a member of the League to Combat Zionism, front for the illegal Reds. Next day, we learned exactly how he died—and also that he'd been a Jew.

The man who now lay dead—a Communist and anti-Zionist—had supposedly continued marching after he'd been told to halt, and an overwrought policeman had blown his head half-off, screaming as he squeezed the trigger, *"Ibn'lkalb! Yehudi nijis! Sahyuni nijis!"* Son of a dog, filthy Jew, filthy Zionist.

Communism hadn't entered into it. He'd been killed because he was a

Jew, but because he was a Communist, his final words had been "Long live Arab Palestine."

Even when a Jew was anti-Zionist, even when he cheered the *M'silmin* in their holy war, he wasn't safe. This single death, however, was an isolated incident, and *Shura* felt the heat was off us. Temporarily, at any rate, Palestine had been displaced by Portsmouth.

For the next few days, the city seethed and smoldered. Then, on January 26, fifteen students died in further demonstrations, and Baghdad boiled over. Fearing for his life, Jabr resigned and fled to Cairo; his patron, Nuri, who'd been heavily involved in negotiating with the British, left hurriedly for Beirut. On January 31, a proclamation by the new Prime Minister informed us that our government had reconsidered; it wouldn't ratify the Portsmouth Treaty.

The people had achieved a victory, or so they thought. In point of fact, the treaty had been rather beneficial, but Iraq was on its own now, and now that all the foreigners were leaving, the marchers would expect improvement in their lives, as promised for so many years by so many of their lying leaders. When everything remained the same, and children still went hungry, another surge of rage would sweep them.

As I looked ahead, my pessimism mounted. Without a treaty to protest, Palestine would once again become the burning issue. And once again, I feared, the government would fuel the fire. It was easier to feed a hate than fill three million stomachs.

24

For the next six weeks, the city was at peace, the papers printed news of sorts instead of purely propaganda, and Baba said that business was improving every day. With elections close at hand, attention turned from Palestine to Parliament, and as for Holy War, I hardly heard the *jihad* mentioned. In spite of all, however, my instincts still insisted that we stay alert. Alone among the High Command, I couldn't loosen up and let myself enjoy life day by day.

Both the *Shura* and the *T'nu'ah* were becoming lax. With partition won, the *sh'lichim,* recently arrived from Palestine, were overly complacent. Coming, as they had, from bloody battlefields, Baghdad looked to them like Shangri-la. Strangers to the city, they could only see the surface, and the surface was serene.

Our trips outside the city, planned so we could practice shooting, were turning into little more than pleasant picnics. Our cells of six, restricted security, had been expanding; already some had escalated to as many as a dozen members. When I protested to Gidon, the new commander of the *Shura,* he patted me paternally and told me not to worry, sounding quite a bit like Baba.

The air of calm seemed even eerier to me when weighed against the war in *Eretz Yisrael*—for war it was, though still officially described in terms of individual attacks. By now, the roads between the major cities had been blocked, and many convoys had been cut to ribbons. In the Negev, the isolated *kibbutzim* were savagely assailed.

Theoretically the keepers of the peace until their Mandate ended, the British didn't interfere with such assaults. In truth, they aided them by turning over outposts to the Arabs as they left. Had I still retained a spark of admiration for the English, the nightly newscasts of the Haganah would now have snuffed it out. With every move the British made, the situation of the settlers worsened.

After much discussion at the General Assembly, the British had decided that the date of their departure would be August 1, 1948. Weeks later, in the interests of their Arab clients, they revised the time to May 15. By accelerating their evacuation, they left the Jews in Palestine with ten weeks less to lay in stores and arms against the coming conflict.

Everyone was well aware that full-scale war was in the offing, and the British were determined that the Arabs were to win it. A Jewish victory would mean commercial losses for the English, but more than money was involved. Foreign Secretary Bevin had declared a personal vendetta. Never fond of Jews, he'd been foaming at the mouth for months; the Jews, he raged, had schemed against him in achieving the partition. The Germans, he informed the world, had taken lessons in atrocities from Jews.

Under his explicit orders, the ban on Jewish immigration was ruthlessly maintained until the day the troops departed. Most of those refused admittance were survivors of the death camps. Palestinian accounts in British banks were frozen when partition was effected; almost all was Jewish money, made unavailable by this decree for waging a defense.

Hunted down by British troops, civilian-soldiers of the Haganah were stripped of weapons. At the same time they disarmed the Jews, the British sold a vast array of weaponry to Arab states. British army installations in strategic spots in Palestine were either sold or simply given over to the Arabs, accompanied by all the "secret" details of withdrawal. This enabled them to occupy the posts immediately upon evacuation by the English, thus maintaining pressure on the Jewish settlements without a moment's pause. By the end of March, the British were predicting that the Jews were finished . . . this while English troops were still in Palestine, still pledged to keep the peace.

On April 7, some *happy* news was broadcast from Jerusalem. The Haganah had captured Kastel. A natural fortress, 2500 feet above the only roadway, Kastel commanded access to Jerusalem. The Mufti's men entrenched there had been clobbering the convoys, and with nothing getting through, the Jews were starving in the city. The battle had been fierce, and in the fight, the terse report continued, the nephew of the Mufti had been killed.

My pencil faltered and every vestige of my pleasure vanished. Reaction of the Arabs to Husseini's death would be volcanic. Even if he hadn't been related to the Mufti, his own position as a leader of the Arab Liberation Army would assure their rage. The only area of doubt was in the form and the ferocity of their reprisals.

The answer wasn't long in coming. The following day, the Iraqi government declared a week of mourning, and a silent state of war against Iraqi Jews began. There weren't any edicts or announcements, but suddenly there weren't any jobs for Jews within the Civil Service. Then, for any trumped-up reason, those Jews already holding jobs were fired. Next, without announcing it, came confiscation of incoming mail. It was weeks before we realized that anything addressed to Palestine was also intercepted.

While tightening our operation and restoring former safety measures, the *Shura* also fattened up its bribe fund and cast about for more informers. Any minor functionary might be useful. We already had a great variety of contacts, but we needed ears in every agency of government. Had we, for instance, known about the intercepted mails earlier, we might have saved my father's partner from a prison term.

In the middle of the night, their favorite time to call, the C.I.D. had come to question him about some money that he'd sent to Palestine. "To finance the Zionists," they bellowed, but Haguli answered that he'd just repaid a debt. "I owed the money to a relative," he told them. "All you have to do is read the letter." Of course they had the letter, and the money too, but both had been "mislaid."

Without allowing him to waken anyone or call a lawyer, they hustled him away and held him incommunicado till the time of trial; in the meantime, the papers publicized his "treason." The trial itself was such a blatant fraud that even anti-Semites were surprised. In the Quarter, though, we understood. The whole procedure—and the ten-year sentence—had been carefully designed to cow us. What it said was "Jews, beware! We can cut you down at will."

The message came through loud and clear, and Haguli was too close to home for comfort. Baba also wrote to relatives in Palestine. However, in destroying the defendant's alibi, the C.I.D. had shown us how to circumvent such "trials." After checking out the postal system and seeing how it worked, the *Shura* crossed some crucial palms with silver, and sacks of mail, which could have sent more Jews to jail, were forever "lost." It was a fact of life in Baghdad, and a godsend to the underground, that someone could be bribed at every level.

The government used money as a weapon too. When applying for a passport for a trip outside Iraq, Jews had always been required to deposit tidy sums. Should they fail to return, the cash was forfeit. In 1936, fifty *dinars* were demanded. By 1946, it was a thousand. Now another increase was announced: ten thousand *dinars.* That served as well as walls and guns to keep Iraqi Jews from leaving; should permission, by some chance, be granted, no one could afford to go.

While Jews couldn't leave the country, they were disappearing from the city. The vanishings began in May. A man would meet a friend, stroll with him, exchange a little gossip, and some days later learn he'd been the last to see him. Somewhere on the street he'd ceased to be.

At a special meeting of the High Command, we pieced the incidents together and discovered that in every case the disappearances had taken place on Saturday—*Shabbat.*

On a Saturday, observant Jews were on the streets for just two reasons. They were either heading for the synagogue or coming home from services; dissimilar in every other way, all they had in common was the Star of David, engraved on every prayer book and embroidered on each shawl case.

Like writing to a relative in Palestine, the *Magen David* had been made taboo without our being told. The government was playing deadly games again, altering the rules at will—ensuring that we'd overstep them. Unwritten rules. We'd only know we'd broken them when we were seized and sent to jail.

The word went out to every Jewish household that Iraq had redefined this ancient symbol of our faith. Overnight the Star of David had become a sign of Zionism in Iraqi eyes. Its mere possession was proof enough of guilt.

When those who'd disappeared were put on trial, we learned exactly what had happened and how perilous the Star could be. Each of those accused had been carrying his prayer shawl in the customary silk or velvet case, embellished with the *Magen David.* So smoothly as to seem rehearsed—as, indeed, it was—police had stopped each man, snatched his case, accused him of the crime of being Zionist, and swept him off to be arraigned. Under Hitler, Jews had been compelled to wear the Star. Here, it was prohibited to have one. The rules were different, but the game was just the same.

In the synagogues, though sick at heart, we covered up each *Magen David.* In ghetto buildings, all the doorways were examined, and *mezuzahs* bearing Stars were hastily replaced with plain ones. Women hid whatever jewelry they owned on which the emblem was engraved and expunged it from their household items. A family could be convicted by a candlestick.

Crying silently, Nana picked out every stitch she'd sewn on all our prayer shawls, but when the beautifully embroidered Stars had been abolished, their imprints still remained. Streaming tears, she smoothed the silk, trying to eradicate the outlines. When she worked on my *bar mitzvah* shawl, I couldn't bear to watch.

Despite our care, 500 Jews were caught and jailed, and in the course of these arrests, another pattern evidenced itself. The richer men appeared to run the greatest risk of seizure. At sentencing, the mystery was solved. For the crime of being Jewish, the judge imposed both prison terms and fines—fines solely based on what defendants could afford to pay. It was extortion, pure and simple, so why not snatch the wealthiest with most to lose? On *Shabbat,* instead of dressing in their best, Jews began to walk the streets in shabby suits and work shoes.

That spring Nazima's baby was our only joy. I'd set my heart on being uncle to a boy, but since I loved my sister, I pasted on an artificial smile when invited in to view the infant girl. Then I saw my newborn niece and instantly became her slave.

I felt possessive and responsible and, overnight, a good deal more adult. With this baby's birth, I'd suddenly become "the older generation." The world she lived in would be the one we elders left her; at the moment, it was in a mess.

With conditions in Iraq already out of hand, and the day approaching when the British troops would empty out of Palestine, the future of a Jewish infant was, to say the least, uncertain. Whether Zionist or not—and few Iraqi Jews *were* Zionist—my co-religionists had learned the hard way that what went on in Palestine would influence their lives for good or ill.

In early 1948, with hardly 20,000 members, the Haganah was holding out against the whole of Islam. While Jewish victories enraged the Arabs and exposed us to increasing persecution in Iraq, news of them was all that kept our courage up. Though as dangerous to have in one's possession as the Star of David, the demand grew daily for copies of our covert paper.

Sitting in the midnight dark, ear almost *in* the radio, I almost burst with pride that month of May. On the tenth, when Safad fell to Jewish troops, I pounded on a pillow till the feathers flew. The occasion called for fireworks and whoops of joy, but even in the deepest recess of the house, it wasn't safe to risk a beam of light or sound above a snore. The C.I.D. was always on the prowl.

Psychologically, the taking of Safad was of the greatest import, since the Mufti had declared Safad the future capital of Galilee; he'd make Galilee an Arab state. Instead, 10,000 Arabs had been put to flight by 1400 Jews. Four days later, I punched another pillow out of shape. Jaffa had been taken by the Jews.

From Kol Ha Haganah, I heard some news that never would be broadcast here in Baghdad. Eight thousand strong, Iraqi troops had tried to cross the Jordan into Palestine, but they'd been beaten back so badly, they never made another move. Later, Jewish scouts discovered dead Iraqi gunners chained to their artillery to keep the men from fleeing.

As we counted down to May 15, apprehension in the Quarter mounted. Along with it, however, was a breathless expectation. After living with uncertainty so long, on a given date, something *definite* would happen, and whatever happened would be better than this trembling on the brink.

No one knew precisely what the day would bring, but we assumed that when the British Mandate ended, a Jewish state would be proclaimed. Most believed its name would be Judea, but *M'dinat Hay'hudim*—State for Jews—was also in the running. In the last edition of our newssheet before the fateful day, we notified our readers that on May 14, a Friday, at 1 P.M. Iraqi time, "a declaration of extreme importance will be broadcast from Jerusalem." As that time approached, everyone was asked to say the *Shehechianu,* the prayer that ushers in the highest Holy Days. "Blessed art Thou, oh Lord, Who has kept us alive and made us reach this day. . . ."

On May 14, following their normal pattern, most Jews closed their shops at noon and left for home and lunch. Today, however, no one would return at two. The Arabs also listened to the radio, and after 1 P.M., there could be riots.

At the long-awaited moment, groups of Jews were gathered at the sets which drew the strongest signals. We had several neighbors with us, none of whom knew modern Hebrew, so I volunteered to translate. Ben-Gurion began to speak, and because of atmospherics or Arab interference with transmission, the sound was very weak and spotty, but while many words were lost or garbled, the decisive ones were coming through. At 5 P.M. our time, a Jewish state would once again exist! Its name was Israel. The *shofar* sounded, and the interference stopped. The quavering blast was clear and strong, and everyone, I saw, was weeping, including some who'd never been the least concerned with past events in Palestine.

On the radio, they were playing the "Hatikvah," the anthem of the state to be. Explaining what it was, I asked them all to stand. When I began to sing, and Baba heard the kids join in, he understood at once that they were also in the underground. A momentary flicker of the eye in my direction was all that he allowed himself. My father was a realist.

I switched to the Iraqi radio as soon as the "Hatikvah" ended, and music of another sort snapped us to a taut attention. From long experience, we'd learned to dread the drumbeats of a military band. Martial music always introduced important, and generally unpleasant, proclamations. As expected, an official started speaking.

"The glorious Arab armies have entered Palestine at every point."

My lungs constricted, and every face went pasty gray.

"Already our soldiers occupy . . . ," he commenced to name the towns that had been taken by the Arabs, and as he reeled them off, my breath returned. I was chuckling so hard, however, that I almost choked again. The others looked at me as if I'd lost my mind. Every town he mentioned had been Arab to begin with. So far, there hadn't been a single Arab victory.

Relief, though, lasted only till the next announcement.

"Martial law is now in force throughout Iraq."

No longer would there be the *pretense* of a legal process. Under martial law, a Jew could be summarily dispatched. From this day on, life or death for us was solely at the state's discretion.

Despite the chilling edict, as the clock ticked on toward five, our spirits soared. The omens, all agreed, were good for Israel, if not for us. Five o'clock on Friday was a most propitious moment for its birth. Friday, the start of the *Shabbat,* and five, a lucky number. I didn't have the heart to tell them that, in Israel itself, the time would be an hour earlier. Nana, in particular, was happy with the figure five. Each *Shabbat* eve, she lit that many wicks, one for every Father of the faith. This evening, though, with wicks already flickering for Abraham, Isaac, Jacob, Moses, and Aaron, she suddenly decided on another two. As on the highest Holy Days, King David and King Solomon must also be included. She was right, of course.

Israel's rebirth deserved them all—and seven was an even better number.

Once the radio was switched off on a Friday afternoon, ordinarily it stayed off till *Shabbat* was over. On this occasion, Baba looked the other way and let me listen, and he stayed within the sound of it himself.

According to the Baghdad station, Jerusalem was totally surrounded, and Tel Aviv would soon be isolated too. The Egyptian army was advancing from the south, the Arab Legion from the east. Syrian troops were closing on Tiberias, and Safad, the biggest city in the northern Galilee, was threatened once again, this time by the Lebanese. The Iraqi army, along with Arab Legion forces, was moving steadily toward Haifa. Every Jewish stronghold was also being battered from the air.

Allowing for the usual extravagance of Arab speech, and discounting even more because the radio reports were always extra florid, the situation still seemed close to hopeless. And only hours ago, I'd laughed so hard it hurt.

When I spread a map of Palestine, and sketched on it the outlines of the state of Israel, the skinny length of it was scary. The entire population couldn't patrol the crazy borders, much less beat back all the *M'silmin* massed to breach them. If depth was needed for defense, as every strategist I'd ever read insisted, then Israel had been designed for doom. Especially across her middle, narrow as a wasp waist, there wasn't anywhere to go except the sea.

I switched to Kol Jerusalem, the British station, searching for a crumb of comfort, and the first few words provided it. A voice was saying that the station's name was now Kol Israel. At last we had a legal voice.

Briskly and without embellishment, the voice began to give the news. The Haganah had blocked the Syrians before they reached Rosh Pinna. Knowing where Rosh Pinna was—right on the border—I relaxed a bit. They'd been stopped before they really started. In the Negev, although the fighting was described as fierce, we were holding the Egyptians. The "massive" air assault on Tel Aviv, described so vividly in Baghdad Radio's report, had consisted of a single pass. The Egyptian air force would return, however; they'd undoubtedly discovered that the city had no antiaircraft guns.

Jerusalem was ringed completely by the Arab Legion, and in dire straits, and the Legion was entrenched in Lod and Ramle. Laconically the voice reminded us that both had once been British bases. Like so many other installations, these had been delivered into Arab hands.

Accustomed as I was to bombast and flamboyance on Iraqi radio, Kol Israel seemed spare and dry. The bare-bone facts were stated simply and in temperate tones, with no attempt to dramatize events. However, by the middle of the final item, the stoic Voice of Israel was choking with emotion.

Refugees, he said, were pouring onto beaches, dropping to the sand and sobbing as they kissed it. Israelis now controlled the harbor serving Tel Aviv, and ships blockaded by the British, some of them afloat in sheer defiance of the laws of physics, were spilling out their cargo from the death camps. Skeletons, escaped from ovens, danced with joy. Old men and women

wept with happiness at having stayed alive so they could die in *Eretz Yisrael.*
They thought their enemies were all behind them.

25

Since it was Saturday, the shops continued closed, but I was glad to see that just as many Jews as ever were going to the synagogue. Given martial law and the volatility of Arab tempers, I'd half-expected them to hide at home, but while they weren't stopping on the street to gossip, neither were they scuttling along like bugs in fear of being stepped on.

Outside the locker room at school, I started to have qualms, but assuming a facade of confidence I didn't feel, I strode in briskly. Rashid, in a noisy knot of Arab students, was standing at the farthest wall, studying a newly posted map of Palestine. When someone's finger drew the outline of the Jewish state, otherwise not indicated, a derisive roar went up from all the others.

Askari was the first to spot me. A swaggering bully and a rabid anti-Zionist, who also hated Jews in general, he stated loudly that he planned to spend his summer bathing on the beach at Tel Aviv. He was baiting me, of course. "Maybe all of us can go together," I responded.

He deflated like a pricked balloon. If I'd shied and dodged, Askari and the others watching would have seen it as a sign of weakness; like wolves, incited by the smell of blood, they would have closed on me.

Rashid, I saw, had drifted to the outskirts of the group; his face was oddly inexpressive. No animosity, but no approval either. Poor Rashid. He didn't know *what* to think. On the one hand, I'd told him I was pro-partition; on the other, I'd always acted like a loyal citizen. The light touch, the tone I'd taken with Askari, that's how I'd have to handle it. No arguments, no show of special interest in the Jewish state. An Iraqi, what had I to do with Israel? That had to be my attitude.

As I watched, he pressed his lips together, nodded once as if he'd come to a conclusion, and ambled over with a gruesomely salacious story to unfold. Between the two of us, in Rashid's eyes, everything was back to normal.

While school remained a safe retreat, outside of it, existence was in daily doubt. Before the week was over, 3000 Jews had been arrested and shipped without a hearing into limbo. If it hadn't been for Baba's contacts, we wouldn't have heard a word about the camps. Hours away from anywhere, originally selected for their isolation, evacuated British installations had been hastily converted into prison barracks; there was room, we learned, for thousands more of us. In Palestine, where Jewish settlers could have used them for defense, once-British posts were occupied by Arabs. In Iraq, the Arabs used the British camps to keep us in a state of subjugation. There was a certain awful symmetry about it. *Damn* the English! Even in their absence, they were helping those who hated us.

The orders at the start had been to pick up Jewish leaders and the well-to-do, the ones whose summary arrest would be a lesson to the Quarter. At first the aim was to intimidate. Very soon, however, arrests became completely hit-or-miss. Any *Mislim* with a grudge against a Jew could send him to a prison cell. Those whose greed was greater than their malice made a business out of blackmail, extorting money for *refraining* from an accusation. Some tradesmen saw the opportunity to rid themselves of competition and rushed to charge their Jewish counterparts with crimes against the state.

Before this last decree was issued, the legalities that bound us, elastic as they were, related only to religion and political beliefs. Now there weren't any limits, and life assumed the crazy, shifting shapelessness of nightmare. Accusations grew increasingly capricious, and in a case against a Jew, "evidence" was anything an Arab cared to offer. With the wristwatch incident, we discovered just how far the courts had fled from reason.

With very few exceptions, only Jews wore watches. On spotting one that looked expensive, a policeman had approached the owner as if to ask the hour. Once assured the man was Jewish, he relieved him of the timepiece and took him into custody. The watch, he told the judge, contained a tiny wireless; he'd caught the Jew, he claimed, sending military secrets to the Zionists in Palestine. Without examining the "evidence" or asking any questions, the judge pronounced his sentence. The "traitor" went to prison, the watch to the policeman as reward.

When the shock of this had been absorbed, the net effect was strangely beneficial. Who would have thought to worry over something like a watch! It could as plausibly have been a pipe wrench or a pair of pants, and if freedom was dependent on such arbitrary, freakish acts, then worrying was senseless. With recognition that arrests were random, thus impossible to guard against, everyone relaxed a little.

Baba had never lost his cool composure, so I verged on panic when he walked in from the street one morning, crying uncontrollably. Word had swept the market that Jerusalem had fallen to the Arab Legion. Racing to the radio, I was just in time to hear the jubilant announcement. I reminded Baba that they'd boasted falsely in the past, but both of us were well aware that the city had been under seige for many months. We also knew that even the most rabid Arab leaders would shy away from bald-faced lies about Jerusalem. It wasn't simply one more Jewish settlement. Jerusalem belonged to everyone in spirit. For once, the world was watching.

All morning, as more and more exuberant reports were broadcast, we sat in heartsick silence. Slumped, and looking drawn and furrowed, Baba shut his eyes and started fingering his *sibha.* I switched the station off. Everything was over. Two weeks after Israel had been reborn, they'd torn her heart out. And on their Sabbath, as they emphasized in every new announcement. Allah had been good to them. God was with the *M'silmin.*

Out of habit, and too disturbed to settle down and study, I turned the dial to the wavelength of Kol Israel. To my surprise, I got a signal. Through a mushy hum, I heard in Hebrew, ". . . leaving through the Zion Gate."

I lost the sound entirely for precious seconds, then suddenly the voice boomed out, ". . . orderly surrender of the Jewish Quarter." My shout was loud enough to bring the family running from the farthest rooms. "It was the Jewish Quarter, not all Jerusalem," I yelled.

On June 11, the U.N. ordered an immediate cease-fire for a period of thirty days, and as the *M'silmin* were strategically positioned, they complied. When the war resumed, they anticipated early triumph. Rested, well-fed Legion forces would sweep through long-beleaguered, ill-equipped defenders of the city "like a mighty sword through sawdust."

In Baghdad, though the pressure on us lessened somewhat, uneasiness increased within the Quarter. We'd known such interludes too often to misread them; the letup here was merely the civilian version of cease-fire. No one doubted any longer that our fate would be determined by events in Israel.

In the ghetto, sharp divisions made for ugly arguments and deep unrest. Anti-Zionists, silent until now, began to speak up sharply. They hadn't been supporters of partition—why should they suffer for the deeds of others? In the underground, we kept a "can't-be-trusted" list. Not many, though, were that committed to a stance on either side. Most still warred within themselves and suffered for their indecision. Self-preservation pushed them toward the anti-Zionist position, but being Jewish, their hearts went out to other Jews embroiled with the Arabs. And Jerusalem, of course, was ours. That, we *all* agreed on.

On July 6, before the expiration of the truce, Egypt struck illegally at Israel and was repelled. Ten days later, a second halt was ordered by the U.N. Council. In the intervening period, Israeli troops had taken the entire Galilee and Negev and embarked upon the Sinai. Moshe Dayan, a one-eyed colonel, had routed the Iraqi forces from a former British base at Ramle, just eleven miles from Tel Aviv.

Infuriated by the overall advances of the *mashlool* Jews, and especially embarrassed by the sorry showing of Iraqi soldiers, the Iraqi Parliament retaliated with an edict so all-encompassing that every Jew could "legally" be done away with.

Death was now the mandatory sentence for the "treasonous" offense of Zionism, and as defined in this immoral fiat, a Zionist was anyone who thought that Jews should have a homeland—even if he made no effort to achieve that end. And even if he never uttered that belief. A Jew accused of *thinking* of a Jewish state could be convicted.

Not a single Jew remained in Civil Service. Overnight, the few who'd been retained were fired. Our postman, who'd brought the mail since the British Mandate started, was dismissed. His lifework gone, divested of his promised pension, and dependent on the charity of others for his very food, he sank into despondency. Soon, I knew, he'd die, a broken spirit beyond the skill of medicine to save, and as much a victim of the Arab war as any Jewish settler.

Baba was concerned, of course, but not acutely worried for our family.

With all his influential Arab friends, he felt our safety was assured. In July, however, with the seizure of Shafik Adas in Basra, father's confidence began to crumble.

At first, he didn't believe it. No one knowing Shafik would. The Regent stayed with Shafik when he went to Basra, and Adas socialized with all the ministers. The richest Jew in the entire country, Shafik, among his many other interests, served as the exclusive agent for American and British Ford, which meant important foreign contacts to protect him.

If any more was needed to make him absolutely unassailable, Shafik was a caustic and outspoken anti-Zionist. I'd had arguments with him myself. An unequivocal assimilationist, he kept his office open on the Jewish Sabbath, and closed it Friday, when the *M'silmin* worshipped. His older brother, Ibrahim, who lived in Baghdad, even spelled his name the Arab way. Jewish only by the accident of birth, Shafik's position seemed impregnable.

Some months ago, having set his heart on building a palatial mansion for himself in Basra, Shafik had hired Baba as contractor on the job. Then one day—a scorcher in July—a call came in at 5 A.M.; one of father's workmen on the site was on the wire. Shafik, he said, had been arrested. Should they continue with the work? Saying that he'd phone right back because it had to be an error, Baba got to Ibrahim and found him quite composed. A simple mix-up, Ibrahim assured him. It was inconceivable to either one of them that anyone could hold Shafik for longer than it took to reach the Regent.

In record time, however, he was brought to trial by the military, accused not only of upholding Zionism, but of running guns and shipping money into Israel. His attorneys, the four best Arab lawyers in Iraq, were not allowed to speak in his defense. One word, the officer presiding warned, and the four of them would find themselves on trial too.

The witnesses against Adas were also four in number: an unskilled laborer in his employ (who clearly gloried in this golden chance to "get" the boss), a porter, a policeman, and a horse-and-buggy driver. All testified that they had seen Shafik arrange to smuggle armaments and money to the Zionists in Palestine. No one ever said Shafik was stupid, and to win that sort of audience, he'd have had to plot his treason in a public square and send out invitations.

With the outcome predetermined, credibility was unimportant, so the prosecution hadn't even bothered to devise a decent frame-up. Though the "trial" was to take two weeks to squeeze it dry of every drop of propaganda, sentence had been passed on the day his "friends" in government decided to indict him. Sacrificing such a man would serve a double purpose, both pacifying Arabs, angered by the recent routs in Palestine, and paralyzing Jews with fear.

The instant he was taken into custody, the orchestration started; the radio and every paper, regardless of political complexion, insulted and abused Shafik solely on the basis of his race. We rarely heard his name pronounced or saw it printed. He was always called "the Jew," "the Zionist," "the Jewish traitor." There had never been the least uncertainty about the verdict, but not content with hanging him, they also fined him the equivalent of 20 million dollars.

The Regent was required to confirm the sentence, and the country's press, playing out the farce, pretended that reprieve was possible. Front-page stories warned "the traitor could escape the consequences of his evil deeds." Savage editorials, appealing to the blood lust of the mob, insisted that there be no mercy for "the Zionist spy, the serpent in our bosom who betrayed us." The Regent beat his breast about the "perfidy" of one whom he'd embraced—and signed the order. Exultant headlines screamed, THE ZIONIST DIES! Blunter than the rest, the right-wing organ added, DEATH TO ALL THE JEWS!

Baba was completely devastated. His entire way of life had been designed to keep us safe, but if Adas could be killed, then no one was secure. An ambitious man by nature, Baba had deliberately restrained his drive and scaled down his aspirations. For the sake of good relationships with Arab peers, he'd overbid on many contracts that he could have taken, thereby leaving more for *M'silmin.* Because he had a reputation for reliability, he often was awarded work even when his bid was higher; when this occurred, he'd split the job and share it with the Arabs who had lost to him. From the start of his career, instead of squashing competition, he'd always subsidized the other firms' existence. This policy had paid him dividends in peace and quiet on the business scene.

As for the family, Baba had indoctrinated all of us. Since wealthy Jews attracted more attention than was wise, he didn't allow us to be ostentatious in our habits. Our "outside" clothes were casual, our car the kind that any businessman could well afford. Though commanding in appearance, Baba had no arrogance about him, and he never brandished power for the sake of showing he possessed it. When necessary, he still pitched in to lend his laborers a hand. He also lent an ear to all their problems. Universally respected, without a single enemy he knew of, Baba never had a sleepless night until Shafik's arrest.

Stripped of every shred of dignity, Shafik's hanging was designed to be a circus rather than an execution. The site selected was directly opposite his half-built house in Basra. To accommodate the record crowd expected, they'd cleared a mammoth square in front of it, and the night before the big event, the best locations, those closest to the scaffold, were already densely occupied.

By dawn—4 A.M. in summer—the area was packed with happy celebrants and vendors doing splendid business. Whole families had come to see the fun. A carefree, picnic air prevailed, and the freshness of the morning made them ravenous. Having emptied all the baskets brought from home and filled the chinks with sweets and soft drinks from the enterprising vendors, they impatiently awaited the event itself. When the children clamored that they couldn't see, indulgent fathers swung them up and set them on their shoulders.

Look now! See the Jew!

As Shafik dropped, the mob, as one, erupted in a long-protracted shriek of satisfaction. Moments later, claiming that Shafik still lived, the hangman propped the corpse in place and dropped Adas a second time. The second time was even more appreciated. The howl that split the sky was heard by Jews in Basra's ghetto, where they huddled deep within their homes, behind the heavy doors now newly braced with extra iron bars.

To prolong the pleasant outing for his fellow citizens, Shafik was left to hang till 9 A.M. On the following morning, the full front page of every paper in Iraq consisted of a single picture. Shot up close, it showed Shafik swinging by his broken neck, his eyes half-bursting from his head. They hadn't even offered him a blindfold.

On the Sabbath after Shafik's death, every Jew in Baghdad went to services, including some who hadn't seen the inside of a synagogue for years. The prayers that day were desperate, disjointed pleas, and many of the men sat dumb, staring at the Ark unseeingly, their eyes still blinded by the horror of the hanging. Those of Baba's generation looked shrunken in their prayer shawls, as if they'd flinched so often that they'd physically contracted.

The killing, so carefully contrived, had worked exactly as the government intended. The deliberation of the act, its icy inhumanity, was more effective than a frenzied onslaught. Passion could be met with passion, but this cold, machinelike killing killed the spirit. And no one cared. How *could* they care? No one even knew.

Outside Iraq, even coreligionists were largely unaware of us. To the Christian world we were entirely unknown. The pogrom against us seven years ago had gone unnoticed by the Western press. Since then, we'd seen the Jews of Europe almost decimated by the Nazis, also unprotested by the press or other powers.

Still, until Shafik, everyone believed, like Baba, that somehow he and his would be preserved. Broken now, convinced of the futility of any effort, they wouldn't lift a finger in their own defense. I recalled a line from one of last year's lectures: "Extreme despondency often leads to mental apathy and physical inertia." My own community could be a textbook case. In this condition, whole congregations could be led to slaughter.

I wished that I could tell them that an underground existed. If they knew the size and scope of it, the measures we had taken, the defiant life force of their sons and daughters, they might be horrified, but maybe heartened too. At least they'd be aroused, and *something* had to shake them up. It was an aimless train of thought, however. Sworn to secrecy, I couldn't say a word about the *T'nu'ah* or the *Shura.*

I was free to speak for me, though. What I was speculating on might not accomplish anything except invite undue and dangerous attention. Still, someone had to break the silence. In the synagogue today, I'd been praying for a sign of leadership, but not a single word was uttered on the subject uppermost in every mind. Of necessity, I'd have to speak.

I asked my father if he wanted *aliyah;* if not, I said, I'd like to have the honor. Each Saturday, seven *aliyot* were open to the congregation; until now, I'd never bid to "rise and read the Torah." *Aliyot* were usually employed to honor loved ones or events of great significance in Jewish life such as births, *bar mitzvahs,* and betrothals. Though taken by surprise, Baba told the usher that "the Doctor" wished to read.

At the *teba* on which the Torah rested, I inhaled deeply to control my trembling. Soaked with sweat before I even reached the rostrum, I plunged right in without a pause. If I stopped to say the customary prayer, I'd lose the drive to do what must be done.

"I have taken *aliyah,*" I started, "in memory of someone who has died. . . ."

Since commemoration was a common reason, no one stirred until I added, "someone who has died for the heinous crime of being Jewish."

Heads snapped up in unison; I heard the hissing sound of breath sucked sharply in.

"The Dreyfus trial gave us Herzl," I continued. "Let the Shafik Adas hanging make each of us a Herzl."

After the initial gasp of disbelief, the synagogue was silent as a tomb. Throughout the prayer I said for the deceased and my reading of a passage from the Torah, not a soul had stirred. Baba's face was ashen when I left the *teba* to rejoin him. Under current law, my speech could send me to the gallows. And—as I realized only after sitting down among them—I'd implicated the entire congregation. If they didn't denounce me, their silence would be deemed agreement, and sympathy with such remarks was treason.

As I hunched back in my seat, Baba held me to him briefly in a hard and loving hug. "Someone had to say it," he admitted, echoing my very argument, but he stopped himself before "Why you?" escaped him. He already knew the answer, and it shamed him for his abject generation. Shafik's death had truly made these Jews *mashlool.*

When the service ended, some friends of father's nodded at me as they hurried by, but many kept their eyes averted. All I'd done, apparently, was compromise myself and make myself an outcast. They were afraid of contact and contamination, and the way they picked up speed in order to escape me provoked a slight hysteria. I ought to wear a little bell, I thought, like ancient lepers. Then they could scatter when they heard me coming. I'd never been as pessimistic as I was that night. These men had given up already.

To my astonishment and joy, I was shown to be in utter error. Much to Baba's consternation, in the weeks that followed, almost everyone who'd heard me, and some who'd only heard *about* me, came to call, and whatever pretext each employed was soon abandoned. Everyone expressed the wish to go to Israel. Like me, each thought the others were incapable of action, so each one kept his private counsel and came alone to seek advice on leaving.

By now, of course, the borders had been sealed like safes, but insofar as secrecy permitted, I encouraged them with hints about the exit plans in preparation. Although the *Shura* was investigating emigration via Persia, no routes had been approved to date.

Shafik's death in August also cast a shadow over school that fall. The Jewish students, some of whom had shied away from me for being much too Jewish, approached me at the start of the semester. Apparently every family in Baghdad had had a friend or relative sitting in our synagogue that Saturday. Looking rather rueful and subdued, they asked if I would teach them Hebrew, and twice a week I stole the time to lead a class. They soaked the language up like sponges, much faster than my former pupils. The smartest of the smart to start with, they also found the dangling body of the late Shafik a strong incentive. What a thesis one could make of that. *Excellence Through Apprehension:* an explanation of why Jews do well in school. They're *scared* into an education.

In Palestine, following a long cease-fire, fighting started up once more in mid-October and continued until January 7, when the U.N. intervened again to halt it. On February 24, 1949, Israel and Egypt signed an armistice agreement. One month later, Lebanon withdrew from active combat, and in early April, Jordan also ended its aggression. No final peace was made, no pacts or treaties sealed, but to all intents and purposes, the Jews had won the *jihad.* By midspring 1949, only Syria, Saudi Arabia, and Iraq were technically at war with Israel.

By a tacit understanding, Rashid and I avoided speaking of the issue and were almost as before. In school and out, external tensions eased as fighting slowed and stopped. While martial law continued and all restrictions that applied to Jews remained in force, the harshest concentration once again was on the Communists. Life for us seemed almost normal.

The calm, of course, was superficial. Latent hatreds boiled just beneath the surface, seeping through a thousand tiny fissures. We felt its heat in all the small indignities of daily living and stoically endured it as the price of peace. Up to a point.

Mahmud Abdul Wajih was one of those who seethed with unremitting enmity, and anything could cause it to erupt. An instructor in the Clinic on Internal Medicine, he was undersized and scrawny, also greasy skinned and prone to pustules. With liver-lips and lashless eyes, his ears and nostrils sprouting mossy mats of hair, he was as loathsome in his manner as he looked—a man-shaped sac of venom. Poisonous toward everyone, he saved his worst for Jewish students.

In the middle of a discourse on a medication recently discovered by a doctor in a Cairo clinic, he stopped to point at me and yell, "You there! What are you grinning at? You think that only Jewish doctors can discover things!"

I'd been smiling at a joke my seatmate told me, but before I could explain, he screeched, "You Jews are all alike. You . . . ." He trailed off into a strident squeal of disbelief as I rose and left the room. The Jew was being insubordinate! He'd been less than subtle many times before, but this display was too offensive and overt to bear.

Four other Jews were in the clinic overseen by Wajih. Deciding that we couldn't continue, we requested that he let us transfer to another unit. Almost frothing at the mouth, as friends informed us, he went to Dr. Witri, the College Dean, ranting that "the Jews are in rebellion."

Fatherly and mild-mannered, the Arab Dean was fond of students and had always acted fairly. Therefore, when he said we'd have to stay with Wajih since we only had a few weeks left of clinic service, we assented unprotestingly.

Leaving lab that evening, on the run as always, I heard Rashid call to me to wait. Catching up to me, he shook his head impatiently and asked, "Why didn't you *tell* me you were having trouble? Wajih and I are both Nationalists. I could have smoothed it over."

I was mystified. The trouble *had* been taken care of. When I told him not to be concerned, he shook his head again and led me to the posted reprimand signed by Dr. Witri; it listed all the "troublemakers" who had asked to be transferred. The original was in the College files and would forever blot my heretofore unblemished record. And one more incident of any sort would mean expulsion. No matter what a Wajih said or did, we'd have to take it. The Dean himself had been afraid to buck an active Rightist, even in so small a matter. If Dr. *Witri* was intimidated, I knew that we were overdue for further aggravation.

"No matter what, I have to finish school."

I thought I'd said it to myself, but Rashid nodded.

"Next time, come to me."

26

All summer, working in the clinics, I exercised meticulous control, as careful of my every move as if I walked among a million land mines. One false step and I could be expelled—for me, about the same as being blown to bits. I couldn't conceive of any life for me except in medicine. My first concern, beyond my safety, was finishing my education, and my major fear was that a Wajih might succeed in stopping me. Then, too, the government could always kick me out of school. If loyal civil servants had lost their "lifetime" jobs, I couldn't assume that Jewish students were exempt from such injustice. The likelihood was that they'd just forgotten our existence, but tomorrow we could come to their attention. In view of the unrest again in evidence among the *M'silmin,* they'd soon be needing further scapegoats.

Food shortages were stirring up the *fellaheen.* In the cities, unemployment was heading toward an all-time high, and the downward dip in the economy had turned into a headlong dive. Parliament was powerless to halt it, and with the British gone, Jews, as usual, would be the scapegoats. In the Quarter, many others had arrived at that conclusion, and requests to emigrate were doubling almost daily. Led by *Shura* members, a small but steadily increasing number trickled toward the east and into Persia. From Teheran, the refugees were flown to Israel. That escape was closed to me, however. I still had one more year of school, and as yet Israel had no facilities for teaching medicine.

On an impulse, I addressed a letter to the University of Geneva, asking for admission data and including details of my academic background. The response was quick and comforting; if my scholastic records were as I described, they'd be happy to accept me. Naturally, they wanted copies of the records; when that request sank in, the glow began to fade. By bribery I might be able to obtain them since the secretary to the Dean was known to be a mercenary man. However, he also had an appetite for flattery that scared me off. He might decide to be a hero and denounce me; I'd need such transcripts only if I planned to skip the country.

He knew that as a Jew, I'd never get an exit visa, so I'd have to leave illegally, and if the secretary tipped the C.I.D., they could stumble onto *Shura.* Even if I did receive permission, there was still the stiff deposit demanded by the government. With business bad, Baba's cash was low; everybody owed him, and 10,000 *dinars* would be hard to borrow. More troubling still, by putting up the money for my passport, he'd be suspect.

If I pursued the matter, I'd impoverish the family and also place them in a perilous position. I could add the new Swiss stamp to my collection, but otherwise the letter to Geneva was a total loss. Until I won my sheepskin, I'd have to stay in Baghdad.

When you haven't any options, I discovered, it's easier to toe the line. In school that fall, I didn't deviate an inch on either side of it. I was obedient but not obsequious, industrious but not excessively intense, intelligent but not so innovative as to ruffle feathers. Avoiding conflict while still maintaining marks and self-respect became a game, and I was getting very good at it.

In class and lab and clinic, I hung on the instructor's every word; if he looked at me, my eyes were on him. There were no asides to schoolmates, no more smiles, nothing to be misconstrued or used maliciously against me. When called on, I responded swiftly and succinctly, careful to confine myself to textbook answers. Debate was dangerous, and overzealousness made enemies. If I disagreed with anything a teacher said, I swallowed hard and kept my mouth shut; my face didn't show my feelings either. I'd practiced, and perfected, an expression of sincere respect. They could have made a cast of me and called it "Perfect Pupil."

On the whole, life was simpler in the *Shura,* where the idea was to go *entirely* unnoticed. Take now, for instance. As prearranged, Gidon, the new commander, would stroll by any second. Two boys with books, walking briskly off to school, could chatter all they wished without awakening suspicion, but standing on the street alone invited undue interest. However, Gidon didn't appear, and by *Shura* law, I had to leave. Five minutes was the longest we could linger.

At school I found a message from my mother: "An emergency. Call home at once." Outside the ghetto, we used "emergency" to mean "arrest," and I raced to place the call, convinced that Gidon had been caught. Through a flood of tears, Nana told me otherwise. Aunt Gourgia and her husband had been taken to the hospital, she said. Agitated as she was, she'd remembered to say "hospital" and hang up quickly. "Hospital" was also code; translation, "stationhouse." We cut our conversations short because the phones were government-controlled and often tapped. And we used them cautiously, concealing what we really meant in commonplace allusions.

As neighbors told the story, the police had come at one that morning. They'd pounded on the door, and happily, Aunt Gourgia got there first. My uncle was a zombie for an hour after waking up, but she always had her wits about her. When they asked for Sion Hinkali, their eldest son, she answered loudly, in pretended anger, that they'd argued, and he wasn't living with them any longer. She thought he'd left the city, but she wasn't sure. Her strident voice awakened Sion, as intended, and he crossed the roof to safety. Aunt Gourjiah didn't know it, but Sion was a *madrich* in the *Shura.* As often happened now, the police had seized the parents when the son escaped them.

I had to get a go-ahead from Gidon before attempting anything to aid my aunt and uncle, but I couldn't reach him anywhere. I couldn't find *any* of his staff, and increasingly alarmed with every failure, I tucked the little Mauser deep inside my sock and set off for the ghetto to investigate.

As I passed the tailor shop, a few doors up from Gidon's home, the old man stopped his sewing and asked if I was heading for the Nahom house. When I said I was, he wagged his finger, warning me to stay away, then signalled me to move in closer to his stool. The *shurta,*" he murmured softly, "they may still be there. They took the mother, but the boys were gone. It was the boys they wanted."

The C.I.D. had had a busy night, and if Gidon's name was known to them, the chances were that mine was too. They might be waiting for me now at home. Nana would be scared to death—literally to death, I thought. With a mental picture of her pressure shooting for the moon, I fled toward Baba's place of business, thinking he could call the house or send a man around.

I circled warily, prepared to dart off into one of the bazaars if the *mamzerim* had Baba's place staked out. For a fugitive, his shop was in the best location in the whole of Baghdad, surrounded as it was by all the major sprawling markets. I could lose myself in seconds if the need arose. Everything looked normal, though, and all the news was good. No one had been asking for me, either here or at the house, and my aunt and uncle had already been released. Aunt Gourjia could outbrazen anybody. For hours on end, she'd wailed that her son was never home and she hadn't known what he was up to "since the boy left school."

I laughed in sheer relief, but Baba was unsmiling. Fifty homes, he told me, had been raided in the night. "Fifty that I *know* about," he emphasized. It was hardly more than ten o'clock, and more undoubtedly would be reported as the day went on. At Hanoon, he said, the word was that the sweep was on for members of a Zionist group, the *Tannua'h.*

Father's eyes were fixed on me, watching for a sign of recognition. *Tannua'h* was Arabic for *T'nu'ah,* but I didn't blink. My stomach flipped and my intestines braided into one big knob, but my face remained a blank. If Baba didn't know for sure, why saddle him with one more worry?

Before I had a chance to ask, he beat me to the answer. "They found out from a Communist. A Jewish boy. He told them in return for his release." When Baba mentioned the informer's name, a flicker must have given me away. "You know the boy." It was a statement, not a question, but seeing I was lost in thought, he didn't pursue it.

Sai'id. Prior to his Communist conversion, he'd been in the *T'nu'ah,* but I couldn't remember when he'd been recruited. Was it when security was loose, when cells were larger? How many of us had he met and offered up, and how many like him had we harbored? It would be the height of irony if purging Communists resulted in destruction of the underground.

Baba broke the silence, and I came to with a start.

"You *are* involved with all of this, aren't you?"

I may have erred in thinking that I heard an underlying hint of pride in Baba's voice, but I had no doubt whatever that the disapproval of the past was missing. When he said, "Don't tell your mother," it was like an affirmation of my manhood.

On mentioning my mother, he remembered that she'd called and left a message for me. "Another of your 'classmates' is waiting at the house," he said. "She's been there quite awhile." And even now, there weren't any questions. Now silence was my father's way of showing faith in me.

Awaiting me at home I found a youngster, Osa's age. A courier for both the *Shura* and the *T'nu'ah,* she'd been sent by staff to brief me. The original informer, a sixteen-year-old Communist, was acquainted only with the members of his six-man cell, and in the three years since he'd left the underground, the name of one had faded from his memory. The other four had been arrested. By a stroke of luck, the four had never left the cell for leadership positions, so they knew no other names. However, when the older brother of a captured boy inquired for him at the C.I.D., Sai'id had recognized him as an underground official.

When an hour passed without the brother's reappearing, his waiting friends reported to the *T'nu'ah.* By bribery and infiltration, we discovered that the C.I.D. was torturing the older brother. Beatings hadn't broken him, nor had the slivers pounded underneath his nails, so they trussed him up, attached him to a generator, and sent electric currents screaming through his testicles. In time, of course, he cracked, and Gidon's name was one of those that he'd revealed.

Some, like Gidon, had escaped the roundup, but many *madrichim* were now in custody, undergoing torture as I listened to the courier. More names would certainly be shocked and savaged out of them, followed by another sweep and further sessions with the generator, ad infinitum. Eventually they'd have us all.

The courier concluded with instructions from the High Command. A committee had been formed to deal with the emergency, and I was on it. All rosters were to be destroyed. Sanctuaries were to be established for the fugitives. Every code word was to be replaced. We had to work on the assumption that the C.I.D. knew everything. An enlarged and completely new communications network was a prime requirement. We wouldn't meet again until the word went out that we were once again secure. Except for the committee, everyone was on his own.

Other couriers, the youngster said, were spreading through the ghetto, and everyone they reached would pass the information on to all his normal contacts.

Unbelievably, in light of all the running back and forth, it wasn't even noon when I walked the courier out the door and strode off in the opposite direction, toward the College. I couldn't afford to take too many cuts. Not only would my absence be observed, perhaps exciting speculation, but missing one too many classes meant expulsion.

My mind was whirling like a disconnected cogwheel, and just as unproductively. Of the thousand racing thoughts, none meshed for more than seconds. With enormous effort, I regained control, and proceeded to examine my predicament as clinically as I'd approach a patient.

The analysis was not exactly cheering. In a medically equivalent condition, I'd have to tell a patient he was terminal. Even now, someone might be naming me. With every raid on Jewish homes, and every tortured howl, the probability of being hunted down grew greater. It seemed to me that I knew everyone in both the *T'nu'ah* and the *Shura.* I'd been in at the beginning, enlisting others, attending endless meetings, teaching countless Hebrew classes, conducting an infinity of first-aid courses. Thousands could describe me, even if they didn't know my real identity.

The underground aside, I'd spoken up at school and openly declared myself in synagogue. To save himself, or spare his family, any congregant could point a finger. And I had to add Rashid to the inventory of conceivable informers. Foolishly, I'd let a *Mislim* know my sentiments. No matter where I looked, I was open to attack.

When I laid it out like that, logically, I knew I had no choices. All that I could do was continue doing what I'd always done—until the day I was identified. Any change in my routine, especially at school, would stir up curiosity, and curiosity invited questions. As long as I remained unknown to the authorities, school and home were just as safe as any other place that I could think of.

At the College, like a grain of sand in the Sahara, I could lose myself among the other students. At home, if I had to run, our roof gave access to a half a dozen different streets. My "wolf-dog" was another argument for staying put. Lassie looked the part now, and could keep a minimum of three men occupied until I got away. As a last resort, I had my Mauser and my own supply of ammunition. If I couldn't make it off the roof, some others would remain with me. Forever.

In school, immersed in trauma and disease, and at the hospital among the sick and dying, life, eerily enough, was normal. In the "healthy" world outside, the nightly sweeps and torturing continued. As the pace of raids accelerated, more boys were leaving home, often only steps ahead of C.I.D. enforcers. On the pretext that I had to study even later than before and didn't want to bother S'hak (who still believed that "all of this" would soon blow over), I moved into the storage room and started sleeping in my clothes.

Despite my subterfuges, Nana knew that something ominous was hanging over me. Every evening now, I noticed, she lit a special wick. The *kindeel,* she said, was for Ezekiel, "my" Prophet, the one for whom she'd named me.

"Yitshifa'alak."

He would bow before the Lord and plead for my protection, she assured me. If anyone had influence, it was Ezekiel, and Nana's confidence was comforting. Like a cool hand on a fevered brow, it eased although it couldn't cure. At the very least, the act enabled her to get some sleep. Until enlisting him, I'd heard her moving restlessly around the house for half the night.

As of today, however, we'd *all* be losing sleep. Our Emergency Committee had finally agreed on tactics. The second that the C.I.D. arrived, everyone within the house was to rush up to the roof and yell for help. "Really yell," I stressed in passing on instructions to the family. "We're telling the entire ghetto. We want to know who goes and when. No one will be sneaked away in silence any longer."

"But they'll still be taken," Baba shrugged.

"We'll scream so loudly that no one can ignore it. No one—and that includes Kh'dhouri."

At Kh'dhouri's name, dawn began to break in Baba's eyes. *Hakham* Sason Kh'dhouri, who controlled the Jewish Council, was so adamantly anti-Zionist that even after Shafik's hanging, he wouldn't admit that all our difficulties didn't stem from Zionism. As the representative of our community (though only candidates approved by the Iraqi government could be elected), he had a certain leverage, which he hadn't so far exercized on our behalf. Even the most militant Iraqi rulers were influenced, to some extent, by world opinion, and through Jews in the Diaspora, Kh'dhouri was in constant touch with other countries. Therefore, when the first arrests had taken place, we'd sent a *shaliyach* to ask for his assistance. Kh'dhouri's answer was that these arrests involved a handful of illegal Zionists, not Jews as such, and he emphatically refused to intervene.

If the entire *Quarter* made an uproar when their homes were raided, we figured that he'd have to pay attention, but though the theory was sound enough, the scheme had no effect, either on Kh'dhouri or the C.I.D. In ten days' time, 700 Jews were taken, most of them the blameless relatives of undergrounders who'd escaped. By October 22, we had a hundred members of the *T'nu'ah* and the *Shura* safely hidden and the jails were full of Jews who'd never even heard of us. Still Kh'dhouri said that only Zionists had been affected.

To show him how the Quarter felt and pressure him to protest to the government, the Emergency Committee ordered two of us to organize a token rally. As originally designed, it was to be a rather small assembly, just enough to fill the area on which the Jewish Council building fronted. Situated as it was at the intersection of Rashid and Kambar Ali streets, thousands could have been accommodated, but with everybody running scared, we'd only asked some fifty activists to show themselves, inviting each to bring along a friend or two. The fear of congregating openly was so engrained, all that we could hope for was a token turnout.

Long before the hour appointed, we began to realize how much we'd underestimated the communal anger. By 8 A.M., so many had already gathered, I knew we had momentum going for a massive demonstration. And the more that came, the more that would come. Acting on the knowledge that a crowd attracted crowds, I dashed across the street to the entrance of the Textile Market. Composed of several hundred little stores, the market was the largest source of Jews in the vicinity. Zigzagging back and forth, informing everyone in earshot, and asking them to join the demonstration, I could hear the iron shutters banging down behind me as the owners shut up shop.

When the dimensions of their exodus became apparent, and I recalled the Regent's daily ritual, a strategy occurred to me. He'd be driving from the palace to the Parliament—right down Rashid Street—and I rushed to head the merchants and their workers off. I knew exactly where I wanted them and when.

I barely made it; the Regent's motorcycle escort was already passing. Since we'd kept our crowd confined to Kambar Ali Street, the escort signalled to the motorcade that Rashid Street was clear and the Regent could proceed. As the vehicles approached, I dropped my arm. The market emptied as if I'd swung a sluice gate open, and the textile people streamed into the street, completely blocking it. The Regent's car couldn't move an inch, and I was close enough to see the beads of sweat spring out on Abdul Ilah's forehead. The Regent of Iraq was terrified!

When the police moved in and started breaking up the bottleneck, I slipped into an alleyway and disappeared. I was home and on the phone, reporting to the *T'nu'ah,* before the Regent reached the Parliament and stopped perspiring.

Later in the day we learned that twenty-five protestors had been taken into custody, but all had been released. It would be embarrassing for Arab courts to prosecute a group of Jews for demonstrating peacefully against a Jewish agency.

I was thankful that none of those I'd talked into the streets was taken, though a fine of ten *dinars* was imposed on every merchant in the Textile Market. Though this levy was just another instance of the "legal" looting that was part of Jewish life, I felt responsible. However, coming home that evening, unsuccessfully attempting to restrain a smile, Baba eased my mind; he had a message for me from the textile tradesmen. Tell your son, they'd said, that it was worth a hundred *dinars* to see the *mamzer* sweat."

Within a day, Kh'dhouri's resignation had been tendered and accepted, and a sympathetic Council member took his place. To celebrate the new regime and convince the Council of our unity, the *T'nu'ah* quickly organized a novel show of solidarity. Every Jew was asked to fast for one full day, and on that day, every Jewish shop would shutter. We'd all be in the synagogue, out of sight, annoying no one. Since there wasn't any law against not eating or not making money, even our resourceful C.I.D. could hardly say, "He looks poor . . . he looks hungry. Put the handcuffs on."

With the city's commerce at a standstill, the Council finally spoke up for us. Of course they couldn't criticize the seizure of the Zionists or the right of legal government to make arrests. All that they could do was register a strong objection to the scope and the gestapo style of the early morning sweeps. Little as this was, it seemed to work.

Suddenly, there weren't any raids, and the Council was accepting all the kudos. Though we knew better in the underground, if the "power" of the Council was a comfort to the people of the Quarter, they were welcome to the credit.

Actually, however, it was one American, a famous female journalist, who caused the government to curb itself. We had tipped her to our demonstration, told her how arrests were made, and helped her in her own investigation. On her horrified discovery of torture tactics, she threatened to disseminate the story "in every paper in the world" unless the terror ended. Politically pro-Western, the last thing Abdul Ilah wanted was a blast of bad publicity abroad, so the C.I.D. was ordered to desist.

I used the respite to get out and scout the ghetto. Safe houses for the fleeing *T'nu'ah* members were in short supply, and after school I wore my shoes out searching. One afternoon, having stopped to rest at uncle's coffee shop, I was starting off again when I saw a woman down the street who seemed familiar. The moment that I placed her, I ducked back into uncle's, praying that she hadn't spotted me.

It was Evlene's mother, who'd blamed me with such stridence for her "baby's" flight to Israel. She was smiling now, which is why I hadn't recognized her right away. She was staring straight at me and grinning, an insanely wide and imbecilic smirk! She swooped on toward me like a bird of prey, her talons out to pin me down. The woman was demented. She'd gone mad with grief! I'd trapped myself by backing into uncle's shop, and braced myself to meet the onslaught. When she grabbed my hand and spoke, I understood; she was off her head with happiness.

"Heskel! We just heard! She's married. My baby's married!"

Her baby. My Evlene. I wanted to be stricken, but what hurt the most was that I hardly hurt at all. Evlene and I had shared a tender episode, and the episode was over.

Much more difficult to face than Evlene's loss was the growing likelihood that medicine might also slip away from me. If I had to leave the country now, minus my scholastic records, years of work would go to waste. With transcripts unavailable, Lindsay Rogers was my only hope; he could validate my claim that I'd completed the curriculum with honors.

Long past the student-teacher phase, the two of us were truly friends. Despite the differences in age, religion, ethnic origin, and all the rest, we'd formed a very real attachment to each other. Those very obstacles, in fact, by forcing us to exercise uncommon thought and effort, probably accounted for the strength of our association. And there was something else. Alien to each other at the start, both of us were also alien to the Arab culture. We illustrated a phenomenon I'd often read about and thought contrived—that staple theme of fiction, the ill-matched strangers in a foreign land who ally with each other.

Sometimes we were poles apart, but each discussion ended in consensus and reinforced our strong rapport. Oddly enough, our friendship had been buttressed by the testy words between us at the time the Portsmouth Treaty was inciting riots.

With anti-British feeling running high among the *M'silmin,* police had been assigned to guarantee the safety of the many Englishmen who staffed the school. Rogers was outraged that students might attack their teachers. I was sitting in his office, having just reported to the *Shura* that the streets would be unsafe for Jews and that we'd better mount patrols, and he was pacing back and forth, complaining. The police intruded on his private life; they were an inconvenience. "You students ought to be restricted." He said "you students" once too often, and I heard myself responding sharply, "*I'm* a student. Who's protecting *me?*" I'd never spoken as combatively before, and it startled me as much as it did Rogers.

On seeing his bewildered look, I checked my anger and explained, as to a child, that when Arabs built up rage enough against the British, they generally discharged it at the Jews. "England is a long way off," I pointed out. "They can't loot homes in London, and those of you who live in Baghdad are protected by the government, but they can always get at us."

He'd begun to look abashed, but I was too wound up to end it there. "We've *always* been the safety valve for Britain. Without the Jews, this country would have blown up in your faces." I stopped then, and the silence hung between us.

"I didn't know." And with those three short words, Rogers broke the barrier forever.

His willingness to listen and to learn distinguished him from most adults I'd met. What I thought of as the "stamp example" proved his attitude in this respect. Shortly after the establishment of Israel, I presented him with all my stamps from Palestine, but protesting that he couldn't take so valuable a gift, he held the box out, trying to return them. I clasped my hands behind my back, responding that they weren't worth my liberty or life. At his baffled look, I went on to enlighten him.

He was horrified to hear that anything and everything that had to do with Palestine was deadly dangerous for Jews. When I told him that the cancelled stamps could "prove" that I'd been spying for the "enemy," his eyes went wide. Sounding very English, and somewhat snobbishly amused, he snorted, "How utterly absurd! We collected German stamps all through the war."

I'd responded hotly that nothing was "absurd" if people died of it. His smile had faded, and from that point on, he seemed to understand what being Jewish meant in Baghdad. I was counting on that knowledge now.

Ordinarily, when I wished to see him, I'd rap at Rogers' door; if he was free, he'd ask me in to chat awhile. This was too important, though, for such a casual approach. When I asked him for a firm appointment, he perceived at once that this entailed more than idle talk.

I told him everything, except that I was with the underground—and it wasn't just the oath of secrecy that kept me silent. In Iraq both Jews and Arabs held the firm belief that every foreigner, whatever his profession, was spying on the side. Having firsthand knowledge through the *Shura* that many English merchants were "observing" for the Foreign Office, I was more convinced than most. I'd questioned Rogers once about his being with Intelligence. He'd laughingly denied it, but naturally an agent would. As close as we'd become, if he was an agent, and if he ever had to choose between his feelings and his duty, I'd be afraid to put his friendship to the final test.

As with Rashid, I discovered that I couldn't trust myself entirely to foreign or non-Jewish friends. I could relate to them and truly love them, but trust was always tinged with fear of ultimate betrayal. Jews had been betrayed so often and by such a great diversity of "friends" that everyone was suspect. That tiny seed of doubt, product of the centuries of persecution, was the heaviest of burdens that I had to bear. Someday, perhaps, I'd slough it off. For now, however, Rogers needn't know about the underground.

After listening gravely, he assured me of his willingness to help. "If you have to leave Iraq, write to me at once," he ordered, "and I'll send you what you need." When I began to thank him, he waved my gratitude away. "You've earned your doctorate. You're entitled to it." Thinking we were through, I rose to go, but Rogers motioned me to wait, and scribbling on the back of a prescription blank, he said, "I'm writing my address for you."

His address? The college name would be enough for any mailman in Baghdad, but what Rogers handed me was a long address that ended in "New Zealand."

"It hasn't been announced yet," he informed me, "but I'm leaving at the end of the semester."

First Evlene, then the friends who'd had to flee the country, now my mainstay at the school. One by one, the pillars of my life were disappearing. Soon nothing would be left to cling to. I clutched at the address—a solid rock in the center of a raging maelstrom. Whatever else I lost, I'd salvage medicine.

27

Time was running out. An hour after my leaving Rogers, the *T'nu'ah* warned me that the C.I.D. was searching for a doctor by the name of Hiyyim. Hiyyim was phonetically too close for comfort to my code name, Haim. And since I wore a stethoscope, the tipster had assumed I was a practicing physician. When the registry of doctors failed to reveal a Hiyyim, it might occur to someone that students at the Royal College also used the instrument. Investigation at the school would eventually unearth me. On matriculating at the College, I'd signed in with my first and family names, eliminating Haim Ma-Sha-Allah. However, my middle names were on many other records. Add to that the fact that the Regent could undoubtedly identify me. I'd been near enough to see him sweat, so he'd been near enough to see me smile.

With an active search in progress, I couldn't risk another night at home. The safe house I selected for myself was one of those I'd scouted in the southern part of Baghdad. Our sanctuaries ranged from run-down rabbit warrens in the ghetto to the stately mansions of the *nouveaux riches.* Aside from willingness to aid another Jew and the self-control to keep from asking questions, all our "landlords" had in common was a lack of ties to any Zionist activity. To the C.I.D., no *Yehudi* was above suspicion, but some were more remote from it than others. And those—the last they'd choose to check on—were, naturally, the first we looked to for assistance.

In order to protect our hosts, we provided simple and convincing cover stories for our refugees and never used their names. In case of inquiry, my host would say, for instance, that I'd asked to stay with him until my father's temper simmered down. No, he didn't know the details. The fight had been "a family matter." By sheltering an activist, the owner of a safe house eased the guilt of noninvolvement, but the less he knew, the more he liked it.

School required no decision. Since my absence would attract attention and also put an end to my career, I continued to attend. Unwittingly, the secretary to the Dean assumed the role of early warning system. I told him that my mother was extremely ill and a message might be left for me at any moment, telling me to hurry home. Could I count on him to see that I received it quickly? As I discreetly dropped a *rial* on his desk, he assured me that he'd see to it himself.

"Sinking fast" would mean the C.I.D. was onto me—my cue to exit.

While running scared myself, I still retained responsibility for those I'd stashed away. Waiting to be taken to the border, my cousin Salih and some others had been cooped up for a month or more and were restless to a desperate degree. Salih, in particular, was acting up. His sole companion in the safe house was a deaf and doddering old lady, who was driving him insane with her incessant, senile chatter, and he spoke of breaking out just as if he were in jail.

In some respects, the shelters *were* like prisons. Once identified and on the "wanted" list, fugitives were under orders to remain in place until a plan to quit the country was approved. If the house was small or overcrowded, or often filled with company we couldn't screen, the refugee was faced with even more severe restrictions. For weeks on end, some had lived entirely in storage rooms, without a slit of a window to the world. Apart from members of the household, with whom they had to exercise the utmost caution, I was the only one they saw or spoke to for the length of their seclusion.

Before each round of visits, I'd arm myself with all the latest news about their families and friends, and with ever-less-persuasive promises that they'd be getting out "probably within the week." The truth was that predictions were impossible. The rule was that the high-risk refugees went first, but each arrest would rearrange priorities. From one day to the next, we never knew whose turn it was until the time arrived to hit the trail.

As everyone grew either more obstreperous or more depressed, depending on his personality, I had to make the rounds more often, encouraging and calming them—and cutting into class time. Whenever I requested them to do so, the other Jewish students signed me in and asked no questions. Luckily we registered our own attendance; a roll call by instructors would have done me in.

Sipora was my major worry. A nineteen-year-old *madricha,* she'd been in hiding even longer than Salih and was clearly on the verge of cracking up. Sipora was a nursing student and gregarious by nature. People-oriented and accustomed to activity, she couldn't stand the silence and the sitting still. The walls, she claimed, were closing in on her, and every time I left, she cried a little more hysterically. I began to think she might do something drastic, like diving out a window and shrieking down the street.

All the signs were pointing to an imminent explosion. Slim to start with, she now looked almost anorexic, and from lack of sun and exercise, her skin was white as newly quarried marble. Her face had hollowed, and her eyes, immense in it, were too electrifyingly alive. To many men, she might have been exotically alluring. As a doctor, the main emotion she aroused in me was worry.

She did, however, make me feel important; my visits were the high spots of her life, and unhealthy as it was, I half-enjoyed the whole affair. I tried to tempt her appetite with sweets, and took to spending my allowance on little gifts to ease her boredom, but with every meeting, my departure was a stiffer struggle. She'd cling to me, weeping with her eyes wide open, begging me to stay a while longer.

One day, her back against the door, she swore she'd leave the house alone if I refused to take her out. "Just for an hour or two," she pleaded. Eyes spilling pearls, she said that she was going crazy. Yes, she knew the streets were swarming with police and that they probably had pictures, but she couldn't remain inside another second. With me or without me, she was heading out.

When I said I'd take her to a movie, her face lit up as if I'd pulled a switch. In the dark, wrapped up in a black *abaya,* her features shadowed by the folds of fabric, she ought to go unrecognized. Before I could direct her, she'd dropped her eyes and tucked her chin well in. With head and shoulders bent, she was suddenly a middle-aged, submissive housewife, and I marveled at her acting—until we reached the street. I saw then that it wasn't any act. Outside, she shrank back even deeper into the *abaya,* and the docile stoop became a crouch. She was petrified with fear.

I'd planned on taking her to see my favorite actress, Ingrid Bergman, whose film was showing several blocks away, but instead, I steered her to the nearest theatre. I'd already seen the picture, but I also saw police patrolling. Once seated, she relaxed and the worst, I thought, was over. Getting home again should be a cinch. When the show was over, the audience would empty out in one great stream; the crowd would carry us, submerged in it almost to our doorstep.

In the middle of the sad, romantic movie, with Sipora sobbing happily beside me, the lights went on throughout the theatre, and a male voice commanded that we all stay seated. Sipora gasped and half-rose from her seat. I yanked her back and held her down by force. She heaved spasmodically against me, then collapsed, quiescent in the grip of terror.

To lend support for the encounter soon to come, I put my arm around her shoulders. The contact triggered an idea. The police, I knew, inclined to look on loving couples more salaciously than with suspicion. Whispering, "Don't say a word, no matter what, and we'll get out of this," I pulled her closer, turning her to hide her face.

The *shurta* were walking slowly down the center aisle, scanning everyone on either side. Excellent! If we'd been pointed out, they'd have known precisely where we sat. As the men approached, I started talking to Sipora in the Arab dialect. As stricken as she was, when I hissed at her to giggle, she managed to emit a squeak. A policeman was abreast of us by now, and deciding on a bold attack, I signalled him impatiently. He bent to hear me ask, "What's going on?" in the plaintive tone of one whose pleasure has been interrupted. He explained that they were after a reported rapist. Noting how I held Sipora, he jabbed at me, one lusty roué to another, rudely joking, "It wasn't you, I guess. You've already got one."

Just a search to catch a rapist, not a Jewish roundup!

Sipora's body had gone limp in my embrace, and I thought she might have fainted. I rather hoped she had. Having reached the first row of the movie house, the officer was heading back. When he paused in passing, as I'd bet myself he would, I had my hand beneath Sipora's black *abaya,* doing who knows what and where. Her face was hidden in the hollow of my neck, and all the *shurti* saw was in his own imagination. We exchanged a manly wink, and he went leeringly about his business as the lights blinked out and film began to grind again.

Sipora came alive and let the air escape her lungs in one great exhalation. Weak and nauseous from the fear and strain, she wanted us to race right out, as anxious to return to hiding as she'd been to reach the street. Once again, I physically restrained her. If *I* commanded that unfruitful search, I'd station men at all the exits, and anyone who hurried out would have to answer for his haste.

All this time my arm had stayed around Sipora. She didn't object. Indeed, she nestled into me, and I began to think about another outing. It was idiotic but intriguing, and I might have carried out the fool idea except that she was winnowed from my list that very evening. In our absence from the house, arrangements had been made for her departure. Even as I heard about it, she was on her way to Persia.

Along with other women and the older, weaker men, Sipora would be moving south; past Basra, near the Gulf, they'd escape Iraq across the Shatt al'Arab river. At any rate, they would have used that route the week before. Overnight, it might have changed. Eventually the border guards discovered and patrolled each trail, but once committed to the trip, we couldn't turn back; the guide would have to improvise. However, since any unplanned detour substantially increased the danger, we preferred to keep our refugees impounded until other fully researched routes were opened up. The climate also played a part. Soon, for instance, we'd lose the northern route across the mountains.

In November, the need to find additional escape routes became especially acute, but not because of weather. We woke one morning to find that martial law had been abolished. Oddly, though, instead of quieting the Quarter, the abrupt cessation of hostilities unnerved it further; we couldn't account for it, and anything that couldn't be explained was suspect. Then, too, we'd all become so acclimated to living in a state of tension that the sudden easing of the strain was as psychologically unbalancing as if the spinning world had stopped. The sense of insecurity intensified tremendously, and in this period of peace, more Jews than ever asked to leave Iraq.

Completely in the dark as to the government's objective, we floundered for the reasons; a thousand rumors eddied in the air, ungrounded in a single fact. One finally was given substance by our paid informants in the Civil Service. The Prime Minister himself, they said, took credit for the plan, the initial stage of which was due for execution any day now. Simply put, Iraqi Jews would first be stripped of all their assets—pauperized—and then expelled. Two aims would be achieved. A *Mislim* country would acquire all that Jews had earned and owned, and in the same inspired stroke, it would put an end to Israel.

With nowhere else to go, Iraqi Jews would surge into a land already sinking under waves of refugees from Hitler's Europe. The flood of penniless Iraqis, all of them in need of *everything,* would finish off the Jewish state by drowning it in debt. Already ravaged by the Arab war and endless streams of other victims, the economy of Israel would crumple so completely that the country couldn't exist. What the *jihad* couldn't accomplish, the Jews themselves would do. Israel would be destroyed.

This blueprint for the killing of a country only made it more imperative to leave at once, while something could be salvaged. According to my uncle, whose coffee shop was frequented by several well-established smugglers, everyone who could was converting what he owned to gold. Carried in from Persia, where its purchase price was low, gold had heretofore been snatched up mainly by Baghdadi jewelers, among them, another of my mother's brothers, Uncle Dahoud. Now, my uncle said, the market was expanding daily, and the cost was spiralling to the sky. Since cars and houses couldn't be hauled away, everyone intending to go "out" was bidding on the contraband.

While making rounds and keeping all my refugees in order, I still had school commitments to contend with. Lecture halls and clinics could be managed, but Obstetrics posed a problem. Like all the fifth-year students, I'd been assigned to do deliveries for two weeks straight, and since our days were fully occupied with other work, we always drew the night shifts. My stint was due to start on Monday. At night, however, the secretary to the Dean was somewhere on the other side of Baghdad. With no one in the office to relay a message, I wouldn't have a moment's warning if the C.I.D. was on its way. Adding to the danger, the doors to both the College and the hospital were guarded after dark. Escape would be impossible. Under these conditions, doing my obstetric service would be tantamount to sitting on a ticking bomb, and I doubt I could have concentrated on the intervals between contractions.

For the benefit of both the birthing women and myself, I reassigned my two-week service to a half-starved Arab student. Except for special duty such as this, the school had no facilities for living in, so Ahmed, far from family and friends, was sleeping in a hovel and scraping by on scraps. By taking my two weeks, he could eat himself into a stupor—at hospital expense—and also save on room rent.

For fourteen days I signed the register at 5 P.M., then slipped away. The delivery room was really run by midwives, and the Arab birthrate being what it was, they were much too busy to bother with the niceties of introductions. Ever-changing, the students blended into one vague, nameless blur, especially as they weren't underfoot that much. When giving birth, many Arab women wouldn't permit a man to be around. It was a factor that I'd figured on. In the main, a student hung around the fringes, out of sight, observing everything he could if he was conscientious, otherwise catching up on sleep and intervening only if and when a medical emergency occurred.

As I hoped, the births in my appointed period were all routine; the midwives handled everything. To celebrate, and since the raids had not resumed and the search for Doctor Hiyyim had apparently just petered out, I began to sleep at home again.

I returned to find my mother frantic. In my absence the house had been beseiged by people who had seen me either in the synagogue or at the demonstration. Nana estimated that she'd told at least 200 callers that I wasn't home. "They wanted you to help them out," she said; still innocent of my activities, she thought they'd come to me for medical attention. Nana only heard the "help"; I knew that "out" was what they wanted.

Antithetically, I found my father freshly optimistic. They were foolish to abandon everything, he argued, on the basis of unproven information. At the very thought of exile from the city and the life he loved, Baba had reverted to his previous position, stubbornly insisting that the Jews were too entrenched in Baghdad to be rooted out for any reason.

The old debate resumed, although I realized now I'd never win. I was finding out that where a deeply felt emotion is involved, wishful thinking more than matches rude reality, and Baba wished with all his heart to stay in Baghdad. His last rebuttal was the fact that Nuri-es-Said was known to keep a Jewish mistress, "so how could he dispose of Jews?"

"The same way that his great good friend, the Regent, hanged Shafik," I might have said. It wouldn't have helped, however, so I simply let it pass.

It was academic anyway. Baba couldn't have left, and neither could the others. I was apprised of that when I approached the *T'nu'ah* on behalf of my 200 applicants for passage out. Israel, I learned, was asking that we stem the exodus "for now."

Deluged with Jews from German concentration camps and from the holding pens in Cyprus established by the British, the immigrants had far outstripped available resources. Israel, as es-Said surmised, was running out of everything essential for survival. Therefore, Jews with homes, however hazardous, were urged to put off *aliyah.* In accord with this request, the *T'nu'ah* would extend its aid only to the most endangered.

I discovered something else, as well. Since the northern route was not traversable in late November and our border crossings in the south had been detected, this decision by the High Command was mere redundancy. While individuals could still be smuggled through, though at greater risk than ever, no groups had been dispatched for weeks. When Israel was ready to receive them once again, our backlog would be staggering. Since they'd sought me out, I felt especially responsible for "my" 200, and with the *T'nu'ah* abdicating, for the moment, from the emigration business, it was up to me to find new means of leaving.

Indirectly, S'hak led me to the answer. A *Mislim* named Ahmed, the younger brother of one of Baba's best employees, had approached him with a proposition predicated on the heavy flow of traffic between Baghdad and Basra. The train, he pointed out, ran only once a day, at a pace that would disgrace a snail, and with stops at every little hamlet on the line. Moreover, it was heavily policed, and more police could board at any point. Once underway, a passenger was at the mercy of the *shurta.*

He didn't have to spell it out. Anyone with anything to hide—which included half the businessmen in both the cities—would much prefer the freedom of the road, for which they'd gladly pay a premium. Therefore, he suggested that he and S'hak offer them a faster, privacy-protecting shuttle service. If my brother bought the limousine, he'd act as chauffeur and find him other drivers as required. Calculating quickly, S'hak struck the bargain then and there; it sounded like a solid business venture.

It also sounded like my new escape route. All the drivers for the underground were *Mislim* smugglers. Professionals who spent their lives in carting contraband across the border, they knew the country better than the men who'd mapped it. Like gold and opium, Jews were just another form of merchandise, but one for which the charge was larger. Whatever the religious scruples of the drivers, cash in hand could always overcome them.

Naturally, we'd built in safeguards, such as making money payable at destination, subject to the safe delivery of "merchandise." And if a smuggler should be apprehended, he knew we had the contacts and the cash to come to his assistance—contingent on his keeping quiet. We could buy a minor bandit out of jail as easily as flies find honey. If a driver talked, however, he was equally aware we'd let him rot. Of course it was impossible to tell ahead of time if our hired hand had sold us out and if the *shurta* had arranged an ambush. The government could offer bigger bribes and far more fearsome penalties. In the last analysis, everything depended on our judgment of the individual. Ahmed looked good to me.

When S'hak talked to me about the shuttle and its huge success, I steered the conversation toward a family trip. We hadn't been away together since I'd started school, I said, and with his service working out so well. . . . I left the idea dangling, and S'hak snapped it up. Soon all of us were off to Basra, Ahmed at the wheel. For at least eight hours, or maybe ten or twelve, depending on what stops we made to picnic, I'd have him to myself. As always, I sat beside the driver. From earliest infancy, I'd been subject to excruciating motion sickness, much worse when seated in the rear, especially if the car was hot and crowded. After throwing up the first few times we'd taken trips, a seat in front was automatically assigned to me. Alone, alongside Ahmed, I could sound him out and come to a decision.

Under everyday conditions, he and I would never have a normal conversation. When people of our disparate status spoke, one issued orders and the other acquiesced. At the start, as I expected, he was overly obsequious, intimidated by his brother's boss in back and by a *dektor* at his side. To someone like Ahmed, a doctor was a godlike being. And this one was the boss's son.

When I initiated a discussion, he looked positively panicked. Extremely nervous, he let his steering waver for a second, and S'hak's yell increased his apprehension even more. We were heading back to Baghdad before I really broke the barriers. By then, we talked as easily as any two acquaintances. The time had come to test him.

Offhandedly, I drew my Mauser and asked where we could stop so I could do some target shooting. It was illegal for a Jew to own a gun, and I was interested in seeing his spontaneous reaction. He didn't even blink. A moment later, though, he mildly suggested that my gun would serve me best if I concealed it. I was pretty sure I had my man!

Nearing home, with both of us relaxed now, I led up to my real objective. In a joking sort of way, I said, "Don't tell my brother it was my idea, but you ought to go in business for yourself." Instead of laughing, he cocked his head receptively, and I continued. "If you had a client with some valuables to smuggle, this would be the way to do it."

Catching on at once, he answered, "As you say! And, *b'Allah, Dektor,* you could depend on me to get them through." When Ahmed swore by Allah, it was safe to speak of anything. He nodded when I told him what I wanted, and we struck a bargain. In the next few months, in groups of five to ten, we took a total of 120 men and women to an isolated stretch of river south of Basra, then across by fishing boat and into Abadan. There, a sizable community of Persian Jews took over and arranged for them to reach Teheran.

In March, however, security was tightened once again, and this way, too, was closed to us. I put Ahmed on alert and started still another search for an alternative. Before I found one, a law was passed which, on the face of it, appeared to obviate the problem. As of March 1950, emigration of Iraqi Jews was authorized by Parliament. For a one-year period, a Jew would be allowed to exit simply by renouncing his allegiance to Iraq.

Expressed that starkly, as it was in all the first announcements, it sounded like the answer to a lot of prayers. Our elation lasted only till we read the law itself. Its built-in ambiguity—a conscious, crafted kind of vagueness—shrilled a loud alarm. It said "allowed to leave" all right, but not "immediately," "within a week," or anything like that. No element of time was mentioned, nor did it specify the status of those who, seeking exit, were no longer citizens but still resided in Iraq. From the day they signed to go until the day the government permitted their departure, they'd be stateless persons and completely unprotected.

There were other ominous omissions. Nowhere did the statute say that we might opt to go wherever in the world we wished, or by any means available. Conceivably they could restrict us to a single exit on the Syrian or Saudi border, even send us out on foot, "authorized" to perish in the almost endless stretches of the western desert.

In view of past experience, each government pronouncement gave automatic rise to paranoia. Was this one purely propaganda—or worse, perhaps? It well might be a lethal trick, contrived in its entirety to flush out those the government could then call traitors. Who but traitors would want to leave their native land? If the rulers of the country could kill a friend, a superpatriot like Shafik, outspokenly and scathingly an anti-Zionist, what would happen to an average Jew who stood before a government official and formally renounced Iraq?

I wasn't skeptical about it; I was sure. The statute was another trap, the word "permission" the perfect bait to tempt a law-abiding people. However, even this equivocal "permission" excluded anyone engaged in "criminal"—that is to say, Zionist—activities, as well as relatives of anyone the C.I.D. was seeking. Since warrants weren't issued and most arrests were absolutely arbitrary or made on nothing more than unsupported accusation, that clause alone could easily eliminate the whole community.

Two Jewish doctors volunteered to test the law. The responses they received, though evasive as the law itself, nonetheless revealed a pattern: No professionals would be permitted to escape. If anyone was given leave to go, it wouldn't be anyone of use to our economy.

The *T'nu'ah,* more dubious with every reading of the edict, sent its couriers throughout the Quarter to denounce it as a hoax. The ghetto, as we soon discovered, had independently arrived at that conclusion. Strangely, though, requests to leave illegally abruptly dropped, and many who'd been driving me insane, demanding that I get them out, decided to sit tight awhile. While no one would admit it, they were secretly convinced that *some* would be allowed to leave, just to make the law look valid. Once again, they'd wait and see.

In the underground, we'd long ago dispensed with such illusions. Since the law had failed in its aim, they'd simply sweep it into limbo and fabricate some other, and less subtle, scheme. Angered by its failure, they'd undoubtedly revert to force and further roundups.

Convinced another crackdown was in store, the *T'nu'ah* sent the word to Israel: "Iraqi refugees will shortly be arriving." We couldn't wait; when raids resumed and more arrests were made, we anticipated mass migration. Whole families would be applying. Along with healthy adults, we'd be dealing with the aged and infirm, infants at the breast, and restless children. Completely new techniques would have to be evolved.

In the meantime, the underground had offered me a route suitable for able-bodied men. Shorter than some others, it was physically more difficult than any we had undertaken. We'd be crossing the Amara plain, a treeless, close-to-desert tract, then making several steep ascents. On every trip, as I scrambled for a handhold, feet sliding out from under me, I conjured up a mental image of my roly-poly little mother, clinging to a rock and crying.

Between March and May I emptied out my sanctuaries, taking twenty-one "most-wanted" men from Baghdad to the Persian border. One day soon, I wouldn't be waving them goodbye and turning back. Even if the law had been authentic, I'd have had to leave illegally; an official application would instantly expose me. The *T'nu'ah* had ordered all of us on search lists to effect our own escapes. As a highly visible commander whose capture could imperil many others, I knew I was a source of worry, but nonetheless, I made excuses, stalling my departure. If I could hang on one more month, I would walk away with my diploma, the passport to my future life.

In itself, this fifth and final year of school had been an uphill battle. Now, in addition to a killing load, exams loomed just ahead. I was averaging three hours of sleep each night, and even when asleep, I dreamed that I was studying.

A day or two before exams began, I was checking out a hernial incision in the men's ward when Rashid gestured me to join him in the hall. He wasn't smiling, which was rare for Rashid, so I hurried out as quickly as I could. He raised a cautionary finger to his lips and nodded toward an empty room. I trotted after him, alarmed by his behavior. Matters must be grim indeed if Rashid couldn't openly address me.

He rapidly advised me that there might be trouble at exam time. "You and the others"—elliptically alluding to the other Jews—"had better come *exactly* when they're due to start and get away as fast as you can finish." All he'd add was that he'd heard "some talk." Translation: "Ambush Jews and beat them up." Though embarrassed for his fellow *M'silmin,* he also felt that telling me had been betrayal. I understood and sympathized. Each of us had ethnic loyalties, binding us to others of our tribe even when at odds with them. Sorry for us both, I didn't press him, and, separately, we left the little room.

Remembering the baccalaureate exams, I hadn't really needed details of the trouble. Laying for the Jewish students and beating them to jelly was an old and well-known Arab trick. We used to joke that Jewish kids would always test out best because being dumb was just too dangerous. If you hadn't studied quite enough and had to sit there, slowly sweating out the answers, the *M'silmin* would be waiting when you finally got through. It behooved a Jew to finish first and flee the hall. Inside the hall itself, well monitored by staff instructors, we were safe.

I warned the others. We entered as the doors were being shut, then turned our papers in, and scurried out again well ahead of any Arab students, and in time to save our skins. As I passed his desk, I saw that Rashid, who usually completed tests as quickly as the Jewish pupils, was writing with deliberate languor. Understandably, he didn't want to leave with us.

Knowing I'd done well, I spent the afternoon at home, trying to relax. Marks would be announced tomorrow, and in a week, the Dean would hand me my diploma. As soon as it was safely in my grasp, I'd be on my way to Israel by way of Persia.

Having lost the knack of doing nothing, the lolling hardly lasted long enough to muss my bed. I was on the roof, prowling restlessly, when footsteps on the stairs sent me rushing toward the roof abutting ours. The stairwell door was opening before I reached it, and I'd already drawn my Mauser when my sister's head appeared. Two men—"Jewish men," Osa added hastily—were in the downstairs hall, asking for Haim.

We didn't need introductions. They were members of the Aliyah Division of the *T'nu'ah;* I'd met them in the course of work. Without preamble, they told me that the C.I.D. was at the College, scouring the school for Doctor Hiyyim. The net was closing, and the man I knew as Sabah said, "You'll have to go at once."

"You mean tonight?" I asked, and he shook his head impatiently. "I mean right *now.* You don't need anything except a blanket."

I bargained for an extra hour. Impossible, they said. Thirty minutes then? Sabah was reluctant but agreed to give me fifteen minutes.

For months I'd mentally rehearsed my exit, hoping I'd be here at home when time ran out. I'd been luckier than many others. Not everyone had even fifteen minutes for a final look around. I ran up to my room, slipped into my newest suit and shoes—just bought for graduation—borrowed S'hak's winter coat in lieu of blanket, packed my *tallith* and phylacteries, and stuffed my shaving brush and razor in a pocket. Two minutes, as per practiced run-through.

This cool efficiency evaporated on my picking up a picture of the family. To protect them in event of capture, I couldn't take it with me, and precious seconds passed before I forced myself to put it down. Resuming the rehearsed routine, I checked myself for anything that could incriminate another person. All my ties to everyone and everything I'd ever loved would have to be eliminated. The only piece of paper that remained on me bore Rogers' street address. I'd ripped off both "New Zealand" and his name.

Outside my door, Osa softly called my name. Having grown up in the underground herself, she'd sensed that something of importance was afoot. When I asked her in and said, "Take care of Lassie," she understood at once that I was leaving. Though tears welled up, she turned away to spare me and sped downstairs. Halfway down myself, I doubled back and grabbed my stethoscope. They'd tear up my diploma, but the learning that it took to earn it was forever mine. I was a doctor.

In the kitchen, Nana was sitting at the *takhta,* cutting crescent shapes of dough to fill for dinner. How to tell her that I wouldn't be there to eat it? When she heard me enter, she raised her eyes and looked at me inquiringly. This wasn't my domain. Ordinarily, if I wanted something from the kitchen, I'd either call for it or send Avram to fetch it for me. Then she registered the suit and shoes and knew the answer.

Rising too abruptly from the floor, she almost fell, and I grabbed at her, holding her against me while she wept, "Who will feed you? Who will wash your clothes?" I tried to comfort her, telling her I'd see her soon in Israel. Over Nana's head I saw Avram and Daisy gaping at us, wide-eyed, as, our roles reversed, I rocked my mother in my arms. "Tell everyone goodbye for me." With the words, I began to edge away, but Nana pushed away from *me.* Running for the phone, she wailed, "Your father . . . your brother . . . you have to say goodbye to them."

S'hak wasn't to be found, but Baba reached the house in minutes. Fearful, angry, crying, and cajoling all at once, he pleaded with me not to go. "I can fix it," he assured me. "I have friends." And he followed with a litany of names, important people who could help. In the midst of his appeals, the men from Aliyah returned. When Sabah tapped his watch, Baba broke off in the middle of a word and reached for mother. Her bitter sobs were muffled by his body, then silenced by the shutting of the massive door behind us. It sounded like the clanging of a coffin lid.

On the street outside, I stopped to take a final look. Everyone, I saw, had raced upstairs to watch me from the windows of the winter floor. As I stood there, staring at the row of faces, Nana's disappeared. Afraid she'd fainted, I swiveled back, but Sabah tugged at me, tight-lipped now and not to be entreated. He'd been more lenient already than his schedule allowed. At the corner, though, before the turnoff that would hide the house from view, he paused to fish a piece of paper from his pocket and inspect it with elaborate care. Stony Sabah was giving me this extra moment for a final glimpse of home.

Nana hadn't fainted as I feared. She was standing at the open door, flinging something from her doubled fist in the same direction we had taken. As I strained to see more clearly, she stooped to lift a pitcher, then poured a stream of water over what it was she'd thrown. Suddenly I recognized the ritual, one as old as Jewish history in hostile lands, where every step away from home was full of hazards. To blind the Evil Eye that might be on me, my mother had been tossing salt in it, and while the Wicked One was sightless, she'd washed away my footprints so that evil couldn't pursue me.

I gasped like someone wakened from a sleepwalk, as shocked as if the ewerful of water had struck my face instead of Kambar Ali Street. I thought that I'd been braced to go, but it hadn't really hit me that my going was for good. The ceremony of the salt and water drove it home, right to the heart of me. I'd never be returning from this trip. Farewell to everything I'd ever known. The house that I was born in. The country of my birth. Everything. Farewell to everything forever. And when I said the word, I finally confronted what I hadn't wished to face. This parting from the family might also be forever.

Sabah's voice said, "Hurry now," and blinded by the salt of unshed tears, I followed close behind his swiftly moving blur.

28

A short drive in a horse-drawn buggy brought us to the southern end of Ghazi Street, on the outskirts of the ghetto. We left the vehicle some distance from our destination, walking the remaining way and entering the safe house from an obscure alley. From the street, the huge old building seemed an empty shell, unworthy of attention. It looked, and was, unoccupied. In the *hosh,* however, a mob scene spread before us, eerie in its immobility and spectral silence. The only movement was provided by the flickering of the candles in the corners of the courtyard.

The scene remained unreal until a muffled shriek cut through the quiet, and a figure flung itself at me with such velocity I almost fell. With my arm already raised for a karate chop, just in time I saw that my "attacker" was Claireed, Aunt Gourjiah's teen-aged daughter; she'd enlisted in the *T'nu'ah* with my sisters, but no one had the least idea that she was also going out.

Claireed fell silent when the senior of my guides—Naji, by name—suggested that we settle down to sleep. "We'll be leaving long before the dawn," he warned. He beckoned me to follow him inside.

Off by ourselves, in the hallway of the house, Naji told me this would be the biggest group ever to attempt escape across the eastern desert, and I, he said, would be its leader. There were thirty-six of us in all, twelve of whom were women; seven of the eighteen men were over fifty, and all six kids were under ten. On hearing this, my immediate reaction was to ask about the first-aid kit. With that assortment and with the temperature already in the nineties, we'd need some digitalis, lots of antidiarrhea drugs, and belladonna. As Naji's partner slipped off to obtain the pharmaceuticals, I settled back, expecting that we'd talk about the trip. So far I only knew the general direction. Naji's eyes were closed, however. "Sleep now," he mumbled. "I'll tell you when the time arrives."

I was wide awake all night, unable even to relax enough to lie full-length. The responsibility was awesome, and despite the heat, I huddled in my coat against an icy chill inside me. Around me, the thirty-five whose lives were in my hands slept like the dead, and I shuddered at the simile. A dozen times I heard the sound of an approaching motor, but each one passed and died off in the distance. I wished that "dead" and "die" didn't keep recurring.

While the sky was still soot-black, something rumbled to a halt at the entrance to the alley. At the sound, others stirred around me. I heard Naji in the *hosh,* already crisply in command, ordering that everyone relieve himself before embarking.

"Quickly, use the bathrooms. The trip will be a long one, and the truck has no facilities."

We found each other in the dark, and nodding at the swiftly moving queues, Naji said, "So far, so good. I'll get them out of here, and then they're yours. It's time we talked."

By 4 A.M., he told me, we'd be taking off inside a truck which was customarily employed to carry watermelons. Squeezed hard, the thirty-six of us would fit, but barely. Since produce commonly was sheathed against the searing sun, our canvas cover shouldn't excite suspicion, though lashed a lot more tightly than was usual. At the open loading end, two crates would shield the occupants from view. Of course, they'd also cut off any flow of air. Inside, I thought, our bodies would be baked like loaves of bread. I'd planned for diarrhea, but dehydration was an even greater danger. Anticipating me, Naji pointed out the porous jug already lashed in place. Evaporation would keep the water cool. Ten canteens had also been provided, plus a burlap sack of bread and smaller bags of seeds and dates.

The truck would take us to Amara, several hundred miles south of Baghdad. From there the group would walk its way across the border to a Persian army post where we'd be welcome. On the final leg, we'd travel north to Teheran.

I felt another presence, and in the darkness of the alley, Naji introduced a deeper shadow by the name of Mahdi. The glint of one gold tooth was all I saw of him. Mahdi was the Arab guide who'd ride with us, then steer us past the armed patrols and checkpoints.

Taking me aside, Naji handed me a slip of paper. "That's the password," he informed me. On our safe arrival at the Persian post, I was to give it to the guide.

"He'll get paid only when he tells it to me on returning here. Then we'll know you made it over. Oh, you may need this," he added, handing me a heavy metal object. Recognizing and refusing it, I pulled my sock down and, in the circle of a shaded light, showed him that I had a gun already. The little Mauser didn't impress him, but my secreting it reminded him of something still to do.

Though expressly warned against it, some members of the party would attempt to smuggle cash or jewels. While understandable—starting over strange and penniless was scary—we couldn't allow it. If the guide smelled money, he'd be tempted to entrap us and abscond with it.

When directly questioned and threatened with a search, most complied, pulling little stashes from concealment in their clothes. Others, mainly women, tried to bluff it out, but seeing that we really meant to probe their persons, they turned their backs abashedly and hauled the contraband from hiding. Suspicious of some extrabulky belts, I found the final holdouts. Several of the younger men had razor-slit the leather and stuffed the fissures full of paper money. Everything we confiscated was labeled for delivery to relatives, and we were ready now to load.

Naji thrust me forward, and addressing the assemblage, announced that "Heskel here will be in charge." For the first time in the underground, my code name was ignored; the significance of this was overwhelming. If we were caught now, names wouldn't matter.

The body of the truck was built of horizontal slats spaced at three-inch intervals. When we were moving briskly, I figured that the breeze would belly out the canvas canopy; the men, at least, might urinate between the tarp and slats. The verticals to which the slats were fastened were only five feet high, so here the women had the best of it. Smaller, they could stand upright; the rest of us would have to crouch.

Boarding last, I helped to hoist the boxes filled with fruit meant both to feed and hide the human cargo. Wedged in, with only space enough to plant our two feet on the floorboards, none of us could fall. None of us, in fact, could even lift an arm to scratch an itch, and after lacing down the canopy our heads were hitting canvas. Within minutes, the atmosphere was steamy, and this before the sun was up.

Worse, I knew, was yet to come, but sooner than expected. In the central part of Baghdad, the streets were smoothly paved, and we adapted to a rhythmic swaying motion. On the outskirts of the city, we suddenly hit red-dirt roads; quagmires when it rained, now late in May, like surf turned stone. Rattling over sun-seared troughs and peaks, we bounced erratically in place like rubber balls. The overladen lorry crushed the ridges of the ruts, and dust seeped through the smallest openings.

An hour after setting out, everyone was floured, head to foot, with pinkish powder. Shortly it was mud as perspiration poured from us. Inside the van, the air itself was visible. The children, who'd been good as gold, were now beginning to be cranky, and since breakfast had been skipped to speed departure, I decided to distract them by dispensing snacks. They fell voraciously on everything I handed out—peaches, dates, dried apricots, and tiny, sour apples—but many of the adults, already squeamish from the jouncing up and down, waved away their rations.

One woman retched and vomited, spewing out her last Iraqi dinner. I'd meant to ask for motion-sickness medication, but everything had moved so fast that I'd forgotten. One upheaval generally incited others, so I shouted out that anyone who felt the least bit queasy should refrain from drinking. "Soak a handkerchief and suck on it instead," I said, "and breathe as deeply as you can." No one paid me much attention until Claireed called out, "Heskel is a doctor!" After that, everything I said was gospel, and a heaving epidemic was averted. From that point on, I noticed, they addressed me only by my title.

A restless stirring soon gave notice of another problem. Knowing that the truck had no facilities had no effect on natural functions; bladders kept refilling. I poked a peephole through the tarp, and everytime the road was empty, allowed another man to urinate between the slats. The women, unequipped for such a finicky adjustment, simply had to exercise their self-control. In the company of men, especially male strangers, an Iraqi Jewish woman couldn't express the need, much less do the deed itself. In time, however, even iron will and modesty were not enough.

"For the sake of God, please stop!"

The writhing woman looked to be in labor, but since no one on the truck was pregnant, I knew her need could only be to move her bowels.

I plowed my way past thirty-five packed bodies to the window of the cab. Rapping hard, I finally attracted the attention of the guide and explained the situation. His head was shaking "no" before I finished. We couldn't stop. Patrols, he said, were thick as flies. I'd have to find my own solution.

A little privacy was all I could provide. To furnish even that, I asked that every man move forward to the front end of the truck and face ahead. Somehow the squirming mass got sorted out by sex, and, surrounded by the other women, the lady in distress tore a square of cloth from someplace on her person and eliminated onto it. From the center of her guard, I heard an almost sensual groan of sweet release.

After eight, as the sun climbed higher in the sky, the heat became intense. At least 106 outside, I estimated; inside, I wouldn't attempt a guess. Everyone had peeled as much as decency permitted, and most were in a semistupor from the fetid air. Fresh sweat already stank, and the smell of urine said that someone must have missed the space between the slats. Not having slept the night before, I wasn't in the best of shape myself. To stay alert, I sent my mind back to more stimulating scenes.

I was back at school again, in the outer office of the Dean, speaking to his secretary. It was two days since I'd taken the exams, and though results were strictly secret, he whispered that I'd passed "and with plenty left to spare." The memory was marred, though, by the thought that followed. I was officially a doctor, but without credentials. When the Dean was handing out diplomas, I'd be far off in a foreign land.

The road unwound behind us and stretched endlessly ahead. Seeking some distraction, at intervals I used my peephole, but the flat unchanging landscape offered no relief from deadly boredom. My watch alone marked progress, and the steady ticking of its sweephand suggested a diversion. I began to count the road bumps like a human pulse.

My charges only roused themselves to swat at flies or ask for water. The person charged with dipping and dispensing it was overgenerous, and I had to curb his impulse to be kind; we couldn't replenish our supply until we crossed to Persia. At noon, I meted out a second meal, but skipped my own. More than ever, I missed the motion-sickness pills, this time on my own account. As the leader of the group, I felt I couldn't allow myself the luxury of heaving or even, for that matter, moaning.

About four that afternoon, when Amara should have been in sight, I scanned the landscape through my peephole in the canvas, but saw no signs of habitation. By checking out the sun's position, I judged that we were southeast of the city, closer to the border than we'd ever taken trucks before. Score one for Mahdi. Veering off this way meant miles less to walk, and having stood for twelve straight hours, I was painfully aware that breaking in my brand-new shoes hadn't been among my *best* ideas.

It was 6 P.M., still bright as noon, before we slowed and stopped. Peering out again, I saw Mahdi leave the cab and leaped to join him. On my other trips, our arrival had been timed to coincide with darkness setting in. Daylight traveling had always been considered much too dangerous for larger parties.

Mahdi's explanation sounded credible, and I couldn't do much but take him at his word—and watch him every minute. He'd found a shorter, safer route, he claimed, one which lay exactly equidistant from the two police posts in the area. He'd timed their regular patrols and planned our reaching here precisely at this hour. We'd be slipping past the posts between patrols. By midnight, he assured me, we'd be with the Persians.

Stiff and sore, legs and ankles swollen from the prolonged standing, the party slid by inches off the truck. After handing down the ten canteens and what little bread was left, I got my first good look at all my fellow travelers. My heart contracted at the sight. Pasty gray and sagging like disjointed puppets, they seemed readier for stretchers than the risky hike ahead. On close examination, Mahdi didn't enhance my spirits either. Back in Baghdad, in the blackness of the alley, I'd gotten only glimpses and sitting in the truck cab the tail of his headcloth had been draped across his face to keep the dust out.

A Bedouin with a built-in squint, Mahdi looked both sly and stupid. The only brightness in his aspect was the golden tooth. His other teeth were carious and broken, and a few day's growth of patchy beard did little to improve his overall appearance. Instead of a *dishdasha,* the normal garb for such a guide, he sported an incongruous *z'boon,* a gala floor-length garment, elaborately embroidered, which closed kimono-fashion, and was kept in place around his body by a heavy, studded belt. Of a rich and closely woven fabric, fully lined, it couldn't have been less suitable for someone of his station, doing what he did. Flapping open over it, he wore a worn and soiled jacket out of Saville Row. His sandals, Yemenite in origin and blazing red when new, were now so cracked and stained and sand-buffed, I could barely tell where they left off and feet began. His headgear was an equal horror. Badly wrapped, with dangling ends, it was neither Bedouin nor city style. And this strange assembly of ill-matched messy bits was making critical decisions, controlling thirty-seven lives, including his and mine!

I turned to the terrain and, if possible, felt even more depressed. I'd forgotten since the last trip just how flat and drab it was. When the haze of dust from the departing truck had drifted off, there was nothing left to look at. Except for flies and fleas, the land looked lifeless. The clayey sun-baked earth was covered by what seemed to be a layer of tiny pebbles. In reality, the stones were bits of soil, resulting from the whipping of the surface by torrential rains, followed by a rapid drying out. Crystal-hard but brittle, they could trip you up when trod on, rolling underfoot at first, then blinding you by pulverizing into powder. Otherwise, all that met the eye were multitudes of stunted dull-green desert shrubs.

When I began to line the group up in parade formation, Mahdi motioned me aside and suggested that I spread them out. From a distance, he explained, they'd appear to be a herd of sheep, but in perfect lines, they could only be a group of people marching.

The man was right. I regrouped the party, assigning someone to the rear to round up stragglers. On more advice from Mahdi, I also passed out bits of staling bread, suggesting as I did, "Just hold this in your mouth. It increases the saliva flow and cuts the thirst." They murmured their appreciation of my expertise, and I felt a total fraud. However, Mahdi, with exquisite tact, had turned away.

For the next few hours we plodded silently across the trackless clay. On both my feet the blisters formed and burst and bled. I'd have to peel the shoes off like a plaster. Someone turned an ankle; another fell and jarred an elbow. Limps grew more pronounced and groans less smothered. Laggards in the rear increased, and those around me begged to take a rest. Catching up with Mahdi, I suggested that we call a halt, but he was adamant about our moving on. I couldn't argue; he knew the schedules of each patrol, and if safety lay in movement, we'd simply have to move.

With the setting of the sun, the plain grew cold, and the sudden loss of body heat sapped our last remaining strength. At 9 P.M., when I warned him of our imminent collapse, Mahdi said that we might rest; his acquiescence wasn't due, as I discovered, to recognition of our deep fatigue, but rather to the fact that the falling darkness would require realignment. As Mahdi laid it out for me, even Bedouin could lose their bearings in the lightless desert night, and with such as us, a straggler could be miles away before we missed him. We'd have to figure out a new formation while the others took a break.

When we rose to go again, I arranged the group in nine tight rows, each four abreast. By holding hands, the four in every line maintained continued contact, and the lines, in turn, were linked together by lengths of cloth and belts; one end of each was fastened to a marcher's waist, with the other firmly clutched by whomever was behind him.

As the cold increased, I began to understand why Mahdi wore so many and such heavy and unlikely clothes. Suddenly, the sloppy headgear also made great sense. All day the dangling ends had kept his neck and ears protected from the searing sun, and in the nighttime's icy air, they now provided insulation. The practicality of the *z'boon* was evident as soon as darkness had descended. When Mahdi crouched, the long ballooning garment made a kind of tent; under it, he could safely use his lighter, though what clues he found to guide him on the stony ground I couldn't see at all.

At 11 P.M., estimating that we only had another hour on the road, I distributed the last of our provisions. Since Mahdi was examining the ground again, the entire caravan had had to stop in any case. While he was peering at the surface, a loud dispute erupted in the ranks. Two boys were arguing, one claiming that the other had received a bigger piece of bread. Mahdi raised his head and hissed at me, "Tell them to keep quiet. We're in trouble."

Reaching for my gun, I ran to where the boys were battling. There wasn't time to arbitrate. "Shut up!" I snapped, *sotto voce* but with bite. "I have a Mauser in my hand, and the next to say a word gets shot."

Stunned, the boys fell silent. All murmuring among the others also stopped. My threat had been too softly uttered to be overheard, but everyone was conscious of an atmospheric change, as if the air itself was charged with danger.

Back with Mahdi, I found him squinting off into the distance. "Look there," he said, and following his pointing finger, I saw a brilliant pinpoint. In muffled, deep disgust, he swore a string of awesome oaths. "We're too far south," he finally explained. "That's the post."

We were close enough for me to hear the horses neighing. If we were spotted, the police patrol could run us down and round us up in minutes.

Rag-doll limp, everyone was on the ground—still, however, hanging onto hands and belts, obeying my instructions. I felt a rush of pride in their endurance as I bent to tell them, one by one, that silence must be absolute from this point on. Would they be able to suppress a groan, I wondered, when I ordered them to rise again? I had doubts myself about resuming; my muscles thought my mind had gone berserk. Acting as both leader and liaison, assigning duties, settling minor arguments, overseeing water distribution, running back and forth to answer questions, attending cuts and bruises, I'd walked the actual distance covered four times over. My body wanted to rebel, but with trouble out in front of us, adrenaline was shooting through my system, flushing out fatigue.

Mahdi steered us past the station, and soon we felt a difference in the ground beneath our feet. These rocks were real, and treacherous to tread on. By three that morning, the sole of my left shoe had separated from its upper and flapped with every step, exacerbating all my blisters. At last, reluctantly, I tossed away half a pair of brand new shoes and bound my foot in borrowed handkerchiefs.

For awhile now, I'd noticed I was leaning slightly forward when I walked. The incline told me that we'd reached the foothills of the Zagros Mountains. The route, arrow-straight till now, became circuitous. At intervals I'd ask how far the border was, and Mahdi always answered, "*Matrahassa.*" A stick's throw. Some stick, I thought, as the twists and turns grew ever more precipitous.

When dawn began to break, we'd been walking for about ten hours. At every step, the pebbles slithered trickily beneath our feet, and I was so intent on staying upright on the steep ascent that the scenery made no impression. I only saw the trail before us. When we stopped to take a breather, I looked around and promptly closed my eyes to keep from keeling over. We were half a mile high, and my head was whirling like an ungeared wheel. Along with motion sickness, I also got vertiginous on any elevation. Safe behind a barrier, I could bear to stare straight down, but here there wasn't anything to bar a fall. Nothing stood between me and the earth below but empty air, and I felt myself sway forward. Digging in my heels, I sat down hard and inched back from the edge, shaking inwardly and pouring out more perspiration than my water ration would replace.

On our feet again, we wound around and ever up. A final pretzel turn opened on a flat plateau. Peaks surrounded us on every side, and Mahdi swept his arm around, exclaiming, "*Hena.*" We are here.

None of the others understood, which was just as well, seeing that no signs of life were evident. Certainly there wasn't any Persian army post. Smiling for the first time since we'd started off, Mahdi looked distinctly sly and unreliable. Grinning emphasized the foxiness of his expression. Was he laughing at us for believing he would bring us safely through? Physically and mentally exhausted, remembering the perfidy of other Arab "friends," it was easy to assume the worst.

Mahdi might have sold us out to the Iraqis or to other smugglers. In leaving home forever, he'd assume that we'd be carrying our cash and antique heirlooms. Which group, I wondered, would swarm around the bend to steal from us or take us back to Baghdad and to prison or the gallows? In the last analysis, it wouldn't matter much. Thieves would either slit our throats or leave us here to die of thirst. An hour back, anticipating our arrival, we'd emptied out the last canteen.

Mahdi spoke again, this time asking for the password. In as cool a voice as I could muster, I responded. "You were to take us to the army post. That was the arrangement."

Impatiently, he jabbed his finger into space, repeating, "*Hena, hena.*"

At that, I drew my Mauser and, aiming it between his eyes, announced that I would kill him if he didn't lead us to the camp. Dropping to his knees and turning ashen, Mahdi swore by Allah that we really had arrived. The plateau marked the border. This *was* the place, he kept insisting, even when the pistol touched his skin. As my finger tightened on the trigger, an unseen someone shouted, "Stop!" The order was in Arabic spoken with a Persian accent, and looking up, I saw a row of rifle muzzles pointing down from a projection not fifty feet away. Mahdi had been telling me the truth. The riflemen were Persian, so we had to be across the border.

Intimidated by the guns, however, Mahdi turned and ran before I handed him the password. Probably he figured that the rifle sights were set on him. As I discovered later, he had cause to be concerned; Mahdi smuggled more than Jews across the border.

"It's *sayara. Sayara,* Mahdi." I yelled the word as loudly as I could. What the Persians thought, I couldn't imagine, but my own Iraqis looked at me as if I were insane. Why else would I be bellowing, "Automobile, automobile," to a Bedouin I'd been about to shoot?

The figure, small now in the distance, stopped and turned; as Mahdi grinned, his tooth threw golden glints at me. He'd get the fee to which he was entitled and Naji would be told that we'd arrived intact. Without the word, which meant his money, Mahdi wouldn't have any reason to report. Rather sheepishly, I explained the situation to the thirty-five, who sighed in unison, relieved to hear their leader hadn't suddenly gone loony.

Four Persian soldiers scrambled down the steep embankment, led by a lieutenant. Addressing me, he issued what were clearly orders, but since he spoke in Farsi, I didn't understand a single word, and "stop," apparently, was all the Arabic at his command. When I conveyed my lack of comprehension, he made sweeping and impatient gestures toward a narrow pass. We were to file through, and swiftly.

Two cliffs towered above the slit—a classic ambush setting—so I shook my head, told my people to stay put, and started off alone to reconnoiter. Though I didn't know it at the time, a soldier was detailed to trail me.

The pass was only slightly more than one man wide, sloping upward as sharply as a flight of stairs. Past the peaks and in the clear, I was ready to return when I almost took a final step into oblivion. As if lopped off by a giant razor, the left side of the path was cleanly, sheerly cut, dropping off abruptly to the desert floor. Taken by surprise, I had no defense against the sudden surge of vertigo that swept me. If the soldier at my back hadn't seized my arms and hauled me from the edge, another instant would have seen me over. A deep breath later, I was calling to the group to come along.

Once through the pass, we came upon a one-room, rude stone building, with unshielded openings instead of proper doors and windows. One of the smallest and most isolated of the border stations, its fourteen men had never hosted any refugees before. In proceeding too far south, we'd overshot the installation that expected us, and if Mahdi hadn't known this other post existed, we'd undoubtedly have wound up as a mound of bleaching bones.

However, no one here knew what to do with us. Luckily, a sergeant spoke a little English, but just enough to deepen my dejection. No, there wasn't any telephone. No wireless either. And the nearest post that could communicate with Teheran was a day away on foot. At the moment, walking on was inconceivable. Every ounce of energy had long since been expended, along with food and water. Before we took another step, we needed sustenance and sleep. The soldiers, spartanly supplied themselves, offered more than they could spare, and after eating, everyone collapsed in place, nodding off as soon as they were horizontal.

Noting that the English-speaking sergeant had an eye infection, I offered to administer some sulfa drops, and having done so, fell asleep myself. Twenty minutes later, the sergeant shook me urgently awake.

"Come! Come!" Almost pulling me upright, he entreated me to follow him. Stumbling after, I stopped when he approached the pass, and asked him to explain. Pleading, "It's important. I owe you for my eyes," he persuaded me to navigate the narrow slit again.

Once again the Persian officer was standing on the elevation overlooking the plateau, this time talking to a group of mounted men. All spoke Farsi, but I recognized the horsemen as Iraqi even as the sergeant whispered, "They want you back."

The lieutenant, I could see, was decidedly ambivalent, and I couldn't really blame him. Here he had some strangers on his hands, with no instructions from superiors. He didn't know who we were, and we'd already eaten deeply into scarce resources. Few but smugglers braved the rugged Zagros range; there might be thieves and murderers among us. He was in a quandary, and accustomed to obeying orders, he responded to authoritative intonation. The Iraqis sounded sure of their position and insisted that he turn us over.

As an Iraqi spoke again, the sergeant made a swift translation. "He says that they can settle this right here, and they'll never hear a word in Teheran, not unless he lets you stay. But if he protects you, Baghdad will protest to Teheran, and he'll be in a lot of trouble."

Smart! First soothe his fears, then stir them up. An old police technique, and the strategy appeared to be effective. The officer was wavering, his uneasy shift from foot to foot foreshadowing surrender. I'd have to scare him even more than the Iraqis or he'd give us up for sure.

I sent the sergeant with my message, and watched while he delivered it. The lieutenant listened, blanched, and looked my way. His swaying stopped abruptly and he stiffened into military posture. The sergeant had informed him that the highest government officials, the commander of the Persian army, and the Shah himself, were all aware of our existence and our imminent arrival, and that anyone who hindered us in any way would have to answer to the whole shebang.

The lieutenant answered the Iraqis, and before the sergeant smiled at me, I knew that we'd be staying.

A step across the border, I took a last, long backward look. Knowing that I'd never see Iraq again, I expected waves of sadness to wash over me. Instead, I was surprised—and sad—to find I felt no sadness. The only feeling was of emptiness or, rather, *blankness.* The love I'd borne my native land had been obliterated, erased as if it never was, entirely expunged by Jewish blood. I'd mourn my home, but not my homeland.

29

Awakening refreshed from my first night's decent sleep since leaving, I wanted to start off at once. It would have to be on foot since the camp lacked any transport, so I shook some powdered sulfa on my bloody broken blisters, and set about to borrow shoes.

At the post we'd overshot, an emissary of the Mosad Aliyah awaited our arrival. Illegally, but with the sufferance of the Shah, the Israeli agency in charge of immigration was aiding Jews escaping from Iraq. By now, the representative assigned to us was probably convinced that we'd been caught; he'd leave unless he heard that we were here, and on our own, we'd never make it north to Teheran.

The lieutenant refused to let me go, afraid, perhaps, I'd flee for good or fall and break my neck, thus sticking him with thirty-six to feed and shepherd. He'd send a courier instead, he said. Familiar with the trail, he'd make the trip in half my time, he argued; the messenger, in fact, did return the following morning, riding in a lorry.

With evident relief, the lieutenant loaded us aboard. Midway to the other post, an axle cracked, and my announcement that we'd have to walk was greeted with a universal groan. Sleeping in the open on the stony, icy earth had worsened all our aches and pains; muscles, once relaxed, actively protested a return to work. Our stomachs also started to rebel. Excited by the truck's appearance, we hadn't stopped to eat, and since the camp was just an hour's drive, we hadn't taken food or water.

Ten hours after starting out, we straggled in. The encampment, much larger than the one we'd left, almost filled a flat plateau. Unaccountably, the stench of rotten eggs was in the air. Otherwise, the post was most impressive, its structures well designed and strongly built of local stone.

As soon as we appeared, a sentry waved us toward a central square; clearly, he'd been briefed about our coming. I'd expected that the Mosad Aliyah man would be there to greet us, but instead it was a Persian soldier who approached me on instructions from the camp commander. In basic Arabic and in an agitated tone of voice, he said the *Sarhang* wished to see the doctor "as soon as he arrives." Ordering the group to stay together, I allowed the *Sarhang*'s aide to lead me toward the Colonel's quarters.

Encountering the scrubbed and barbered officer, trimly uniformed with buttons brightly glinting in the sun, I was suddenly acutely conscious of my own obnoxious state. I hadn't bathed since leaving Baghdad, and shaving without water had left my face a patchwork quilt of scraped raw flesh and coarse black stubble. My once-white shirt was sixteen shades of stain, from sweat to swatted insects, and the reeking rags around my feet were indescribably offensive. The accumulated odors of so many people crammed together in the small space of the truck had paralyzed my sense of smell. All at once it came alive and almost bowled me over.

The *Sarhang* didn't seem to notice. On close inspection he had a bleary look himself, like someone who'd spent several sleepless nights in sequence. All he saw before him was the only doctor within days of long, rough riding. His baby daughter, he explained, was deathly ill. Would I hurry, please, and see her. I asked for soap and water first, and focusing at last on my appearance, he hastened to comply. The clayey dust deposits had hardened into sort of an enamel shell; it required half a dozen separate scourings to cut through all the baked-on grime and get to skin again. I felt as peeled as a banana.

The *Sarhang*'s three-month-old was suffering from diarrhea and screaming stridently enough to terrify a pair of recent parents, but I saw at once that she wasn't really very sick. While not exactly saying so—it might be useful for the Colonel to feel grateful—I reassured him and his pretty wife, measured out the proper dose of paregoric, and gave directions for the baby's diet. When the mother turned away, I took a longer look at her. Though unveiled and very lovely, it was her copper-colored hair that made me stare. Never seen among Iraqis, it reminded me that Persians might be *M'silmin,* but they weren't Arab. In the days ahead, I'd be adapting to a thousand little differences.

Relaxed now that the infant was asleep, the Colonel led me to his office and offered me a cigarette. Another first. I'd never smoked before, but then again, I'd never climbed a mountain either, so I took a light and tried to look at ease. The news he had for me, however, ended the pretense. The man from Mosad Aliyah had been and gone. Since we were two days late in coming, he'd given up on us and taken off this morning.

On seeing my distress, the *Sarhang* hastily went on to say that everything would be all right; a message had been sent the moment we arrived. Until arrangements could be made to take us north, he'd do his best to solve our basic problems. Some tents were up already, and even as we spoke, food was being portioned out. Thanking me effusively for tending to his daughter, he invited me to eat with him that evening.

On returning to the group, the women greeted me as if I were another Moses. I'd led them from the wilderness to food and water. More than satisfying thirst and hunger, though, they wished to wash—themselves, their clothes, their offspring. I had the soldiers string some ropes and sling our blankets over them for privacy. Behind the barrier, almost orgiastic in their avid soaping, the women squealed and splashed with shrill abandon, sloughing, for the moment, all their woes. Women, to my wonderment, washed the way men fought, with absolute emotional involvement, and I envied them their outlet.

At dinnertime, the *Sarhang* sent an orderly to fetch me, and I followed him in borrowed shoes. Having fed for days on bread and fruit, I salivated at the smell of cooking meat. At first it didn't occur to me to wonder what the meat would be—or whether it was *kasher.* When I thought about it, though, I knew of course it couldn't be *kasher.* The rice would be permissible, but not the lamb. (By now, I recognized the odor.) The lamb required ritual slaughter, and that luscious, aromatic little creature had simply had his throat cut or his head bashed in. What should have been more loathsome still, a bowl of yoghurt stood beside the steaming platter, and milk in any form is forbidden at a meal containing meat.

"Thou shalt not cook the lamb in its mother's milk."

I thought I'd feel revulsion, but my appetite remained. The text reverberated in my mind, but my stomach ruled to strike it out. In special instances, I told myself, God forgives transgressions, and this, I swore to Him, was special. I was *starving!*

I took a good-sized serving of the rice, spooning onto it some charcoal-broiled lamb strips, Baghdadi style, and attempted to ignore the yoghurt. Assuming that I hadn't seen it, the Colonel leaned my way and ladled out a healthy portion, which ran into the rice and joined the meat juice. At the juncture, I half-expected that the mixture would explode.

The *Sarhang*'s wife, as solicitous as he, offered me a bowl of uncooked eggs. The Colonel had already taken two, and I watched to see what he would do with them. Using just the yokes, he dropped them on a dune of virgin rice, mixed them through the mound, added meat, and spooned some yoghurt on the side.

"Tchelo-kabab."

He named the dish, then demonstrated how to eat it. To my utter consternation, he dipped a forkful of the meat stew in the milky yoghurt, briefly swirling it before he brought it, dripping, to his lips. Though refraining from the final step, I polished off a man-sized meal—my first non-*kasher* food.

After dinner I looked in on the baby, who was playing with her toes and plainly better. Beaming with relief, the *Sarhang*'s wife asked me if I'd like to use her extra room. When I said I'd like it for the women, her smile faded. "Can they be quiet?" she inquired. Iraqi women, like their menfolk, were known as extra noisy, and Jews were no exception. Exulting in the water, they'd outdone themselves today; even from the farthest edge of the encampment, the clamor must have reached her ears.

Seeing my embarrassed blush, the Colonel interposed. "It's only that we haven't slept . . . you understand . . . the baby. . . ." Now he was flushing, and we both began to laugh. In one way or another, women were a problem.

Assuring them the room would be as silent as a tomb, I hurried off to tell the news. On hearing that they'd sleep indoors, on rugs instead of dirt, the women screamed with joy. Wincing at the sound, I warned them of the stipulation; they'd have to speak in whispers, if at all. Claireed suggested that I sleep with them and keep them quiet. The others clamored their approval, creating so much noise again, I knew I'd have to do it. At any rate, I didn't much relish bedding down on dirt myself. As it happens, I didn't have to hush them up at all; bone-weary, the women went to sleep as soon as they stretched out.

In the morning, before the sun had cleared the mountains and while the air still held an icy edge, the Colonel's orderly was rapping at the door. In the jeep awaiting us, I jumped on contact with the frigid seat and came awake completely. When I asked where we were heading, he answered, "Ein Kibreet." Whatever Ein Kibreet might be, an awful smell surrounded it—the same I'd noticed coming into camp. The stench grew ever stronger, and stopping at a rock-rimmed pool, my nose informed me that I'd found its source. Ein Kibreet, the orderly confirmed, meant "sulfur spring." The Colonel thought that I'd enjoy a swim; he was too well-bred to urge a bath.

As eager as I was to wash, I didn't really want to wash in anything that stank far worse than I did. However, others of the colonel's men were in already, seemingly indifferent to the frosty air and reeking fumes. They appeared, in fact, to find it fun. I couldn't refuse to join them without losing face.

To get it over with, I grit my teeth, shucked my clothes, and dove in almost in a single motion. The water was as warm as blood. The spring was hot as well as sulfured, and a blissful glow seeped through me. Someone tossed a cake of soap, strong enough to overcome both sweat and sulfur, and I nearly scrubbed my skin off, then settled in to soak.

Eyes closed, I didn't see the courier approach. Calling out that I was wanted back in camp at once, he disappeared before I could collect my thoughts and question him. Reluctantly, I left the peaceful pool, loath to reassume my duties and my dirty underclothes. Fresh shorts and shirt appeared as if by magic: With the Colonel's compliments, the orderly announced.

Refreshed in flesh and spirit, the *Sarhang*'s news completed my recovery. A message had come through from Teheran; the Mosad Aliyah had sent a man to see to us. By evening he'd be here.

Ziadi, a Persian Jew, arrived on schedule, bearing vouchers for the train and orders for our transportation. A convoy of supply trucks would be coming through, two of which would take us to the depot. We were packed and ready when the call came from the Corps of Engineers; the trucks would be "a little late."

The hours dragged, becoming days, but Ziadi, though impatient, wasn't worried. "It's the way things are," he shrugged, confiding that a dozen bribes had been involved in making the arrangements. "And everyone will blame somebody else." Ziadi's calm impressed me; for a messenger, I thought, his calibre was quite exceptional.

The convoy came at last. Four hours later we were at the Dizful station, and soon thereafter, still chewing on a pick-up dinner, we stepped aboard the train for Teheran.

Until the wheels began to turn and I could temporarily relinquish my control, I'd put aside the problem of my own peculiar status. On the truck it had occurred me that I could be conscripted by the Persians for several years of military service. Technically I was a Persian—or enough of one to raise the issue.

Naturally, I'd always known that my mother's and my father's parents had been born in Persia. When they'd headed west, to what was then the Baghdad Region, the entire area was under Ottoman control. While the Persians were acknowledged by the Turks to be an entity apart, Iraqis as a national group didn't exist at all. Therefore, because their fathers had been Persian, my parents were considered Persian too, though both were born in Baghdad.

When Iraq became a nation, Baba prudently retained his Persian status, and at every birth had legally declared each kid was also Persian. In the restless Middle East, it was wise to have a haven in reserve. If I gave it any thought at all, I guess I just regarded it as evidence of Baba's extra conscientiousness on our behalf; every possible contingency was planned for. As for me, however, I was all Iraqi, notwithstanding what a card in Baba's strongbox said.

My identity was never questioned until I went to college. To satisfy a routine school requirement, I'd applied to the police for a certificate attesting to my sterling character; in order to matriculate, every student had to prove he was a citizen in good repute, without a record. Only then did I discover that I wasn't an Iraqi. A born Baghdadi, I'd just assumed I was a citizen. At worst, I figured I had dual identity, or so I argued, but to no effect.

I wasn't an Iraqi, the police insisted, but I *could* be one. All I had to do was raise my hand, renounce a land I'd never seen, and swear allegiance to the land I loved and lived in. A moment later, no longer Persian, I had my precious statement and was set for school.

On the train to Teheran, I remembered that I'd kept the card identifying me as Persian—and subject to at least two years of military service. Pulling out my wallet under cover of my coat, I extracted the incriminating card and tore it into tiny bits. Slowly, one by one, I let them float out through the open window over forty miles of lonely landscape.

30

We arrived at Teheran at ten the following morning, to be met by someone named Said. Smiling at my evident surprise, since Said was a *Mislim* name, he hastened to assure me he was one of us. His pseudonym was necessary, he explained, to give him greater latitude in helping groups like ours.

"You must remember," he advised, "Iran is part of the Islamic world. The people may be Aryan, but they worship with the Arabs. While the Shah will let us in, he doesn't want to advertise our being here, especially that we fly from here to Israel."

Of course—Israel, the enemy of all Islam. Even Persia had not as yet extended recognition, and aiding immigrants would certainly sit badly with the Arab states surrounding it. The situation was a sticky one. We were suffered here, I gathered, but out of sight, consigned to silence. Still, the Shah deserved our deepest gratitude. He, at least, allowed us to exist.

Other explanations were in order. I'd expected to be met by someone from the Mosad Aliyah, but Said had been sent by something called the J.D.C. The Mosad, Said told me, only handled the clandestine end of refugee escapes. Now that we were in the clear, the J.D.C. assumed responsibility for us. At his second use of these initials, I asked him what they stood for, and astonished that I didn't know, he spelled them out: Joint Distribution Committee. That conveyed as much to me as J.D.C. We'd never heard about the "Joint" at home.

In the bus on the way to the Mahane, the refugee encampment on the outskirts of the city, Said held me fascinated with the story of the J.D.C. Delightedly I learned that Jews had brought a worldwide body into being, big and strong enough to be a major influence on our behalf. Accustomed as I was to small and secret cells, each dependent on itself and all of it illegal, the scope and openness of Joint procedures staggered me.

Said was a fount of information, which I pumped without a pause. When the J.D.C. had been exhausted, I asked about the Persians. "First of all," he started, "stop saying 'Persia.' It's now Iran. And the people are Iranians, or Irani. There's still some argument on that."

Describing them as touchy and intelligent, he said they were a subtle people, but addicted to insane exaggeration. So far, they sounded like Iraqis. "They tend to be pretentious," he continued, "and they're quick to make excessive promises. Probably they're summed up best by what they say about each other. 'All promise, no performance.' "

Too engrossed in listening to look outside, I didn't see anything of Teheran. As Said finished speaking, we stopped and idled at a massive gate, the only opening in mud-brick walls that stretched out endlessly on either side. We'd arrived at the Mahane, once a Jewish burial ground, abandoned when a new one opened.

The iron portals swung apart and, passing through, we rolled on to a barren clearing where we disembarked. Rows of temporary wooden barracks ringed the square, slapped hurriedly together to house the maximum of bodies in the minimum of space and comfort. Baba would have shuddered at the sloppiness of the construction.

Observing my reaction, Said was apologetic. "Some are only here a day, and everyone will go within two weeks, but for each who leaves, another one arrives. We always have about 600." He'd told me what I wanted most to hear. I'd be gone from here in two weeks at the worst. With luck, I might be flying off to Israel tomorrow. In light of that, who cared about accommodations? Defensively, however, Said pointed out some more substantial structures which served the camp as offices, bath facilities, and food-dispensing centers. "We even have a clinic," and he nodded toward a smallish but a solid-looking building. If I didn't leave too soon, I'd make a point, I thought, of stopping in; perhaps I'd even know the doctor.

Camp personnel had taken over, and no longer needed by my people, I welcomed Said's walking me to meet Akiba, the Director of the Mahane. As a courtesy, Said informed me, he always registered the leader of a group himself. The Director, though initially appearing rather gruff, greeted me as warmly as an uncle, and from this excellent beginning, everything continued to improve.

"You're the lucky one," he boomed. "Someone who was scheduled to go tonight took sick. You can take his place. You'll be in Israel by dinnertime."

Amused by my expression—my jaw had come unhinged—he clapped me on the back and handed me a piece of paper. "For our records," he explained. "Once you fill this out, off you'll go."

My fingers were so nerveless, I could hardly hold the pen, and Akiba snorted with delight at my excitement. I was handing him the registration when I sensed another presence; at my rear, a voice I recognized exclaimed, "It's Haim! How lucky you have come!"

Sipora sounded absolutely ardent, and when she spoke again, in the middle of our warm embrace, the reason for her superfervent welcome was revealed.

"Our doctor left us yesterday. How lucky you've arrived!"

Akiba's eyes popped wide, and something warned me that I wasn't all that "lucky."

"So you're a doctor." Akiba sounded like a drowning man who'd stumbled on a sandbar. "Well, that's a different story." With that, I knew I wasn't going.

Happy as he was to have a doctor dropped from Heaven, my stricken look distressed him. "It's only for a little while," he assured me. "Israel has promised an immediate replacement, but for now, we really need you."

My Achilles' heel was being needed, and the change in my expression didn't escape Akiba. To hearten me still more, he said I'd get a salary, "the same as doctors earn in Israel itself." I'd also have a room in the dispensary instead of sleeping in a barracks bunk.

Intrigued now by the prospect of a "practice," I pretended more dejection than I truly felt. Akiba could have ordered me to work the clinic, but preferring to persuade me, he'd put me in the driver's seat. From that position, I argued for some further "perks." My clothes were little more than rags, and my shoes, indeed, *were* rags. Saying that I couldn't see patients in that sorry state, I asked for an advance, and an escort who could help me shop.

Aware he'd been maneuvered, but entertained by my audacity, Akiba shook his head in mock despair and headed for the office safe. "Your first month's salary," he said, counting out a sheaf of varitinted tissue paper inscribed with characters I'd learned in kindergarten but which didn't add up to any words I'd ever seen. The alphabet was Arabic; the language wasn't.

At my baffled look, Akiba fanned the currency and pointed out the figures. "They call it *tuman.* Here you are, 400 *tuman.*" Seeing I was still confused, he made another stab at explanation. "It's equal to a hundred pounds, Israeli." Israeli pounds were just as much a mystery as *tuman.* Sipora, who'd been silently observing, finally spoke up, stating the amount in money I could comprehend. Translated into *dinars,* I'd be making more than any intern in Iraq. A spiteful and altogether gratifying glow suffused me.

Since Sipora knew the city, Akiba sent her off with me. In the taxi, careening into Teheran, we could have been in Baghdad. As at home, every driver seemed intent on either suicide or slaughter. Flinching in my seat and getting slightly carsick, I suggested that we leave the cab and stroll while still some distance from our destination.

We were heading for the intersection of Lalazar and Istanbul, in the central business zone, where the Jewish shops were concentrated. Sipora trotted by my side in silence, understanding that my every sense was wholly focused on the scene before me. The sights and sounds, I knew, would never have as strong an impact as at this first encounter.

On the jam-packed streets, pushcarts vied for space with Cadillacs and loaded donkeys. Wagons, floridly adorned with painted patterns, were hauled along by horses hung with tinkling bells and braided necklaces. Some had manes and faces stained with henna, others flaunted red-gold legs and tails. Blue beads on every harness warded off the Evil Eye.

Farther down the avenue, a string of camels tied up traffic—Kashgai camels, according to Sipora, directing my attention to the high flapped hats and thick felt vests of those who drove them—migrant tribesmen, here to trade, having come up from the Kuh-i-Dina, where mountain winds drove fiercely down the treeless slopes. Too warmly dressed for Teheran and homesick for the heights, they dripped with sweat and loudly cursed the city and their stubborn, spitting camels.

We stopped a moment to see a wrestling bear and then again to buy some sunflower seeds and glacéed fruit. Tiny, open-fronted stalls offered everything from socks to spice cakes, and the sidewalks swarmed with peddlers, many selling lottery tickets, loudly shouting that they had the winners. Our appetites were whetted by luscious smells from charcoal braziers at the corner snack bars: cumin-scented sizzling lamb and ibex, roasted eggplant, saffron-crusted rice with raisins.

As in Baghdad, music blared from radios in every shop, and, also as in Baghdad, I watched the headgear of the world pass by. Tarbushes, fezes, turbans—some green, proclaiming that the wearer was descended from the Prophet. I saw kepis, skullcaps, even homburgs. All I missed was a *sadara,* like the one that Baba wore. The thought of Baba made me look more closely at the buildings, opening my eyes to other similarities, such as crooked builders who cheated on construction for the state. The lavish opera house, I saw, was already half-collapsed.

But there were differences as well. Throughout our walk, not a single beggar whined and held a hand out. As I later learned, derelicts were rounded up routinely and shipped to rehabilitation centers to be taught a trade. What really staggered me, however, was the overall civility.

Take the waiters in the streets. Rushing steaming cups of tea to shops, they looked exactly like their counterparts in Baghdad. The huge brass trays, cups teetering, one atop another, were identical. When I saw a briskly striding walker accidentally strike a tray, causing all the cups to crash, I caught Sipora by the arm and pulled her back, out of range of the anticipated battle. In Baghdad, the waiter would have done his best to kill the bumper. To my astonishment, the two men stood and talked. What most impressed me was that each politely called the other "*Agha,*" a title of respect, the Middle East equivalent of "Sir."

In general, the mass of men resembled Spaniards or Italians, and seemed to share their temperament as well as their appearance. Said had ticked them off, correctly, as mercurial and vocal, but he hadn't mentioned noncombative.

The other sex was also a surprise. In the downtown area, mostly populated by the more sophisticated city women, the great majority were wearing Western dress and walked about unveiled. When, inadvertently, I met a woman's eye, she didn't look away. *I* did. I also blushed. Such contact was taboo where I grew up. Even older women seemed much freer than Iraqi Arabs. Unlike the full-length, all-encompassing *abaya,* their *chadors* only reached the shoulders.

My conversation with Said had primed me for another, much more vital, deviation. Where Baghdad looked to Britain as a model, Teheran had taken to the U.S.A. Movies from America were advertised on most of the marquees, and Mickey Mouse was everywhere. "Nylons from New York" were hawked by sidewalk vendors, and the coiffures of the smartest women were copied from the films. I'd seen them on my favorite stars, but never on a human head. Some suits the men were wearing also looked familiar from the movies, and many, it developed, were authentically American—secondhand and somewhat shabby, but snatched up nonetheless by admirers of all Americana. The year before, I learned, a million dollars' worth had been imported.

In the middle of the day, with Sipora at my side, and almost in the center of the city, a girl accosted me and said a few soft words in Farsi. From the way she spoke, and from Sipora's smothered giggle, I understood that I'd been propositioned by a pro. When I waved her off, she in turn waved off the horse and buggy keeping pace with her as she paraded. Sipora said the drivers and the walkers worked in teams. If the harlot hooked a client, they'd climb into the carriage to be taken to a section of the city entirely inhabited by whores. The profession was permitted, the performance area restricted.

In the Jewish mercantile sphere, where I thought I'd feel at home, I was just as much at sea as on the avenue. Everyone spoke Farsi, and my only Persian was a little nature poem I'd learned from Baba. "Birds" and "baby lambs," however, had little application to my current needs.

On my first foray, for shorts, Sipora briefed me on the basic terms and waited on the sidewalk as I went inside to shop. When I asked to see the underwear, the clerk asked me a question. I could tell because his voice went up. At my Arabic response, he shook his head and tried again in stilted English. He was asking me my size, and while I understood his words, I couldn't answer. I didn't *know* my size, not in underwear or any other article. In my entire life I'd never had to buy a piece of clothing. Nana and Nazima had always made my shirts and shorts, a tailor cousin cut and sewed my pants and suits, and my shoes were custom-cobbled. Every place I shopped, the merchant had to measure me.

Back in camp, Sipora took me on a tour of the facility I'd supervise. My "quarters," which had sounded so impressive when Akiba said the word, were scarcely big enough to hold a bed. My bedroom door opened on a slightly larger space, which held a cabinet containing our supplies and an improvised examination table. Eight narrow cots completely filled the third and final room. When necessary to segregate the male and female patients or to isolate a case, Sipora said they simply draped some bedsheets. To my dismay, there was almost no equipment, not even basic instruments other than syringes and a set of scalpels. This medical facility was merely an inflated first-aid station.

At the moment no one occupied the cots, so I could vent my views without restraint. An aide, faced away from me, folding towels, was startled, so I thought, by what I said and how I said it, and she gave a little shriek. It was my voice, however, not my vehemence, that shook her up. Shouting, "Heskel!" she was almost in my arms before I recognized Aziza. Another cousin!

I hadn't known she'd left Iraq, and only now did I discover that Aziza, too, had been an active member of the underground. With Sipora due to leave soon, she told me she'd be taking over as my chief assistant. We whooped like kids, and when I said Claireed was also in the camp, she screamed again. Sipora cleared her throat, reluctant to disrupt our glad reunion, but time was short, she said, and before she went, she had to teach me the routine. "The grind begins tomorrow morning," she explained.

I'd be examining each new arrival; before the government permitted us to fly a person from Iran, I had to certify that he or she was fit. The requirements included tests for syphilis and active lung disease, a smallpox vaccination, and an antityphoid shot. Those alone would eat up all the day, with no allowance for emergencies or treatment of the chronic illnesses I'd certainly encounter. The older refugees all had some condition that demanded care, but the camp itself cried out for most of my attention.

Overall, the situation was horrendous, and this, of course, affected health. That put the matter squarely in my province. In its current state, the place was on the very edge of epidemic. Swarms of flies surrounded stinking heaps of garbage. Collection was erratic, and provision for disposal nonexistent. One look inside the privy informed me that a latrine squad had never been assigned. Sanitary measures were my first priority.

With a list of what was needed, I went to see Akiba, and walked in on his meeting with a tall, blond man. Lounging at his ease, the fellow looked relaxed and quite at home. On being introduced and learning that this Lova was the J.D.C. liaison, I unloaded all my problems. My abruptness didn't bother him at all, and nodding his approval of the points I made, he jotted notes. Minutes after finishing, we'd formed a plan of action. Lova was another hyperactive, but an older, more experienced, and shrewder man than I. I knew at once that we'd do well together. He undertook to organize the health squads, and said he'd see to our incinerator.

With Lova as an ally, I decided I could take some time to catch up on my own affairs. Since Aziza had most recent news of home, I headed off to track her down and talk. She'd left Baghdad three days later than Claireed and I, but her group of four young people could safely navigate the northern route, so the trip to Teheran had taken just a day.

Naturally, I asked first for the family; everyone, she said, was fine and praying for me daily. As for school, she'd heard from friends about the goings-on at graduation. The custom was to call the students' names in the order of their academic standing, and the first name called was mine. When there was no response, the Dean repeated it again. As he said my name in Baghdad, I was scrambling up a Persian mountain.

A voice had called out from the audience, "He's left for Tel Aviv," and disquieted by this, the Dean had dropped my medical degree, which slowly rolled across the dais. The audience exploded into laughter, and the ceremony turned into a shambles. On the following day, when Baba showed up at the College and asked the Dean for my diploma, he'd been coldly told I'd have to come for it myself.

While I was gratified to hear that I had headed up my class, I mourned the missing parchment. Then Aziza told me that the day I left, Lassie had been struck down by a truck. She'd run into the street, seeking me, no doubt, and died for wanting to be with me. Feeling tears well up, I turned and ran, trying not to cry until I closed the door behind me in my tiny quarters. In the loss of my companion, a living creature who adored me, the lack of a diploma was suddenly of no significance. Not then.

31

When I wakened to my first full day as camp physician, I was pleasantly surprised to find the morning air invigorating. This time of year in Baghdad, the heat would be unbearable, the air opaque with suffocating dust, and my sinuses completely clogged. Here the sun was screened by drifts of downy clouds, constantly evolving in the Elburz range which towered over Teheran. Supine in bed, I could see the summit of Mount Demavent, thrusting more than three miles high. The altitude of Teheran itself, 4000 feet above sea level, induced a slightly giddy feeling on arising.

Light-headedness was pleasant, I was thinking, when my bowels grumbled and the day turned grim. Bloody diarrhea announced that I had dysentery, probably acquired at the Persian army post. As I was soon to find, almost the entire camp was suffering the same complaint. If not for that, I surely would have figured it as punishment for eating meat with milk. However, the scope of the disease pointed to contaminated water.

Baghdad was distinguished in the Middle East for the sweetness of its drinking water; our intestines had no tolerance for Teheran's polluted soup. The city had no sewage system. Tumbling from the mountains, fresh and clear, the water was directed into rough stone gutters, open to the elements and to anyone for any purpose. Children waded in these *jubes,* workers washed in them, and in them, animals relieved themselves. Along with drinking water, the ancient ditches also doled out typhoid and diphtheria.

Everyone who could afford it brought *abshah.* This "water of the King" was hauled down from the hills in metal hogsheads, and hawked about from horsecarts. The containers, though, were so eroded that even much *abshah* was suspect. At least we had supplies of drugs to ease the diarrhea. Almost at once, I had more pressing problems.

Sipora was about to leave, but since she was on duty till the moment of departure, her farewell celebration was a picnic-style lunch in the dispensary. In the midst of it, an office clerk came gasping in, "They're bringing her—you'd better come!"

Lying on a doubled blanket borne by frightened bunkmates, Selima was so cyanotic she was turning blue, and so short of breath she couldn't speak. She was also very, very pregnant. Her heart was failing, and her labor was about to start. Without a history, I had to guess at what had done the damage. Rheumatic heart disease seemed likely.

Before I got the orders out, Sipora had syringes at the ready, and Aziza was preparing to insert a tube. The digoxin took effect upon injection, and once the oxygen was flowing and the patient started turning pink, I left to see Akiba.

We were unequipped for anything but upset stomachs and simple lacerations. If delivery required even forceps, or—God forbid!—a surgical procedure, we'd lose Selima and her baby. And in her condition, we could almost count on complications. A solution was at hand, however. Sipora was about to leave for Israel. We could put Selima on the plane with her. I assured Akiba that should labor start en route, Sipora was as capable of coping with its early stages as I'd be myself. (Or even more so, though I didn't add it.) First pregnancies were apt to be prolonged, so by the time of birth, they'd likely be in Israel and safely in a hospital. As a dividend, the baby would be born a *sabra.* To my intense relief, Akiba nodded his agreement and began at once to make arrangements.

With Selima on her way, I settled back to read in bed that evening with an unaccustomed sense of true tranquillity. I'd faced and solved the first real problem of my practice. About 10 P.M., when I estimated that Selima's plane was setting down in Israel, I fell peacefully asleep. At 1 A.M., a haggard, spent Sipora was shaking me awake. For a moment I thought it was a nightmare, which indeed it proved to be.

Engine trouble had delayed the take-off. Then, several hours out of Teheran, they'd lost an engine, and limped on back in lieu of landing on unfriendly soil. Sipora had returned to camp to brief me and to bring Selima in. Her water had already broken; birth was imminent. My problem had come home again.

Murmuring "Goodbye, I'm sorry, but I have to get back to the airfield," Sipora said she'd wake Aziza while I got my pants on. Aziza and I were both still buttoning up when we burst into the ward. As we entered, Sipora slipped away; even at the risk of being left behind, she hadn't left her patient.

The baby's head was visibly engaged, and the mother's face was bluer than before. More digoxin stabilized her heart, but Selima lay inert. Trying to induce contractions, I administered the standard shot of Pitocin, to no effect. Her pulse was speeding up, the baby's heartbeat growing weaker. Sweat pouring down my back, and as close to panic as I'd ever been, I cursed whoever hadn't ordered forceps. I'd have to use the only tools I had. My own two hands. There wasn't even time to scrub.

Pulling on some rubber gloves, I had Aziza stand where she could instantly apply firm pressure, pushing on Selima's abdomen to help expel the infant when I gave the order. I'd only read about the next procedure, but I summoned up the illustrations in the textbook and slid my left hand into the vagina. On encountering the baby's head, I gently probed on past the soft eye sockets and the nub of nose to find the infant's mouth. I introduced my index and my middle fingers, my ring and little fingers resting on the baby's cheekbones for support. With my right hand in the birth canal, I cupped the fragile skull and began to ease the baby out.

"Now!" I gritted at Aziza, and with her pressure on the uterus, the infant's head emerged. Shifting hands, I helped the shoulders through, and it was over. Before I could administer the little spank for respiration, the boy gave out a healthy squeal and started turning pink. All of him was absolutely perfect, and Selima's uterus was also acting as it should, contracting normally, expelling the placenta in a single stringy clump. A textbook birth, by any standard, and to top it off, the mother named the baby after me!

That evening, at the first of what would be our daily meetings, Lova and Akiba seemed to view me in a slightly different light. The emergency had subtly changed my status from that of clever but unseasoned kid to capable adult. As warm as both had been to me before the birth, they'd acted with a certain condescension stemming from their senior years. We were speaking now as equals.

Aside from medicine, however, I had much to learn. In my innocence of Persian politics, I asked if we could borrow some equipment from the city's health facilities. Akiba hooted loudly. "Don't bother learning 'lend' in Farsi," he advised. "The authorities don't lend. They only sell."

At my startled look, Akiba laughed again. "Did you think, by any chance, that all of this"—he swept his arm around, encompassing the camp—"is out of love of Jews or justice? We pay for everything. We pay and pay and pay."

Lova leaped to the defense of Shah Pahlevi, and Akiba grudgingly agreed that the Shah had shown a genuine goodwill toward Jewish refugees. "All right. Okay." He gave some ground. "Let's all be grateful to the Shah. But aside from him, admit it, everyone is out to fleece us."

Lova countered, "Not just us, everyone robs everyone. Larceny's a way of life here. Without a little something extra, no one lifts a finger, not a workman, not a government official. *Especially* not a government official." Now *he* was getting heated. "And they aren't even honest crooks. They'll take the bribe and double-cross you. Or not do anything at all. I don't know which is worse, the lazy bastards!"

Lova sighed, "I try to keep my temper, but sometimes I could kick their tails, and of course I can't say anything but 'Please' and 'Thank you.' "

Frustrated in his daily efforts and seldom able to relieve his feelings, Lova seized upon my presence to unload. I learned that nothing had been given us except by other Jews. Nothing but asylum. The land we camped on was the property of Persian Jews, and every stick of furniture, every bite of food was dearly bought and paid for by the J.D.C. And even our asylum was restricted. Once a refugee arrived at the Mahane, he couldn't leave until he took the plane to Israel. Only camp officials who had business in the city were exempt, and only on condition that they make no mention of the camp to anyone except their Persian counterparts. Few ordinary citizens even knew the place existed.

Lova grumbled, "But it sometimes seems that *everyone* is in the government. It's not overstaffed, it's overstuffed!"

Politicians paid off debts by putting people on the public payroll, sometimes on several payrolls. He described departments "padded like a mattress." Typically, the total of employees on the books might be two hundred, but only fifty ever showed up at the office.

Summing up the system as corrupt, undisciplined, and devious, Lova made a glum prediction that Iranis would, in time, explode. Except for the bureaucracy, the landlords, and the moneylenders, the average man earned something less than $50 annually. Right now, he said, in famine-stricken Azerbaijan, where the major share of Persia's grain was grown, the tenant farmers slowly starved. What harvest was achieved went almost wholly to the owners of the land, who lived palatially in distant cities. Food shipped in to feed the children had been looted by officials, and usurers made stingy loans at interest rates ensuring endless servitude. The debts survived the debtors, legacies to those they left behind.

"We'll be out of here before it happens," Lova said, "but someday soon . . . kaboom!"

To change the subject, I asked about the messenger who'd put us on the train to Teheran.

"Some 'messenger,' " Akiba twitted me. "Like Muhammad was a messenger of God!"

Ziadi, it appears, was one of Mosad's most outstanding men. A "wonder boy," according to Akiba, he could conjure up an exit visa out of air. So my instincts had been on the beam; I'd sensed Ziadi's strength. Though I filed his name for future reference, it was unlikely, Lova said, that we'd ever meet again.

For the next few days my time was occupied entirely with duties as a doctor. New refugees were streaming in, and all of those already resident were suffering, in some degree, from diarrhea. Except for hasty meals and tending to my own distress, I hardly left the clinic or had a thought beyond our most immediate concerns at camp. In a situation such as ours, clean latrines were far more vital than the rise and fall of empires. The Mahane was a world within a world. Self-contained and spinning in restricted space, it tended to contract into an ever-smaller orbit.

I was shaken back into awareness at the first of weekly meetings with officials of the J.D.C., the Mosad, and the Jewish Agency. On arrival, I overheard some talk about "the bombings," and assumed, of course, they'd taken place in Israel, where terrorists continued their promiscuous attacks. A moment later, someone mentioned Baghdad.

Some ten days after my departure, the quarters of the Jewish Council had been hit. Three days after that, Kahwat el-Shat was blasted. That bit of news was like a bombshell. A riverside cafe, a rendezvous for Jews after their attendance at the synagogue, Kahwat el-Shat was one of Baba's favorite places.

Apparently the main objective hadn't been to murder Jews. Within an hour of the incident, the government was on the air, announcing that "reactionary elements among the Zionists" had planted the explosive; their aim, or so the propaganda said, was to scare Iraqi Jews into scuttling off to Israel. The ghetto now believed that the government itself had backed the bombing. This time, perhaps, it *wished* the Jews to go but didn't want to say so. They'd used the Zionists instead.

In any case, the man from J.D.C. concluded, most Iraqi Jews were finally convinced that going was a good idea. Following the second detonation, 500 had applied to leave. On orders from the government, the Jewish Council was setting up assembly centers in the synagogues, from which departing Jews would be transported to their planes. At Nicosia, the emigrés would transfer to another plane for Israel. The route was so arranged to satisfy the phobic loathing for the Jewish state. A wheel which touched Israeli soil would never be permitted to return and taint Iraq.

The son of the Prime Minister was getting rich on refugees. As a reward for assigning it the right to ferry Jews, the selected airline paid him a percentage based on passengers. Every Jew aboard meant money.

As usual, the allegations of the government aroused the students, and the student demonstrations stirred the populace. The same old game was on again, and more pogroms might well be in the offing. If Baba still persisted in remaining, I feared for the entire family, and since no one ever said I couldn't call home, I simply went ahead.

I walked into the central office, scrawled the city and the number for a stolid clerk, counted out the fee, and fidgeted for half an hour, almost hoping that they couldn't make connection.

It belatedly occurred to me that I could be a danger to the rest of the Haddads. All officials weren't stupid, even in Iraq. The mails, I knew, were monitored, so it also stood to reason that the phones were tapped—not all of them, not always, since they couldn't spare the personnel—but some of them, sometimes. I'd have to trust to luck and also edit every word I uttered. And as much as possible, of course, I'd speak in code.

I could trust the others to contain themselves, but if Nana heard my voice, she'd certainly shriek, "Heskel!" Fortunately Nana was afraid of phones and only answered ours if no one else was in the house.

As it happened, Baba answered, and heartened by this good beginning, I spoke up briskly. To my horror, no sooner had I said, "It's Hassan here," than Baba fell apart. Without allowing me to get another word in, much less warn him to be circumspect, he plowed ahead, not about his problems but only of his worry over me "until the guide got back and said that you were safe." In a single breath, unstoppable as flood tide in the Tigris, he told me that I'd topped my class at college. To be sure I understood, he said it twice, and twice I shuddered. An *idiot* listening in would have to be suspicious. Just "guide" would trigger close attention. Couple it with "safe" and we were really in the soup! Baba's breaking down would indicate that someone very near and dear was on the phone. All they had to do was tick off all the family members. The only one they wouldn't find was me . . . the Hiyyim sought for "Zionist activities against the state." In the present climate, that could hang them all. The charge would be they'd "aided and abetted" me.

My time was up before I'd asked a single question, but at least I knew the family was still intact. I'd sorted out the voices in the background, and everyone was present and accounted for. However, I was just as ignorant of Baba's plans as when I'd placed the call.

Though more concerned about the family with every passing moment, my restlessness was drained away by eighteen-hour workdays. In the following weeks the intermittent trickles turned into a flood of worn and frightened refugees, and I fell into a set routine, checking out the emigrés on their arrival.

In the camp, the populace at one point reached a staggering 6000, and the days and nights blurred one into another. Since Akiba only kept responding that "they promised," I stopped inquiring about the other doctor. My stay, I saw, was doomed to be indefinite, but once the crush was over and some time remained for me, I made every minute count.

Through Lova, I acquired every street map of Jerusalem and Tel Aviv obtainable in Teheran, and spent off-duty hours committing them to memory, along with distances from place to place and means of public transportation.

When I *did* arrive in Israel, I wouldn't waste a second in floundering around to find my way.

When I could manage an entire afternoon, I'd take a cab to Teheran, each time to a different section of the city. Teheran was rags and riches. Pretentious villas spilled into the northern suburbs, while off the main road south—in an area referred to as "the Pit"—people lived like animals in caves carved out by nature.

Practicing my Farsi, I explored the five-square-mile maze of markets in the city. The largest of the world's bazaars, the Sabzeh-Midan smelled of every spice on earth, all overlaid, however, with something sharply acrid that was strange to me. In several trips, I couldn't identify the odor, which no one else appeared to notice.

On my initial visit, hair was being hennaed brilliant orange in a tiny alley, while a turn away, artisans were sheathing teeth in gleaming gold. The clang of coppersmithing hammers cut through donkey brays and porters' curses. Bent double by their burdens, some men would never stand erect beyond the age of thirty; their spines were ankylosed for life.

The sick and maimed bought amulets to cure their ills. Leaves and seeds were parceled out, both to brew as medicine and burn as incense. Shavings, paper-thin, of sun-dried snake and lizard sold for more than gold. One supposedly restored the strength to shriveled limbs, another cleansed the lungs. The most expensive promised superpotency and many sons.

Outside the city, in one day's aimless walking, I saw a hillside strewn with patches of exotic brilliant blooms, such flowers as I'd never seen except in dreams. Coming closer, I discovered them to be of more substantial stuff, the finest wool, in fact. Nearer now, I recognized the acrid odor. Here, as in the Sabzeh-Midan, it emanated from exquisite Persian rugs; the dyes, all vegetable in origin, mingled with the ovine reek of fleece that only time and water would dispel. Our rugs at home were old and therefore odor-free. In a shallow pool at the bottom of the slope, the carpet washers plied their trade, treading out the dirt, then spreading out the richly colored rugs to dry.

In the main, however, my days were dull and colorless; I hadn't planned to specialize in diarrhea. The news from home continued to be gloomy, with the only welcome word about my brother. A friend of one of S'hak's friends, just recently arrived, informed me that my brother had acquired a brick mill and was doing very well indeed. The government itself was buying S'hak's bricks. So normality of sorts persisted. If the price was right and the payoffs properly distributed, even now a Jew could operate. And S'hak certainly could operate! If I knew my brother, as long as he did business he'd remain in Baghdad. Conceivably, he'd be the last to leave the city.

The thought provoked a kind of perverse pride. Foolhardy he might be, but gutsy, and I'd bet on him to beat them at their game. When we met again in Israel, I'd have to tell him how he'd cheered me up.

32

Since Lova was our liaison with everyone outside the camp, we saw him daily. When just the two of us were talking, at my request the conversation was entirely in English. Mine was textbook British, self-consciously correct and somewhat nineteenth century in style; his was looser, more colloquial than mine, spiced with slang and Yiddish, which at first I found it difficult to follow. Under Lova's tutelage, however, my speech freed up and flowed.

Despite the pleasure of his company, I balked one day at his suggestion of an outing in the newest Jewish cemetery. There was something there he thought I ought to see. "We're *living* in a cemetery," I protested. "Even if the other's new, what could be so novel?" But Lova was unusually insistent, and finally I climbed into the car beside him.

Inside the gate, instead of quiet gravesites, we came upon a tattered, milling mob, its members oddly dressed and alien in their every aspect. Certainly they weren't city people—but Jewish peasants? Whoever heard of Jewish peasants? Or were they even Jews at all? I turned to Lova for an explanation, but he shook his head and raised his hand to halt me. "Just listen."

We were close enough by now for isolated snatches to be heard above the hum. Though neither Arabic nor Farsi—not Hebrew either—something in the language struck a chord. Single words were understandable, or almost, and all at once I knew their source. This motley ragged mass was speaking a derivative of Aramaic, the language I'd encountered in the Zohar! Impure, admixed, distorted, but unmistakably the ancient tongue!

On spotting us, the entire teeming swarm came surging toward the car, stopping only feet away to stare in sudden silence. Lova thrust his head out to ask if anyone spoke Farsi. An arm shot up, and someone in the rear began to wriggle forward. While he worked his way, Lova seized the opportunity to shed some light.

These, he said, were Kurdish Jews, 2000 here, 4000 more dispersed among the city's synagogues. Too soon for me, the Farsi-speaking volunteer commanded our attention, leaving me a thousand questions clamoring for answers. Clearly, though, Lova wanted me to see things for myself before he said much more.

Mordechai, our would-be aide, was short and thin, with sunken cheeks and heavy, overhanging eyelids, leaving only slits for him to see through. Still, he looked alert, and certainly spoke Farsi—faster than my ear could follow. In response to something Lova said, he shouted out a message to the churning mob. "*Aghai Dektôr,*" I understood. "Mr. Doctor."

The title elicited immediate respect in Baghdad, but from all appearances, it commanded something that approached idolatry among the Kurds. All speech ceased, all movement was suspended, and every eye was fixed on me.

Lova pushed me on ahead of him and pointed to the chapel. "That's the place," he said, without explaining further, and almost bursting with importance, Mordechai again addressed the crowd, and again he mentioned "*Aghai Dektôr.*" A path appeared as if he'd waved a wand, and I felt a bit like Moses must have when the Red Sea split before him. The transient glory faded swiftly in the misery I now encountered, only inches off. The skin of every face I saw was parchmentlike in tone and texture. Skull-bare bones seemed just about to burst their sheathes, and radiating cracks around anemic lips were added evidence of dangerous nutritional deficiencies. Hollow, fevered cheeks . . . swollen red-rimmed eyes . . . wheezing aspiration . . . hacking coughs and constant spitting. . . . With every step, I diagnosed a new disease. Only hunger, filth, and apathy were common to them all.

In the chapel, another human sea receded under Mordechai's instructions, revealing, at the far end of the room, a huddled heap of rags, from which a moan arose. I ran to find a woman dying—not in a bed, not even on a blanket, but on bare and splintered boards. Her head lay cradled in a weeping woman's lap. Her own emaciated flesh was all the ease she had to offer.

Anticipating my eruption, Lova hastily informed me that the Kurds had just arrived. "They took us by complete surprise," he said.

Hopeless as I knew it was, I turned back to the dying woman. Even in the best of hospitals, I couldn't have helped, but that was little comfort. Moribund, she struggled for each shallow breath, and on her brow, my fingertips felt scorched by fever. She was burning up and burning out. Terminal pneumonia.

When I shook my head and said that nothing could be done, Lova stated that he'd thought as much. He'd only brought me here to see how matters stood.

"If I'd described it, would you really understand?" he asked. Even seeing, hearing, smelling it, I didn't understand. How could such conditions be permitted to continue?

Staving off my questions, Lova said that he had more to show me. On a tour around the cemetery, I grew more incensed at every turn. Not even tents had been provided. The refugees had housed themselves in every sort of makeshift shelter, mostly improvised from random lengths of stained and rotting canvas, stretched across some upright sticks, at best providing stippled shade but no protection from the other elements or any privacy at all.

The "residential" area was as wide and long as several city squares. Unlike the other cemetery, where ancient trees created cool and pleasant enclaves, all here was open to a torrid sun. In the Iraqi camp we had a fountain and a pool, and grass grew green and soft. Here, the barren ground grew rocks. Table-flat, with nothing but some scraggly shrubs to stop the eye, the sheer monotony was mind-destroying. There were no distractions, nothing to engage the senses, no amenities of any kind. A vegetable might feel at home here, except that even vegetables need food and water.

Too furious to hold it in a minute longer, I turned my wrath on Lova, demanding that he tell me where these people ate. *What* were they eating? Where were the toilets? In the entire area, I hadn't seen a water tap, much less a place to wash. The camp was asking for an epidemic. Poor Lova. I blasted him with accusations and he let me rave without attempting a defense.

When I'd blown off all my excess steam, he steered me to the car, saying that I had to see the synagogue as well. On the way, he'd tell me everything he knew.

For the last 2000 years, he started, these Kurdish Jews had lived among the *Mislim* Kurds, although in separate settlements, in the farthest northwest corner of Iran, in a wedge of land with Turkey on one side of it and Russia on the other. According to the Kurdish Jews, they were direct descendants of the ten lost tribes of Israel. Since the first dispersion, they'd been awaiting the return of the Messiah, so when word had reached the region that King David was again in Israel, they gathered to begin the journey back to join him.

My startled grunt made Lova grin. "It's logical. An Israel reborn, with a David at its head. All they heard was David, not Ben-Gurion. To them, King David. After all, they've been expecting him."

Word had also spread that scattered Jews from every outpost of the world were being borne to Israel on eagles' wings. I worked out that allusion on my own. God had said to Moses "and I will carry them on wings of eagles." Their eagles were our airplanes, awaiting them in Teheran. With only what they wore and what pots and pans and small religious relics they could salvage from marauding mountain tribesmen, they'd come en masse to mount the eagles.

As Lova toured me through the seven synagogues, each crammed so far beyond capacity that most within had only room to stand, he acquainted me with Kurdish Jewish life. Despite the centuries of sharing territory with the *Mislim* Kurds, the Jews remained a race apart, forever prey to other mountain people. They were the merchants of the mountains and also acted as accountants to the tribal chiefs. Once farmers, their land had long since been expropriated by the local sheikhs, and their existence was dependent on the sheikhs' protection.

Among their neighbors, anti-Semitism wasn't only inbred, but actively encouraged as an outlet for aggression. While tribal feuds were everyday affairs, with each group always warring with at least one other, when complete and utter chaos threatened, the leaders called for common cause against the Jews, and all joined arms to crush the "enemy of Islam." Excess energy drained off, as if vented through a steam valve.

In self-defense, the Jewish Kurds built sturdy stone and timber homes, consolidated into tight-knit hamlets, clinging to the hillsides. The *M'silmin,* mostly nomads, lived in tents. Nonetheless, once night had fallen, no Jew would venture out of doors without an urgent reason. To do so was to risk a certain robbery and often death.

And still these Jews had made the journey here to Teheran. Responding to the promise of their ancient prayers, they'd left without a backward look and braved their enemies to reach the eagles. Caught completely by surprise when the horde swept through the outskirts of the city, the Persian government had called the Jewish Council in. The Kurds, though Persian citizens, were suddenly a strictly Jewish problem. Lova said, "They told us to take care of it, and turned away."

Knowing more now of conditions in Iran, I could understand, if not condone, their sloughing off responsibility. Economically, and every other way, the country was disintegrating. In the face of two successive failed harvests, even those who farmed the land were going hungry. The entire feudal system was in dire straits. Though illiterate and almost slaves, the peasantry was finally protesting. The same 200 families, obscenely affluent already, were growing fatter by the minute while millions went to bed with empty bellies. Entire villages were owned by city dwellers who had never even seen the land, and now the starving peasants were streaming into Teheran to see if they could wrest a living from its riches. At the last assessment, almost 80,000 were already here, with more en route. The officials, whose long collusion with the landlords played a major part in bringing this to pass, were all wrapped up in quelling a rebellion. We couldn't hope for any help from them.

Among our own, as Lova laid it out for me, we also had dissension. At the insistence of the government, the Jewish Council acted swiftly to corral the Kurds and sweep them off the streets and out of sight. Temporarily, they emphasized, they'd feed and shelter them, but funds were low and spread too thin already. They sympathized, they even agonized, but in the last analysis, they owed their main allegiance to the Jews of Teheran; all responsibility for other Jews lay with the J.D.C.

The Joint contested this position, declaring it could only be accountable for foreign Jewish refugees, not native Persians like the Kurds. And while each establishment argued that the other ought to do the job, 6000 Jews were almost totally abandoned.

Indignant as a human being, I was almost apoplectic as a doctor. Already weak and harboring endemic ailments, some Kurds would never leave the cemetery, and the synagogues were hardly more than holding pens. Under these conditions, the old and frail would soon succumb to any one of ten diseases I'd seen evidenced already.

Lova watched me mutely. He knew me well enough to spot the signs of imminent explosion. When I boiled over, steaming that I'd take this on myself, he looked a little smug. Of course! The entire expedition had been planned for just this purpose, and he'd really roped me in. As a paid employee of the J.D.C., he was honor-bound to back up their decisions, so his hands were tied. He couldn't act himself, but he could spur *me* on, make me mad enough to take the bit between my teeth, then steer me to the proper people. Almost as important, he had a car at his disposal; in the next few hours, we almost ran its tires off.

Since the J.D.C. controlled the flow of funds, I started out by seeing the Director. A prime example of bureaucracy in fullest flower, his answer was "We have no allocation." Not "We have no money," but "No one has decided that we'd spend it this way." There wasn't time enough to argue. Before they drew a new agenda, drafted a prospectus, and neatly dotted every i, the Kurds would cease to be.

The Jewish Agency was sorry, but "our budget has already been approved." Without much hope, I tackled Mosad, and the story here was slightly easier to swallow. Mosad *had* no money—the only sane excuse.

In a single afternoon I'd exhausted all my sources. Heading back to camp, I was too depressed to talk, and Lova, also silent, drove as if he'd like to cause some carnage. When the rain began, though safe and dry inside, a shudder ran along my spine, and Lova's shoulders hunched involuntarily to hold it off. Both of us were thinking of the unprotected cemetery square.

In bed that night, exhausted by my efforts, I fell asleep at once. The air grew chill, the summer storm intensified, and solid sheets of water beat the roof above me. Awakened by the sound, well-blanketed and warm, I started weeping.

Obsessed with what I'd seen, I couldn't have been less interested in Lova's news. He came rushing to the clinic to tell me that a wire-service correspondent from the U.S.A. was coming to the camp. Whatever story she sent back would spread across America, he said. Since she was read by millions—tens of millions, he corrected—it was terribly important that we make a good impression. To underscore how vitally this visit could affect us, he stated that the highest Joint officials would be at her side every second that she spent with us. At that, a scheme emerged, full-blown in every detail, from my up-till-now infertile musings. For his own protection, I kept my Kurdish plan from Lova.

The visitor arrived in style, escorted by a corps of brass. Educated by the movies, I'd braced myself for someone on the jaded side, impervious to pain or pleasure. When I saw our correspondent, my civil little smile widened and I could have whooped. Middle-aged, dressed sensibly, with shoes selected more for comfort than for style, and just overweight enough to look maternal, her appearance made my plan seem truly possible. All it needed was another human being.

Normally Akiba would have been the host within the camp, but since he didn't speak English—a factor which I'd counted on—the duty fell to me.

The reactions of the correspondent were exactly what we wished; impressed with the entire operation, she promised us a glowing story. At the crucial moment, with the car drawn up for her departure, I said that there was something else I'd like to show her. Obligingly, she turned back toward the camp, but I shook my head and motioned toward the car, "I mean the *other* camp."

The Joint Director nearly had a stroke. "I'm afraid we don't have time for that," he interposed.

I countered with, "I'll take her there myself," and drawing on my film lore, added, "No one else has been there. It would be a scoop—exclusive!"

Amused no doubt by my naiveté, but impressed as well by my intensity, she said she'd like to see this special place. Swallowing his fury, the Director issued orders to the driver. We were off to tour the Kurdish camp, and the worst the Joint could do to me was kick me out of Persia. Tonight would not be soon enough!

Her sentiments were obvious, but only on her face at first. For half an hour we walked about without a word. When she spoke at last, she lit into the Joint Director in a voice that rasped with rage.

"How can you *allow* this!"

When he fumbled out, "Our budget . . . ," she stared him into silence.

"That's no excuse. Nothing could excuse this."

I was standing to the side and back of the Director, and she must have seen me nodding in agreement. A tiny smile twitched her lips. Smart lady. Having seen right through my little scheme to use her, she now became an active co-conspirator.

"I'll make a deal with you." She spoke again to the perspiring Director, and her tone this time was brisk and businesslike.

"This is quite a story," she began, and paused to let the threat implied sink in. He blanched and she continued, "However," and he brightened at the word, "I'll kill it if you promise that you'll help these people—and I mean today."

I thought his head might come unhinged from so much nodding in abject assent.

How well she'd played the scene! Behind his back, I pantomimed applause. To wind it up, she said she'd keep in touch. "I have sources," she advised. "I'll know what's going on, and I can always take the story off the spike."

If they noticed it at all, the others must have thought she'd had a sudden nervous tic, but the fleeting wink was meant for me. We'd won it for the Kurds!

33

The promises were implemented, and so promptly we were almost unprepared. Basic building was begun at once, with several crews at work. Medications asked for in the morning were delivered by the middle of the afternoon, and instead of shipping me to Israel, as I expected, the Joint requested that I stay and serve the Kurds in addition to my other duties.

Until another doctor came to the Iraqi camp, I'd split my time between the two, but spend my nights at the Mahane. Eventually, I'd move completely to the Kurds. Instead of disappointment at postponing my departure, I felt elated at the new assignment. If ever medicine could make a difference, it was here and now.

In my first official hour at the "other" cemetery, I made the chapel my dispensary and supervised its scouring to an antiseptic state. Before the day was out, the beds were in, with some already occupied. At my request, Lova had been tapped to act as temporary camp commander, with Mordechai as aide. Together we sorted out our refugees by strength and skills. Those few who spoke a decent Farsi were assigned to translate. Many of the Kurds were craftsmen and were put to work on building projects. Others, like the herdsmen, unskilled with tools or words, would serve as a policing force to keep the camp as clean as possible.

If time allowed, I hoped to teach the Kurds some basic Hebrew, but my first concerns were health and housing. Barracks rose like mushrooms after rain, and pipes were run for water taps and showers while the structures still were shells. As we dug latrines at one end of the open square, a food facility, complete with all equipment, came together at the other. I'd been dubious about the Joint's ability to follow through, but every pledge was honored. Help had been recruited from the Jewish Council, and inside the Joint itself, screws were turned to squeeze the funds required out of other channels into ours. Our lady correspondent had them running scared!

Before the walls had dried, the dispensary was doing booming business. Since I wasn't due to start my doctoring until the clinic was complete, no announcement had been made of my arrival, but everyone appeared to know that I was on the scene already. By the hundreds they came streaming toward the chapel, and it wasn't idle curiosity that urged them on. Every single one of them appeared to need attention.

Appalled by the dimensions of the problem, I wondered where to start and whether there would ever be an end. The mere evaluation of their ailments might take a month, and only the acutely ill could actually be treated. Almost sick myself with fear of failure, I gave the order to unlock the door, although alone, I knew, I couldn't even make a dent in such a multitude. And then another miracle occurred. Out of nowhere I had nurses. Three of them, all competent, accredited, and two days earlier than I'd expected.

Following the sketchiest of introductions, I situated two of them outside the building to control the flow. Acting as a triage team, they'd screen the crowd and send the sickest in to see me first. Feeling better, rather pleased, in fact, with my efficiency in setting up a system within seconds, I braced myself for one long ceaseless surge of Kurds. The flow shut off as soon as it began, however. My initial patient was a flushed-faced man with obvious pneumonia—and a million healthy lice. In legions, they meandered in the creases of his clothes. His scalp was seething with the creatures, his beard alive with them.

I wasn't unacquainted with the louse, having met up with *pediculus humanus* in the course of clinic duty in Iraq; never, though, had I encountered shoals and galaxies of lice like these. And not, as I discovered with a shudder, just the hordes of common head lice. Every crevice of his body crawled with several other species.

Aside from qualms about my own contamination, alarms went off about the camp in toto. If the other Kurds all carried equal cargo, we could wind up with a typhus epidemic. A quick spot-check of other Kurds confirmed the infestation. All of them were overrun. And with all my careful planning and compiling, the one thing I'd omitted from my many lists was DDT. Via Lova, enough came in that afternoon to start delousing individuals. Supplied with spray guns, the nurses "shot" each patient as they passed him in to be examined. This, of course, was simply stopgap; the entire camp would have to undergo extermination, and we didn't have the means. And more omissions soon became apparent.

That day alone, I saw bloody dysentery, enormous streptococcal boils, extremes of dehydration, disabling rickets, five cases of trachoma, uncounted hacking coughs, a fractured femur, and a score of festering, unsutured wounds.

As the Kurds kept passing through, I kept adding to my "must" list. Surgical equipment, the materials and implements for blood and stool and sputum tests, a new array of medications. In short, a hospital facility. Compared with the conditions here, the Iraqi camp resembled a vacation spa. The refugees from Baghdad had been fairly healthy when they started, since only those thought fit to travel had been cleared to take the trip. Among the Kurds, entire villages had come, including ancients on the brink of death and babies newly born. Leaving anyone behind would be consigning him to certain slaughter. In any case, however sick a man might be, he meant to mount the eagle.

On a break to grab a hasty sandwich lunch, I sought out Lova to unload my woes. With all that we'd accomplished, it wasn't half enough, I warned. I was simply letting off some steam, not anticipating further miracles, but once again I'd underestimated Lova. Within an hour, he was back to me, trying unsuccessfully to stem a grin. Aha, I thought, he's gotten me an X-ray. More than that, I found. He'd gotten me a meeting with the Minister of Health. Though prominent in Persian Jewish circles, I hadn't known that Lova moved so easily among exalted *M'silmin.*

Past eight that evening, after cleaning out and stitching up a lacerated leg, I called it quits. Outside, as many people milled around as in the morning, but told they must return tomorrow, they melted off without a murmur. Starved so long for some attention, they would have stood there through the night if not dismissed.

Until I stopped and slumped back in my seat, I hadn't really seen my nurses; they'd merely been some blurs of white. 'Ster and Hanna, both chubby, short, and rather flat-faced, were so alike they looked as if they'd split off from a single ovum. Eliza was another matter. Taller than the other two, she was roundly slim and creamy-rose in coloration. Half-Russian, her heritage was evident in gold-flecked, greenish eyes, slanted slightly upwards by distinctly Slavic cheekbones.

All three appealed to me as people, but Eliza was attractive as a woman. I hadn't felt such stirrings since Evlene. However, the circumstances weren't too propitious for flirtation. Not only were we both exhausted, but every evening we had to spray each other, head to foot, with DDT. Sex ran second to a shower and sleep.

The meeting with the Minister of Health produced immediate results. While Lova and I were sitting in his office, he made a string of phone calls to the city's leading hospitals and lab suppliers. Anything I asked for was to be provided. Top priority. To my astonishment, he there and then appointed me "consultant" to the government, and said that I'd be paid a fee for "aiding and advising in connection with the Kurdish Jews."

When I started to dissent, he waved aside my protest, piously asserting that the Kurds were Persian citizens "and our responsibility." At this late date, I murmured to myself. Embarrassed as I was at reaping benefits from altruistic actions, I was also, I admit, elated. The sum he named was more than the Mahane paid, and at the moment the money looked like manna from the Lord Himself.

Yesterday, I'd spoken to a new arrival from Iraq, a businessman who'd often dealt with Baba. My father had applied to emigrate, he told me, and his application had already been approved. That meant the family would probably reach Israel before me.

On exiting Iraq, I learned, each emigré would only be allowed a single suitcase, this to hold just intimate belongings, such as shoes and clothes. Everyone was searched, and all expensive or attractive items confiscated.

"If it had a silver handle, the thieves would steal a blind man's cane."

My informant, by coming out illegally, had saved "a little something," and he let me see a tiny sack of uncut stones. When he arrived in Israel, he'd have a stake. Baba would be starting off without a cent, and with nothing to convert to cash. My unexpected extra fee was positively providential.

I was feeling rich as Croesus when we left the office, but Lova brought me back to earth. "In Israel, everything's imported and costs twice as much," he told me. That being so, he said, I ought to buy whatever we required here. As an immigrant to Israel, anything I bought abroad for one full year after my arrival would be free of import duties. In Israel, large appliances, I learned, were hard to come by and insanely priced, so with Lova's aid I ordered a refrigerator to be sent to Tel Aviv. I also purchased several Persian rugs.

"A good investment," Lova was approving, but I'd bought them solely for their beauty, and for Nana. She'd have to leave our own behind in Baghdad, which would break her heart.

Gradually all the Kurds were transferred to the cemetery from the seven scattered synagogues. From the outset, I had a daily average of twenty patients bedded down with serious disease or disability, and attended anywhere from seventy to ninety of the walking sick and wounded.

Dehydration, in at least one instance ending in a woman's death, appeared repeatedly, scaring me because I couldn't account for it. To a born Iraqi, acclimated to a summer temperature which often hit 100, Teheran seemed almost cool. It didn't occur to me for quite some time that it was ovenlike to Kurdish epidermises and Kurdish lungs, accustomed to the crispness of the mountain air.

With their sensitivity to heat, I expected that the showers would be overcrowded. I'd complained to Lova that we'd built too few—but those we had were proving to be wasted pipe. The Kurds preferred to bathe, as always, from a bucket. The best that I could do was encourage them to sluice themselves a dozen times a day.

In time the women found a use for showers. We discovered what it was when all of them stopped working; the lines were clogged with solid lumps of gritty soil. As at home, the women had been scrubbing out their pots with sand and, in lieu of setting them in mountain streams, were rinsing them by turning on the shower spigots.

From the first, even as a filthy horde, outlandish in appearance and alien in their culture, the Kurds exerted an intense appeal to my emotions. My interest and concern became obsessive, and I resented time away from what I soon began to call "my" camp. Whenever I could spare a minute, I walked around and simply watched.

A clothing distribution had improved the look and spirit of the camp, and a regular and decent diet also made a difference. Instead of sitting apathetically, as on arrival, the women dug their spindles out and started whirring strands of woolen yarn. While the men assembled looms, they dyed the stuff with herbs and berries carried down from Kurdistan, and soon were sewing up the rugged homespun into new apparel, now subtly influenced by Western styles.

They also supplemented food that we supplied. The yoghurt cultures, kept for generations, had come with them, and a spoonful saved from every batch was used to turn another bowl of milk to creamy clabber. The culture was contained in rough stone pots, none of which was ever washed. The showers came in handy for another Kurdish staple. Milk left to sour would become a sticky mass of curds and whey, which the women strained through homespun. In the mountains, the solid residue was tied into a square of cloth and sunk into a running stream to rinse and harden. Here they used the showers, and since the milky water wasn't damaging to drains, we pretended not to notice.

While I soon picked up some Aramaic phrases, I couldn't hold a casual conversation with a Kurd. Their great respect for doctors verged on reverence, and on meeting me they'd drop their eyes and almost bow, as if to face me, man to man, would be a blasphemy.

As they settled in, the Kurds regained their normal lively spirits. Ecstatically devout, unlike the solemn scholars I grew up with, they reveled in religion with incessant song and dance. I left the camp each evening to the sight and sound of stamping, shuffling feet and joyful male voices. Not allowed to join the dance, the women clapped in cadence, but looked just as lost in rapture. I wouldn't have recognized them as the same dejected spectres that Lova had insisted on my seeing.

The Kurds were camped on acreage adjacent to existing gravesites, on land intended for expansion of the cemetery. The space that we were occupying would one day house the dead. For the moment, though, our tenancy was uncontested. A temporary gate, south of our encampment, gave access to the active burial grounds without intruding on the Kurds, but to reach this gate, anyone approaching from the city had to pass the camp.

The cemetery visitors had eyes and ears, and friends and relatives, and every Jew in Teheran soon knew our situation. One by one, and then in groups, influential Persian Jews appeared to offer aid. We were sent a slaughtered lamb for *Shabbat* dinner, and crates arrived packed tight with childrens' toys. Small sums of cash and clothing came in almost daily.

When Khudepur, a wealthy dentist and a major donor, invited me to dinner, I accepted with alacrity. With the exception of the Colonel's quarters in the army camp, I'd never been inside a Persian home. He called to pick me up in a large, expensive auto from America, and we sped, in splendor, toward the richest residential area in Teheran. The dentist pointed out each showplace as I happily anticipated our arrival at his own imposing home.

Unexpectedly, the car veered sharply off, and a moment later we were inching through a mean and grubby neighborhood of narrow, shadowed streets. I thought that Khudepur was taking me around to see the sights; this would be a *Mislim* quarter, much like one of Baghdad's least alluring.

When the car stopped cold, I thought he'd braked it to avoid a street obstruction. Then my host hopped out, unhooked an iron gate, and returned to take us through it. Pulling up again inside a courtyard, he announced, "We're home." Unbelieving, I looked about the dismal scene, and when my eyes came back to meet my host's, he smiled at my stunned expression. "This is where we *all* live," and he flung his arm out to embrace the ghetto.

Aghast, I realized that it *was* a ghetto, and worse than any that existed in Iraq. Until that instant, I'd imagined that the Jews of Persia were completely integrated.

In the course of dinner, my dentist friend enlightened me. Officially, he said, no restrictions were in force. Nonetheless, the schools maintained a rigid quota, and in the military and administrative services, Jews could rise to just a certain level. On the surface, and in the lower echelons, Jews enjoyed equality. Discrimination was so subtly practiced that few outsiders ever spotted it at all, he said. Among the Jews themselves, a substantial number had Moslem-ized their names and assimilated even to the point of doing business on *Shabbat.*

Khudepur was openly contemptuous of his Jewish countrymen. "The great majority," he said, "are scared to step on any *Mislim*'s shadow. They're so humble and submissive that, of course, they're kicked around. The way they act would bring the bully out in anyone."

In view of my reception at the Ministry, his statement seemed extreme. "The Director couldn't have been more cordial," I protested. "He was almost deferential. You should have heard him."

Khudepur responded wryly, "I'm not surprised. He didn't treat you like a Jew because you don't *perform* like any Persian Jew. You're not subservient. You stand up like a man. He's so accustomed to the stereotype that when someone doesn't fit it, he reacts to him as just another individual and not a Jew."

Later, over tea, he shook me up again, asserting that in some respects, Iraqi Jews were better off than Jews in Persia. "The government is openly against you in Iraq," he said. "The enemy is plain to see. Here, everything is hidden. The tensions are the same, and we're also second-class, but because they haven't killed us, we can kid ourselves that everything will be all right. We just can't be too Jewish."

Face twisted with the pain of this outpouring, he paused a moment to compose himself, and then resumed: "You Iraqi Jews who left *remain* Iraqi Jews—in exile, but intact—but we sit still and keep diluting our religion. If this goes on much longer, what sort of Jews, if any, will we have in Persia?"

Khudepur was under forty, but his voice was like an old, old man's. It was a more informative, if less enjoyable, excursion than I'd planned on.

Back at camp, Akiba had another, more agreeable, surprise in store. Finally a doctor had arrived to take my place, and I was free to leave for Israel—tomorrow, if I wished. In my mind, I was already at the airport. No! In Israel itself, with Nana in my arms, and the family all clamoring to hug and kiss me.

No obstacles remained. Both camps were running smoothly. Baruch, the new physician, would be stepping into well-supplied and fully staffed dispensaries. As morally committed as I was to aid the Kurds, I could leave now with my conscience clear. Baruch could easily assume my role.

But Baruch dissented, and the vehemence of his refusal shocked me. No sooner had I uttered "Kurd" than he sputtered out a string of "no's" as sharp as rifle fire. Apologizing for the violence of his reaction, he explained.

He'd been drafted in Iraq, and sent to serve in Kurdish territory as a captain in the medical corps. Though he was stationed among *M'silmin* and never saw a Jewish Kurd, he lumped them all together as the agents of his exile, rapping out, "I'm only here because of those barbarians!"

Shortly after his arrival in their area, two Kurdish men had come to fetch him; a woman of their family was sick, they said. Both had guns, "or else I wouldn't have gone. I'd been briefed about those bastards." Baruch leaned forward and a vein began to throb. "They said that I'd be fairly safe among the settled Kurds, but that the hill men had some nasty habits, like slaughtering the doctor if the patient died. So when we reached the woman, I was very glad to see that she was only pregnant—about six months' worth, I figured—and otherwise appeared to be in perfect health."

The men, who'd proved to be her father and her brother, had waited by the bedside for his diagnosis. "I expected them to be delighted at the news," Baruch went on, "and I wondered what the father meant by his remark to me. 'If you're right about the baby, you'll go free,' he said. And before I knew what he was doing, he unsheathed a knife and plunged it in his daughter's belly, slashing up and down to make an opening. Then he shoved his hand inside her and lifted out the infant; one little arm was almost severed. Both the mother and the baby bled to death. I couldn't have done a thing, even if they'd let me."

The girl, who was unmarried, had brought shame on them, the father said; in silence, the son had walked Baruch back to the village. "Luckily, it was convenient to the northern crossing. After that, I couldn't stay on, so here I am in Persia," he concluded.

Awful as it was, I reminded him that ordinary *M'silmin,* not only Kurds, would consider what was done a cleansing action, not a killing. "Koranic law," I started, but he stopped me short. "I know," he said impatiently, "but knowing it and seeing it are not the same. As far as I'm concerned, the Kurds—all Kurds—are savages."

No argument would sway him. Since he broke out in a sweat if he even *saw* a Kurd, he could hardly lay a healing hand on one.

I'd have to stay.

Baruch assumed my duties and inherited my quarters at the Mahane. I slept, thereafter, in a house the Joint had rented in the city for its personnel. From this point on, I'd work exclusively among the Kurds, six days a week, twelve hours at a stretch.

Soon after starting this regime, I noticed an increasing restlessness; the Kurds, heretofore so easygoing, were getting edgy. Though remaining docile patients, they squabbled constantly among themselves. The separate groups were clearly feuding. No major clashes had occurred, but arguments were breaking out about such trivial matters as the allocation of a foot of space or the ownership of sticks of kindling.

I attributed this fidgety behavior to the length of time we'd all been living in a state of limbo, and since the incidents were always trifling, paid them only scant attention. To tell the truth, I too was on the skittish side.

It was already August—the Hebrew month of Av—and commemorating *Tisha B'Av* underlined how long I'd been here. No day was more conducive to despondency than *Tisha B'Av.* In somber mourning for the First and Second Temples, we fasted, sitting on the floor and singing dirges. I read from Deuteronomy, Jeremiah, and the Book of Lamentations, missing the inflections of my father's speech and the feeling of the family around me. Clothed in black, marking the destruction of the Temple and the exodus of Jews from Old Jerusalem, I wondered if the wandering would ever end—specifically, *my* wandering.

The intensity of my emotions should have told me that the quarreling among the Kurds was also more than superficial. Right after *Tisha B'Av,* a boy came racing in to see me. Panting that there'd been a brawl and someone had been badly injured, he pulled at me to follow him.

Mordechai was cowering in the middle of a sullen mob, bleeding from the battering inflicted by the inner ring of men. His lip and scalp would need some stitches, probably his nose was broken, and judging by the careful way he held himself, his rib cage would require X-rays. As I helped him stagger to his feet, his attackers drew ashamedly away. One muttered that they hadn't meant to do him any lasting damage.

Back at the dispensary, Mordechai related what had happened. The turbulence had started building long before I was aware of it. At first the Kurds had been too sick and scared and hungry to be anything but passive. However, as the weeks went by, and minds and bodies normalized, they questioned why we kept them in the camp. Where were the eagles that would carry them to Israel?

Early on, Mordechai explained about the metal birds, pointing out each plane that passed. With surprising ease, the Kurds accepted them as eagles, but grew ever more impatient as they saw how many "birds" flew by without a pause to pick them up.

They'd learned that Mordechai was making up the lists for emigration, and assuming that the names of those he wrote down first would be the first to ride the eagle, those who weren't highest on the roster ripped it up. He'd already made a dozen lists and lost them all. This time, instead of simply starting over, Mordechai decided to defend his last-made manifest; in doing so, he was beaten into mincemeat.

After patching up his wounds, I picked my best interpreter and started talking to the large assemblage drawn to see the fray. Agreeing that there *were* a lot of planes, I said the number should be reassuring; there'd be room for all. Everyone, I guaranteed, would get to Israel, but everyone couldn't go at once, and *no* one would be going if they didn't allow a list to be submitted. To still whatever doubts remained, I said that I'd be staying on until the Joint assigned another doctor, "and when I do go on to Israel, I'll fly aboard an eagle which will carry only Kurds." Shouts swept the crowd; my promise made the rounds of camp, and quiet reigned again.

Two weeks later, a physician came to take my place. On August 30, 1950, the Kurds and I were off to *Eretz Israel.*

34

Parked out in the sun all morning, the plane became so oven-hot that bounding up the metal steps to board it almost set my socks afire. Inside the Constellation, I shrank from air so heavy that it seemed a solid. The cabin door clanged shut behind me; luckily I was the last; another body wouldn't have room to breathe.

Ahead of me, every inch was packed with people and possessions. Rope-tied boxes shared the seats with bulging baskets. Tucked between and teetering uneasily atop them, strings of pots and pans, hand-sewn canvas sacks, and every size and shape of cloth-bound bundle threatened imminent engulfment of the human cargo, for the Kurds themselves, unused to seats, were squatted on their haunches, sealing off the only aisle. A haze of heat and sweaty emanations hovered closely overhead, and wisps of steam from cooking pots curled up to feed the fog. The Kurds were building little fires on the floor! I screamed to Mordechai to stop them.

Passage was impossible. With my bags between my feet and a bulging hamper biting through my arm, I braced my back against the door, prayed that someone had secured it, and resigned myself to standing up until the plane set down again in Israel. Unless, of course, I fainted. I'd never flown before, and had no idea of how my acrophobia would take to air. Although I'd made it through the mountains, there, at least, my feet had been on solid soil. Sky-high, standing on a flimsy metal skin, aware that only miles of empty atmosphere supported it, I might just come unglued. In fact, I felt some queasiness already.

Instantly erasing the unwanted thoughts, exactly as I would a blackboard, I substituted images I'd rather see—and I could really *see* the things I summoned up. Most people think that "mind's eye" is an idle phrase, but such an "organ" always did exist in me.

This time I drew myself a mental map. From Teheran, the heading would be northwest into Turkey, the pilot careful not to overfly Iraq. Well into Turkey, we'd take a sharp turn south, swooping down past Cyprus with the sea beneath us, skirting Lebanon, until we reached the coast of Israel. Banking east, it would only be a minute to the airport. Indeed, the country was so narrow that some extra seconds in the air would signal an alert in Jordan.

In order to avoid unfriendly skies, a trip that ought to take at most two hours would take six instead. After twenty centuries, those extra hours would be unimportant except for my extreme fatigue and phobic tendency. I'd planned on falling to my knees, not on my face, when I finally arrived in *Eretz Yisrael.*

A familiar voice recalled me to the cabin. Mordechai, still acting as my aide-de-camp, was waving frantically for me to meet him at the far end of the aisle. At the same time, he was shouting orders to the others, and a path began to open through the press of bodies.

Scooping up their cooking pots and crawling infants, and squirming to the side, the Kurds freed inches for my feet, and as I edged ahead, my luggage followed close behind, traveling from hand to hand. At my journey's end, I found a small oasis. Three empty seats! All mine, a grinning Mordechai informed me. The Kurds had saved them for *Aghai Dektôr.*

My thanks were smothered in the sudden roar of engines . . . the sound of eagles. The plane was moving . . . the miracle beginning.

For the following hour the singing and the chanting never stopped, nor did the eating. Between hosannas, I watched the Kurds scoop up and swallow masses of their spicy rice with lamb and chicken. Everyone was dipping into pickled mangoes or tipping up the skins of sour milk. They spat out streams of pomegranate seeds and scattered eggshells till the cabin had a snowy carpet. For them it was a feast day, and while my heart and soul were with them, my stomach shuddered at the sights and smells.

I envied them their equilibrium, but it wasn't merely that they had no fear of heights. Their whole approach to life was simple and accepting. Unlike me, they welcomed what the moment offered, enjoying all they could of it. I never had been able to relax like that, but always looked ahead, always sacrificed the here and now for "when. . . ." Now, more than ever, all my senses were directed toward the future.

First, of course, I had to find the family. We'd have a home again, if not the kind of home we'd had. I'd thrust the thought away a thousand times, but finally I faced it squarely. We wouldn't even have a scattering of old, familiar objects to ease us through the change. Everything was gone. Baba's Isfahan, Nana's precious candlesticks, so heavy that she couldn't hold them, the ancient clock Haddads had owned since time began. I'd long since reconciled to the largest loss—the house itself. It was the loss of little things that caused the pain—the priceless things that money couldn't replace; my *bar mitzvah* shawl, my medal for Biology. . . .

I brightened when I thought about my love poems; at least I'd kept them safe from hostile eyes. I'd always had to keep them hidden, since a single word of Hebrew was enough to hang a Jew. They were buried in my bedroom, in a groove I'd gouged to hold them. Recalling that, I felt a little better, but it didn't last.

I'd never see my strange black stone from Babylon, or hold again my hand-bound book of scrupulous dissection sketches. They'd taken me a year to do, but to the *Mislim* who'd inherited our house, they'd simply be some scraps of paper. Even now, they might be wrapped around a fish. The mental picture made me sick, so sick I came within an inch of throwing up. On opening my eyes, however, I found the cause was more than my imagination.

A woman standing over me was shyly offering to share her food. So close to me my eyes crossed, I could see, and smell, what once had been the choicest chunks of lamb. By now they were a grayish mass of beaded grease. I declined as graciously as nausea would allow.

The stifling air had turned to ice, or else I had the world's worst chill. I shivered and my stomach spasms worsened. The stench was unbelievable. I recognized the sulfur smell of stale eggs, the stink of rancid oil, and the gaminess of goat's-milk cheese gone bad. Or the goat itself might be aboard. I wouldn't put it past a Kurdish herdsman.

My ears felt stuffed. I realized that the cabin wasn't pressurized; that's why the temperature was dropping. Gradually the singing stopped. Then the prayers. Bundles tightly bound to last the trip were torn apart for extra layers of clothing. I was already wrapped in everything I owned.

Soon the only sounds were muffled groans and smothered whimpers. I noticed that a sharp new smell was slicing through the old miasma. Urine. Since the plane had several washrooms, at first I blamed the babies, but the few aboard couldn't possibly account for such an odor. Too late it struck me that the Kurds had only been exposed to camp latrines; no one had thought to teach them how to flush the toilets, so the piercing reek of piss would undoubtedly be followed by an awful wave from active bowels. Even as I forecast, it arrived.

My stomach undulated, but I kept its contents down, thankful that I'd eaten almost nothing. In front of me an old man heaved, erupting like Vesuvius and spewing forth a lava made of lamb and dates and cheese and rice and chicken, all identifiable. As I feared, it set off wholesale vomiting throughout the plane. The prayers were starting up again, but these were ululating wails—cries for help, and not to Heaven. Dear Lord! They were calling for *Aghai Dektôr.* In my own distress, I'd clean forgotten that I *was* one.

I inched along the aisle, dispensing pills to sweating, wretching mounds of utter misery, and with half the sick still holding out their hands, I reached the bottom of the bottle. All I had to give was good advice: Sit still and draw deep breaths, I said. If they escaped asphyxiation, that would hold the heaving down.

The moans and groans were growing fewer, and soon I heard the snoring start. These simple, hardy souls were falling into peaceful sleep, trusting in the hands of God to set them safely down in Israel.

Numb with cold and physical depletion, I stared up at empty space and down at empty sea for almost four more hours. No one stirred, and the droning engines never changed their pitch. Half-hypnotized, I wondered if another human being in my orbit was awake, or were the Kurds and I the only ones aboard? The Constellation had no intercom, and I couldn't have sworn it had a pilot. I'd read about remote control, and in my present state of mind, anything seemed possible. The door between the cabin and the crew had never opened, and I'd heard no voices other than our own since taking off.

Dozing for an instant, I dreamed that Israel was just a dream, that I was doomed to fly forever. I woke up in the frigid cabin, wet with sweat, and willed myself to stay awake.

Close to 8 P.M., I felt the plane bank sharply left and start a slow descent. Gradually the air grew warm again, and by straining, I could see the faintest, far-off smudge, the merest streak of sandy ocher. *Eretz Yisrael!*

I sat poised to leave the plane the moment that it skidded to a stop at Lydda airport. After that, I knew exactly what I'd do. When you loved a land so much and the wait had been so long, could one do less than kiss the ground?

The changing pitch of the propellers wakened Mordechai, who hastily aroused the others. The prayers began at once, and when the wheels touched down, a shout went up that surely reached to God's own ears. Laughing through their streaming tears, the Kurdish men were dancing in the aisle, while the women, ever practical, repacked their pots.

When the Constellation slowed and stopped, the Kurds fell silent and stillness filled the air. Outside the plane I heard no sounds of jubilation, saw no banners waving. No committee was on hand to welcome us. I don't know what I *thought* would happen, but I'd not expected simply *nothing.*

Inside, we sweltered in a tropic, humid heat. Every surface dripped, and I was sopping up the perspiration when an agonizing earache struck. In the excitement of arrival, I'd forgotten that I should have swallowed. Since I hadn't told the Kurds, they too were clapping at their ears and crying out in pain.

At last I saw the flight crew emerging from the forward hatch. So we had been flown by flesh and blood. In some respects, however, they resembled robots. At the very least, human beings would have *looked* at us; these walked away without acknowledging that we existed. We might have been a cargo of manure.

I was wriggling toward the exit when the door flew open. Through an interstice between the crush of Kurds, I caught a glimpse of yellow hair and pink-fleshed, youthful face. As our odor hit, the face went chalky white. I saw a flash of uniform and part of an insignia before the officer was buried in an avalanche of loving bodies. The Kurds were kissing him—his face, his feet, whatever they could reach of him—and wailing in the ecstasy of their arrival. To him they must have looked like madmen.

I leaped up on a seat so he could see me, yelling out in Hebrew, "Let them kiss you. All they want to do is touch you."

Only slightly reassured, he shouted, "Silence!" and as an afterthought, *"Shalom."* At that, the din around him doubled. *"Shalom"* was the single word they understood.

Then two more men appeared and raised their arms, I thought, in greeting. At last—the welcoming committee! They carried objects in their arms that looked like rolled-up scrolls. But the scrolls they bore were spray guns, and without a word of warning, we were drenched with disinfectant. They pumped until the walls were wet, until our alien smells were overpowered by official stink.

The doctor in me knew that it was necessary, but the man—the Jew—the exile being "gathered in"—knew only shock, and then acute embarrassment, but not for us. For Israel. This procedure was for animals in cattle cars, and not a way to welcome brothers.

The Kurds were philosophical; they simply hid their faces from the disinfectant. Perhaps they thought it was some sort of special blessing. Again I envied them their innocence—or was it total trust? Far from all they'd ever known, afraid and sick, they still had such implicit faith—the eagle had delivered them.

Their spirit shamed me. The end was all that mattered, and what happened on the plane was unimportant. The end was Israel, and Israel was right outside. That's where the good began.

Somehow I was off the plane, almost at the bottom of the steps, about to set my foot on holy soil. In seconds I would kiss the earth of *Eretz Yisrael!*

My pulses drummed. I paused to etch this moment in my memory (and also to enjoy the drama!); then, stepping off the final tread, my foot, at last, touched—asphalt! I could have cried. Could anyone kiss asphalt?

To eyes still smarting from the acrid spray, the WELCOME sign was just a smudge. The queue, however, was impossible to miss; it stretched the length of the arrivals building. I'd forgotten there were other emigrés from many other countries.

The Kurds kept urging me to move ahead of them, but this time I refused the favor since all of us were equally fatigued. Instead, I asked that oldsters and the nursing women be allowed to head the line. In the first five minutes, we advanced a foot. According to my calculations, we'd be creeping in this queue at least an hour, and there wasn't any cabin wall to hold one up. My shoulders slumped, some of those ahead of me were almost on the ground already, and while we sagged, the officer in charge—the one who'd process us like cans of peas—was sitting like a sheikh.

My blood was up again, and anger pumped enough adrenaline to starch my spine. Head held high, I'd show them how a Jew should enter Israel.

As I stretched myself to ramrod stiffness, a hand fell on my shoulder and a shouted "Heskel!" almost burst my eardrum. It was Ziadi, the Mosad messenger, and my dignity went down the drain. We clutched each other's arms and whooped and kissed and danced around like dervishes. In a land of strangers, someone known as slightly as I knew Ziadi seemed a brother; those moments in the mountains were equivalent to years of normal life.

"But stop with the 'Ziadi,' " he commanded. "At home I'm Dov."

In record time, he had me cleared through Immigration and was buying me a cup of coffee. He offered food, but I was filled with too much turmoil to be hungry. I could hardly taste the coffee, but the caffeine helped. So did fresh, sweet air and being able to communicate without the aid of Mordechai.

Out the window, I could see the side of the Arrivals building. One by one, the Kurds were drifting out the door, duly processed. As they found each other, they huddled close for comfort, like a flock of freezing sheep. Then suddenly the sheep were rounded up and herded brusquely into open trucks. Before I fully comprehended what was happening, the trucks had left. I never even got to say goodbye.

It was probably a sense of guilt that set me off, and I vented all my pent-up rage on poor Ziadi—pardon—Dov. Why, I stormed, why is everyone so clipped and curt, so self-important that they never stopped to say a word that wasn't strictly necessary? Why, I fumed, was every face so grim and every voice so grating?

Dov didn't answer. Instead he pointed to a rumple-shirted man, sitting at a table with his eyes shut. The man looked sick. His skin was prison-sallow, and everything about him sagged, as if his flesh were falling off his bones from sheer fatigue. He needed sleep, I thought, and lots of sitting in the sun.

"There's your 'self-important' immigration officer." Dov sounded older than his years and infinitely weary. His exuberance had fooled me, but I should have seen beyond it to his pouchy eyes and badly bitten nails. Though he wasn't in the best of shape himself, I now perceived, his immediate concern was my perception of the others.

He jabbed his finger toward the officer again. "He's been working here since six this morning, and he'll stay until the last plane lands tonight, whenever that will be. And it's been like that since *aliyah* began."

Then quietly he questioned me.

"Do you know how big it is? Do you know that 30,000 have arrived this month already? You're just the latest. Half a million came ahead of you. God willing, there'll be half a million more."

He smiled to take the sting out.

"We're brusque because we're tired and we're always short of time. We're short of everything except for Jews with empty hands—and that reminds me. Have you any money? Israeli money?"

When I shook my head, he pushed some coins and paper in my pocket, checked the airport clock, winced at what he saw, and steered me to a taxi. Dov held the door but didn't join me, and smiling wryly, he explained.

"It's not polite, I know, to send you off like this, but at the moment, we're also short of etiquette. As my mother used to say, 'When you're hungry, you don't worry how you hold your fork.' As soon as possible, we'll hold our forks politely." And with that, he waved farewell.

When the driver asked where I was going, I was stumped. Past the point of my arrival, I hadn't thought to make a plan. I suppose I'd hoped a miracle might happen, like maybe having S'hak meet me. S'hak always had connections and a car. Or, even better, a car might come for me with Baba at the wheel. At worst there would be messages. If not—but this I'd buried so far back, I'd half-forgotten—I could always go to uncle. I gave the driver uncle's Tel Aviv address.

I'd never seen my father's brother; Uncle Eliahu had been living here in Israel since 1929. Perhaps the family was home with him. I tried to tell myself that I'd be seeing them within the hour—"if I live," I added, as I pressed myself against the cab seat.

Experienced as I was with both Iraqis and Iranis at the wheel, the maniacal careening didn't upset me overmuch, but I wondered if the *car* could take it. Its decrepitude surprised me. With the fare so high—six pounds, the driver said—it should have been a sleek and shiny limousine. Leaving quality aside, if everything in Israel was this expensive, my money wouldn't last a week.

Trying to ignore the swerves and bumps, I examined the Israeli coins contributed by Dov. Although I knew their names and worth, I'd never actually encountered them before.

In contrast with the satisfying clink of silver *rials,* richly heavy in one's hand, these scarcely rustled. Made of lightweight, inexpensive alloys, they felt unnervingly like counterfeit and forcefully reminded me that Israel was almost bankrupt. The mint didn't have the money to make proper money.

At today's exchange rate, my ready cash should come to . . . but I couldn't concentrate on figures. Concern about the family intruded on my calculations, and the ifs and buts broke through the wall I'd tried to build against them.

They might not be at Uncle Eliahu's. They might not even be in Israel. All I had was thirdhand information. All I knew for sure was that the government had opened up an exit for Iraqi Jews, but I also knew how quickly they could snap it shut.

Deep in thought, I didn't hear the driver's voice until he braked the cab and turned impatiently to me. Did I know where that address was? He was speaking very slowly, enunciating every syllable, and clearly not too optimistic that I'd understand. I was an alien, and that's the way one spoke to strangers.

I responded in a swift and polished flow of perfect Hebrew, informing him exactly how to reach my uncle's. His grunt of sheer surprise was as visceral as if I'd poked him in the solar plexus, and afforded me the same degree of satisfaction.

He couldn't know that I'd been studying this country since the age of nine. For the last eleven years I'd been collecting maps and committing them to memory. I could draw the whole of Israel, complete with all historic sites and geographic features. I could ink in each *kibbutz* and lay out every major avenue in every major city.

After all this effort, I expected to find Tel Aviv familiar. I thought I'd feel at ease and right at home the moment I arrived, but I hadn't figured on arriving in the dead of night. I couldn't see a single landmark, and was just as lost as any other immigrant.

It was almost midnight when we pulled up at my uncle's place. In the faint illumination of a distant streetlamp, I saw a squarish, quite substantial-looking structure. Five stories high, of ocher-colored brick with concrete columns, it seemed dully institutional and boringly devoid of any detail. While not exactly squalid, it was even less than second-rate. A slum, at least, had character, but this was simply commonplace. In the entrance hall, the walls were flaking and the tiles of the floor were cracked. On checking the apartment number, I found I had four flights to climb.

The balustrade was broken and the treads so deeply rutted that I wondered at the safety of the stairs. Halfway up, it suddenly occurred to me that I hadn't seen a single light in any window. Either everyone was sleeping, or the whole damn place had been deserted. I almost hoped it was the latter. Haddads didn't live in such abysmal settings.

On uncle's landing, I hesitated at the door, then pressed the buzzer lightly and listened for some sound of movement. No one stirred within the flat, so I pushed again, more firmly, but again to no avail. Now leaning on the button, my index finger bearing all my weight, I almost fell inside when someone flung the door wide open. A furious, mustachioed man confronted me with fists upraised. He looked like Baba, much diminished, and was bellowing in Baba's voice.

"Who the devil are you? Are you mad, waking people in the middle of the night?"

He broke off suddenly and stared at me, struck dumb by my appearance. I could feel what he was seeing, and I sympathized with his confusion. I knew that I was grinning idiotically from ear to ear; I could also sense the glassiness that glazed my eyes and smell the disinfectant I'd been doused with. When he was just about to slam the door, I shouted out, "I'm Heskel!" It didn't register.

"Your nephew!"

Uncle wrapped his arms around me, hugging till my ribs hurt. Past his cheek, I saw a pinch-faced little woman peeking round a doorjamb. My aunt, no doubt. Those other three behind her would have to be my cousins. I looked for other faces, listened for some other footsteps, but my heart was sinking. Had Baba been in the apartment, he'd be out by now.

Misreading why my body slumped against him, uncle said, "The boy's about to drop. Go back to bed. We'll talk tomorrow."

Silently they all embraced me, and my aunt made up the sofa that I'd sleep on. She asked, "Will you be staying long?" I saw a flicker of relief when I responded, "Only for the night." The tiny flat could hardly hold the five of them.

I refused the cup of tea she offered; I didn't think I had the strength to swallow. With my last reserve of energy, I asked the crucial question, and uncle answered swiftly and succinctly, "Your family is fine."

Inside me all the knots unwound.

They'd arrived in Israel six weeks ago, he said. After coming through Sha'ar Aliyah—Sha'ar Aliyah, "the Gate," was the major entry point for immigrants—they'd been sent to live at Lyd. A camp, my uncle called it.

Lyd. I closed my eyes and conjured up the proper map. Lyd. Near the coast. The closest town, Natanya. Now I had a goal; I'd go tomorrow.

The sofa was a slab of stone and full of bumps and hollows, but to me it felt like baby-duck down. I began the bedtime prayer, "Hearest thou, oh Israel . . . ," and on that word, started the descent to sleep. My mouth went slack. The litany remained unfinished. Other words, however, were breaking through the barriers I'd consciously erected—words I'd been repressing since arrival. Half-asleep, I lost control and now they were escaping. Bursting free, they filled my head. Whispering insistently inside my skull, I heard my own voice saying, "I wish I hadn't come."

35

I could always set my mind to wake me when I wished. It was 4 A.M. exactly when I hobbled off the sofa like an old arthritic and crept into the kitchen for a quiet wash. I was soaked with sweat and streaming mucus. The old rhinitis, temporarily relieved in Teheran, had returned full force in Tel Aviv.

I tried to snuffle *sotto voce.* No one else was up, and I hoped to get away without advice or explanation. Later I'd apologize, but all that mattered now was reaching Lyd.

As I bent to pull my pants on, a dozen separate spear points pierced my spine. What the sofa hadn't bruised, the sticky damp had swollen. For someone from Iraq, humidity like this was almost inconceivable—like living in the center of a soaking sponge.

To add to my distress, my empty stomach started rumbling, but the kitchen offered no relief. The sum of all I found would scarcely make me one square meal, with nothing left for any of the others. Last night a glance had told me that the flat was much too small for five and that the furniture was scant and shoddy. Now I saw the family was also short of decent food. I settled for a glass of water, and even that was disenchanting. To me it tasted salty, not like sweet, soft Tigris water.

Sipping it, I thought about my uncle's situation. Everything gave evidence of penny-pinching poverty. The light bulbs were the lowest wattage, the water heater wasn't on, and the towel I was using was so thin from wear that it was sopping wet before my face was dry. I had to wipe my hands along my pants.

So all these years, uncle had been lying in his letters; to save his pride, he'd written sagas of his great successes. Knowing Baba, my father would be on his feet in no time flat, and as soon as we were settled, we'd be back to help without my uncle's asking.

I folded up my sheet, plumped my pillow, propped a thank-you note against it, and picked up both my bags. Hereafter I'd be staying with my parents. Buses left for Lyd from Central Station, and I'd be on the earliest.

From my poring over maps, I knew the way. The walk would be a long one, but I welcomed it. So far all I'd seen were streetlamps and a lot of asphalt. I had to get out there and let it all wash over me, immerse myself in sights and sounds and smells. In the daylight, rested and with hope renewed, and on my way to find the family, I marveled at my feelings of the night before. Anxiety and plain fatigue, I told myself, but all of that was over. I was back where I belonged, where everything began.

Long before the birth of Christ or Islam, Haddads had lived in Israel. My early images were shaped by family legend at least as much as by the five books of the Bible. The land of my imagination was a green oasis in an arid world, with air as sweet as *Shabbat* wine.

Reality, in the form of uncle's flat, impinged already. Outside, it set in with a vengeance. The air was like a wall of water, and walking was an effort. The heavy cases didn't help, and unaccustomed sweat streamed down me. My nose still dripped, my skin began to itch, and the message from my eyes was "ugly!"

When I'd looked about a little longer, I amended that assessment: not ugly but unbeautiful. The place was ordinary, *worse* than ugly. In Tel Aviv everything was square, cement, and "modern." I ached to see an arch or dome, but all was blunt and angular. A baby might have laid it out with building blocks.

Each cube, however, had a saving grace—some earth around it. In Baghdad, every house was jammed against another, and I rather liked the airiness of this approach. To all appearances, the openness applied to people too. Across the street a boy and girl were walking with their arms around each other's waist. You wouldn't see that in Baghdad. But on the other hand, here you didn't hold hands with men friends. Keeping customs straight could be a problem.

Fluttering against the sky, some scraps of cloth attracted my attention. Squinting brought them into focus and shivers iced my spine. In Baghdad, what I saw so boldly flying would have led to certain bloodshed. Even hidden in the house, the smallest Star of David was a danger. Now here I was, surrounded by the brightest, bluest, biggest Stars I'd ever seen, streaming from a score of flagstaffs.

Unhappily, however, the splendid ensigns were like fresh, sweet frosting on a stale cake. At a casual glance, the city looked immaculate, if undistinguished, but close-up observation showed extensive damage and decay—neat gardens gone to seed, flaking paint and sagging shutters, windows paned with wood, and many roofs with tiles missing. For awhile, the gashes in the stucco walls remained a mystery; I'd never seen a bomb scar.

The evidence of war was also in the cracked cement of sidewalks and the patches, like gigantic pockmarks, in the asphalt of the streets. The vehicles traversing them were plain pathetic. Sputtering and creaking, antique buses barely kept abreast of me. Two taxis passed, and both had broken headlights; the remaining glass bore flecks of blackout paint. The tires on an heirloom truck were baby-bald, and where it stopped for lights, it left behind a little pool of oil.

The traffic lights were also new to me; at home we had police at intersections but no signals. From my reading, I understood that green meant "go," and since the light was green, I left the sidewalk. A van careened around the corner, nearly clipping me, and the driver shook his fist and screamed a curse. That they did in Baghdad, too.

Though Baghdad woke up early, here they beat the birds up! At home, at this hour of the morning, a few men, early for the market, might be strolling on the street, but no one seemed to stroll in Tel Aviv. Both sexes stepped out briskly, and the streams of both were swelling while I watched. I'd never seen so many, and such varied, women, all unveiled. As for the men, their approach to dress was casual, to say the least, and lots of them looked downright derelict. Austerity again. I remembered Dov remarking over coffee, "The war was won a bullet short of bankruptcy."

I noticed that the worse a man was dressed, the more he swaggered when he walked, as if to show contempt for outward trappings; clearly, more was on his mind than clothes. Army tan appeared to be a favorite shade, and I suspected that the shirts and pants had all been army issue. Many of the men had grown the most aggressive brown and black, and even red, mustaches that I'd ever seen. What I'd never seen, though, were the earlocks worn by all the strictly orthodox. In Iraq, they weren't even worn by rabbis.

The streams converged on Central Station.

Inside, I joined the line waiting for the bus to Lyd, and, more to practice Hebrew than to gain the information, I asked the man ahead of me if there was always such a mob.

"Mob?" he echoed. "This you think is mobbed? Try some morning when it's *busy!*"

He pointed to his paper and commanded me to look.

"You're worried over crowds?" He jabbed his finger at a front-page story. "*This* is something you should worry over!"

At first, I didn't understand why he was so upset; it seemed like just another article on economics. However, following his finger, I saw that yesterday, as I was taking off from Teheran, the pound had been devalued. I was practically a pauper.

My stomach hurt and I could hardly breathe. I was sick with loss, but with a greater loss than pounds and grush and pruta. Everything I'd figured on was false. Even money was illusion. *Nothing* was the way that I'd envisioned it.

I don't remember boarding, but the bus was on its way when I returned to full awareness. I'd been staring out the window with my eyes turned inward. A jolting bump refocused them. The pits and ruts ahead and under us looked deep enough to trouble tanks. Pushed off to the side, stranded cars were commoner than trees, and everything that sputtered past seemed headed for the trash heap. Casualties of battle—I could spot the scars. The war was over but its legacies would linger for a long, long while.

Calmer now, I tried to see my problems in this new perspective. What war didn't kill, it crippled. The devalued pound was merely one more victim. Even uncle's sorry flat could be accounted for by shortages. And then of course, I was extra edgy. When your sinuses were stuffed, your muscles stiff, your mind conflicted, and your stomach empty, it wasn't easy to be tolerant and even-tempered. All in all, perhaps I hadn't been completely fair. In view of everything we'd both been through, perhaps both Israel and I might be forgiven for our faults.

I relaxed with that and settled down to watch the passing scene. Along the highway, squads of dark-skinned, bearded laborers were swinging picks and tamping tar. They looked to me like Yemenites. Edging past each grimy, sweating gang, the bus rode smoothly for a moment on another stretch of newly surfaced asphalt. A flash of red or yellow sometimes pierced the weary sameness of the sandy landscape, and from my botany books, I recognized the clusters as anemone and mustard.

According to the schedule, we still had twenty minutes' traveling time to Lyd. In twenty minutes . . . fifteen . . . five . . . the family would be together.

Technically the schedule was correct. We reached the sign for Lyd exactly on the dot. The sign, however, pointed toward an unpaved road: 1 km, it read. Off the bus, I squeezed my eyelids to a slit to see against the sun, but nothing broke the bleak horizon.

As soon as I set foot on the approach road, a dust storm swirled around me, and with every step I started up another flurry. The bus had been an oven and we'd baked inside, but suddenly my skin was broiling. Undeflected now, the sun was striking me with flights of flaming arrows. Pools of sweat collected in my crotch and armpits, then overflowed in creeping crawls of itch. The Baghdad sun could suck a person dry; this would drown me in my own outpourings. So this is how the Kurds had suffered. At last I understood.

At ever shorter intervals, I had to set my luggage down and dry my hands. The blisters were already rising. For all my education, a desert Arab would be doing better. A Bedouin *woman* would be doing better. She'd be walking with the cases on her head, not courting blisters. Though I couldn't do that, any cover on my head might ward off sunstroke. Stripping off my sport coat, I draped it like a sheikh's *kaffiyah.*

If there *was* a camp ahead—and I'd seen no sign of one so far—I wondered how inhabitants went in and out, especially the old and sick. I was only twenty, with a swimmer's legs and lungs, and I was panting like a pulmonary case. Except to cross the *hosh* or shop in shaded arcades, my mother hardly ever walked outside. I'd have to pick her up and carry her away.

The dust had settled in the time I'd taken to adjust my headdress, but what the clearing air revealed only added to my apprehension. I was standing in the center of a sea of sand—not yet quite sand, perhaps, but long-dead soil. Dish-flat and desolate, it stretched for miles on every side of me, uninterrupted by a bush or tree or blade of grass. The path aside, I couldn't see any sign of human presence. There had to be another Lyd. I was looking for my family, and this was only fit to harbor sand fleas.

I was about to turn and trudge back to the road when something kicked up dust clouds in the distance. Gradually, a group of men emerged, and more men followed, scores of men, laborers, from the look of them, and heading for the highway.

I stopped the first and asked for Lyd. He answered, "Just ahead. You're there."

36

Every camp I'd ever seen bore some resemblance to a normal settlement. Not Lyd, however. So vast it seemed to sprawl into infinity, I couldn't find its start or finish, and my senses were confused. No walls, no gates, no boundaries, and—inconceivably—no buildings!

Squatting on the snuff-brown sand and almost melting into it, Lyd was long, low lines of khaki-colored tents. The camouflage was rendered perfect by the clouds of dust that hugged the ground, obscuring every outline. After uncle's place, I'd been prepared for sorry housing, such as army-style huts, but something structured, something solid. The thought of Nana under canvas stood my hair on end.

I walked in from the road, but I could have entered anywhere. Whatever the perimeter of Lyd might be, one could wander in and out at any point on it. Rather than affording me a sense of freedom, this lack of any kind of real containment disconcerted me. Lyd proliferated like a cancer, radiating out, unchecked, in all directions. On the bus, I'd pictured how I'd stroll inside and spot the family right off. In this enormity, I knew that I could search a month and miss them.

As I was standing there slipping on my jacket and deciding what to do, an old but wiry Kurd approached me; pointing to my cases, he made carrying motions. Apparently he earned some money acting as a porter. For all I knew, he might also be the camp's official greeter, since no one else appeared. Slipping him a coin, I refused his aid, while praying that my parents had received a warmer welcome.

In the distance, a shard of light arrested my attention. I shifted and it blazed again, this time at a different angle. Sun reflected from a roof, a metal roof, and metal roofs meant buildings. A building in a canvas city would have to be the seat of power and a source of information.

Arriving at the long, one-story wooden barracks, I saw an old and faded sign in English; something clicked. Lyd had been a British army camp. Another freshly painted signboard, this in Hebrew, read HEADQUARTERS.

Even as I brightened at the sight, I staggered at the smell. It was just as bad as on the plane, and one look told me why. In this central area alone, I could see a thousand bodies, each contributing its quota of decay. More approached the square each moment, and every new arrival joined a queue. There must have been a dozen lines, all long and growing longer.

Watching, I began to understand at last the true extent of emigration from the Eastern countries. A parade of nations passed before me. In addition to Iraqis, Kurds, and Persians, I spotted Libyans, Lebanese, and Syrians, also Turks, Tunisians, Greeks, and others from Morocco, Egypt, and Algiers. And there were costumes, looks, and languages I couldn't identify.

In all the high-pitched babble, I only heard a word or two of Hebrew. The apparel of the refugees, most of it familiar to my eyes, looked alien and garish in these glum surroundings. Coins and bangles, beads and bright embroidery—and every dialect of Arabic extant. Coincidence, no doubt, but all I saw and heard were Africans and Orientals. Even those in Western dress had Eastern faces. Had the influx from the continent abated so completely? From what Dov had said, I wouldn't have thought so.

I was distracted by the actions of a little fellow in the line in front of me. Afraid to lose his place, he'd been squirming for the last ten minutes, and finally, shamefacedly, he'd squatted down to defecate. And from the pungent odor of ammonia that engulfed me, the ground was also soaked with urine. The queues were barely moving, and if lines like these were everyday occurrences, those stuck in them would *have* to empty bursting bladders.

Luckily for me, the line before the office building was the shortest and the swiftest-moving. Closer to the queue, I saw, to my amazement, that the head of every person in it had a halo, and I blinked my eyes to dissipate this odd illusion. The rings were real, however. Alive, in fact, and formed by swarms of small black gnats. Soon I had a halo of my own. Circling just too high to swat, the midges swooped like tiny Messerschmidts, strafing any naked skin.

At least I had two hands to scratch with. Those standing in the longer lines could only twitch and try to shake the creatures off. Their hands were fully occupied with cups and bowls and cardboard booklets. Intermittently, the smells of cooking wafted through the other odors; out of sight, but close behind the office building, the commissary of the camp began to come alive. I wondered if the whole camp queued for breakfast. My brother Avram was always front and center when it came to food, and while searching for his face, I saw a ripple run the length of every line. As if on orders, everyone had shuffled one step forward, and suddenly the cups they carried looked like beggars' bowls. Intellectually, I understood that such a system might be necessary. Food was fuel, and these were solely fueling stations, stoking up the needy, nameless stomachs; nutrition *had* to rank ahead of social niceties. Not much evidence of good nutrition was apparent, though. The adults all looked drawn and sallow, with signs of definite deficiencies. Even more disturbing, the youngsters looked as listless as their elders.

This sun, of course, could slow down almost anyone. My head felt incandescent, each hair a filament of flame, and the perspiration stung where I'd been digging at the bug bites. From the next line to my left, a wizened little *bibi* reached across to me and shrilled, pointing to her own swathed skull. She spoke a dialect I didn't know, but Nana lashed at me like that when I was doing something stupid.

The thought of Nana made me smile, and the *bibi* threw her hands up in reproof, rattling off an even louder volley. It must have seemed that I was mocking her. I made apologetic motions, but a male arm encircled me and cut them off.

"She's telling you the sun has broiled your brains. She says a sane man doesn't leave his head uncovered."

He was huge, he was overjoyed to see me, and his accent was Iraqi. I knew him but his name escaped me. However, the incision on his neck told me where we'd met. I'd sewn him up in Persia, and his name was in the neighborhood of—Enos? Maybe Amos?

Stalling him, I touched the scar and said, "It's healed up nicely," at which he hugged me once again and trumpeted, "I always tell your father that his son will be the finest surgeon in the country."

Ehud. His name was Ehud. And he knew where Baba was.

Tent P-7, he informed me, and scratched directions in the sand. Shouting back my thanks, I shot off like a bullet, the little *bibi* screaming after me to stop. Running in this sun *was* crazy, and I had to slow in any case to count the rows. Since the camp was laid out alphabetically, P-7 would be sixteen alleys down and the seventh tent along.

Avram saw me first, then Osa screeched and Daisy squealed, and all of us raced headlong for reunion. The noise brought Nana out to shush the kids. Peering through a tangled web of arms, I saw her face, and prayed she couldn't see mine. I couldn't keep the shock from showing.

My mother looked just like a Bedouin woman. An older, tinier-than-ever, brown-baked, dried-out Bedouin. The house in Baghdad had screened her from the dessicating sun. Here the sun had seamed and shrunk her. When I ran to hold her, instead of plump, soft flesh, my arms enfolded bird bones, barely covered. I was afraid to hug too hard, afraid of breaking her, but Nana clutched me fiercely with the strength of desperation. Weeping bitterly, she wailed against my chest, "Why did you come? Why did you come?"

An hour ago, it would have cut me to the heart to hear her say such words. Before the dust and stench and dreariness, I wouldn't have understood what my appearance here would mean to her, but now I knew. How could a mother bear to see a son she loved in Lyd, or have a son see her? From the way she hid herself against me, I knew that Nana was aware of how she'd aged and changed.

I could feel the tremors as she tried to stem the sobs. Finally succeeding, she straightened up, kissed me once again, and took control. Urging me toward Tent P-7, she sent the girls to look for Baba, and Avram flew to find Nazima.

At that, my breath blew out in one big sigh; I hadn't realized that I'd been holding it, awaiting word that everyone was here. Now all had been accounted for but S'hak, and if the rest had safely exited, then S'hak was all right. "All right" undoubtedly was understatement. I'd bet that at this very moment, he was either with a pretty girl or adding to his assets in some fashion. S'hak could do business in the Gobi Desert.

My brother's machinations always made me laugh, but Tent P-7 wiped the smile away. Inside, it was a sultry, swamplike cave of canvas. The humidity and heat seeped in, but there was no escape for old and breathed-out air. Suspended, still and dead, saturated with the sour reek of mildew, a gray miasmal haze hung overhead.

At my second step, before my eyes adjusted to the semidarkness, I scraped my shin against an angled edge, and Nana warned belatedly, "You have to watch yourself. There's hardly room to move."

In point of fact, there wasn't *any* room to move. Three beds abutted on each other, like three sides of a square, and in the small space left around the center pole, Baba's big black box was serving as the only other furniture. Something vaguely bothered me about the dishes on this "dining table," but while my eyes were on the box, my mind flew back to Kambar Ali Street. The surface of our massive table gleamed; often it reflected fifty faces. Its four scrolled feet each rested on a different flower in the richly patterned rug. The Isfahan, my father's favorite. Behind my mother's seat, an ancient silver candelabra shimmered.

I blinked, and there was Baba's box again, sitting on the hard-packed sand. A saucer held a candle stub.

The box was real. The rest was fantasy. Until this very second, I'd been nurturing some fairy tales, but finally I faced up to the cold, hard, total truth. Our house was lost. Our line was ended in Iraq. Everything we owned was in this tent. Our only hope was Israel. Our only home was here.

We were taught in school that shock is sometimes therapeutic. I'd also heard that drowning men must hit the very bottom or they'll never rise again. Some jolts, it's said, can energize; and the bottom is a solid one can push against, impelling upward movement.

Those adages were proving out. Smaller shocks had merely muddled up my thinking, but this one cleared my mind and activated my adrenals. For the first time since I'd entered Israel, I really felt myself.

Mother was still warning me to watch my step, so only seconds had elapsed. I sat down on the nearest bed and tried to see P-7 with unbiased eyes. The only word for it was "awful." Facilities of any sort were nonexistent. Nana's stove had been concocted from tomato tins, and the tea she brewed reeked strongly of the kerosene.

Avram's voice was calling us to come outside. Through the open flap, I saw Nazima with a child in her arms and her other two behind her. Four more safe and well.

Hugging me, she murmured, "Oh, Heskel, not you too." Like Nana, my sister sounded stricken. She was thrilled to see me, but sick to see me here in Lyd.

"We're over on the other side of camp. That's why we took so long," she said.

She'd been assigned to CC-64, she told me, while strangers drew the tent next door to Nana. Separating families seemed stupid, and when I said it didn't make sense, both Nana and my sister shrugged. "You'll find that *nothing* here makes sense," this from Nazima, the eternal optimist. In my entire life, I'd never heard her speak so.

What, I wondered, would my father have to say? I strained my eyes, but Baba wasn't to be seen or S'hak either. Maybe both would come together, and what a meeting *that* would be! However, Nana dashed that hope by worrying aloud.

"I don't want Abu S'hak to leave the line until he gets his laxative."

Laxative? Baba? We used to laugh and say that Baba could eat bricks. Everyone in camp, my mother claimed, was either constipated or excreting all the time. "The food and water don't agree with us," she told me, "and the latrines smell so bad, you try to stay away as long as possible."

All the toilets had been clustered in the center of the camp, which meant a good long hike for all those on the outskirts, and after that, a good long wait; only half the number needed had been built. As I'd seen myself, many just eliminated where they were. At first, Nazima said, the families with children fought for tents close to the facilities; then, nauseated by the stench, they'd fought as hard to get the quarters farthest from them. For bathing, the camp provided running water, but faucets only, no tubs or sinks or showers.

"How many are there here?" I interrupted and was staggered when she answered, "Fifty thousand."

While several doctors were on call, not a single one had quarters in the camp. After Baba stood in line until he almost dropped, a nurse would hand him what he asked for. Lord help him if his bellyache was really an inflamed appendix; a laxative could kill him.

Crowding down my anger, I questioned them on other matters. Was it coincidence, I asked, my seeing only Africans and Orientals in the queues? Was the camp divided? Different hours, perhaps, for different segments of the population? I couldn't make myself say segregated, but Nazima knew what I was after, and she shook her head. "It's not like that," she said. "There aren't any here but us."

No German Jews or Polish Jews? No French or Dutch or Danish? Was it possible that no one from the Western world was emigrating? Or were the *Ashkenazim* somewhere else?

I spared my sister further inquisition, but stored the questions up for someone like a Dov to answer. The family was miserable enough already without my calling more attention to their sorry state.

Deprived of any proper home to care for, Nana was disoriented and adrift, and the kids complained of constant boredom. No provision had been made to exercize their minds or bodies. It was the Kurdish camp all over. When Avram said what I was thinking—"There's nothing here to *do!*"—Nana chided him, but gently; she must have heard the words a thousand times by now. "You can wash," she ordered. "It's almost time for lunch."

He made a face and flung out "Lunch!" as if he'd just ingested something live and squirming.

That really shook me. From infancy, my brother's appetite had been a legend. We used to say that others spooned but Avram shoveled. The memory amused me, but Nana was reproving. "It's nothing you should smile about. Yesterday they gave us sliced *salami!*" Like Avram's "Lunch!" she said the word with loathing.

Salami was a *Mislim* thing, taboo for Jews. That sort of sausage was like filth to us. Still, trying to be fair again, it wasn't such a tragedy. One uneaten lunch was hardly worth such agitation. Now that they'd been told we didn't eat it, something else would be supplied. I said as much, and saw my sister's face contort.

"Tell who?" I'd never seen Nazima so incensed. "Try to find someone to tell! No one ever talks to us. And we get salami every Wednesday, sometimes even twice a week. And for Friday dinner, they gave us *regel karush!*"

Nana pressed her lips together and looked sick. I felt a little ill myself. In the West, they called it *kishke* and considered it a treat, but to us, the mere idea of eating stuffed intestines was unholy. And on *Shabbat* yet!

Stupid! Stupid! Stupid! How could even bureaucrats be so damned dumb? No wonder Baba had a bellyache.

Nazima fished for something in her pocket, and I recognized the cardboard booklet of the breakfast line.

"These," she waved them angrily, "these are three months' worth of coupons for our food, but it's food for *Ashkenazim.* Most of it we have to throw away."

The catalogue of errors was positively awesome. Lamb, the staple meat for Eastern Jews, was unavailable at Lyd, and the salted herring that replaced it was repellent to Iraqis. In describing bread, disgust became despair.

"It's so hard, you have to *cut* it! With a *knife!*"

In Nana's eyes, the act was almost sacrilegious. The Bible spoke of "breaking" bread, and how did one eat bread that couldn't be broken. More than anything, they missed *khibz.*

Tzimmis—prunes and carrots cooked together—turned their stomachs. As for the soup, Nana shrugged it off with, "Once they may have washed a chicken in the water." I'd already tasted the insipid tea, so Nana simply pointed to the cup and shrugged again. Even "they" should know that strong black tea was *the* essential of the Eastern diet. Instead, the camp got mostly coffee.

I steamed to think that just one lazy bastard with a shopping list could cause such misery among so many helpless people. A minute spent with any kid in camp could have straightened out. . . . my train of thought was interrupted.

So far off I hardly heard it, a voice was shouting "Heskel." There had to be a hundred Heskels here at Lyd; unhesitatingly, however, I vaulted up and out. He was still two alleys down when I flung myself at Baba's neck. It isn't possible to laugh and cry and kiss and hug and howl with joy, not all at once, but that's precisely what I did.

Baba's arms were strong as ever, and his back as straight. His voice, his smile, the way he shook his head at my exuberance—all exactly as before. The same exactly, I exulted.

I backed off for a better look, and subtle changes struck me. Seeing him, a stranger would have said, "A handsome figure of a man." Baba still looked fine, still bronzed and leanly muscular, his hair still thick and black, his stride still longer than my own. And yet I saw a difference.

He was *looser* than he'd been. Not as crisp. Not—I searched to find the word—not as "kempt." His clothes were clean but rather rumpled, as if he'd lain about in them, and he didn't have a tie on; Baba *never* went outside the house without one. This small defection from his standards was disturbing.

On our arrival at P-7, he stopped and waved me sweepingly inside.

"Won't you join us in the Promised Land?"

In his own wry way, Baba was reminding me that Israel was my idea.

"Here, at least, you're free to be a Jew," I answered, but even to myself, I sounded flat and passionless. Before I'd seen this place, I'd said it in a stronger, surer voice. I had to get them out, and fast. First, a decent flat for Nana. And to be the man he was, my father had to find some work. The kids, of course, must go to school. After all these things had been accomplished, I could see about my own career.

I was twitching in my skin, impatient to depart this place and start. The sooner I could get away, the quicker I could see to their release. I almost said "escape." I was only waiting now for S'hak. Wheeler-dealer S'hak—what had *he* been doing all these weeks, I wondered. Impatient to be off, I asked, "Isn't S'hak *ever* getting back?"

Nana clapped her hands together and began to cry. S'hak wasn't here. He'd never left Iraq. I knew now what had bothered me about the "table"—five places had been set instead of six.

Baba brought me up to date. To keep its own economy in order, Iraq had eased a little in its anti-Jewish stance. Certain Jews with special talents might elect to stay, and others, like my Uncle Ezra, were *compelled* to stay; they needed him to run the gasworks.

S'hak had an option. Since his mill made more and better bricks than any other, he'd been given special dispensations and guaranteed a handsome profit. As long as he was safe and making money, he'd remain.

"Even with a yellow card. . . ." Baba didn't continue, but the ending was implicit, "maybe S'hak's better off."

I didn't trust the government, and carrying a yellow card was odious, but even so, I felt a twinge of envy. S'hak was at home, on Kambar Ali Street. The hopes I'd buried earlier began to stir. Something might be salvaged after all.

But S'hak wasn't at the house. When Baba had to tell me what had happened to the house, he aged before my eyes. Arabs occupied our home and every other once the property of Jews.

"The day before we left, this *Mislim* scum arrived 'to look about.' He said the house had been assigned to him, and ordered me to show him everything. I didn't expect such arrogance, not even from a filthy peasant farmer." Unexpectedly, my father grinned.

"Well, I showed him!" And he winked at me.

I could picture Baba's booby traps. I saw the kitchen ovens spewing kerosene, the cesspools stopping up and spilling over, and the ceiling fans come crashing down. I smiled, but only fleetingly. With all the cash they'd confiscated, plus every other Jewish asset, the Arabs had the final, lasting laugh.

Remembering, however, had a good effect on father. Soon, he said, we'd be together in a house again. Maybe not a house, exactly—actually a shack—but, with solid walls instead of stinking canvas. Some of Baba's friends had moved from Lyd to *ma'abarot,* and if the quarters weren't much to look at, at least a man could make a living in a work camp. It was only unskilled labor—"black labor" was the term he used—but anything was better than this vegetating.

I recalled the road gangs, stepping back to let the bus go by, the heavy picks burnished by the scorching sun, the faces caked with filth. Black indeed. At Baba's age, and with his background and ability, he'd settle for a shovel and a tin-roofed shack?

I rose to go without announcing my intentions. Baba wouldn't be working on a road gang. I'd find a place for us and a proper place for him. Until I did, however, I'd have to stay with uncle.

My suitcase had been shoved beneath a bed, and Nana still was searching for a place to stow my satchel. She thought, of course, that I was moving in.

I took the satchel from her hand, and without a word between us, Baba bent to get the suitcase. He understood that I was aching to be on my way, and quieting my mother's questions, motioned me to leave.

I had to go before I either bellowed like a bull or burst out crying. From this day on, even my emotions must be wisely spent. I couldn't afford to spill them out solely for my own relief. I had to hoard my anger, keep it hot and under pressure, ready to release as needed. It was all the power I possessed, all I had to fuel me for whatever I might have to do.

There were a *thousand* things to do, and suddenly it struck me that I didn't know where to start.

37

At dawn the following day, I again left Uncle Eliahu's flat to board a bus. Bumping toward Jerusalem, the road was just as bad as that to Lyd, and I had to stand and lurch the whole three hours. After 1400 years, what a mean, prosaic way, I thought, to make the grand re-entry.

Since my forebears had to flee the city, every generation of Haddads, like all the Jews of the Diaspora, had prayed in its direction, pledging to return, and while a worn-out and plebeian bus was not the vehicle I would have chosen, at least I'd make it *almost* home. Old Jerusalem—*our* Jerusalem—was still in alien hands.

My mind was in the city long before the bus arrived, recalling its geography and juggling my agenda to make the most of every moment.

The Joint in Teheran had given me the names of people I should see here, from the Minister of Health to Ari Bernstein of the Jewish Agency. With their assistance I hoped to wrap up everything within a week. A flat to house the family, employment for my father, and a place for me to practice, as well as leads on all my aunts and uncles from Iraq.

Everything was urgent. The decision as to what came first, however, had long since been determined—and by the Talmud: As soon as I got on the bus, the words began resounding in my brain: "If I forget thee, oh, Jerusalem. . . ." From infancy I'd known what I must do. On entering Yerushalyim, a Jew must make directly for the Western Wall and pray.

The *Kotel* was in Arab hands, but even that contingency had been foreseen.

If the Wall itself was out of reach, we were to offer up our prayers at the closest point approachable.

On Jaffa Road already, we crossed the intersection with King George Street and pulled up at the station. Having memorized the maps, I knew I'd soon be seeing massive walls . . . the walls entirely enclosing Old Jerusalem. And deep within them was *the* Wall, the sole remaining remnant of the Second Temple. The *Kotel.* And even that was now denied us. About the closest I could come was David's Tomb, just outside the Zion Gate that led into the ancient city. Above me, on the monumental battlements, soldiers kept continuous patrol, and I recognized their red *kaffiyahs.* King Hussein's legionnaires, armed and on the lookout.

On Mount Zion, facing the *Kotel,* and under Arab guns, I said the designated prayer. Wanting, needing more, I went exploring in the Tomb itself and found an exit to the roof. From up above, I thought it might be possible to see the Western Wall, but I was still too low; I looked about in search of some place higher. By then, the Tomb's custodian had tumbled to my enterprise. Peering up at me but careful not to show his head, he screamed a warning.

On the ground, I'd felt completely screened and safe because Mount Zion was so lushly full of greenery, but belatedly I realized that on the roof, my silhouette was sharply etched against the sky. The Jordanians could pick me off with slingshots. Although I strained my eyes, I couldn't see a stone of the *Kotel.* What glittered back at me, instead, was the bulbous golden dome belonging to the Mosque of Omar. For the sight of that, constructed on the Mount that once belonged to us, I didn't want to die. Scrambling down, I shot away, the sexton screeching imprecations after me.

I decided to begin with Ari Bernstein at the Jewish Agency, which was far enough away to warrant riding. On the bus, I lucked into a window seat, the only way that I could sightsee without wasting any time.

Having listened to illegal broadcasts back in Baghdad, I could picture what the city looked like while the war was on. At this very moment, though no vestiges of ruin remained, we were going past a scene of bloody carnage. Arab terrorists had packed a truck with high explosives, parked it in the center of this shopping district, and set it off to maim and murder innocent civilians. Since then, the area had been rebuilt, and I couldn't detect a single sign of devastation. To conceal the scars, construction crews had gone to the surrounding hills to match the damaged stone. Already ancient when King David's men had quarried it, the sun-tinged golden granite bound Jerusalem together in a glowing, healthy whole.

The city was serenely ageless, but the Agency was strictly here and now. Bernstein pumped my arm, once up, once down, announced that he was Ari to his friends, and briskly stated that Iran had briefed him. "I know all about you, so let's get down to business. Do you have a place to stay?"

Unprepared for such dispatch, I shook my head, as much in sheer amazement as response; in Baghdad, the initial greeting would have gone on for an hour. Dov said that they were short of time here, and Ari more than saved his share. He was on the phone already, snapping out, "Someone here from *T'nu'ah.* Baghdad. Needs a bed. Better get on over."

Hanging up, he swiveled back to say, "His name's Hanoch. Last name, Temple. Has an office right next door. Mizrachi House. Youth Aliyah. He runs it." His staccato style made everything he uttered sound important, and most of what he told me was.

Before Hanoch arrived, Ari summarized the housing situation. While I knew about the shortage and I'd heard of Histadrut, a sort of super-union for almost everyone who held a job in Israel, I had no idea that Histadrut had anything to do with housing.

"Simple. Histadrut controls the labor, labor does the building." Ari shrugged expressively. "And then there's politics." The major parties, he explained, each had someone representing it on Histadrut's Executive Committee, and naturally each scrambled for its own constituents. For shelter, then, you joined a party which could push your case.

I'd informed myself about the four main factions, and like any other citizen, expected to enroll in one as soon as I was settled, but it seems I had the sequence wrong. Apparently you settled on a party first, and *then* you found a place to live. I ran them over in my mind, resenting the necessity of making such a swift decision on so serious a matter.

The Mapai Party was middle of the road, Poel Mizrachi's main concern was keeping Israel an orthodox and strictly "kosher" country. Members of Mapam, the most radical of all the four, were accused of being communistic, and *L'achdut ha'aboda* was to the left of the Mapai and to the right of the Mapam.

But there were splinter groups I'd never heard of—at least eight or nine, Ari said—which operated independently of Histadrut and each of which had influence in certain spheres. My head began to spin, and he shook me up completely by telling me I'd set my sights too high to start with.

"Forget a flat," he counseled bluntly. "We're talking temporary housing: *shikunim*—that's the best that you can hope for."

He spelled out names of party representatives for me to see, and as I wrote the last of them, the doorknob rattled, and a hearty, freckled man with flame-red hair burst in. If Bernstein was informal, you'd have to call Hanoch outlandish, at least in his appearance. His pants were rump-sprung and his shirt misbuttoned. A hand-crocheted hot orange *yarmulke* was barely clinging to his head, skewered by a huge black hairpin.

A minute after shaking hands and booming out "*Shalom!*" he had me taking down his office number and his home address "in case we miss connections." His hospitality extended far beyond the bed requested.

"What luck!" he beamed. "Tonight we have a wedding. You'll enjoy it."

Not "would you?" but "you will." I loved his positive approach, and my spirits took an upward turn. Already he was more than an acquaintance. At noon, it was agreed, I'd meet him at Mizrachi House and eat with him at home. As in Baghdad, the working day began at seven, so lunch was long and leisurely.

Next, I headed for the Ministry of Health, only minutes from the Agency. To my delight, not only was I ushered in at once, but the Minister appeared to be expecting me. Someone had been briefing him about my background, because he pumped me dry of everything I knew that had to do with anything Iraqi. Although an hour passed before I could allude to my predicament, I was happy he showed such concern for all my fellow emigrés. On the street, it was easy to forget that there were any Jews but *Ashkenazim.* Most of "us," it seems, were still sequestered in the camps.

Finally his appetite was sated, and he asked at last how he could help me. I compressed it to a single sentence.

"I'm a doctor, but I don't have my diploma. What do I do?"

Like Ari, he answered me by picking up the phone—and he was asking for the General Director of the Health Department! Right to the top! God was being good. Everyone I'd had to see so far was either sitting in his office, seemingly awaiting me, or instantly available by telephone.

By the rising "Oh?" and the startled lifting of official eyebrows, I could tell, though, that the seamless stretch of luck had started shredding. The Minister was hearing something that surprised him, and he wasn't pleased. According to the General Director, my case was far from novel. Israel was full of doctors who had fled without credentials.

"He says that doctors by the boxcar are coming in without their records, many from the death camps."

If that was so, I thought, surely he'd arrived at a solution. Apparently the Minister was of the same opinion, and with a hearty handshake, he dispatched me to the G.D.'s office.

"Unhappily," the G.D. started, and my stomach muscles tightened. What followed, though, at first seemed less unpleasant than perplexing. "While we haven't yet set up a full-scale medical establishment, you'll be pleased to hear the school. . . ."

School? But what had school to do with me? The man was maundering! He continued talking, telling me the school had been envisioned back in 1946, before the state itself came into being, but the plan, he said, had been aborted by the Orthodox community because dissection was required in the study of anatomy and religious law forbade the "desecration."

"But now," his tone turned hopeful, "we think we have a way to get around it, or at any rate get started."

Since I could hardly interrupt him, I consciously relaxed and listened. Even if it had no application to my own dilemma, what he was going on about was really quite inventive.

Israel's first school of medicine was being brought into existence upside down. Instead of starting up with first-year students, the institute would open at the sixth-year level, enrolling those who'd taken their Anatomy abroad. Israelis studying elsewhere could now come home to finish up their final courses.

But avoiding controversy over cutting into corpses was only partially responsible for setting up the school in such a way. When he mentioned "other doctors who had trained abroad," I began to realize that the G.D. wasn't aimlessly meandering. In some way or another, this establishment pertained to me.

"Its whole name," he was saying, "is the Hebrew University Hadassah School of Medicine, and it's right here in Jerusalem. You'll have to see if they'll accept you."

When it hit me that I'd have to go to school again—if, that is, they let me in—I shot up from my seat, and forgetful of my manners and my very junior status, shouted out, "But I'm a doctor!"

The G.D. made some sympathetic sounds. "Sit down. Let's see if I can make you understand. You're not the only one, you know. This rule applies to every doctor trained abroad who comes without impeccable credentials. Our standards here are high. To be absolutely sure that everyone is fully qualified, some must suffer inconvenience."

What a way to put it! "Catastrophe" would be more accurate.

Thinking of the family curtailed my tongue, and I thanked him for his courtesy, said I'd check into the school that afternoon, and asked if I could ask another favor. "Right now, I need a job," I said. Could he suggest some avenue I might explore? He saw my struggle for composure, and appreciating what it cost me, scribbled off a letter introducing me to Dr. Bruner, director of the hospital in Givat-Aliyah.

"I'll get in touch with him," the G.D. offered. "I think that he can use you until school begins."

My depression lifted slightly; his words implied I'd be accepted. Walking home with Hanoch also helped. If men like these accepted me so readily, how could Bruner or Hadassah turn me down?

Though larger and in better shape than uncle's, Hanoch's apartment still was far from lavish, and less than I'd expected for a top official. Much as I loved luxury, it was somehow comforting that everyone in Israel was equally deprived.

Lunch proved the deprivation also stretched to food. The soup was thin and hardly had a taste at all. My portion had a slice of carrot and some skinny noodles. Considering its low caloric value, it was hardly worth the energy expenditure to spoon it up. The "butter" was an oily imitation. The main dish was a medley of the vegetables in season, mixed with cubes of salted cheese. Some wrinkled, unknown objects, almost black in color, were interspersed among the edibles I recognized. Although I'd never seen one, I suspected they were olives. And that's when I discovered that I hated olives.

At home, we would have dressed the dish with vinegar and oil; here they squeezed a slice of lemon over everything. Instead of Nana's rice, Hanoch's mother passed me roast potatoes, and throughout the meal, everyone drank carbonated water squirted from a siphon.

"Tonight," Hanoch announced, "we're having meat. We've been saving all our coupons for a month." The others looked ecstatic, but my puzzlement was plain to see. I'd thought that only refugees required coupons.

"No one told you?" Hanoch was incensed. "If you expect to eat in Israel, you'd better register." My "must do" list was getting longer.

Almost everything, Hanoch explained, was on a quota, and he pulled a copy of the morning paper from his pocket. Under "Ration News" I read, "For Tel Aviv: Eggs, coupon 8. Poultry for the sick, zones 6, 7, and 8. Potatoes: zone 7 and 8, 3 kilos." Every sort of foodstuff was included, and there were points for clothes as well as coupons to contend with.

"You'll catch on," Hanoch assured me. "Most of us get sixty points a year. Shirts, for instance, start at seven. For pants and jackets, you'll pay over thirty. Even putting soles on shoes will cost you points. Leather's very scarce, and so is paper. Writing pads and typing bond are very hard to come by, and expensive. Our imports keep increasing, and our economy can't stand the strain."

Hanoch walked me partway to Hadassah, and much as I despised the whole idea of temporary housing, I asked about *shikunim,* and how best to go about applying—just in case, since anything was better than the camp. As I suspected, Hanoch had connections with a major party, and he scrawled a name. "See Mizrachi. Say I sent you." When I returned to Tel Aviv, it was the first thing I would do.

Walking on alone after dropping Hanoch at his office, I wondered if I'd ever grow blasé about the scene around me. To an old inhabitant, undoubtedly it looked prosaic, even dull perhaps. Nothing much was happening—no bombs exploding, no bloody accidents or even street brawls to attract attention. To me, however, the sight of Jewish soldiers, displaying Stars of David, speaking Hebrew openly, and strolling on the avenue with rifles slung so casually across their backs, was more astonishing than men from Mars. In Iraq, any of these "crimes" would have sent them to a jail cell, if not a cemetery.

Even more astounding was the Arab in Israeli battle dress. Then I realized I'd seen a Druze. I'd read about the sect, which had allied itself with Israel; its members were the only Arabs who were serving in Israeli forces.

On arriving at the wing in which the school would be established, I was shown into the office of the Dean without delay. Dr. Pryves, a Polish Jew who'd earned his medical degree in France, had just arrived to take the post. Most correct in manner and almost military in his stance, he still exuded something so receptive that I let myself speak out with no restraint. Intending to relieve the pressure, Dr. Pryves said, "It's not a major problem. I'll accept a letter from any one of your professors in Iraq."

I put my situation to him in the briefest, flattest terms. In Iraq, I was high up on the "wanted" list, an enemy of Islam. In view of that, what government-employed professor would risk his neck to write and send a letter of endorsement?

The Dean's requirement would keep me out of school, and the state required that I go to school before allowing me to practice my profession.

It seemed hopeless; staying longer made no sense, but when I pushed up from my seat, Pryves waved me back. Staring fixedly at me, he tapped his fingertips together; finally he offered an alternative. He'd accept the testimony of at least two doctors who had known me in Iraq. Letters signed by them, stating that I'd finished school successfully, would be sufficient. "After I receive them, you can take the test."

Now all I had to do was dredge up several doctors acquainted with my school career in Baghdad. The trouble was, I didn't know anyone in Israel who qualified.

Where next, for what, and how and when? Did I start to look for doctors first or try for the *shikun?* Spring the family from Lyd or start to make a living? Sometime soon, I had to go to Givat-Aliyah, near Jaffa, to investigate the job with Bruner, but the school year for the kids was also starting soon, and someone had to see to registration. Except they couldn't be registered until they had a place of residence. And there were ration cards. And relatives.

Tel Aviv was central for everything I had to do, and tomorrow I'd be up at dawn and on the first bus out. Tonight, though, I was going to a wedding.

Since I'd worn my best to see the Dean, I didn't have to change on my arrival at Hanoch's. That was fortunate because the family was almost out the door when I appeared. Unlike Iraq, where the ceremony would be held at home or in a synagogue, here the parents of the bride had hired a hall. Few Israeli flats were large enough to hold a wedding party, and the houses had no *hosh.*

In the hall, I saw my first Hassidic Jews up close, their *peot* curling lushly past their ears and their long, black caftans lending dignity to drab surroundings. Remembering my uncle's wedding and the rainbow richness of the layers of Persian rugs, this place looked extra plain and bare. The ritual itself was barely recognizable. While in Hebrew, it was Hebrew with a heavy Western accent, the cadences of which were so outlandish that without a *chupah* hanging overhead, I wouldn't have known it was a wedding. Not that the *chupah* wasn't odd as well. It was round at home, of fine embroidered fabric dripping heavy golden tassels; this canopy was square in shape and stripped to the essential cloth. With the crushing of the wineglass underfoot, however, everything got back on track.

The shouts of joy were just the same, and someone started singing. The singing spread, and a moment later, all the men were circling the groom, shuffling in a sidewise dance step. By now I knew there wouldn't be any orchestra or entertainment, but I didn't expect what *did* occur. The nervous bridegroom, seated on a common kitchen chair, was hoisted high above the dancers' heads and swayed there in the center of the circle. I couldn't believe my eyes. That's how *M'silmin* acted at a wedding, except that Arabs didn't bother with a chair, and *ba'abitzed* the embarrassed groom. Even in the absence of the Arab goosing, the exhibition struck me as undignified.

The biggest shock had come before the ceremony even started, when I found a woman sitting in the seat alongside mine. I'd never sat through any service with a female, and certainly I'd never instigated small talk with a female stranger—nor did I this time. She began it with a bold *"Shalom,"* and by the time we went to dinner, I was past the point of blushing, but still so ill at ease that I never even heard her name. Too shy to ask her to repeat it, she remained, for me, "the Polish girl."

When she discovered this was just my second day in Israel, she shook her head in mock despair. "You've got some sticky times ahead. You'd better let me fill you in."

"Everyone of us has strange ideas about the others," she began. "For instance, I'm from Wolyn, and the saying is 'After shaking hands with anyone from Wolyn, it's wise to count your fingers.' All of us, supposedly, are thieves. And take Rumanians," my Polish girl continued. "No one ever merely mentions that someone is Rumanian. He sneers it. Among the other Europeans, saying that a person's from Rumania is equivalent to calling him a crook."

She kept a "hate list" in her head, she said. "It's a sort of rating system. No one knows who started it, but everybody has one. It's the only way you know where people stand."

I was totally at sea. If I understood what she was saying, and accepted it, Israel was more like India than Eden. I hesitated, but I had to ask, "Are you saying that the state condones. . . ?"

"No, not the state," she cut me off impatiently. "It's purely something *people* do. They put each other in the proper box and paste on labels. Right now, the lowest box belongs to the Moroccans. *Everybody* loathes Moroccans. The other 'Africans' are just above them." She paused a second, sorting out her thoughts. "After that, it gets a little trickier. The Poles and the Rumanians are equal in the eyes of all the others, and they also see Hungarians and you Iraqi Jews as just about the same."

The equating of the latter two was so insane, I had to laugh, but she persisted, "I mean the same in the degree that they're disliked. Both the groups are clannish, and the others say they're egotistic, that they think they're something special."

She concluded with the Yemenites and Kurds: "They tie for last." What happened to the bottom-of-the-heap Moroccans, I inquired, and she made a face. "They're still exactly where I said. They're so far down, they aren't even *on* the hate list. They're too submissive to detest, and since they're not considered competition, they're simply looked on with contempt. If there was a 'nothing' list, they'd lead it."

Ending with an impish grin, as if she'd just been making jokes, she switched the conversation to the food before us. Perhaps she *had* been twitting me. More probably, she only meant to entertain. Clearly, though, an element of truth existed in her listing, and I wasn't sure how much was fact and how much mere embellishment to make a better story. If I only half-believed her, the country simmered with conflicting castes and classes.

Right now, however, my conflict was with food. Much of what was placed before me was in urgent need of explanation, and the Polish girl obliged.

That braided item, for example, four feet long and as brightly gleaming as enamel, was—implausibly—a loaf of bread. A *challah.* She identified the round and rather rubbery objects in my soup as matzo balls and the floating doughy shells with meat inside as *kreplach.* With the gefilte fish, which at least I could identify as coming from the sea, she suggested that I try a dark-red relish, but failed to tell me what amount to take. I introduced a healthy forkful on a bit of fish; immediately, my eyes brimmed over and I blindly groped for water. I felt as if I'd swallowed flame. Through the roaring in my ears, I heard her say approvingly, "That's really good horseradish."

Accustomed as I was to bite-size lamb, the beefsteak in a single slab looked gross, and with it, once again, there were potatoes. Had no one in this country ever heard of rice? Dessert was one big blob of brilliant red, which my tutor said was jello. I found it less than appetizing, trying to ingest a substance that seemed to flinch and suffer when you touched it.

Despite my ending up still hungry after dinner, I was smiling when I went to sleep in Hanoch's house. For someone newly come, I felt that I was coping rather well.

At dawn, finding me awake, Hanoch asked if I would care to join him at the synagogue. When he said, "It's in 'the Hundred Gates,' " I eagerly accepted. Although the gates were, for the most part, gone, nothing else had altered since the first inhabitants had built their homes in this, the oldest Jewish settlement outside the walls. Mea Shearim remained the stronghold of the ultra, ultra Orthodox in Israel, operating almost as a separate entity within the state.

From Hanoch's flat, Mea Shearim was only minutes off, and all downhill. Turning at the bottom of a steeply sloping street brought us right into the center of the section. The main road of this enclave was only two blocks long and twelve feet wide. At its eastern end, a U.N. flag identified the border. Since the War of Independence, the land beyond had been out of bounds for Jews. Having shelled and otherwise abused Jerusalem, Jordan claimed it now as "holy" to Islam.

Some Jews, of course, weren't even welcome where we stood; the Orthodox stood guard against the "desecrators." On the Sabbath, since riding was forbidden, every road was blocked by rocks and timber, and sometimes stones were thrown at cars attempting entry. Tourists were expected to be "properly" attired, and women wearing anything provocative were sternly warned and sent away.

No house was more than two floors high, and either age had darkened them or different stone had gone into construction. Whereas a golden glow suffused the other sections of the city, this was somber as the atmosphere within it. Much of the architecture had a Moorish look, and there appeared to be a synagogue on every street, and on some streets, every corner.

Even at this early hour, we were under the surveillance of the "Guardians of the City." Where Hanoch worshipped, one of the *Neture Karta* looked me over, nodded at Hanoch, and let us in. It was the smallest, darkest synagogue I'd ever seen. Squinting in the gloom, I couldn't spot a single window to the outside world, and while my eyesight soon adapted to the dimness, I thought my hearing might be damaged by the din. My eardrums positively quivered.

The level of the noise was probably no higher than I'd often heard in Baghdad, but it bothered me because the sounds were strangely dissonant, the inflections unfamiliar and eccentric. The scene around me was reminiscent of an overcrowded epileptic ward. Every member of the congregation was convulsing and appeared to be in pain. All were bobbing back and forth, to and fro, up and down, pouring out their prayers in perfect cadence with their spastic seizures. When I turned to Hanoch for a clue, I discovered, to my consternation, that my friend had also been afflicted. Eyes shut tight, he was bobbing with the best of them.

Later he described what they'd been doing. "Davening" he called it. Even praying here was odd and somewhat alien. In Baghdad, worship was the one thing that we didn't do at highest volume. Once seated, we stayed put and communed with God in quiet murmurs.

Despite the great disparities, however, I was swept up by the words themselves; the rhythms might be different, but the meaning of the service was the same. The same, then, must apply to people. All of us were people of the self-same Book. Jews might be dissimilar in customs and appearance, but where it counted—at our core—we were surely all alike and equal. But thinking of the Polish girl, I added, "in the sight of God." Even his anointed people might not see so clearly.

38

On the bus to Tel Aviv, my stomach ground uneasily away at breakfast. After synagogue, we'd gone back to Hanoch's place, where I dug into the *dag malouach,* though just the thought of salted fish so early in the morning made me queasy. The yoghurt, called *labaniya,* which I seized on to erase the taste, was sweeter and more liquid than our own, and I missed the tang and crusty topping. Most of all, I missed my morning tea. My heart might be Israeli, but my taste buds and digestive tract stubbornly retained their old allegiance.

After two full hours in a bus queue, fighting down the fish, I felt I was entitled to enjoy the trip; I wiped a patch of window clean and settled back to sightsee like a tourist.

Approaching Bab el Wad, on the outskirts of Jerusalem, I began to note the skeletons of cars and trucks abandoned by the roadside. When the few became a score, I looked at them more closely. None was an ordinary wreck resulting from an accident or over-age. They'd been firebombed and blasted by a thousand bullets.

I suddenly remembered then. When Jerusalem was under seige, citizens contributed their private cars to form a convoy. Unarmored but for homemade metal plates, exposed and helpless on the single highway snaking through the hills, and under heavy *M'silmin* fire every mile of the way, they'd saved the city from starvation. The lifeless hulks were left exactly as arrested, monuments more graphic than the finest shaft of marble.

At Latrun, within a yard of where the asphalt ended, a signpost marked the border. Over there was Jordan. The Judean hills were now behind us and the road lay flat to Tel Aviv. I'd planned to drop my bags at uncle's place and take right off to tend to business, but since lunch was set when I arrived, my aunt insisted that I stay and eat.

Uncle knew I'd been to Lyd, and I expected a barrage of questions, but they never came. On thinking back, I realized that he hadn't said a word about the family except in answer to my inquiry the night I first appeared. I'd always thought that Baba and his brother were extremely close, and couldn't bring myself to ask about this obvious estrangement. I'd had my share of arguments with S'hak, so my father and my uncle were entitled to their own disputes. Still, it bothered me. Now was not the time for interfamily antagonism.

Whatever caused the friction, the quarrel evidently didn't extend to me. Uncle Eliahu said that I was welcome for as long as I would like to stay, and escorted me to what would be my room. It was on the roof, "just an old tin shack we use for storage, but it's big enough to put a bed in." Every inch of it was crammed with junk. Not the slightest bit abashed, uncle said, "Once we clean it out, that is. And no one will disturb you here."

Ousted from the flat, I felt unwanted, but with no place else to go, I proceeded to make space while my uncle brought the cot up.

That settled, he asked if I had any leads to living quarters. I knew, of course, how hard it was to find a flat? I did, indeed, I told him, but in a week or two, if nothing better offered, I thought that I could swing us a *shikun.* Uncle snorted at my innocence.

"Don't count on it," he warned. "You'd better figure that they'll be at Lyd at least three months, and maybe six. After that, the *ma'abarot.* Tin shacks. "Eventually they'll pull them down and put up more *shikunim.* Then they'll tear *those* down and build for real, but that won't be for years yet."

I waited for suggestions, but all he offered was a cynical "good luck" as I started on my "hopeless" quest. I decided that I didn't much like my uncle.

I knew that Histadrut had great prestige and power, but I hadn't comprehended just how huge it was until I checked it out. Depending on the source, either seventy-five or eighty-six percent of all Israeli men and women working for a wage were under its umbrella. As ubiquitous as it was big, Histadrut was much more than a labor union. It published and distributed a paper, operated reading rooms, and provided an extensive range of top-flight lectures, concerts, and scholastic courses for its members. In addition, Histadrut administered Kupat Cholim, thereby overseeing almost all the clinics, convalescent homes, and hospitals within the country. And the officials I was off to see had all that strength supporting them—that, and their political affiliation with the four main parties.

At Mizrachi headquarters, Hanoch's name evoked the utmost cordiality, but no *shikun.* The other parties were just as affable and just as unaccommodating—and each employed the same excuse: The average wait for housing was from three to six years' time . . . even worse than *uncle's* estimate. However—and each one also offered me the same however—since I was "special," my family might possibly be placed in months instead of years. By "special," I assumed they meant my service in the underground, but my major merit, it appeared, was in my origin, specifically, my being an Iraqi with some reputation. These fellows were on top of all the figures, and the figures showed that 40,000 of my countrymen were already here, with many thousands more to come. A major voting bloc, and thus far uncommitted. If I were so inclined, I could help them vote "correctly."

In offering his aid, each official of course, expected me to propagandize for his party. Along with applications for *shikunim,* they whipped out forms for me to sign, making me a party member. While indicating interest, I held back, requesting literature to study at my leisure. A political affiliation was important, too important to be sold for a *shikun.* Anyway, *shikunim* were, admittedly, a stopgap sort of housing. It wasn't good enough. Somehow, I'd have to solve this on my own, unless. . . .

Yes, Dov was in, they told me in the outer office, and when he clapped me on the back, the words began to gush as if the friendly blow had freed a long-stuck bung. Like a filled-to-bursting barrel, I spouted all the rancor I'd been holding in since Lyd.

Why were the camps so bleak and barren? Why, with willing hands to work, was living space so scarce? Why were we building big hotels, wasting short supplies on tourists? And overriding all the rest, why didn't *Ashkenazim* ever talk to us as equals and ask for our opinions, if only in connection with our own affairs?

When I finally ran out of accusations, Dov didn't respond at once. Really looking at him now, I noted deep new creases etched across his brow, and he raised his hand to rub exhausted eyes. The action seemed to ease him. With thousands of us streaming into Israel, it belatedly occurred to me that everything I'd thrown at him, he'd heard before, who knows how many times.

Before I could apologize for my eruption, he began to speak. "It's an old, established *Ashkenazi* custom to answer every question with a question, so let me ask you this. Right now, we're spending $1600 we don't have on every refugee who enters Israel. Shall we spend a little more on those already here, give them softer beds and better food, and tell the others not to come? You're a scholar. When it comes to Jewish history, I'm sure that you could teach about the last 2000 years, but you don't know beans about the last *two* years. Now let me tell you." I listened, mesmerized, as he proceeded.

"You've only seen one camp. We have more than thirty operating at the moment. And in addition to the camps, we're running 140 *ma'abarot.* In the last six months . . ." he stopped to flip a folder open and consult it briefly, ". . . in the last six months, 72,515 immigrants arrived. In July alone, we registered a total of"—head down again to look—"14,380, and at least another 20,000 will be in before October. As for willing labor, God knows we need it, but half the heads of families who came here are either physically depleted or untrained. You want to hear some other cheery figures?"

The question was rhetorical; he went on without a pause.

"In the average *ma'abarot,* forty percent of all the residents are school-age kids or infants. In the future, all of them will work. In the meantime, all of them are eating, and they all need shelter. Nearly seventy-five percent of everything that we can scrape together goes to agriculture and to housing.

"The Germans and the Arabs send us Jews with just the shoes they stand in. Already, all of us—*all,* not just the immigrants—eat fewer calories per day than the minimum the U.N. recommends. And the mouths we have to feed also come with tongues we have to teach to speak in Hebrew. We speak a hundred languages, and everyone is mad as hell in all of them."

A grin destroyed his carefully composed expression, and I had to smile back. A host of questions still remained, but the seething need to spit them out had been extinguished.

"We welcome those no other country will allow to enter," he began again. He spoke about the special camps for those who suffered with such illnesses as syphilis, bilharzia, and every sort of parasitic malady endemic to the Arab world. "Do you know," he asked, "about the village for the blind? Mostly Yemenites, mostly from trachoma. No one ever treated them." I *hadn't* known. Near Gedera, he informed me. An entire village, and I hadn't known.

Addressing my attack against the tourists, he explained, "They're worth their weight in gold. Or—just as good—hard currency." Most were from America, and while Dov admitted that they used up scarce resources at a fearful rate, they more than paid for them, he said, in U.S. dollars. "Internationally, our money isn't worth much. Without those dollars, we couldn't buy necessities abroad."

But of even more importance, he continued, the tourists served as ambulating billboards when they went back home. "They talk about their trips; each one tells a thousand others. And they talk about both good and bad. We *want* them to do that, to tell the world it's not all milk and honey here."

His grin broke through again. "It's not as if we had to make an effort. When a tourist steps into a shower and searches for a cake of soap that isn't there, he sees, firsthand, how short we are. Sometimes there isn't even toilet paper. If we want their dollars, we have, at least, to give them toilet paper, so someone has to be deprived. Some poor Israeli will have to find another way to wipe his butt."

Dov grew serious once more. "They come because they care. For comfort, they could go to any of the grand hotels in London or in Paris, but they come to us instead. They see that they eat better and are better dressed than we are, and if they feel a little guilty, and want to buy an extra bond or pledge an extra hundred bucks . . . ," he heaved a sigh, "how else do we exist?"

Back to briskness, Dov began to churn out other facts and figures; everything was in his head and clearly in the forefront of his mind. With every word he uttered, I could almost see the furrows deepen. Finally, abandoning his temperate approach, he spoke with passion of the problems and the possible solutions—of all the things that troubled him and some that made him swell with pride. I listened as intensely as he talked, aware that I was getting in a single gush the sum of all his study and experience.

Shelter occupied his thoughts as much as it did mine. This year, he said, 40,000 housing units would be built, but 100,000, at the minimum, were needed *now,* and more with every ship and plane disgorging displaced people. Compounding the financial squeeze and scarcity of labor, lumber was in short supply. Our earth had been denuded, and Israel was planting trees, not axing them; wood was one more import item.

An estimated twelve percent of all Israelis would spend the winter under canvas, and even canvas was in scant supply. Because of the Korean war, most of it was earmarked for the Western armies. Before the rains set in, 20,000 children would be sent to winter homes with strangers to escape the cold and start their schooling.

"What's really sad is that the more the parents love their kids, the faster they consent to let them go."

I was relieved to learn the school reopening had been delayed until the middle of September. That gave me two more weeks to find a flat before the kids could be assigned to class. "Since last semester," Dov informed me, "the student population has increased a third. We're even pinched for pencils."

In another area, however, we were very well prepared. Since the Arabs specialized in sneak attacks, every frontier settlement was furnished with a ring of searchlights. "At night, it looks like Hollywood. Our people have to learn to sleep with open eyes."

Even as we talked, he said, another fifty settlements were going up on both sides of the road between Jerusalem and Tel Aviv, the convoy route on which I'd seen the rusted, twisted wreckage. It was more than possible that Dov had driven it himself. "They'll never isolate Jerusalem again." He swore it softly, and his eyes had shut me out. He wasn't saying it to me.

His body stiffened as he spoke about defense. "Our army—unbelievable! In a single unit, soldiers born in thirty different countries. Being here and being Jewish is all they have in common. Until we teach them Hebrew, hardly any two can talk together. As for military discipline—salutes and such—we mostly do without it. When you have Yemenites, for instance, who don't know how to *sit,* who never saw a *chair* before. . . ." Dov shook his head in disbelief, then deadly serious again, resumed.

"Some *Ashkenazim* from the German camps still tremble when they see a gun. Israeli officers don't click their heels; the sound would cause a mass psychosis. We have psychologists for sergeants. It's one sweet way to run an army!"

The grin returned. "It's one sweet way to run a *country!* Craziness! Except it works. A few years back, you know what they exported? Oranges and trinkets made from olive wood. Now it's leather goods and pharmaceuticals, false teeth and textiles, fresh-cut flowers and precision instruments. Our diamond industry will one day be the biggest in the world. We send out all the beautiful and useful things we can't afford to own ourselves, just so we can keep importing immigrants we can't afford to feed. Did I say crazy? *Meshugah!*

"So God didn't give us oil. Instead, he gave us plants that grow where no sane plant would drop a seed. *Sabra* plants. With no petroleum, we're making plastics out of castor plants."

I was baffled by the reference to *sabra.* Naturally I knew the word for native-born Israelis; derived from Arabic, it meant a cactus fruit, but the analogy escaped me.

As Dov explained it, the human *sabra,* like the fruit, is prickly and forbidding on the outside, but sweet and soft within. "The cactus and that castor plant are stubborn forms of life. Defiant forms, but able to adapt, and nicer than they seem at first."

Dov's eyes had strayed, and I saw that he was looking at his watch. Only friendship had prevented him from saying at the outset that I had no claim on any of his time. Officially our interaction ended with my safe arrival. Mosad served endangered Jews as lifelines, leading them from sinking ships. Once in Israel, however, we couldn't continue clinging. All Mosad aid was needed by the thousands still adrift.

I rose to say farewell and placed the pounds I owed him on his desk. My finding him today had been a stroke of luck; it was unlikely that we'd meet again, at least until the "gathering in" was over. A quick *"shalom,"* a hard and final hug, and another cycle ended.

Dov had drawn a starkly honest image. Now I knew the best and worst, and knowing, I could cope. Life wasn't easy here, but everything was in the open, even animosities, and that alone would balance out a thousand hardships.

I didn't envy Dov. Unlike him, I was done with false identities and constant pretense. No more secret codes for me. No more scheming just to stay alive. And maybe best of all, no more swallowing of insults. However pungent my retort, here I only risked a blackened eye.

One thing about Israelis—they encouraged self-expression. "Speak out!" could be the slogan of the state. The answers to my questions often shook me up; in the long run, though, their sharpness served me better than more soothing ambiguities. Illusions wasted time and effort. Dov had swept the last of mine away, and in spite of what he'd said, I'd never felt as confident about the future or as perfect an affinity with Israel. Both it and I were minus almost everything but opportunity and dedication. Who could doubt that we belonged together? And where was there to go but up?

I lingered in the street, seeking to delay the moment when I'd have to tell my uncle he'd been right about *shikunim.* To my great relief, he didn't rub it in, and after dinner he even started up a pleasant conversation, in the course of which I told him of my work in Persia. At mention of a salary, he sat up straight.

"You were paid?"

Behind his widened eyes, I could almost see my status shift; Uncle Eliahu was advancing me from poor relation liability to up-and-coming family asset. Enjoying his surprise, I confided that I'd even saved a little. When he heard the sum, he spilled his coffee. While only half of what it was before devaluation, it was still a healthy figure.

"You should have let me know at once," he sputtered. "There are several places that I could have sent you."

It was my turn now to stare. When last I heard, my uncle was a working plumber. Since when did plumbers have such pull? And even if he swung some weight, why wait till now to offer aid?

Of course. My nest egg was the inspiration for his sudden helpful spirit. As he now revealed, my uncle and his son had long since switched from plumbing to construction, and their business was the building of apartment blocks. They could buy and sell my father! If I hadn't said that I was solvent, uncle would have kept his little secret. Heaven knows, no one would suspect his wealth from seeing how he lived.

"How could your father leave with *nothing?*" he exploded.

So that explained the curious estrangement. I'd thought that uncle might be envious of Baba and his great success in Baghdad, but the answer lay in Baba's present poverty. Eliahu hadn't gone to Lyd because he feared he'd have to help!

The salt fish of the morning meal had come alive inside me and was threatening to swim upstream. Repressing anger always hit my innards. For now, however—for the family—I had to swallow down disgust and rage. Uncle Eliahu had some information that I needed.

I prodded him, and with a profit in the offing, he went on at length about the building business. My ears picked up on hearing that apartments were available for rent, and seemed extremely reasonable. "But then, of course, you've to pay the *dme-mafteyach,*" he added. *Dme-mafteyach:* key money, and in astronomical amounts.

Uncle steered me off this sort of deal. "You don't have any equity for all that money," he advised. "Better if you buy a flat and own it outright."

I hadn't known apartments could be purchased, and his telling me had solved my problem. I'd simply have to find and buy a flat for us—but it wouldn't be from uncle.

39

I was up and out the following morning long before the others stirred, determined not to be indebted to my uncle for as much as one more breakfast. Buying every paper published that might carry ads, I settled in a coffee shop to search for an apartment. The entire stack of newsprint didn't weigh as much as one good mango; each was only four sheets thick and ads were scarce, and scary. For most apartments, the money asked was scandalous, and many flats were unavailable until some future time.

With so much else to settle, I had to get us anchored down, and on the double. My target date was Rosh Hashonah, just a week or so away. The 11th of September, 1950—5711 by the Hebrew calendar. The date would make my mother very happy, since all the numbers, especially the 5 and 7, were the best of omens. Five symbolized the name of God, and seven was the seventh day, *Shabbat.* Yes, Nana in particular would find the time propitious.

According to my mother, odd numbers had the power to repel the Evil Eye, while even numbers screamed for its attention. When I'd come from school, tearing in to tell her that my test score was 100, Nana had been horrified by my announcement. "Say 95 plus 5," she'd plead. Not only would the Evil Eye be driven off, but the double five would add some extra glory to the grade.

I wasn't superstitious, still I reached for my *k'tibeh*—and I saw the ad the moment that I clasped it!

On the final page of the last remaining paper, two lines of type leaped out at me, and I knew I'd found our flat.

"2½. Immediate occupancy. 2900 pounds. Good terms available."

Two and a half bedrooms was the biggest flat I'd seen described, and while the price for it was frightening, in relation to the others, this apartment was a steal. I couldn't come close to meeting the required figure, and undoubtedly some major flaws would show up on inspection, but still I felt euphoric.

Fifteen minutes later, I was striding up a wide and pleasant avenue in Giva'atayim, a quiet residential section of the city. The building, hedged around with half-grown greenery, was spanking new and built to stand for several generations. The construction would appeal to Baba. Climbing up the common staircase, I walked into an airy third-floor flat. By the nameplates on the other doors, I knew we'd be the only "Orientals," but that could also be a plus. With *Ashkenazim* for their neighbors, my parents would be pressed to pick up Hebrew.

Inside, of course, there wasn't any *takhta* in the kitchen, but on the other hand, there was a sink of gleaming porcelain and taps that read both "hot" and "cold." On Kambar Ali Street, modern plumbing meant a single faucet screwed onto a length of pipe plugged in the wall.

The boiler in the bathroom bore a sticker, requesting residents to turn it off at 6 A.M. and not to switch it on again till midnight. For the other eighteen hours, industry had prior claim to power.

Before partition, this part of Palestine had drawn its power from Transjordan. Since statehood, Israel had generated all its own electric current, and fuel for doing so was just as short as food and shelter. Every bath and shower was a planned event.

Even when the water wasn't hot, the bathroom would enchant the children; in fact, I played in it a bit myself. The bright white toilet flushed out clean; one merely had to push a lever. Until now, the finest plumbing I'd encountered had required that one pull a chain. This was much more elegant!

The tiled floors throughout would be easy for my mother to maintain, and the rugs I'd bought in Teheran would fit them to a tee. So far almost faultless, yet something marred my pleasure in the place. Despite the spaciousness of all the rooms, I felt confined. It was the absence of a *hosh* and private roof that hemmed me in. The roof in Baghdad had served us almost as a summer home; here we'd have to do with just a narrow terrace. Having said that, I knew I'd sold myself on this apartment.

I closed the deal within an hour, putting down less cash than first requested, and arranging for a bigger loan and better mortgage than I could have hoped for. I'd introduced myself, quite properly, as Doctor Heskel M. Haddad, and that, no doubt, affected my financial credibility. Even here the title "Doctor" seemed to work its special magic. Handing me the keys, the builder asked when I'd be moving in. I hadn't thought that far ahead, but I heard myself responding in the firm, sure tone affected by physicians, "We'll be in tonight."

It was an off-the-cuff decision, but excited at the prospect, I left at once for uncle's to retrieve my suitcase. Why *not* tonight? To my regret, uncle wasn't home to hear my news, so I thanked my aunt politely, and was heading out the door when he walked in. Looking at my bags, he asked the very question that I ached to answer. "Where are you off to?"

"To our new apartment," I replied.

His jaw was still unhinged when I gently shut the door between us.

With so little left to us, packing took no time at all, and, ecstatic at the news I brought, not even Baba stopped to ask for hows and whys. For now, it was enough that they were leaving Lyd. Later, settled in his own establishment, Baba could be told about his brother—if, that is, he didn't already know.

Our swift departure was only slowed in signing out of camp. The administrator tried to talk us into staying on, warning Baba that he'd lose his benefits by leaving. If he continued here, he'd be helped to find a job and for one full year he wouldn't have to pay a tax on earnings. And, the manager reminded us, everyone in camp was covered by insurance.

"Should you get sick . . . ," he focused on my father, and remembering how Baba had to stand in line for laxatives, I snapped, "If he gets sick, there's a doctor in the family."

The word appeared to work again. Abandoning the fear approach, he tried another tack. If we moved to a *shikun* from Lyd, necessary furniture would be supplied. Otherwise, you're not entitled to a stick," he said.

I meant to stay aloof, but that business of the furniture was more than I could bear. Our enterprise in finding our own flat would save the state substantial sums of money, but the officer in charge, instead of thanking us, was working hard to keep us wards.

There wouldn't be time to buy us any beds tonight, and picturing my mother on the cold, bare tiles of Katznelson Street, I vividly expressed myself. Steam was almost streaming out my ears. Having seen me storm so often, my family paid scant attention, but the officer was shaken. I'd barely hit my stride when he surrendered, meting out two iron cots and mattresses. I held out for some extra blankets; we could improvise the other beds with them. By now, he couldn't wait to see us go, and when our cab pulled up, he even helped us with our baggage. No goodbyes were ever more sincerely said.

After living in a tent so long, the family found the flat palatial, and pointing out amenities, I basked in everybody's approbation. It was Nana, ever practical, who brought us back to earth.

"How am I to cook our dinner?" she inquired.

I'd been showing off the kitchen, but the kitchen, as was customary, came unequipped with anything but sink and shelves; buyers brought in all their own appliances. Forgetting that we had no stove, I'd left the makeshift tin contraption back at Lyd. Not that it mattered much, since I'd also failed to stock the shelves with food.

Embarrassed at my oversights, and assuring Nana that she'd have a stove tomorrow, I was rushing out to buy our dinner when I bumped into a woman at our door. Come to welcome us, Israeli-style, she held a steaming pot, and something in it smelled delicious. Others in the building followed, and soon the cots were covered with the edibles each carried in. With no place left to sit, our neighbors sent the kids for chairs and offered us the loan of any furniture we needed. I interpreted for Baba, who expressed his thanks, but asked if he might borrow tools instead.

At dusk, I flipped a switch and nothing happened. We had no lights because I'd clean forgotten that we had to be connected. As I blushed my richest red, everyone rushed off for candles.

The evening ended in a friendly glow. As a microcosm of Israeli life, it couldn't have been improved on. Emergencies, improvisation, speech we didn't understand, warmth and smiles we did. A great good will, and yet a certain wariness. I'd caught the sidelong glances at our sparse belongings and our slightly darker skins. So, I saw, had Baba. Overriding all, however, were the outstretched hands, the effort to express accord as Jews. For tonight, at least, our differences didn't matter.

I began the day by buying us a hot plate and some beds and putting down a whopping big deposit with the power company. It frightened me to see how fast the money melted. At the Customs House, I found that my refrigerator had arrived, and I arranged to have it trucked to the apartment. The rugs, for unknown reasons, had been routed via Haifa, and my presence was required to release them. However, other things were more essential at the moment, such as signing up for ration cards and seeing to the children's schools. Once the family was settled, I could get to other matters. That job with Bruner, for example. It wouldn't wait forever.

By my return, Baba had already built a table and some stools and a *takhta* for my mother. With Nana chopping in the kitchen, the flat began to feel like home, and Baba seemed himself again. The time in camp had sapped his self-esteem, even altering his physical appearance, but a single day of doing something useful had restored his old authority. I couldn't know the next day would destroy it.

The following morning, without informing anyone of his intentions, Baba left to find the local hiring office, confident that Histadrut would offer him immediate employment. From all we'd seen and heard, men with his construction skills were sorely needed. Baba meant to bowl us over with the news that he was back in business.

Walking in, he looked instead as if they'd bowled *him* over—with a ten ton truck. Sounding stunned, he said they'd offered him a shovel—the lowest form of labor—"like they were doing me a favor."

Yes, he said, he'd told them that he'd owned his own contracting firm in Baghdad. He'd even told them that he'd put the plumbing in the royal palace. He hadn't asked to start off at the top, but considering his long experience and skill, he expected that they'd snap him up for something supervisory. Their reason for rejection was that foremen needed fluency in Yiddish.

Why Yiddish? The question came in chorus from us all, and Baba said he'd asked the same. Why Yiddish, when Hebrew was officially our language? Unhappily for Baba and the others like him, the placement people had a valid answer.

Almost all the carpentry and plumbing crews were *Ashkenazim,* and from many different countries. A common language was required, and only Yiddish fit the bill. Wherever on the continent they came from, these immigrants could speak and understand at least a little *mamaloshen.* Naturally, the foreman had to know it too. For Eastern and Sephardic Jews, however, the mother tongue was Arabic, not Yiddish.

What seemed like bias was probably just common sense, I said. Communication was essential; it was only Baba's Arabic that held him back.

While not entirely convinced, he grudgingly admitted that it might be true. To distract him from his "failure," I insisted that he come with me to Haifa to help me with the Persian carpets.

By his silence on the bus and the twitching of his lips, I could tell he was debating with himself. His pride was battling with his need to be the family provider. Should he hold out for more suitable employment, or settle for a shovel and a salary to start at once? He hadn't reached a resolution when the bus arrived at Haifa.

The area around the port was packed with people, many of them *M'silmin.* Heading for the Customs shed, I walked among more Arabs than I had since Baghdad. Near the water and away from the refineries and factories in which they worked, the *M'silmin* disappeared, and the screaming of the harbor gulls was almost smothered by a babble of excited Western voices. With a raucous screech, a P.A. system came alive above our heads, blaring out announcements in a dozen different languages, each one greeted by another burst of jubilation. Caught up in the laughing, crying crowd, we were swept along until restraining ropes contained us at the dockside. Everyone was gazing seaward, waving frantically to specks aboard a vessel steaming in.

Barely audible at first, a melody was floating from the ship. As it neared the shore, the sound grew stronger, silencing the swarm around us. On recognition of the song, they exploded in a shriek of exultation.

Lined along the rails of the ship, the refugees were chanting the "Hatikvah"; one by one, those waiting joined the anthem. The song of hope swelled Heavenward and out across the water. I was unaware that I was also singing until Baba broke the spell, speaking with a bitterness that struck me dumb.

"Even how they *come* is different." "They," of course, were *Ashkenazim,* but the import of the other words escaped me.

"Of course," I said. "They come by sea."

Baba's face was set in stone; his reference was not to route. "Look there," he ordered, pointing to a row of buses and a banner reading WELCOME!

"They get padded seats. We stood in trucks like cattle."

I suggested that the camp for these arrivals was probably so close at hand that using city buses would be less expensive. Even to me, the explanation sounded lame and Baba didn't buy it.

"And the WELCOME sign?" he snorted. "And maybe you'll explain the music too. There wasn't any music when Iraqis came."

What could I say? The Kurds and I had also been unwelcomed.

Elbowing our way in silence, we left the celebrants behind to greet their relatives and friends. In the Customs shed, I gave a clerk my copy of the documents. He sent me to a second counter, where another civil servant slapped them back at me and pointed to an inner office. For careless inefficiency, we could have been in Baghdad.

The officer in charge was pasty-faced and grossly fat. When he swiveled at the sound of our approach, the floorboards creaked in protest. Grunting an acknowledgement of our existence, but with no *"shalom,"* he snatched at my receipts and slowly, very slowly, scanned them. From his meticulous, suspicious manner, he might have been in search of secret messages in microdots. Once or twice he raised his eyes and peered distrustfully at us.

He could have processed fifty papers in the time that he was taking, but he plainly liked to exercize his power, discomfit people, make them sweat. He'd like to see us bow and scrape before he did his duty, so with great deliberation I slid back in my seat and closed my eyes as if to nap. My nonchalance annoyed him into rasping out, "Which one of you is Moshe?"

Baba answered and the officer shot forward to accuse him.

"You didn't declare these carpets!"

When I snapped right back that Baba hadn't bought the carpets, that I'd purchased them and put them in his name, the doughy face flushed purple. His rage was out of all proportion to the circumstances; something else was eating at the man. Almost apoplectically, he shouted out the answer:

"How do *you* come by such carpets? *I* don't have a Persian carpet."

All that fury rising out of simple envy, or so I thought. I tried to mollify him by explaining how I'd worked to earn the rugs and what they meant to us. Unless he simmered down and stamped the papers, they'd remain right here in storage.

"They're all we own," I told him. "Everything we had was lost."

"We didn't have such things to lose," he countered.

In as calm a voice as I could muster, I requested that he validate the documents or give them back.

"Don't tell me what to do!" he shrilled. "We treat you Africans like human beings and you act like wild animals."

Africans! So that was it.

Beside himself with rage, he snatched a pen and scrawled a word across the bill of lading: CONFISCATED.

The exchange had been conducted in colloquial Hebrew, but Baba got the sense of what was said. The sounds of bigotry are much the same in every language. His fists, I saw, were balled, but still he gestured to restrain me and rose to make a dignified departure. There was nothing to be gained here but additional abuse.

Picking up the papers, I trailed out behind him, determined that I'd have the carpets if I had to get Ben-Gurion himself to take a hand. Through questioning a clerk, I found I had a closer recourse. Customs headquarters was halfway up Mount Carmel, just a healthy walk from here. And, yes, a dockside ruling could be countermanded.

Angry and impatient as I was, I paused at intervals along the way to look below me. With every step of our ascent, the panorama grew in breadth and beauty. Solomon had sung about this view, but even his descriptive powers scarcely did it justice.

The refineries and storage tanks were hidden by the swelling slope, and the arc of Haifa harbor was the purest curve, the clearest and most brilliant sweep of blue. The city rose above it, strewn across the hillside like a gentle spill of sugar cubes. The air was sweet with foliage and flowers, and straining eastward, I could almost see the fertile Plain of Yizra'el.

Though I tried to shut them out, some ugly memories impinged upon the peaceful scene. Down there, the *Patria* had sunk, taking with it several hundred refugees from Nazi terror. Down there, illegal immigrants in leaky tubs had braved the British gunboats. The internment camps were also there for those they caught.

While Baba paused along with me, his mind was somewhere else. Undoubtedly, the Customs episode had further undermined his low morale, and he was sinking back to where he'd been at Lyd. One more defeat, however minor, might be more than he could handle at the moment. We had to win the carpet war.

Without a firm appointment, they refused to let me see the head of Customs, so we waited in the outer office. When the door to the Director's sanctum opened and the pace of work increased among the clerks, I knew it was the boss emerging. Approaching him, I held out my receipts and he reached for them reflexively.

In his hyperbolic wrath, the dockside officer had pushed his pen nib through the paper, ripping it in several places. The tattered document supported what I said to the Director, and apparently amused by my initiative, he promised an immediate investigation. Of course, we still didn't have the carpets, but his courteous attention acted on me like a tonic. I felt invigorated, up to any further challenge, and even Baba's face had brightened.

We weren't through with the bureaucracy in Haifa. Sha'ar Aliyah was next on the agenda. Whether fleeing from the slaughterhouse of Europe or the Arab states, almost all of us had lost some family or friends along the way. The Central Registry was where one went to find them, and we'd come today to locate missing relatives.

Baba lagged a step behind, once again allowing me to lead. It was disquieting—no, *more* than that—unnatural. When Baba was around, I wasn't used to being boss, and I discovered that I didn't like it. Way down deep, I think, every son's the same about his father. From infancy he looms so large, and we struggle toward adulthood, trying hard to equal his achievements; in our hearts, however, we really hope he'll always be a little bit beyond us, a bigger, stronger, wiser man than anyone on earth.

While Baba stood aside, I stepped up to the counter. Supersensitized by what had happened at the dock, and determined not to suffer any insolence, I gave my name, stared glacially across the counter at the clerk, and almost dared him to show any sign of disrespect. Incredibly, the bland official face cracked open ear to ear.

"Dr. Haddad!" He could hardly speak for smiling. "It's Dr. Haddad!" he said again, making an announcement to the room at large. I knew I didn't know the man, but he knew me—and so did half the office staff. Sha'ar Aliyah, they told me, had handled my reports from Persia. For seven months these people had been reading what I wrote from both the camps, and they'd also heard my name from former patients who had plainly sung my praises.

Baba was adoring all the fuss. Couched in Hebrew, the compliments escaped him, but he understood the patting on the back and pleased expressions. I would have bet on what was running through his mind: "At least the *Ashkenazim* know my *son* is special."

The tide had turned, and now it seemed that nothing could go wrong. One, two, three, the Registry disgorged the information we were after. Most of Nana's closest kin were here and well, living all together in a section called Sh'chunat Hatikvah—Quarter of Hope. I liked the sound of it and decided, on the spot, to seek them out.

Baba had begun to sag, so telling him that I was tired, I suggested that we stop for coffee. We were in the small cafe, seated and already served, before I saw that it was strictly Arab. Ordinarily, it wouldn't have mattered, but I suddenly remembered what had happened here in Haifa, and the sweet black brew turned acid in my mouth. Only four short years ago, at the refinery we'd seen that morning, the Jewish workers had been massacred by *M'silmin,* and here they were, perhaps the murderers themselves, more prosperous than ever in their lives and smugly at their ease, so much more so than my father. They were safe from us, as Jews were never safe from Arabs in the Arab lands.

Israel was ours. Jews should feel secure, and Arabs just the least bit apprehensive. I wasn't out for blood, but let them be a little anxious. Their complacency enraged me . . . their casual and overnight acceptance of those freedoms that we'd never won in centuries among them.

In my dreams of Israel, before arrival, Arabs hadn't played a part. Now they were a weighty and a painful presence. Perhaps we should have sent them packing. When the *M'silmin* threw us out of all the so-called Arab countries—some of which we'd occupied since long before Islam evolved—perhaps we should have shipped these back to take our place.

The *Ashkenazim* spoke of peaceful coexistence with "our Arab brothers," trying to convince themselves that Eden was at hand. "Just give it time," they urged, even as the terrorists continued killing. For a thousand years, my family had felt the same. Some million Jews knew better now. Coexistence hadn't worked. *Both* sides had to want it, and the Arabs wouldn't settle for a less than ruling role. Where they let Jews live at all, it was only on a *dhimmi* level. Where were *Arab* spokesmen for this phantom "coexistence"?

I hadn't known I harbored such a deep disquiet. I'd thought, in fact, that I was *through* with Arabs, that I'd never have to think of them at all, and here I was, as roiled up as ever in my life, and growing more so with my every glance around.

The cafe's clientele was mostly of the merchant class, well dressed, well fed, speaking freely with their friends, expansively enjoying their existence. In clashing contrast, Baba sat in silent gloom, brooding over fellow Jews who'd made him feel a failure. The final blow would be for him to focus on these brisk and thriving *M'silmin.*

Before the coffee roused him from his tired trance to look around and come to my conclusions, I hustled him outside. Walking toward the station, I told him I was taking off for Sh'chunat Hatikvah.

"Don't you think you ought to head for home?" I asked, expecting him to argue, but Baba only nodded, even closer to the end of his reserves than I'd supposed.

Toward the southern end of Tel Aviv, the streets grew ever narrower and more congested, and by the time I left the bus, I was thoroughly dismayed by what I saw. No Jewish Quarter in Iraq was half as squalid as this slum. Garbage overflowed the sidewalks, and from the moment I alighted, I was beating off the buzzing swarms of flies, the only ones I'd seen since Lyd. As I picked my way along, pools of stagnant water washed my shoes with greenish slime.

The buildings, uniformly squat and square, were mostly made of poured concrete, now cracked and pitted; among the shabby cubes, some few of brick looked almost ostentatious. Minus glass, many of the window frames were filled with cardboard. Every sort of food stall spilled its own detritus, but the odor of putrescent fish outdid all others.

In tiny open shops—little more than stalls—bent and bearded Yemenites crouched low above their workboards, loupes as firmly screwed into their eyes as if the sockets had been threaded, the lacy filigrees they fashioned unbelievably incongruous in such a setting. In a few short strides, I passed a tinsmith and a sandal-maker, a carpenter and several cross-legged tailors. Except for higher density and greater dirtiness, the sights and sounds were much the same as Baghdad's, even to the coffeehouse I spotted down the street.

Except for size, the establishment I entered could have come intact from home. The tiny room contained a mere four tables rather than the fifty in my uncle's place in Kahwat el-Zyaghghi. All else, however, was identical. The cane-seat chairs, the round brass serving trays, the gleaming copper pots, the thin black streams of coffee, each jetting out to just exactly fill a cone-shaped cup. The slender spout required artful aiming, and the waiter here was up to even uncle's rigid standards. That wasn't so surprising since the waiter *was* my mother's brother.

I yelled out "Uncle!" Kh'dhouri spun around, and the coffee, for the first time ever, missed the cup. Exceedingly emotional, he laughed and cried with such abandon that he almost strangled. Breath restored, he asked a thousand questions, and each response was greeted by another bout of joyous weeping. By now, every patron in the place had turned to face us, and a face among them looked familiar.

But it *couldn't* be Baruch. I'd left him back in Teheran, tending to the camp.

It *was* Baruch. Whereas I'd been stuck for seven months, someone had been sent to spell him after only seven days. He'd almost beaten me to Israel. In the midst of our reunion, I realized that I also knew the fellow sitting with him: Selman—with a new mustache. He'd been a class ahead of me in college. The three of us were wallowing in reminiscence when it hit me. *They* could be the witnesses the Dean demanded. Before we parted, both had scrawled the letters that would get me into school. Only then did

I remember Rogers. Professor Rogers in New Zealand. In all the flurry of arrival, he'd somehow slipped my mind; I'd never thought to write to him, and now it wasn't necessary.

At home, Baba matched the news I brought with tidings of his own. Stoically, but looking more relaxed and like himself again, he told me he was taking on the pick-and-shovel job. A man, he said, must earn a living, and he wouldn't allow himself to be demoralized by doing menial work. He knew his capabilities, and someday "they" would too.

I'd never been as proud of him as at that moment, and I was strengthened in my own decision. *Whatever* Bruner offered when I saw him, I'd accept. If Baba could begin again, then so could I. A job and school. Both were equally important. Though I had the letters for the Dean in hand, in order to make *sure* I'd be admitted, I decided that I'd also write to Rogers.

Think "interim," I told myself. Think "temporary." Better days are on the way. I wished that I could bide my time as well as Baba. Sitting in the chair he'd made himself, restored to confidence and reconciled to his present humble state, he looked serene. I envied him his new composure. He was truly reconciled. I was just resigned.

40

In Israel nothing had a mere two sides. Everything was faceted with unsuspected, tricky angles. No question had a clear-cut answer, and any argument was subject to a range of strong rebuttals. Issues, which elsewhere would be starkly black and white, were present here in subtle shades of gray, each having just as staunch support as every other.

I'd always dealt in absolutes, but total certainty was something else I'd lost along the way. Since my arrival, I realized now, hardly anyone had ever said, "You're wrong," when I reproached him on the handling of a problem. The response was always on the order of "You're absolutely right—except . . . ," or "True, but for the fact that. . . ." Life was so much simpler when the rights and wrongs were rigidly defined.

I floundered more than usual on the forty-minute ride to Givat-Aliyah, fluctuating up and down between a buoyant optimism and the blackest, deepest blues; every bump provoked a change of mood. On the upside, a euphoric state . . . I'd be working in my field. On the down . . . it would only be a sort of scut work, only marking time until I took the tests for med school, which wasn't really school at all, but sort of like a melting pot, designed to make us doctors more homogenous.

Every student would already have a medical degree, earned elsewhere in the world—everywhere from Baghdad to Berlin. And therein lay the problem. Each of us had a training different from the others, and common sense required that the country have a single standard. The year we had to do would smooth out our discrepancies.

Though still unhappy at the prospect, I accepted the necessity of spending still more time in study. After that, however, I'd have to do a year's internship before I could present my thesis and finally become accredited in Israel. It was now September 1950, and my life was all tied up until the early summer 1953.

Back and forth. Up and down. I'd seesawed since we left the station. Disgusted . . . grateful. Hostile . . . hopeful. I was anxious to begin and angry that I had to make a new beginning. I *was* a doctor, but I couldn't *be* a doctor. Even if the Dean and Minister had doubts about my lost credentials, they were well acquainted with the work I'd done in Teheran and with the fact that I'd been drafted into doing it. Now, in Israel, the same administration that had wooed me disavowed me.

To complicate the matter even more, I could also make a case for them. With no one else available in Persia, they'd *had* to take a chance on me. It was different here. Here they *drowned* in doctors. Israel, per capita, had more physicians than any state that ever was—with more arriving every day—and even those with all their documents in perfect order had to put that extra year in. Since I didn't have proof that I'd attended kindergarten, much less college, I could hardly hope for quick, unquestioning acceptance. The difficulty was—I *did.* Hardly anyone had ever doubted me or my ability before.

When the driver called my stop, I thought at first he'd dropped me at the wrong address. The hospital, a single-level sprawl of bright white stucco, looked exactly like an Arab house, expanded to enormous size. A stretch of soft green lawn and flowerbeds along the borders made it even more inviting. Though the sea was hidden on the far side of the building, its susurration reached me as I neared the office wing.

The Director was expecting me, and accustomed now to Western ways of greeting, I shook his outstretched hand. Baghdadis didn't shake hands, and taking back my damp, crushed digits I didn't really feel we'd been deprived.

While Dr. Bruner had a grip of steel, he couldn't have been more affable in speech and manner. That he was Viennese and elegant was obvious, and judging from the shrewdness of his questions, he was well informed about my background. Discussing my ambiguous position, his sympathy seemed heartfelt. The job, he said, was mine.

Perhaps it was the too-quick snap of tension, plus his almost fatherly approach, but when Bruner offered "any help that I can give," everything dammed up inside me suddenly discharged. In one long breath, I spilled out all my hopes and fears. Though he responded with a repetition of his offer, I knew I'd made a serious mistake. He'd shrunk from my emotional outpouring, and his second offering of aid was stiff and formal.

My feeling was confirmed when Bruner spoke again.

"Oh, by the way, you'll work in B."

He tossed this off as if it were of little consequence, but both of us knew better. The hospital incorporated two departments. Department A was

Bruner's own, and by assigning me to B, he'd shunted me aside. Or had he? Was it just my ego acting up again, or perhaps a little paranoia setting in? If Department A was fully staffed, he *couldn't* fit me in. In any case, I couldn't do a thing about it. I couldn't even brood. Turning brisk, Bruner ordered me to make myself familiar with my new surroundings.

The hospital consisted of two separate structures, with several private homes between them. You had to walk a public thoroughfare to get from A to B. In light of what I'd heard, their physical division seemed appropriate. Departments tend to mirror chiefs, and where Bruner was *le grand seigneur,* Fryd, who headed B, was oftenest described as "nice." Everybody's Baba. The boss, but not imperial about it.

Fryd was fiftyish, owl-eyed, and stout, and everyone adored him. He beamed when Bruner introduced us. When the Director left, I waited for his smile to fade, but Fryd, if possible, enlarged it. "You'll do fine with us," he said—and I believed him.

To acquaint me with the operation, he told me just to tag along. By noon, I felt that we'd been friends forever, but that, of course, was simply wish fulfillment. A department chief and pseudo intern like myself exist on different planes; they're just about as equal as a king and palace cook. We couldn't be friends. Fryd, however, didn't appear to know the rules. When I spoke, he listened as intently as he had to Bruner, and my battered ego started to expand again.

Everything about the man appealed to me. I even liked his shabbiness. Fryd was frayed around his every edge. His collar points were threadbare, his cuffs were overlong and badly scuffed, and his pants seat sagged exactly like the underbelly of a nursing sow. Next to Bruner, I'd felt countrified; alongside Fryd, I was a fashion plate.

However, walking through the lunchroom, I saw that everyone was staring at my feet. I'd never noticed that my shoes made so much noise. In Baghdad, everyone had metal plates attached for extra wear, and mine were clanking like hydraulic hammers. Since Iraqi hospitals were almost as uproarious as the streets outside, there the sound was lost amid the other hubbub. I made a note to pry the plates off. In the meantime, I tried to deaden the tattoo by sliding on my way instead of striding. Dr. Fryd didn't bat an eye or miss a beat, but slowed his pace to match his steps with mine. I could have hugged the man. Better yet, I'd break my back for him in B.

At the thought, my feet froze to the floor. I'd clean forgotten that I'd set a scheme in motion to release me from the need to be here. I might not see Department B or Fryd again.

Since we'd landed at the food line, and Fryd had also halted, my stop, midslide, went unremarked. I couldn't believe that I'd forgotten so completely, but the frenzy of the last few days undoubtedly accounted for the lapse. The enterprise was too far under way to stop. When and if it worked, I hoped that Fryd would understand.

Eating lunch, I followed every move he made. Soup was easy—I was used to spoons—but the meat required cutting, and knives and forks were still a novelty to me. In Baghdad, forks were owned by just a few sophisticates, and only used to push what they were eating onto spoons. Ordinary people used a piece of bread to serve the purpose. And we had no use for table knives at all since food was cut to fit the mouth before it ever hit the stove.

But after all, I told myself, I was a surgeon, and these were only instruments, and simple ones at that. Outwardly at ease, but breaking sweat, I picked them up and plowed right in. Dr. Fryd looked startled, and I thought I'd made some frightful error, but all he had to say was "How extraordinary! You eat like an American."

I filed this for Baba's benefit. He'd often chided me for wasting so much time in movies, but Hollywood had taught me Western table manners. Baghdad's major movie houses played only Arab pictures, but many smaller theatres in the Jewish section showed captioned films from both America and Britain. Six cinemas had Baba's plumbing, so I never had to pay.

Whenever I could spare the time, I sat until my bottom ached, cracking pumpkin seeds and staring wide-eyed at an odd, exotic world where flakes of white, like shreds of fleece, fell straight down from the sky, and every man was six feet tall and either wore a set of tails or else a set of spurs. I'd learned a lot from movies. Along with fork manipulation, I'd also learned that girls had legs.

Despite my grand success with fork and knife, it was good to see a spoonable dessert. When I asked him what it was, Fryd looked mildly surprised; that was nothing next to my astonishment on hearing him reply, "Rice pudding."

Rice! Incredible! For twenty years my favorite food, eaten every day in every way—or so I'd thought. It was the staff of life to all Iraqis—and even this, in Israel, was unfamiliar. Rice with sugar was unheard of, but delicious. This I filed for Nana.

On finishing, I fumbled for my handkerchief to wipe my lips. So discreetly that no one else took notice, Fryd nodded toward a rack of paper napkins. Napkins, too, were new to me.

In the course of lunch, a dozen doctors drifted over. From Fryd's reaction, some had come solely for a look at his companion. Me. The strange new specimen. While they were very civil and stuck their hands out to be shaken, they either glanced at me and quickly looked away or stared too long and too intently. Clearly, they considered me a sport, a sort of freak of nature. No one here had ever seen a doctor from Iraq. Was it possible that someone from an Arab country could be qualified? The question glinted out of every eye.

Busy as he was, Fryd walked me to the bus stop and waited till the 31 arrived. As I climbed aboard, I felt that twinge of guilt again. This sweet, good man had spent such warmth on me, and how would I repay him?

He knew, of course, that med school was my main objective and that this job with him was merely marking time. Should I find a swifter, smoother route to school, surely he'd forgive me if I took it. Still, he'd be expecting me the following Monday, and chances were, I wouldn't be back.

41

If not for Fryd, I wouldn't have felt the least deceitful. It wasn't my fault that I hadn't been informed of all my options before I sought the job with Bruner. I learned about the other possibility by chance only hours after he'd agreed to see me. If I enlisted in the army, I discovered, I could ask for an assignment to a medical facility. Service was compulsory for all Israelis, so in any case, I'd face induction someday. Therefore, I decided that I'd volunteer immediately. The time I'd serve before I passed the tests for med school would apply to my entire tour of duty.

These facts in hand, I'd gone to take the physical at once. Head to foot, the army doctor put me through the same procedures that I'd practiced on so many others. I knew, of course, he'd find no abnormalities.

At the end of his examination, I began to rise, but he motioned me to stay in place. When he tipped my head and probed my neck a second time, his touch set off a faint reverberation; it felt as if he'd triggered an alarm. Distant, indistinct, and unaccounted for—but all the same, slightly worrisome. Then he called in two more doctors, and the small alarm became a klaxon. Each checked my neck and nodded at the others. Apparently they all agreed, but what about? I knew better than to ask, but ask I did, as reflexively as any anxious layman. Not knowing I was one of them, naturally they'd answered, as I had myself on such occasions, "You mustn't worry" and "You'll hear from us."

At home, following my interview with Bruner, I found a letter from the I.D.F. which ordered my return for further testing.

This examination was conducted by another, older doctor, and was even more exhaustive. On finishing, he scrawled some notes I couldn't see and ordered me to pick up all my papers at the desk.

Handing me my service folder, the clerk on duty grinned and said, "Congratulations!" I thought it was a welcome to the army, but the open book explained his rather envious expression. EXEMPT—in big red letters—was stamped on every page, which to me spelled defeat.

The clerk repeated his congratulations as I walked away. Some, I knew, exulted at escaping service, but all I felt was deep despair, compounded of frustration fed by new-born fear. Not only did the verdict block the Army route; it also raised the spectre of still other detours. It might even stop me dead.

Yet this disease of mine had never slowed me down a second. Quite the contrary. In the underground that extra surge of energy, that supertaut alertness had often saved my hide. I could thank my hyped-up thyroid for my life.

Until I took the physical, I'd totally forgotten that I'd ever had a glandular enlargement. When I was twelve, there'd been weeks and weeks of X-rays. They said the therapy had been successful. "Dismiss it from your mind," they said, and so I had. Eight years later, by some peculiar yardstick, I was well enough to work at any hospital in Israel except an army hospital. Or was I? Would I have to undergo another physical for Bruner? Or would the army record reach his eyes, and if it did, what happened with that now-so-needed job?

I didn't draw a peaceful breath all week, but nothing negative occurred, and I reported Monday, as arranged. My exam results were safely buried in some army file, and for once, I blessed bureaucracy.

I'd been assigned a cubicle all to myself, and unpacking only took a minute. Aside from toothbrush, shirt, and shorts, and the stethoscope I'd had since Baghdad, all I'd brought were my phylacteries and *tallith.* Among the other interns, prayer shawls were far exceeded by pajamas, but all my life, I'd worn my underwear to bed and said my prayers on waking. In time, perhaps, pajamas would replace the shorts, but morning prayers were permanently part of me.

There were three like me in B, and for eight pounds every month, plus room and board, we'd work a six-day week, from 8:00 to 6:00, except on Friday, when they turned us loose in time to reach our homes before the sun set and *Shabbat* began. Every fifth day, each of us would take his turn on call for twenty-four unbroken hours; except for on-call days, we were free to leave the hospital and sleep at home. The routine was familiar. I'd done it all before in Baghdad.

To give me time to settle in, Fryd excused me from the early rounds. I hit the laundry first. The hospital required us to wear a long white cotton coat, and like every such facility I'd ever seen, the laundry offered just two sizes. One was big enough to satisfy an Arab smuggler, and the other bound me like a body cast. So far I felt at home.

However, little else resembled Baghdad, and my spirits soared, observing the disparities. Not only were the bedsheets snowy white, they were white all over. In Iraqi wards, the grayish sheets bore darker ghosts of bygone blood and pus and puke. In time, we got to recognize the individual designs.

The walls here were as spotless as the sheets, and the surfaces were smooth and whole. At the Royal Hospital, falling plaster was a hazard from above, and we also had to watch where we were stepping. These floors were clean enough to eat from. Best of all, there weren't any roaches, flies, or maggots. And the building didn't stink of ancient blood and old excreta, or even of the sort of disinfectant used to smother all the other smells. The differences delighted me.

The staff was equally dissimilar. Passing by Pathology, I overheard two German accents. One technician in the X-ray room could only be from Britain, with the others from Vienna and either Brooklyn or the Bronx. The latter I distinguished from the films. In the group I later joined for rounds, I found an even wider range.

Marmer, a resident on B, had come from Hungary, and Katz was unmistakably a Russian. I wasn't sure about the other intern, but she was certainly from central Europe. Maybe Czech. Or perhaps she was a Pole, like Dr. Fryd. She might also be a psychic: As I stared at her, Naomi startled me by saying, "I'm Roumanian." The second resident, named Rednick, was that *rara avis,* a native-born Israeli, but since he'd been to school in France, even *he* spoke Hebrew with an accent. Amid this crew, any doubts I entertained about my Hebrew disappeared. Compared with theirs, mine was pristine pure.

Bearing out my expectations, rounds were quite routine. As for Fryd, I'd never seen more sensitivity to patients' problems or such patience with a flock of fledgling doctors. Everyone expressed himself without constraint, even to the point, at times, of questioning their Chief's conclusions. In any *Mislim* country, such conduct would be cause for instant discharge.

On concluding rounds, Fryd led us to his office, for what Katz referred to as "the cookie klatch," where we reassessed the cases we'd just come from seeing. Dispensing juice and gingersnaps, Fryd actively solicited opinions from us all, according each of us his courteous, complete attention. One more plus for Israel. Aside from giving orders, Iraqi doctors rarely spoke to interns.

Even in that single session, I learned a lot about my colleagues. Marmer, about forty, I sized up as a very suave and worldly fellow, quick and clinical at work and supremely self-possessed. Every female patient preened at his approach, and he adored it.

Rednick, the other resident, seemed destined to be that and that alone. "The other resident" is what the patients called him. He was competent enough, but could never come to any firm conclusion. On his own, invariably he'd say, "Let's wait and see." The man had no charisma, no self-confidence, and certainly no special skill, but I warmed to him at once. He might not cure his patients as expeditiously as Marmer, but he cared about them more.

Among the interns, Katz attracted my attention by virtue of his being so flamboyant. Formerly a captain in the Russian army, he seemed so much a stereotype, I thought at first he might be acting out a role for our amusement. No one *really* swilled such quantities of liquor or carried on with such a wide—and weird—array of women. But according to the others, Katz outstripped the tallest of his tales.

Right after rounds, I heard him say to Marmer, "A real Ramat came in this morning." He leered and Marmer laughed. Standing by, Naomi also laughed, then, observing my bewilderment, explained.

"It's a system Katz invented. He claims that he can pigeonhole a woman with a single look."

Three categories were involved, she said, each associated with a town in Israel. Ramat-Gan, or "elevated garden," was a lushly lovely place, and thus a Ramat was a gorgeous girl. A *real* Ramat was extra sensuous.

The average female rated only "Zichron-yaakov," a typical if undistinguished settlement. Respectable, but nothing special. And in Katz's code, "Beersheba" was a warning of disaster. The woman so described was flat and drab and arid, as sterile of all pleasure as the desert town itself.

By Katz' reckoning, Naomi would be halfway up the road to Ramat-Gan. Because her hair was silver-blonde and silky, and her color fresh, she looked far younger than her thirty years, and she belied her age still further by a certain air of innocence. I loved the way she laughed—open-mouthed and unself-consciously, exactly like a kid—but what I liked the most about Naomi was that *she* liked *me.*

On the other hand, there was *Achot Raschit* Bilah. With her, I didn't even *hope* for friendship. All I asked was that it wouldn't be open war between us. Head Sister Bilah was a breed I'd met before. In Baghdad, and probably in Boston and in Timbuktu, an intern quickly learns how low a place he holds in many hearts. If, indeed, a head nurse *had* a heart, he'd rank in hers about the same as snakes or spiders. Or make that worms. Snakes at least inspire fear, but worms—like student interns—are solely to be stepped on.

At being introduced last week by Dr. Bruner, Head Nurse Bilah had impressed me as the iciest and most austere of martinets and one to shun whenever possible. Today, however, instead of taking detours to avoid her, I had to seek her out and ask for information on the new admissions. At her desk, I cleared my throat and said a low *"shalom."*

Her head jerked up, just like a snapping turtle's, but the "turtle" smiled widely and asked if I'd enjoy a glass of orange juice. Astonished, I took a backward step and blushed, and Bilah broke up laughing.

"Am I so intimidating? Last week, you caught me coming from a very dismal meeting. This expression," she said, assuming it, "is sometimes useful in such sessions. But I almost never eat an intern. Not even young and tender ones." And she shook so hard with laughter that she spilled her juice.

Not wishing to impose too much, I mentioned the admissions, but Bilah shrugged and told me to relax. "Just two today," she told me. "A jaundice and the other with abdominal discomfort." Urging me to drink my juice, she ordered me to come to her for any help I ever needed. I walked away as happy as I'd ever been in Israel.

The patients whose histories I had to take were at the far end of the female ward. To reach them, I had to run the dreaded gauntlet, head down and hurriedly, between two rows of bed-bound, bored, and very vocal women. At their insistence, the screens intended to ensure their privacy had all been folded back. Except for intimate examinations, the "girls" delighted in their access to each other and to anyone who wandered in.

Immediately on entering, I was assaulted by soprano voices. "Doctor, did you see my X rays?" "Doctor, they didn't take my pressure." "Doctor, will you tell them that I can't eat fish?" One complained she couldn't "go"; would I order her a laxative? Another one was "loose": "Please, doctor, something that will stop me up!"

I'd been in female wards before, of course, but never by myself, and I'd never been as nervous, not even in the underground. Nodding noncommittally to everyone and no one, I walked as quickly as I could, compatible with my position. No matter what, a doctor must act dignified in front of patients. The jaundice case, I saw, had gotten out of bed and the bathroom door was clicking shut behind her. I could only hope she didn't have a sluggish colon; a touch of constipation and she'd still be there when I was finished with the other woman.

I dispatched the first case quickly. When I pressed above the navel, to the left, the lady e-ee-e-ked in pain. Some further probing and I had my differential diagnoses. An ovarian involvement, trouble in the urinary tract, or diverticulitis. The last I thought the likeliest. Having marked her chart for all the indicated lab procedures, I folded back the screen and started for the jaundice case.

The sheet extended past the patient's shoulders, and both her arms were under it. She was staring up at me unblinkingly, but whether stunned with fear or simply curious, I couldn't say. I was slightly stunned myself on seeing her close up. Canary-yellow eyes are disconcerting, even if they aren't staring, and except for dark-brown irises, her eyes were altogether yellow. Cat's eyes. Incredible!

Her skin and hair were both the same topaz-y shade, so much alike, I hardly knew where each left off. I'd never seen a more spectacular display. Professionally, as well as in her coloration, this patient was the purest gold. A classic textbook case, and her icterus was altogether mine.

I anticipated learning quite a lot from Miss—no, Mrs. Ada Falke—but my spirits fell when she addressed me in a dissonant and wholly unfamiliar language. When I asked if she spoke Hebrew, she shrugged beneath the bedsheet.

"M'eat." A little.

English? Again the answer was "a little." She asked if I spoke French, and it was my turn now to say *"un peu."* German? No. There went the early bus I'd hoped to catch, but all at once I wasn't all that anxious to absent myself. Setting hue aside, Mrs. Falke was still exceptional.

Her fine-drawn face was angular, with hollows under high-arched cheekbones. The fluting of the groove above her upper lip was absolutely fascinating. Except in ancient sculptures, I'd never seen a philtrum as defined as hers. Her ears were works of art, carvings executed in the purest, polished quartz. For my aesthetic taste, the average female face was oversoft and unresolved, but every part of hers was perfectly determined.

Deciding I could manage by myself, I didn't call for an interpreter. In fits and starts, in the little of the languages we had in common, I began to fill the empty spaces on her case sheet. She'd been born in Hungary; her mother was alive and here in Israel; her husband was deceased.

I wrote in "Widow"—sufficient for the record, but stirring up some questions of my own. With an effort, I returned to the routine. *Profession?* Violinist. *Childhood diseases?* She'd had chicken pox and measles . . . no allergies, . . .

no chronic aches and pains . . . no surgical procedures . . . no moles or wens or birthmarks.

Pointing to herself, but staring up at me with citrine eyes, she said, "I'm perfect." I think I saw her wink. I know I saw her lips twitch. Was she making fun of me, I wondered. I told myself it wouldn't matter if she was. If she aroused some special interest, it was easily explainable. Although I'd figured her for twenty-three or four, she said that she was only twenty. My age exactly. And, like me, she was a refugee. All refugees shared certain basic sentiments, so of *course* I'd feel a slight affinity for her. Because she'd cracked my cool veneer, however, I proceeded to be extra crisp in my examination.

Finished with the questionnaire, I folded back the sheet to hear her heart, and promptly turned to solid stone. She wasn't wearing anything except that little smile. From clavicle to lacquered toes, the girl was bare. Completely bare and utterly enchanting.

In the convulsive jerk preceding my paralysis, I'd pulled the sheet entirely away. Too stunned to drop it, I gaped at one long gleaming sweep of golden flesh, the same fantastic tint from head to foot. And she hadn't lied. Her body *was* perfection. Not the smallest bruise or scar or faintest blemish marred the small but thrusting breasts, the flat and silken-looking stomach, the rounded thighs and sweetly curving calves. She extended like a cat, lazily and slowly tautening until she arched all over. I tried to look away. When my eyes refused to leave her, I focused on her feet; the articulation of her ankles made me catch my breath. Her very *bones* were beautiful!

My feet were anchored to the floor, and I felt my face on fire. I'd seen—and Ada *knew* I'd seen—her one deception. While her hair on public view was blonde, clearly she'd been born brunette.

At the sound of smothered giggles, I dropped the sheet, which draped itself across her lower legs. Since she didn't reach down to pull it up herself, I grabbed the sheet a second time and yanked it up so far that when it floated back, her head and face were under it—but little else. Her entire body rippled, trying to contain her laughter.

While her face was hidden, I seized the opportunity to hyperventilate; it helped a little. It wasn't that I'd never seen a woman. I'd examined every segment of the body before, but each one separate and apart from all the others. Ada was my first full nude. And yellow yet!

Her head emerged, and Ada flung the sheet away. I lunged for it, and at the same time snatched a towel from the bedside stand. By using both to cover her, I managed to complete my work, more or less conforming to the custom. Although I never looked above her neck again, I knew her eyes were on me every moment. When I turned aside to write my notes, my hand was trembling so, I doubted that my shaky scrawl would ever be deciphered.

Plowing toward the door, I was totally unconscious of the fourteen other females crying "Doctor!" The only sound that reached me was her stifled laugh, and a spot between my shoulder blades was burning—the spot at which her cat's eyes were converging. Or was it merely my imagination?

At the threshold of the ward, with my hand already on the door, I risked a backward look and saw her wink. This time there wasn't any doubt about it, and I hit the door so hard, I almost ripped it off its hinges. At least, thank God!, she'd covered up.

Later, on the bus for home, I finally caught on; Ada Falke was Katz' "real Ramat." I blushed at intervals until I went to bed—and then I dreamed. In color. And everything was yellow.

42

As soon as I checked in the following morning, Marmer chewed me out for missing something on the jaundice case.

"Your history was incomplete," he said, proceeding then to tell me of the two abortions Mrs. Falke had owned to on admission. They weren't in my workup, and the word he used was "sloppy." Stung by his assessment, I protested that I'd asked the proper questions, and she'd answered in the negative.

To justify myself, I insisted that he come with me to set the matter straight. At the bedside of this aggravating girl, and too indignant now to blush, I put it to her bluntly: "Have you ever in your life been pregnant?" To my great relief, she once again rebutted with a fast and firm denial. Her head, in fact, was shaking back and forth before I finished. Then she spoke herself—in the same eccentric language I remembered from my first approach. Marmer seemed to understand. Of course. Our house physician also came from Hungary. When he turned to me, he was trying to suppress a smile.

"When she shook her head at you," he snickered, "she wasn't saying 'no'—only that she didn't know what you were saying. 'Pregnant' isn't part of her vocabulary. In Hungarian, the word is *'terhes.'* Maybe if you'd tried *'enceinte'* . . . ."

Yes, *enceinte* she understood. A flush of red rose through the jaundice, and this time, when I left the ward, she didn't wink. Her embarrassment was brief, however. At staff rounds, right in front of Dr. Fryd, she flirted shamelessly with me.

I had to see her twice a day, and every time I tingled more and liked myself a little less for letting her upset me so. Formality was no defense. A clinical approach only spurred her on to ever more outrageousness, as if I'd offered her some sort of challenge. I couldn't tell for sure if I attracted or amused her, or if, bored by her confinement, she was simply playing games with me to pass the time.

Because she flustered me, I fumbled like a lummox anywhere around her. I could hardly count her pulse for the pounding in my ears. Far from shrinking from my stethoscope, she'd fill her lungs and rise to meet it. During intimate examinations, where other women looked away, her eyes would fix unswervingly on mine.

Her favorite trick involved my ocular examination. Though she'd start by sitting bolt upright as I instructed, so I could peer into her pupils from a dignified position, she'd slip down by degrees, obliging me to bend until I almost tumbled into bed with her, and then she'd laugh delightedly at having done it, uncaring that the other women in the ward would speculate about the sound. A wail, a sigh, a sob they'd understand. At a cry of pain, they'd hug themselves in sympathy, but a laugh behind a screen was suspect.

I couldn't decide if Ada's open show of her emotions was immodest and abandoned or the candor of an impish kid. However flip she acted, she was honest in her aims. She didn't pretend that touching me was accidental, or that a sheet had "slipped" to let me see a golden leg. She was irresponsible, no doubt, and indiscreet, but as unafraid to show her feelings as her flesh. Her directness both invited and appalled me.

Every time I saw her, I acted more besotted. But her jaundice was abating, so my misery—and ecstasy—were almost at an end. She's an addiction, I decided. An addiction I could kick.

I didn't have time or energy to waste on any woman, and I wouldn't have picked an Ada if I'd *wanted* an alliance. She violated every code of ethics I could think of. First, of course, doctors don't pick playmates from among their patients; at any rate, they're not supposed to. The standards set at the *yeshiva* were even more imperative. There, women were defined for me as wives "and others."

And "others" were discouraged, but since sex is necessary for survival, abstinence was not exalted as it is in some religions. Rabbi Ezra never preached repression. The carnal urge, like any other appetite, was given us by God, he said, and at a certain stage of life, it was natural to want a woman. To satisfy that need, he taught, a proper Jewish man must take a wife.

In normal times, in Baghdad, I would probably have been a bridegroom by the age of twenty, but here, with all the fresh beginnings to be made, marriage was a long way off. And even if I could afford it, Ada was, by any measurement, among "and others." A non-Iraqi, twice-aborted, somewhat wanton widow wasn't what I had in mind. Away from Ada, all I had to do to damp my ardor was think of introducing her to Nana as the woman that I wished to marry. My mother would have fainted dead away.

If I'd been alone in Israel, Ada might have overcome my scruples, but going home to sleep each night strengthened my resistance. In the bosom of the family, I saw her as an alien and intruder. Once outside her orbit, I was safe. At home, she dwindled to a shadow, like a movie star who didn't exist except when I was staring at the screen.

The family, on the other hand, was always on my mind. With the Hebrew that I'd taught them in Iraq, Tikva and Avram had integrated easily, and Daisy, who remained at home, had learned enough *Ivrit* at Lyd to translate for my mother. Actually, Nana knew as much of modern Hebrew, but she doubted her ability and didn't attempt to use it. When we moved into the flat, I'd lectured her severely. "You *must* speak Hebrew," I insisted, "or you won't have any friends at all."

Within a week, without a word, Nana was the darling of the building. Almost doll-like in the midst of all the taller, broader *Ashkenazim,* she appealed to their protective instincts, then surprised them with her strengths. Unsummoned, Nana would appear wherever needed. Baby-soother, kitchen aide, or sympathetic sounding-board, she made herself available to everyone. She also offered *me* to all and sundry. After dinner, the living room became an unofficial "clinic"—free, of course—and rarely did an evening pass without a neighbor's stopping in with some complaint, exactly as our neighbors had on Kambar Ali Street. Except for intervals with Ada, life was almost back to normal.

They'd given me the whole day off to travel to Jerusalem and take the tests for med school. Returning earlier than I'd expected, and confident I'd more than made the grade, I headed for my favorite spot behind the hospital. When tension had me tied in knots, the wide blue sweep of water and its soothing sound unwound me.

Today, however, tension waited at the seawall in the person of my cat-eyed patient. Now able to get out of bed, she was standing, with her back to me, precisely at the spot I always chose myself. Coincidence? I wondered if she'd spied on me. On second glance, I wondered if the girl *was* Ada. The figure looking seaward was surely too petite to be the woman I'd examined. Then she turned around as if she'd sensed me. Now milky-skinned and softer looking than when sharply etched against a sheet, she seemed altogether different—but Ada all the same. Her size astonished me. Till now, I'd only seen her lying down, and since every part of her was as perfectly proportioned as a classic Grecian goddess, I'd just assumed that she was statuesque. When I said, "You're looking well," she whipped back swiftly, "Are you speaking as a doctor or a man?"

Big or small, lying down or standing up, the woman was too much for me. "You'll soon be going home" was all that I could think to say, and I said it with a mingled sense of loss and great relief. But she rattled me anew with "When I leave, will you take me to the movies?"

"It isn't done. Doctors mustn't socialize with patients."

Even to myself, I sounded pompous, but Ada laughed delightedly and clapped her hands. "I've got you now," she gloated. "After I'm discharged, I'm not your patient anymore. Wiggle out of *that!*" she challenged. I fled, instead, leaving her still laughing.

By the time of Ada's checkout, I'd been reassigned to Surgical, but she tracked me down to say goodbye. Luckily she found me in the course of rounds—the safest place, I figured; since I was ringed about by other doctors, even Ada would be decorous. In accordance with the custom, she shook the hand of each physician, skirting me and leaving me for last. When she clasped my hand, she clung to it—in front of everyone. Amputation was the only way I could have freed myself.

Fryd tactfully withdrew a step, and nodded for the rest to follow suit. I half-expected her to ask again about the movie, but what she said instead was that she'd miss me; her mother wanted her to rest, and was taking her away from Tel Aviv. Could she call me at the hospital when she got back?

Got back? I'd thought her going was forever!

I guess I said she could, because she squeezed my nerveless hand and slowly let it slip from hers. Behind me, someone whistled long and low, but no one made a comment, not even Katz.

Weeks went by without a word. At the very moment I concluded that she'd never meant to call, her call came in. She'd just returned to town, she said. Without preliminaries, and certainly without premeditation, I asked her out that evening. We made a date to see a movie, and agreed to meet at 7:00, at Mughrabi Square, a favored rendezvous for couples in the theatre district.

I don't remember anything I did that day except observe how slowly every second passed. Late that afternoon, however, a new admission in Emergency engaged my full attention. Her breath was acetonic, and diagnosing diabetes, I called for Rednick to attend in accordance with established order. When she slipped into the coma I expected, he, in turn, called Fryd.

Fryd ordered an i.v. at once, but the patient was enormously obese, with every vein imbedded deep in fat; and her circulation had been slowed so much that the sunken, bloodless veins were impossible to palpate. When Fryd inquired if I'd ever done a cutdown, I assured him I could do it. If I'd never dug a vein out, I *had* removed some major organs. Time was much too short to specify my surgical experience.

Thrilled to have a scalpel in my hand again, I incised the elbow, lifted out a threadlike vein, slipped the needle in, and started up the flow. It was textbook-smooth, and Fryd, I saw, was pleased with my performance.

My only problem was the hour. My date with Ada was at 7:00. It was now 8:10, and even if I didn't stop to wash, and didn't have to wait too long to catch a bus . . . but it was hopeless. She'd be gone, and everything was over.

Nonetheless, I ran out like a madman. Hours late, I reached the city and Mughrabi Square. Since all the shows had started, the square was almost empty. I'd known she wouldn't be there, and still I felt abandoned. Behind me, a woman's footsteps sounded on the pavement, and I didn't have to turn. A sudden prickling, or perhaps a never-noticed scent, informed me it was Ada.

Inside the theatre, my eyes were fixed on Ingrid Bergman but my nerve ends were receiving only Ada. When *Stromboli* ended, I couldn't recall a scene of it to save my life. By then, however, I'd regained at least a measure of control, and in the coffeehouse across the square, as composed as I could ever be with Ada, I carried on what started as a normal conversation.

Beginning with the movie, we both agreed that Bergman was a marvel. "But as an actress, not a woman," I asserted and continued with a discourse on the evils of divorce; she was just then at the center of a scandal. Ada interjected in defense of Bergman, but I wouldn't allow it. "She's immoral," I announced. My lady bit her lips and lapsed into an unaccustomed silence. I, on the other hand, was all wound up and spouted off on several more of my aversions, including my antipathy toward seeing women smoke, my distaste for any sort of face paint and my horror of exaggerated fingernails. Ada wore mascara and a vivid lipstick, her fingers ended in the longest, brightest nails ever seen on human hands, and she'd smoked right through the film.

When I finally ran down, she resumed our conversation just as if I hadn't been an utter boor. Pretending not to see my flaming face, she changed the subject; for the first time, she spoke soberly. With her mother still in transient camp, she felt adrift; the cousin that she lived with wasn't too compatible, nor was her work. An apprentice diamond-cutter, she found the dust so irritating that she didn't intend to stay. As for music, she missed it dreadfully, but in Israel, violinists—just like doctors—were a dime a dozen. And then *she* flushed, fearing she'd offended me. "It's just a phrase I picked up in the hospital. I didn't mean. . . ."

She was adorable! Once again, I was a one-man tug-of-war. My heart said she was unalloyed delight, and more than anything, I wanted to be with her. Then my mind took hold; she was also the antithesis of everything I'd always wanted. Until now. Pulled equally in opposite directions by my own divided self, I was firmly stuck in indecision.

"Yes" and "no" meant "maybe," but "maybe" always tipped, in time, toward one side or the other. Perhaps the answer lay in seeing Ada, but in such a way that I could study her objectively. Study. That was it! Scholarship was my domain, emotion hers. In the atmosphere that I envisioned, *Ada* would be disadvantaged. I'd be more at ease than she, more capable of steering matters my way. And what an irreproachable excuse for our relationship! Not sensuality, but education. Conscience clear, integrity intact, I'd be acting in the best tradition of the Torah, which encourages the quest for knowledge. Ada knew a lot that I could learn. For example, I hardly knew a word of German, which she spoke so well. It would almost be a sin to skip this chance to study.

The argument came easily, as if rehearsed; it had really slipped my mind that I'd set up this scenario before. First Evlene, and Avram's French instruction, now Ada and another language. At worst, I'd wind up with a smattering of German. Though startled by the proposition, Ada readily agreed to teach me, and we set a date to start.

Ada showed up for our first appointment bare-faced, both the lipstick and mascara missing, and her nails had been filed short and left unpolished. She told me that she hadn't smoked since seeing me, and never would again, and all at once I understood why peacocks strut and roosters crow. Officially, I'd entered manhood at *bar mitzvah,* but now I felt completely male. No Iraqi woman could be more compliant.

Our women were subservient to men, but I'd been much too young in Baghdad to experience the thrill of such surrender to my every wish, except, of course, by Nana and my sisters—and it wasn't in the least the same! Still shy with girls, I found the women here were overly audacious. They didn't defer to men in *anything,* as far as I could see, and none appeared to know what all Iraqi girls were weaned on: "Weakness is a woman's strength." They wanted to be strong the way that men were, insisting they were "equal" as if "equal" meant "the same as."

Admittedly, I wasn't any expert, and listening to the Katzes and the Marmers made me all the more aware of what I'd missed. They'd gone to school with girls, held hands with them, and danced with bodies touching while their parents watched with pleasure. Half-naked (Katz had pictures), both sexes even sported on the beach together. This sort of open dating was unheard of in Iraq, and if a daring couple met, they did so in the deepest secrecy, knowing that they risked a scandal that could ruin their lives.

Certainly no mother in Iraq ever bragged about how popular her daughter was, how often she "went out." For my sisters, and for every other decent girl, "going out" meant shopping or the synagogue or seeing relatives, and always in the company of elders. I wondered fleetingly about my sisters and their new-found freedom. Was it gratifying or confusing?

Fleetingly, I say, because I couldn't keep my mind off Ada more than minutes at a time. Her bowing to my wishes had affected me profoundly, the more so since they'd been so casually expressed. I hadn't made demands; she'd capitulated at my slightest comment. My every word was like a law to her. It was delicious!

I approached our second lesson still ecstatic but prepared for disappointment. Nothing lasted at that level of elation, and no one could be quite as wonderful as I'd imagined Ada. Except it did . . . she was. And so I entered on a period of nearly perfect bliss.

For the next few weeks, we saw each other almost every evening. On occasion, a tinge of doubt would cloud my rapture, reminding me of Ada's status as an *Ashkenazi* widow. From Nana's standpoint, I knew she'd seem the worst of aberrations—but why did Nana enter in at all unless . . . ? I was amazed to find that I was entertaining even the *idea* of marriage. Much as I adored her, such a match with Ada was impossible for many reasons. Even if she'd been a virginal Iraqi and acceptable to Nana, I still couldn't marry now because of school. If nothing else, I simply couldn't afford a wife, but in spite of conscious efforts to eradicate the thought, it kept recurring.

43

Aware now of the depth of my involvement, I was riding on that old familiar seesaw of despair and exultation. Admitting that I loved her didn't alter the realities, but every time I took her call, the obstacles evaporated into nothingness again.

The Rama, our favorite rendezvous, was a cinema in Ramat-Gan, the suburb in which Ada's cousin and his wife had settled. Waiting for the show to start one evening, she idly mentioned that the two of them were out of town. I nodded an acknowledgement, but Ada looked at me expectantly, as if awaiting some additional response. I thought she wanted me to show concern, and since she needed affirmation of my feelings, I assured her that I'd worry at her being all alone.

While the film was on, I caught her looking at me sidewise several times. That entire evening, she was out of sorts, and when I walked her home, she seemed so spiritless, I stopped to feel her forehead. That made her giggle, and insisting that she wasn't sick—"in any way," she said, with more emphasis than seemed essential—she brightened up and chattered as before. But when I left her at her cousin's house and turned away, I saw her face go blank again. I said, *"Shalom"*; she answered, "So you're going. So *'Shalom' to you,"* and banged the door behind her.

Rescheduling at the hospital required me to call off several lessons. I expected her to pout about it but she didn't appear to care, and her change of attitude was all the more distressing because I couldn't trace the cause. When next we met, she'd sunk into a state of numb passivity so different from her normal *joie de vivre,* I felt acute alarm. When I asked her bluntly what was wrong, she wouldn't admit to anything. In an atmosphere more melancholy by the minute, we closed our books and headed for the bus.

As always, she slipped her arm through mine, but she walked a bit apart from me. Acting on the purest impulse, I whirled around and kissed her. Taken unaware, she pulled away, but only for an instant. Then Ada kissed me back, mouth and body bound to mine. Involuntarily, I moved against her, gasping, and her lips moved under mine again, this time, though, to speak. She was asking me how many girls I'd slept with.

Too abashed to answer "none," and none too sure that I could speak at all, I shook my head and felt the flutter of her starting smile as she slowly let me go.

"I thought so at the movie, but I wasn't sure," she said.

On fire, more confused than ever, the most that I could manage was a strangulated "Why?" which she interpreted correctly as "What tipped you off?"

Still clinging like a limpet, she responded, "When I said my cousin was away, the apartment would be empty—I'd be all alone—you didn't take the hint."

I hadn't known it *was* a hint, and Ada laughed delightedly at my expression as I pulled away to stare at her. Though stupified and feeling foolish, which with anyone but Ada would have seen me in a smoking rage, I found I wasn't angry. Her laugh had only love in it. Love—and great relief that all that stood between us was my lack of practice.

Now the same ebullient Ada as before, she explained her strange behavior by confessing that she feared rejection. When I'd failed to accept her "invitation," she'd felt that I was spurning her.

Holding her against me, I dispelled whatever doubt remained. What she thought of as my innocence was, more precisely, inexperience; I wasn't unenlightened, merely uninitiated, and with Ada in my life, my time had come. I couldn't be continent much longer. Way ahead of me, she whispered in the middle of a kiss, "Let's go away this weekend."

On the day we were to leave, she called to say that she was home in bed with "just a little chill and headache." By quitting time that evening I was almost crazy, speculating on the umpteen thousand dread diseases that announced themselves with "just" a chill.

I reached her cousin's home in record time, with a pocket full of pills and a mental picture of her racked with pain and broken out in some repellent pox or other. In a flimsy nightdress, looking perfectly enchanting, she opened up the door herself. Apparently her cousin and his wife were hardly *ever* home. I saw at once she wasn't sick enough to warrant any apprehension. The degree or two of fever only added brilliance to her eyes and brought her cheeks a rosy and becoming glow. All of her looked flushed, but the color was reflected from her flesh-pink gown. Propped on two pillows in the dimly lit antechamber, she looked so lovely I couldn't tear my eyes away.

Ada greeted me as if unconscious of her dishabille. My blood began to pound, but the sight of her dishevelled bed reminded me that she was sick. "Lie down," I ordered, and, much to my relief, I sounded like a self-possessed physician.

The flat was small, and with no place else to put it, her folding cot was set up in the center of the foyer. In the hospital, behind a screen, she'd had more privacy than here. Without examination, I could tell at once her trouble was a touch of grippe, but her temperature was only slightly elevated, and she said she had no chest pain. In all good conscience, though, I thought I ought to check her out. I'd do it automatically on any house call, and she certainly deserved the same attention that I'd show a stranger.

Step by step, I followed the approved procedure. At first, her heartbeat through the stethoscope was steadier than mine, but a moment later both were beating a tattoo in tandem. I bent to kiss her, but she held me off, protesting that she was infectious, that she wouldn't forgive herself if I got sick. When I insisted, saying that a kiss would more than compensate, she hugged herself and laughed elatedly.

Now she clasped her hands behind my head, and pulled me down to meet her. Catching fire from her fevered grasp, my already-heated blood began to boil. Awkward in my inexperience, I fumbled for release but only fanned the flame, intensifying my frustration. I couldn't find the way, but Ada seemed to know it so I held her tight and let her take the lead.

In the afterglow, incandescence tamed to warmth, I floated—free and incorporeal—at perfect peace. I didn't want to move a muscle—indeed, I wasn't sure I could—but the rattle of a key aroused me. I had barely time enough to pull myself together when the front door opened, and Ada's cousin entered.

Distinctly disadvantaged, I didn't know what to say or do; the tangled sheets and blankets told the tale. A flicker crossed her cousin's face, and I tensed myself to meet his righteous anger, but all he did was swiftly walk around us to an inner room. I couldn't believe he'd gone until he closed the door behind him with a solid thud. Braced for his abuse, if not an actual attack, it took a minute for the truth to penetrate. The flicker had been quickly curbed amusement. He'd found the situation funny!

Disconcerted by his strange behavior, my goodbye kiss was passionless, perfunctory, and fast. I fled the flat, not so much embarrassed as bewildered. His attitude unnerved me. What kind of man could possibly condone our conduct? If I were he, I would have killed me! What sort of family was I involved with? And I was involved. Despite my many other doubts, that I knew decisively. For good or ill, Ada was my woman.

Of course it wasn't quite that simple. Still awake at 2 A.M., and caught between the memories of Ada's cot and the qualms aroused by Ada's cousin, I was just as full of conflict as before we'd slept together—even more so, since I'd made the move from wanting her to taking her. While Jewish law imposes no particular proscriptions on the sexual act outside of marriage, except, that is, when virgins were involved, I'd fallen short of even stricter standards that I'd set myself. They were overly austere perhaps for any but a bloodless saint, but all the same, I blamed myself for not resisting. And yet, the thought occurred to me, if shame, in fact, attached to what had happened, the shame should be assigned to the aggressor—even if the "victim" had been thoroughly entranced by the experience. As for violation of a virgin, the only virgin on the scene was me.

Though physically depleted almost to the point of stupor, my brain refused to let me sleep. Was there fault at all, I asked myself, and if so, was it mine or Ada's? Hours after falling into bed, I finally arrived at a conclusion. God Himself bore all responsibility. After all, the Lord created us, complete with every urge, including sex. If He'd made it irrepressible, succumbing was expected. Our conduct was ordained by Him, and what He'd destined us to do could scarcely be a sin.

To my tired mind, the argument was practically Talmudic, but not entirely to my liking. God-willed or not, it made me out too much a weakling in the hands of women. However, all it needed was a minor switch of emphasis to fix it—a stress on strength instead of weakness. The basic premise still applied: God had given me this urge, so powerful that nothing could oppose it. Having put such passion in me, how pleased then He must be to see how *long* I'd stayed a celibate!

Satisfied at last, I shut my eyes and instantly fell fast asleep.

I intended to call Ada as soon as I arrived at work, but she reached the phone before me. Sounding agitated, she said she had to see me, "and if you care for me at all, you'll come."

If I cared? How could she question it! Had I been clumsy? Had I hurt her? Alarmed by her intensity, I asked to have the day off, and was knocking at her door before I noticed I was still in whites. Seeing that I hadn't even stopped to change, she flung her arms around me, begging me to hold her hard. Once in my embrace, Ada started weeping.

"I love you and I lied to you."

She loved me! Until now, neither one of us had said it. But loving me, what monstrous lie could make her cry so? Pressed against me, she confessed the awful truth. She was older than she'd told me.

With a shout of sheer relief, I lifted her and swung her crazily around, finally collapsing on the cot. "I was afraid you wouldn't like an older woman," she began, but without a word, too avid to undress or ask her cousin's whereabouts, I quickly disabused her. Later, lying quietly at peace, for the first time in my life, I told a woman that I loved her.

After that, every aspect of my life improved. Sex, while inexpressibly exciting, was only one of many doors that Ada opened. She stimulated all my senses. Through her, the city, which had simply been a place to *be,* became a boundless source of unsuspected pleasures.

Until she redesigned it, the pattern of my days in Tel Aviv had been dully repetitious, involving only hospital and home. Routine had worn a rut so deep, I'd sunk too far to see the world around me. From a neutral blur, Tel Aviv, with Ada, became a sharply etched and brightly animated panorama. Like someone blind and deaf who's suddenly restored to sight and sound, I reveled in the smallest and most commonplace of objects and events.

Through Ada, I was sensitized to atmospherics: the dynamic hum of business being done; of sidewalks packed with people briskly elbowing from enterprise to enterprise; the muted but eternal murmur of the tideless sea a block or two away.

Side by side, a hundred different cultures coexisted, all contributing to make the city a seductive place to stroll. We walked incessantly, people-watching, window-shopping, pausing for a bite to eat, browsing in the many bookstores, or examining the work of all the new Israeli artists. Galleries were springing up on every street, and Tel Aviv already had more bookstores than any other city of its size.

Ada also introduced me to the unknown world of Western music. All of Israel was passionate about the arts, and seats for everything were always in as short supply as eggs and butter. I never saw an empty seat in any cinema or concert hall, and the opera was impossible for any but the most alert and passionate of patrons. Long before the season started, the subscription list was closed.

Together we discovered the Kamari and Habimah theatres, the first performing in the modern realistic style, the latter in the strict tradition of the Russian drama. And, true Israelis, we argued, with the utmost fervor, every nuance of an onstage speech, every movement of an arm or lift of eyebrow. As brusque and irritating as they often were, I began to have a better understanding of the *sabras* and the older settlers. On casual contact, they exhibited a rough facade, like Tel Aviv itself, but showed a wholly different aspect to initiates.

A sprawl of squat and stodgy concrete cubes, relieved of total insipidity only by the shrapnel scars, the city had impressed me as innocuous at best. Rushing, always rushing, I hadn't really looked at it since first arriving. In wandering with Ada, I could feel the energy that charged its very air, investing otherwise prosaic buildings with an aura of importance.

Harshly angular by day, their stiff precision liquified in moonlight. Business done, the dynamism drained away, and fragrance filled the soft night air. From scores of coffee shops and tiny cabarets, all open to the street, the strains of every sort of ethnic music floated out and intermingled.

On hearing that I'd never been to Dizingoff, Ada was insistent that we spend an evening in "society." A Circle in the residential center of the city, its spot-lit fountain visible from radiating avenues in all directions, Dizingoff attracted the elite of Tel Aviv. Promenading slowly, greeting friends, stopping for a moment's gossip, snacking at an endless string of open-air cafes, then ambulating on, again they seemed a breed apart from people of the daytime Tel Aviv.

I preferred Mughrabi, the smaller, less imposing plaza at the always-busy intersection of Allenby and Ben Yehuda. Served by many bus routes, surrounded by the major cinemas and shops, it was a coming-going kind of place for people with a purpose. Instead of sauntering, Mughrabi's people strode. More attuned to aimless wandering than I, Ada was at home in Dizingoff. Striding, though, was more my style.

In this, as in all we did together, Ada gracefully deferred to me, and every day edged deeper into every area of my existence. If I felt we had no future, I also knew I never wanted *now* to end.

Our biggest current problem was the lack of any private place to satisfy our passion. Snatching quick embraces where we could, our nearness only fed frustration. Wordlessly one evening, we walked behind a boulder on the beach, and sheltered on the landward side, made love on still-damp sand. Another time, we took each other in a hollow of the little park, a block from where she lived. Ada didn't complain, but on discovering the deep-blue bruises stamped into her back and buttocks by the stones—and me—I made my mind up. I had to find my own apartment.

A letter from Jerusalem, telling me I'd passed the tests for school, strengthened my resolve. I'd receive a stipend for that final year of study, just big enough to rent a modest room—but the smallest room was big enough to hold a bed. And we could even do without a bed if we only had a door to shut behind us. "We" and "us." How warm the words were!

Out of habit, to ensure continued fortune, I fumbled at my neck before remembering that what I reached for wasn't there. Tired of explaining to the other staffers, I'd tucked my old *k'tibeh* in a drawer at home, but now I wished, with all my heart, I had the talisman to touch. So much new was happening, I needed the security of something from the past. As far as Ada was concerned, my parents couldn't provide it. At the thought of them, the warmth subsided. While it was Heaven *loving* Ada, *explaining* Ada would be sheerest hell.

44

For now, the fates were with me. Daily, Ada was increasingly adoring and adorable, my future was assured, and a smiling fortune even rectified a grievance from the past. I finally received an answer from New Zealand, and though I'd won admittance to the school already, my hand was shaking as I opened the response from Lindsay Rogers.

The formal letter, written for the Dean, was practically a paean to my intellect and medical attainments, and of course I felt a flush of pride. It was the second letter in the envelope, however (addressed to "Dearest Heskel") that healed the wound he'd once inflicted. Distance had improved his vision; half a world away, his view of Zionism had more, much more, than moderated. Rogers had become a convert!

Immediately on hearing that I'd been accepted by the school, the family began to plan a party. Everyone participated in the preparations, but as the guest of honor, my only obligation was to be there. I'd be there, all right, and with me would be Ada. No better opportunity would ever be afforded. At such a celebration, I could introduce a man from Mars, and if my mother didn't faint, she'd feed him. To save her soul, Nana couldn't be less than gracious to a guest, and Baba was his warmest, most expansive self at family affairs. My *Ashkenazi* "friend" would be received politely at the very least.

The shopping had begun already, and Baba, as in Baghdad, did the bulk of it. Thereafter, though, he went beyond the normal bounds for most Iraqi males. Few men at home would dream of even entering a kitchen, much less cooking in it, but pastry was my father's forte, and our parties were considered incomplete without his flaky, rich confections. His baklava was indecently delicious, his diamond-shaped *luzina* unsurpassed. A perfectionist, he picked out every walnut one by one, and while Nana was allowed to blanch the almonds, he'd peel and mince the orange rind himself. His *ben safan,* full of freshly shredded coconut, was cooling in the pan already. In Iraq, he would have cut it into varied shapes, but in honor of the state of Israel, whose school I'd be attending, Baba said this *ben safan* would all be Stars of David.

On the evening of the party, Ada waited at the downstairs door while I went to pave the way for her appearance. From the foyer just outside the flat, I called to say a friend was with me, and speaking Arabic, employed the gender which informed them that the friend was female. Several seconds ticked away before my father answered, "Bring her in," and I beckoned Ada up the stairs.

Inside we faced the family en masse. The kids were staring wide-eyed, and next to Baba, a flustered Nana tried to hide her floury hands behind her back. She'd rushed in from the kitchen when I called, and clearly wished that she'd remained there.

On entering, in accordance with Israeli custom, Ada said, *"Shalom,"* and as I introduced her, the family examined her, transfixed. By this time, in the ordinary course, Baba would have asked a visitor to sit, and Nana would have offered food, but nothing of a normal nature happened. I'd never heard the house so silent or seen the kids so motionless so long. Caught off guard, the sight of *any* unknown girl clutching at my arm might momentarily have taken them aback, but a girl with sun-gold hair and snow-white skin was more than merely startling.

Unexpectedly, my mother broke the spell, timidly inquiring, "Is she Jewish?" Laughing with relief, I said she was. The highest hurdle was behind us. She wasn't an Iraqi, but she was the right religion.

Though still a bit reserved, Baba soon relaxed into his role as host. Between them, he and Ada had enough vocabulary to communicate, but pleading that her Hebrew was inadequate, Nana mostly smiled and served. Ada, for all her tiny size, could eat along with any laborer. Nothing made my mother happier than feeding someone with a healthy hunger, and Ada's obvious appreciation had a positive effect on Nana's feelings toward my "friend." I saw, though, that her smile kept slipping.

I realized that my mother was adrift in conflict. Though I tended to be secretive, she knew that what I *did* confide was true, so Ada certainly was Jewish. On the other hand, her eyes and all her experience informed her that she *couldn't* be Jewish. To this very day, Nana still had doubts about my Polish soldier. In Baghdad, every Jew was an Iraqi Jew and looked and spoke like us. Here, people who professed to be of our religion looked and spoke like Aryan strangers. While she accepted them as bona fide *Yehudim* with her head, in her heart and soul, the only genuine, authentic Jew remained exclusively Iraqi.

Nonetheless, I saw her warm to Ada, who reciprocated with a brave attempt to compliment the menu in the tattered scraps of Arabic I'd taught her. The result was so hilarious, with Ada laughing even harder than the rest of us, that Nana was inspired to attempt some Hebrew. By the time we left, everyone was thoroughly at ease.

Back from seeing Ada home, I was glad to find the family had gone to bed; I wasn't in a mood to be interrogated. By morning, I'd be on my toes and ready to riposte.

At breakfast, Tikva twitted me about "your girl" and Baba glared at her, but the only other reference to Ada was my mother's "she seemed sweet." Baba's eyes bored into me and saw my "friend" for what she was, but the comments I was primed for never came.

Perhaps he figured she was just a passing fancy and that time would take the edge off my obsession. Or maybe he supposed that seeing her among us had already made me sane. He knew that if he pried and stormed, he'd only heighten her importance in my eyes. How well he understood me! This time, though, he'd started from a wrong assumption. Ada was already of supreme importance, and she wouldn't go away. The family would have to learn to live with her.

Our holiday had been arranged, and I left at noon on Friday to rendezvous with Ada at the depot. Transportation stopped when *Shabbat* started; from dusk on Friday until Saturday at sundown, not a wheel would turn in Israel, so we had to be at Nahariya by the time the drivers braked their buses. Since work began again on Sunday, we'd only have a day together, and I didn't want to spend it stranded. The religious laws required careful planning, and running late, I raced to reach the station.

Central Station always teemed, but Fridays were by far the worst. In much too small a space for so much traffic, the overloaded buses lumbered to their docks, often scraping sides in squeezing past each other. I spotted Ada waiting where they turned in from the street, and rushed to meet her.

Just yards apart, she screamed and hurled herself at me, felling me and falling with me to the hard cement. The bus I hadn't seen careened around the corner which had hidden it, missing us by inches. She'd risked her life to save me.

As if primed for this occasion, the words "I want to marry you" shot out of me. Ada's face was still contorted with her fear for me, and she showed no sign of having heard. When I repeated it, even more resoundingly, she shook her head and whispered, "Not with everyone around." A staring circle had surrounded us. I didn't care, however. The moment that the words popped out, I knew that I'd been forcibly suppressing them, almost from the start. Despite the valid arguments against it, taking Ada as my wife had always been inevitable.

On the bus, she said she loved me and would wait for me forever—but she wouldn't marry me, at least not now. All the arguments I'd used myself, she used against me. This wasn't any time for me to take a wife. For the sake of both our futures, school was first and foremost. Until they got to know her, the family would be against it. She'd go with me wherever I would have to be, but she wouldn't burden me with more responsibility than I could manage.

Before the trip began, I thought I loved her wholly, but her manner of refusing me inspired such emotion as I'd never felt before. I'd never dreamed of such unselfish adoration. Offering her all to me, she asked for nothing in return, and ashamed of having harbored any doubts about her, I determined to be just as generous in spirit as she'd shown herself today.

Nahariya proved to be exactly as described by Ada. A lovely little town, some ten miles south of Lebanon, it lived on visitors, providing quick relief from both the pressures of the city and the barrenness of raw and sandy settlements. In contrast with the blocky sameness of the city's buildings, every small hotel and *pension* was architecturally unique, and none was more than minutes from the sea. Bright pennants flying over beach cabanas lent a festive note, as if always in a state of celebration.

Looking rested and relaxed, people ambled slowly on their way to nowhere. The scent of honeysuckle mingled with the rich perfume of pastry made with plenty of the best ingredients. Ada said they never seemed to suffer scarcity of anything in Nahariya, and promised me a taste treat; she'd introduce me to old-fashioned German cheesecake. The thought of cake from cheese appalled me, but I let it pass. For Ada, I might even eat it.

In Tel Aviv, on Friday night, nothing would be open, but the cafes here were all lit up and doing lots of business. At the place we chose to stay, the desk clerk's accent stirred some memories that lessened my surprise at this. Years before, my uncle had informed us in his letters that Palestine was overrun with Germans. From his description, they didn't seem like Jews at all. They didn't observe the Sabbath, and hardly spoke a word of Hebrew. "Among themselves—and how they stick together!—they grind away in German," my uncle had objected.

The more I saw of Nahariya's residents, the better I could understand the bitter note that uncle struck. All the businesses were owned by Germans. Those early refugees from Hitler—those who'd gotten out and settled here before the major massacres began—had brought with them their capital as well as culture. We Jews from Arab countries had been less perceptive; overloyal to our native lands, we'd stayed too long. If our best had left for Israel much sooner and in more substantial numbers, arriving here both self-assured and solvent, we *Mizrachim* would be the ones who ran things.

In the restaurant, on seeing what was on the menu, I almost lost my appetite. Except in Persia, where it couldn't be helped, I'd never eaten anything that wasn't *kasher,* and even there, the food had been familiar if "unclean." Recognizing nothing that was offered here, I let Ada give the order. While she pondered over every item, weighing which would please me most, a new misgiving suddenly emerged. Ada wasn't in the least religious. Would she keep a *kasher* house for me? Could she, even if she wished to? And ignorant of all the old traditions, could she teach our children to be truly Jewish?

If not, I could. I dispatched this latest scruple as I did the food. With Ada watching anxiously to see if I enjoyed it, I resolved to swallow if it sickened me, and smile as I did so. For a girl who'd saved my life. . . .

But the meal was marvelous, my smile genuine, the stroll back "home" to our hotel a long-drawn-out, deliberately extended interval of rapturous anticipation. Unhurried, uninhibited, for once without the fear of interruption, reacting only to unspoken signals from each other. Inexhaustibly, the whole night long, we loved each other.

The day went by so quickly that the sight of traffic on the street surprised us. *Shabbat* was over, and our short hiatus from the working world was almost ended. When I said we should be starting for the station, Ada begged to stay a little longer. We were opposite an ice cream shop, and seizing an excuse to linger, she insisted that we have some. As anxious to prolong our stay as Ada, I acceded.

I was puzzled by the mob of people in the place until I saw that customers were streaming from the synagogue across the street. The sundown services had just concluded. We stood behind a group of boys with bronzy skin and curly, coal-black forelocks. From their accents and appearance, they were Yemenites.

When their turn arrived and their spokesman asked for half a dozen ice creams, the tight-lipped clerk behind the counter snapped, *"En glida,"* followed by a barely smothered *"Schwartze!"* From my German lessons, I knew not only that the word meant "black," but that used as she was using it, it was also an invective—like "nigger" in the U.S.A. And from where I stood, I could see that her *"en glida"* was a lie; the tub still held a quantity of ice cream.

Bridling with anger, I prepared to act, but Ada beat me to it. As steely-eyed as Baba, she snatched the money from the stricken youngster and repeated his request. Aware that she was overmatched, the clerk complied, and murmuring their thanks, the boys slipped out. I would have gone as well, but Ada wouldn't leave without our ice creams.

Since her emotion ran so high, I was all the more astonished when she later said she understood the woman's feelings. My head snapped up, and seeing my aghast expression, Ada added hastily, "Not that I excuse her for the way she acted," and fumbled for an explanation.

The woman was afraid, she said. And what was she afraid of? That "they" would change the neat, clean character of Nahariya. I answered that the Germans didn't own the town. "Every place in Israel is Jewish," I reminded her, and "they" were just as Jewish as the Germans. Maybe even more so.

Inadvertently, my spine had stiffened with my speech, moving me away from Ada. Her eyes welled over, and wiping tears away, she whimpered, "*I* don't feel the way they do. All I said was that I understand how *they* feel."

If she hadn't said that word again, I think I could have exercised restraint. I really wanted to embrace her, but "they" stood firm between us.

"Another 'they'!"

Instinctively, she shrank away from my explosive outburst, seeming to be spurning me, reinforcing what I'd always feared, for—exactly like the clerk's—my anger *also* stemmed from fear. *My* skin was bronzy and my hair as black as ink.

Frightened as she was at my intensity, Ada straightened up and stepped back toward me. I tried to turn away, but she cupped my face in both her hands, and forcing me to see her tear-streaked cheeks and swollen eyes, apologized abjectly for anything she'd said that even hinted at intolerance.

Regaining equilibrium, my own "I'm sorrys" mingled with her self-reproach. All she'd been was honest, but she'd struck a nerve—one supersensitive to even the suspicion of a hostile touch. Warned and painfully aware now, we'd both be on our guard against a repetition. For our love affair, our love itself, to last, we had to learn each other's hidden scars and sore spots in order to avoid them. In a way, I told myself, the incident had worked to our advantage.

Against whatever good it did, however, I measured what was gone. Except in bed, we'd never be as joyously abandoned as we'd been before it happened. From here on in, we'd both be extra careful, examining and censoring a chancy word before we said it, always on our guard a little. Guilt and shame had gained a foothold. The ice cream was our apple, and the Eden days were over.

45

On the surface, everything was as before, but the episode made me even more alive to the mass of *Ashkenazim* who "understood" the ice-cream lady. The minority who didn't despise us or consider us inherently inferior felt at minimum that we were "different." I'd been confident that I could change some attitudes around the hospital, if nowhere else, by dint of doing more and doing better than the other interns, but something happened shortly after Nahariya that discouraged me as much as the encounter at the ice-cream stall.

Ordinarily, we interns were exempt from clinic service, but when patients who spoke only Arabic came in, I was often called to translate. Since this always interfered with other duties, I was overjoyed when several Arab doctors were appointed to the clinic staff. As soon as I was able, I introduced myself in Arabic, and expressed my satisfaction that so many educated *M'silmin* had decided to remain in Israel.

My civility fell flat. The expected smiles failed to appear, and one man in particular responded with extreme resentment. When the British held the Mandate, he haughtily informed me, he'd served as the director of this whole establishment, and he considered his assignment to the clinic a calculated insult. He continued to make claims of persecution, but in the course of time, as doctors tend to do, we turned away from politics and clashing doctrines to discuss our own affairs. From wherever they begin, physicians always end up talking medicine. And that was his mistake. The man was years behind in every area and barely adequate to treat the simplest traumas. His appointment by the British had plainly been a matter of expedience, but justified or not, he believed with all his soul that bigotry had brought him down.

I thought the reason for his speaking up so freely was my Baghdad origin and fluent Arabic. I soon discovered, though, that his feeling of affinity was founded on a premise that repelled me.

"We're both the same to them," he stated bluntly. "Don't they look at you as if you were an Arab?"

As often as I'd said it to myself, I couldn't accept it from a *Mislim.*

"I'm a Jew, just like other Jews," I shot back hotly, and our interchange was over. *I* could criticize Israeli conduct; members of a family may privately oppose each other, but we always stood as one against an enemy attack. But when other *Jews* became the enemy. . . .

Where I hadn't thought to find hostility, especially so openly expressed, was in the hospital among my own. Since every supervisory nurse I'd ever known—except for Bilah—had been anti-intern, I wasn't too perturbed, at first, to feel the iciness that rolled my way from Miriam, Bilah's counterpart on Bruner's ward.

While short of charm, she was efficient in her duties—at any rate while working with the other doctors. As time went on, however, I noticed that while aiding *me,* she slowed and stalled to just this side of insolence.

One day I asked her for a certain new device, and she responded that the hospital didn't have it, adding in the smirkingly obnoxious style she employed with me, "You can't be saying that you had such things in *Baghdad?*"

I held my tongue until the afternoon she treated me with undisguised disdain in the presence of a patient, and even then I tempered my objection to a moderate reproof. All my self-restraint elicited was further scorn.

"Who asked you here?" she hissed. "If you don't approve of how we do things, you can always leave! We'd manage very well without you."

As baffled as I was affronted, I finally told Bilah what was going on. What had I ever done to Miriam, I asked, and though my question was emphatically rhetorical, she answered, "You were born!"

And I saw she wasn't joking.

Solemn when she said it, she was fighting not to smile now as she went on. "You see, it isn't *you* she hates. It's *all* of you, all you 'savages.' "

She leaned across her desk and, winking at me, whispered, "You should hear her on the subject of the *Marocani!* In comparison, she's *crazy* for Iraqis!" Bilah's lips were twitching, and both of us began to laugh. After that, I simply didn't react at all to Miriam's harassment.

First Dov had hinted at the problem; then the Polish girl had fleshed it out; and slowly since, from personal experience, I'd evolved into an expert on the subtleties of social bias. But insight in this instance only made me more resentful. Oneness of the Jews had been the dream, and I'd awakened to a nightmare of disunity. Disunity, perhaps, was overstating it, but even if I substituted fragmentation for the harsher word, the end result would scarcely be affected. Either one could only lead to chaos, and this time, there'd be no escape. No other Israel awaited us.

In Iraq the *M'silmin* had been splintered into sects, but Jews were Jews, diversified as individuals but not divided. Truthfully, of course, we couldn't take all the credit for remaining so cohesive; our history had made us more homogenous than most. All stemming from the same reserve of antecedents, we'd settled into place, for centuries a self-contained community, hardly drawing from outside ourselves for anything. While other Jews were wandering and taking on the coloration of a hundred different countries, our mores and our customs stayed the same. *We* stayed the same. In Baghdad, someone might be richer or of more imposing presence, but not better by an accident of birth.

Now home at last in Israel, gathered in from all the scattered places, together, we were worlds apart. Separate and unequal. At the top were those who'd lived in Palestine pre-Statehood; next, the *sabras,* born and bred in Israel; and in descending rank, the *Ashkenazim,* the *Sephardim,* and last and least, the Easterners. The Orientals. "Arab" Jews. *Mizrachim.* And all of these, in turn, were subdivided into smaller units. Though disavowed by everyone in public office, the pecking order, based on origin alone, was all-pervasive. Where Arabs spat *"Yehudi!"* in Islamic states, Israelis of an upper class would utter *"Marocani!"* or *"Tunisai!"* with the same contempt.

In fairness, from the standpoint of these upper castes, there was cause to be concerned. While crime and vice were insignificant compared with those of other countries, both were on the increase here, indicating widespread, deep disruption of established order. Customs common to communities of African and Eastern Jews were often strange and sometimes evil in the eyes of *Ashkenazim.* Insupportable, for one, were child marriages, completely orthodox among the Yemenites and Kurds. A law forbidding them in Israel had quickly been enacted.

Bigamy was also a divisive issue. Should his mate be barren, a male Yemenite had always been allowed to take another wife and even wed again if his second choice was also sterile. Quoting the commandment to be fruitful, they insisted on the right to keep remarrying for purposes of procreation. Those who entered Israel possessed of several wives already were permitted to retain them; once here, however, they couldn't acquire more than one, and both sides ended up unhappy and at odds. What was Law to some was both illegal and uncivilized to others, and in the wake of every judgment, the loser Jews alleged injustice. Not always, but too often, the complaint was valid.

I understood that all of us, including me, daily made decisions based to some degree on bias. I struggled, though, to recognize my leanings and allow for them. Conscious of my tilt to one side or the other, I could more or less correct for it in coming to a fair conclusion. Not every time, perhaps, and not completely, but at least I made the effort. What worried me was that so many didn't. A few, of course, were hard-core haters, but most were ordinary, decent people who would angrily deny that they were biased.

In the great majority of instances, the *Ashkenazim* weren't out so much to hurt us as to hang on tight to what they had. From elite positions, I suppose it's only normal to look downward, and looking down on us, they flinched to see us reaching up, scrambling for some status of our own. Every day more refugees were fighting for a foothold. Feeling threatened, those already on the upper rungs flailed out reflexively at everyone beneath them.

But there were others, less forgivable because they had no cause to be concerned; their status was assured and unassailable. The men who held these prominent, secure positions, safe from our encroachment, were middle-aged or older, so their attitudes were fully formed before they ever met us. Now able to examine us, however, and maybe alter their inherited ideas, most opted not to be enlightened. Life was easier with firmly fixed convictions.

Bruner was a prime example. On the weekly rounds that he and Fryd conducted jointly, he rarely called on me, convinced I couldn't perform as well as Western Jews. Fryd included me routinely. One day he asked me to interpret X-rays on which several of the others disagreed, and though the radiologist confirmed my reading, Bruner's smile remained disdainful. As the weeks went by, I proved myself a score of times, yet he clung as stubbornly as ever to his *idée fixe:* Iraqis couldn't be first-rate doctors. I could make a *miracle* and not convince him.

On a date with Ada, I mentioned my unhappiness with Bruner, but instead of the solicitude that I expected, she insisted that I hear *her* story, excitedly exclaiming, "You'll be so proud of me, you won't mind him!"

I'd given her a picture of me in an Arab headdress, and on the bus that morning, she'd pulled it out to show a friend. A woman standing over them had rudely interrupted the display. "It's not allowed to go out with an Arab," she declared. "It's against the law." No such civil law existed, but Ada didn't dispute her, saying only, "He's not an Arab. He's a Jew from Baghdad. An Iraqi Jew." To this, the woman had retorted, "What kind of Jew is that!"

"And did you tell her?" I inquired. Indignantly, she answered, "Well, of *course* I did! I said, 'A Jew, just like other Jews.' " And delighted with herself, she smiled sunnily at me, anticipating my approval.

Instead of hugging her, I scared her half to death, spewing out a reservoir of boiling rage. Unaware of how much fury had been building up, fed by all the Bruners, I was almost as surprised as she was by the vehemence of the eruption.

Hardly anyone, including Ada, knew anything about Iraq, but everyone felt free to comment, even strangers on a bus. Though angry that she'd been attacked because of me, a part of me was also mad at Ada. While she swore it wasn't so, I still suspected that like all the rest she really saw the *Ashkenazim* as superior to other Jews, and by saying that Iraqi Jews were "just the same," she was "raising" us to their exalted level. Lady Bountiful, doing me a favor!

And ignorance was no excuse. She hadn't ever asked about Iraq. Did she think we were ashamed of what we were, or maybe that we weren't much of anything? Jews from France, shipped to stoke the Nazi ovens by their fellow Frenchmen, still spoke in Israel of French sophistication. German Jews, bearing numbers branded on their arms, still mourned the loss of German *kultur.* Only those of us from African and Eastern countries were assumed to be without a background, as if we'd sprung from sterile heaps of sand.

In a nonstop spate of random data, surging out of raw emotion, I overloaded Ada with Iraqi legend. Seven thousand years ago, I shouted, when her Hungary was wild wasteland, our Sumer was already called "the cradle of the world."

I flung out disconnected facts as fast as I could form the words, without regard to how they hung together. She had to hear it all. How the science of astronomy had started in Iraq. That the twelve divisions of the clock had come from us, and so had Hammurabi and his code of law. Even Eden, where *everything* began, was believed to be where two Iraqi rivers met: the Tigris and Euphrates, not the Danube and the Elbe, I added pointedly.

Iraqi Jews had lived in Babylonia since long before the Christian era, arriving there in 586 B.C., when the Second Temple fell and we were driven from Jerusalem. Most triumphantly of all, I told her, *we* could trace our lineage directly back to ancient *Eretz Yisrael*—without a detour.

Ada's eyes had widened when I mentioned Babylonia; she hadn't known that Babylon of old was now Iraq. I proceeded to inform her that my birthplace, Baghdad, dated back to 762 A.D., and for much of its existence had been home to more—and more important, more respected—Jews than any other place on earth. Jews, I said, had inhabited Iraq for centuries before the Arabs started to arrive, and to this very day—and till the last of us departed—Iraqi Jews remained the oldest recognized *continuing* community of Jews in the entire world. We hadn't known diaspora till now. Unlike the *Ashkenazim,* our history had been unbroken.

Out of breath, emptied of my stored-up anger, I ended as abruptly as I'd taken off, but I couldn't look at Ada for the waves of shame that washed me. The blast had been engendered by the Bruners and the Miriams, the ice-cream seller and the stranger on the bus but Ada, in all innocence, had triggered the explosion and suffered the entire impact.

Too disgusted with myself to speak, I sat gingerly beside her. No apology was possible. What could I say? After lashing out in all directions, I was finally remembering what set me off.

She'd said "a Jew, just like other Jews," precisely what I'd said myself in answer to the Arabs at the clinic.

The next few months were blissful, mainly due, I must admit, to Ada's efforts. She even bought herself a *kaf* "to ward off evil spirits since I'm almost an Iraqi." Visiting the family, she soon became a favorite with the kids, and was slowly winning over both my parents. Aghast at how unlearned she was in our religion, Baba lectured her and Ada listened avidly. She captured Nana by watching wide-eyed while she cooked. Bursting with importance—in her kitchen she was queen—my mother promptly taught her to prepare my favorite foods.

Despite the cultural abyss between them, my quiet Nana and my lively Ada were compatible in all that really mattered—until it came to marriage. Much as Nana liked her as an individual, she decidedly didn't want her as a daughter-in-law. My wife must be Iraqi.

Given time, however, I trusted Ada's gaiety and charm to overcome this obstacle. They'd worked so well with me that my only second thoughts, these days, were focused on finances. Eventually, without a doubt, we'd meet beneath the *chupah* and be married. At the moment, though, I didn't have the wherewithal to house or feed a wife, much less the family I'd father. Ada certainly was fertile—I pushed the thought of the abortions back—and once I could afford them, the babies couldn't come fast enough for me. But for now, birdseed would have strained my budget.

On my own, even with my meager earnings, I was more or less removed from most privation. The hospital, for instance, was exempt from rationing. "Civilians," on the other hand, hardly had a mouthful more than bare subsistence. Aware of the discrepancy, I only took the skimpiest of servings when I ate at home.

I was constantly amazed at how my mother managed. Unable to obtain real eggs, she made herself a powdered-omelet expert, and deprived of lamb, she'd learned to turn the tough and stringy beef, in the miniscule amounts allowed us, into plattersful of filling and delicious dishes. Our finest fruit was sent abroad, but half of all our other foodstuffs were imported. *Dag* fillet—frozen cod from Denmark—was a staple; the saying was that "fish is the Israeli's meat." Nana knew a hundred ways to make the icy, bony block not only edible but appetizing.

The actual cooking of the food was just as complicated as the process of obtaining and preparing it. The limits set on power usage made both cooking and the washing up a matter of strategic planning. Here again, I had it easier than most. All day long, the hot taps at the hospital ran hot.

Until the rainy season started, I hadn't had a really rough encounter with the rationing system. Clothes were "on the coupons," but I'd bought enough in Teheran to tide me over. The one thing I'd forgotten was a mackintosh, and already soaked to sponginess by three straight days of rain, I fumed on hearing that the rest of February would be wet.

When I discovered what a coat would cost in pounds and coupons, I slammed into the house announcing that I'd have to wear a blanket "like a horse." The family, as one, offered all their clothing books. If I accepted, none of them would have new underwear for one full year. If I declined, with the old rhinitis already showing signs of acting up, I'd probably be sick in bed until the season ended. Nana solved the problem by buying sheets and making undershirts and slips and shorts exactly as she had in Baghdad, allowing me to buy the coat without too many qualms.

For a variety of reasons, I didn't discuss such needs as these with Ada. Like the family, she'd have tried to force her coupons on me, and her eyes would fill with tears when I refused. The main complaint I had about her was the extra easy way she wept. And she'd have cried the harder if I voiced my spleen about the system, as of course I would, once started. Every time I said that something was unfair, and it was something run by *Ashkenazim*—as was everything in Israel—she'd take it as a personal affront.

Of course it wasn't her fault, but it was unfair for everyone to have identical allotments. Some refugees had left their countries with both clothes and cash. Some were sent whatever they required by their relatives abroad, and still collected clothing coupons. Those, like us, who'd left their all behind were *still* behind in Israel. At times, equality is less than equal. Though I knew it was bureaucracy in fullest flower rather than a form of bias, I raged inside on ripping out each coupon.

46

We were all aware, of course, that conditions in Iraq were worse than ever. Insofar as possible without official access, the Israeli press was covering the country, and acting independently, the Union of Iraqi Jews issued special bulletins when anything of consequence occurred. However, I depended more on private sources to supply me with the sort of trivia that really told the story. Of late, these scattered bits and pieces were adding up to something awful.

Recent refugees, the strain still showing as they spoke, told us of the shame and degradation suffered at the hands of the Iraqi officers at Baghdad airport. At the very end, heaped on all the ignominy undergone already, they were pillaged of their last possessions. The Customs men were stealing openly from emigrants about to board for Israel, breaking what they didn't wish to take and beating those who dared complain.

We'd never written to our friends and relatives directly, knowing that receipt of anything from Israel could place their lives in peril. Now we couldn't write at all, even through an intermediary. No matter what the postmark, every piece of mail to a Jew was being monitored. The most innocent of statements, we were warned, would be examined by an enemy intent on seeing treason and assigning it to the receiver. With a sentence, I could seal my brother's doom.

The last I'd heard, S'hak's brick mill was a huge success with S'hak still in favor, but weeks had passed since that dispatch, and everything had worsened. All Jewish shops were closed without exception, and there wasn't any question of a Jewish quota; no Jews at all were now admitted to the public schools.

The allowance any refugee could leave with had been slashed from fifty *dinars* to an absurd five. So far, the total wealth Iraqi Jews had left behind was estimated at a quarter of a billion dollars.

Every day the grapevine carried news of fresh disasters. The worst had taken place about a month ago. It was on *Shabbat,* on January 14, 1951, that a long black car containing bombs had sped through Bataaween, slowing only long enough for two bombs to be tossed at one of Baghdad's biggest synagogues. One worshipper was killed and twenty-five were wounded.

This, though, wasn't simple terrorism of the type we'd known so long. The police were on the scene in seconds and had clearly been a party to the plot. Without investigation, they said the Jews themselves had been responsible, and the official word, broadcast within minutes, was that Zionists had thrown the bombs to scare their fellow Jews into joining them in "Palestine." The name of Israel was never uttered.

It was obvious to those of us who'd dealt before with its deceptions that the government had planned the bombing for the very purpose they ascribed to unnamed "Zionists." In the ten months since the declaration that Jews would be allowed to leave, many fewer had requested exit permits than the government expected. The "voluntary" emigration was a fraud from start to finish, and most Iraqi Jews had recognized the scheme for the monstrous snare it was.

Merely making a request to leave meant automatically relinquishing all assets to the state. Also required was that Jews renounce allegiance to Iraq. And after all of this, there was absolutely no assurance that the government would ever let them go. Stripped of all they owned, they could easily be stuck in limbo their entire lives. No longer citizens, they had no status or recourse to civil law.

Four days after the initial offer, to *force* Jews into flight, the government had issued an amendment: Jewish emigration would only be allowed until the first of March. Then this too was amended, and the "final" edict ordered that anyone who wanted out would have until the end of May.

When the stampede they expected hadn't taken place, they decided on the double-barreled bomb approach. With one strategic blast, they could smear the hated Zionists and also scare those stubborn Jews into a mass evacuation.

I'd been able to protect the family from some of the alarming facts, and when we spoke of S'hak, it was still in terms of *when* he would arrive, not *if.* Since the bombing hadn't worked and nothing further was reported, I settled back into my normal spring-wound state—tense but under tight control. Though still disturbed enough about my brother to be extra touchy, a more immediate concern demanded my attention.

I was on a break, flat out on the beat-up sofa in our triple-duty office, lounge, and conference room, when a call for me came through the central switchboard. The voice was Daisy's, and she sounded apprehensive.

"Nana said to phone you. She said to tell you that she's sick."

Since Nana was the least complaining woman in the world, I knew there must be something really wrong. Later I could be a son; now I spoke to Daisy as a doctor.

"Describe her symptoms," I demanded.

Daisy said that she was pale and sweating and also that she couldn't stop coughing. Almost as an afterthought, she added, "And she's spitting up a little blood."

Shocky certainly, and maybe bleeding from an open lesion. Automatically I ticked off differential diagnoses. With TB rampant in Iraq, that might be it. Or in view of Nana's elevated pressure, the symptoms could be warning of a stroke ahead.

Snapped back by Daisy's wailing "Heskel! Heskel, are you there?" I told her what to do. By the time I got to Fryd, I was less the cool physician than the frantic son. Before I asked, he ordered me to leave at once, insisting that I take a taxi, and his hand was in his pocket when I said that I could swing the fare myself.

At Nana's bedside, I noted that her pallor had diminished, and neither pulse nor pressure was alarming. The blood was fresh, probably originating in the nose or throat. If from the stomach, particles of food and acid would have given it a muddy cast, and lung blood would be sputum-filled and frothy.

Fryd had ordered me to call the moment I completed my exam, and on hearing my report, suggested that I bring her in as soon as possible for comprehensive studies. That wasn't quite as simple as it sounded, and I approached the task with trepidation.

My mother had a morbid fear of hospitals; in her youth a hospital had been a place where people went to die. Anticipating tears and protest, she astounded me—and frightened me—by nodding her immediate agreement. That could only mean that what was happening inside her scared her even more than entering the "death house." The only fear she voiced was that she wouldn't know how to eat. The fork, for Nana, was still an ugly and unnecessary implement, one she never chose to master. I assured her that the doctors and the nurses knew our customs and that no one would look down on her for spooning up her food. Satisfied, she smiled up in utter trust. Her doctor-son could do no wrong.

Bilah went all out for Nana. Along with special foods, she ordered that her trays be forkless, and popping in to see her as often as she passed the ward, she beamed at her benignly and even made a stab at speaking Arabic. Fryd also treated Nana with tender, loving care, and Marmer winked at her and held her hand, flirting as outrageously as only Marmer could. While professing to be shocked, she blushed and bloomed at each of his appearances. These extra courtesies, of course, just strengthened her conviction that her Heskel was a most important man. Had she walked in unannounced, however, she would probably have wound up with as much attention. I'd often seen it happen. Strangers looked at her and started smiling. Nana had the same effect on people as a small and cuddly puppy.

The pleasant aspects of her stay ended with the X-rays. Though a mass was plainly visible, we couldn't make a positive assessment. In the left lung's lower lobe, it could have been a tumor or a cyst, perhaps hydatiform. Such cysts were commonplace in Baghdad, and resulted from the presence of a dog-borne tapeworm. When I thought of it, I winced. Please, I prayed, almost anything but that! My Lassie was the only dog that Nana ever let come near.

A conclusive diagnosis would require that the lump be excised, and the mere idea of saying "surgery" to Nana sent me into deep depression. More than hospitals, she feared the "knife."

Fryd reprieved me for a little while. Since we couldn't go in until the flare-up was contained, he suggested that I keep the surgical decision to myself until she stabilized. When she was back at home, I'd break it to her somehow. She'd have to know the truth, but not the whole unvarnished truth. That would be my father's burden.

Within a week, she was happily at home again. After toasting her "recovery" with cognac—in reality, to bolster up my courage—I broached the subject squarely. She was fine, I said, except for one small problem. Before it grew into a bigger one, I told her that we'd like to take it out. I made it sound like easing out a splinter. After that, I promised, she'd be well and strong forever. She wanted to believe me so she bought it. Baba, though, knew better; I'd had to tell him what was actually entailed. This lobectomy meant opening the body, front to back, and wrenching ribs apart to reach the lung. I'd tried to soften it but father understood. It was a very major operation.

Resigned to surgery, Nana had insisted on a single stipulation. She'd go in without a struggle, but not before the holiday. Who'd prepare the seder? On this she was immovable, and since her life was not immediately endangered, Fryd accepted the postponement until after Passover.

I kept my mother reassured, but as the time for surgery approached, I grew ever more depressed. Knowing I had never seen an opera and hoping it would cheer me up, Ada bought two seats for *Samson and Delilah.* She must have spent an afternoon in line and sacrificed her lunches for a month to try to give me one good evening.

At the theatre, she apologized because we had to climb so high to find our seats, but I liked the balcony and looking down at one great sweep of happy people. Then the overture began, and from the first sound floating up, every note seemed targeted at me alone. I was so entranced that Ada had to shake me free at intermission.

Before the opera started, she'd been telling me about the prompter. Intrigued by her description of his duties, I said I'd like a close-up look, and now she led me down to see the box he stood in. At the center of the pit, she pointed out the prompter's little cubbyhole. "At home," she said, "I always sat behind it."

"Because you were a violinist?" I supposed those front row seats were the amenities accorded fellow artists, but Ada seemed uneasy at my casual assumption.

"Am I wrong?" I asked. She didn't answer, and accustomed to her lightning-quick responses, I teased, "*You* need a prompter," but a warning signal sounded in my mind. It wasn't like her to avert her face, or speak, as she did now, so low, and slowly.

"In Budapest, my husband is a leading tenor. As his wife, I always sat up front."

So that explained her manner. She hadn't wanted to remind me she'd been married. Relieved, I laughingly corrected her mistake. Ada's English had improved, but tenses still caused trouble.

"You mean your husband *was* a leading tenor."

My tutorial voice always made her smile, but her mouth remained a straight and narrow slash, and her lips had lost their color.

"No," she said. "He's singing now."

I was still at work on that when she hit me with another.

"Naturally, he's not as good as before he tried to kill himself."

My head was reeling, but she *couldn't* have said he tried to kill himself. "Tried" could only mean he'd failed, and she'd said that he was dead. But dead men didn't sing. Either I was going crazy or her spouse was still alive.

She'd said she was a widow. Adultery was heinous in the eyes of God, and I'd been bedding with a married woman.

I could feel my mask begin to form—that glacial face with blanked-out eyes and lips stretched thin, allowing no expression. Always in reserve, it snapped in place to hide my private pain from public view. She hadn't seen this face before, and for an instant, she recoiled. Recovering, she reached out toward me.

"But I'm divorced!"

When I flinched away, she looked as if I'd struck her. Did she really think that made a difference? Divorce just didn't *exist* among Iraqi Jews. Aside from how I felt myself, no decent son would stigmatize his family by introducing anyone in Ada's state. The existence of her husband was insuperable. If his suicide attempt had been *successful* now. . . . Now she had me wishing someone dead!

"Why did he try to kill himself?"

I noted that my voice was quite dispassionate and cool. So the mask, this time, was tight enough to keep my speech in check. Haltingly, she started to divulge the story, but I cut her short just seconds after asking. The way things were, I wouldn't believe a word she said, so why prolong the agony of parting?

Trying to get up the aisle and away from Ada, I was bucking the entire audience attempting to return. With a shoving mass in front of me, and a sobbing woman clutching at my coattails, I couldn't make any progress. The exit to the street was blocked, and by the time I'd struggled to the bottom of the stairs, I was too embarrassed by the situation to continue pushing. Close to tears myself, what I wanted most was darkness and escape from all those eyes, so I allowed the crowd surrounding me to sweep me up. Huddled in my seat again, I could scarcely hear the music for the sound of Ada's sobs. As if afraid that I might flee again, she clung to me throughout the rest of the performance.

My armor had a chink in it. All through the second half of *Samson and Delilah,* her eyes brimmed over, and every tear that fell etched deeper into my defense. Much to my dismay, I felt it melting. The long walk to the bus afforded her another stretch of sobbing time, and on the ride itself, open now to anything she threw at me, I was easy prey to Ada's explanations.

She swiftly told the tale of a failed marriage. In a scant six months, her husband had lost everything they jointly owned, and soon she found he was a thief, stealing to support his gambling habit. So deep in debt, he couldn't face the future, he'd put a rifle to his head and pulled the trigger.

"And even *that* he couldn't do right."

Her comment jarred me but she did have some excuse. Already almost bankrupt from his "borrowing," both families scraped bottom for the best of medical attention. Following a long, expensive convalescence "when I served him like a slave," she said, he again began to sing . . . and once again began to gamble.

"I stayed until I knew he'd never stop, until I nearly had a nervous breakdown. And it was only then I left him," she declared.

Unable to condone divorce, and equally unable to condemn her, I could only say she should have told the truth. I couldn't manage more until I'd sorted out my mixed emotions.

As bad as disillusionment with Ada was my new distrust of *me.* The woman was unwidowed, un-Iraqi, unreligious, and untruthful, and in continuing to want her, my confidence in *me* was undermined. Her biggest fault was her ability to fog my mind. For that, I couldn't forgive her.

47

Normally high-spirited and self-assertive, Ada sank now into willing serfdom, submitting to my every whim without dissent. Instead of basking in such vassalage, enthralling as I would have thought it, I found it difficult to deal with. When she'd yielded to my views before, I'd been ecstatic. Women were supposed to be subordinate to those they loved. I was finding, though, that total abnegation was unhealthy for us both.

As long as it was under some control, our arguing and making up had added liveliness to love and life. I missed the little friction that excited sparks between us, but fearful of another of my flaming outbursts, she was snuffing out her slightest show of spirit. By smothering her own emotions and appeasing me on every point, she managed an uneasy peace between us. As time went on, however, her humble knuckling under only made me angrier and more ashamed, inciting me to ever more despotic actions.

Our relationship was slipping into sadomasochistic channels, and I couldn't seem to stop it, even while admitting that the major fault was mine. What Ada was or did before we met was none of my affair, but since I couldn't accept that simple premise, I should have said so at the start and sent her packing.

My basic nature barred an Ada. From boyhood on, a flaw in anything I owned had bothered me unduly. I wouldn't tolerate a knife blade with a nick in it, and if Nana sewed a crooked seam where no one else could see it, I wouldn't wear that shirt or pair of shorts. Perfection was impossible, and still I sought it, but where knives and underthings were easily disposed of when their faults became apparent, I couldn't part with Ada.

Unable to surrender her myself, I often wished she'd walk off of her own volition, and as agonizing weeks went by, I gradually began to shift the burden of the blame to her. More and more, I had the feeling that her meekness was, in fact, manipulation—that, consciously or not, she was playing off my weak point. Tears, she knew, unnerved me, and Ada made an art of looking woebegone and weeping softly. Acting like a doormat, she insisted that I step on her.

Those days preceding Nana's surgery were rough on everyone, but I alone was conscious of the real and scary risks. Of all the patients undergoing the procedure, up to one in five would die. Our rate in Israel was better than the average—only one in six or seven—but that one could be Nana.

Frightening figures were assaulting me on every side, and once again I worried actively about my brother. From late reports, survival odds for any Jew still living in Iraq were even worse than Nana's surgical statistics. On March 11, the Parliament in Baghdad had approved a bill that froze *all* Jewish property and bank accounts, not just the assets of the emigrants. Eight days after that, Kahwat el-Shat was bombed again. The riverside cafe, patronized exclusively by Jews and always crowded after services at sundown, had first been targeted when I was still in Teheran. Three died this time and thirty more were wounded.

Three days later, still continuing its cat-and-mouse game, the government called off its terrorist attacks. Those Jews, fewer than 5000 now, who'd somehow managed to remain Iraqi citizens, were told they'd be accorded equal status with their *M'silmin* countrymen.

At the end of March, however, new brutalities were authorized against the ghettoes. As before, bombs thrown from bicycles and cars were attributed to Zionists. Valuable as propaganda, the other purpose of these bombings was to instigate a further exodus, another "voluntary" flight of fearful Jews. By "abandoning" their property, they'd save the government the slight embarrassment of stealing it outright. The fundamental aim, though, was to strip Iraqi Jews, then dump them, indigent, on Israel. Militarily, the *M'silmin* couldn't destroy the Jewish state, so the plan again was to drown it in a sea of starving refugees.

Our relationship had so corroded that I couldn't confide my fears to Ada, especially about *Sephardim.* I didn't encourage her to ask about my mother either, but in this, she stubbornly persisted. Uninvited, she was at the hospital and at my side throughout the whole ordeal.

As she'd promised, Nana went without a protest when the holiday was over. Baba had stayed home to pray, and for six eternal hours, Ada stood with me, a step outside the operating theatre, a silent and consoling presence.

I didn't acknowledge her at all until I heard and saw that Nana had survived. Her peaceful, sleeping face then snapped the tension so abruptly that I sagged as though supporting cords had suddenly been cut. Ada caught me in her waiting arms, and for the first time since this nightmare started, I hugged her lovingly, not out of angry need.

The spot on Nana's lung had been a harmless cyst. The lung would heal itself, and everything would soon be back to normal. With Ada too, I vowed. Our hurts would also heal, and even as we stood there, I felt the process start.

Except for lack of news from S'hak, life, overnight, was on the upswing. Nana mended faster than I'd dared to hope, and the winning streak extended to my work as well. A call informed me that I'd been accepted at Hadassah Hospital, the foremost teaching institution in the state. Every student hoped to be assigned there, but only eight of us had won appointments. Bursting with the news, but cut off for the moment from the family and Ada, I told a beaming Fryd and an equally exultant Bilah.

In the midst of the rejoicing, Bilah, ever practical, brought me back to earth by asking where I'd live. The hospital didn't house its students. According to my calculations, the subsidy provided would scarcely be enough to rent a room. Even eating at the hospital, I wouldn't have a *grush* to spare for such necessities as haircuts or a pair of socks, much less any money to send home.

The glow began to dim. With five to feed, and the expert manager, my mother, out of action, Baba's wages wouldn't begin to meet expenses. The little I contributed was sorely needed. And Ada had her job here. Was this a time to leave, I wondered?

The appointment to Hadassah was a dream, but dreams were fragile stuff, while duty pressed on me, a massive burden that I couldn't put down. Weighing both, the scale tipped intractably against Hadassah.

Before I lost the will to do it, I called the office of the Dean and spoke to his assistant. Shocked at my decision—no one ever turned Hadassah down—she said she wouldn't accept my "no" as final; I was to think about it overnight and call her back.

When I got home that evening, Ada was already with my mother. Since Nana's operation, all our dates were by her bedside. More in love than ever, our ties were even tighter than before, and tacitly acknowledged by the family, though not without some lingering reluctance.

Ada's servile days were over, and I happily resigned my tsarist role—except for one last ultimatum. She was never to articulate the word "divorce," in any language, anywhere around my parents.

In Arabic, with a quick aside to Ada, I broke the news about Hadassah, playing down the honor and stressing the importance of the training rather than the place I took it. I could choose to go, I told them, or stay right here in Tel Aviv, implying that all hospitals were much alike. The family assumed, of course, I'd stay at home.

Ada's Arabic was limited to simple phrases. However, hearing "Tel Aviv" recur so often, with Jerusalem just mentioned once, she began to get the drift. Unlike the others, Ada understood the opportunity Hadassah offered and how painful it would be for me to pass it up.

Other evenings after dinner I'd sit awhile with Baba while the women did the dishes. Along with Tikva, Ada always cleared the table, but tonight she didn't insist, eager to be off to talk with me. Once outside, she stated firmly, "You're going to Jerusalem. If you don't," she said, "I'll never speak to you again."

Then tempering the threat to an offer that was almost irresistible, she said that she'd go with me. Anticipating my response, she hurried on, "I can always get a job, and with Michi in Jerusalem, I also have a place to stay."

That was a sacrifice; she'd mentioned brother Michi only once before, describing him as "aggravating" and "impossible." Still she'd live with him to be with me.

I had qualms as well about her quitting work in Tel Aviv. She was training as a diamond-cutter, and with Ramat-Gan rapidly replacing Amsterdam as the center of the industry, her future was assured. Leaving now would put an end to all her prospects. She swore, though, that she would have quit in any case, and I remembered her complaints about the irritating diamond dust.

Swayed in the direction that I wished to go, I called Jerusalem again, cancelling my cancellation. The Dean's assistant said I'd made the only sensible decision; I trusted that the family would also see it our way.

I planned to keep my leaving quiet until very near the date of my departure. While school didn't start till June, housing in Jerusalem was hard to come by, so I set my going for the first of May. Along with living quarters, I also hoped to scout out something I could work at when I wasn't at Hadassah. It wouldn't completely salve my conscience, but sending money home would help.

I called Hanoch as soon as I decided. Swearing him to secrecy, I broke the news. His instant "Marvelous!" encouraged me to ask about the possibility of part-time work. Promising he'd keep an eye out, he called me back before the day was over. Shaare Zedek, a hospital supported by Mizrachi, could use me for the month of May to cover for vacationing physicians. After that, they'd need me nights and weekends. Would I be interested? I may have burst his eardrums with my answer.

The last essential was a place to stay. About to ask for Hanoch's aid in this as well, I had a sudden second thought and snapped my mouth shut just in time. He'd undoubtedly have fixed me up, and with the finest, most respectable of families. That, of course, would cook my goose. With Ada coming, the last place that I wanted was with people who would see me as a son. My main requirement was absolute, inviolate aloneness, and a landlord who cared only to collect the rent.

Having packed my case in secret, I informed my parents I was going as I went, and was out the door and on my way before my mother's eyes had more than misted over. If I'd lagged a moment, and she thought she had a chance to change my mind, she'd have clutched at me and cried herself into a state of sick exhaustion. Cruel as it might seem, this quick, clean break was kinder.

Jerusalem and Tel Aviv were only hours apart; I could practically commute. On leaving, I'd assured her that she'd see me just as often as before. Nana knew, however, that the move this time meant more than miles between us. Except in exile, when I'd had no choice, I'd never lived away from home. Of my own volition now, I was setting up a separate household, if only in a single room.

I found that room on Prophets Street. The owner of the house was old, uninterested in me, and on the deaf side, and my room was angled off the entrance hall, a step beyond the street door. Anyone could slip inside and out again without attracting notice. I couldn't have asked for any place more perfect.

All that I remember of the next three weeks is aching loneliness for Ada. I'd anticipated missing her, but not this much. My happiness was so much in her hands, it scared me.

Today was the third anniversary of Israel's statehood, and the sky above the city was a zinc-white ceiling, holding in the molten heat. The scorching desert wind, the one we called the *khamsin* in Iraq, sent swirling clouds of sand and dust down every street, and still the streets were crowded. Nothing could have stopped the celebration.

Tanks rumbled by the hospital and fighter planes roared overhead. Every upturned face was smiling, and I felt myself the only sad and lonely soul in all Jerusalem. I could have been with others, but I wasn't in a social mood. Mostly, I was missing Ada and the family, but some of my despondency was strictly physical in origin. During the *sharav,* the Hebrew name for *khamsin,* anyone with weather sensitivities was actively unhappy. Throughout the Middle East, as every doctor knew, the driving desert winds increased insomnia and raised the incidence of stomach upset and asthmatic wheezing. The ceaseless soughing nagged at ragged nerve ends, and ferocious fights erupted over niggling nothings. The oppressive heat and bone-dry air affected everyone to some degree, but those, like me, with easily exacerbated nasal problems were the most acutely miserable.

With everyone determined to participate in celebrating statehood, Shaare Zedek was threatened with a shutdown. On the festive day, desperate for staff, the hospital administration offered a substantial bonus to anyone who'd stay and work. I seized the opportunity, not only for the extra money, but to lose myself in doing something useful.

I was with a patient when a nurse appeared to say that someone wished to see me. It was Ada in the office, but an Ada that I'd never seen before, slack of face and looking sicker than she had with jaundice. Rising slowly, she began to sway. I rushed to catch her, and against my breast she burst out crying. Well acquainted as I was with Ada's easy flow of tears, these frightened me. They weren't for effect, and they clearly offered no relief.

What but death could cause this kind of agony? Her mother? *My* mother? Had she come to break some news so terrible it couldn't be told by phone? Frantic now, I shook her; she tried to speak but strangled sobs distorted what she said. When I caught the words, they were "I'm pregnant."

I roared out my reaction, and she flinched away, misinterpreting my howl of joy for fury.

"It's wonderful!" I yelled. "I couldn't be happier."

Briskly, as befit a man about to be a father, I announced that we'd be getting married. Ada's mouth dropped open and she flung her arms around me. Hugging her, I wondered briefly why she'd been so worried. Even *Ashkenazim* ought to know that every Jewish man was meant to be a father.

I felt ten feet tall and strong enough to take on every Arab in Islam. Above us, another squadron of our planes swooped sharply down to show its skill, and looking up, I laughed out loud. On Independence Day, I was giving up my independence, and I couldn't be more elated. Ada's news had made it all so simple. The existence of a tiny mass of living cells eliminated every trace of doubt. Suddenly the path ahead looked clear and unencumbered.

Because it was a holiday, the office of the Rabbinate was closed, but if Ada stayed the night, we could see him in the morning, early, and arrange our marriage. More urgently than ever, I wanted to be with her and was tempted to invite her to my room. Yesterday, I would have, but the baby had effected change already. My approach to Ada, as the mother of my child, would be Rabbi Ezra orthodox from this point on. No more sneaking sex, no more surreptitious snatching at each other. Soon we'd be a family, an Iraqi family, in strict accord with custom, so Ada would be sleeping at her brother's house instead of in my bed. Despite her strongly voiced objections, I sent her off to stay with Michi. Then I called Hanoch, and swearing him to secrecy again, said that Ada had accepted my proposal. Could he find us an apartment?

At the Rabbinical Court, the desk clerk asked, "What language would you like?" and pointed to the piles of forms behind him. I asked for Hebrew; Ada picked Hungarian. When I completed mine, I looked across at hers, and though Hungarian was Greek to me, by counting down the lines, I could see the question stumping her was "Do you have a *get?*"

Was it possible she didn't? With a sinking heart, I recognized another possibility: She might not even know the word. "Get: a certificate legitimizing a divorce in accord with Jewish law." I'd never thought to ask about the *how* of her divorce. In Iraq, as here in Israel, civil marriage among Jews was nonexistent, so when divorces did occur, they were always by rabbinical decree.

My fear solidified when Ada asked me what a *"get"* was. So that easy, pleasant path ahead was still obstructed, and the stumbling block was big. We couldn't marry till she got a *get.* In *halachic* law, her civil-court divorce didn't count. In Jewish eyes, she remained the singer's wife.

In shock, I recognized a second and stupendous block. Since she was still his wife, I'd been sleeping with a married woman, engaging in adultery, a heinous sin. But there was even more to this offense than falling from the grace of God. By the same *halachic* law, we'd made ourselves *psulai hitun:* unable to be married to each other. Properly divorced or not, a woman may not wed a man she slept with while she had a husband. If I married Ada, I'd be flouting the religious law. If I didn't, my baby would be born a bastard. My baby won. No one knew about us. No one would.

When we were ushered in to see a rabbi, all I told him was the truth about the civil-court decree. Sympathetic to our plight, he spoke to Ada in an olio of Yiddish, Hebrew, French, and English. Our situation came as no surprise, he said; it was all too common, especially among the emigrants from Iron Curtain countries. In the past, rabbinical divorce had been accepted as sufficient by their civil courts, but since they now insisted on a secular decree, many Jews just skipped the *get.*

While promising to contact Ada's husband and ask him to cooperate, he couldn't predict the time the *get* would take. "That depends on how and when your husband answers," he explained, and I could hardly plead with him to expedite our case because the bride-to-be was pregnant.

Ada, as expected, was wet-eyed when we left his office, and I hastened to assure her that whatever happened, we'd be a family and live together, legally or not. For our child's sake, God, I said, would certainly forgive us, but the words I'd meant to ease her mind only made her more unhappy. She'd never heard of the *halachic* law, so how was she to blame, she asked. "Can you break a law you never heard of?" Still pleading for an answer when I put her on the bus, she was weeping as I waved her off to Tel Aviv.

Unwanted and unbidden, my earlier anxieties came crowding back. Could even Ada, nonobservant as she was, not know about a *get?* And even now, did I know for sure which "truth" she'd told about her husband? No matter how I tried to blank them out, the many inconsistencies of Ada's "explanations" kept recurring; what she didn't omit, she edited to suit her ends. Finally, I fell back on the same excuse she'd thrown at me. If not innocent, exactly, I felt my ignorance entitled me to gentle judgment. Was I really guilty of adultery, believing that she *was* a widow?

Sanely reasoned, our relationship was doomed to failure, but the fact remained that I adored her and already loved the infant in her womb. Doubts be damned. We'd stick it out together.

We arranged to meet at Natanya on the following weekend. Ada, as I saw at once, was far from being back to normal, but while pale and drawn, she didn't look as shaky or distraught as in Jerusalem.

After lunch, we detoured to our favorite park before returning to the city. Very possibly, conception had occurred there. The thought excited me. Though I steered her to the park today, intending only talk, once we settled in our private place, I started to caress her; but when I pulled her to the sandy ground beside me, she rolled away and sat up straight.

"I can't," she said.

For the first time ever, she'd refused me, and I stared at her in disbelief. Often it was Ada who initiated sex, and she was never not prepared when I proposed it. Uncomprehendingly, I asked her why. "You're not *that* pregnant," I reminded her.

Back turned to me, she answered in a strained but steady voice. "It's for the best. Believe me, Heskel."

The hair had risen on my neck, and I snapped her head around, forcing her to face me. "Explain yourself!" I ordered.

Ada quietly responded, "There is no baby. Yesterday I went for the abortion."

I couldn't speak, but my entire body shook. She couldn't have done it. Not my son. Ada tried to take me in her arms.

"It was for you," she started, and I flung her from me. Sprawled where she had dropped, and as dry-eyed as the dead, she watched me stumble to my feet and blindly run from her. This time *I* was crying.

48

In Jerusalem again, too steeped in my despair to see an inch beyond it, I passed Hanoch without a sign of recognition. He grabbed my arm, announced that he had news for me, and pressed a slip of paper in my hand. "An apartment," he explained. "For you and Ada."

The paper floated loose from nerveless fingers, and I groped about so clumsily to pick it up that Hanoch cackled, "I figured you'd be pleased, but I didn't think you'd fall apart." Happy that he'd overwhelmed me, Hanoch strode off smiling.

The searing irony of it! Finding an apartment *now!* I crumpled the address and threw it from me as I'd flung off Ada. The only ray of hope was that I had none. If nothing else, I'd been unshackled from that fitful seesaw. I was done with all the ups and downs. Done with could we/should we marry. Finally, emphatically, she'd settled that. I didn't want Ada for my wife, but as a woman, I still wanted her as much as ever.

In the first few days that followed on the bombshell, I deliberately established an exhausting schedule, designed to drain my every ounce of energy. I fixed it so I didn't have a second to myself to think. Control escaped me only when I slept, and then the baby who was not to be obsessed me.

My unconscious mind harked back to Zohar, and to what it said about the soul of the aborted infant. The *nefel,* torn from life, waited in the afterworld to greet its guilty parents and to haunt them to the end of time. Abortion, says the Zohar, is a crime without a possible requital. In other killings, expiation is exacted by the civil code, but of even more importance, the slain are known by name and each may be lamented as a singular remembered soul. The unborn are anonymous, however. Denied existence, thus identity, the *nefel* is deprived of even special prayers. No name or face can ever be attached.

Awake, I was starting to feel free of Ada when I found a letter from her waiting on my bedspread. Seeing the familiar scrawl was sufficient to arouse me to a state of excitation, as if Ada's very body lay in bed. So warned that I was still susceptible as ever, I decided not to read what she had written.

The envelope was heavy in my hand—three sheets, at least, stained, no doubt, with tears, and studded with extravagant endearments and another set of "explanations."

With my fingers worrying the flap, I forced myself to drop the letter. If it stayed in sight, however, I knew I'd open it eventually. I could tear it up, of course, but pieces could be put together. I simply didn't trust myself. Fire would destroy it past redemption, but I didn't smoke, so had no matches. The communal wastecan in the kitchen was another way. Once I stirred it down among decaying rinds and rancid fat, I wouldn't retrieve it—but the mere idea revolted me. The thought of flushing it also made my stomach turn.

Exhausted, I dropped it on the dresser. Half-asleep by now, I figured I'd be safe with it until tomorrow, and in the morning, early, I'd dispose of it in some way less disgusting than the garbage can or city sewer. After all, I'd loved the author.

At 3:00 A.M., I ripped it open.

Four pages, smeared with the expected tears and crammed with the anticipated explanations—but arguments and not excuses.

"If I live to be a hundred, it was the hardest thing I'll ever have to do," she wrote, "and I could only do it because I love you even more than my own flesh and blood." Until that moment, I'd only thought about the baby's being mine.

Everything I wouldn't listen to, she laid out in the letter. If she'd had the child, she'd have ended my career, she argued. I wouldn't have let her work and leave our baby, and I couldn't support a family and still remain in school. I found she knew precisely how the family perceived her. Given time, she said, she felt that they'd accept her. However, if she'd gone ahead and had the baby, they'd surely think she'd trapped me into marriage, and in standing up for her, as she knew, of course, I would, I'd alienate the others in my life I loved. "And how long would you love me then?" she asked.

"I'll be coming to Jerusalem," she ended. "If you want me, I'll be with you. If not, I'll understand, but in any case, I'm coming."

Shortly before my internship was due to start, I was summoned to the school; the Director wished to see me. I assumed that it was standard policy to welcome students, and that Dr. Mann would shake my hand and offer me a minute's worth of warm encouragement.

An hour later, I was sitting in his office in a daze. Dr. Mann was asking if I'd help him out. "You'd be doing me a favor," the Director said. He'd been speaking of the TB hospital, operated by Hadassah, whose resident had just been drafted. Would I care to substitute for several months? Of the eight new interns, he went on, I appeared to have the most experience.

It wasn't just the compliments that left me speechless. What stunned me into silence was the opportunity itself. Everything about it seemed designed to solve my problems. Mistaking my bedazzled look for indecision, he added hastily, "The time, of course, will count toward your internship, and you'll be drawing doctor's pay."

I had to bite my inner lip to keep from grinning like a pinhead. Going to Tz'fat—Safad—would get me physically away from Ada, and allow me time to straighten out my weirdly mixed emotions. And the money! The astronomical amount of money! Four hundred pounds a month instead of eight. Even two such paychecks would provide a cushion large enough to last until I left Hadassah.

Dr. Mann, supposing that reluctance made me slow to answer, volunteered additional inducements. "Naturally your room and board will be included, and your travel costs, both up and back, and any necessary outlays."

Rather than responding with an honest cheer, I nodded graciously, saying that I'd like to be of service but was more or less committed elsewhere. One quick call effected my release from Shaare Zedek, and Dr. Mann was suitably impressed with both my dignified deportment and my ethics.

Instead of calling Ada, I sent a telegram, saying that I wouldn't be in the city for the next eight weeks. I meant to keep the message short and noncommittal, but on reading what I'd written, I realized how curt and cold it sounded. Since I had some words to spare, I added, "Working in Safad. Sorry not to see you."

An hour later, I was packed and on my way to Tel Aviv; I'd asked to have a day at home before proceeding to my post. In the upper Galilee, distanced equally from Lebanon and Syria, Safad would take me far away from family and friends. I wouldn't be seeing them again until my two-month stint was over.

The visit home was uneventful. Nana's health was much improved, and only Baba seemed to notice my subdued behavior. All he said, and only on my leaving, was "There's lots of time, so take it slowly. You're only twenty-one."

Past Haifa, heading north and east, the trip through ever-hillier terrain introduced me to the lushest scenery in all of Israel. After Tel Aviv, Safad felt almost frigid, and the air was piney fresh. A room had been arranged for me, and waking from a good night's sleep, I found the hospital was straight across the street from my hotel.

An old and sturdy building in the British style, the facility was much like those in Baghdad. Rested, full of breakfast, and invigorated by the bracing mountain breezes, I launched into my duties with the lightest heart I'd known since leaving Ada. Here I'd have the breathing space I badly needed, detached from both my past and future problems. If not escape, these sixty days were necessary respite.

Aside from the Director, I was the only doctor on the staff. With a therapist, three nurses, and some aides, we attended to 120 patients. The first day started swimmingly; I slipped into the hospital routine without a hitch, and remained until my eyes began to glaze. At eight that evening, I crossed to my hotel, tired but free of tension, and convinced that I was over Ada. I hadn't thought of her for twelve straight hours.

She was sitting in the lobby, eyes glued to where I'd enter. At the sight of her, my isolationist philosophy dissolved in sheer desire. At 8:10 by the clock, we were in bed, and the whole affair was on again—but with a difference. "We" had no future. It was back to "she" and "I" and here and now—and now that was enough for me. It struck me then that even when I had a wife, medicine would be my mistress.

Medicine claimed more of me with every passing day, and I found that I preferred the company of people in my own profession to purely social contacts. For an hour's relaxation, Safad itself sufficed.

Historically a center of religious study, the splendid setting of the town was rapidly attracting artists too. On the shortest walk, I'd be sure to hear a scholarly discussion or stumble on a painter, trying to commit the purple hills to canvas. High and cool and green, Safad had still another rare distinction. I never saw a single Arab on its streets. Since I knew that *M'silmin* had resided here before partition, I asked about their absence. My inquiry at dinner was greeted with a shout of glee from all those at the table, and Amos, a native of Tz'fat, explained.

In 1929, as he reminded me, the Arabs of Safad had butchered almost every Jew then living in the city. Fearing retribution for the bloody massacre, they were understandably a little edgy when the war broke out in 1948. The fact that Jews had guns this time was bad enough, but when a rumor surfaced that the Haganah had atom bombs, they'd fled in panic at the first big bang they heard.

Amos cackled. "And all we had were *davidka!*" *Davidka* were homemade mortars, pieced together out of pipe lengths. "Of course we couldn't machine them," he continued, "so lots of flash escaped, and they made an awful racket. One salvo and the last we saw of Arabs were their rear ends disappearing in the distance. And they never did come back."

As the end of my appointment neared, the thought of leaving Safad saddened me much more than I would ever have expected. I'd slipped into the sort of free and easy friendships that I hadn't known since early boyhood. Once started with the underground, I'd never felt secure enough to let myself relax with strangers. In Safad, I rediscovered camaraderie, and left the town renewed by the experience, and entirely convinced that I was "cured" of Ada.

In Jerusalem, I moved back to my room, and explained to Ada why her staying with her brother would be best for both of us. Living openly with me, I said, would ruin her reputation, horrify my family, hold me up to censure from the hospital, and even risk my stipend. Unhappy as she was, she couldn't rebut a single statement.

Michi, Ada's younger brother, was a bachelor, by trade a leather craftsman, and too shrewdly smooth to suit my taste. By mutual consent, we rarely saw each other, and whatever he suspected, he kept strictly to himself.

Before Safad, when I was out with Ada, another woman could have walked by naked and I wouldn't have noticed. Now I noticed, and Ada *noticed* that I noticed. I glanced at someone in a coffee shop one day and Ada cupped my cheeks and turned me forcibly to face her.

"How would you feel if I looked at every handsome man?" she asked.

This time she'd overstepped; I couldn't ignore it. Coldly answering that she could look at anyone she liked, I watched her eyes fill up, as always, and she wept the whole way home.

In the early days, totally engrossed in one another, we'd made no mutual acquaintances. Now I was forming friendships, and she bitterly resented it. If I spoke of anything outside our shared experience, she curled up small and sulked. Yet she insisted on her isolation. When I wanted to include her with a group, her standard answer was "I want to be alone with you."

As my private life grew more conflicted, my professional career made steady progress. Safad had sent an excellent report, and my standing at Hadassah was heightened even more by a series of "perceptive" diagnoses—so described by my superiors.

With diarrhea rampant among kids from backward countries, the tiny Yemenite had been admitted as a routine case. On examining his stool, however, I saw it was "tomato soup," indicative of dysentery, but supposedly amoebic dysentery only hit adults; it was unheard of in a three-month-old. My department head had hooted at my diagnosis, but looking at the smear I'd taken, his derisive smile faded, and he called for his assistant. "Come see what Heskel found!" Then he rolled my name out richly.

"Haddad—it suits you."

I flushed bright red, of course. "Haddad" in Arabic is "smith," but in Hebrew, it means "sharp."

Some weeks later, while on call, I was sitting over dinner with the house physician, Dr. Sabo, when a nurse burst in to say that we were needed, stat. A six-year-old had just arrived in shock. Somehow he'd fallen in a barrel full of powdered plaster. Headfirst and deep, she said. While striding toward Emergency with Sabo, I urgently suggested that he order up a trach set. Sabo scoffed. "A tracheotomy for shock? That's crazy!"

I was trying to convince him that edema of the pharynx could develop.

When we reached the boy, we found him traumatized but not the least congested. With a mocking look at me, Sabo set about examining the youngster, and I slunk away, unneeded. I should have kept my mouth shut! Up till now, Sabo had respected my proficiency; it wasn't smart to overstep, and so insistently, when serving with the house physician.

When he slumped beside me twenty minutes later, I braced myself for censure, but instead he said, "It happened. Just the way you said it would. Suddenly he started turning cyanotic—then stopped breathing. I didn't have a set, so I had to trach him with a pair of scissors. I should have listened."

When he asked me how I'd known, I said my father was a builder, so I'd been around construction all my life; I'd seen what gypsum did when wet. The boy, like anyone who falls head down, would automatically have gasped and sucked up powdered plaster. He'd expel as much as possible, but what he couldn't spit out, when saturated by his mucus and saliva, would expand and harden, forming an effective air block.

Sabo told the story on himself, and for the next few days, I basked in glory. However, what really firmed my reputation started with a standard workup.

The woman had been diagnosed as having an ovarian hernia. I dissented, stating that I'd found a bifid uterus. In this condition, which was hardly ever ascertained except by opening up the patient, the womb is separated into two lobed "horns." In spite of everyone's raised eyebrows, I wrote my note and signed the chart.

When the schedule for surgery was posted, I was down as third assistant for her herniorrhaphy. As the country's top practitioner in women's problems, the patient's doctor didn't expect to find dissenting diagnoses on our workup chart. Skimming it he stopped at my boldly written "bifid uterus."

How, he asked, had I arrived at that "most interesting" conclusion? The locus of the uterus had tipped me off, I told him. If the womb had been a normal one, the herniation would have pulled it much more sharply to the side. To resist displacement, the uterus, I reasoned, would *have* to be divided. The split had let the organ "give."

He thrust the chart at me. "Draw it," he commanded, and after studying my sketch, startled me by saying, "You'll assist me." First assistant. Instead of holding a retractor, I was actively engaged again!

The patient's uterus proved to be exactly like the drawing. When the former first assistant, angry at my elevation, muttered, "Lucky guess," the surgeon glared at him. "Perceptive diagnosis," he corrected crisply. I walked a foot above the floor for weeks.

Happy at the hospital, I lingered when I could have left, reluctant to engage with Ada. Once again, she was acting almost slavish, anticipating any possible displeasure, soothing hurts before they happened, inviting me to wipe my feet on her. The more she said she loved and "understood" me, the less I liked or understood myself.

Though still emotional about her, I was infinitely less involved than she was. While my world was growing larger, she was busy shrinking hers so that she and I would be enough to fill it. The walls were closing in on me; smothering, I struggled to escape, wounding both of us in every such attempt.

Bed remained the arbiter of every quarrel. Our bodies were as much attuned as ever, and despite the other screaming discords, sex was still a perfect blending.

If my emotions couldn't be trusted, my instincts were infallible. Take Schwartz's case, for instance. Somehow, sometime, my intuition told me, this man would make a difference in my life. Aryeh Schwartz had been admitted with a bleeding ulcer, and no one else on duty spoke sufficient English to attend him. Although a government official, about the only word he knew in Hebrew was *"shalom."* He claimed he never had the time to learn. The truth was that he had no gift for languages, but his other talents were so valuable to Israel that everyone accepted the excuse.

South African in origin, educated in Great Britain, Aryeh was a master strategist in every area of economics. His specialty was cultivating overseas investment in Israeli enterprises, and he concentrated on Americans, with notable success. Few businessmen or manufacturers—or *anyone* who influenced the flow of funds—escaped from Israel without a Schwartzian sales pitch. A good percentage of the time, it coaxed a signature on something that would aid the state.

A most important man, he was accustomed to the finest that the country had to offer, including medical attention. Stricken suddenly, however, he'd been stuck with me. On my appearance at his bedside, he'd made his feelings known, exclaiming, "But you're just a kid!" Looking even younger than my years, I'd long since learned to deal with that reaction. Responding, "I'm a doctor," I shut him up by shoving a thermometer between his lips. Comments on my age annoyed me, but wanting to impress this man without yet knowing why, I set about the Schwartz exam with extra crisp efficiency.

The blood loss was apparent in his pallor, and his pulse was racing, but sick or not, I felt him sizing up my moves and making judgments. I must have satisfied his standards because I later found he'd asked that I continue to attend him for the two weeks he was with us.

Although our ages and our interests, to say nothing of our social and financial standing, were much too far apart for normal friendship, by the time he left, Aryeh had elected to become a kind of patron. He kept telling me I had potential, and hinted at some future help. On his checkup visits to the hospital, we talked at length, but only on the subject of my medical ambitions; I don't recall our touching on another topic such as soccer scores or family affairs. As far as I could tell, Schwartz *had* no interests outside work; that's why he had his ulcer. Since I spoke of medicine with much the same intensity, he must have sensed a kindred spirit.

Once I dropped a casual remark about my going to America "sometime" to take more training. Schwartz seized on this with thunderous approval and enthusiastically insisted that I think of him as my "American connection." When I was ready for the U.S.A., he said, I was to call him, and on his final visit to Hadassah, he wrote the number that would reach him. Appreciating that the gratitude of patients faded once the pain was gone, I shouldn't have placed much stock in Schwartz's offer. My instinct told me, though, to keep his number safely tucked away.

49

If Ada was content with what she got from me, I decided that I'd go along and leave off struggling to escape her. The guilt I'd fought against was almost gone. She had to know by now that we were going nowhere but to bed together.

Oh, we did get out, but always by ourselves. If not *alone* alone, she saw to it that we remained an isolated island in a sea of people. Once I'd thought she might be phobic, but it wasn't fear of people in the mass that made her antisocial. Holding hands with me, she was perfectly at ease among the hundreds in a concert hall or milling at an exhibition. She only shied away from smaller and more intimate environments where, in Ada's eyes, any one of my acquaintances was competition. If my attention strayed for just an instant, her anxiety was nakedly apparent. Since anyone outside my family awakened apprehension, my time with Ada was restricted to a tiny circle—mainly us.

Leaving her one evening, I was too distressed to settle down and study. I tried to walk away the tension, and striding blindly, slammed into a stanchion; I hardly felt the impact, but I did feel foolish. Luckily, the streets were almost empty. Unlike Tel Aviv, Jerusalem was not a "late" town, so I was quite surprised to see an unescorted woman coming toward me, and more startled still to hear her say, "Good evening, Doctor." Out of uniform, I hadn't recognized Tzivia.

A nurse in Pediatrics, she was darkly beautiful, and I'd noticed her, of course. When I learned her father was from Iraq, I'd been eager to engage her in a conversation, but at the hospital, she was the target of the whole unmarried staff, and I stayed away, afraid she'd figure me for just another male on the make.

Face to face now, I asked where she was heading at this time of night, assuming she was off on some emergency and needed aid. Single women just didn't wander in the streets so late. Her response was that she'd had a sudden urge for ice cream. Intrigued, I asked if I might join her.

Licking cones, conversing like the best of friends, we walked along without a destination. With a pleasant shock, I realized I was having fun. For the first time since the early days with Ada, I wasn't weighing every word. And also for the first time ever, I was holding a protracted talk in Hebrew with a woman. With Ada, our exchanges were in snips of several languages, none of which were native. Linguistic nuances were difficult between us, and while feelings could be acted out, humor was impossible. Now Tzivia had me telling jokes!

Submitting to another impulse, I suggested that she walk me home. All she asked was "Why?" with no fluttering of eyelids or pretense of shock. I answered as succinctly. "I write poetry. I'd like to read you some."

In my room, riffling through my verses, I quickly recognized that most—my finest efforts—were much too passionate to speak aloud, especially on such short acquaintanceship. I found a poem on social justice, then segued into several odes to nature. Inspired by her rapt attention, I read the least emotional of my effusions, and in step-by-step progression, finally arrived at those which throbbed with love.

When she shifted on my only chair to circumvent a broken slat, I invited her to sit beside me on the bed. With a blissful sigh, she swept her legs up under her. First our arms brushed lightly, then our shoulders touched. When she didn't withdraw, I said I'd like to sleep with her. Bluntly, as before, she asked me why. "Because I like you," I replied. She searched my face, apparently approved of what she saw, and slowly started to remove her clothes.

When I walked her to the hospital, we parted with a friendly kiss. The episode was over. Passing in the hallway of Hadassah, a dozen hours after bedding down together, we exchanged a chaste *"Shalom."*

Uncommon happenings continued to occur. That very afternoon, Dr. Bromberg, Chief of the Obstetric Section, called me to his office. Abruptly, he began to pay me compliments, and suspicious of such fulsome praise, I waited for the axe to fall. When he finally got down to business, and delivered the expected "blow," I almost burst out laughing.

Bromberg had been fawning to fill another vacancy; I was wanted in Beersheba, and the "sacrifice" he asked of me was much more like a godsend! If I agreed, I'd be replacing the Director of Obstetrics for about eight weeks. Would I take it on? Would I! Full doctor's pay again, chief of a department, and a second chance to cut the bonds connecting me with Ada. Safad was too inviting, but even Ada would be daunted by Beersheba.

The only flaw in this arrangement was the town itself. Leaving *here* for *there* was like trading in a diamond for a lump of dung. That's why Bromberg felt compelled to flatter me so much. Beersheba was a blemish on the map.

In 1948, swarming northward in its first attempt to scuttle Israel, the Egyptian army occupied the area. Until that time, Beersheba had been Bedouin. Outfought by the Israelis, the Egyptians had retreated, and the residents had fled with them. The few who weren't scared away by warnings that the Jews would drink their blood were living on the edge of town in tents. Now a dingy, sandy Jewish city, stuck down south of anywhere you'd want to be, it had the hospital alone to recommend it. The sole facility in the entire Negev, it served about 10,000 people.

With a week to go before I left, I made a date with Ada—if all went well, our last. The episode with Tzivia had put affairs in crystal-clear perspective. Before our night together, I'd never had a standard of comparison, not only in the sphere of sex, but in the normal interaction of the sexes.

With Tzivia, conversation had been unconstrained. We'd been free and easy with each other, falling into step—and into bed—as instinctively and easily as drawing breath. Nothing had been plotted out ahead, but the smallest move involving Ada required the most careful planning.

Take now, for instance. Here I was, sitting in a movie house, oblivious to what was on the screen, mentally composing a scenario: "How to Break the News about Beersheba." Before we went to bed or after? Loving first might make her more receptive. Or I could tell her first, then stop her tears with sex.

At Michi's, with my arms around her, I told her I was off again. As a guarantee of isolation, I only said, "The Negev."

When the time arrived, I wouldn't let her take me to the station, but on leaving her to make my bus, my tongue and brain lost contact for a moment, and unthinkingly I said, "I'll see you when I get back from Beersheba." Ada smiled blindingly. In mentioning the town, I'd as much as issued her an invitation.

Beersheba was even drabber than described to me. The hospital was purely functional. Prefabricated, like the temporary, shacklike structures of the camps, it offered nothing but the basics. There were no amenities to ease the workload. A shabby and abandoned mosque on one side of a dusty central square was the only evidence of pre-Israeli occupation. On the bright side, there'd be nothing to distract me from my studies. Exams were coming up the end of May, shortly after this assignment ended.

The range of work surprised me; for so small a hospital, we handled a heroic load. Though I'd been sent specifically to manage OB-Gyn, with only eight of us to deal with all complaints, we often had to spell each other, overlapping into everything. The atmosphere reminded me of Persia and the Kurdish camp.

Other memories were stirred when I discovered that the great majority of patients were Iraqis who'd been settled in Beersheba. Since they'd never had a doctor who could speak their dialect before, everyone insisted on my services no matter what their symptoms.

At times, the Hippocratic oath was hard to live by in Beersheba. At 2 A.M., just days into the job, I rushed into Emergency to find a dead Israeli soldier on a stretcher, another with a superficial bullet wound, and a gravely injured Arab terrorist who'd shot them both. The pull of blood struggled with the oath I'd taken. My impulse was to tend my fellow Jew, but in my first decision of the sort, emotion bowed to ethics. As I started on the Arab, a lecture from my freshman year echoed in my mind.

"Put politics and personalities aside. They have no place in medicine. The sickest must be cared for first, with no exceptions."

A noble sentiment—but still Haron had died. I hadn't thought about my cousin since Iraq, and the surge of hatred toward his killers made me extra careful with the Arab.

In Beersheba, I called on all I'd ever learned, even practicing psychology. Outside Emergency one night, some thirty Kurds were noisily involved in interfamily feuding. The fight was mostly verbal, but as fists began to fly, I intervened in the little of the language I remembered. As far as I could tell, the family of the ailing girl was saying that her husband had brought about her illness. His side screamed his innocence. Effecting a cease-fire for the moment, I went to see the wife.

Sixteen at most, she lay there like a corpse. Keening shrilly, her mother hovered over her; the husband, a scared young teen himself, was wedged into a corner with his head between his knees.

I knew at once my patient wasn't comatose. What I *didn't* know was why the girl was faking. I could have stuck a pin in her, exposing the deception, but instead of solving what was probably a minor problem, that could escalate the fight into full-scale family warfare. To gain some time, I ordered everybody out except the nurse. Sounding as stentorian as possible, I said, "Let's get her clothes off." Before we even touched the sheet, still less her outer wrappings, the youngster's eyes shot open and she sat upright.

The modesty of Kurdish women is excessive, so I figured that a threat to strip her was the surest, fastest way to end the farce. On my promise not to bare her fraud, she told me how it came to pass.

Her new young husband had spoken to her sharply, and to scare him out of doing it again, she'd fallen in a "faint." Since the families were both at odds before she could "recover," she was stuck with her unconscious state.

Honoring my promise, I told her husband that I'd brought her back; from the look of him, he wouldn't yell at her again for years. As for the families, I informed them that the fault was nature's, not her husband's. She needed peace and quiet. No more arguments, I ordered, and everyone subsided.

Right after that, when I was feeling most expansive and at peace, Ada made her first appearance at Beersheba. For eight long hours, every other weekend after that, she'd travel on a sprung-seat, bumpy bus to see me for a single day. As in Safad, she'd decided on this schedule herself; ending or extending it was strictly up to her.

With the Beersheba stint behind me and back to finish out the last few weeks before exams, I intended to spend all my extra time with textbooks. Until I took my finals at the end of May, I told Ada that I wouldn't be around.

The tears were swimming on the surface of her eyes, trembling on the lid, and I tried my best to stop them. "Just weeks," I pleaded. "I have seven years invested in these tests. I have to pass them."

"I know," she choked, but when and if I wanted her, she said, all I had to do was drop by Michi's.

True to form, and much to my dismay, I found myself at Michi's far too often. Though I never gave her any warning, she was always in and eagerly expectant; if her brother wasn't out already, he'd be on his way in minutes. For a little while, I'd forget exams and everything but Ada; and every time I left her, I said it was the last time I'd be over.

With sixty other students from half a dozen hospitals I took the tests, and passed with flying colors. As soon as the results were posted, Hadassah offered me a bona fide internship. With scarcely any change except in status, I went back to work. At last, Israel acknowledged me as what I'd been since Baghdad: a graduate physician. Still, one final step remained.

In Israel, a thesis was required before a medical degree was granted. However, I had a year in which to do it, and with the pressure off, my rapport with Ada gradually improved. Earning money, socially at ease, and surer of myself in all respects, I was more relaxed with her and less inclined to prickle at the least annoyance.

In some areas, we never argued; as much as bed, music was our meeting ground. The Heifetz concerts, just announced, naturally excited our attention, but only two had been arranged, and seats were unobtainable. However, we participated in a way by wearing out his old recordings, and we planned to pick up all the papers for reviews of both recitals.

Last night, he'd played the first of them in Tel Aviv but critiques, as such, were absent. Instead, the concert had made headlines.

Heifetz had performed a Wagner piece, and the audience had indicated its displeasure. Most Israelis had defended him at first, assuming simple thoughtlessness, but public outrage had exploded when Heifetz stated that his program would remain unchanged; he intended to play Wagner in Jerusalem, as well, though every high official had asked him to eliminate the work. Revered by Hitler, Wagner's music was the leitmotif of every German victory and mocked each Jewish victim. Many refugees would sicken at the merest strain of it, but Heifetz had refused to budge. Unencumbered by their memories, he'd only say, "Music has no ideology."

Over lunch with Ada, our conversation centered on his thesis. It might be valid in a perfect world I granted, or in a vacuum, but it wouldn't work where human feelings were involved.

Unexpectedly, Ada backed the Heifetz view. Color high, and rather haughtily reminding me that music was her area of expertise, she repeated his contention that art transcended politics. Heating up myself, I responded that the great majority of Europe's Jews were less sophisticated. "Not all of them are violinists," I retorted, arguing that visceral reactions were more honest than her own approach. "It could be they were closer to the ovens," I concluded.

Our discussion was rapidly degenerating into real contention when someone poked his head inside the coffee shop and shouted to his waiter-friend, "Heifetz has been wounded."

Dispute forgotten, I ran to grab a paper and read with great relief that he'd only suffered scratches. At the table, Ada's face was ashen and her lips looked thin as pencil lines. Before I could assure her that it wasn't serious, she spat, "My God! It must have been a *Marocani!*"

I stopped dead-still. What shocked me most was how she'd said the words. They'd been so instantly available. The very lack of adjectives was chilling. No need to emphasize what everybody knew—that those "other" Jews were just barbarians. Loud, uncouth, uncultured *"Marocani"*—or substitute another subdivision of *Sephardim.* Any one of us would do.

I headed for the street, so torn inside I thought I might disgrace myself by throwing up. Through the haze of rage and sickness, I could hear her crying after me, "Come back!" I fled as from a plague.

50

For the third time in a row, I went home to Tel Aviv without inviting Ada, and no one asked about her, probably at Baba's order. He'd known for some time now that our relationship was not the same.

Being with the family was as soothing as a Turkish bath. Nana had effected a complete recovery, and Baba's skill had been rewarded by a slightly better job. At almost sixteen, my younger sister was enjoying every second of existence. Pretty and vivacious, Osa had a host of friends and happy prospects for the future. After finishing her business training, she could pick and choose among a multitude of lucrative positions.

Daisy had some problems. Older, less convivial than Osa, and acclimated longer to a different kind of life, she had difficulty fitting in. A skillful seamstress, she chose to stay at home and earn some money sewing. Close to twenty, and by Iraqi standards more than ready for the *chupah,* she bristled at the idea of a marriage broker, but while shying from the old ways, she wasn't up, as yet, to mingling on her own with adult men. Caught between the cultures, Daisy had withdrawn a little, but I thought I saw some signs of her emergence.

Avram, on the other hand, was altogether integrated. The highest-ranking student in his class and just about to graduate from grade school, his optimism knew no bounds. According to my brother, *everything* was possible in Israel. The only hurdle here was money. Elementary school was free, but tuition loomed ahead for higher education, and all of us would have to help.

On the whole, I was proud of our substantial progress. Certainly the worst was over; with all of us advancing and continuing to add to our resources, the future of the family seemed finally secure enough for me to concentrate entirely on my career.

With my internship half over, I hadn't yet decided on a specialty. The trouble was that almost every one of them intrigued me. Like a kid who had to pick a single cookie from a storeful, I couldn't make a choice. At last, I lopped the list to two. Surgery or ophthalmology.

Of the other interns, all but Spelnick opted for the fields that I'd foreseen, but Spelnick had selected Pediatrics. I couldn't believe my ears! Spelnick was money-mad, gregarious, and oversexed; the only "babes" I'd ever seen him smile on were several years past puberty. But being Spelnick, naturally he had an angle. Babies were increasingly big business.

"They're money in the bank," he gloated. "Good as oil wells! All you have to do is look around you."

And he was right, of course. The swarms of kids were everywhere, and every other girl, it seemed, was only days away from parturition. Pregnancy, in Israel, was epidemic.

"The *land* should be as fertile. . . ."

Spelnick's mouth was moving, but in my head I heard a voice that wasn't his, and Kurdish words seeped through the Hebrew. Gradually the landscape of the Kurdish camp obliterated Spelnick. The second camp in Teheran. The woman I was seeing in my classmate's stead was seventeen at most, a child herself, but old enough to have an infant of her own.

I knew so little Kurdish that at first I thought I hadn't heard correctly. The bundle she had handed me was much too light to be a living baby. Perhaps a baby's toy, a little puppet made of sticks and covered with a kind of parchment. And then I felt the "puppet" twitch.

A tiny, wizened mummy, the boy was drained so dry by diarrhea that his very eyes were arid. He was mewling like a kitten but he couldn't cry. Tears require moisture. With the gentlest touch, his skin would crease and hold the folds.

I ordered glucose and saline solution, knowing he was too far gone, but praying for a miracle. We had no intravenous rig—not that it mattered. The baby's veins were shrunken into strands the size of spider silk, slimmer than the finest i.v. needle. I'd have to pump the fluid through the skin.

The syringe was fully half the infant's length. I moved to shield the mother from the sight, but as the needle pierced her son, she screamed. I felt the tip touch bone and grate on it. There wasn't any flesh, and the liquid lumped beneath the dermal layer. Frantically, aware of how it had to hurt, I dug my fingers in, breaking up the solid ball to send the fluid through the shriveled tissues. The baby was so close to death, I couldn't tell exactly when he slipped away.

Somehow, he looked less ravaged, and when I picked him up and turned to her, she took him with a cry of joy and cradled him. Between her thanks to God, she blessed "the *Dektôr.*" That much I understood, and I shriveled like the son she thought was sleeping. I had to tell her, but I didn't know how. I knew few words in Kurdish—none of comfort. All that I could say was *"met."* Your son is dead.

As I forced the image from my mind, and Spelnick and the hospital returned to view, my throat remained constricted, the deadly word still stuck in it. But words would never stick in Spelnick's throat. Right through my passage back to Persia, he'd been peddling Pediatrics like a hot new stock. When I picked it, as I now intended, he'd undoubtedly take credit for converting me. I couldn't care less, though of course it wasn't Spelnick or the soaring birth rate. I'd had to summon up the little mummy to remind me that prolonging life had always been my prime objective, and of all the sick and suffering, the youngest, at the start of life, had most of life to lose. Helped by modern medicine, they also had the most to gain. Since I'd come down on the side of life while struggling with the drowning *Mislim,* how better could I serve than taking care of kids?

Early in December, shortly after making my decision, I received a call from Aryeh Schwartz. No, his ulcer wasn't acting up; his health, he said, was excellent. He was phoning to invite me for a drink. "I have friends here from America, people you should meet."

Perhaps I should have said again that such a meeting would be premature by many years. Someday, indeed, I hoped to study in America, but certainly not now, nor very soon. Since Aryeh knew my plans, however, I concluded that he'd probably just called me on the impulse of the moment, and only for the drink he offered. At the bar, therefore, I was wholly unprepared for Schwartz's sales pitch. Following the introductions, he fell to work at once, informing the Americans of my ambition to study in the U.S.A. Would they aid me in obtaining an appointment?

The five men sitting at the table nodded. Naturally they'd help a friend of Aryeh's, but he should have spoken sooner. A residency really worth my while wasn't easily arranged. Still, I shouldn't worry, and they winked at me.

My head was whirling. Americans moved even faster than Israelis. Before I could explain, they were on their feet as one, and off to do another deal.

Though I was sure that Aryeh's friends were simply being civil, I sent them resumés, as they requested, and promptly put the matter out of mind. America was someday . . . maybe . . . far off in the future, if at all. For now, and as far ahead as I could see, I'd be practicing in Israel, in Pediatrics.

If everything panned out as planned, I'd be working under Dr. Berman. A residency was about to open up in his department. Of course I needed his endorsement, and probably he'd sweat me some, but in the end, he'd certainly confirm me. In my three months on his service, he'd indicated more than ordinary interest in my progress and had even said I had a special aptitude for Pediatrics.

Walking toward the cafeteria to catch him on his coffee break, I thought back to our first encounter. His comic multicolor mustache and halo of electrified and orange hair almost blinded one to what he was—the shrewdest, most discerning diagnostic expert at Hadassah. While his approach to medicine was strictly orthodox, his habits were as wildly offbeat as his appearance.

For one thing, you could find him anytime by following his trail of burned-out cigarette butts. A zone of stale smoke surrounded him, and every pair of pants he owned was honeycombed with holes from falling sparks. Spelnick, fresh from service in the Psych ward, said that Berman sucked on cigarettes for oral satisfaction. He also analyzed the way he sat, with skinny legs wrapped twice around and locked together at the ankles.

"It's plain as day! He masturbates through every lecture!"

Watching closely, I could half-believe it, but it didn't bother me a bit. Whatever else the rubbing of his thighs accomplished, the action seemed to stimulate his brain. I'd never listened to such trenchant, lucid lectures.

However, I was less forgiving of another of his quirks. While he called the other interns by their given names, me he called "Iraqi." The first time he addressed me so, I figured it was just a friendly joke. With repetition, though, the "joke" wore thin. When I finally expressed my feelings, he looked at me with owl-eyed astonishment.

"I thought you understood," he said, "I'm doing it to sensitize you." He smiled benignly, in the evident belief that everything was crystal clear now. My expression disabused him.

"Perhaps I should have said '*de*-sensitize' you?"

He searched my face again and saw that I was still confused. Lips pursed in disappointment at my slowness, he shook his head and started over.

"An Iraqi doctor is considered 'different,' and in this imperfect world, 'different' almost automatically inspires fear. Depending on the circumstances, such fear gives rise to hatred or contempt."

I recognized his lecture style; this once, I wished that he were less precise and comprehensive.

"Other people think of you as 'the Iraqi,' " he continued, "and they call you that behind your back. Some of them will say it to your face—with malice or contempt. *I* say it so you'll be accustomed to the sound of it. In time, you'll be so used to it, you'll hardly even hear it."

Berman positively preened, completely satisfied with his "solution" to my problem. Before I could articulate my arguments—the main one being that I'd never thought "Iraqi" was in any sense an epithet—he checked his watch, whistled at the time, and loped away, with "Come, Iraqi, we'll be late for rounds."

Thinking of that past encounter, I almost missed his entrance. Berman took his coffee at the counter and was looking for a table when I caught his eye and beckoned to the empty seat beside me. I hadn't seen him since the test results were posted, and his warm "Well done, Iraqi!" encouraged me to say right out, "I'm applying for your Residency."

I didn't expect he'd dance a *hora,* but neither had I figured on a silent stare. When he spoke, he sounded somber.

"Iraqi, are you sure?"

I specified how sure I was, and in rebuttal, Berman talked for twenty nonstop minutes, trying hard to push me into general practice. And not just any general practice, but G.P. on a *farm.* Selling hard, he sounded like a second Spelnick.

"The good that you could do!" He positively glowed. "Take an agricultural community. A *moshav.* Maybe a *kibbutz.*" Leaning forward in his seat, he sprinkled ashes in my applesauce. "You'd do wonders, and you'd love the *kibbutz* life!"

How had he arrived at that, I wanted to inquire. He knew that I'd been born and bred in Baghdad, and Baghdad was about as far from a *kibbutz* as you could get, but he continued to expound the theme: The noblest, healthiest, most patriotic practice I could hope to have was "with the people."

I tried to stem the torrent with "What about the people in the cities?" My interjection didn't even slow him down. In a settlement, he said, I wouldn't "sink into the rut of any single specialty."

He hadn't sunk in *his* rut, but he brushed off all my arguments, saying that he only wanted what was best for me. I believed him—but I also knew that I knew better what was best for me. I steeled myself to ask the crucial question.

"Don't you think that I could do the job?"

Looking stricken, he spent another twenty minutes assuring me of his belief in my ability, but made me promise to consider what he'd said. After due reflection, if I decided I still wanted it, he'd write the letter recommending me for Pediatrics.

Of course he couldn't know, but the promise he'd exacted had already been fulfilled. I'd already looked into the life he thought I'd love. The moment Berman said *kibbutz,* memories of Gidon and Geva swamped me.

Gidon, a boyhood friend and fellow member of the underground in Baghdad, was now a member of the Geva settlement. He was living there when I arrived in Israel, and as soon as possible, I'd spent a weekend with him. Like every immigrant, I felt obliged to visit a commune, and judging from his passionate portrayal, Gidon's was almost Eden.

While knowing that the northern Negev wasn't really desert like the Sinai, the greenery of Geva still proved startling. Made possible by subterranean springs, this improbable oasis sat squarely in the center of a stony wasteland. The edges of the settlement were so precise, the angles so exact, it seemed not merely man-made but machined. Each patch of planted land abruptly ended in a line of green against a straight-ruled edge of ocher. From a distance, it appeared that not a single grain of sand encroached upon the growing crop, and not a spear of green extended into sterile space.

The buildings, barracklike and graceless, were also green, as if the color, even painted, was a comfort to the eye of the *kibbutzniks.* Little lizards, identical in hue, sunned themselves on every surface, invisible until a sound disturbed them and they scuttled off to safety. For the safety of the settlers, a lookout tower loomed above the other structures, and all were ringed about by man-high rows of heavily barbed wire.

Except for Gidon's face, everything I saw was strange. Ever the enthusiast, he grabbed my arm and dragged me off to gaze on Geva's wonders. Evangelically intense, he exhibited, with equal fervor, an irrigation ditch, a kindergarten class, a chicken hatchery, and a huge and steaming compost heap at which he sniffed as if it were perfume. At an intricate assembly in the pumping system, he pointed out the perfect welds and positively beamed. In Baghdad, even in the throes of love, I'd never seen him so excited.

In the combination meeting room and mess hall, loaded weapons lined the walls; on entering, everyone would stack his rifle, but not so far away he couldn't reach it quickly. At lunch that afternoon, I stuffed myself on better food than any of the cities had to offer. Gideon kept filling up my dish, filling me, as well, with all the relevant statistics of each serving. With the carp, he instructed me on raising fish in reservoirs, and passing bread, he bragged that they were growing twice the wheat the Arabs ever harvested from equal acreage. The bowl of grapes elicited the information that their yield of fruit was five times more abundant than before. "You should have come last week," the others at the table chorused. "We had wild duck for dinner." The lushness of the land was bringing back the migratory birds. As Gidon put it, "They flew right over Palestine, but they stop to feed in Israel."

"And they wind up fat and happy—and filling our Israeli stomachs," but expressing what I thought would have been ungracious. While my stomach was content, the rest of me rebelled.

The story of the birds had merely emphasized that everybody pays a price. You get, you give. What irked me here at Geva was the lack of options. What if I'd been hungry when it wasn't time to eat? Everything was too well organized by others to appeal to me. A committee laid your life out, and that's the way you had to live it. I understood the reasons for the strict regime and was honestly impressed with all my countrymen had done, but a weekend was enough. This style of life was simply not for me.

Aside from all the rules and regulations, the commune was much too quiet, much too uniform, and just plain too predictable to keep my juices flowing. I liked variety and ferment and the feeling that I might find something strange and wonderful around a corner. The unexpectedness of city life was like adrenalin. I was stimulated by the noise of city streets, and I thrived on competition.

As promised, I'd examined the alternative and found it wanting. I wanted Pediatrics and Hadassah. Now it was Berman's turn to honor our agreement.

I waited overnight and caught him as he left his office in the morning. On hearing my decision, Berman blinked and nodded briefly. The letter would be sent. All he said was "Please don't pin your hopes on it. Anything can happen."

The final phrase disturbed me, but I satisfied myself that it was merely a conventional disclaimer. With his endorsement and the grades I'd gotten, what could possibly go wrong?

51

Only five months of internship and a thesis now stood between a certified, completely kosher medical degree and me. Though the dissertation wasn't due for months, I'd already done the research and was halfway through the writing. "Intravenous Angiography in Congenital Heart Disease" would soon be ready for submission.

With prices ever rising, and Avram's education to finance, it was imperative that I start earning more than intern's pay. I therefore asked the Dean if there was any way an earlier degree might be awarded. By March, I thought my thesis would be finished. Might I submit it then instead of waiting until June? The Dean agreed, and in deference to my experience in Teheran, also waived my last few months of service, "providing that your paper is acceptable, of course."

Aware that Berman was a member of the *concours* committee which would pass or fail the paper, I honed and polished endlessly, intent on making it exceptional, not merely adequate. The paper, plus endorsement by the *concours* was my pass to the post in Pediatrics. Study as I would, I couldn't find a flaw in my projection.

Slaving at the thesis, I saw less and less of Ada. With an unimpeachable excuse for my neglect, for once I felt no guilt.

In early March, I turned my thesis in; on the 23rd, the Dean informed me that the committee had accepted it "with honors." Since no diplomas had as yet been printed, the certificate they issued me was marked "provisional," and typed out on an ordinary letterhead. Holding it, I had to laugh. I'd graduated for the second time and *still* had no diploma. In June, however, I could trade this makeshift in for something more official. In the meantime, formal document or not, I was the first to earn a doctorate in medicine in modern Israel.

On the following day, a letter from Hadassah brought me back to earth. I'd forgotten that receipt of a degree meant automatic termination as an intern. I was a full-fledged doctor, and I was also unemployed. Mechanically, I opened up a second letter, only to be stunned anew. Children's Hospital, Boston, Massachusetts, wished to see my resumé. If it satisfied requirements, I'd be invited to submit my application for a Pediatrics residency.

So it hadn't been just idle talk! Aryeh's friends had intervened, not only on the highest level, but at supersonic speed. In the Middle East, a project that entailed paperwork could easily take months to move from one desk in an office to another.

While buoyed by the show of interest, I also felt abashed at having put the men to so much bother. Over drinks that day, I should have made my plans a whole lot plainer. I wasn't ready for America. Not even close to ready. Study in the U.S.A. was for the future—maybe five years off. Nonetheless, courtesy demanded that I answer Children's Hospital. Out of curiosity, I would have done so anyway, just to see if I could qualify for the appointment. Berman's sermon on the joys of general practice had eaten at my absolute assurance.

Not that Berman worried me. I told myself that there were valid reasons for his rather negative reaction. Senior interns were notorious for switching specialities. Remembering the other disciplines I'd almost picked, I figured he was testing my fidelity to Pediatrics. If I wavered in the face of opposition, naturally he wouldn't want me. "Dedication" was among his favorite words.

By now he knew I couldn't be swayed; my grades were close to perfect, and my thesis had been highly praised. By all criteria, I was better qualified to fill the post than any other applicant.

Though the *concours* as a body made the ultimate decision, it always backed the candidates endorsed by the department heads. In light of that, I thought of something that would show the strength of my commitment.

Berman's staff was overworked, and I decided that I'd offer him my services. I'd have several months in which to slide into the resident's routine before the *concours* met and made a permanent appointment. When named, I'd already know the job from A to Z, which would surely be to Berman's benefit.

Under *any* circumstances, I'd have picked this post with him, but the system made a staff position almost mandatory. Through Histadrut, nearly everyone in Israel was covered by a health plan, leaving little of the populace to private practice, and the great majority of doctors apparently approved of the arrangement. Competition for a staff appointment in a top facility was fierce. Once acquired, such a job was safe for life. Those eliminated by their first-choice institutions would wind up lower down the line, in less prestigious clinics, convalescent homes, *kibbutzim,* and so on.

I could understand why middle-aged physicians sought the safety of a state-supported post; an older refugee, uprooted once already from a well-established practice, would look on lifelong tenure as a dream come true. As for me, however, staying anywhere forever—even here—was the most appalling prospect I could possibly imagine. Like a limb immobilized in plaster, my spirit withered when confined too long.

After qualifying at Hadassah, perhaps I'd teach part-time or branch out into pediatric research. I might even take a second specialty. All these airy plans were perfectly achievable as long as they were anchored to a firm foundation—the hospital affiliation that I sought with Berman.

At Hadassah, ostensibly to say goodbye and gather up my personal belongings, I was really there to waylay Berman. Relaxing with a smoke and coffee when I caught him, he offered his congratulations on my thesis and invited me to join him. Some small talk later, I asked if I could work for him until the *concours* met and made its choice.

The beaming face turned blank. "We've been over this before," he snapped, and firmly shut the door on more discussion. As I rose to leave, he softened his abrupt dismissal by saying that he'd sent the letter I requested. "Now let's leave it to the hospital committee."

Hearing that, my hopes revived. A stickler for the rules, Berman was reluctant to advance me as a candidate too strongly. I could see his point. If he hired me, the other members of the *concours* might feel pressured. It would appear that he'd already picked me, almost forcing them to ratify his choice. They might be so resentful they'd exclude me in revenge. Of course he couldn't hire me, and thanking him, I hurried off.

Though convinced of my eventual appointment to Hadassah, I nonetheless decided to pursue some other avenues "in case." For future reference, I'd already written to the A.M.A., asking for a list of U.S. hospitals, but my current concentration was on Tel Aviv.

Without a job, staying in Jerusalem was senseless, so I moved in with the family again, telling Ada to continue where she was since I expected to be back in June. In Tel Aviv, I made appointments with the Pediatric chiefs of all the leading hospitals; from each I got the same reaction. Why here with me? Why not with Berman? No one from Hadassah ever went elsewhere by choice.

What answer could I give without an hour's worth of exposition? Each meeting also came to the identical conclusion: "We don't have any openings."

In the midst of this, the booklet from the A.M.A. arrived, and only deepened my depression. In addition to the list of U.S. hospitals accredited for residency training, the catalogue included all the foreign and domestic schools of medicine which met with A.M.A. approval. Naturally, I looked for Israel.

Ireland was there, then Italy. There wasn't any Israel. Our school of medicine was unaccredited. Two degrees and *still* shut out? It wasn't possible! Panic swept me and I ran to find a phone. Exhorting me to calm myself, the Dean himself explained the system, and the fist that squeezed my stomach slowly opened.

Our curriculum, he said, had been examined and was satisfactory in all respects; the A.M.A. would list us when enough degrees had been awarded. Having earned the very first of them was proving more a handicap than help. So even if I'd wanted it, America was also out for now. Everything was at an impasse until June, when the entire class would graduate and get us recognition. Then too, of course, the *concours* would convene. In the meantime, I was going crazy.

Ada had been writing to me every day, clearly angling for an invitation. Nervous and depressed, I needed her and wanted her, but knew that in my present mood, I'd only make her miserable. Hyperactive to begin with—with all the pent-up energy undrained by work—I felt myself a ticking bomb, apt to detonate at even tender touching.

Constitutionally I couldn't sit still, but only empty days awaited me. Too tense to read or eat, I couldn't even sink myself in study. Aware of how such marking time affected me, Nana kept inventing errands, and Avram suddenly required help with homework. Everyone was extra careful not to ask me questions. Even Osa treated me as if I were an invalid.

Ten days after leaving, I returned to job hunt in Jerusalem and headed for Hadassah, intending to apply to Personnel for anything at all that might be open. For the six-week stretch before the *concours,* I could stand the dullest drudge work.

In the old familiar atmosphere, my appetite returned, and I dropped into the cafeteria to have some breakfast. I was dawdling over coffee when Dr. Davis stopped to say *"shalom"* and ask what I was doing with myself. Davis was a research man, currently investigating vascular disease, and my paper had impressed him. When I told him I was looking for a job, he said, "Well, you can stop. You have one. Report to me at 8:00 A.M."

Dumbfounded, I could only nod. By the sheerest luck, I'd landed not just work, but work with someone who was sitting on the hospital committee. The way I'd slave for him, I'd have him telling all his colleagues on the *concours* (of course including Berman) what a dedicated worker Haddad was.

Settled in my room again, gainfully employed and with my goal in sight, I felt serene enough to start up, cautiously, with Ada.

Davis supervised a special section of the clinic. We dealt entirely with cardiovascular disease, and my time was mainly spent in taking pressures, issuing the usual prescriptions, and scolding obese patients when they gained a pound. While not my dream of medicine, it more than served its purpose as an interim assignment.

Everything was breaking right. Five days after starting on the job, I received another letter from America; despite Hadassah's lack of listing, I was acceptable to Children's Hospital. In my response to their offer of a residency, they asked me to include a letter from the Israel Medical Association, stating that I stood in good repute. I hadn't joined the I.M.A. as yet, but membership was almost automatic on submission of an application.

Calling Aryeh Schwartz to acquaint him with the news, I fought down shame. My gratitude was real enough, but I didn't intend to take the offer. I'd be using it—and using Aryeh—and though no one would be hurt, I hated the deceit I planned to practice.

The idea had occurred to me the moment that I read the letter. This Boston job could guarantee the job I wanted—in Jerusalem. When Berman saw the letter . . . when I told him I'd rejected the appointment . . . that I'd rather work with him . . . he'd *have* to be impressed. Children's Hospital was probably the most prestigious pediatric institution in the world, and my choosing to remain with him would make him realize how much his residency really meant to me. I knew my aptitude had never been in question, and this gesture would convince him of my single-minded and unswerving purpose.

Long white envelope in hand, I was on my way to Berman's office when I skidded to a stop. Technically, I realized, the offer was conditional. To make the strongest impact possible, I'd do better holding off until I got the I.M.A. endorsement, sent it on to Boston, and received, in turn, a final and unqualified commitment. *That's* the one I'd wave in Berman's face.

At the Medical Association, I filed the proper form, explained the situation to the Secretary, and asked for the confirmatory letter. Since the residency started on July 1, time was growing short, and the Secretary promised that he'd expedite my application. Relying on his word, I wrote to Boston, stating that the I.M.A. endorsement would be sent posthaste.

When notified of my admission, I called to thank the Secretary of the I.M.A. and ask again about the letter. His attitude this time was strictly formal. Yes, he'd seen the chairman on the matter, and, no, the letter wasn't ready. No letter would be written. My request had been refused.

When I pressed him for an explanation, he icily informed me that he had none. The ruling made, the matter was completely closed. Every trace of friendliness had disappeared, and giving up on him at last, I insisted on an early meeting with the chairman and executive committee. I stressed the urgency, but the first appointment he would give me was a month away. By then, the *concours* would have met. Still, I heard myself agreeing to the date. At the very least, I'd find out why they wouldn't support me.

I could still make do with what I had in hand, what I thought of now as the "original" Boston letter. In itself, it was sufficiently impressive. To ensure its being fresh in Berman's mind, I decided that I wouldn't display it until just before the all-important meeting.

In his office by appointment on the designated day, I whipped the letter out and watched his eyes sweep down the page. When they reached "Sincerely yours," I launched into a well-rehearsed oration. Boston wanted me, but all I wanted, I reiterated, was to work with him.

When I took the letter from his hand, and crumpled it to emphasize my spurning of the offer, his brows shot up, and staring at me with an indescribable expression, he stood to leave on rounds. His only words were "You'll do well, Iraqi!" But he shook my hand and clapped me on the shoulder.

As soon as I was posted to Hadassah, I'd have to send a letter of withdrawal to the hospital in Boston. I had it framed already; the vital phrase was "for the present." I'd be studying abroad some distant day, conceivably in Massachusetts. My strategy was something that the underground had taught me. "Always have an exit in reserve."

By the morning of the meeting, I'd psyched myself into a state of stoic calm. A hundred feet from where I worked, a group of men would be deciding on my destiny, and there was nothing more that I could do to influence the outcome. I could, however, shorten the suspense. With any luck, the news would reach me within minutes of its being made.

I hoped, of course, to hear it first from Berman, but my second line was Dr. Davis. At the conclusion of the *concours,* he'd be heading for the clinic, and since the conference room was at the far end of our common corridor, my ally, the receptionist, would buzz three times on seeing him emerge.

I was listening to a diastolic murmur when I heard her signal. With the stethoscope still in my ears, I sprinted for the hallway and almost into Dr. Davis. Interrupting my apologies, he addressed me with an unaccustomed gruffness.

"Why didn't you tell us you'd been accepted in America?"

Before I could collect myself, Davis disappeared. His office door clicked softly shut, but his final words were roaring in my ears. "Well, that eliminated you, of course."

I hadn't even lost. I'd been eliminated—if I was ever in the race at all. It hit me like a thunderbolt; Berman had always meant to stop me, one way or another. The "Iraqi" slurs, the G.P. ploy, and then the Boston job—the simplest, surest way to cut me out. And I'd handed him the scalpel for my own excision.

He'd told the others that I'd been accepted, but not that I'd refused the offer. Or perhaps he had. It wouldn't have mattered, as I found out later. My applying elsewhere had given them a reason to reject me. But *everyone* applied for several places. If you lost out on the spot you'd set your heart on, at least you'd have a shot at something else. A violation, it was all the same the universal rule, and never questioned by authority. Except, that is, in some specific cases. I kept forgetting that the rules were only rigidly enforced for certain citizens. If your origin was wrong, your rights were at the mercy of the rulers. Finally, I faced up squarely to the facts I'd been attempting to ignore.

It wasn't chance alone that every chief of service was a European and that every member of the *concours* was also *Ashkenazi.* Or that it was the German—Berman—who made "Iraqi" sound like something shameful. No, it wasn't chance alone. I hadn't had a chance to start with.

52

Now it was imperative to get the letter from the Medical Association. Swallowing my pride, I called the Secretary of the I.M.A. again, pleading for an earlier appointment. "Impossible," he answered curtly. End of conversation. No "sorry," no *"shalom,"* no courtesies accorded every *Ashkenazi.* A click and he'd dismissed me—like the *concours.*

The line was dead, like my career, and for an awful, fleeting instant, I felt capable of killing. The blood-red rage was out of all proportion to the Secretary's slur, and I recognized my overwrought condition even as I smashed the phone down on its cradle. I slammed it hard enough to hurt my hand and send a shock wave traveling to my shoulder. Piercing through the fury that enveloped me, the pain restored my reason. I only hurt *myself* in lashing out like that in futile anger, but another week of idle waiting would be even more destructive. Action was the only antidote against this sort of sick despair.

I decided to proceed as if the letter had been posted and would soon be here, in hand. I had to start with that assumption or abandon any hope of reaching Children's Hospital. To leave, I'd need an exit visa, and whatever was required for admittance to the U.S.A., as well as reservations on the ship and train and plane that would take me to America. Those weeks before the I.M.A. appointment, heretofore so endless, seemed suddenly inadequate for all I had to do.

After queuing up and waiting at the passport office, I was waved off toward a seat and told to wait again. For fifty-seven slowly ticking minutes, a lumpish clerk behind the counter pushed around some piles of paper. At last he crooked a languid finger.

I sprinted to the counter, expecting him to send me somewhere else within the office—else why the wait? Instead he shoved two sets of forms at me and said I was to fill them out, "then bring them back to me." For that, this civil "servant" had kept me twitching on my seat edge for an hour! I forced myself to walk away before I flung the papers in his face and suggested where he file them. All I had to do was make an enemy of someone who could "lose" my application.

Instructions called for filling out a set of forms in English for the U.S.A. The applications for internal use called, of course, for Hebrew. On finishing, I rapped, politely, for the clerk's attention, handed him the documents, and stood there, silent, while he scanned them.

The Hebrew application passed inspection, but at the first line of the English form, his head snapped up; he thought he'd found an error, and clearly it afforded him enormous satisfaction.

He waved the sheet at me, exclaiming loudly that my name was wrong. For America, I'd written "Heskel," which is how I'd always spelled it. At birth, however, "Yeheskel" had been recorded, and I used it on the Hebrew forms. The discrepancy disturbed the clerk.

Without consulting me, he said, "We'll use 'Yeheskel,' " and struck a line through "Heskel" on the sheet in English, obliterating most of my existence—and my monogram. I'd always liked the symmetry of H.M.H., and in destroying it, the tyrant overreached himself. No matter what, I was and would be Heskel, and an argument ensued. I heatedly insisted that I damn well knew my name.

The clerk strategically retreated. If I could prove that I was "Heskel," he'd allow it, and, yes, my medical diploma would be proof enough. Still tasting gall, I took off at a gallop, back to school to get a copy of my medical degree in English. At my current rate of progress, I'd arrive at Boston with a long gray beard and ulcers. And everything so far had simply been preliminary to beginning. What I was doing now was just applying for permission to make application for a passport.

To stem the flow of emigrants, the state was tightening the tourniquet, and getting out was getting tough. The economy required workers, and the constant threat of war necessitated strong defenses; between the labor force and army, all of us were needed. To obtain an exit visa, travel had to be essential, and I honestly believed my going was. Stymied here, I'd be just another general practitioner. After Boston, though, I'd be coming back a pediatric expert, trained at no expense to Israel. And my absence would be offset by the thousands I had helped escape. Then, there was my service in the Persian camps. I felt my debt had been repaid already, but I wanted to give more. Boston would allow it. However, proof would be required that my trip abroad was in the interests of the state. A letter from the I.M.A. would more than do it.

I was certain that the bottleneck had been the Secretary. Probably he hadn't put my case correctly, and to cover up his own ineptitude had tried to shift the blame. He knew I'd find him out on facing the committee; that accounted for his hostile turn-about as soon as I requested an appointment.

The I.M.A. didn't awe me. As impressive as it sounded, the Medical Association was essentially a Histadrut for doctors. Empowered to negotiate for my profession, it was, for all its dignified facade, intrinsically a union. A union might command respect, but certainly not fear. A recent piece of news had left me even more relaxed about the outcome of our meeting. Only yesterday, a former classmate at Hadassah had taken off for Boston, also to become a resident. Except that he was heading for a different hospital, our situations were identical. If Schmuel had been allowed to leave, they'd have to let me go as well.

Arriving at the I.M.A., I found myself in lush surroundings. Unlike the spartan ambience of all the other offices I'd seen in Israel, the room I entered was imposing in its airy size and elegance. Three men, the youngest in his middle sixties, sat behind a stately, polished table. The atmosphere was frigidly correct, as formal as a court of law, and perching on the armless chair opposing them, I felt on trial for my life.

Quick introductions and their cursory *"shaloms"* did nothing to relieve the tension. The chairman said that he alone would serve as spokesman. He opened the proceedings swiftly, and in a single sentence also brought it to an end.

"After carefully reviewing your request," he said, "we must continue to refuse permission."

On that he snapped the file shut with such finality, it should have rung like steel. The breath whooshed out of me, leaving just enough to wheeze out, "Why?"

The old man was already half-erect. Officially the interview was over, and habituated as he was to the unequivocal acceptance of his every word, he clearly felt imposed on by my "Why?" Sinking back, and sounding very spleenish, he proceeded to explain.

"In effect," he said, "anyone who goes abroad becomes an emissary of the state, and we simply feel you aren't ready yet to be a representative of Israel."

I stared at him in stark amazement. Did he really think he'd given me a reason? Did he honestly expect me to be satisfied with such a slick and oily circumvention? From the look of it, he did indeed. All three of them were rising when I blurted out, "When *do* you think that I'll be ready?"

Openly astonished at my stubborn perseverance, the ancient fixed me with a flinty eye and answered shortly, "When you've learned to be a Zionist."

Now *I* was on my feet, and careless of the repercussions, I plucked my file from his fingers and slammed it on the table, scattering the papers it contained.

"You can't have even opened it," I charged him. "I've been a Zionist since age eleven, and it says so there."

Once started, I went on in one great gush about the underground and all the rest. Wholly unprepared for my emotional outpouring, the three of them exchanged uneasy glances. I loosed my final bolt right at the chairman, reminding him about my classmate, Schmuel, even then approaching Massachusetts.

"You gave *him* a letter, so how can you refuse the same to me?"

When he responded, "That was different," the others bobbed their heads in perfect harmony; unlike me, apparently they seemed to understand his cryptic comment. The chairman amplified, but briefly.

"Schmuel was born here."

The four words were enough; unhappily, they did explain the difference. Schmuel was *sabra,* so even worthier than *Ashkenazim,* and a world removed from me.

Forestalling any possible rebuttal, the chairman had adjourned the meeting. One committee member lingered for an instant, and had the decency to say that he was sorry, adding with a shamefaced air, "It's not that you're Iraqi." Overhearing him, the chairman glared, and all three made a hasty exit, leaving me alone.

Dropping in my seat, immobilized by hopelessness, I sat and stared, unable to do anything but think my bitter thoughts. They'd put me in my place, and I was stuck in it. Literally, they'd stopped me where I sat; and not because of any crime that I'd committed, or even any flaw of character. And it wasn't that they'd hated me on sight, as sometimes happens. They'd never even seen me till the moment they demolished me, and that was more appalling than a personal vendetta. I couldn't defend myself because my *self* had never been the issue. My "kind" was in the dock, not me.

Since Boston was his baby, I called on Aryeh Schwartz to tell him that the baby had aborted. Swimming in despondency, all I wanted was some sympathy, but Schwartz was more pragmatic.

"Their excuse is that you're not yet Zionist enough? So think! Who knows how Zionist you are?"

I didn't think fast enough for Aryeh, and he shook his head in mock despair.

"The Jewish Agency, you numbskull! They know your background. You have friends there. Let *them* take on the I.M.A."

The paralyzing apathy had disappeared before he finished. Aryeh pushed the phone at me, but too itchily impatient now to place a call, I shook his hand and shot right over to the Agency. The receptionist informed me that everyone from Teheran was on assignment, out of Israel and out of reach.

Irresolutely standing in the center of the anteroom, gloom again descending, I was slow to move when someone barrelled through the door. A briskly striding man bumped solidly against my arm, apologized, and disappeared. As abstracted as I was, I couldn't help noticing his air of great authority. He reminded me of Baba. I was walking out the door, without a destination, when the pleasant young receptionist recalled me.

"The man who just came in—that was Bar-Giora." The way she spoke his name was almost reverential. "Do you think, perhaps, that he could help?"

It was *kibbutz* time if Bar-Giora couldn't so why not try the man? He was a prominent official of the Agency, primarily involved with immigration from the Arab countries, and on top of that, *Sephardic.* I fought to keep this slender hope from burgeoning too high and wide. At the moment, another major disappointment might unravel me for good. However, it was hard to keep my hope contained when Bar-Giora pumped my hand, proclaiming that he'd always hoped to meet me. My whole career was known to him, and heartened by his interest, I told him all my troubles, ending with the Medical Association.

As I spoke, my spirits rose. A man with Bar-Giora's influence could surely pressure someone in authority. Then he shot me down by saying that he couldn't intervene in connection with the I.M.A. On hearing his "however," though, I bounced back even higher.

Smiling to himself, but saying nothing of his scheme to me, he scrawled a two-page letter, tucked it in an envelope, licked the flap, and flipped it at me with a look of satisfaction. "That ought to do the trick," he said. A second later, he retrieved it with a laugh. "I forgot to tell you where to take it." When he gave it back, the envelope had been inscribed: GENERAL DIRECTOR, DEPARTMENT OF HEALTH.

Bar-Giora ordered me to go at once; he'd call ahead to say that I was coming. With a hearty handshake and an impish grin, as if we'd been conspiring like schoolboys, he sent me on my way.

Still dazed by his performance, I arrived at the Director's office to find myself expected. Rising from his seat to greet me, B'tesh was a most impressive figure. Extremely tall, he towered so far above me that he had to bend to keep in visual contact. His face and freckled arms gave evidence of too much sun for someone with so light a skin, and his Nordic look was emphasized by pale eyes and red-blond hair, now going gray. In my newly optimistic frame of mind, I'd figured on his also being *mishilanu,* but everything about him screamed out *Ashkenazi.* From the warmth with which he welcomed me, however, it was obvious that he and Bar-Giora were the best of friends.

I handed him the letter, and halfway through, he paused to study me intently, the sort of scrutiny that would have set me sweating had it lasted just a second longer. What was *in* that letter?

"I see you have a problem," he remarked.

Before he finished, he stopped once more to scan my face. Rills of perspiration rose and slithered down my spine. Since Rabbi Ezra, no eyes had pierced so deeply. Pale they might be, but sharp. I stiffened when he put the paper down, tightening my muscles like a boxer bracing to withstand a blow.

"A Jew like you should *have* no problems."

He smoothed the letter on his desk and smiled widely, laughing when my breath escaped in one great exhalation; I hadn't known that I'd been holding it.

After asking me to tell him more about the meeting with the Medical Association, during which recital his amusement faded, B'tesh called his secretary in. The letter he dictated grimly was a single sentence long, hardly longer than the sentence that the chairman of the I.M.A. had passed on me.

"To Whom It May Concern:

Dr. Haddad's trip to the United States for specialized training is essential and is thoroughly endorsed by this Department."

No poetry had ever moved me more. A second sigh of sheer relief burst out of me, and B'tesh, who'd regained his grin, laid Bar-Giora's letter in my field of vision, pointing to the postscript. The P.S., written large and underlined, read, *"Mishilanu"*—"one of us"—embracing all the so-called Oriental and *Sephardic* Jews.

"You?"

B'tesh's grin grew even wider. With a finger to his lips, he cautioned, "Let's keep it to ourselves. Anyway, I wouldn't have done it if I didn't feel you were deserving."

53

Before the day was over, the original of the endorsement was on its way to Boston. With a copy, I applied for and obtained a passport. Another duplicate netted me a visa for America. In addition to unlocking every door with dizzying speed, the magic document was also saving me a ton of money. The tax imposed on ordinary travel was as much again as actual transportation, but since my trip was now officially essential, the entire tax was waived.

Within a week, I was booked the cheapest way to Massachusetts—by boat to Marseilles and train to Paris, and for the final leg, a flight to Boston. I didn't believe that everything had really come together until I had the tickets in my hand. However, the biggest, hardest jobs were still ahead of me; I couldn't avoid them any longer, and here I'd have no help. How I'd tell my family and Ada was strictly up to me.

I hadn't dropped a hint that I was going, afraid, perhaps, that something might dissuade me. As I was ready to admit at last, that something was my weakness when it came to Ada. As long as she was readily available and ever-willing to accede to my demands, I'd never make the final break I'd known so long was needed. Only oceans and a continent between us could sever the connection.

In isolated sexual bouts, we still reached heights together, but in ordinary intercourse, we walked on eggs. Always, and at ever-shorter intervals, my voice would rise, her tears would fall, and one more joyous memory would be erased. I wanted us to finish while the ecstasy we'd shared outweighed the pain.

I'd given up my room, settled up my bills, and said my hospital goodbyes before I phoned her, asking her to meet me at her brother's house.

I'd steeled myself to tell her I was going, but I couldn't get a word in. Ada prattled without pause from the moment she arrived, and though her artificial animation only fooled me for a moment, I couldn't break through with less than brutal force. Somehow she knew this was a showdown and was staving off the grand finale in the old, surefire way. Inevitably, her efforts led to bed.

Close and warm, I was uncertain as to how, or if, I could inform her of my leaving. She settled it by whispering, "I know you're going."

In guilt and gratitude, I asked her if she'd like to come to Tel Aviv.

My last stop in Jerusalem was Hanoch's house. I'd deliberately arranged it so I'd have to run as soon as the farewells were said. Hanoch was the only one who knew me well enough to see through my assumed elation.

My arrival home was always greeted with a flurry of excitement, no more so this time than any other. I'd be staying for the next two days, then taking off, I told them, on another trip. By now, the pattern was familiar, and everyone assumed that I was simply on a medical assignment. I didn't intend to tell them until just before I had to go. Memories of home would have to last me for a long, long time, and as far as possible, I wanted everything to be as everyday and unconstrained as always.

One problem still remained. My cardboard suitcase, carried from the Persian camps, had finally collapsed. I had to purchase luggage and pack the things I'd kept in Tel Aviv. Bringing in two bulky bags, gathering together all my treasured bits and pieces, then slipping out, unseen, to take them to the travel agent's office necessitated scheming—and assistance. Normal traffic in the house was heavy and erratic, and someone had to call the signals. Nana, in particular, would have to be diverted. Osa, more adventurous than any of the other kids, had always been my closest ally, and after misting up and hugging me on hearing I was leaving, she volunteered to serve as spy and decoy "like the old days in the underground," she smiled through her tears.

That breached the dam I'd built, and all my tightly curbed emotions slipped restraints, engulfing me in crazy tides of wildly conflicting feelings. Excitement fought with fear of the unknown, and anger at the reason for this exodus mingled with anticipation. Shortly, though, a sense of loss expunged all other feelings. For the second time, a land I loved was forcing me to leave, driving me from family and friends, from all I cared for. More than anything, I felt alone.

Over tea, on the night before departure, Nana fussed about my packing. "You'll be starting early. You shouldn't put it off," she scolded. Then, affording me an opening I had to take, she asked, "Where is it this time?"

"America," I answered. Having held it in so long, it shot out so explosively that midway through, my voice changed pitch, cracking like a kid's. Everyone at the table laughed at my tomfoolery. Almost everyone, that is.

When Baba saw that Ada wasn't smiling and that Osa had begun to cry, he straightened so abruptly that his heavy chair screeched jarringly across the tile floor, turning off the laughter. Bewildered by the silence that descended, Nana looked from Baba back to me. Surely it was just a joke. Her eyes implored me, "Tell us it was just a joke." When I dropped my own, she knew that it was true. A strangled moan escaped her, and I caught her in my arms before she fainted, a fraction of a second faster than my father moved to break her fall. Face to face, his eyes, I saw, shone diamond-bright with unshed tears; I knew what he was thinking. His eldest son was still in Baghdad. Now I'd be even farther off, each of us a world away.

Nana moved between us, struggling back to consciousness. A moment later, over the initial shock, she took command, not only of herself but of the situation. No son of hers would sneak away without a proper send-off. Baba was dispatched to tell the relatives. The kids were sent to fetch our friends and neighbors. The flat began to fill, and soon the small apartment was humming like a hive of bees. Within an hour of my uttering "America," there was hardly room enough to pump a hand and say hello—goodbye.

Grateful for the opportunity to greet them all, and glad to hear so many wish me well, I was even happier to have them here because of Nana. Scrounging up enough to feed the mob, preparing and dispatching heaping platters from the kitchen, completely occupied with welcoming our guests, she wouldn't have time enough to weep—not really weep, the way that Eastern women wailed when their hearts were broken.

Furtively, at intervals, she'd blot her brimming eyes, unseen by anyone but me and Baba. When the last guest drifted out at dawn, Nana disappeared. Instinctively, I knew where she would be.

The kitchen door was open just a crack. I watched and fought back tears as Nana touched a match to the *kindeel.* She was praying that Ezekiel the Prophet would protect me on my journey.

My ship was docked at Haifa; by 7 A.M., I'd have to be aboard the bus from downtown Tel Aviv. At 5 A.M., never having slept at all, I shaved and showered, packing every item as I finished with it for the final time in Israel. Razor, comb, and toothbrush—all evidence of me would be erased.

Exhausted as she was, Nana had prepared my favorite breakfast omelet. I kissed her for the *ajja b'kerrath,* and though my stomach strained against it, swallowed with a show of zest. My tears were too close to the surface to restrain for long, so when Baba said that he was taking me to Haifa, and the kids began to beg to go along, I resisted their entreaties. "No, not to Haifa. No one. Not even to the bus. I want to say goodbye at home."

The moment had arrived, and as Ada silently embraced me, I began to come unstuck. To spare ourselves and others added pain, we'd pretended to each other—and the others—that our parting was a temporary matter occasioned only by career needs. The implication of our conduct was that when the year was up and I returned, all would be exactly as before with us.

This act of ours had never been discussed between us. We'd arrived at it, each independent of the other. In a sad and eerie way, we were the closest, most at ease, we'd ever been. Now that she had cause to weep, when everyone would sympathize and understand, her eyes were desert-dry.

Ada stepped inside. The last embrace belonged to Nana. Holding mother in my arms, I felt her hand creep up and drop a hard-soft something in the pocket of my shirt. "Keep this with you always," she implored, by which I knew the packet was a tiny sack of salt.

When trouble threatens, throw it in the devils' eye!

I hugged her till the squeal of tires told us that the taxi had arrived. Time had run completely out.

Brisk and businesslike, helping with my heavy bags, Baba took me to the taxi. Nana was already sobbing in the background, but he, I thought, was strong enough to send me off with cool composure. After opening the cab door and tossing in the luggage, he turned to say a last *"shalom."* Straightening from his stoop and uttering an inadvertent bleat of pain as muscles pulled, he was smaller and more fragile, for a second, than I'd ever seen him.

Except for one brief period, just after my arrival and the Lyd ordeal, I hadn't even thought about my father's growing old, and now I almost choked on seeing evidence he *wasn't* an immortal.

Suddenly he hugged me hard, his arms encircling me like hoops of steel, and breathless, I could breathe again. He wasn't old and never would be. Not in any way that mattered. Murmuring the blessing of a father for a son, he held me hard against him for another instant, then shoved me toward the taxi.

Twisting for a final glimpse of all the gathered family, I saw my mother hurling water like a fury, washing out the car tracks to confound the Evil Eye.

Around the corner, out of sight and free to weep at last, I found that I was smiling. No devils did pursue. The good was going with me and the bad I'd left behind. And coming back, I'd help to make it better.

Index